THE
COMMON THREAD

1905 to 1941

Harry Sterne

The Book Guild Ltd.
Sussex, England

This book could not have been written without the invaluable help in research, typing and corrections made by my wife Margaret who died on 11th December 1987.

The Book Guild Ltd.
25 High Street,
Lewes, Sussex

First published 1992
© Harry Sterne 1992
Set in Baskerville
Typesetting by Kudos Graphics,
Slinfold, West Sussex

Printed in Grat Britain by
Antony Rowe Ltd.
Chippenham, Wiltshire.

A catalogue record for this book
is available from the British Library

ISBN 0 86332 696 X

CONTENTS

ACKNOWLEDGEMENTS

I would like to take this opportunity of thanking the following people and the various organizations and libraries for their help in the writing of this book.

To Mr David Elliot, without whose help and experience, together with that of my wife Margaret, this book could not have been written. And to Mr Gordon Schaffer and his invaluable experience as a former Political Editor and author, who patiently checked through the manuscript and made many valuable suggestions, particularly concerning events during the 1920s and 1930s. To Mr Phillip Knightly who read through the manuscript and made a number of wise suggestions and corrections and whose book *The First Casualty* had given me a deep insight into the military events of the relevant period.

I would also like to thank Dr Fred Cowley, until his recent retirement, chief librarian at Swansea University, together with his many colleagues and the invaluable help from staff at the Colindale Press Library in North London.

Madame Francine Frey of Boulogne-sur-Mer was particularly helpful during my research into French history covering the relevant events concerning Franco–British relations and their effect upon the rest of the world. My thanks and best wishes to the chief librarian and assistants in the beautiful old town of Boulogne.

I particularly wish to include that of a dear friend of more recent years, the late Lord Elwyn-Jones, P.C., C.H., who as a comparatively young Q.C. was a prosecuting counsel at Nuremburg when Rudolf Hess was in the dock. His help and experience was invaluable in my assessment of the career and background of Hess until his final end.

I had a number of meetings with the late Professor Eric Burhop, F.R.S. and former President of the World Federation of Scientific Workers. Professor Burhop was an eminent Australian scientist who was a witness at the testing of the first Atomic Bomb at Los Alamos.

I also wish to thank Mrs Peggy Williams, who read through parts of the manuscript, Mrs Ann Seroka of Ystradgynlais library, the chief librarian and assistant of the excellent Brecon library and Mr Peter Williams, my solicitor and legal adviser. I would also like to thank the chief librarian and staff at the Swansea General Library.

But last, but not least, to the late Fanny Carlin, a life long friend of my family, who died at the age of 91. She read through many of the chapters covering the 1920s and had a vivid memory of the events concerning the Zinoviev Letter and the Arcos Raid.

INTRODUCTION

At 8.15 a.m., 6 August 1945, a B-29 of the United States Air Force, flying over a provincial town in the northern island of Japan, dropped a bomb.

During the six years of World War II tens of thousands of bombs had been dropped upon military targets, upon armies and cities – in Europe, Africa and in Asia. But this was no ordinary bomb. In a blinding flash and amid a cloud of dust and debris 80,000 human beings were killed. Three days later a second bomb was dropped upon a similar town in the southern island of Japan. In all, just under 200,000 Japanese civilians, old and young, men, women and children were killed by those two bombs and thousands more were to die in a long drawn-out agony. The names of the towns, Hiroshima and Nagasaki, previously unknown to millions of people in the Western World became symbols of the new atomic age, to be identified with mass slaughter, devastation, radiation, leukaemia and new forms of cancer. Their inhabitants were the guinea pigs of a macabre development in the fields of science and technology.

According to General MacArthur, United States Commander-in-Chief, SE Asia, 'The selection of Nagasaki as the second objective of the atomic bomb was caused by unfavourable weather conditions. After circling for fifty minutes above the smoke-obscured city of Kokura, which was the primary target, the bombing plane flew on to drop the bomb over Nagasaki, the alternate target. Kokura was spared by a blind miracle of chance, but in Nagasaki 100,000 inhabitants died within seconds.'[1]

Robert Alvin Lewis, an American Army Air Force Captain, was the co-pilot of the plane which dropped the

15

first atomic bomb and as he watched Hiroshima disappear in a mushroom of cloud he cried out, 'My God what have we done.' He told an interviewer in 1982,

'I'll never forget that feeling. You could see a good-sized city, then you did not see any more. It was simply gone.'

The American President, Harry S. Truman, was at the time on board ship, returning from the summit meeting at Potsdam with Churchill and Stalin. According to those present, he exultantly exclaimed: 'This is the greatest thing in history.'[2]

I was then a young man, one of a number of ordinary soldiers recently returned from the Second Front in Europe. We were in Hull when news came on the BBC of the atomic bomb being dropped on Horishima. We were stunned. It was incomprehensible.

I can vividly remember my own reactions at the time. The war in Europe was over. The Nazis had surrendered. Italy had been out of the war for quite some time. It was just three months since we had been celebrating VE Day, and were awaiting news of arrangements for our demobilization. It did not make sense.

The news of the past three months had been full of optimism. The German army had been smashed. Hitler and Mussolini were no more and the Americans had been bombing the hell out of the Japanese navy and had Japan almost on its knees. The general impression that one gathered through the BBC and the press was that Japan was on the verge of collapse.

A few days later the news was full of the Red Army sweeping the Japanese out of Manchuria – fulfilling its wartime obligation of helping to bring the war in Asia to a rapid end. I can remember the press reports of the speed with which the Russian tanks were driving the Japanese out of mainland Asia and into the sea.

The first impact on hearing the news of the atomic bombing of Hiroshima was one of shock and amazement. Only after further news began to filter through during the following week and the effects of the shock had worn off did suspicion and doubt begin to enter some of our minds. Why, we asked? Why bring about such senseless slaughter? What have these innocent human beings done to warrant such action?

16

I can recall during my early training days – bayonet training – being told that the important thing to remember was to kill the enemy, if not, he will kill us. That *we* only attacked military targets. That there was a Geneva Convention on human behaviour in warfare, which did not include the bombing of innocent civilians, and that it was the Germans and Japanese who continually broke the Geneva Convention.

President Truman said on 9 August 1945 that the bomb was used 'to shorten the agony of war in order to save the lives of thousands and thousands of young Americans.'[3] Yet the Chief of the United States Army Air Force, General Henry H. Arnold, wrote in his book, *One World Or None*, 'the fact is that the Japanese could not have held out long because they had lost control of the air.'[4] It was also known in the middle of July that Japan had been in contact with Stalin to discuss peace proposals and Churchill had accordingly been advised. He in turn passed the information on to Truman.

On 8 August 1945 *The Times* reported that:

> 'a correspondent in the Baltimore Sun, writing from an authority which seems unimpeachable, says that until early in June the President and military leaders were in agreement that this weapon should not be used, but a reversal of this high command policy was made within the last 60 and, possibly, the last 30 days.'

Professor Blackett, eminent nuclear physicist and British Government adviser, posed two very pertinent questions in his book, *The Military and Political Consequences of Atomic Energy*:

> 'If the saving of American lives had been the main objective, surely the bombs would have been held back until
> (a) it was certain that the Japanese peace proposals made through Russia were not acceptable.
> (b) The Russian offensive which had for months been part of the Allied Strategic Plan and which Americans had previously demanded, had run its course.'[5]

17

Two Americans, Norman Cousins and Thomas K. Finletter*, took the mystery a little further. On 15 June 1946 in an American magazine, *The Saturday Review of Literature*, they ask:

> 'Why then did we drop it? Or assuming that the use of the bomb was justified, why did we not demonstrate its power in a test under the auspices of the United Nations, on the basis of which an ultimatum would be issued to Japan – transferring the burden of responsibility to the Japanese themselves? . . . '†

This book will attempt to explain why.

Notes

1. MACARTHUR, Douglas General, *Reminiscences*, p. 263
2. LIDDEL-HART, B.H., *History of the Second World War*, p. 696
3. FLEMING, D.F., *The Cold War and Its Origins, Vol. I.*, p. 296
4. ARNOLD, Henry H. General, *One World or None*, p. 28
5. BLACKETT, P.M.S., *The Military and Political Consequences of Atomic Energy*, p. 120

---

*Finletter was later chosen by President Truman to be Chairman of the US Air Policy Committee. He afterwards became head of the Marshall Plan mission in London.
†From Professor Blackett's book, American edition, *Fear, War and the Bomb. Military and Political Consequences of Atomic Energy*, p. 137.

1

THE AWAKENING

On the 22 January* 1905 over 200,000 workers gathered in the streets of St Petersburg – which was then the capital of Russia – to demonstrate against an appalling standard of living and terrible working conditions.

It was a Sunday, and bitterly cold. Many believed that they should appeal to the Tsar for justice.

The inside of the Tsar's Winter Palace was deserted, outside were hundreds of soldiers and artillery. That week there had been an outbreak of strikes throughout the capital. They began at the Putiloff Iron Works and at the Franco-Russian Semiankoff Works, spreading rapidly to other engineering and industrial plants, not only in St Petersburg, but also to many other industrial cities. In Lodz,† a leading textile town, an estimated 100,000 were on strike. According to a report in the British *Daily News* of 19 January 1905, which described the city as the 'Manchester of Russia', 'a crowd was fired on by the police . . . and many were killed and wounded.'

Russia was on the verge of a revolution, its workers were no longer prepared to tolerate the long hours of work – as much as fourteen hours a day in the textile mills; the primitive housing with its terrible overcrowding and the meagre wages, the purchasing power of which had been undermined by inflation.

In the preceding decade the cost of food had risen by around twenty five per cent but the Russian factory workers' wages had only increased by five per cent. With

*9 January in the Russian Calendar.
†It was actually in Poland, then part of the Russian Empire.

five million unemployed in the rural areas and only two and a half million workers employed in the factories, the existence of a massive 'reserve army' of labour reinforced the belief that the employer regarded himself as a 'benefactor' for agreeing to pay any wages at all. Collective bargaining was denied to the steadily increasing class of industrial workers, the majority of whom were employed in factories and mines owned and controlled by foreign companies and foreign managers. Even the foremen were brought in from abroad.

'In 1900 there were said to be 269 foreign-owned companies in Russia, of which all but 16 had been founded since 1888 . . . Foreigners owned 67 per cent of the shares in all metallurgical companies in 1900 and no less than 85 per cent in those making iron and steel in the Ukraine.'[1]

That Sunday, thousands of workers and their families trying to enter St Petersburg's main square were prevented by mounted troops who had blocked the openings at each end. The first clash came at around eleven o'clock when, according to the *Daily News* report under the heading 'MASSACRE IN ST PETERSBURG',

> 'the military tried to turn back some thousands of Putiloff strikers at one of the bridges connecting the island, which is the great industrial quarter, with the central portions of the city . . .
>
> The Cossacks at first used their knouts, then the flat of their sabres and finally they fired. The passions of the mob broke loose like a bursting dam. The people seeing the dead and dying carried away in all directions, the snow in the streets and the pavements soaked with blood, cried aloud for vengeance . . .
>
> Meanwhile the situation at the Palace was becoming momentarily worse. The troops were reported to be unable to control the vast masses which were constantly surging forward. Reinforcements were sent, and at two o'clock here also the order was given to fire.
>
> Men, women and children fell at each volley, and were carried away in ambulances, sledges and

carts. It was no longer a workmen's question. The indignation and fury of every class was aroused. Students, merchants, all classes of the population alike are aflame.'

In his comments the paper's foreign correspondent wrote:

'The die is cast, the Czar has not the courage to receive the workmen of St Petersburg, and a revolution stares him in the face.'

and in its editorial the paper referred to the events of that Bloody Sunday as 'the baptism of revolution'.

'Hundreds of the Czar's subjects, defenceless, unarmed, were shot down by the Czar's soldiers. It is a crime that will send a thrill of horror and anger throughout the civilised world. It is a crime that marks the Russian despot as the enemy not only of his own subjects, but of the human race.' (*The Daily News*, 23 January 1905)

The 22 January 1905, 'Petersburg Bloody Sunday', sparked off a movement throughout the whole of Russia. Strikes spread at such a rate that by the middle of April 122 towns were affected and over a million workers involved. The Government had failed to terrorize them into submission. The strikes, instead of coming to an end, continued to spread from region to region reaching a total of close on three million workers by the end of the year.

Towards the end of August Government authorities mobilized the 'Black Hundreds', counter-revolutionary gangs used by the Okhrana* for anti-Jewish and anti-revolutionary pogroms, to attack the workers who had gone on strike in the Baku oilfields. It was against this background that local strikes erupted during the second half of September. There was the strike of the Moscow printers, followed by the bakers, then the tobacco workers and the tramway men. On the 6 October the railway men in Moscow and Kazan joined in.

---

*Political Police. Employed both detectives and special agents, as well as informants and agents provocateurs.

The workers' response to the Petersburg massacre spread to Poland and the other Baltic States (then part of the Russian Empire). A general strike and street demonstrations in Poland ended in a massacre second only to that in the Russian capital. Martial law and executions without trial were frequently brought into operation. In Warsaw there were four general strikes up to the end of 1907. To make matters worse, there was the unpopular war in the Far East. The 'impregnable' fort of Port Arthur had surrendered to the Japanese with most of the Russian Far Eastern Fleet: four battleships, two cruisers and their armaments, together with 32,000 prisoners of war. News of the killed and disabled had yet to arrive.

In the meantime, Manchuria, which the Russian Imperial Army had been illegally occupying (for it was part of China) fell into the hands of the Japanese. The Russian Army was forced to retreat from Mukden, the capital, in complete disorder. Broken, humiliated and with losses, including prisoners amounting to 120,000, the Far Eastern venture had been a total failure.*

Disaffection soon began to spread within the armed forces. In June 1905 there was a mutiny aboard the battleship Potemkin of the Black Sea Fleet. Four months later the revolutionary movement spread to the Baltic Fleet where hundreds of seamen were arrested. Two artillery equipped regiments were sent to Kronstadt and it was only with their aid that the movement was crushed after a desperate resistance. But no sooner was this mutiny put down than reports came in of a rebellion in the Black Sea port of Sevastopol. The revolutionary movement reached its peak on 11–12 November with the fraternization of the Sevastopol Army garrison soldiers and the seamen, culminating in a joint demonstration. The leader of the revolt and three seamen were court martialled and shot. The naval barracks were bombarded and taken and the mutiny crushed. Meanwhile, news of military disorders poured in from all parts – from Rostov – from Kursk, from near

---

*Throughout the whole war against Japan Russian losses were 41,000 killed and 57,000 disabled – in addition to 12,000 seamen who lost their lives and the thousands taken prisoner.

Warsaw and from Riga, from Viborg in Finland – from Vladivostock, from Irkutsk and from Harbin, the Manchurian seaport. In spite of the peace treaty signed with Japan earlier in the year, there had been no demobilization.

The overwhelming majority of non-commissioned soldiers were conscripted from the rural areas and many villages had lost up to fifty per cent of their able bodied men, thus adding to the poverty and misery of an already intolerable life. Disorder was rife in these regions too, and flogging was used both to quell the unrest and to stifle disrespectful remarks directed against the Tsar and his administrators. As in the towns, there were peasants who refused to be cowed. Some refused to pay the oppressive taxes and others began to loot estates and mansions.

The disorders continued throughout 1905 – in Central Russia, Georgia, Transcaucasia and in areas around the Volga. A telegram sent to the Governor of Kursk at the beginning of 1906 advised him that in order:

> 'To put an end to the disorders take the most ruthless measures; it will be found useful to raze to the ground the rebel villages and to exterminate the rebels by force of arms without mercy.'[2]

From August 1906 until April 1907 field court martials were introduced throughout the whole of Russia. 'Between 3,500 and 4,500 persons, not peasants only, are estimated to have been executed.'[3] The discontent was so widespread that even some sections of the nobility who had expressed gentle hints for constitutional reform were banned to remote areas.

The bitterness and hatred for the Tsarist regime reached out into the heart of the many nationalities within Greater Russia. Out of a population of 170 million, about 100 million were described by Lenin as 'aliens without rights' – people who had been living in Russia for generations – Armenians, Georgians, Jews, Tartars and other minorities. Their mother tongue, newspapers and books were all suppressed. Schools which used their languages were shut down. Jews were not allowed to live in the Greater Russian provinces, whilst in other regions, such as as the Ukraine

23

and White Russia, they were restricted to the towns. A Government 'percentage norm' kept nearly all Jewish children out of the schools. They were allotted only three places in every hundred. Pogroms and a war against the 'infidels' fitted neatly into the Government's plans. It provided the Tsarist administrators with 'potent measures to direct the rising tide of revolution in another direction.'

> 'Pogroms were recorded in 110 localities . . . From 3,500 to 4,000 people were killed and some 10,000 mutilated. The worst pogroms took place in the outlying parts of Russia – at Odessa, where the number killed amounted to 700, and at Tomsk, where in the presence of the Governor and a Bishop, over 1,000 people were locked up in the theatre, set fire to and burned alive.'[4]

To take the sting out of the widespread revolts and general discontent, the Government eventually set up what it described as a 'Representative Body' – a Duma.* The original intention was to limit its powers to consultative status only, but on this occasion it had to succumb to pressure from abroad; to at least present an image of some kind of democracy that might improve its standing in the countries which were bolstering its economy.

The first Duma opened on the 10 May 1906. According to M.N. Pokrovsky 'the Duma was convoked in fulfilment of an agreement with the Paris Bourse which had just lent (Tsar) Nicholas money to help him recover from the war'. Although the terms of the loan did not stipulate that it should be approved by the Duma, the French Government, nevertheless, 'wanted a fig leaf to show the petty bourgeois, who invested their savings in the new loan . . . that they were not lending money to an autocrat but a "Constitutional Russia". M. Poincaré, at that time French Minister of Finance, advised the Tsar not to remove the useful decoration too early, and to stage the promised play – "the meeting of the people's representatives".'[5]

---

*The Duma was a National Assembly

This loan, 'the largest of all the Paris loans, was issued after the French Government had made certain of Russian support at the Algeciras Conference on Morocco.' It was also used 'to strangle the revolution' and 'was bitterly denounced by all groups in Russia from liberals leftwards.'[6]

The Duma lasted only ten weeks. It was dissolved under the pretext that it had interfered in matters which were not its business, such as the question of land tenure. The 'useful decoration' was put into cold store. it was resuscitated in 1907 and then with the help of agents-provocateurs was dissolved with even less ceremony than the first.

An article in a British publication, *The Socialist Annual for 1908*, by Theodore Rothstein, describes the events which led up to the dissolution of the Duma. The leaders of the Social Democratic Group were arrested by the Government 'under the plea of an imaginary plot'. The Duma was dissolved and the Government then decided 'to change the electoral law in such a way as to preclude for ever the return not only of Socialists, but even of the opposition in general.'

The franchise in cities such as St Petersburg or Moscow was extended only to citizens who paid a minimum rent of 1,320 rubles for lodging, which meant an income of at least five to six hundred gold pounds annually. 'Not only the teachers of the Municipal schools, but those of the High schools and even the Junior University teachers were left outside the franchise. Petersburg with a population of one and a half millions would have only 9,500 votes. Moscow with one million – 14,000 votes, Odessa with 405,000 inhabitants – 7,000 votes and so on.'[7]

While the Tsar and his administrators had been busy preparing their 'fig leaf' the Russian workers were creating their own representative body. During the summer of 1905 they established their first Soviet of Workers Deputies. It lasted only a few months, but the principle had taken root and it led eventually to the formation of an All Russia Soviet.

There were a number of factors which contributed to the failure of the 1905/6 Russian revolution, not least of which was the 'huge international loan from Western Europe to the Tsar's Government . . . enough to finance the suppression of the revolution and to make the government independent of the new Duma before it could meet.'[8]

An uneasy calm settled over the country but the scars of the abortive revolution still remained. The years between 1912 and 1914 marked the beginning of a new revolutionary upheaval in Russia, with a million and a half workers on strike in 1913, rising to over two millions in 1914. The industrial unrest spread even to the remote areas of Siberia where in April 1912 troops were called in to break a strike at the Lena Gold Fields. The company was 70 per cent British owned.* B.H. Sumner relates in his *Survey of Russian History* that 'A storm of protest, not from the workers only, followed the ghastly shootings in the far distant Lena goldfields, when a strike, which was in essentials purely economic, ended with a casualty list of over 500.'[9]

Notes

1. WESTERN, J.R., *The End of European Primacy*, p. 119
2. POKROVSKY, M.N., *Brief History of Russia, Vol. II*, p. 237
3. SUMNER, B.H., *Survey of Russian History*, p. 132
4. POKROVSKY, M.N., *Brief History of Russia, Vol. II*, pp. 91, & 170
5. POKROVSKY, M.N., *Brief History of Russia, Vol. II*, p. 254
6. SUMNER, B.H., *Survey of Russian History*, p. 358
7. POKROVSKY, M.N., *Brief History of Russia, Vol. II*, p. 151
8. FLEMING, D.F., *The Cold War and its Origins, Vol. I*, p. 9
9. SUMNER, B.H., *Survey of Russian History*, p. 370

Russia and Europe, Reinhard Wittram, p. 98. (Thames and Hudson, 1973).

2

PRELUDE TO WORLD WAR I – THE DRIFT TO WAR

At the beginning of this century a few minutes' glance at a map of the world would have seen how this planet had been carved by a handful of countries into areas denoting their imperial possessions. The largest was the British Empire, embracing an area of between eleven and twelve million square miles; the Russian Empire with over eight million square miles, followed by France and her colonies with just over four million. The United States, a comparative newcomer to the imperial scene, together with her colonies, covered three and three quarter million square miles. The declining Turkish Empire had shrunk to one and a half million and the latest imperial aspirant, Germany, had accumulated just over one million.*

The imperial picture would not be complete without including the lesser empires of Austro-Hungary and Italy, and the scramble for colonies and the penetration of capital into one another's territories. Economic rivalry led to the hardening of political attitudes between some of the imperial powers.

Germany had been expanding her heavy industry far more rapidly than either Britain or France and German capitalist development was steadily moving ahead of her European rivals. Furthermore the German economic and political challenge was being reinforced by a massive build-

---

*'Between 1870–1900 Great Britain acquired 4,754,000 square miles of territory adding to her population 80 million people. Between 1884 and 1900 France acquired 3,583,580 square miles and 36,553,000 people and in these same years, Germany, a bad last, gained 1,026,220 square miles and 16,687,100 people.' (FULLER, Major General, *War and Western Civilisation*, p. 134)

up of her navy which the British Government, in particular, regarded as a serious threat to its own supremacy of the oceans of the world. It was the emergence of this new industrial power upon the imperial scene which precipitated the patching up of the old antagonisms between Britain and France and led to the signing of the Entente Cordiale Agreement in April 1904 – a deal between two of the oldest imperial powers, covering their respective spheres of influence in North Africa and South East Asia.

Both countries also had a considerable economic stake in Imperial Russia, and a vested interest in propping up the Tsarist regime after its disastrous war against Japan, and its well-nigh collapse under the blows of the 1905/6 revolution. The Paris Bourse rescue loan of some £80 million was supplemented by £11 million raised by the London Stock Exchange with the blessing of the British Foreign Office. By 1914, of the French investment overseas which totalled around £1,600 million, just over a quarter was in Russia, mostly in the Crimean and Ukrainian Iron and Coal industries, whilst British investments were mainly concentrated upon Russian oil in the Caucasus. 'Of Germany's pre-war investments, amounting in all to about £1250 million, not far short of £500 million was invested in Russia, Austria-Hungary, Bulgaria, Roumania and Turkey.'[1]

The Entente Cordiale was followed in 1907 by an Anglo-Russian Agreement, and in the same year the three countries drew closer together into an alliance which became known as the Triple Entente, not to be confused with the Triple Alliance of Austria-Hungary, Germany and Italy established some twenty-five years earlier.

The inevitable German reaction to the Triple Entente was to seek allies wherever it could. It found them in the ailing Austro-Hungarian and Turkish Empires. Italy, allied to Germany during the era of the Triple Alliance, was won over to the Anglo-French side by being promised a free hand in her occupation of Tripoli and Cyrenaica in Africa, and the Dodencanese islands, including Rhodes, in the Aegean.* This led to the Italo-Turkish war of 1911 and the

---

*These territories had been part of the Turkish Ottoman Empire since the sixteenth century.

eventual crumbling of the once formidable Turkish Empire.

In the nineteenth century, the scramble for colonies had led to the outbreak of military conflict all over the world. In Africa, Asia and Latin America people had been killed and many deprived of their homes in the drive for raw materials and the cheap labour that went with it. The increasing demands of the rapidly developing industries of Britain, France, Germany and the United States of America and the fierce competition for the expanding markets of the world continually brought with it 'the need of financiers to find a new outlet for the investment of their surplus capital' . . . 'British investments overseas, for example, rose from £785 million in 1871 to £3,500 million in 1911.'[2]

J.A. Hobson wrote in 1902, in his book *Imperialism*, that the

> '. . . foreign policy of Great Britain is primarily a struggle for profitable markets for investment. To a larger extent every year Great Britain is becoming a nation living upon tribute from abroad, and the classes who enjoy this tribute have an ever-increasing incentive to employ the public policy, the public purse, and the public force to extend the field of their private investments, and to safeguard and improve their existing investments.'
>
> '. . . what is true of Great Britain, is likewise of France, Germany, the United States and of all countries in which modern capitalism has placed large surplus savings in the hands of plutocracy.'[3]

It was therefore inevitable that financial interests would be followed by strategic interests, and the consequent acquisition of naval and military bases.*

It was out of the economic and political rivalries of the imperial powers and their alliances that military conflicts broke out in the Balkans. The heat, generated by the Balkan

---

*Japan and Russia came into the Industrial-Imperial competitive conflicts to a lesser degree globally towards the end of the 1800s and the beginning of this century.

countries, manipulated by the imperial Austro-Hungarian, Russian and Turkish Governments, together with the struggle of the subject peoples for national independence and self-determination, provided the combustible material to start a major war. All that was needed was a 'spark' to set it alight. Both France and Germany played their parts in the drama of the Balkans – but behind the scenes. Both had their investments to protect, their political influences to preserve, and the need to bolster their allies. Shifts in the overall balance of power between the countries of the Triple Entente and the Triple Alliance were therefore affected, not only by the activities of the Balkan countries themselves, but also by what went on inside those countries.

In 1903, the King and Queen of Serbia were assassinated and, as a result of a Palace revolution carried out by a group of officers, Serbia, which had been receiving arms and financial aid from France, replaced its pro-Austrian foreign policy with one that ensured closer ties with Russia.

In October 1908, Austria-Hungary annexed Bosnia-Herzegovina.* The plans for the annexation had originally been part of a deal between Austria and Russia, with the latter getting the help of the other Entente countries, and Austria using its influence to persuade Germany in a combined effort to force Turkey to open the Dardenelles Straits to Russian shipping. But the plan misfired. Neither of the three major powers felt inclined to get involved. There was no response from the British and French Governments, nor from the Germans. Nevertheless the Austro-Hungarian Government went ahead with the annexation. The neighbouring country, Serbia, became disturbed and looked to Russia for support. Although the annexation was immediately condemned by Britain, France, apprehensive of Russia's intentions, discreetly reserved her judgement in spite of the subsequent German support for the Austro-Hungarian action. The German Chief of Staff, General von Molke, wrote to Conrad von Hotzendorff, the Austrian Commander-in-Chief 'The moment Russia mobilizes, Germany will also mobilize and

---

*Bosnia-Herzegovina had been part of the Turkish Empire but had been administered by Austria since 1878.

will unquestionably mobilize her whole army'. The German threat was sufficient to compel the Tsarist regime 'to accept the situation and the only remaining formality was for Turkey to receive an indemnity of £2,400,000.'[4]

The imperial conflicts in the Balkans and the danger of a major war breaking loose were reflected in the statements made at the International Socialist Congress held in Stuttgart, April 1907, where a resolution was passed in which it warned that:

> 'The struggles against militarism cannot be separated from the Socialist class struggle in general. Wars between capitalists are, as a rule, the outcome of their competition on the world market, for each state seeks not only to secure its existing markets, but also to conquer new ones. In this, the subjection of foreign peoples and countries play a prominent role.'

The resolution then went on to appeal to the working class and their leaders in the countries involved, that it was their 'duty' – 'to use every effort to prevent war' and that if war should break out, 'their duty is to intervene and bring it promptly to an end.' But to no avail, the drift to war continued.

A further warning of the danger of the eruption of imperial rivalries into a major war was issued at the 1910 Copenhagen Congress of the Socialist International,* which called upon all Socialist Members of Parliament in their respective countries to vote against the granting of War-Credits.

The connivance of Britain and France in the following year in encouraging Italy to carve slices out of the Turkish Empire and the attack on Turkey, in October 1912, by Bulgaria, Greece, Serbia and Montenegro inevitably had its repercussions in Germany.

With a considerably weakened Turkey, the first of the Balkan wars had resulted in a swing of the balance of power from Germany to the Triple Entente.

The dangers inherent in the potential threat of the

---

*The Socialist International was also known as the Second International.

Balkan wars spreading to the rest of Europe, prompted the International Socialist Bureau to call a special congress. The delegates met in the Swiss border town of Basle on 24 and 25 November 1912 where a Manifesto was issued which re-affirmed the policies of 1907 and 1910 and appealed to the working class of all countries to

> 'exert all its energies to prevent the annihilation of the flower of all peoples threatened with the horror of mass murder, starvation and pestilence . . . Congress therefore appeals to you . . . to make your voices heard in this decisive hour.'

Such was the state of tension in 1912.

A year later, on 29 June 1913, the Balkans flared up again into a second war. On this occasion it was provoked by Serbia (Russia's protégé) in an attempt to enlarge its territory, so that it could escape from its land-locked position, have an outlet to the sea (the Adriatic), which meant the occupation of Albania, and less dependence economically upon Austria-Hungary. Serbia had long nursed the grievance that it was entitled to compensation for the loss of territories it had to secede in the creation of an independent Albania,* which was established under the joint sponsorship of Austria-Hungary and Italy. It therefore felt that it was entitled to the coastal region of Macedonia which instead was to be handed over to Bulgaria as part of the victor's spoils gained at the expense of Turkey in the first of the Balkan wars. When Bulgaria refused to concede the territory, Serbia formed an alliance with Greece. Fighting once more broke out with an attack by Bulgaria on Serbia and Greece. Roumania and Turkey joined in the counter-attack on Bulgaria and the Bulgars suffered a heavy defeat.

The Imperial powers had throughout the Balkan wars been sitting it out in the wings, anxiously watching their protégées engaged in bitter fighting. Eventually, the wars were brought to an end by a treaty signed in Bucharest, in August 1913, leaving a vulnerable Austro-Hungarian

---

*Albania had been part of the Turkish Empire.

Empire encircled by subject peoples seeking their liberation.

Serbia came out of the war with an enlarged territory which was not to the liking of the Austro-Hungarian Government, and a plan was worked out by the Austrian Prime Minister and his Commander-in-Chief with the support of Kaiser Wilhelm of Germany to embark upon a 'short war, followed by the partition of Serbia.' The Kaiser told the Austro-Hungarian Government that 'you can be certain I stand behind you and am ready to draw the sword whenever your action makes it necessary.'[5] German preparations for a military show-down were well under-way. In January 1913 military conscription was authorized by the Reichstag to be increased from 280,000 to 343,000 and in France a political battle was being waged to increase the period of conscription from two to three years. Meanwhile, Britain concentrated on strengthening her naval bases. As explained earlier in the chapter, danger of a major war was constantly present. All that was missing was the 'spark'. This came on 28 June 1914 at Sarajevo, the capital of the annexed Bosnia-Herzegovina, with the assassination of the heir to the Austria-Hungary throne, Archduke Ferdinand, and his wife. The assassination was the work of the Black Hand, an underground organization based in Serbia. Most of the conspirators involved were captured, and although there was no proof that they had links with the Serbian Government, nevertheless the event was exploited by the Austro-Hungarian Government.

At the time of the assassination the Austrian Government was planning Serbia's diplomatic isolation. The murder had now given it the additional incentive to remove a threatening Serbia by creating a political climate which would justify going to war against that country. Once defeated, Serbia would be split up and portioned out among its Balkan neighbours.

The Austrians were not unaware of the dangers of precipitating such a war, but nevertheless believed that it could be contained.

On 27 July 1914 the Austria-Hungary Government declared war on Serbia. It immediately set off a chain of events starting with a mobilization in Russia on 28 July.

According to Denis Brogan 'if mobilization did not mean war in France or Russia, it did mean war in Germany', and that once 'the news of the Russian mobilization' was announced, it 'made German mobilization inevitable.'[6] This began on 31 July and on the following day Germany issued a declaration of war against Russia.

'On the eve of the war', comments William Carr, in his *History of Germany*, 'real wages were falling, prices rising, unemployment growing and the State authority were dealing more ruthlessly with strikers than ever before, as political tensions mounted in Imperial Germany. Capitalism was plainly on the eve of a crisis.'[7] The plans for mobilization included the arrest of the Socialist leaders. However, the Social Democrats, with a few notable exceptions, supported the war wholeheartedly. Only Karl Liebknecht, in December 1914, voted against the Reichstag's Bill on War-Credits. In fact the preparations for a major war between the rival alliances, and the patriotic ballyhoo that accompanied them, had the same effect upon most of the Social Democrat leaders. No sooner had war been declared, than the overwhelming majority of Socialist MPs in the belligerent countries cast their votes in favour of War-Credits.* In Russia, the Bolshevik members of the State Duma, who were known opponents of the war, were arrested and banished to Eastern Siberia.

The drift to war had been accelerated by a rapid intensification of an arms build-up within the Imperial countries. This, together with the propaganda which was used to 'persuade the ordinary citizen that the growing risk of war justified additional military expenditure', played a prominent part in encouraging 'the growth of bellicose nationalism in all lands.'[8]

France too, in 1914, had been going through a period of industrial unrest. 'In the first seven months of the year there had been 654 strikes involving some 160,000 workers, but in the remaining five there were no more than 18.'[9] French public opinion was being pressed to believe that 'if war came, it should be seen to be the result of intolerable

---

*From then on the Second International ceased to exist.
There were two Serbian Social Democrat Members of Parliament who voted against their Government's granting of War-Credits.

German provocation.' The French people 'would not understand a war which resulted from some obscure issue in Morocco, or in the Balkans, unless it were made abundantly clear that France's vital interests were at stake.' For there were 'strong pacifist and anti-militarist feelings, which were by no means confined to the socialists.'[10] A considerable section of the French Radical Party came into this category, but their sentiments, together with those of the socialists, were soon stifled by the proclamation of the 'Union Sacrée'.*

To many British politicians and journalists war appeared inevitable. And most of the national press had very little to offer, except to create an atmosphere of acquiescence towards the drift to war. Nevertheless, the British section of the Second International did take the initiative in alerting people to the danger of the impending war. A mass demonstration was held on 2 August 1914 in Trafalgar Square, passing a resolution which stated:

'That this demonstration representing the organized workers and citizens of London, views with serious alarm the prospects of a European War, into which every European power will be dragged along owing to secret alliances and understandings which in their origin were never sanctioned by the nations, nor are even now communicated to them;'

'We stand by the efforts of the international working-class movement to unite workers of the nations concerned in their efforts to prevent their governments from entering upon war, as expressed in the resolution passed by the International Socialist Bureau . . . '

The German Government having declared war against

---

*War-time coalition of the major French Political parties.
Clemenceau was the leader of the Radical Party.

Russia immediately set into motion the Schlieffen Plan* which was to avoid a simultaneous war on two fronts. The plan was to attack on the Western Front through Belgium and Northern France by a 'knock-out blow' (the fore-runner of the 'blitzkrieg'), to encircle the French forces, and then, having destroyed the French army, hopefully in a matter of weeks, rush the victorious armies by rail across Germany and attack the Russians, whom it was assumed would take much longer to mobilize. As France was a key member of the Triple Entente, the Schlieffen Plan automatically came into operation. Germany declared war on France on 3 August and when the Germans invaded France through Belgium, the British Government announced its declaration of war on the following day.

No sooner had Britain declared war on Germany than the members of the British section of the Second International moved into line with the Government. 'So far from intervening "to bring it promptly to an end" they were joining in a recruiting campaign together with the capitalist parties. The overwhelming majority of the labour movement abandoned its previous standpoint and swung in behind the Government.'[11] The honourable exception was the Independent Labour Party which maintained its anti-war stand. Its leaders, which included the young Fenner Brockway, were imprisoned for their refusal to 'bear arms' against their socialist comrades. In their Manifesto of 13 August 1914, they sent their 'sympathy and greeting to the German socialists' who 'have laboured increasingly to promote good relations with Britain, as we with Germany. They are no enemies of ours but faithful friends.'

Notes

1. KEYNES, J.M., *Economic Consequences of the Peace*, p. 15
2. WOOD, Anthony, *Europe 1815–1945*, pp. 273–274
3. HOBSON, J.A., *Imperialism – A Study*, pp. 53–54
4. WOOD, Anthony, *Europe 1815–1945*, pp. 319-320
5. WOOD, Anthony, *Europe 1815-1945*, pp. p.324

*The Schlieffen Plan was devised by Count Alfred von Schlieffen, German Commander in Chief, 1891 to 1906.

6. BROGAN, D.W., *The Development of Modern France 1870–1939*, p. 458
7. CARR, William, *A History of Germany*, p. 212
8. CARR, William, *A History of Germany*, p. 237
9. BURY, J.P.T., *France 1814–1940*, p. 236
10. WATSON, Robin, *Georges Clemenceau*, pp. 222–223
11. PAGE ARNOT, R., *The Impact of the Russian Revolution in Britain*, p. 53

3

THE WAR OF EMPIRES (1914 to 1918)

War and preparations for wars have invariably provided the environment for inflation and profiteering. World War I was no exception.

> 'Thus [for example, in Germany] 1914, paper money issued by the Reichsbank was not more than 2.5 milliard* marks. At the close of the war, the paper money in circulation was 22 milliard marks which was roughly the annual issue of the Reichsbank to meet the Government war accounts. With the paper money thus obtained the Reichsbank bought war materials and issued war loans . . . 20 milliards annually found its way into the pockets of the war industry captains and, as the war lasted four years, these annual war loans amounted to rather over 80 milliard. This artificial method of financing was the sheet anchor of the Central Powers war finance . . . Since no taxes, no war-profit taxes could be collected, there was nothing left but to finance war by inflation, that is by throwing the whole of the burden on the masses. Obviously after four years of this an *impasse* was reached.'[1]

The position of France in 1914 was even more complex to the average Frenchman. Internally the French Government concentrated on selling treasury bonds, squeezing various sectors of the economy, but did not float its war loans until

---

*Milliard = 1000 million. Today the term used is Billion.

1915. Most of its external borrowing was financed through Great Britain and the United States of America but the loans were, in the main, tied to purchases in either country.

As in Germany, the French Government made good use of its printing plant, and stepped up the circulation of its paper currency.

'At the outbreak of the war, the note circulation was 5,900 million francs, by the end of 1919 it was 37,000 million' an increase of over 600 per cent and, as Brogan points out in his book, *The Development of Modern France*, 'it was in 1919' after the war was over 'that the biggest increase in the note issue took place.'

Inflation became one of the most widespread diseases of World War I.

'By the end of the war, the external debt of France alone' was 'almost double the total pre-war debt – which was in 1914, the highest in the world.'[2] In 1914 the French national debt was around 27,000 million francs. Four years later, its foreign debt alone was 43,000 million. The United States was owed just under $3,000 million and Britain close on £620 million. Yet, in spite of these massive debts, French farmers and the wine growers had been able to make very large profits during the war. The farmers, in particular, 'were legally as well as practically, exempt from the excess profits tax' and 'escaped from the curiosity and rapacity of the [French] treasury.'[3]

But, of course, it would be unfair just to single out farmers who profited out of the war. Many branches of industry were saved from extinction by the outbreak of the war and a number of industrial concerns, by the end of 1918, had made very fat profits indeed out of war contracts.

In Britain, the economic and social effects of the war were mainly determined by the Government's financial policy. To pay for the war it borrowed upon terms which, for most of the 1914–18 period, had become so inflationary that by the end of 1918 the purchasing power of the British people had been cut by over sixty per cent. As a result of loans to the Dominions and other allies and indebtedness to the United States it was confronted with a major financial crisis. 'By the end of 1919 such loans by the British

39

Government to other Governments totalled some £1,825 million, and its borrowing amounted to £1,340 million.'[4]

At the same time, apart from the massive loss of military equipment, a third of the British fleet had been sunk, and there were pensions and benefits to be paid to the millions of war-widows and war veterans.

The National Debt which stood at £1,105 million in the financial year 1914–15, escalated to £7,435 million four years later.

In the United States, just prior to the outbreak of war, the economy had slipped into decline and much of its industry was on the verge of stagnation. With the industrial countries of Europe unable to fulfil the needs of their normal trade around the world, the vacuum was eagerly filled by American manufacturers and farmers. The United States economy experienced a boom, the like of which was unparalleled in their history. Within three years steel production almost doubled and the gross national income had increased by 12,000 million dollars.

Until 1916 the United States had been trading with the belligerents of both sides. It was only when German submarines started sinking American ships and American citizens were losing their lives that United States public opinion began to swing away from isolationism. The Government's position of neutrality was being questioned.

Eventually, on the 2 April 1917, after an appeal to Congress by President Wilson, the American Government decided to join the Allies and four days later declared that it was at war with Germany. The trade vacuum in the Far East was in turn eagerly filled by Japanese manufacturers and shipbuilders, while in Latin America, the Argentine had been thriving on greatly increased exports of beef, canned meat products and cereals.

Of all the countries involved, it was Russia which provided the largest number of military personnel. Ill-equipped – often without rifles, boots and adequate clothing and meagre food rations – the Russian soldiers soon lost their will to fight. By the end of 1915, over four million Russians had been killed, maimed or taken prisoner. 'Cannon fodder', a term which was to become part of the international vocabulary, would not be an exaggeration to

40

describe the methods employed by the Tsarist generals in the feeding of their war machine. Their tactics were simple. They 'were to send their troops against the Germans in wave after wave in the hope that what could not be won in any other way could be won in sheer weight of numbers.'[5] The conscripted Russian workers and peasants were simply used as human battering rams.

It was not surprising therefore that the Russian soldiers fled from the front in their thousands. Army discipline had broken down. The transport system, the provision of military and civilian needs and the general economic life of the country had deteriorated into a state of utter chaos. The long queues for bread, milk, sugar and other bare necessities, often in the bitterest of weather, the carnage at the front, the Government's toleration of speculators and war profiteers, built up a hatred of the war and of the Tsarist administration even deeper than that in 1905.

By the middle of 1917, the Russian Army had suffered more killed and wounded than all the other Allied armies combined, after having mobilized close on fifteen million men.

The anti-war propaganda at the front, the poverty and deprivations in the towns, and increasing social and political awareness, initiated by the leaders of the Bolshevik Party, re-kindled the revolutionary fire which had been dampened during that early period.

The war of attrition produced nothing but mass slaughter, demoralization and despair. The cheapest commodity was human life. The French offensive launched on 14 August 1915 resulted in 300,000 casualties. The battles around Verdun, the Somme and Ypres cost the Allies and Central Powers combined over two million killed and wounded, and the four month slaughter around Passchendaele in 1917 resulted in 400,000 British casualties alone. German losses were put at 270,000.

Frank Owen in his book, *Tempestuous Journey*, reveals some of the crazy obsessions of British army leaders in their efforts to break down the military stalemate.

'To the yellow, slimy swamp of Passchendaele trudged a million British soldiers. The roads

41

across it were early smashed to rubble by the bombardment (24 million shells were poured there in a month) and buried beneath the oozing tide. Burdened with 60lb of "fighting kit" . . . Sodden to the skin, holding their rifles high above their heads to keep the mud clear of the magazines, stumbling in file along the slippery corduroy tracks, every one of which was ranged by the enemy's field batteries, mortars and machine-guns, and periodically scythed by his low-flying aircraft, the fine flower of the greatest army that Britain ever raised went resolutely up to death and mutilation and suffocation in the mud.'[6]

While this unprecedented slaughter of human beings was going on, Allied politicians, including Russian, were meeting to put their signatures to a number of secret pacts. The first was the Treaty of London, signed on 12 February 1915, by Sir Edward Grey, Britain's Foreign Minister, and Russia's Ambassador in London. Their two governments had secretly agreed that, once the war was over, Constantinople and the Dardanelles Straits would be placed under Russia's control, with a proviso that 'the aspirations of Great Britain and France in the Ottoman Empire as well as in other regions are realized.'

A month later, the French and Russian Governments entered into a similar agreement.

The London Treaty was also used to induce Italy to enter the war on the side of the Allies by promising her Istria, Dalmatia and the Southern Tyrol, which were then part of the Austro-Hungarian Empire, and Albania, a former Turkish colony, but independent only since 1912.

A further agreement was made on 9 May 1916 by Sir Mark Sykes of Britain and Georges Picot of France with the assent of Russia. It provided plans for a post-war dismemberment of the Ottoman Empire. Russia would acquire the Turkish occupied Armenian provinces and some Kurdish territory. France would acquire Lebanon and the coastal region of Syria, and Britain would take over Southern Mesopotamia and Palestine, including the ports of Haifa and Acre.

The war of attrition on the Western Front with its millions of casualties inevitably began to cause severe problems. There was an eruption of mutinies in the French army. Between May and June 1917, 115 French regiments had been affected.:

> 'the cry was peace, peace, down with the war, if anybody sang, it was not the "Marseillaise", it was the "Internationale". The form the mutiny took varied from unit to unit; whole battalions refused in some places to re-enter the front line ... Some groups planned a march on Paris; others simply deserted and went to live like vagabonds upon what they could find; some turned upon their officers.'[7]

The news of the mutinies was heavily censored although some information, and rumours, filtered through to the French public. In addition, there was considerable industrial unrest. The rapid increase in food prices and general living costs led to violent demonstrations and there were many strikes. This, together with the discontent in the army and the withdrawal of the French Socialists*, brought down the Painlevé Government and brought back the veteran Clemenceau as the new Prime Minister. In 1917 there were 696 strikes, involving close on 300,000 workers. By the end of 1917 the Union Sacrée had ceased to exist.

> 'As early as the Autumn of 1914, a handful of Syndicalist leaders, including the Secretary of the powerful Union des Métaux had protested against the collaboration of the Socialist Party in the Government of National Defence. During the following two years Socialists and Syndicalists in neutral states had begun to organize propaganda denouncing the "imperialist war" and calling for a speedy peace without indemnities and without annexations.'[8]

The conference of representatives of Socialist parties in the belligerent countries, which met in Zimmerwald,

---

*The Socialist Deputies withdrew from the Government in September 1917.

Switzerland, in the Autumn of 1915, issued a declaration that 'This war is not our war'. Although the delegates only represented the left-wing of their parties, the call from Zimmerwald had a stimulating effect upon many pacifists and left wing militants in their countries who were becoming increasingly active in opposition to the war.

By the end of 1916, 'it was significant that nearly half the delegates of the French Socialist Party's annual congress voted in favour of resuming relations with socialists in other (including enemy) countries, and that nearly half also opposed the continued participation of the socialists in the Government.'[9]

The cry from Zimmerwald that 'this war is not our war' was inevitably confirmed whenever soldiers in the belligerent countries returned home from the front and were able to see 'how many behind the lines were living in comfort and making handsome profits, while boasting of their patriotism.'[10]

In Germany most of the Socialist deputies were what the press and other forms of media describe in later years as 'moderates'.

> 'Men of the centre seeking the best of both worlds' who 'did their best to damp down the revolutionary feeling of the masses . . . at the same time in the interests of party unity' maintaining 'a facade of revolutionary respectability. Seeking the best of both worlds, they ended up getting the worst of both.'[11]

From 1913 onwards, much of German public opinion had been influenced by the philosophy put forward by General Bernhardi in his book, *Vom Heutigen Kriege**, which declared 'that war was a biological necessity and a convenient means of ridding the world of the unfit. These views were not confined to a lunatic fringe but won wide acceptance especially among journalists, academics and politicians.'[12] This was a convenient diversion exploited to mask the real

---

*'War of Today' – The Bernhardi philosophy reappeared and was put into practice some years later in the master race (herrenvolk) policies of Nazi Germany.

nature of Germany's war aims, for the Prussian landowners hoped to lay their hands on the rich agricultural areas of Poland and the Baltic countries, whilst the industrialists aimed to take over Belgium's coal and metallurgical industries.

By the autumn of 1916, German losses in killed, wounded and missing was over two and a half million. The German working class had begun to despair of ever seeing an end to the war, let alone victory. They had become increasingly critical of 'the ineffectiveness of many price controls, the growth of the black market and the ostentatious display of wealth by the new class of war profiteers'.[13]

There were sharp divisions within the German Parliamentary Socialist Party which led to a breakaway group. An independent Socialist Party committed to peace without any annexations of territory was established.*

From the very outset of the war, the Reichstag had played a very minor role in German affairs. 'It met at intervals largely to vote credits for the prosecution of the war', and when Karl Liebknecht and a colleague voted against the granting of War-Credits (in April 1915), they were supported by a group of thirty Socialist Deputies, who walked out of the Reichstag before voting took place, expressing the view that the war 'had ceased to be a war of self preservation and was being used by the Imperialists as a means of carrying out a widespread plan of Imperial conquest.'[14]

The Spartacus League, a forerunner of the German Communist Party was formed in January 1916 under the leadership of Karl Liebknecht and Rosa Luxemburg. It was the first to campaign against the war and to react militantly against the imperial war aims of Kaiser Wilhelm and his administrators. Although initially part of the Socialist Party, it eventually joined up with the Independent Socialists. Both Liebknecht and Rosa Luxemburg were imprisoned in 1916. In June of that year there was an outbreak of strikes in the Metallurgical industries, the first of many that were to continue in the years to follow. Those remaining in the Parliamentary Socialist Party – the Majority Socialists

---

*Seventeen members of the Socialist Party broke away in the Spring of 1916.

– continued to give their support to the prosecution of the war and the imperial aims that went with it.

The common denominator in all the belligerent countries was the colossal loss of life, the enormous military expenditure and the general misery and deprivations that were foisted upon the mass of ordinary people.

Beginning as a European conflict, it had developed into a global war. Homes, farms, towns and villages were destroyed under the cloak of patriotism and the defence of Empires, with millions of families broken up, never to be re-united.

Notes

1. PRICE, Morgan Phillips, *Germany in Transition,* p. 16
2. BROGAN, D.W., *The Development of Modern France,* p. 519
3. BROGAN, D.W., *The Development of Modern France,* p. 517–518
4. THOMSON, David, *England in the 20th Century,* p. 58
5. KNIGHTLEY, Phillip, *The First Casualty,* p. 139
6. OWEN, Frank, *Tempestuous Journey – Lloyd George His Life and Times,* p. 398
7. LOFTS, Norah and WIENER, Marjorie, *Eternal France, A History of France 1789–1944,* pp. 254–255
8. BURY, J.P.T., *France 1814–1940,* pp. 245–246
9. BURY, J.P.T., *France 1814–1940,* p. 246
10. BURY, J.P.T., *France 1814–1940,* p. 247
11. CARR, William, *A History of Germany 1815–1945,* p. 212
12. CARR, William, *A History of Germany 1815–1945,* p. 237
13. CARR, William, *A History of Germany 1815–1945,* p. 257
14. BITHELL, Jethro, *Germany – A Companion to German Studies,* pp. 116–117.

4

THE RUSSIAN REVOLUTION

In Tsarist Russia, the revolutionary cauldron that had been simmering ever since the eruptions in 1905 and 1906 blew up during the latter part of February 1917. As in previous years, it started in Petrograd.*

On 23 February there was a massive lock-out by the Petrograd employers of around 100,000 workers, many of whom had joined in a demonstration calling for an end to the war, food shortages and corruption. In the meantime, rioting had been going on around the long queues outside the bakers' shops. The next day nearly 200,000 workers came out on strike, followed by further demonstrations. On this occasion the demonstrators included many sections of the middle class, government employees, teachers and students. On Sunday, 26 February, a regiment of the Imperial Guard mutinied and joined up with the demonstrators. They were followed by other units on the next day. One unit, the Volhynian Regiment, nevertheless, continued to obey orders and opened fire with machine-guns, killing forty of the demonstrators. However, by Tuesday of that week they too had joined the ranks of the mutineers.

On 27th, the factory and shopworkers of Moscow came out on strike and on 28 February there were massive demonstrations, reinforced by the presence of soldiers from various regiments in the Moscow vicinity.

The revolution then began to gather momentum and spread to other cities.

'In Nizhi-Novgorod thousands of workers gathered around the city Duma building ... After a speech from the

*Petrograd, formerly St Petersburg.

Mayor the workers marched off with red banners to free the politicals from the jails. By evening, eighteen out of the twenty-one military divisions of the garrison had voltuntarily come over to the revolution.'[1]

By 28 February, the Tsarist administration had lost control of its capital city. Their instructions to dissolve the State Duma were ignored and a provisional committee was set up composed mainly of Mensheviks, Socialist Revolutionaries, the Right Wing Cadets and Liberals. Leading Bolsheviks, including Lenin, were either abroad or in exile.

On 2 March the discredited Tsarist regime came to an end. Tsar Nicholas was forced to abdicate and a new provisional Government took over from the Duma Committee. At the same time a Petrograd Soviet was elected, dominated by Socialist Revolutionaries and Mensheviks.

After the February revolution leaders of the Bolshevik Party were able, for the first time, to carry out their work openly. Under the Tsarist regime they had been compelled to go underground or go abroad. The Party was illegal and all their publications had been banned. Nevertheless it had continued to operate. The banned publications were read and had influenced Russian workers, soldiers and others in various walks of life.

On 17 April, Lenin, who had been living in Switzerland, returned to Russia after many years in exile. The significance of his return was reflected in the tumultuous reception that he received on arrival in Petrograd. On the following day he presented his famous April Theses in which he set out the type of revolution which he believed the country should follow. The Theses were founded upon the links between the revolution and the war, the development of capitalism in the twentieth century, and of Imperialism. They provided the guide-lines for converting the Bourgeois Revolution into a Socialist Revolution.

On his arrival in Petrograd, the membership of the Bolshevik Party was no more than 45,000. According to the *History of the Communist Party of the Soviet Union*:

> 'Lenin was not calling for a revolt against the Provisional Government, which at that moment enjoyed the confidence of the Soviets, that he was not demanding its overthrow, but that he wanted,

by means of explanatory and recruiting work to win a majority in the Soviets, to change the policy of the Soviets, and through the Soviets to alter the composition and policy of the Government.

This was a line envisaging the peaceful development of the Revolution.'[2]

A national congress of Soviets was held in June, with the Socialist Revolutionaries gaining 285 representatives, the Mensheviks 245 and the Bolsheviks 105.

John Reed, the American journalist, who had been covering the events in Russia during the latter part of 1917, has described how the Menshevik and Socialist Revolutionaries in their belief 'that Russia was not economically ripe for a social revolution' and that it 'must pass through the stages of political and economic development known to Western Europe' had 'insisted upon the collaboration of the propertied classes in the Government. From this,' said Reed, 'it was an easy step in supporting them' and 'so it resulted in the Socialist Ministers being obliged to give way, little by little, on their entire programme, while the propertied classes grew more and more insistent,' until in the end, 'the Mensheviki and Socialist Revolutionaries found themselves fighting on the side of the propertied classes.'[3]

At the same time, the Russian people's earnest desire for an end to the war had been ignored. The Provisional Government, mindful of the secret treaties, already referred to, and of the economic dependence upon Allied financial assistance, especially French, obstinately clung to the belief that if it continued to provide armies for the Allied war effort, it might eventually receive its share of the winner's spoils, as agreed to in the Treaty of London.

The Bolsheviks, from the very outset of the February revolution, reiterated their opposition to the war which they had attacked ever since August 1914.

When Milyakov, the Provisional Government's Foreign Minister, reaffirmed to the Allies in May 1917 that Russia would continue its prosecution of the war, the news created a furore in the streets of Petrograd. Milyakov was forced to resign and the Government was brought down, but only to the extent of a re-shuffle which kept the same Prime Minister, Prince Lvov, and brought in Alexander Kerensky as the new Minister for War. As has often happened in more recent times, a change of government does not necessarily imply a change of policy. Kerensky continued where Milyakov left off. The new Government also took measures to try and curb the influence of the Bolsheviks. But without success. On 18 June, in Petrograd, nearly 400,000 people demonstrated against the war.

Since taking office, Kerensky had been presiding over the preparations for a massive offensive which was to be launched in July. He toured the fronts in attempts to whip up what he believed were dormant patriotic feelings. The offensive was an utter failure, and ultimately brought about the end of the Government's war policy.

On 17 July there was an even larger demonstration of workers and soldiers in the streets of Petrograd, demanding an end to the war. This was quickly suppressed on instructions from the Provisional Government. Tsarist officers, directing their fire into the crowd, killed over 400 people. Mensheviks and Socialist Revolutionaries, in co-operation with White Guard officers, thereupon seized the opportunity of wrecking the premises of the Bolshevik Party and, in particular, the printing presses of *Pravda* and other Bolshevik publications.

Warrants were issued for the arrest of the Bolshevik leaders, who had to go into hiding or seek refuge abroad. Lenin escaped to Finland. Meanwhile Kerensky had taken over as Prime Minister.

Forced once again to go underground the Bolsheviks, nevertheless, managed to hold their 6th Party Congress in secret from 8 to 16 August. Lenin, although still in hiding, was elected chairman and through the ingenuity of close associates was able to direct the proceedings. The Congress called for the preparation of an armed insurrection.

Support for the Bolsheviks was rapidly gaining ground, and by the end of September they had achieved an overall majority in the Petrograd Soviet. With majorities in most of the Trade Unions and in the Moscow Soviet, membership of the Party had increased during the summer months to nearly 250,000.

Realizing that existing army units in Petrograd could not be relied upon General Kornilov, who had just been appointed Commander-in-Chief, decided to reorganize the garrison by drafting into the capital reliable military personnel. However, the plan failed to materialize for the troops did not even reach their destination. They mutinied en route, refused to accept orders from their officers and set up their own Councils with the help of members of the Petrograd Soviet.

On 23 October, Lenin, who had secretly returned from Finland, and the leaders of the Bolshevik Central Committee decided that the time had come to implement their plans for the armed uprising. They were carried out on 7 November. The Bolsheviks, backed by most of the army in the Petrograd area and the crew of the battle cruiser, *Aurora*, which was at hand nearby, with its guns trained on the Winter Palace, stormed into the Palace and arrested most of the Provisional Government's ministers. Bolshevik supporters at the telephone exchange, the central post office and the key railway stations had completely paralysed the functions of the Kerensky administration. By nightfall, Petrograd, Russia's capital and seat of government had passed over to the control of the Bolshevik Party. Kornilov was arrested, but Kerensky managed to escape to the United States. Other Tsarist generals were arrested, but were soon afterwards released on parole.*

The Manchester Guardian's correspondent, Morgan Phillips Price,† in his account of the fall of the Provisional Government states that:

'The Government of Kerensky fell before the Bolshevik insurgents because it had no supporters in the country. The bourgeois parties and the generals and the staff disliked it because it would not establish a military dictatorship. The Revolutionary Democracy lost faith in it because after

---

*'The parole was promptly broken in the case of Generals like Krasnov and Dutov who did not believe in keeping faith to the 'canaille' [rabble] for they did not regard it as a matter of honour to keep their word given to the lower classes.' (ARNOT, R. Page, *The Impact of the Russian Revolution in Britain*, p. 85).
†He was afterwards replaced by a less objective correspondent, and joined the *Daily Herald* in 1919 as their correspondent in Germany.

eight months it had neither given land to the peasants, nor established State control of industry, nor advanced the call of the Russian peace programme. Instead it brought off the July advance without any guarantees that the Allies had agreed to reconsider war aims ... The Bolsheviks thus acquired great support all over the country.' (*Manchester Guardian*, 20 November 1917)

The following day, 8 November, after an all night sitting of the Second Congress of Soviets, foundations for a socialist Russia were laid. Two historic decrees were adopted that night. One on peace and the other dealing with the ownership of land. The decree on peace was presented by Lenin and it declared that:

'The Workers' and Peasants' government, ... proposes to all belligerent peoples and their governments the immediate opening of negotiations for a just and democratic peace ... '
' ... By such a peace the government understands an immediate peace without annexations (i.e. without seizure of foreign territory, without forcible incorporation of foreign nationalities) and without indemnities ... '
'... The government considers it the greatest crime against humanity to continue this war for the sake of dividing among the powerful and wealthy nations the weaker nationalities which they have conquered.'

Lenin then dropped his bombshell. The secret treaties, he said, concluded by the Tsarist administration and endorsed by the Provisional Governments of Lvov and Kerensky will be published in full. Furthermore, he declared that the new government

'... denounces absolutely and immediately all the provisions of these treaties, designed as they were in the majority of cases, to secure profit and

privileges for Russian landowners and capitalists
. . .'

'The provisional Workers' and Peasants' government of Russia appeals also in particular to the class conscious workers of the three mightiest states taking part in the present war – England, France and Germany' who, 'by their resolute and vigorous activity will help us to bring to a successful end the cause of peace, and, together with this, the cause of the liberation of all who labour and are exploited from every kind of slavery and exploitation.'[4]

The Decree dealing with the tenure of land set out proposals for the abolition of all landed estates without compensation. The landed estates which included those belonging to the Crown and Church, together with their properties, were to be handed over to the control of the land committees and to the representatives of the local Soviets and peasants. In future, ownership of land was to be taken over by the State or public authorities. However, the decree emphasized that 'The land of ordinary peasants and ordinary cossacks shall not be confiscated.'

In addition, it was proclaimed that all nations within greater Russia would have a 'genuine right to self determination' and that capital punishment in the army which had been re-introduced by Kerensky in July would be abolished.

Out of this Congress was formed the first Soviet Government, with the election of Lenin as Chairman. The government became known officially as the Council of Peoples' Commissars.

From then on the revolution began to spread rapidly throughout the whole country.

The secret treaties were published in *Izvestia*, the organ of the National Council of Soviets, and *Pravda*, the organ of the Bolshevik Party, on 23 November 1917. The following excerpts relating to those treaties concluded in 1915 and 1916 were quoted in the *Manchester Guardian* on 12 December 1917 which highlighted the planned carve-up of Turkey's Ottoman Empire and of the countries of the Middle East and Asia Minor.

'The (Russian) Imperial Government completely shares the view of the British Government that the holy Moslem places must (also) in future remain under an independent Moslem rule. It is desirable to elucidate at once whether it is contemplated to leave those places under the rule of Turkey, the Sultan retaining the title of Caliph, or to create new independent states, since the Imperial Government would only be able to formulate its desires in accordance with one or other of these assumptions. On its part the Imperial Government would regard the separation of the Caliphate from Turkey as very desirable. Of course the freedom of pilgrimage must be completely secured.'

'The Imperial Government confirms its assent to the inclusion of the neutral zone of Persia in the British sphere of influence. At the same time, however, it regards it as just to stipulate that the districts adjoining the cities of Ispahan and Yezd, forming with them one inseparable whole, should be secured for Russia in view of Russian interests which have arisen there. The neutral zone now forms a wedge between the Russian and Afghan frontiers, and comes up to the very frontier line of Russia at Tulgager. Hence a portion of this wedge will have to be annexed to the Russian sphere of influence. Of essential importance to the Imperial Government is the question of railway construction in the neutral zone, which will require further amicable discussion.'

'Towards the end of 1916 the British Foreign Office had privately elaborated proposals for "the creation of a Polish Kingdom" which would include much of the Polish population then within Germany as well as the Silesian coalfields and would be ruled by a member of the Russian Royal Family – "under a Russian Grand Duke".'[5]

The carving of the Ottoman Empire, under the Treaty of London Agreement 1915, and the Sykes-Picot Agreement, a year later, included the portioning out of Constantinople and the Dardenelles Straits to Imperial Russia, most of Mesopotamia, (now Iraq) and Palestine to Britain, and Syria and the Lebanon to France.

Suspicions about the imperial nature of World War I were now being confirmed, and the revelations created quite a stir in the belligerent countries.

No sooner had the Soviet Government announced its plans for peace and disclosed the contents of the secret treaties, than a rigid censorship was imposed by the belligerent governments upon all news emanating from Russia 'which took a line different from that of their governments'. The handful of Journalists 'who did realize the impact the revolution would have on world affairs' and who tried conscientiously to report what was going on in Russia 'were silenced – by the censor or some other authority. The others made little effort to see beyond what they were told to see. They accepted as fact not only the propaganda of their own governments, but also the obviously suspect reports of the Czarist agencies in exile.'[6]

When the Soviet Government announced plans to nationalize the Banks, the Railways, the Merchant Fleet and all the major branches of industry, a rumour, which originated in the United States, was circulated through the press soon afterwards that the Bolsheviks were planning to introduce the 'nationalization of women'.

Phillip Knightley in his book, *The First Casualty*, has shown how sectors of the news media have deliberately falsified or distorted the news over many years. Referring to the 'gross misinformation' of news about the new Soviet Russia, Knightley says that 'one of the main reasons was a growing apprehension as to the nature of bolshevism which encouraged wishful thinking about its early demise. As details of Lenin's new social order filtered through to the West, the first signs appeared of the strong anti-Bolshevik sentiment that was soon to become fanatical ... So when the delegates at the Soviet Congress spoke of the "coming world revolution of which we are the advanced guard", *The Times* responded with an editorial saying "The Remedy for Bolshevism is Bullets", and *The Times* readers began to regard the Bolsheviks as a gang of murderers, thieves and blasphemers whom it was almost a sacred duty to destroy as vermin.'[7]

'Lenin's revolutionary decrees were still being announced', says Knightley, 'when the British Secret Intelligence Service (SIS) sent its first agents into Russia with the express aim of overthrowing the Bolsheviks. They were involved in an abortive plot to assassinate Lenin.' Lenin was shot* by Dora Kaplan, a Socialist Revolutionary. The assassination was planned to concide with 'risings in Moscow and Petrograd organized by the notorious spy Sydney Reilly.' The plot nearly succeeded. Lenin was shot twice but, although critically wounded, just managed to survive. 'There was soon in existence an S.I.S. dining circle called BOLO (for Bolshevik Liquidation Club).' Churchill's dream of 'strangling Bolshevism at birth' was no idle fantasy. It was taken very seriously indeed by 'at least one section of the Allies.'[8]

Although thousands of German, Austro-Hungarian and other troops of the Central Powers were in occupation of large tracts of their territory, the Soviet leaders had no alternative but to negotiate the best terms that could be obtained in the given circumstances. From the very outset, Lenin had insisted that their most urgent need was 'breathing space'. Time to tackle the immediate threats of famine, counter revolution and civil war; to build their own army as quickly as possible and to proceed with the construction of a new country, founded upon their own 'blue-print' or Socialism. To achieve this 'breathing space', he was prepared to pay almost any price, if only temporarily. The Bolshevik leaders knew that there was increasing international working class sympathy for their cause, especially in Germany, and a general war-weariness and desire for social change in all the belligerent countries.

There were reports of riots in both Germany and Austria over shortages of bread and other basic foods. In January 1918, strikes and anti-war demonstrations had broken out in Austria, and in Hungary a state of emergency had led the Government to requisition food supplies, creating severe disturbances in some of the provincial areas. Disaffection had by now spread to the armed forces, and on 1 February

*31 August 1918.

there was a mutiny in the Austro-Hungarian Navy.

It was also known that the Austrians were desperately anxious to get corn from the Ukraine by the Spring. But to Lenin, these factors were heavily outweighed by the situation as it was in November and December 1917, and not what it might be some months hence.

On 30 November 1917 Trotsky, the Soviet Foreign Minister, announced the end of all military operations on the Russian Front, just two days after the German acceptance of the Soviet proposals for the conclusion of an Armistice.

The headquarters of the German Eastern Front High Command was in Brest-Litovsk, a town near the Polish and Russian borders and it was there, on 20 December 1917, that a Soviet delegation opened negotiations with the representatives of Germany and other Central Powers.

During the initial stages the Soviet representatives put forward six points which incorporated two main conditions. Firstly, there must be 'No Annexations' and 'No Indemnities' and secondly, the negotiations must be held in public. The latter was accepted by the Central Powers, but their spokesmen were careful at this stage to 'side-step' any commitment to the Soviet demands concerning annexation and indemnities. The German Government chose instead to interpret the plea for non-annexation of such areas as Lithuania and Ukraine as a recognition of their desire for independence, but under German protection. The Soviet representatives requested an adjournment and there was a recess to enable them to consider the German conditions. Negotiations were resumed on 9 January; but this time the Germans took a much tougher stand and laid out their terms. They had decided to extend their frontiers to include Lithuania and Western Latvia, most of Poland, and included an arrangement with an independent Ukraine which would come within their protection.

The talks were once again adjourned but on this occasion Trotsky, on Lenin's initiative, was instructed by the Council of Commissars to take charge of the negotiations and to drag them out for as long as possible. In view of the Bolsheviks' weak negotiating position he was instructed to sign a Peace Treaty should the Germans resort to issuing an ultimatum. On resuming the talks, the German delegation immediately pressed the matter of a separate peace. Their demands, followed by Trotsky's report to the Council, created a serious split in the Bolshevik leadership, the majority of whom believed they could still challenge the Germans and continue the fighting until the workers of Germany and Austria took over their countries and threw out the imperial leaders. Lenin nevertheless remained steadfast in his belief that they had no option but to get out of the war immediately and use the 'breathing-space' to avert famine and civil war, and strengthen their political and military base as quickly as possible. The building of their own army, the Red Army, became the number one priority. Lenin warned his committee colleagues that 'Germany is only pregnant with revolution . . . The second month must not be mistaken for the ninth. But here in Russia we have a healthy, lusty child. We may kill it if we start a war.'[9]

The opening up of the Brest-Litovsk peace talks to the whole world inevitably created an increased awareness of the imperialistic nature of the war. Questions were being raised not only in the belligerent countries but also in the United States of America about the war aims of the belligerent governments. Reports of the open discussions were commented on by United States President Woodrow Wilson during his presentation to Congress on 7 January 1918, of his Fourteen Points which dealt with matters relating to the aims of war and peace, and a proposal for a League of Nations to guarantee the independence and sovereignty of its member states. Wilson praised the Soviet representatives who, he said, 'have insisted very justly, very wisely, and in the true spirit of modern democracy, that the conferences they have been holding with the Teutonic and Turkish statesmen, should be held within open, not closed doors. And all the world has been audience, as was desired. . . . Moreover', said Wilson, 'there is a voice calling for these definitions of principle and of purpose . . . It is the voice of the Russian people.' (*The Manchester Guardian*, 9 January 1918)

Within the Fourteen Points the American President included his famous 'Acid Test' – point six – which called for 'the evacuation of all Russian territory and such settlements of all questions affecting Russia as will secure the best and freest co-operation of the other nations of the world in obtaining for her an unembarrassed and unhampered opportunity for the independent determination of her political development and national policy, and assure her of a sincere welcome into the society of free nations under institutions of her own choosing; and, more than a welcome, assistance also of every kind that she may need and may herself desire. The treatment accorded Russia by her sister nations in the months to come will be the acid test of their goodwill, of their appreciation of her needs as distinguished from their own interests, and of their intelligent and unselfish sympathy.'

Although President Wilson's 'Acid Test' on its face value appeared sympathetic to the enormous problems that faced Soviet Russia, he nevertheless made little effort to convince the Allies that Russia was in no position to continue the war. According to Colonel House, Wilson's roving Ambassador, the President was anxious to secure from the Allies a 'manifesto on war aims that might serve to hold Russia in the war and result in an effective diplomatic offensive against the Central Powers.'[10] This he failed to achieve and the United States, faced with the decision of the Soviet Government to withdraw Russian forces from the war; the attack on its shipping by German submarines, and the heavy commercial interests, which were far greater within the Allied countries than in Germany and the other Central Powers, eventually joined in the war to tip the balance of forces in favour of the Allies.

It became quite clear that the Allies had no intention of recognizing the Soviet Government as the legitimate representative of the Russian people. To maintain contacts, yes, but diplomatic recognition, that was quite out of the question. They were '"willing to reconsider their war aims in conjunction with Russia", as soon as she had a stable government with whom they could act.'[11]

Meanwhile, an Anglo-French 'Spheres of Influence' Convention, held in Paris on 23 December 1917, adopted proposals in a British Government memorandum which was to assure the Bolsheviks, 'that we have no desire to take part in any way in the internal politics of Russia, and that any idea that we favour a counter-revolution is a profound mistake. Such a policy might be attractive to the autocratic Governments of Germany and Austria but not to the Western democracies or America.'

The document then went on to recommend

'that we should continually repeat our readiness to accept the principle of self-determination and subject to that, of no annexations or indemnities.'

While the Allies were trying to convince the Soviet leaders of their honourable intentions, plans were being put into operation to supply

'money to reorganize the Ukraine, to pay the Cossacks and the Caucasian forces and to subsidize the Persians.'

The memorandum, which was accepted as the basis of future Allied policy towards Soviet Russia, then emphasized the importance of having

'agents and officers to advise and support provincial governments and their armies. It is essential' it declared 'that this should be done as quietly as possible, so as to avoid imputation – as far as we can – that we are preparing to make war on the Bolsheviks.'[12]

History has invariably shown that actions speak louder than words. This kind of duplicity and double talk justifiably confirmed the suspicions of the Bolshevik leaders. Wilson's 'Acid Test' did nothing to sweeten the atmosphere. Plans for intervention went ahead, together with a series of back stage manoeuvres to entice the Americans to join in the anti-Bolshevik crusade.

When Trotsky returned to Brest-Litovsk to resume the peace talks, the Central Committee had agreed to give his

'No War, No Peace' policy a chance. The aim appeared to be a policy of spinning the talks out as long as possible as an aid to Lenin's 'Breathing Space', while at the same time challenging the Central Powers to break the Armistice and invade, with the consequential effects upon public opinion, not only in Germany and Austria, but also in the Allied countries. It was a desperate gamble and it misfired. Trotsky refused to sign on the German terms, stating that his Government would, in spite of German threats, continue to demobilize their own forces. On 10 February 1918, he broke off the talks and returned to Petrograd. On 16 February the Germans threatened to end the Armistice within forty-eight hours unless their terms were accepted. And on the 18th, massed divisions of German troops moved into Russia. 'Later that night, after hours of argument', an emergency meeting of the Central Committee, 'agreed by only one vote, seven to six, to surrender.' Lenin signed the telegram of surrender just one hour before the ultimatum expired. 'But the Germans were in no hurry to stop their advance. For five days they swept on, covering 150 miles and capturing over 2,000 guns, thousands of prisoners and most damaging of all, hundreds of motor vehicles, railway locomotives and trucks.'[13]

A harsh lesson had been dealt to Trotsky and a group within the Central Committee through the logic of Lenin's policy. The gamble had only served to whet the imperial appetites of the German Government and their High Command.

The Treaty of Brest-Litovsk* was signed on 3 March 1918. Under the terms of the treaty, Russia had to concede Poland, Lithuania, Latvia, Estonia and some islands in the Baltic. She had to recognize the independence of the Ukraine, which was at the time under the control of a German backed puppet administration – the Ukrainian Rada (Council), as well as that of Finland and Georgia (which still had troops on its soil). The overall result was that Russia lost 32% of her agricultural land, 34% of her population, 54% of her industry, 90% of her coalmines and

---

*The Treaty was abrogated by both the Soviets and the Allies when the Armistice was signed on 11 November 1918.

84% of her best sugar producing areas. She was cut off from the Black Sea and from most of the Baltic. In addition, she had to pay an indemnity of 6,000 million marks in gold.

The revelation of the harshness of the Brest-Litovsk terms aroused bitter hostility from the German workers towards their government and High Command. Basil Davidson, the British journalist, in his book *Germany, What Now?*, apportions blame to the 'Social Democrats in the Reichstag', whom he said, 'did not utter one word of condemnation of the terms of Brest-Litovsk. They were persuaded – that what was good for Imperial Germany was good for Europe' and 'that what was good for the German monopolies was good for them.'[14]

The Soviet Government had provided a golden opportunity for both the Allied and Central Power governments to sit round the conference table and bring this murderous war of attrition, which neither side looked like winning, to an end. Instead, although the Central Powers still retained over a million soldiers on the Eastern Front, most of whom were still in Russia, the German High Command, nevertheless, was still able to transfer forty divisions from this area for operations on the Western Front.

Despite the hostility of the German workers, the demonstrations and the massive strikes against it, in which over a million workers were involved, the Brest-Litovsk Treaty was passed in the Reichstag by a large majority. 'Only the Independent Socialists voted against it. Even the Majority Socialists abstained. Scheidermann [Majority Socialist leader] admitted that the treaty was probably incompatible with true self-determination but declared bluntly that the party could not vote against a treaty bringing peace. In reality the abstention was a tactical manoeuvre to disguise the fact that the party was divided and that some members were ready to vote for the treaty.'[15]

Britain's Prime Minister, Lloyd George, was fully aware of the effect the war was having upon the workers and soldiers in all the belligerent countries, including his own, when he admitted that 'the squeezing process in Germany of the last few months of the war was driving tens of thousands into desertion and ere many months passed it drove hundreds of thousands into rebellion which overthrew the throne. Some of the more powerful Trade Unions were showing signs of becoming resistant to the pressure for combing out more of their men for the front.'[16] Most of his observations could have included France, where opposition to the war had spread to the army. Reports of mutinies in sixteen divisions were recorded, and in Italy the majority of the population had from the very outset opposed their country being dragged into what they regarded as somebody else's war.

Lloyd George recalls how the 'determination to make peace on the basis of "no annexations and no indemnities" was also having its effect on public opinion amongst a considerable section of the industrial population in Britain and France' and how the 'attitude of the Workers' Government in Russia was having a very disturbing effect on the artisans in our workshops.'[17]

This, together with the steep rise in the cost of living and the shortage of many basic foods, was beginning to undermine the general support which the majority of the British people had been giving to the coalition war-time government. Winston Churchill, who in 1917 was Minister of Munitions, urged the Government to issue a statement which would effectively counter the influence that the Russian revolution was having upon the workers of Britain's munition factories.

This was at a time when the British and French Governments were secretly preparing plans to abort the Russian revolution by military intervention, and by aiding and abetting the counter-revolutionary forces.

Notes

1. TROTSKY, Leon, *The History of the Russian Revolution*, Vol. I, p. 155
2. *History of the Communist Party of the Soviet Union*, p. 186
3. REED, John, *Ten Days That Shook the World*, Preface
4. *Soviet Documents on Foreign Policy* Vol. I 1917–1924 (ed. Jane Degras), pp. 1–2
5. ARNOT, R. Page, *The Impact of the Russian Revolution in Britain*, p. 111
6. KNIGHTLEY, Phillip, *The First Casualty*, p. 138
7. KNIGHTLEY, Phillip, *The First Casualty*, p. 149
8. KNIGHTLEY, Phillip, *The First Casualty*, p. 151
9. SILVERLIGHT, J., *The Victors' Dilemma*, p. 21

10. *The Intimate Papers of Colonel House* (arranged as narrated by Charles Seymour), p. 324
11. KENNAN, George, *Soviet-American Relations – 1917–1921*, p. 137
12. LLOYD GEORGE, David, *War Memoirs*, Vol. V, pp. 2582–5
13. SILVERLIGHT, J., *The Victors' Dilemma*, p. 20
14. DAVIDSON, Basil, *Germany, What Now?*, p. 123
15. CARR, William, *A History of Germany (1815–1945)*, p. 264
16. LLOYD GEORGE, David, *War Memoirs*, Vol. V, pp. 2648–9
17. LLOYD GEORGE, David, *The Truth About the Peace Treaties*, Vol. I, pp. 66–67.

5

THE WARS OF INTERVENTION

Three and a half years of a murderous war and all the deprivations that went with it had considerably reduced the manifestations of nationalist fervour which had been so prevalent in 1914 and 1915. The Russian Revolution, a Bolshevik Government, and now the official withdrawal of the Russian army had created an entirely new political situation and the opening of a new era. The old imperial and feudal regimes were beginning to crumble, not only in Russia, but in other European countries. No sooner had the Soviets announced their proposals for an armistice than the Allied Governments began to prepare public opinion to acquiesce to their policy of intervention. 'The newspapers were loud in their condemnation of Russia's treachery in leaving the Allies faced with a Germany freed from Russian pressure on the Eastern Front . . . So intervention was justified at the beginning on the grounds of the German peril.'[1]

Morgan Phillips Price, the *Manchester Guardian*'s Foreign correspondent, was one of the few British journalists who had tried to report, honestly and objectively, the historic events that were happening at that time. In his book, *My Three Revolutions*, he recalls that 'a conspiracy of silence had been decided on about the War of Intervention which the Western Allies were waging against Soviet Russia. Only reports favourable to the intervention were allowed and these were being retailed extensively in the press of Lord Northcliffe and Horatio Bottomley.'[2]*

---

*Horatio Bottomley was sent to prison in the twenties for fraud and corruption.

65

Once the armistice was signed (11 November 1918) and the war was over, justification for military intervention by the Allies became more difficult. They were in need of a pretext. A pretext, moreover, which would influence President Wilson and American public opinion that intervention was the way to save Western civilization.

On 1 January 1918 there was a meeting of the British Cabinet; among the points raised was the matter of 600,000 tons of Allied stores lying idle in Vladivostok. The meeting was just a few days after a report had come in of 'Bolshevik atrocities against the inhabitants of Irkutsk' an important town in Western Siberia, astride the trans-Siberian railway. The substance of the report 'later turned out to be false.'[3] Vivid details were circulated of how 'the Bolsheviks were bombarding the town, murdering and plundering inhabitants, raping women, killing children . . . Severe fighting in the town had taken place and some foreigners may have been hurt; none were killed.'[4]

The true facts were not known until many weeks later. But the report arrived at a very convenient time. It fitted in nicely with the rumours about the safety of Allied prisoners of war in Russia, and fears about losing the 600,000 tons of stores in Vladivostok. As a result of the Cabinet discussions, a telegram was sent through the British Ambassador to President Wilson, urging him to consider their proposal to join with them in landing an expeditionary force in the Far East to protect Allied supplies and commercial interests. A week later 'the French Ambassador told the Americans that in view of Bolshevik atrocities in Irkutsk, they were considering sending in an expeditionary force to protect French citizens, support those groups "that have remained true to the cause of the Entente", secure the use of the Trans-Siberian railway in order to help the forces in South Russia, and to protect the supplies at Vladivostok.'[5]

The Anglo-French appeal failed to move the American President at that time. He remained firmly against United States involvement in Allied plans for intervention, but the pressure to make him change his mind nevertheless continued. The initial stage of the Allied plan was to back and encourage the Russian counter-revolutionary groups with arms, money and anti-Soviet propaganda. The next was to entice the Japanese to land troops in Siberia as part of an overall plan to put pressure on Wilson and the US Congress, by exploiting the fear of Japanese expansionism in the Far East.

Colonel House has given an indication of some of the subtle steps that were used to make President Wilson change his mind

> 'The British Government considers that it is neces
> sary
> for the Allies to unite in order to bring about a
> Russian national revival, in order to adopt a pol-
> icy of freeing Russia from foreign control by means
> of Allied intervention. The Allies must, of course,
> avoid taking sides in Russian politics.'[6]

Lloyd George suggested that if President Wilson feared Japanese support of reactionary forces in Russia, he should join the Allies in the Far East in their intervention and

> 'dominate its developments . . . If, finally, Wilson
> was ready to send an important political mission
> to Siberia I would certainly see that a Liberal or
> Labour representative from this country accom-
> panied it.'[7]

What apparently clinched President Wilson's support were the sensational reports of 'Red atrocities' and their effect upon American public opinion.

Valdivostok in 1917 had a population of around 350,000. It was, and still is today, one of the most important commercial and naval ports in the Far East. Founded by Tsarist Russia in 1860, it became Russia's chief seaport and naval base in the Pacific ocean. At the beginning of this century its commercial importance was greatly enhanced when it became the eastern terminus of the newly con-structed Trans-Siberian railway.

The value of the strategic importance of Vladivostok was therefore not lost upon political leaders and service chiefs in those countries which believed in the strangulation of Bolshevism at birth. Vladivostok was, after all, Russia's main 'back door', a gateway into Siberia, and the great natural wealth which had yet to be fully exploited.

It did not need a great deal of encouragement from Britain and France to entice Japan, whose northern island was only about 180 miles from Vladivostok, to ally itself to their plans for intervening in the Russian civil war. Ever since the Russo-Japanese war in 1904–5, Japanese commercial and military expansionism in the Far East had been steadily going ahead.

Towards the end of March 1918 the struggle between the pro-Bolshevik forces and the counter-revolutionary elements in the Far East had been reaching a climax. In the Vladivostock area the Bolsheviks were beginning to get the upper hand. 'The fact that the Bolsheviks had not yet taken over was due in the main to the presence of four warships lying off the town; two Japanese cruisers, the British Cruiser HMS *Suffolk* . . . and the American Crusier USS *Brooklyn*.'[8]

The significance of this gun boat diplomacy was soon to be realized when on 4 April 1918 two Japanese clerks who were employed in a Japanese controlled shipping office, were murdered by masked gunmen. On the following day, without making any attempt to investigate the matter, the Japanese Naval Commander in the area seized upon the incident as a pretext for landing his marines to safeguard Japanese citizens and property. Whereupon the British Government decided that it too had property to protect and proceeded to exploit the situation by landing fifty marines from HMS *Suffolk*.

At that time there were in Russia some 45,000–50,000 Czecho-Slovak prisoners of war and deserters from the Austrian army. Through the initiative of Dr Thomas A. Masaryk and with help from the Allies they were kept together and formed into an independent volunteer Czecho-Slovak army.

Masaryk was a professor of Philosophy and before 1914 had been a prominent member of the small Czech Party in the Austrian Parliament. His main objective was national independence for the Czecho-Slovak people. In 1916 he went to France and with French encouragement helped to establish a Czecho-Slovak national Council. It was not until the overthrow of the Russian provisional Government in

November 1917 that Masaryk and his colleagues in the National Council were faced with their first major dilemma. The greater part of the Czecho-Slovak army was stationed around Kiev and there was a restlessness among its troops to get out of Russia and either join the Allied forces on the Western Front or go home. They were aware that the Soviet Government had declared its neutrality and had taken its army out of the Imperial War. Many senior officers in the Czecho-Slovak army were Russian – Tsarist and anti-Bolshevik – and after the November revolution had persistently tried to involve them in the civil war that had been raging in the Ukraine between the German backed Rada and the pro-Bolshevik forces. After Brest-Litovsk, the Czecho-Slovaks were brought under the control of high-ranking French officers.

On 26 March 1918, Soviet and Czecho-Slovak leaders, together with Colonel Vergé of France, representing the Entente, signed an agreement for the evacuation of the Czecho-Slovak troops to France via the Trans-Siberian railway and Vladivostock. Under the terms of the agreement, endorsed by Stalin, Commissar for Nationalities, the Czecho-Slovaks would be travelling armed 'not as fighting units, but as groups of free citizens, who carry with them a specified number of weapons for defence against counter-revolutionary attacks'.

According to W.H. Chamberlin's history of *The Russian Revolution*, 'Every train load of troops was to have with it an armed company of Czech soldiers to the number of 168 with one machine-gun. Three hundred bullets were to be allowed for every rifle, 1,200 for every machine-gun. The remainder of the arms were to be turned over to the Soviet authorities in Penza and some of the Russian officers were to be dismissed.'[9]

Tragically for the Czecho-Slovak troops, for the Russian people and Allied servicemen, neither the terms nor the spirit of the agreement was carried out. There was no surrender of any arms whatsoever.

Dr Benes, a leading member of the Czech National Council, had on 1 April 'received a message from the French military attaché to London expressing some doubts about the Czechoslovak army ever reaching Europe by the proposed route. The War Office in London had told the military attaché that there was a severe shortage of shipping facilities, and that if the army was a military factor at all it could operate best within Russia.'[10] The hint was not lost on Benes. He has recalled that the 'French military representatives, Vergé and Guinet*, who had received urgent telegrams from Paris, refused to guarantee the transport of the troops to France.'[11]

Morgan Phillips Price was under no illusion of what were to be the real functions of the Czech Legionaires. In his *Reminiscences of the Russian Revolution*, he records:

'After the November Revolution these volunteers were left high and dry, and two alternatives were before the French Mission. Either it could transfer the Czecho-Slovaks to the west front or else it could use them to suppress the Soviets and re-establish the east front.

'After examining all the evidence connected with the conflict between the Czecho-Slovak volunteers in Russia and the Soviet Government, I am convinced that the former were nothing more than unconscious tools of French militarism in the East, which was exploiting to its own advantages the strong anti-Austrian and patriotic sentiments of these Czecho-Slovak exiles.'

He submits as proof 'the fact that important documents, bearing on the relations between the Czecho-Slovak National Council and the Allies during the war, were discovered by the Extra-ordinary Commission for the Fight with the Counter-revolution in June 1918 in Moscow.' It was:

'After the seizure of Pensa and Tchelyabinsk† by the Czecho-Slovak Legions, the Soviet authorities searched the premises of the Moscow branch of

---

*Head of the French Military Mission attached to the Czecho-Slovak army in Russia.

†Strategic towns astride the Trans-Siberian railway.

the Czecho-Slovak National Council. In this bureau they found the correspondence which had been going on during 1917 and the first part of 1918, between President Masaryk, and Dr Maksa, President of the Moscow Czecho-Slovak National Council*. The correspondence disclosed the fact that during 1917 secret negotiations for a separate peace had been going on between the Allies and Austria with a view to secure the isolation of Germany. Austria was attempting to get, as one of the conditions of a separate peace, the recognition of the principle that CzechoSlovakia was an integral part of the Dual Monarchy. This news greatly alarmed the National Council in Paris and Moscow, for it was realized that this would jeopardize their hopes for the independence of Czecho-Slovakia. During the summer of 1917 Masaryk emphasized in communications with Maksa in Moscow that the situation in Paris was very dangerous for the future of Czecho-Slovakia, which was constantly on the point of being sacrificed by the Allies to plans of a separate peace with Austria. After the November Revolution the French Military Mission in Russia seems to have taken the initiative in opening negotiations with the Czecho-Slovak National Council. The French military agents in Russia knew that the independence of Czecho-Slovakia had not been definitely decided upon in Paris, because the hope of drawing Austria out of the Central Alliance was not yet abandoned. They therefore played upon this uncertainty and on the fears of the National Council in Moscow to levy blackmail on the Czecho-Slovak volunteers.'[12]

The November Revolution had completely altered the

---

*The author says that he had 'read a summary of this correspondence in December 1919 when the material was about to be brought forward at the trial in Prague for high treason of the Czech Communist leader in Russia, Muna. The trial, however, never took place and Muna was released on political considerations. The full texts were never brought before the public.' (Morgan Phillips Price, FN, p. 291)

financial status of the Czecho-Slovak volunteer army. Having previously been financed by the Russian Provisional Government, it had now become financially dependent upon the Allies and in particular France. The Czecho-Slovak National Council received eleven million roubles through the French Consul in Moscow and £80,000 from the British. 'The money was paid to members of the National Council, M. Shiep and M. Bogumiltchermak, and through their hands it went to the commanders of the Czecho-Slovak detachments in various part of Russia.'[13]

Meanwhile, propaganda had been carefully dispensed for the Czecho-Slovak troops by the French Military Mission. They were told that 'the Soviet Government had refused to allow them to return to France, and was about to deliver them to the Austrian military authorities, who would hang them all as deserters.'[14] Cut off from the outside world, the Czecho-Slovaks had thus become easy prey for rumours and propaganda. Their suspicions were further aroused by rumours 'that the Soviets were arming Austrian and Hungarian war prisoners in Siberia. The rumours', says Professor Fleming, 'had no real basis.'[15] Their own publication, *Cechoslovak*, a newspaper of the Czech National Council had on 26 July 1917 referred to 'Kerensky's charges against Lenin and his comrades' and wrote that '"a band of paid agents of the German Government succeeded in stirring up unrest in Petrograd."' According to Zbynek Zeman, in his book *The Masaryks*: 'It mattered whether the Allied representatives in Russia saw Lenin as an agent of Germany, because such a view would make it possible for them to take action against him and his régime; more important, Lenin was, before their very eyes, taking Russia out of the war.'[16]

On 14 May 1918, a train carrying Hungarian prisoners of war drew up alongside carriages of another train which contained soldiers of two of the Czech regiments stationed at the Siberian town of Chelyabinsk. The Czechs had been stuck on the railway sidings for some days awaiting instructions to continue on the way to Vladivostok, and they were not in the best of moods and the sight of Hungarian soldiers, whom they had regarded as part of the Austrian enemy, did not improve their frayed tempers.

Insults were exchanged and a Czech soldier was wounded by a piece of metal thrown by one of the Hungarians. Immediately there was an uproar and the Hungarian soldier was seized and promptly lynched. An investigation into the affair was conducted by the Soviet authorities and while this was going on some Czech soldiers who had been called as witnesses were detained. Two days later, a Czech delegation sent 'to demand their release' was arrested. The Czechs had by now become so enraged that they marched into the town, 'released the prisoners by force, disarmed the Red guards, and took possession of the arsenal.' The situation was further inflamed by a telegram from Trotsky which instructed the local Soviets on 25 May to disarm the Czechs. He warned that 'every Czech who is found armed on the railway is to be shot on the spot'. On the following day an attempt to carry out Trotsky's instructions led to bitter fighting between Czech and Soviet troops. The Czechs had by then gained control of the important town of Penza and on 8 June took over Samara. It was here, writes James Bunyan, that

'their activities became closely linked with those of the anti-Bolshevik elements of Samara ... Similar developments took place in Siberia. Cheliabinsk fell on 26 May, Omsk was captured on 7 June, and a local anti-Bolshevik government known as the Siberian Provisional Government, came into existence at Omsk.'[17]

When the Soviet forces re-occupied Samara during the Autumn of 1918, they discovered a 'proclamation of the Siberian section of the Czecho-Slovak National Council to their military forces in East Russia.' It was dated Samara, 9 September 1918 and stated:

'The Siberian section of the Czecho-Slovak National Council informs all fellow citizens at the front that it has just received a telegram, giving the text of a conversation which has passed between the commander of the Vladivostock forces, General Diederichs, and the commander of

73

the Czecho-Slovak forces, Colonel Gaida. Professor Masaryk has sanctioned our activities in Siberia and Russia, and the Allies have now agreed to recognize the Czecho-Slovak National Council as the constitutional Government of the Czecho-Slovak Republic. The Allies have also decided to assist us, and Englsh, American, French and Japanese troops have landed in the Far East under the command of the Japanese Marshal, Otani.'[18]

Troops based in Allied colonial territories were to play an important part in the Far Eastern venture. On 10 July 1918, the British Government had 'announced that the 25th Battalion of the Middlesex Regiment would be transferred from Hong Kong to Vladivostock . . . Within 48 hours 1,150 men of a French Colonial Infantry Battalion had also arrived from Indo-China and on 16 August the 27th United States Infantry was transferred to Vladivostock from the Phillipines. They were followed by the 31st US Infantry a week later.'[19]

The United States had eventually been cajoled into joining the 'crusade', when on 17 July it notified the British and French Governments that although it was opposed to armed intervention it 'would join the Japanese in landing troops at Vladivostock.' The Japanese had been landing thousands of troops throughout the summer.

The American forces were commanded by General William S. Graves who soon showed that he had no sympathy for the counter-revolutionaries led by the Allies' nominee, Admiral Kolchak. General Graves limited the United States commitment to guarding parts of the Trans-Siberian railway. He and his troops had become disgusted by the barbaric atrocities of Kolchak and his aides, Semenov and Kalnikov. 'These villains were protected by the Japanese who poured 72,000 troops into Siberia, in violation of their pledges to the United States, and conducted themselves in a manner that the Soviet peoples never forgot until they smashed Japan's armies in Manchuria in 1945.'[20]

General Graves has since countered some of the fabrications of the press. He states in his book, *America's Siberian Adventure*:

> 'There were horrible murders committed, but they were not committed by the Bolsheviks as the world believes. I am well on the side of safety when I say that the anti-Bolsheviks killed one hundred people in Eastern Siberia to every one killed by the Bolsheviks.'[21]

It was not until 29 September 1919, that the final orders for the evacuation of all Czecho-Slovak military units were announced, although the actual evacuation did not in fact commence until the following April – almost a year and a half after the end of hostilities between the Allies and the Central Powers, and two and a half years since the Soviet Government withdrew from the war and had, by its peace proclamation, declared its neutrality.

To understand more fully the background to the events in Russia during 1918, one should not forget the Anglo-French 'Spheres of Influence' Convention of 23 December 1917 and the subsequent agreement reached between the two countries. Russia's withdrawal from the war after the establishment of a Bolshevik Government had introduced an entirely new dimension into the War of Empires. Britain, for example, had been assigned 'the Cossack territories, the territory of the Caucasus, Armenia, Georgia, Kurdistan'[22] and it was within this 'sphere' that Baku and the oil wells were situated. But it was not only the oil which was at stake. Both Britain and Turkey also had an interest in the strategic importance of the region; Britain because of its proximity to Persia* and India, and Turkey because it was near her borders and contained territories that were formerly part of the Ottoman Empire and which she still coveted. A weakened and divided Russia, especially a Bolshevik one, would not have been unwelcome to either country. The contestants for Baku oil were Britain, Turkey and Germany. The latter's interest was linked to that of her ally, Turkey, but there was a dispute over distribution

---

*Persia had been dominated by British Imperial interests since the middle of the last century.

75

should Turkey win the contest.

Within twenty four hours of the Convention, secret instructions were transmitted to Major-General Dunsterville, at that time stationed just inside India and along the North West frontier. He was to prepare a Military Mission for service in Russia in order 'to prevent German and Turkish penetration'. The Mission was made up of 400 officers and NCOs, 41 Model T Fords and some Russian officers.[23]

During the early months of 1918, the Russian Civil War in the region had developed into a bitter struggle between the Bolsheviks, among whom were *Left* Socialist Revolutionaries, and counter-revolutionaries which included a combination of Mensheviks, *Right* Socialist Revolutionaries, Tsarists and an assortment of local and regional breakaway independence movements. By the spring, the Bolsheviks had gained ascendency in Baku and some of the surrounding territory and on 25 April established the first Baku Commune, but it was to remain in existence for only three months. In that period decrees were issued for the nationalization of the banks, the oil industry and the Caspian merchant fleet. There were also decrees for the reform of the Court system, confiscation of the land of the Beys and Khans and its distribution among the peasants, and the institution of an eight hour working day. But all their plans for a new social and economic order were aborted, for on 26 July the Baku Commune was destroyed from within, and from without.

Meanwhile Dunsterville and his troops had moved into the area. In his book, *The Adventures of Dunsterforce*, he records:

> 'I was now in touch with Baku by almost daily messenger and our friends the Social Revolutionaries seemed likely to bring off shortly the coup d'etat which was to throw out the Bolsheviks, establish a new form of government and invite British assistance.'

and then adds later:

> 'The long expected coup d'etat took place at Baku,

the Bolshevik Government were thrown out and replaced by a new body calling themselves the Central-Caspian Dictatorship.'[24]

Following the collapse of the Baku Commune, fighting flared up in the town at a time when the Turkish Army was preparing for its first major attack. Colonel Keyworth, who was already in Baku, telegraphed Dunsterville on 7 August 'that the Dictatorship was in a precarious position and might come into conflict with the Bolsheviks'. Dunsterville thereupon authorized the Colonel to 'support, if necessary with force, the Dictatorship against the Bolsheviks.' He in turn had been authorized by the War Office 'to eliminate any remaining Bolshevik influence at Baku, assuring him that he could rely on the full support of the War Office in carrying out these instructions.'[25]

A few days later, the Baku Commissars and a detachment of Red Army troops left by ship for Astrakhan, a northern Caspain port, then under Bolshevik control. After two days at sea, the ship was stopped by a warship of the Central-Caspian Dictatorship and forced under escort to return to Baku where the troops were disarmed and the Commissars, thirty five in all, were imprisoned awaiting a court martial.

During the last week in August the Turkish Army began a fierce and brutal attack upon the city and thousands of its inhabitants were slaughtered. The battle continued until the middle of September and on the morning of 14 September the Turks launched what eventually became their last onslaught upon the beleaguered city.

Ronald Grigor Suny, whose book, *The Baku Commune 1917–1918*, has given a vivid account of what went on in Baku during those tragic days and nights, writes: 'That night British troops left Baku ... The Dictatorship had abandoned the city and the imprisoned Commissars left to the mercy of the Turks.' Baku was in a state of utter chaos 'with thousands leaving the city under Turkish fire.'[26]

Through the initiative of Anastas Mikoyan and some colleagues who had not been imprisoned, the Commissars were released and taken through the inferno down to the harbour and on to a ship to sail once again to Astrakhan, but instead of sailing north the ship was diverted eastwards towards Krasnovodsk which was controlled by Right Socialist Revolutionaries and bolstered by a detachment of British troops. According to Soviet sources, 'The Baku Commissars were arrested in the presence of Colonel Batin and other English officers.'[27] Suny has confirmed that the Colonel was there for he writes that 'on 17 September the British Intelligence Officer, Battine, telegraphed Malleson from Krasnovodsk that among the arrivals from Baku were the arrested Bolshevik Commissars.'[28] Major-General Malleson was the head of another British Military Mission with headquarters in Meshed, just over the frontier in North Eastern Persia. According to Robert Jackson, he 'had been keeping a close watch on events in Transcaspia through a network of agents.'[29]

The Governor of Krasnovodsk was a Socialist Revolutionary named Kun, a Caucasian Cossack officer who 'had subordinated himself to the executive committee in Ashkhabad, largely made up of Socialist Revolutionaries and nonparty anti-Bolsheviks. The Ashkhabad Committee headed by F. Funtikov, a Socialist-Revolutionary worker, was in turn closely associated with the British military mission of General Malleson.' Close links between Malleson and the Ashkhabad Committee were maintained through Dokhov their 'liaison official in Meshed' who, on 18 September, also 'informed Malleson of the arrival of the Baku commissars in Krasnovodsk.'[30]

Captain Reginald Teague Jones, an intelligence officer, was Malleson's man in Ashkhabad. He had been assigned to maintain close contact with the committee and records:

'I first learned of the arrival in Krasnovodsk of the Bolshevik commissars on the 17th September 1918 and immediately wired and informed General Malleson. On receipt of my telegram General Malleson discussed with Comrade Dokhof the question of the captured Bolsheviks and expressed the desire that they should be handed over to the British authorities.'

He further states that on the same evening the President of the committee, Funtikov, asked him:

'to go to a meeting to discuss the matter, as the Government were undecided as to what action should be taken. I attended the meeting.'

A statement was made by the committee:

'that they had been informed from Meshed that General Malleson had declined to take over the prisoners, or, at any rate, had expressed his disinclination to do so, and had told the Ashkhabad representative that their Government must make its own arrangements.
It was then argued that the local prison was full, that Krasnovodsk had refused to keep the prisoners for the same reason, and that therefore there was no alternative but to shoot them.'

Teague Jones says that he:

'left the meeting before anything had really been definitely decided.
It was not until the next evening that after closely questioning Funtikof, the latter informed me in confidence that it had been finally decided to shoot the prisoners, and that he, Funtikof, had dispatched Kurilef to Krasnovodsk the previous night to make the necessary arrangements. On hearing this, I immediately wired General Malleson accordingly.'[31]

The following morning, 20 September, before daybreak, twenty six commissars were taken out of Krasnovodsk by train to a deserted spot some 130 miles away and murdered. 'Some shot, others mutilated by swords.'[32]
Soviet accusations of British complicity in the murder of the twenty six commissars have been persistently denied by members of the Military Mission who were operating in this sphere of influence at the time.
According to Richard H. Ullman:

Teague Jones 'does not indicate that he made any

effort to contradict Funtikov's statement that Malleson declined to take responsibility for the Commissars. Yet he says that he knew at the time that the reverse was true. Moreover, he left the meeting of the Ashkhabad Committee before any decision had been reached.'

Ullman points to the fact that:

'We do not know how strongly worded Malleson's instructions to Teague-Jones were, but if the latter had chosen to make an issue over the fate of the twenty-six Commissars, Funtikov and his colleagues would surely have found it difficult to refuse the British request. Upon British good-will depended British military support, and upon British military support depended the future of anti-Bolshevism in Transcaspia.'[33]

Many years later a letter appeared in *The Times*, 10 October 1961, signed by C.H. Ellis (a member of Malleson's Military Mission). It was in reply to a reference made by the Soviet representative to the Disarmament Talks in Vienna earlier in the month concerning the murder of the Commissars. Ellis says 'No British officers or officials were present or in any way involved in the arrests or shooting of the Commissars.' In his book, *The Transcaspian Episode*, published in 1963, he further states that 'Funtikov's action in disregarding Malleson's advice completely destroyed any reputation he may have enjoyed in the General's eyes.'[34]

Another book which refers to this tragic affair is *The Youngest Son* by Ivor Montagu in which he relates what Sir Robert Hodgson,* HM Chargé d'Affaires, told him in Moscow in 1925 when he 'asked him about the twenty six Commissars claimed on their memorial to have been shot by the British.

---

*He was asked by the Foreign Office to investigate the matter as a result of enquiries made by a Labour delegation during their visit to the Soviet Union.

'"Oh I went into that" said Hodgson. "The Foreign Office asked me to when the Labour delegation got home.

"We did not give the order I'm certain, but I can understand how these people thought we were responsible. There was a local government of Mensheviks in the town and when we caught this shipload of Commissars we naturally put them into their hands. We don't interfere with what an administration does more than we can help in these cases, our object is just to be sure of the place strategically and give a chance to the locals to get the government they want.

"A British officer was in fact assigned to attend all the meetings and see no one got up to anything silly, but the records show quite clearly that when they held the meeting that decided on the execution our fellow wasn't there. He was rather junior and I don't know why it was; he may have been playing the fool of course but on the other hand he might just have had a cold."'[35]

Suny's assessment of the fate of the Commissars was that:

'While the more exaggerated claims by Soviet historians of British responsibility in the death of the twenty-six cannot be substantiated, there is enough evidence to conclude that the British agents in Transcaspia could have prevented the execution if they had been interested in doing so. This they simply were not, and British protests were filed only after the fact.'[36]

Although the Armistice for World War I was signed on 11 November 1918, there were British troops still in Transcaspia until 1 April 1919 but by the summer of that year Soviet troops had regained ascendency in the area and within a few months had driven out the counter-revolutionary forces. Baku was eventually retaken by the Bolsheviks on 28 April 1920.

The ink had barely dried on the signatures to the

Armistice Agreement when, on 12 November, warships of the Allied Fleet passed through the Dardenelles and sailed into the Black Sea. French troops were landed in Odessa, Russia's principal Black Sea port, gateway to the Ukraine and the 'granary' of Eastern Europe. According to Pichon,* the French Foreign Minister, French and British forces employed in Southern Russia alone totalled 280,000 and they were supplemented by troops from Italy, Roumania, Serbia and Greece. In all, some 850,000 soldiers, sailors and marines were involved in the Southern anti-Bolshevik crusade. The French Government 'generously' disposed of Russian property to the White anti-Bolshevik leaders by concluding agreements by which the White leaders would be given 'control of Russian railways for 50 years and of economic and military policy for five years.'[37]

In spite of this massive intervention Soviet Red Army troops captured Kiev, the Ukrainian capital, on 3 February 1919. John Silverlight in his book, *The Victors' Dilemma*, describes how hundreds of innocent civilians were slaughtered by interventionist forces. Kherson, a port in the Crimea, had come under the control of Greek troops. Towards the end of February it had become almost encircled by the Red Army. The Greek troops retreated towards the dock area and in their withdrawal, a warehouse, in which 2,000 men, women and children were being held as hostages, was set alight by an incendiary shell fired from an Allied warship which had been lying offshore. Amidst panic and confusion, the helpless victims frantically 'clawed their way out of the flames' only to be mown down by the Greek machine-guns. 'At least 500 people were killed.' News of the massacre had reached the attacking Red Army troops and when they captured the town Nikifor Grigorev, their Commander, issued instructions for every Greek prisoner of war to be shot.[38]

The battles for the ports in the Crimea eventually became a one-sided affair. The interventionist forces were more interested in being demobilized than in fighting. As far as they were concerned the war ended on 11 November 1918.

The French High Command had become alarmed by the

---

*Stephen Pichon, *Allied Policy in Russia – May 1919*, Vol. 10 Part 1.

fraternizing of their troops with the pro-Bolsheviks and when mutiny broke out in the French Black Sea Fleet, instructions were issued for the withdrawal of all Allied forces in the area. The mutineers, who were inspired by a young seaman, André Marty,* were court-martialled. When news of the court-martial reached France it sparked off a wave of disorders throughout the French Navy as well as in the dockyards.

French led intervention in the Crimea lasted less than four months. It was a disaster of the greatest magnitude. Four years of war, news of the mutinies, and under pressure from hostile public reactions, both at home and abroad, the French Government announced on 29 March that they had decided not to send any more troops to Russia and that plans were afoot to evacuate those already there. The 'crusade' had collapsed into utter chaos. One hundred and forty thousand men had been sent to Odessa, Sevastopol and the rest of the Crimea 'in an effort to recover some part of the great sums by which' successive French administrations had 'bolstered the Tsarist regime for more than twenty years.'[39]

There had been attempts by both Lloyd George and Wilson to work out some form of negotiations to end the Russian Civil War earlier in the year but the 'Tiger', Clemenceau, with the help of Winston Churchill, had 'pulled the rug from under their feet'. The French Prime Minister vetoed the Anglo-American proposal for representatives of the Bolsheviks and anti-Bolsheviks to meet in Paris. He was vehement in his opposition to having any Bolsheviks in Paris. Eventually, he reluctantly agreed that invitations be sent to all Russian Parties – including the Bolsheviks – to meet in Prinkipo, a Turkish island in the Sea of Marmora, just off Constantinople. Clemenceau was convinced that the Bolsheviks would refuse the invitation and his Government 'assured the Whites, the anti-Bolsheviks that they need not accept, as they would go on receiving allied support in any case; from the British side Churchill gave the same assurances. Not surprisingly, the invitation was rejected.'[40]. But it was rejected only by the

---

*Was in later years a leading member of the French Communist Party.

leaders of the counter-revolutionary movements who were being subsidized financially by millions of francs and pounds sterling. The Bolsheviks not only accepted the invitation but, according to a secret report which had been compiled by President Wilson's agent in Stockholm, 'after an intimate conversation with a certain Mr Litvinov' the report claimed that 'the Soviet Government of Russia really earnestly sought peace, and were prepared to protect existing foreign enterprise in Russia, to grant new concessions and even to discuss Tsarist Debt.' Wilson had produced this report in the presence of Clemenceau, 'To which the Tiger snapped, "Who is Litvinov?"'[41] He refused to accept any form of diplomatic recognition of the Bolshevik administration.

Clemenceau had made his position absolutely clear from the very outset of the Russian Civil War. His fanatical hatred of the Soviet Government was only surpassed, in the political world, by Winston Churchill. Less than a fortnight before the collapse of the armies of the Central Powers, Clemenceau had sent instructions to his Commander in Chief in the Balkans, General Franchet d'Esperey:

> 'The main line of the plan of action which should be adopted is not only to continue there the struggle against the Central Powers, but also to bring about the encirclement of Bolshevism and to provoke its downfall.'[42]

Noulens, his Ambassador to Russia during the latter Tsarist and Kerensky periods, on his return to France had, in his address to the Deputies of the French Chamber and members of the press, told them that 'with regard to the Bolshevists, we must consider ourselves "as if in a state of war".'[43] But of course, without the international legal niceties of a declaration of war.

The damage caused to the Russian people and their property by the French intervention alone, during their four months in the Crimea and the Ukraine, was estimated at 125 million roubles.

Britain's involvement in the Southern crusade ended almost as disastrously. In support of the anti-Bolshevik army, under General Denikin, according to Winston Churchill:

> 'A quarter of a million rifles, two hundred guns, thirty tanks and large masses of munitions and equipment were sent through the Dardanelles and the Black Sea to the port of Novorossiisk; and several hundred British officers and non-commissioned officers as advisers, instructors, store keepers and even a few aviators.'[44]

They were hastily dispatched in the hope that the Red Army would disintegrate and the route to Moscow*, the capital, be prised open. Denikin did achieve some millitary success during the early months of 1919, but by the end of October the Bolshevik armies were advancing on all fronts.

The disintegration, in fact, came within the counter-revolutionary Whites, who had become thoroughly discredited; riddled by corruption, imcompetence and dissolute officials and by the restoration of the old landlords. Major-General H.C. Holman, Commander of Britain's Military Mission in Southern Russia has given an indication of the scale of the corruption, particularly to that relating to the misuse and misappropriation of British military supplies and equipment. On 3 September 1919 he presented an aide mémoire to Denikin stating:

> 'At a time when between 150,000 and 200,000 complete sets of clothing and equipment had been issued to your supply service and armies, I found not a single Russian soldier with a complete set of British equipment; soldiers barefooted and in rags, fighting on cold nights without greatcoat, blanket, or waterproof sheets, and on hot days without a water-bottle; sick and wounded lying on the ground in their filthy rags without the first necessities of treatment, while a rich store of British medical equipment lay at the base; British guns without buffer or lubricating oil, or the

---

*Moscow became the capital after the November Revolution 1918.

necessary tools or spare parts, all of which had been delivered at the base . . . I should be guilty of the gravest dereliction of duty if I failed to state clearly that this state of affairs, if continued, can only lead to disaster. Against all this is the proof positive of what can be done by the proper use of the material which His Majesty's Government is so glad to put at your disposal.'[45]

It had been reported that petty officials and bureaucrats in Southern Russia were wearing British uniforms, 'while at the front, although the supply of uniforms far exceeded the number of Denikin's troops, only twenty-five per cent of the troops wore them. Officers often drew a double issue of clothing and sold the surplus at lucrative prices . . . Hospital beds and bedding were appropriated by officers and officials for their own homes. During the battle in which the Red Army captured Kharkov in November 1919, British anti-freeze fluid was sold across the bar of the Hotel Metropole while lorries and tanks froze for lack of it.'[46] While at the same time thousands of refugees died of cold, hunger and disease.

Denikin and his counter-revolutionary army were ultimately destroyed as an effective fighting force. Together with some of his senior officers he was taken aboard one of the many Allied naval ships lying in the bay of Novorossiisk and escaped. Thousands of refugees had crowded the quayside but only the remnants of Denikin's army, the British Military Mission and 'only those civilians who had been actively engaged in helping the White cause were to be taken off. As the ships loaded, the crowds on the wharves and quaysides were kept back by British troops with fixed bayonets. Some broke through the cordon and rushed the vessels; machine-guns on the docks opened up and more corpses joined the debris that covered the surface of the harbour.'[47]

Among press reports, the most prejudiced and ill-informed came from a section of Allied journalists. Harold Williams, war correspondent for *The Times* and *The New York Times*, had become part of the Denikin entourage. A fanatical anti-Bolshevik, Williams had convinced himself that the Russian people in the South were so wholehearted-ly behind Denikin that when he 'passed in his car through the streets of Kharkov women weeping for joy pressed forward to kiss his hand and those who could not do that, kissed even the mudguards of his car.'[48] His anti-Bolshevism and his euphoria over Denikin's early victories had blinded him to what was really going on in Russia at the time. Denikin's army was riddled with disillusioned men, and the lack of support from the local populations and the appalling conditions under which they were expected to uphold a system in which they no longer believed, soon drove many of them into desertion and some into support of the Red Army; 'the "demoralized" Red Army of the "tottering" Bolshevik Government – according to Williams, almost devoid of guns and troops – drove the Whites into the sea, with Williams shouting to the end, "This can't be true".'[49]

Even the Prime Minister, Lloyd George 'believed that though the vast majority of Russian people were not Bolsheviks, they preferred the Reds to the Whites, for they were certainly sick of the war and they did not want the old landlords back either.'[50] But his view was that of a minority within his own Cabinet.

The Allied victory and the signing of the Armistice was promptly exploited by Lloyd George for political gain. A snap election was held in December 1918. Most Labour MPs who had opposed or had been critical of his Coalition Government and its conduct of the war lost their Parlia-mentary seats, but it was not many months before the British working class began to recuperate from the euphoria following the Armistice. The demobilization of over five million servicemen had created problems which the re-elected Coalition Government was unable to tackle. The search for work in a 'land fit for heroes', the pre-war conditions of labour and the influence of the Russian Revolution were all factors which contributed to a general unrest leading to strikes and massive demonstrations up and down the country. Intervention in the Russian Civil War and the use of British troops, money and equipment had begun to unify all classes of people against the Government in the 'Hands Off Russia' campaign.

Secrecy which surrounded the Government's plans to withhold demobilization of thousands of British troops, and then to re-direct them to the far flung corners of Russia in a suicidal attempt to prevent the emergence of a new Russia, eventually sparked off mutinies.

'As early as 10 January 1919, before he had been appointed to his new office, Churchill* was urging the War Cabinet to consider seriously "whether we should now decide to bolster up the Central Powers if necessary, in order to stem the tide of Bolshevism".'[51]

This was to reinforce what he had already expressed at a Cabinet meeting just a few hours before the signing of the Armistice:

> 'It was important that we should not attempt to destroy the only police force available for maintaining order in Germany. We might have to build up the German army as it was important to get Germany on her legs again for fear of the spread of Bolshevism.'†[52]

Frank Owen, in his biography of Lloyd George, explains many of the reasons why the British Prime Minister was so luke-warm in support of his Cabinet colleagues' plans for intervention. His main fears appear to have been aroused by the mutinies and general disaffection within the armed services, as well as mounting opposition from the Trade Union movement.

---

*Churchill became Minister for War in the new Coalition Government.
†Churchill cannot be accused of inconsistency, for in 1945, nearly three decades later, he was to re-embark upon the same 'Crusade'. At a meeting in Woodford, 23 November 1954, he revealed:
> 'Even before the war had ended and while the Germans were surrendering by hundreds of thousands and our streets were crowded with cheering people, I telegraphed to Lord Montgomery directing him to be careful in collecting German arms, to stack them so that they could easily be issued again to the German soldiers whom we would have to work with if the Soviet advance continued.' (*The Times*, 24 November 1954)
In his memoirs, Field-Marshal Montgomery says 'I had been told that these weapons were to be kept intact. I pressed that this order be cancelled so that I could destroy these weapons.' (The Memoirs of Field-Marshal Montgomery – *From Yalta to Potsdam*, p. 384)

'On 3 January 1919, several thousand British troops quartered in Rest Camps at Folkestone and Dover refused to re-embark for France, and marched into the centre of these towns to demonstrate against the delay in demobilization. At Osterley Camp, Royal Army Service Corps drivers got into their lorries and drove to London, where they staged a mass protest meeting in Whitehall under the windows of the War Office. In the camps at Kempton park and Grove Park, "Soldiers' Councils" were set up. At Luton, a military mob set fire to the Town Hall. At Calais, the leave boats returning from England were picketed and angry soldiers, broken loose from all discipline took over the town . . . ' Meanwhile 'trouble had spread to the Navy in the minesweeper flotilla at Rosyth; it flared into the Royal Air Force, too, on the Kent airfields.'[53] There was also rioting in the streets of Glasgow and a general strike in Belfast.

The Labour Movement's opposition to intervention and its solidarity with the Russian workers was reflected in the number of Trade Unions which had come out against the Government's anti-Bolshevik crusade; none more so than the Miners' Federation of Great Britain which, at its Annual Conference on 26 March 1919, called upon the Government:

> 'to immediately withdraw all British troops from Russia, and to take the necessary steps to induce the Allied Powers to do likewise.'

The resolution was moved by Herbert Smith of the Yorkshire Miners' Association who told delegates:

> 'that if we had no capitalistic money invested in Russia we should have no troops in Russia . . . It is not for us to interfere and land troops to protect capitalist interests.'

It was seconded by the South Wales Miners' vice-President, James Winstone:

> 'This Government of ours are controlling the

89

press of this country, and not allowing the truth about Russia to come out; if they did, possibly there would be almost, if not quite, a revolution against the treatment that has been meted out to the men who have been fighting for liberty, and for justice, and democracy. I think it is one of the great scandals and one of the greatest reflections upon what we sometimes call this free British country of ours, that our troops should be sent there in order to prevent these men and these women, who like ourselves, are endeavouring to work out their own social salvation.'

The resolution was carried unanimously and was adopted, not only by the Miners, but also by the National Union of Railwaymen and the Transport Workers' Federation on 16 April 1919, on a motion put forward by the Triple Industrial Alliance, which covered these three unions.

A 'Hands Off Russia' Committee was formed in London in January 1918 and in September a national committee was established. Many meetings and conferences were held all over the country culminating in a National Conference, held jointly by the TUC and the Labour Party in London on 3 April 1919, in which it also called on the Government 'to take immediate steps to withdraw all British troops from Russia.'[54]

Mutinies, strikes and the militancy of the Labour movement not only in Britain, but throughout Europe, had created a deep impression upon the thinking of the British Prime Minister. His confidential Memorandum to the other Heads of State at the Paris Peace Conference in March 1919 reflected his state of mind at the time when he warned them that:

'The whole of Russia is filled with the spirit of revolution. There is everywhere a deep sense not only of discontent, but of anger and revolt amongst the workmen against pre-war conditions. The whole existing order in its political, social and economic aspects is questioned by the masses of the population from one end of Europe to the other.'[55]

But although Lloyd George saw the pitfalls in getting bogged down in an interventionist war in Russia, which he instinctively knew would end in failure, he nevertheless felt inhibited from doing anything about it. His main pre-occupation was how to stifle the Bolshevik Revolution without resorting to military intervention. In his Memorandum, he goes on to say that:

> 'The greatest danger that I see is that Germany may throw in her lot with Bolshevism.'[56]

Notes

1. KNIGHTLEY, Phillip, *The First Casualty*, p.151
2. PRICE, Morgan Phillips, *My Three Revolutions*, p. 132
3. JACKSON, Robert, *At War with the Bolsheviks*, p. 51
4. SILVERLIGHT, John, *The Victors' Dilemma*, p. 17
5. SILVERLIGHT, John, *The Victors' Dilemma*, p. 18
6. *The Intimate Papers of Colonel House* (ed. by Charles Seymour), p. 404
7. *War Memoirs of David Lloyd George* Vol. VI (from a note to Lord Reading), pp. 3191–2
8. JACKSON, Robert, *At War with the Bolsheviks*, p. 53
9. CHAMBERLIN, W.H., *The Russian Revolution 1917–1921*, Vol. II, pp. 3–4
10. ZEMAN, Zbynek, *The Masaryks, The Making of Czechoslovakia*, p. 106
11. FISCHER, Louis, *The Soviets in World Affairs*, p. 78
12. PRICE, Morgan Phillips, *My Reminiscences of the Russian Revolution*, pp. 290–291
13. PRICE, Morgan Phillips, *My Reminiscences of the Russian Revolution*, p. 293
14. PRICE, Morgan Phillips, *My Reminiscences of the Russian Revolution*, p. 293
15. FLEMING, D.F., *The Cold War and its Origins*, Vol. I, p. 17
16. ZEMAN, Zbynek, *The Masaryks, The Making of Czechoslovakia*, pp. 100–102, 103
17. BUNYAN, James, *Intervention, Civil War and Communism in Russia April–December 1918*, pp. 86–87
18. PRICE, Morgan Phillips, *My Reminiscences of the Russian Revolution*, p. 292
19. JACKSON, Robert, *At War with the Bolsheviks*, p. 59
20. FLEMING, D.F., *The Cold War and its Origins*, Vol. I, p. 21
21. GRAVES, Gen. W.S., *America's Siberian Adventure*, p. 108
22. ULLMAN, Richard H., *Britain and the Russian Civil War, 1917–1921*, Vol. II, p. 54
23. SUNY, Ronald Grigor, *The Baku Commune 1917–1918*, p. 275
24. DUNSTERVILLE, Major Gen. L.C., *The Adventures of Dunsterforce*, pp. 182 and 207
25. SUNY, Ronald Grigor, *The Baku Commune 1917–1918*, pp. 327–328
26. SUNY, Ronald Grigor, *The Baku Commune 1917–1918*, pp. 335–336
27. *Great Soviet Encyclopaedia*

28. SUNY, Ronald Grigor, *The Baku Commune 1917–1918*, p. 338
29. JACKSON, Robert, *At War with the Bolsheviks*, pp. 125–126
30. SUNY, Ronald Grigor, *The Baku Commune 1917–1918*, p. 338
31. British Sessional Papers, House of Commons, Cmnd. 1846 Russia No. 1. Vol. XXV (6–10), pp. 491–495
32. SUNY, Ronald Grigor, *The Baku Commune 1917–1918*, p. 342
33. ULLMAN, Richard H, *Britain and the Russian Civil War, 1917–1921*, Vol. II, p. 324
34. ELLIS, C.H., *The Transcaspian Episode*, p. 64
35. MONTAGU, Ivor, *The Youngest Son*, p. 299
36. SUNY, Ronald Grigor, *The Baku Commune 1917–1918*, p. 341
37. FLEMING, D.F., *The Cold War and its Origins*, Vol. I, p. 22
38. SILVERLIGHT, John, *The Victors' Dilemma*, p. 203
39. FLEMING, D.F., *The Cold War and its Origins*, Vol. I, p. 22
40. WATSON, Robin, *Georges Clemenceau*, p. 374
41. OWEN, Frank, *Tempestuous Journey, Lloyd George – His Life and Times*, p. 509
42. OWEN, Frank, *Tempestuous Journey, Lloyd George – His Life and Times*, p. 506
43. BONNEFOUS, Edouard, *Histoire Politique de la IIIe Republique*, p. 7
44. CHURCHILL, Winston, *The World Crisis: The Aftermath*, p. 250
45. ULLMAN, Richard H., *Britain and the Russian Civil War, 1917–1921*, Vol. II, p. 214
46. ULLMAN, Richard H., *Britain and the Russian Civil War, 1917–1921*, Vol. II, p. 213
47. JACKSON, Robert, *At War with the Bolsheviks*, p. 188
48. KNIGHTLEY, Phillip, *The First Casualty*, p. 158
49. KNIGHTLEY, Phillip, *The First Casualty*, p. 159
50. OWEN, Frank, *Tempestuous Journey, Lloyd George – His Life and Times*, p. 507
51. OWEN, Frank, *Tempestuous Journey, Lloyd George – His Life and Times*, p. 507
52. CAB. 23/14 10 November 1918, 500A, p. 300
53. OWEN, Frank, *Tempestuous Journey, Lloyd George – His Life and Times*, p. 508
54. ARNOT, R. Page, *The Impact of the Russian Revolution in Britain*, pp. 147–150
55. LLOYD GEORGE, David, *The Truth About the Peace Treaties Vol. I*, p. 407
56. LLOYD GEORGE, David, *The Truth About the Peace Treaties Vol. I*, p. 407

6

REVOLUTIONARY UPHEAVAL IN CENTRAL EUROPE

Lloyd George was too astute a politician not to anticipate the effect that the Russian Revolution would have upon the working people of the war torn countries of Europe, especially in a defeated and disillusioned Germany. The German servicemen were just as anxious as their counterparts in Britain and France and the other belligerent countries to get home to their wives, children and families. The Armistice to them, as in the other countries, was the clarion call for demobilization. The imperial aspirations of Kaiser Wilhelm and his ministerial liutenants had been demolished and there was widespread demand for an end to his autocratic rule.

The revolutionary movement in Germany began to gather momentum at the beginning of 1918, with the strike of munition workers in January inspired by the Spartacist movement and a minority group in the Socialist Party. By the end of the summer the Allied offensive in Macedonia brought about the collapse of Bulgaria and the virtual collapse of Turkey, and by 15 September 1918, Germany was isolated. Its main ally, the Austro-Hungarian Imperial Government, had sued for peace. From then on, disaffection began to increase within the German forces. Fraternization with the 'enemy' in Russia, and with Anglo-French forces had been an edifying experience for the German troops. There was much sympathy for the Russian people in their overthrow of Tsarism, for they too had a despotic ruling class carved out of the same mould. Mutinies in the German navy broke out at Wilhelmshaven in October and by the first week in November had spread to Kiel and Hamburg. Soldiers sent to put down the mutinies stayed to join in. Federal Germany began to break apart. In the south, on 7 November, Kurt Eisner and the 'Independent Socialists' proclaimed Bavaria a republic. Other regions were trying likewise to break away from the heavy hand of Prussian autocratic domination. There was a concerted effort by nearly all sections of German political life, with the exception of the die-hard monarchists, and some of the military, to get rid of the Kaiser. On 9 November there was a general strike, followed by a massive demonstration in Berlin clamouring for an end to the war and the removal of the Kaiser and his administrators. Later that day it was announced the Kaiser had vacated the throne. Prince Max of Baden, the head of the Imperial Cabinet made the announcement. He was far too discreet to admit that the Kaiser had refused to renounce his position and had been forced to abdicate. The post of Chancellor was taken over by Friedrich Ebert, the leader of the 'Majority' Socialists.

Reports of mutinies and of a Germany in revolt sent shudders down the spines of Britain's political leaders, but they were not alone in their fear of a real socialist revolution in Germany.

On the night of 9 November 1918, there was a telephone conversation between Ebert, the new Chancellor, and a high ranking officer of the German High Command.

Earlier in the day, Karl Liebknecht the Spartacist leader had proclaimed Germany a Socialist Republic. To counter this move by the Sparacists*, the Social Democrat leaders were, according to Sir John Wheeler-Bennett in his book, *The Nemesis of Power*, 'forced into "making a revolutionary gesture in order to forestall a revolution"', and that afternoon, 'in a moment of mingled exultation and panic proclaimed the German Republic from the window of the Reichstag building.'

Ebert had 'cast about desperately for the means to buttress his flimsy authority. On whom could he depend? What of the Officer Corps?' The telephone to the Chancellor's office 'was connected by a private and secret line' to the military headquarters at Spar. 'Ebert was alone. The windows were closed, the curtains drawn.' Outside in the streets, from the direction of the Wilhelmstrasse and the

---

*The Spartacist Movement – officially known as the Spartakasbund – became the German Communist Party in 1920.

Unter den Linden came the shouts of the demonstrators and singing of the 'Internationale'.

Suddenly the telephone rang. The call was from Lieutenant-General Wilhelm Groner, first Quarter-Master General:

> '"Was the government willing to protect Germany from anarchy and to restore order?" enquired the crisp military voice ... "Yes," said Ebert, "it was." "Then the High Command will maintain discipline in the Army and bring it peacefully home." "What do you expect from us?" enquired the Chancellor. "The High Command expects the government to co-operate with the Officer Corps in the suppression of Bolshevism, and in the maintenance of discipline in the Army. It also asks that the provisioning of the Army shall be ensured and all disturbance of transport communications prevented."'[1]

This historic telephone call laid the foundation for the future role of the German Army, not only in the Weimar Republic, but also that of Nazi Germany. The establishment of a 'Freikorps' to deal with German Bolsheviks or Socialists, or those who were prepared to lead in the struggle for social change, emanated from Ebert's submission that fateful night. It 'enabled the German Officer Corps to establish itself in a position of virtual independence in the Weimar Republic, a State within a State. As such it was to bear a heavy share of the responsibility for Hitler's rise to power.'[2]

Workers' and Soldiers' Councils had sprung up throughout most of Northern Germany and in a few regions in the South. The new President of the Berlin Police was Emil Eichhorn, an Independent Socialist, and he proposed the formation of a people's militia to be comprised of 'two thirds out of organized workmen, trade unionists, and the rest out of former soldiers of the rank resident in Berlin. The Council agreed. But the Minister of the Interior objected to this plan, and especially the majority Socialists' representative in the Ministry, Herr Ernst, who demanded that the old police force should be reinstated and armed.'[3]

The many discontented and frustrated officers and rank and file servicemen, unable to find jobs, provided a first class breeding ground for the 'Freikorps', which were formed all over the country. Their frustrations found expression in brutal attacks upon workers' demonstrations and meetings. Although 'neither irregular nor yet a regular force' they were nevertheless used by the Ebert administration in its 'Law and Order' campaign. His chief aide was Gustave Noske, whom he appointed Minister of Defence, 'a right-wing socialist whose suppression of the naval mutiny at Kiel in November 1915 had made him acceptable to the General Staff.'[4] The word socialist hardly seemed to apply to Noske, who was known by those who were struggling to bring socialism into German political life as the 'Bloodhound', the Social Democrat or 'Majority' Socialist who was responsible for the shooting down of hundreds of workers in the streets of Berlin.

On 15 January 1919, there was a meeting in Essen of a group of German industrialists. It included such well known names as Kirdoff, Krupp, Stinnes and Voegler. 'On the same day, several hundred miles away in Berlin, German officers murdered the Spartacist leaders Karl Liebknecht and Rosa Luxemburg, by shooting them through the head. It was for these and other German officers, organized in 'Free Corps' that the anti-Bolshevik League and similar bodies made generous provisions.'[5]

Karl Liebknecht and Rose Luxemburg were arrested in the Eden Hotel, Berlin. J.P. Nettl, in his biography of Rosa Luxemburg describes how these two courageous pioneers of the German Socialist movement were murdered.

'Karl Liebknecht was led out first before the curious and unsympathetic eyes of the soldiers and a few hotel guests . . . As he emerged from a side door into a deserted street, Runge carried out his instructions, and hit him hard over the head with his rifle butt.

'Liebnecht was then half dragged, half hustled into a waiting car, which went off in the opposite direction to that of the prison. In the Tiergarten he was made to get out of the car and was shot within a few yards. The fatal shot was actually fired by Captain von Pfflug-Hartung. The body was delivered to a local mortuary as that of an unknown man found by the road side. On return to the Eden Hotel this section reported to their Chief that Liebknecht had been "shot while trying to escape".'

[One of the earliest examples of the use of this form of wording as a cover-up]

'Shortly afterwards it was Rosa Luxemburg's turn. Already in the lobby of the hotel some of the soldiers had been exercising their muscles on her . . .

'The transport of Rosa Luxemburg was in charge of a Lieutenant Vogel. Runge punctiliously performed again and, half dead, she was dragged into another waiting car. There the messy proceedings were quickly brought to an end inside the car by a shot in the head from the officer in charge. The car stopped at a bridge over the Landwehr Canal and the body was thrown into the murky waters, where it remained until 31 May. Here the story was that an angry mob had stopped the car and carried Rosa Luxemburg off to an unknown destination . . .

'However, long before her body was found, the real facts began to emerge and were published in *Rote Fahne* [Red Flag]. Certainly by April the government knew the facts if not the motives, but still refused publicly to amend the statement of 16 January . . .

'Demands for a civil as opposed to a military court to try the murderers were refused by the government on the grounds that this would interfere with the process of justice already in motion . . .

'The minimal sentences actually handed out

97

were based on the derisory charge ... of failing to report a corpse and illegally disposing of it, and against Runge of attempted manslaughter.'

The author relates in a footnote how he had met Pfflug-Hartung in a prison camp at the end of the second World War. He was unaware at the time of his role in these events. Pfflug-Hartung had told him 'of the significant role he had played in freeing Europe from Bolshevism, and suggested this as a valid reason why he should instantly be released from captivity.'[6]

Although the Ebert administration did not issue orders for the murder of the Spartacist leaders, no attempt was made by Noske 'to restrain his bloodthirsty auxiliaries. The Freikorps members at that time, and later, felt they could rely on Noske's support in any subsequent proceedings, should these arise.'[7]

Noske and the Ebert administration had much to answer for: 'In March 1919 some 1,200 people were put to death in Berlin after martial law had been proclaimed, on the unfounded pretext that fifty policemen had been murdered.'[8]

It was as a result of the inflamed situation in Berlin that the National Assembly decided to meet in Weimar; dominated by reluctant Republicans who were committed to the old economic and political system slightly adjusted to include a little more democracy – but a capitalist democracy – in which socialism was a word to be used but not implemented in deed.

The repercussions of the Russian revolution had the greatest impact upon the workers and peasants of Central Europe, where the war, plus the Allied blockade, had reduced the German and Austrian dominated areas to a state of near starvation. Former rivals and enemies had now become allies in the attempts to crush the campaigns for social change. Admirals, Generals, autocratic statesmen and capitalist entrepreneurs, especially those who had made their fortunes out of the War of Empires, led the onslaught upon the revolutionary movements that were struggling to get rid of the old despotic ruling class, not only of the Habsburg and Hohenzollern Dynasties, but of the whole privileged social system. Allied plans for the re-defining of the European frontiers were designed not only to weaken the military and economic potential of their former imperial rivals, but was to play its part in the undermining of anti-imperialist and anti-capitalist movements.

The creation of Czechoslovakia, under the auspices of the victorious allies, was partially realized at the territorial expense of Hungary. The Slovaks were encouraged to combine with the Czechs into a federal state in which they were promised complete national autonomy. The Czechs were, at the end of the war, allowed to occupy Bohemia and Moravia, carved out of the Austrian Empire, and Slovakia, which had for many years been part of Hungary,. But the Hungarians were not prepared to let their country be sliced up piecemeal and within days of the signing of the Armistice, Hungarian troops moved back into Slovakia and drove out the new occupants.

The collapse of the Austrian Empire and the establishment of an independent Hungarian Democratic Republic under Count Karolyi in November, 1918 had instilled within the country a revolutionary fervour that had not been experienced since the 1840s. The initial change had been brought about fairly peaceably. A bourgeois revolution in which the first steps that Karolyi introduced were a move towards some form of land redistribution, commencing with the break-up of his own extensive family estate. But the effects of inflation, mass unemployment and sheer poverty could not wait for the implementation of some of the well intentioned reforms of the Karolyi administration. The Anglo-French anti-Bolshevik plans had taken into consideration the use of former enemy troops; while at the same time using the economic weapon, especially the control over food aid to the poverty stricken people of Central Europe to prevent their countries going socialist.

'Food was practically the only basis on which the governments of the hastily created states could be maintained in power' said Sir William Goode, who was at the time British Director for relief in Central Europe. His report frankly admits that 'Half of Europe had hovered on the brink of Bolshevism. If it had not been for the £137 million in relief credits granted to Central and Eastern Europe between 1919 and 1921, it would have been impossible to provide food and coal and the sea and land transport for them. Without food and coal and transport Austria and probably several other countries would have gone the way of Russia ... Two and a half years after the Armistice the back of Bolshevism in Central Europe had been broken largely by relief credits ... The expenditure of £137 million was probably one of the best international investments from a financial and political point of view ever recorded in history.'*

The Karolyi Government was put under great pressure by the Allies. Firstly by trying to get it to collaborate in the interventionist attack upon Soviet Russia and then failing in their first objective, the Allies forced the new republic to commit itself to territorial 'hari kari'. Karolyi refused to submit to the Allied plans and resigned, but not before handing over the running of the country to the United Socialist Party under the leadership of Bela Kun. The Allies, however, were not prepared to be thwarted, and in March 1919 forced the Hungarian troops back into the re-defined areas which they had carved out for post-war Hungary. On the Hungarian eastern flank, the Roumanian Army took over Transylvania, Bessarabia and whole districts astride the Dobruja and Bukovina rivers. It was in accord with Allied policy, for in the 1916 Secret Treaty, Roumania had been allocated large tracts of Hungarian territory. Both Britain and France had endorsed the occupation whilst the wishes of the peoples in those occupied territories were ignored. They had neither a plebiscite nor were they even consulted.

It was against this background that the new Hungarian Socialist Republic was proclaimed on 21 March 1919.

One of its first steps was to abolish the old legal system and set up its own revolutionary courts with a new judiciary. The Judges were elected by local Soviets. It then tackled the power of the Church, by separating its functions from that of the State. On the industrial front, the eight hour day was introduced and the nationalization of all

*The Times, 14 October 1925.

100

factories except the very small ones employing less than twenty people. A national health service was set up with free medical attention, sickness benefits, and for working women a six week maternity leave on full pay. Compulsory education up to the age of fourteen was introduced, as well as an allocation of doctors to the schools. There was a strict form of food rationing in which heavy manual workers received the highest ration, followed by those workers who made their contribution to the state by 'brain and intellect'. The new government followed the Bolshevik pattern by basing their administration upon a national system of Soviets – people's Councils. In Budapest, the capital, the housing situation was tackled by the State taking over the large blocks of flats and houses and re-housing thousands of the poorer working class families. But the greatest challenge to the Bela Kun administration was not in the towns, but in the countryside. Hungary had a predominantly peasant population; over 60% worked on the land, and their hopes of a redistribution of the land were not adequately fulfilled. The Revolutionary Government placed its emphasis upon turning the large estates into co-operative farms. All Crown and Church estates were taken over by co-operatives, as well as other estates of over one hundred acres, and plans were in hand to extend the takeover to estates over twenty acres. Most of the peasants had hoped to farm the land for themselves. Nevertheless, in the main, the Revolutionary Government had, within a space of four and a half months, set in motion many popular fundamental social changes which the Entente powers were determined to stifle. Hungary was attacked on three sides by the Czechoslovaks, Croatians and the Roumanians, with assistance from the French High Command. The Hungarian Revolutionary Government had hoped to receive help from Soviet Russia, but the Bolsheviks were completely committed in their own fight for survival against the counter-revolutionaries and interventionist armies from fourteen different countries. Under the Treaty of Trianon, of 4 June 1920, Hungary was carved piecemeal by the victorious allies, so that its land area was reduced by close on seventy per cent and its population by around sixty per cent.

Of the '325,411 square kilometres which Hungary had before the Armistice, it was now left with only 92,963 . . . Roumania received 103,093, Czecho-slovakia 61,633, Yugoslavia 42,541 square kilometres of Croatia Slavonia and 20,551 of Inner Hungary . . . Of the population [according to the 1910 census] 20,886,487, Hungary was left with 7,615,117. The Treaty required her to pay reparations of an unspecified sum.'[9]

A quarter of a million Magyars were absorbed into the new Kingdom of Yugoslavia, which had been created out of sectors of Serbia, Croatia and Slovenia.

It was the invasion by the Roumanian army which finally put an end to the brief taste of a Socialist Republic. The newly constructed people's militia was not strong enough to withstand the attack. Bela Kun and some of his colleagues were forced to flee the country, 133 days from the inauguration of the Hungarian People's Socialist Republic. The invasion by Roumania was accompanied by the take-over of Budapest by the Hungarian counter-revolutionaries led by Admiral Horthy which embarked upon a wave of White terror against the newly created Soviet Councils and their leaders.

Notes

1. WHEELER-BENNETT, Sir John, *The Nemesis of Power*, pp. 20–21
2. SILVERLIGHT, John, *The Victors' Dilemma*, p. 128
3. PRICE, Morgan Phillips, *Germany in Transition*, p. 26
4. WOOD, Anthony, *Europe 1815–1945*, p. 369
5. DAVIDSON, Basil, *Germany, What Now?*, p. 152
6. NETTL, J.P., *Rosa Luxemburg*, pp. 774–775 FN
7. NETTL, J.P., *Rosa Luxemburg*, p. 774
8. WESTERN, J.R., *The End of European Primacy*, p. 309
9. MacCARTNEY, C.A., *Hungary – A Short History*, p. 205

7

CAUSE AND EFFECT
VERSAILLES AND THE LEAGUE OF NATIONS

Before passing judgement on the conduct of the 1919 Paris Peace talks and the subsequent Versailles Treaty, the factors which led to the War of Empires should be examined carefully. The secret agreements arrived at during the war: who gained and who were the losers? Had any lessons been learnt to prevent such a massive catastrophe happening again?

The liberal economist, John Maynard Keynes, was a member of the British delegation to the Peace talks and in his book, *Economic Consequences of the Peace*, he describes in detail why the Peace Treaty was bound to fail in its endeavours to secure a peaceful, political and economic climate for the future generations of the peoples of Europe.

Many socialist and non-socialist historians have been critical of the Treaty of Versailles and the impossible reparations imposed upon the losing nations. Some have criticized the re-structuring of post-war Europe, but Keynes, who had been a witness for many months to the unsavoury squabbles among the statesmen of the winning side, refused to accept the philosophy of such colleagues as Sir Eric Geddes* who told a Cambridge audience that 'we will get out of her [Germany] all you can squeeze out of a lemon and a bit more. I will squeeze her until you can hear the pips squeak.'

Whether the Bolshevik revelations of the Secret Treaties and their declaration of 'no annexations' and 'no indemnities' had played any part in Keynes' thinking is hard to assess, but his understanding of the role of one imperial country, his

---

*Industrialist and First Lord of the Admiralty during the war.

ownn, was clearly shown in his book when he says:

> 'England had destroyed, as in each preceding
> century a trade rival; a mighty chapter had been
> closed in the secular struggle between the glories
> of Germany and of France. Prudence required
> some measure of lip service to the "ideals" of
> foolish Americans and hypocritical Englishmen;
> but it would be stupid to believe that there is
> much room in the world, as it really is for such
> affairs as the League of Nations, or in any sense in
> the principle of self-determination, except as an
> ingenious formula for re-arranging the balance of
> power in one's own interest.'[1]

Keynes' scepticism of the role of the League of Nations
became fully justified, but one weakness in his analysis was
that the main trade rival, Germany, had been destroyed –
but only temporarily. The number one enemy, since
November 1917, had now become a class enemy, Soviet
Russia. This became clearly evident by the attempts of
leading anti-Bolshevists, such as Winston Churchill, to get
the collaboration of German army units in the wars of
intervention. The imperial and trade rival remained in a
weakened state but, nevertheless, was a potential aide in
the anti-Soviet campaigns which lay ahead.

When the Peace Conference opened in Paris on 18
January 1919, neither the vanquished nor even representatives from neutral European countries were invited to
discuss the restructuring of their own continent; nor were
the colonial peoples of the German, Austrian and Turkish
empires. As for the negotiations, they were confined to the
inner ring of Allied countries, Britain, France and the
United States of America. Japan which had been regarded
as an ally, decided to retire from the talks after the first few
days, and Italy not long afterwards.

Once the conference got under way it soon became
evident what the war had really been about. This was neatly
summarized by Lloyd Goerge when he said:

> 'The truth is that we have got our way. We have
> got most of the things we set out to get ... The

German navy has been handed over, the German mercantile shipping has been handed over and the German colonies have been given up. One of our chief trade competitors has been most seriously crippled, and our Allies are about to become her biggest creditors. That is no small achievement.'[2]

Under the terms of the Treaty of Versailles, 28 June 1919, Germany had to hand over to the Allies all merchant vessels of over 1600 tons gross, fifty per cent between 1600 and 1000 tons, and twenty five per cent of her fishing fleet. This was in addition to the cut back of her military power, reduced to 100,000 army personnel with no tanks, heavy artillery or aircraft, and only a small navy with no submarines.

Alsace-Lorraine was restored to France and the coal mines of the Saar were to be taken over by the French Government for fifteen years although the administration would be under the control of the League of Nations. The colonies were shared out by the victors and their associates: Germany's African colonies went to Britain, France, Belgium and South Africa, and those in the Pacific and South East Asia to Australia, Japan and New Zealand. The establishment of a League of Nations, and the handing over of the loser's colonies, under the League's mandate, provided a cover of 'respectability' in the sharing of the spoils.

'The assigning of the enemies' colonies and dependencies as "mandates" to trustee powers internationally accountable for their welfare' was, according to J.R. Western, 'an Anglo-American idea' and that the 'system of mandates has been decried over since as a contemptible blind for annexation.'[3]

In the Middle East, Turkey's colonial possessions were divided between Britain and France. Britain took over 'mandated' Palestine, Iraq and Transjordania, and France, which was not so squeamish about 'labels' re-colonized Syria and the Lebanon. Britain's ally in the Arabian wars, Sheik Ibn Saud, was entrusted with leadership of the newly created independent state of Saudi Arabia. German South West Africa (now known as Namibia) was 'mandated' to

South Africa.

The League was, in effect, no more than a group of Nations dominated by Britain and France, with Soviet Russia, Germany, Austria, Hungary and Turkey outside the pale of that 'Brave New World'.

Lloyd George even went so far as to suggest that the League of nations should be presented as an 'Alternative to Bolshevism'. In his Memorandum to the Peace Conference, March 1919, he declared that:

> 'If we are to offer Europe an alternative to Bolshevism we must make the League of Nations into something which will be both a safeguard to those nations who are prepared for fair dealing with their neighbours, and a menace to those who would trespass on the rights of their neighbours . . .'[4]

Fear of the spread of socialist ideology, and a socialist revolution on an international scale, appeared to predominate the minds of the League's sponsors. Within days of the cessation of the war, Britain's Foreign Office issued a memorandum (in December 1918) in which it stated:

> 'We have to look forward to a period when Bolshevism – or the religion of the international class war – will be a prominent factor in European policy, and may at any time seize the reins of power in states which are or desire to become members of the League. We ought to lay it down in set terms that governments which promote propaganda subversive of the governments of their neighbours are outside the pale of the League's membership.'[5]

It was inevitable that the conference, based upon such unstable foundations would develop into inter-factional squabbles among its sponsors. British interests, in the main, lay outside Europe. The acquisition of additional colonies, and the undermining of Germany's naval strength became a priority, whereas France concentrated on the destruction of the German army and Germany's industrial potential. The Allies Reparation Commission set a figure for Germany's war indemnities at 132,000 million German marks in gold* – a figure which failed to take into consideration Germany's ability to pay, once its industrial capacity had been well-nigh destroyed.

When the Treaty of Versailles was signed on 28 June, there were 'no provisions for the economic rehabilitation of Europe, – nothing to make the defeated Central Empires into good neighbours', declared Keynes. 'It is an extraordinary fact' he said 'that the fundamental economic problem of Europe starving and disintegrating before their eyes, was the one question in which it was impossible to arouse the interest of the Four. [Allies]. Reparation was their main excursion into the economic field, and they settled it as a problem of theology, of politics, of electoral chicane, from every point of view except that of the economic future of the states whose destiny they were handling.'[6]

The harsh terms of the Treaty brought untold misery and suffering to millions of men, women and children who could not be held responsible for the conduct of the war, or of the war crimes. A statement condemning the Treaty was issued by the National Executive of the Labour Party, and the Union of Democratic Control, a group of Liberals and Socialists whose aim was a democratically controlled British Foreign Policy, 'pointed out that Britain's quarrel had been with the rulers of Germany who had been overthrown and that the apparent purpose of the Allied Governments was to reduce the new democratic Germany to the position of a vassal state.'[7]

---

*Payment of this sum proved impossible and after Germany's financial collapse in 1923, a new reparation scheme, known as the Dawes Plan, was worked out in 1924. It provided for German payments of 2,000 million marks per year without fixing a definite total amount. Even this proved to be too high . . . An international conference at Lausanne in 1932 decided to abolish the reparations altogether. The total payments made by Germany under the various schemes, including deliveries in kind, aggregated about 17,000 million Marks . . . and they were more than offset by the loans granted to Germany by the USA, Britain and other countries in the period from 1924 to 1930. Such loans, including short term deposits, totalled 27,000 million Marks. (*Penguin Political Dictionary*, 1939).

Whatever the problems of the ethnic minorities within the countries of Europe may have been before the Armistice, they were as nothing compared to the problems that were created by the restructuring of Europe after Versailles. Three million Magyars were incorporated into an enlarged Roumania and the newly created state of Czechoslovakia; two hundred thousand Germans in the Tyrol came into the extended Italian territory, and three and a quarter million Germans spread along the Bohemian, Moravian areas were also brought within Czechoslovakia. These latter, together with the two million Germans within a re-created independent and enlarged Poland, were to provide Nazi Germany, some twenty years later, with an excuse to re-capture the 'lost territories'.

The Baltic sea port, Memel, was given to Lithuania, and the Port of Danzig, at the mouth of the Vistula, was declared a Free City and handed over to Poland. A corridor was established linking that country to Danzig. In Southern Europe, the Balkans were re-carved with the creation of the new state of Yugoslavia into which was submerged the Kingdom of Serbia.

It was this arbitrary re-creation of the European frontiers that was to provide seeds of discontent and some of the combustible material for sparking off World War II.

Notes

1. KEYNES, J.M., *The Economic Consequences of the Peace*, p. 30
2. RIDDELL, Lord, *Intimate Diary of the Peace Conference and After 1918–1923*, p. 42
3. WESTERN, J.R., *The End of European Primacy*, p. 318
4. LLOYD GEORGE, David, *The Truth About the Peace Treaties* Vol. I, p. 409
5. ZIMMERN, Professor Alfred, *The League of Nations and the Rule of Law 1918–1935*, pp. 201–202
6. KEYNES, J.M., *The Economic Consequences of the Peace*, p. 212
7. BRANSON, Noreen, *Britain in the 1920s*, p. 48

8

BALTIC COUNTRIES FIGHT FOR NATIONAL INDEPENDENCE

One of the consequences of the granting of self-determination by the Bolsheviks to countries within the Tsarist Empire was the inevitable demand of the peasants and workers to be allowed to participate in the running of their countries. This became evident soon after the granting of independence to Finland and the Baltic States of Estonia, Latvia and Lithuania.

In the case of Finland independence was officially recognized on 4 January 1918 by 'the Council of people's Commissars in full accord with the principles of the right of nations to self-determination.'[1] The Finnish ruling class, however, were determined to stifle any attempts to establish a Soviet type government. After a brief but bitter civil war, in which they had the help of troops from the German Baltic Armies under General von de Goltz, their White Army, led by General Mannerheim,* not only overcame the revolutionary forces in Finland but advanced to within twenty five miles of Petrograd. In recognition of services rendered by the German armies Prince Frederick Charles of Hesse, Kaiser Wilhelm's brother-in-law, was appointed King of Finland but by the end of the year he had been replaced by Mannerheim who was given the title of Regent.

Further south, large areas of Estonia and Latvia were being taken over by local Soviets. German aspirations of

---

*Finnish aristocrat. For many years lived in Tsarist Russia. Married 1892 to daughter of a Russian General. Attached to Tsar Nicholas' personal staff. During the war was Lieutenant General and Commander of Tsarist Russia's 6th Cavalry Corps. Was relieved of his Command after the revolution. Returned to Finland and appointed Finland's Commander in Chief, January 1918. (ex *Three Days to Catastrophe* – Douglas Clarke)

extending their frontiers to embrace the Baltic provinces came to an end on 11 November 1918. Under the terms of the Armistice, Article XII:

> 'The Germans were to withdraw from the territory that was formerly part of the Russian Empire as soon as the Allies should consider the moment suitable having regard to the interior conditions of those territories.'

The German High Command naturally interpreted this declaration as an invitation to remain in the Baltic countries for the time being, as part of Allied plans for stifling the revolutionary forces in those countries in their struggle against the Baltic Barons and the reactionary ruling class. With the help of interventionist forces, White provisional governments were establshed. However, within a few days they were repudiated by the mass of the people, especially in Estonia and Latvia, and Soviet Governments were set up in opposition.

The morale of the German Army was at its lowest point in these areas and when the Armistice was announced many soldiers laid down their arms and insisted upon being sent home. The newly established Soviets were greeted with sympathy and in some cases given active support by units of the German occupation forces.

According to Louis Fischer (*The Soviets in World Affairs*) 'The Allies, who did not wish or were not able to employ their own soldiers in the Russian border states, had decided on making use of the Germans to prevent the spread of Bolshevism westward.' They were afraid that 'the Soviet influence in Lithuania' would spread to Prussia 'and from there join hands with Spartacism in other sections of Germany.'[2]

Britain's role in the Baltic was originally to supply the Baltic White provisional governments with military equipment hoping that, with the help of the German troops, the Baltic Soviets would be overcome. When this plan collapsed, the War Cabinet decided, on 20 November 1918, upon a show of force 'to help strengthen the populations of that part of the world against Bolshevism and to assist

British interests there'. Five naval cruisers, nine destroyers and seven mine-sweepers were sent to the Baltic under Rear Admiral Sinclair. En route, one cruiser, the *Cassandra* struck a mine and sank. Eleven lives were lost and two other ships damaged in a collision.

The following month, two destroyers of the Red Navy were captured and 'handed over to the Estonians together with their crews, forty of whom were executed.' The Commander of the Soviet naval taskforce, F.F. Raskolnikov, and another Soviet prisoner, Ninyuk, a member of the Petrograd Soviet who had been captured earlier by the British 'were exchanged the following May for eighteen British officers' held by the Soviet Government.[3]

British intervention in the Baltic areas was by now beginning to collapse under the attacks of Red troops and disaffection within the Latvian and Estonian counter-revolutionary forces. One Latvian White regiment mutinied whereupon the British decided to take matters into their own hands. 'On the night of 29-30 December, Captain H.H. Smyth, the Senior British Naval Officer in Riga, ordered the Cruiser *Ceres* to open fire on the mutineers' barracks in the town.'[4]

Although the mutiny had been quelled by sheer military intimidation the British intervention naval force was nevertheless unable to prevent Riga from being taken over by the Latvian revolutionary militia. The significance of the failure of this British naval force to tip the balance in favour of the Baltic 'old guard' had not yet been appreciated by Whitehall's intervention strategists. So a few weeks later another naval squadron was instructed to steam into the Baltic and 'show the flag'. The Commander was Rear Admiral Water Cowan. His orders were:

> ' "to show the British flag and support British policy": but no more arms* were to be supplied to local forces unless he was "reasonably convinced that the Estonian or other government is of a stable nature and can control the army". The

*10,000 rifles, machine-guns and ammunition had already been supplied to the Estonian and Latvian governments. (ex Robert Jackson, p. 208)

chief British interest was "to prevent the destruction of Estonia and Latvia ... which is only threatened at present by Bolshevik invaders". Where resistance to Bolshevik attacks was practicable from the sea "we should unhesitatingly do so", and Bolshevik men-of-war operating off the coasts of the Baltic provinces were, as before, to be treated as hostile. On the other hand the Admiral "should not interfere with local politics", nor raise hopes of military assistance other than the supply of arms; and only "under some very exceptional circumstance" was he authorized to land men from his ships.'[5]

Exceptional circumstances were certainly not infrequent during Britain's three years of intervention.

Meanwhile the German army, under von der Goltz, having assisted Mannerheim to crush the Finnish revolution, had been reinforced by volunteers from the newly established German 'Freikorps' and moved back into Latvia. During the Autumn of 1919 White Russian and German troops were joined together in the formation of a North West Russian Army and placed under the command of a Colonel Pavel Milhailovitch Bermondt, who had recently arrived in Latvia. Bermondt had collected his anti-Bolshevik recruits from among the thousands of White Russians who were at the time living in Germany.

Morgan Phillips Price, in his report from Berlin on 31 December 1919, describes the events 'concerning the new Entente-German intrigue against the Russian revolution.'

'The German Foreign Office, according to the official organs here, has petitioned the Entente, on behalf of Bermondt, the Riga adventurer, with the object of getting half his German troops transferred to the North-West Russian front against Petrograd.

The impression has been created, no doubt purposely, that the Entente, when they demanded that Bermondt's troops should withdraw from the

112

Baltic, were serious in their intention of refusing to allow Germans to take part in counter-revolutionary adventures in Russia.

In actual fact, it is now known that the Entente's objection to the participation of the Germans in the anti-Bolshevik armies was not an objection in principle. The Germans are not wanted in Courland and Lithuania because the German government may make claims in these territories which would be troublesome to the 'Tiger' [Clemenceau] and his English supporters in the Northcliffe press. But, of course, there is not the smallest reason why German cannon-fodder should not be used to shoot down Russian workmen and peasants, provided that German capitalists renounce all political and territorial remuneration in the Baltic for the spilt blood of German soldiers.' (*The Daily Herald* 2 January 1920)

The aspirations of the British and French governments to co-opt the Germans into a combined anti-Bolshevik crusade misfired. The remnants of the German Baltic army and the 'Freikorps' under von der Goltz had set their sights on securing a greater Prussian homeland by securing control over Latvia and Estonia themselves. Consequently a clash between the Entente and the Germans became inevitable. Under Allied pressure upon the Weimar Government von der Goltz was recalled to Germany, but Bermondt, with his fifteen thousand troops, showed no intention of being restrained in his aim to 'subjugate the whole of Latvia before his drive into Russia and on 8 October [1919] he marched on Riga.' Warships of the British and French navies eventually decided that the Germans had gone too far and together they issued a joint demand for the withdrawal of German troops. Bermondt and his officers ignored the ultimatum, whereupon the Anglo-French warships opened fire. The Germans fled 'pursued by the Lettish infantry.'[6] By the end of November all German troops had left Latvia.

It is interesting to recall that although a cease-fire and Armistice had been declared between the Entente and

113

Germany in November 1918, the rivalry and, in some cases, military confrontation continued well into 1919 for the control of the Baltic countries even though both the Entente and German leaders had a common purpose in crushing the revolutionary forces in those countries. The Entente's policy was to use the Baltic White armies and Germans as a springboard for a major attack on Petrograd – together with the White and anti-Bolshevik forces of General Yudenitch.

By 21 October 1919, combined Latvian, Estonian and Yudenitch's White Russian troops, aided by Admiral Cowan's warships and six British tanks, had advanced to within eight miles of Petrograd. After a bitter and bloody struggle the Red Army, assisted by the Eastern section of the Red Fleet, having halted the advance, counter-attacked and smashed through the Yudenitch forces. The remnants of the North Western anti-Bolshevik Army were completely routed and driven back into Estonia.

On 31 March 1920 the Admiralty issued instructions to officers of the Baltic Fleet to cease forthwith any further naval actions against the Bolsheviks.

Admiral Cowan, who had returned to Britain on 4 January, disclosed 'in his final report . . . that a total of 230 British warships and auxiliaries had come under his command.' During the period of the Baltic campaign 'British losses amounted to one submarine, two destroyers, two mine-sweeping sloops, seven CMBs (coastal motor boats) and a stores carrier sunk: and 127 officers and men had been killed or were missing . . .

'In addition to the British ships sent to the Baltic', Admiral Cowan also had under his command 'twenty six French, fourteen United States and two Italian ships.'[7]

Peace Treaties were concluded between the Baltic countries and Soviet Russia; with Estonia on 2 February 1920, Lithuania on 30 June, and Latvia on 11 August. But it was not until October 1920, after four months of negotiations, and after the failure of the Allied and German intervention campaigns in the countries around the Baltic, that a 'Treaty of Peace' was eventually agreed upon by the Governments of Finland and the USSR.

Notes

1. DEGRAS, Jane (ed) *Soviet Documents on Foreign Policy*, p. 30
2. FISCHER, Louis, *The Soviets in World Affairs*, p. 135
3. SILVERLIGHT, John, *The Victors' Dilemma*, pp. 294–5; (see also ULLMAN, Richard H., *Britain and the Russian Civil War*, p. 340
4. JACKSON, Robert, *At War with the Bolsheviks*, pp. 207–8
5. ROSKILL, Stephen, *Naval Policy Between the Wars Vol. I 1919–1929*, p. 146
6. JACKSON, Robert, *At War with the Bolsheviks*, pp. 223–224
7. ROSKILL, Stephen, *Naval Policy Between the Wars Vol. I 1919–1929*, p. 153–154

9

INTERVENTION IN THE NORTH

Some months after the Armistice, the British 6th Battalion Royal Marines was informed that it was being sent to Schleswig-Holstein to maintain order during the holding of a plebiscite which was to decide the province's future; instead of which, under cover of secrecy, it was sent to Murmansk, Russia's most northerly sea-port, to be used in the military campaign against the Bolsheviks.

Murmansk, in the Barents Sea, and within the Arctic Circle, was founded in 1915. A creation of the Imperial war, it was connected by a single-track railway to Petrograd, some 800 miles to the south. According to John Silverlight, it was 'built at British instigation and at what must have been a terrible cost in human endurance and suffering to the Russians and others working on its construction: hundreds of war prisoners, Germans, Hungarians, Slovaks and others died miserably while building the railway.'[1] As the Gulf Stream flowed around its shores, Murmansk was practically ice-free throughout the year, whereas Archangel, 400 miles to the south, was ice-bound for six months of the year.

The northern ports of Murmansk and Archangel were to play a prominent part during 1919 in the Allies' intervention plans of prizing open Russia's northern 'back-door'. It was the area where, for the first time, the United States became militarily involved in the anti-Bolshevik crusade.

By the end of May 1918, 520 British troops had been landed in Murmansk. General Ironside, Britain's Commander in the area records that:

'on 23 June an Allied Squadron consisting of two

116

British, two White Russian, one United States and one French warship, under Admiral Kemp, arrived off the port. They brought with them a reinforcement for Murmansk of 600 British infantry and a machine-gun company.'

In addition, there was

'a British Mission of some 70 officers and 500 other ranks, which were labelled "Elope", so as to divert attention from it. It was intended to proceed to Archangel to help in the forming of anti-Bolshevik forces there.'[2]

Archangel was wrested from the Bolsheviks on 2 August. The following day the first contingent of American troops arrived.

Both British and American Governments had been warned by their Consuls in Archangel of the dangers of becoming militarily involved in the Russian civil war. Douglas Young, Britain's Consul in Archangel, had in June 1918, wired his Foreign Minister, Arthur Balfour, 'warning him that military operations without the consent of the effective rulers of Russia, even if locally successful, would commit the British Government to obligations from which they could not free themselves without great loss of prestige.' The American Consul, Felix Cole, cabled his US Secretary of State with an even stronger warning:

'. . . Intervention cannot reckon on active support from Russians' said Cole. 'All the fight is out of Russia.

'. . . The Socialist Revolutionaries, Mensheviks and Cadets who now advocate intervention are discredited office-holders seeking to regain power. The Socialist Revolutionist intellectuals will never rule Russia. Their place is round the steaming samovar not in the halls of government. Their invitation to enter Russia is not an invitation from the Russian people . . . on the other hand, the men who do rule Russia, however badly it is done, are the small Bolshevik leaders . . . No child can ever be convinced that it is spanked for its own benefit . . . Intervention will alienate thousands of anti-German Bolsheviks . . .

'. . . Every foreign invasion that has gone deep into Russia has been swallowed up . . . If we intervene, going farther into Russia as we succeed, we shall be swallowed up . . . '[3]

In May 1919 Churchill presented to 'the House of Commons his optimistic picture of events on the Archangel Front.' He had become so blinded by his fanatical anti-Bolshevism, that it prompted Lloyd George to confide 'to Bonar Law in Paris that sometimes his Secretary of State had "Bolshevism on the Brain" and now he wanted to raise a German force to undertake operations in Russia.'[4]

Morale and discipline among the White and Allied forces were at their lowest ebb.

'Huge supplies of food, intended to feed both the troops and the civilian population were diverted to a thriving free market, and even British officers were caught bartering goods in the streets. The area swarmed with SIS officers in improbable disguises . . . and in February 1919, with still no news of when they were to be withdrawn, the troops started to mutiny.'[5]

Churchill's warning that 'the British Expeditionary Force in North Russia could not leave "that ice-bound shore" until late summer opened the seas for their evacuation'[6] did nothing to appease the British troops.

On 26 February, General Ironside received a wire from Colonel Lavie that his newly arrived Yorkshire Regiment had refused to proceed to the front at Seletskoe. A French battalion on leave at Archangel refused to return to active service and were sent back to France. 'In March a section of the Canadian Field Brigade refused to obey orders, and an American company objected when ordered to return to forward posts.'[7]

This breakdown in discipline led Ironside to report: 'We were drawing terribly near the end of our tether as an efficient fighting force', which must have prompted Churchill's response on 5 April, through Ironside, to the British troops.

> 'Although you are cut off from your country by the ice, you are not forgotten ... You will be back home in time to see this year's harvest in. If you continue to display that undaunted British spirit which has so often got us through in spite of heavy odds and great hardships, only a few more months of resolute and faithful service against this ferocious enemy and your task will have been discharged.'[8]

Winston Churchill had just become Minister for War, and with backing from most of the British press, kept up a campaign to offset the growing influence of the 'Hands-off-Russia' and 'Bring the Boys Home' movements.

The Churchillian policy in Northern Russia was eventually blown wide open when a young South African Lieutenant-Colonel, John Sherwood-Kelly, a Battalion Commander, withdrew his troops from the battle front against the Red Army without so much as firing a shot. Sherwood-Kelly had been decorated on a number of occasions as a war-time hero. He had been wounded five times and among his awards was the Distinguished Service Order and the Victoria Cross. The young Colonel was relieved of his Command by Ironside and sent back to Britain.

On the morning of 6 September 1919, a letter appeared on the front page of the *Daily Express* signed by Sherwood-Kelly, in which he exposed in no uncertain terms some aspects of Britain's interventionist policy.

> 'I have just returned from North Russia under circumstances which compel me to seek the earliest possible opportunity of making known in England certain facts in connection with North Russia which otherwise might never come to light ...
> I volunteered for service with the North Russian

Relief Force in the sincere belief that relief was urgently needed in order to make possible the withdrawal of low category troops in the last stages of exhaustion, due to fierce fighting and the rigours of an Arctic Winter . . .

Immediately on arrival at Archangel, towards the end of May, I at once received the impression that the policy of the authorities was not what it was stated to be. This impression hardened as time went on and during the months of June and July I was reluctantly and inevitably driven to the following conclusions:–

That the troops of the Relief Force, which we were told had been sent out purely for defensive purposes, were being used for offensive purposes on a large scale and far into the interior, in furtherance of some ambitious plan of campaign the nature of which we were not allowed to know. My personal experience of those operations was that they were not even well conducted, and that they were not calculated to benefit in a military or any other sense a sound and practical British policy in Russia. They only entailed useless loss and suffering on troops that had already made incalculable sacrifices in the great war.

I discovered what is now a matter of common knowledge even in England that the much vaunted "loyal Russian army", composed largely of Bolshevik prisoners dressed in khaki was utterly unreliable, always disposed to mutiny, and that it always constituted a greater danger to our troops than the Bolshevik armies opposed to them. This was tragically demonstrated early in July, when the Russians mutinied and murdered their British officers.

I formed the opinion that the puppet government set up by us in Archangel rested on no basis of public confidence and support, and would fall to pieces the moment the protection of British bayonets was withdrawn.

At the same time I saw British money poured

out like water and invaluable British lives sacrificed in backing up this worthless army and in
keeping in power this worthless government, and
I became convinced that my duty to my country
lay not in helping to forward a mistaken policy,
but in exposing it to the British public . . . '

This letter played a major role in precipitating the
eventual evacuation of British and Allied troops from
Northern Russia. Later that month the British contingent,
together with 6,000 White Russians, were evacuated and by
the end of October all the Allied interventionist forces,
around 37,000, had left. The Americans had begun their
evacuation at the end of May, and by the time the last of the
troops had gone their casualities had reached 2,845, even
more than the British.

As for the fate of the White Russians who had not
accepted the offer of evacuation, Churchill placed the
responsibility 'upon the mighty and resplendent nations
that had won the war, but left their task unfinished.'[9]* He
was unable to reconcile himself to the disaster of his
interventionist policy and the collapse of his anti-Bolshevik
Crusades. Military intervention had only temporarily
ceased as far as he was concerned – a 'task unfinished' – to
be taken up again at a more opportune moment.

This anti-Bolshevik obsession was creating many problems for Lloyd George, judging by the letter which he sent
to Churchill on 22 September 1919:

'My Dear Winston,
    Your letter distressed me. You know that I have
been doing my best for the last few weeks to
comply with the legitimate demand which comes
from all classes of the country to cut down the
enormous expenditure which is devouring the
resources of the country at a prodigious rate. I
have repeatedly begged you to apply your mind to
the problem. I made this appeal to all depart-

---

*It will be seen in later chapters, and in Churchill's Fulton Speech of April
1946 how the unfinished task was taken up again.

ments, but I urged it specially upon you for three reasons: the first is that the highest expenditure is still military; the second that the largest immediate reduction which could be affected without damage to the public welfare are foreseeable in the activities controlled by your department. The third is that I have found your mind so obsessed by Russia that I felt I had good ground for the apprehension that your great abilities, energy and courage were not devoted to the reduction of expenditure. I regret that all my appeals have been in vain. At each interview you promised me to give your mind to this very important problem. Nevertheless the first communication I have always received from you after these interviews related to Russia. I invited you to Paris to help me reduce our commitments in the East. You there produced a lengthy and carefully prepared memorandum on Russia. I entreated you to let Russia be for at least 48 hours and to devote your week-end to preparing for the Finance Committee this afternoon. You promised faithfully to do so. Your reply is to send me a four-page letter on Russia. I am frankly in despair. Yesterday and today I have gone carefully through such details as have been supplied about the military expenditure, and I am more convinced than ever that Russia has cost us not merely the sum spent directly upon that unfortunate country, but indirectly scores of millions in the failure to attend to the costly details of expenditure in other spheres.

You confidently predict in your memorandum that Denikin is on the eve of some great and striking success. I looked up some of your memoranda and your statements made earlier in the year about Kolchak and I find that you use exactly the same language in reference to Kolchak's "successes".

The Cabinet have given you every support in the policy which they have laid down, and which you have accepted. I am not sure that they have not once or twice strained that policy in the direction of your wishes . . .

You proposed that the Czechoslovaks should be en-couraged to break through the Bolshevik armies and proceed to Archangel. Everything was done to support your proposal. Ships were promised for Archangel if they succeeded. Denikin has been supplied with all the munitions and equipment that he needed. Still you vaguely suggest that something more could have been done and ought to have been done.

I abide by the agreed policy. We have kept faith with all these men. But not a member of the Cabinet is prepared to go further. The various Russian enterprises have cost us this year between 100 and 150 millions, when Army, Navy and Shipping are taken into account. Neither this government nor any other government that this country is likely to see will do more. We cannot afford it. The French have talked a good deal about Anti-Bolshevism, but they have left us to carry out the Allied policy. Clemenceau told me distinctly that he was not prepared to do any more. Foch is distinctly and definitely opposed to these ventures at Allied expense. Their view is that our first duty is to clear up the German situation. I agree with them.

I wonder whether it is any use my making one last effort to induce you to throw off this obsession which if you will forgive me for saying so, is upsetting your balance. I again ask you to let Russia be, at any rate for a few days, and to concentrate your mind on the quite unjustifiable expenditure in France, at home, and in the East, incurred by both the War Office and Air Departments. Some of the items could not possibly have been tolerated by you if you had given one-fifth of the thought to these matters which you devoted to Russia.'

Referring to Churchill's policy on the Baltic States, Lloyd

George comments:

> 'You want us to recognize their independence in
> return for their attacking the Bolsheviks? They
> would ask us (i) to guarantee it, (ii) supply them
> with equipment and cash to fight with. And in the
> end, whoever won in Russia, the government there
> would promptly recover the old Russian Baltic
> Ports. Are you, Mr Churchill prepared to have a
> war with perhaps an anti-Bolshevik government to
> prevent that? If not, it would be a disgraceful piece
> of deception on our part to give any guarantee to
> these new Baltic States that you are proposing to
> use to reconquer Russia.'

In conclusion, Lloyd George told Churchill that he was well
aware that he 'was willing to spend hundreds of millions of
pounds on these projects.'

> 'For that is what you really desire. But as you
> know that you wont find another responsible
> person in the whole land who will take your view,
> why waste your energy and your usefulness on
> this vain fretting which completely paralyses you
> for other work?
>
> Every sincerely,
D. Lloyd George.'[10]

On 10 February 1920 Lloyd George told the House of
Commons:

> 'It is perfectly clear now to every unprejudiced
> observer that you cannot crush Bolshevism by
> force of arms . . .
>   'I cannot conceive any method which would
> more thoroughly arouse the patriotism of the
> Russian people, and range it so much on the side
> of authority as the advance of a number of foreign
> armies into Russia.' (*Hansard*, Cols. 41, 42, 43)

Britain's Prime Minister had at last decided to face up to
the facts of life, not only in words, but gradually and

somewhat begrudgingly in deeds. Soviet Russia, he knew, was, in spite of military intervention, in spite of the blockade, or of the armed and financially-backed White anti-Bolsheviks, becoming firmly established as a major political and economic factor in the post-war world. Keynes had already warned, in his widely read book, that the need for supplies of Russian wheat and grain 'will be even greater than it was before the war.' The soil of Europe, said Keynes, 'will not have yet recovered its former productivity. If trade is not resumed with Russia, wheat in 1920–21 (unless the seasons are especially bountiful) must be scarce and very dear. The Blockade of Russia, lately proclaimed by the Allies, is therefore a foolish and shortsighted proceeding; we are blockading not so much Russia as ourselves.'[11]

The proclamation Keynes was referring to was linked to the decision of the Allied Supreme Council of victorious powers to 'maintain a "peaceful blockade" of Russia.'

On 30 September 1919 the Supreme Council, who were in session at Versailles, sent out Notes to the neutral governments and the vanquished German Government requesting 'all nations which desire peace and the re-establishment of the social order should unite together to resist the Bolshevik Government.'

'The call was made for complete prohibition of trade, communications of persons, credits or postal intercourse between other countries and Bolshevik Russia. These Notes were not made public in this country nor in the French Republic and only became known later through the publication of the Note to the German Government and in the German press.

'By November 1919, the Blockade Note proposing a universal blockade of Russia had been answered by the countries to whom it had been addressed. Germany and Italy both declined to take part . . . The policy of "intercepting" ships to Russia by British naval forces in the Baltic was stated by the British Government not to be a blockade in the technical sense. Why? Because technically though war was being conducted, Britain was not in a state of war with Russia.'[12] This was a typical example of the Allied use of Versailles and the League of Nations to further their anti-Bolshevik aims. It was obviously too much for Keynes, who

125

not only condemned the excessive German reparation plan, but had become increasingly critical of Allied plans against Soviet Russia. Not just on moral grounds, but also because they made no economic or political sense.*

The divisions within the British Government were by now opening up. Pressure had been accumulating throughout the country and within the Armed Forces for an end to intervention. The clamours had reached such a pitch that some Conservative newspapers obviously felt that it would be prudent to gradually change their militaristic attitude towards Soviet Russia. A leading article which appeared in *The Observer* of 4 January 1920 under the headings 'THE BASIS OF REAL PEACE' 'RUSSIA OR GERMANY?' 'THE GREAT ALTERNATIVE' gives an indication of its change of direction when it declared:

> 'The Bolshevists will soon be in effect possession of four-fifths of the former Russian Empire, including the vast bulk of its agricultural and mineral resources . . .
> We must desire peace with the Bolshevists if possible as with all the world. But not for a moment must we be blind to the difficulty and even impossibility of arriving at any safe settlement with them while Central Europe remains as it is . . . By utterly incompatible policies in the last twelve months, the Allies are surely, steadily driving the German and Russian peoples into each others arms.'

It was thus not only the failure of intervention which had brought about the change.

Statements like this coming from so influential a newspaper would have strengthened the hand of Lloyd George who had seen the danger and futility of the military intervention much earlier than his Cabinet colleagues. He had already announced publicly that intervention against

---

*Keynes resigned from his position of Economic Adviser at Versailles.

Soviet Russia could no longer be carried on effectively. 'The last British troops', he said, had 'sailed for home from Murmansk on 12 October 1919 and from Vladivostock on 1 November 1919.' But there was a very strong rearguard of pro-interventionists within his Cabinet who were still determined, like Churchill, to continue, by whatever means possible, to have just one more 'fling' at the Bolsheviks.

Notes

1. SILVERLIGHT, John, *The Victors' Dilemma*, pp. 30–31
2. IRONSIDE, Edmund, *W.E. Ironside – Archangel 1918–1919*, pp. 17–18
3. SILVERLIGHT, John, *The Victors' Dilemma*, pp. 59–60
4. OWEN, Frank, *Tempestuous Journey*, p. 516
5. KNIGHTLEY, Phillip, *The First Casualty*, pp. 163–164
6. OWEN, Frank, *Tempestuous Journey*, p. 515
7. KNIGHTLEY, Phillip, *The First Casualty*, p. 164
8. IRONSIDE, Edmund, *W.E. Ironside – Archangel 1918–1919*, pp. 114 and 124
9. KNIGHTLEY, Phillip, *The First Casualty*, p. 167
10. OWEN, Frank, *Tempestuous Journey*, pp. 519–521
11. KEYNES, J.M., *The Economic Consequences of the Peace*, p. 274
12. ARNOT, R. Page, *The Impact of the Russian Revolution in Britain*, p. 158

10

THE 'LAST FLING'

On the morning of 24 January 1920, a headline appeared over a report by the *Daily Herald* – '"Z" MEN NOT OUT OF DANGER'*

The report commented upon the 'flood of denials' concerning 'fresh military operations or intervention' that were being 'contemplated by Great Britain.' 'The greatest anxiety' said the *Herald* 'is displayed in official quarters to allay the very natural and widespread alarm and suspicion caused by the War Office communiqué foreshadowing fresh "military commitments on a large scale".'

Who were these 'Z' men? and why were they still in danger?

When the war ended on 11 November 1918 there were still many servicemen being used to fight in the undeclared Wars of Intervention in Russia. Nevertheless, the Government was obliged to set into operation the process of demobilizing the non-professional servicemen who had either volunteered for the duration of the war or had been conscripted. Although they were in theory to be demobilized, in reality they were placed on the 'Z' Reserve List which meant that they were in constant danger of being recalled for service as and when required, once again to be separated from their families and homes.

Just about this time, Palek, the Polish Foreign Minister, had been visiting London and Paris 'to obtain from the Entente much needed aid.' According to *L'Humanité* (18

---

*In 1948 many thousands of demobilized British servicemen of World War II received 'Z' Reserve calling up papers. I was one of them.

February 1920), then the organ of the French Socialist Party, Clemenceau regarded Poland as a bastion of 'European civilization'.

There were powerful elements in Britain and in France who were not content to accept a Soviet Socialist Russia as an established fact. The defeats in the Far East, in the Crimea, in the Baltic and in the North had still not diminished their desires for catching the Red Army unawares and inflicting the mortal blow which would smash Bolshevism once and for all. Within Poland the aristocracy, the feudal landowners and the Army believed they had the support which they hoped could be encouraged to deal the ultimate blow.

In December 1919, Churchill and Clemenceau concocted a plan in which there would be a joint attack by Polish, Finnish and Roumanian troops against the Bolsheviks; the Polish Army to be trained by British and French officers. Their hopes were particularly pinned upon Poland, who only the previous summer had welcomed the return of a 35,000 strong Polish Army contingent, which had been raised in France during the war, and equipped with the most up-to-date weapons. This army, together with the resident Polish national forces had, in May 1919, attacked the Ukrainian White 'independent' forces in Galicia and then went on to capture the Byelorussian town of Minsk. Having achieved their initial objective, the Polish Commander-in-Chief, Marshal Pilsudski, eventually came to terms with the Ukrainian White leader, Simon Petlura.

The disintegration of the White anti-Bolshevik forces on the Eastern, Southern and Northern Fronts, the mutinies and the pressure of the 'Hands Off Russia' movements, had compelled the British and French Governments to re-assess their interventionist policy. They had, for the time being, ruled out direct intervention, but were prepared to support any country that could help in toppling the Bolshevik regime. It was therefore decided to provide Poland with the financial and military backing which, together with the economic blockade, might achieve this objective.

Poland and the Polish people had suffered greatly during the War of Empires. Polish troops, under Marshal Pilsudski, had fought with Germany and Austria against Imperial

Russia and later sided with the Allies against the Central Powers. When the Bolsheviks came to power Poland was one of the first countries to be given its independence. But the ruling elements in Poland were behind Pilsudski in his drive for a 'greater Poland', a Poland restored to its eighteenth century imperial glory. The Soviet Government, fully aware of the aims of the Polish leaders had, between 22 December 1919 and 4 February 1920, issued three appeals to the Polish Government to settle their disputes by peaceful negotiations. The Polish Government had already 'accepted as final' the Curzon Line*, which had been 'secretly drawn by the Supreme Council on 8 December 1919' but apparently had 'successfully defied the Peace Conference in the matter of Eastern Galicia and her politicians did not intend to accept from the world's diplomats less than they thought obtainable by force of arms.'[1]

Although the appeals had placed the Polish leaders in an embarrassing position, they were nevertheless ignored. The Polish Government, in collaboration with the Entente, was rapidly building up its military potential. According to Robert Jackson: 'The Poles had, in fact, begun to create the nucleus of an air force in October 1918, when the 1st Aviation Unit of the Polish Army was formed in Odessa with French help; this however was not transferred to Poland until the middle of 1919, and in the meantime – in October and November 1918 – more squadrons were formed on Polish territory with the aid of some 200 aircraft left behind by the German and Austrian forces of occupation.' Seventeen American airmen had arrived in Lvov and joined the 7th Squadron which 'was equipped with former German Albatross fighters.'[2]

Having just signed an agreement with Petlura, offering him Ukrainian independence in exchange for military help, Pilsudski issued instructions for the Polish Army to commence its invasion of Russia. The attack was launched on 24 April 1920, with a drive into the Ukraine and on 8 May Kiev, the Ukrainian capital, was captured by the

*The Curzon Line defined Poland's eastern frontier, passing through Grodno to Bialostock to Brest-Litovsk and southwards along the river Bug.

Polish troops.

Repercussions of the shock of this latest invasion of Soviet Russia were felt throughout the Allied countries. *The Daily Herald* on 30 April 1920, reminded its readers that it:

> 'for two months past has warned England that the military gamble in the East was not finished; that a new attempt was to be made to overthrow the Soviet Republic by armed force . . . The storm has burst . . . the Polish and Ukrainian armies are advancing towards Kieff. The Finns, newly munitioned from Germany, may at any moment move against Petrograd. The German and Hungarian "Whites" are in reserve. On the South, General Wrangel – Denikin's successor – is moving north from the Crimea, equipped with British munitions . . . The attack' declared the *Herald*, 'has been delivered by the Poles and the Ukrainians, but the real authors of the conspiracy are not all in Warsaw. General Denikin is in London, General Yudenitch has recently been here.'

And a few days later, *The Manchester Guardian*, 3 May 1920, in an editorial demanded:

> 'What is the meaning of the preposterous invasion now being carried out by the Poles against Russia? Poland is devastated by famine and typhus, her people are starving, and she cries aloud to the world for charity. She is utterly bankrupt. She could not carry on her ordinary administration for a single week, let alone an extensive campaign, without foreign aid in money and kind. Yet here she is engaged on vast military operations on a frontier of 250 miles, along which it is vaingloriously announced, her armies have advanced quite a long way and have made handsome captures of men and material. Who is at the back of it? . . . Who is paying for it? What is the motive of it? Who is responsible for this crime?'

131

But the news of the capture of the Ukrainian capital was celebrated by the anti-Bolshevik circles in Britain, as well as in a number of Fleet Street offices. *The Times* led the way with a leading article, euphorically declaring that:

'The fall of Kiev is a great triumph for the Poles and their Ukrainian allies, and it is a heavy blow for the Bolshevists. The city was entered, according to the Russian wireless on Friday, after heavy fighting during Thursday and that day, and by the latest reports the Russians are in retreat followed by the Polish Cavalry. King George expresses the traditional feelings of the British people when he conveys to Marshal Pilsudski on the occasion of the Polish National Festival their "most cordial" congratulations and good wishes for the future of the Polish State.' (*The Times*, 10 May 1920)

The Polish day of National Festival was on 3 May, but it was not until the Poles had eventually occupied Kiev that the King's cable was released for publication.

The Daily Herald, in an editorial, 11 May 1920, 'THE CONSPIRATORS' scathingly comments that:

'The King's message to Marshall Pilsudski has, as we foresaw, been greeted by the war parties here and abroad as one of congratulation to the Polish leader upon his treacherous invasion of Russia . . .

'The Government's policy has, ever since the Prinkipo negotiation been obscure, involved and treacherous. It has professed peace and prepared war . . . Its voice has been the voice of Mr Lloyd George, but its hands have been the hands of Mr Churchill.'

On the very same day as *The Times* announcement of the royal congratulations, a British merchant vessel, the SS *Jolly George*, was being loaded in a London dock, when the dockers discovered that a section of the cargo, destined for Poland, was made up of military equipment including eighteen pounder guns and even military aircraft. The dockers stopped work and refused to carry on with the loading and the coal heavers backed them by refusing to fuel the ship. Meetings at the London Docks had been held some days prior to this incident. Harry Pollitt*, a young boiler maker had alerted dockside workers to governmental intrigues and the plans to ship arms to Poland. The 'blacking' of the *Jolly George* became official when Fred Thomson, London Secretary of the Dock Workers' Union raised the matter with the National Executive. The dockers' leader, Ernest Bevin, in congratulating the men on their action of solidarity, told the delegates at the Union's Annual Conference a week later, 'I am not going to ask the dockers to put a gun in the ship to carry on this wicked venture. The workers have a right to say how their labour shall be used.' (*The Daily Herald*, 19 May 1920). The Union then decided to ban the loading of any military supplies that were earmarked for use against Soviet Russia, unfortunately the pressure was not sustained.

The initial Polish victories were short lived. On 15 May the Red Army launched a massive counter-attack which by the end of the month outflanked the Polish forces, and on 10 June, recaptured Kiev. The Red Army eventually drove the invaders back to the very perimeter of Warsaw. To boost Polish morale, a 'top level mission headed by Lord D'Abernon and General Weygand' was sent to Warsaw. 'At the beginning of August the eagerly waited fresh supplies of French and British war stores began to arrive in Poland . . . The material included new combat aircraft – the first 400 to be supplied to Poland by France, Britain and Italy during the remainder of 1920.' The French contribution was 125, the Italian forty three, and 133 came from Britain. There were also: 'Thirty-eight Albatross D IIIs and twenty Fokker D VIIs . . . from German and Austrian surplus stocks.'[3] General Weygand returned to Poland with 400 French officers to supervise the reorganization of the Polish armed forces.

The British historian, R. Page Arnot, in his book which deals with the *Impact of the Russian Revolution in Britain* describes how

---

*Became General Secretary of the British Communist Party.

'Great Britain suddenly on 11 July, had brought in a new stipulation. This was designed to help their friends, the Poles, who were beginning to lose heavily in their unprovoked war on the Soviet Union, whose Government had already instructed its Supreme Command to enter into Pourparlers with the Poles for an Armistice. Negotiations were to begin on 1 August.

When the delegates met on the night of 1 August, it turned out that the Polish delegates had no powers to fix preliminary peace terms. Negotiations broke down. The British Government now intervened. They demanded that the Russian advance stop, failing which, Lord Curzon said in his Note of 3 August – and Lloyd George stressed in his interview with Kamenev and Krassin* on 4 August – military aid would immediately be given to Poland. Meanwhile newspapers began to report British military and naval preparations. British troops were being used at Danzig to unload supplies to Poland. On Friday 6 August, a British Memorandum was sent to Moscow demanding a ten-day truce under the threat of what they would do if this was not obeyed. Meanwhile however, the Poles had decided to accept the proposals for negotiations with the Russians on the 7th [and] arranged for a meeting at Minsk four days later.

An Anglo-French Conference was held at Hythe on 8 August, whereupon the Russian reply was treated as a rejection. The matter was referred to the military and naval staffs to prepare for action ... once more the country was on the brink of war.'[4]

The 'Z' men were not out of danger.

Arthur Henderson,† Secretary of Britain's Labour Party and a former member of Lloyd George's Coalition war-time

---

Government, decided to alert the Labour Movement to the imminent danger of the outbreak of a new war. On 7 August 1920 Henderson sent a telegram to every Constituency Labour Party throughout the country.

'Extremely menacing possibility extension Polish-Russian war. Strongly urge local parties immediately organize citizen demonstrations against intervention and supply men and munitions to Poland. Demand Peace negotiations, immediate raising of blockade, resumption trade relations. Send resolutions Premier and press. Deputize local MPs.'

Its effect was electric.

Two days later, the Parlamentary Committee of the TUC, the Labour Party National Executive and the Parliamentary Labour Party held a joint emergency meeting in the House of Commons and issued a declaration:

'That this joint conference, representing the Trades Union Congress, the Labour Party and the Parliamentary Labour Party, feels certain that war is being engineered between the Allied Powers and Soviet Russia, on the issue of Poland, and declares that such a war would be an intolerable crime against humanity. It therefore warns the Government that the whole Industrial Power of the organized workers will be used to defeat this war.'

A Council of Action was immediately set up and arranged at short notice for a special National Delegate Conference of all affiliated organizations. They met on Friday 13 August and the Council was authorized 'to call for any and every form of withdrawal of labour which circumstances may require.' The delegates unanimously called for a general strike and pledged themselves 'to resist any and every form of military and naval intervention against the Soviet Government of Russia.'

This threat to the Government inevitably had its effect

135

upon Lloyd George and some members of his Cabinet. The Prime Minister had already tried to de-fuse the national outcry against their policy when he told the House of Commons earlier in the week that the Government was prepared to await the result of the Russo-Polish negotiations which were taking place at Minsk, and would intervene 'only if the independence of Poland was threatened.'

On the evening of 10 August, the same day as the Prime Minister's statement, the Soviet Government's representative in London issued a summary of his Government's Peace Terms. It first of all reiterated its recognition of Poland's independence, and then went on to call for:

'1. Reduction of Polish Army to 60,000 with a civic militia.
2. The demobilization of war industries and the exclusion of war materials or troops from Britain, France or other countries.
3. Unrestricted commercial transit through Poland to the Baltic.

The fourth Russian point was that land should be given to the dependents of Polish soldiers who had been killed or incapacitated.'[5]

The negotiations broke down, and the Poles encouraged by the vast amounts of military supplies still pouring into the country, and confident that the Allies would, if called upon, come to their aid directly, counter-attacked and inflicted a heavy blow upon the overstretched Red Army. The eventual outcome was that the Poles succeeded in gaining 'a frontier hundreds of miles to the east of the Curzon Line with approximately 3,600,000 inhabitants in the intervening area of whom no more than a million were Poles.' A Peace Treaty was signed in Riga on 20 October 1920, defining the new frontier, and ratified on 18 March 1921.

According to Lenin the Soviet Government had made serious political and military errors. It appeared that the lessons of Brest-Litovsk had not been learned:

'what happened in Poland', he told Clara Zetkin,

the German Communist leader, 'had to happen ... our unbelievably brave, victorious advanced guard could receive no reinforcements from the infantry, could receive no munitions, not even stale bread and other prime necessities from the Polish peasantry and petty bourgeoisie. These ... saw in the Red Army soldiers not brother-liberators but foes ... The Polish revolution on which we reckoned failed. The peasants and workers, stultified by the partisans of Pilsudski and Dashinsky, defended their class enemies, permitted our brave Red Army soldiers to die of starvation, and ambushed and killed them.

' ... all the talents of Budenny and of other revolutionary army leaders could not counter-balance our military and technical shortcomings and even less, our false political reckoning; our hope in the Polish revolution.

'Incidentally, Radek foretold how everything would happen. He warned us. I was terribly angry with him, and called him a defeatist – but in the main he has proved to be right. He knows the situation in the West better than we do and he is talented. He is very helpful to us ...

'Do you know that the conclusion of peace with Poland in the beginning met with serious opposition in much the same way as the conclusion of the Brest-Litovsk Peace? I had to fight a hard battle because I favoured the adoption of peace terms which were undoubtedly favourable to Poland and very difficult for us.

'I myself think that our situation made it by no means necessary to conclude peace at any price. We could have carried on through the winter. But I believed that from a political point of view it was wiser to make concessions to the enemy. The temporary sacrifices of a bad peace seemed to me cheaper than the prolongation of war ... We are using the peace with Poland in order to descend up-on Wrangel with all our strength and give him such a crashing blow that he leaves us alone for ever.'[6]

There were still Allied political leaders prepared to have a 'last fling' at the Bolsheviks. General Wrangel, their latest protégé, had been supplied with a wide variety of the latest weapons from Britain and France, including aircraft, tanks and armoured cars; what he lacked was the support of the Russian people. He succeeded in driving his forces through to the heart of the Donbas coal mining area, but he was finally forced into the Crimean peninsular by the Red Army and completely surrounded. Sevastopol and the strategic fort at Perekop were captured by Soviet troops in 1920, and by the end of the year the whole of the Crimea was cleared of White and Allied counter-revolutionary forces. The last fling had failed. The anti-Bolshevik military crusade was over – for the time being. The cost was colossal. Hundreds of millions of pounds, dollars and francs, as well as shipping, manpower and energy that were desperately needed to rebuild a war devasted Europe and, above all, millions of people's lives were sacrificed upon a cause that had neither moral nor legal justification.

The effect of the Allied blockade alone resulted in the deaths of hundreds of thousands, as well as contributing to the millions stricken by chronic disease and malnutrition. The lack of fuel too had had a disastrous effect upon the Russian people. E.H. Carr records that: 'In the winters of 1918–1919 and 1919–20 cold was probably a greater cause of human misery and human inefficiency than hunger.' In addition there was a major crisis in railway transport. 'Of the 70,000 versts* of railway in European Russia only 15,000 versts had remained undamaged in the war or the civil war. Rolling-stock had suffered proportionately; at the end of 1919 when the crisis had reached its most acute stage, more than sixty per cent of a total of 16,000 locomotives were out of order.' The third All-Russian Congress of Councils had recorded that in January 1920 'the productive forces of the country could not be fully utilized, and a considerable part of our factories and workshops were at a standstill'.[7]

Until late 1919 or early 1920, Soviet Russia had been cut off from almost every type of essential raw material. Coal

---

*Verst equals two-thirds of an English mile.

and iron from the Ukraine; oil from Baku and the Caucasus; cotton from Turkestan; flax from the Baltic countries and timber from the great northern forests. This together with the destruction of industrial plant, and the run down of stocks which could not be replaced, had been catastrophic.

In June 1920, a high-level British Labour Party delegation went on a six week tour of the Soviet Union, during which period they

'visited Petrograd, Moscow, Smolensk and the Polish Front, and numerous towns and villages on the Volga, from Nijni-Novgorod to Astrakhan. The marks of the cruel blockade and of war were visible everywhere. In the villages, while food was fairly satisfactory, there was a lack of clothes, coats, household utensils, agricultural implements and machinery. In the towns food was dangerously scarce and the power of work of many workers in the industrial regions was greatly reduced, owing to their obviously miserable physical condition. The transport which should have been bringing food from the country to the towns was taking food, munitions and men to the front. The locomotives, which might have been working stood idle on the rails for want of spare parts for their repair, which the blockade had not allowed to enter Russia. The workshops, which should have been making tools, agricultural machinery and productive machinery, were making guns, bombs and tanks.

'In 1918–19 there were over a million cases of typhus fever and no town or village in Russia or Siberia escaped infection. In addition there have been other epidemics of cholera, Spanish influenza and of smallpox. The soap, the disinfectants and the medicines needed for the treatment of these diseases have been kept out of Russia by the blockade. Two or three hundred thousand of Russians died of typhus alone. One-half of the doctors attending on typhus died at their posts.'

The report concluded with an appeal to the British people

139

'to insist that peace be made now, and Europe be allowed to turn from the terrible spectres of war, famine and disease, to a rebuilding of its homes and reshaping of its shattered civilization. Russia can give much to us from her natural resources, and Russia needs much from us. To pursue a policy of blockade and intervention is madness and criminal folly which can only end in European disaster.' (Report from *The Times*, 8 July 1920)

The signatories to this report were Mr Ben Turner (Chairman), Miss Margaret Bondfield, Mr A.A. Purcell, Mr R. Skinner, Mrs E. Snowden, Mr Tom Shaw, MP, Mr Robert Williams and Mr L. Haden Guest (Secretary).

The report fully confirmed Keynes' criticism of the economic effects of the blockade upon Russia and the rest of Eruope during the War of Empires and Wars of Intervention.

'In the United States', writes Professor Fleming, 'few even remember that terrible time and most Americans never heard of it, but the Russians cannot be expected to forget. Such an experience is burned into the very soul of a nation. Then Red leaders, especially, were given every reason to believe that the Western World sought their extermination and that it would only be a matter of time until the capitalist powers would be back to finish the job . . .'[8]

Notes

1. FISCHER, Louis, *The Soviets in World Affairs*, p. 189
2. JACKSON, Robert, *At War With the Bolsheviks*, pp. 229–230
3. JACKSON, Robert, *At War With the Bolsheviks*, pp. 231–232
4. ARNOT, R. Page, *The Impact of the Russian Revolution in Britain*, pp. 174–175
5. ARNOT, R. Page, *The Impact of the Russian Revolution in Britain*, p. 176
6. FISCHER, Louis, *The Soviets in World Affairs*, pp. 194–195
7. CARR, E.H., *The Bolshevik Revolution 1917–1923*, pp. 192–193
8. FLEMING, D.F., *The Cold War and its Origins*, Vol. I, p. 32

11

THE RUSSIAN FAMINE AND THE CORDON SANITAIRE

The Bolshevik leaders were under no illusions that because the Allied armies had been forced to withdraw and the counter-revolution smashed, intervention was at an end. They believed that their adversaries, although compelled to change course, would not abandon their aim of overthrowing the Soviet regime by whatever means possible. This was made clear when Lenin declared:

> 'We have passed through one period of war and we must prepare for a second. But we do not know when it will come and we must see to it that when it does come we shall be prepared for all eventualities.'*

The Paris Peace Conference was used by the Allied Governments to undermine the Soviet regime and to prevent its diplomatic recognition. They were able to draft the Charters of the League of Nations and the International Labour Organization 'with a view to immunizing the non-Bolshevik Left against the idealogical bacillus of the Bolshevik Revolution.'[1]

By restructuring Europe and creating a chain of anti-Soviet states in the East, together with an enlarged Roumania,† they established a Cordon Sanitaire from the Baltic to the Black Sea, 'a sort of Iron Curtain';[2] at the same time using whatever methods they could to destroy the Soviet regime by frustrating its plans for economic recovery and fomenting discontent between its leaders and the

---

*Lenin – Period of War Communism 1918–1920
†Roumania annexed Bessarabia in 1918 after the War of Empires

people. Their tactics may have varied from time to time, but the objective remained the same.

The terrible Russian famine of 1921–22 was cynically exploited for this purpose. According to W.P. and Zelda Coates, some Allied politicians, 'while paying lip-service to the need to mitigate the suffering of the famine victims, sought to use this fearful scourge as a rod with which to beat the Bolsheviks, and as a lever to wring concessions from the Soviet Government respecting the Tsarist debts, without being prepared to meet the much larger Soviet counter-claims for the losses suffered as a result of the millions expended in aiding the counter-revolutionary generals.'[3]

Between 1920 and 1922 millions died of starvation, malnutrition and disease. Famine was not unknown in Russian history. Tsarist Russia had perhaps the most primitive agricultural and irrigational systems in the whole of Europe. In the 1891 famine it was estimated that seven million peasants, including women and children, had perished. This was in a time of peace. But the 1921 famine had many additional factors which made the situation very much worse. According to the report of an American Commission, under the chairmanship of A.H. Johnson, Director of the New York State Institute of Applied Agriculture, the 1921 famine

'has been due to the destruction of agricultural equipment, loss of draft animals and lack of manpower due to war conditions and finally to the drought of 1920 and 1921'

The Commission had made a thorough investigation of the affected areas. In addition, the war had drastically reduced the manufacture and imports of agricultural implements. The blockade aggravated the situation even further, so that whereas up to 1914 there were some seven to eight million ploughs, 1921 Soviet Russia had to cope with less than three million – worn out – but expected to achieve the same results. Other essential imports such as grain seed had been prevented from entering the country by the blockade.

142

Lenin admitted mistakes had been made.

> 'We made a mistake' he said 'in the distribution of stocks of foodstuffs, although these stocks were considerably larger than in former years. The full crisis is due to the fact that we attempted to restore our industrial life in too large a scale. Agriculture is passing through a crisis not only as a result of the imperialist and civil wars, but because the new state is only gradually working out its methods and therefore makes errors from time to time.'   (*Daily Herald*, 11 March 1921)

As early as April 1919 Fridtjof Nansen, the eminent Norwegian explorer who had become President of his country's League of Nations Society, wrote to President Wilson appealing for help to alleviate 'the present food situation in Russia, where hundreds of thousands of people are dying monthly from sheer starvation and disease'.

Nansen continued

> 'It would appear to me possible to organize a purely humanitarian Commission for the provisioning of Russia, the foodstuffs and medical supplies to be paid for perhaps to some considerable extent by Russia itself, the justice of distribution to be guaranteed by such a Commission, the membership of the commission to be comprised of Norwegian, Swedish, and possibly Dutch, Danish and Swiss nationality. It does not appear that the existing authorities in Russia would refuse the intervention of such a Commission of a wholly non-political order, devoted solely to the humanitarian purpose of saving life. If thus organized upon the lines of the Belgian Relief Commission, it would raise no question of political recognition or negotiations between the Allies and the existing authorities in Russia.
>
> I recognize keenly the large political issues involved, and I would be glad to know under what conditions you would approve such an enterprise

and whether such Commission could look for actual support in finance, shipping and food and medical supplies from your Government.

I have sent similar letters to M. Clemenceau, M. Lloyd George, and M. Orlando in the hope that they will accord the matter the attention which so serious a situation deserves.'

President Wilson's reply, some two weeks later, although expressing approval for Nansen's scheme, carried the proviso that 'provided all Hostilities in Russia ceased' facilities would be offered to carry out the work. This was at a time when the Red Army was being attacked by the Allied backed armies of Kolchak and Denikin. Opposition to Nansen's scheme had already 'been aroused amongst the Russian émigrés; to them and to the politicians of some countries, the feeding of the starving people meant bolstering up the Revolutionary government'.[4] Nansen had also been in communication with Chicherin, the Soviet Commissar for Foreign Affairs. The Soviet leader wrote an appreciative letter explaining to Nansen that

'If left in peace and allowed free development Soviet Russia would soon be able to restore her natural production, to regain her economic strength, to provide for her own needs, and to be helpful to other countries. But in the present situation in which she has been put by the implacable policy of the associated Powers, help in foodstuffs from abroad would be most welcome to Russia, and the Russian Soviet Government appreciates most thankfully your humane and heartfelt response to her sufferings, and ... will be especially glad to enter communication with you for the realization of your scheme of help which you emphasize as being purely humanitarian.

On this basis of a humanitarian work of help to suffering people we would be pleased to do everything in our power to further the realization or your project.'

Chicherin went on to explain why the Soviet Government

would be unable to accept the offer of aid, with its built-in proviso.

'Unfortunately your benevolent intentions which you indicate yourself as being based upon purely humanitarian grounds and which, according to your letter, must be realized by a Commission of fully non-political character, have been mixed up by others with political purposes. In the letter addressed to you by the four Powers your scheme is represented as involving the cessation of hostilities and of transfer of troops and war materials, and we regret very much that your original intentions have been thus fundamentally disfigured by the Governments of the associated Powers.'

It was quite obvious that the Allied conditions would be unacceptable to the Soviet Government; not surprisingly the scheme was abandoned.

Nansen comments in his book *Russia and Peace*

'in 1919 and 1920 Russia was, in reality, only considered from the political standpoint, and this interest chiefly took the form of support, sometimes of a powerful nature, rendered to the attacks made on the Soviet Republic by Kølchak, Denikin, Yudenich, the Polish offensive and Wrangel.'

In 1920 it had been estimated that there were over a half a million prisoners of war, of whom, 'some 300,000 were in Russia, including 40,000 in Eastern Siberian and 20,000 in the Caucasus and Turkestan'.[5] The remaining 200,000, mostly Russians who had been captured during the war, were in France and Germany. Nansen's first great task for the League was to organize their repatriation. After an intensive six months, he was able to report that 'nearly 200,000 prisoners have been repatriated', but before completing his work Nansen was invited by the Council of the League to take on the job of tackling the Russian refugee problem. A problem which, in the main, had been created by the 1917 revolution, and the Allied backed Wars of Intervention.

In August 1921 he was appointed by the Council, High Commissioner for Refugees. Whilst on a visit on behalf of the League, Nansen had been able to see for himself the real nature of the problem, not only of the refugees, but of the even more serious situation caused by the famine. During his visit 'he had been able to make an agreement with the Soviet Government with regard to the transportation and distribution of food supplies which left all authority in the hands of a representative of the Soviets and of a representative to be appointed'[6] by Nansen himself.

At a meeting of the League's General Assembly, Nansen again raised 'the problem of the Russian famine'. E.E. Reynolds, in his biography, describes how Nansen 'put the question clearly in a long speech that evoked great applause but little else . . .' 'To the question, "will the Soviet keep its promises?" he replied "I have worked with the Soviet Government now for more than a year in connection with the repatriation of prisoners, and I must say that, in spite of numerous difficulties, the Soviet Government has actually kept all its obligations and all its agreements and promises it has made to me and to my organization".' He then proceeded to quote examples of his experiences in dealing with the Soviet authorities. 'One organization' he said 'which was a special organization formed for helping prisoners in Russia, sent an equipment for 60,000 prisoners – clothing, shoes, underwear, etc., articles which were of the highest value, and which could have been sold for a fortune in Russia, because they were in great need of them. Yet not one single article was lost inside the borders of Russia.'

Nansen's appeal to the League ended on this note:

> 'We know that at least 20,000,000 people are starving; we know that everything necessary to save them is within a few hundred miles. We know that only one thing is required, that is, for one part of the human race to organize and help the other suffering part. The cost of armaments to the members of the League is hundreds of millions of pounds a year; that is to defend them against

political dangers. Less than ten per cent of this, in the form of a loan only to Russia, will prevent appalling disaster and avert the greatest of all political dangers.

I feel certain that those who think over the situation will find that Europe cannot now stand back; it has to come in and save these lives at once.'

His 'suggestion that the League should relieve the Russian famine by grants in kind, and by guaranteeing a loan, was referred to the Sixth Committee, who decided that, as several governments declined to grant official credits, the responsibility of the League in the matter was at an end.' Nansen was bitterly disappointed. The League, he believed, had missed a golden opportunity. 'For once he spoke out about the difficulties that were being put in the way of even such private relief as had been given:' 'We are doing what we can' he said 'through private charity, but even our charity is being impeded, and it is being very seriously impeded, by the campaign of misrepresentation which is being carried on. There are any amount of lies being circulated.' He went on to remind his audience of the story that had been circulated to the press

'that the first train that Mr Hoover* sent in to feed the Russians was looted by the Soviet Army in Russia. It was a lie: but still the same story is repeated over and over again in the press of Europe. I was abused' he added 'for having sent an expedition to Siberia, and I know it was said that I was bringing arms for a revolution. It was a lie, But I have read it in the papers. It is said that my friend, Captain Sverdrup was in command of

*Chairman of the American Relief Committee in London and then head of Commission for Relief in Belgium. US Food Administrator 1917–19, also member of the War Council. After the war he was head of the American Relief Committee for Central Europe, organized first supplies to ex-blockaded countries. 'The whole of American policy during the liquidation of the Armistice was to contribute everything it could to prevent Europe from going Bolshevik' – Hoover in a letter to O. Garrison Villard, 17/8/1921. (Quoted by Louis Fischer – *Soviets in World Affairs*, Vol. 1, p. 174.)

it, but all that he was doing was carrying agricultural machinery to Siberia . . . . There are many similar stories being circulated . . . . I think I know what is the underlying thought in this campaign. It is this – that the action which we propose, will, if it succeeds, strengthen the Soviet Government. I think that that is a mistake. I do not think that we shall strengthen the Soviet Government by showing the Russian people that there are hearts in Europe, and that there are people there ready to help the starving Russian people. But supposing that it does strengthen the Soviet Government? Is there any member of this Assembly who is prepared to say that rather than help the Soviet Government he will allow twenty million people to starve to death? I challenge this Assembly to answer that question . . . .'[7]

According to Konni Zilliacus, for many years a member of the League's Secretariat, 'the Governments unanimously showed their determination not to pay a penny to save human lives in the hope that they could by helping to starve tens of millions destroy the Communist régime that they had failed to overthrow'[8] by military means.

The withholding of governmental aid did not deter Nansen from his objective; he applied his organizing ability and energy in appeals to the many private organizations and prominent individuals for help. He had already made contact with a number of voluntary organizations and towards the end of August 1921, while in Riga, he cabled the Save The Children International Union:

'Hundreds and thousands of Russian children are dying of hunger and millions of others are threatened with the same fate. Convinced that only an unprecedented effort, immediately undertaken, can save them, I request the Save The Children International Union to appeal to men, women, and especially to children, to give quickly all that they can economize, to save the little famished ones in Russia. Never in the history of the world has help been more desparately needed.

148

Every minute is precious.'

'Within a few months fifteen countries were, through the Save The Children International Union, making a united effort to help the Russian children'. The magnificent response of the voluntary organisations, although making a valuable contribution towards alleviating some of the suffering, 'was a poor substitute for what could have been done if the League had taken his appeal to heart. Five years later, as Rector of St Andrews University he once more expressed his disgust.' He spoke of the

> 'Russian famine in 1921–22 when the Volga region and the most fertile parts of Russia were ravaged by a terible drought – when something like thirty million people or more, were starving and dying . . . .
>
> A heart-rending appeal for help went out to all the world and eventually a great many people in this and in other countries helped, and helped generously. But many more were busy trying to find out first who was to blame. Was it the drought? Or was it the political system of the Russian state? As if that could ameliorate the terrible suffering or make any difference whatever to those who were dying of starvation!
>
> But what was worse, there were in various transatlantic countries such an abundance of maize at that time that the farmers did not know how to get rid of it before the new harvest, so they had to burn it as fuel in their railway engines. At the same time the ships in Europe were idle, and laid up, for there were no cargoes. Simultaneously there were thousands, nay millions, of unemployed. All this while thirty million people in the Volga region – not far away and easily reached by means of our ships – were allowed to starve and die, the politicians of the world at large, except in the United States, trying to find an excuse for doing nothing on the pretext that it was the Russians' own fault – a result of the Bolshevik system . . . .'[9]

The United States, which was not a member of the League and had refused to recognize the Soviet Government, nevertheless felt that something positive should be done. The American Relief Administration, in conjunction with public subscriptions, raised some sixty million dollars.

An example typical of the British establishment's attitude to the Russian famine and starving millions, was reflected in *The Times* editorial of 25 August 1921. Having expressed its sympathy for the victims of the famine, the paper then went on to declare:

> 'The whole conception of providing international credit for Russia demands the most careful scrutiny. For it means one of two things. It may mean unconditional and unguaranteed credit for the relief of the victims of famine and the reconstruction of Russia under the present Bolshevist regime. In other words, it would mean maintaining the Bolshevists in power at the moment when their misdeeds have wrought themselves out in their inevitable consequences and are threatening the collapse of the whole hateful and criminal system. To any such attempt we are most emphatically and resolutely opposed'. (*The Times*, 25 August 1921)

'Careful scrutiny' was certainly in the minds of the Allied Supreme Council when, on the very same day that *The Times* editorial appeared, it 'appointed a Commission to study the question of giving help to the victims of the Volga famine and the French, British, Italian, Belgian and Japanese Governments appointed delegates to it. Later this Commission appointed a Sub-Commission to visit the famine districts and for some reason which was never explained, the former Ambassador to Russia, M. Noulens, was appointed as Chairman'.[10]

The choice of Noulens naturally aroused the suspicions of the Soviet Government. They had not forgotten his anti-Soviet activities during the civil war, or his support for the counter-revolutionary generals and the forces of intervention.

'The Russian people remember' said Chicherin 'how as French Ambassador in Petrograd, M. Noulens worked to bring about Allied intervention, and how he participated actively in the fomenting of the counter-revolutionary rising. He is as much as any living man responsible for the civil war, the foreign invasions and the blockade. The nomination of M. Noulens is in itself a programme. Now the first steps of the Committee justify all our fears.

The Commission does not propose to aid the hungry. It puts forward instead a complicated plan for investigating the whole internal condition of Soviet Russia. Neither the American Relief Administration, which has already begun to send food to the starving children, nor Dr Nansen, as High Commissioner of the Red Cross, has thought it necessary or possible to compel the hungry masses to wait for assistance until those profound researches can be completed. While thousands are dying for lack of food, M. Noulens' Commission proposed, instead of collecting food for the hungry, to collect statistics about Russia'.

Instead of addressing themselves to the urgent task of helping the famine-stricken people, all that the Allied Sub-Commission had done was to apply to the Soviet Government for permission to visit Russia in order to conduct an investigation.

Not surprisingly 'little more was heard of the Noulens Sub-Commission, but the Commission itself later expanded into the International Russian Famine Relief Commission, to which most of the European Governments sent respresentatives'. Its main preoccupation was to provide a platform for warnings to the Soviet Government that 'if it hoped to obtain foreign credits for the relief of its famine stricken areas, it "must recognize the Tsarist debts" and give "adequate guarantees" for all future credits'. Consequently, 'no collective assistance by the Governments of Europe resulted from its deliberations.'[11]

If the famine had occurred under the Tsarist régime

151

declared J.R. Clynes, the Labour MP, during a Parliamentary debate, 'the British Government and the other Governments of Europe would have come more readily to the assistance of the starving people'.

However, the British Government in its financial year 1921–22 managed to spend £300,000 on the maintenance of 5,000 'White' Russian refugees, 'a sum which would have saved the lives of 400,000 peasants in the Volga Valley'.[12]

Notes

1. MAYER Arno J., *Politics and Diplomacy of Peacemaking*, p. 9.
2. COBBAN Alfred, *A History of Modern France*, p. 120.
3. COATES W.P. and Zelda, *A History of Anglo-Soviet Relations*, p. 56.
4. REYNOLDS E.E., *Nansen*, p. 218.
5. REYNOLDS E.E., *Nansen*, p. 220.
6. REYNOLDS E.E., *Nansen*, p. 225.
7. REYNOLDS E.E., *Nansen*, p. 227.
8. ZILLIACUS K., *The Mirror of the Past*, p. 265.
9. REYNOLDS E.E., *Nansen*, pp. 229/230.
10. COATES W.P. and Zelda, *A History of Anglo-Soviet Relations*, p. 57.
11. COATES W.P. and Zelda, *A History of Anglo-Soviet Relations*, p. 58.
12. COATES W.P. and Zelda, *A History of Anglo-Soviet Relations*, p. 59.

12

POST-WAR EUROPE AND THE BARRIERS

In Western Europe, especially France, the devastation caused by the war was enormous. The battle scarred areas were spread over the country's ten northern departments where, out of a population of 4,700,000 in 1914, there remained only 2,075,000 at the end of 1918. Within those four years livestock 'had been reduced to 174,000, about a tenth of the normal. Over 800,000 houses or farm buildings had been destroyed or damaged. In the richest of the occupied departments, the Nord, over 50,000 houses had been completely destroyed, nearly 5,000 miles of roads were seriously damaged; nearly 600 miles of main railway line had been completely destroyed; nearly 600,000 acres of farmland damaged.'[1] It was therefore only to be expected that the French Government and the French people should feel strongly concerning the matter of reparations, especially as Germany had survived, as far as land and property was concerned, comparatively unscathed.

The return to France of Eastern Lorraine and Alsace, with their rich deposits of iron ore, potash and, in the case of Alsace, plant to boost the French cotton industry, provided France with a valuable asset for its programme of reconstruction. But the revival of France, as well as the other war devastated countries, could not be divorced from the urgent need for a world-wide redevelopment of international trade.

In Germany, exports in 1920 were but a quarter of what they were in 1914, and without a rapid boost of its export trade it would be unable to fulfil even a fraction of its reparation commitments. British exports during the corresponding period were down by almost fifty per cent. This must have been among the factors uppermost in the minds of many leaders of industry and commerce who were exerting pressure upon their governments to include Russia in their plans for a European revival.

The Daily News, in an article by its political correspondent on 9 October 1920, warned that:

> 'France cannot prosper by organizing the impoverishment of Germany, and we cannot prosper by creating a famine in Russia. Europe is not a curate's egg that can be good in parts. It lies under a common affliction that will only yield to a common remedy – the remedy of reconciliation and mutual aid. Of that remedy, trade is still the most powerful instrument.'

It was the failure of the Allied Powers to overthrow the Soviet regime, that eventually convinced some of the more far-sighted statesmen that European reconstruction and the redevelopment of international trade could not effectively be realized without the co-operation and recognition of the Soviet Government. This, above all else, determined the Allies to lift the blockade of the Soviet ports, which in turn led to the decision of their Supreme Council to prepare the ground for the reopening of trade relations between Russia and the other Allied states.

Steps for the resumption of trade with Russia had been taken by a number of countries. One of the first was the United States, which lifted its trade embargo on 7 March 1920. This was followed by a Russo-Italian Commercial Agreement on 31 March, which was signed by Litvinov, for the Central Union of Russian Co-operatives, and Cabrini for the Italian National Co-operatives.

During the second week of April 1920 E.F. Wise, acting on behalf of the Allied Supreme Economic Council, met in Copenhagen a Soviet trade delegation led by Krassin, Commissar for overseas trade. The next stage was on 25 April in San Remo where, at a meeting of the Allied Supreme Council, a statement was issued which declared that:

> 'Allied representatives will be prepared to discuss

with the Russian delegates, (who were at the time still in Copenhagen) the best methods of removing the obstacles and difficulties in the way of the resumption of peaceful trade relations with the desire of finding a solution in the general interests of Europe.'

This in effect meant that to pursue trade negotiations with the Soviet Government's trade representatives a de facto recognition of the Soviet Government would have to be entered into. Under normal circumstances full diplomatic recognition, which covers full legal recognition – de jure, would logically follow.

The eve of the San Remo meeting coincided with the Polish Army's invasion of the Ukrain, and during the period when the Red Army was driving the Polish forces back to the suburbs of Warsaw, Soviet trade delegates, Krassin and his deputy Klishko, were in London engaged in negotiations relating to the re-opening of Anglo-Russian trade.

The negotiations were conducted at the highest level. On 31 May 1920, Krassin and his colleague held discussions with the Prime Minister, Lloyd George, and leading members of his Cabinet. They included the Foreign Minister, Lord Curzon, Minister for Trade, Sir Robert Horne, Cecil Harmsworth, Under Secretary of State for Foreign Affairs and Bonar Law, Leader of the House of Commons.

The visit of the Soviet trade delegation was denounced by most of the Conservative press. *The Times* led the way in attempts to prevent the recognition of the Soviet Government by attacking the trade negotiations. Using its contacts with the anti-Soviet elements in France, it declared:

'Our Paris correspondent emphasizes today the strength of French disapproval of the negotiations between British ministers and the Bolshevist delegate, M. Krassin. We understand that this disapproval is by no means confined to France, and that it is shared by more than one Department of State.' (*The Times*, 2 June 1920)

When questioned in the House of Commons about

'French disapproval' the Prime Minister replied that

> 'He was not aware that there was perturbation of
> French public opinion. the mere fact that there
> may be statements in certain newspapers who are
> trying to foment trouble between two friendly and
> Allied countries whose friendliness is essential for
> the welfare of the world, is not proof that French
> public opinion is perturbed.' (*The Daily Despatch*,
> 4 June 1920)

In fact, the C.G.T.* and the French Labour Movement
generally had been energetically campaigning for the promotion of friendly relations with Soviet Russia.

The political and propaganda weapon used most frequently to prevent de facto recognition, and the conclusion
of trade agreements between Russia and the Allied countries, was the matter of repayment of the debts incurred by
the Tsarist Government. Krassin, in an interview with the
French newspaper *La Liberté*, 16 June 1920, explained quite
clearly the Soviet Government's attitude regarding Tsarist
debts.

> 'People who now hold Russian stocks' he declared
> 'ought to have known what risks they were taking
> when they lent their money to the Governement of
> the Tsar. Not only my party, but all Russian
> advance parties had warned the French investor
> from 1905 onwards that the Russian people, it they
> once became masters of their own destinies, would
> never consent to repay the loans which had been
> used to crush their efforts to obtain liberty. Our
> warnings passed unheeded, however, and the
> French continued to lend money for the purpose
> of paying the troops employed to fire on the
> Russian people. French opinion had never be-
> lieved the Russian Revolution would succeed, and

---

*Confederation Generale du Travail.

they ought naturally to pay for their blunder.

We are told on all sides that international financial relations would be impossible if, whenever it changed its government, a nation could repudiate the obligations incurred by the preceding regime. That would be correct in regard to peaceful changes, but history records no instance in which a revolutionary government has paid the debts of a former regime. The French Revolution of 1789 was itself an instance of this. We consider as sacred the obligations which we incur ourselves, but we cannot regard ourselves as bound by the obligations of the former Russian regime. Juridicially, whether you take this word in its broadest or in its narrowest and dogmatic sense, we are not compelled to pay'.

The French Government, although unable to halt moves towards the development of trade relations between the Soviet Government and the other allied countries, nevertheless managed to use its influence in retarding the movement towards recognition.

On 22 June 1920, representatives of the Allied Governments met in Boulogne where it was decided that trade negotiations could go ahead 'on the understanding that there was no question of political recognition of the Soviet Government'.

The linking of trade with recognition had become an anathema to most of the British press as well as dividing the British coalition cabinet. Anglo-Soviet negotiations were persistently being held back because of the reluctance of the Government to officially accept recognition of the Soviet Government. The diplomatic correspondent of *The Observer*, on 4 July 1920, gave an indication of the pressures being applied to abort the negotiations when he pointed out:

'France does not want to trade with Russia, nor does a small section of opinion in Britain. They want more ruin in the blind hope that imaginary enemies will be rendered harmless. It is hard to see what they are afraid of, but they are afraid.'

157

The pro-interventionists really believed, especially during the initial Polish military successes, that to recognize the Bolshevik Government when it only needed one more push to topple it, was the acme of foolhardiness. they were against the lifting of the blockade, and the reports of the wide spread famine encouraged their belief in an early collapse. Most British Conservative newspapers were convinced that the Soviet regime was about to topple.

> 'All the evidence indeed points to the fact that the Bolshevist regime is doomed' said the *Morning Post* 'and there is some ground for belief that the end may not be far off.' (5 October 1920)

Even after the destruction of Wrangel's army in the Crimea this line of thinking still persisted in pro-interventionist circles well into the 1920s.

Throughout the protracted period of the trade negotiations, desperate attempts were made to turn British public opinion against the recognition of the Soviet Government, as well as plots to sabotage the signing of any agreement.

The case of the forged *Pravda* is an indication of the type of campaign that was being waged behind the scenes. A photographed copy of a forged *Pravda* appeared in *The Daily Herald* on 28 February 1921.

> 'The paper itself' explains *The Herald* 'is not the ordinary *Pravda*. It is full of anti-Boshevik propaganda rather clumsily disguised as news. It is, in fact, a Wrangel propaganda sheet, flying false colours and masquerading as an offical Soviet organ.'

According to *The Daily Herald*, the bogus *Pravdas* were printed by a firm of London printers, which, to fulfil its legal obligations, had put its name at the bottom of the last page. The printed copies were then taken to Scotland Yard where the special Branch had its own printing works, and it was there, 'in that secret printing office the tell-tale imprint was cut off by guillotining . . . . Once a fortnight these imitation *Pravdas* (there had been a whole series of them) were taken by Special Branch men to Hull or Harwich and despatched to certain British officials in Helsingfors. Thence through the channels established by the 'Whites' they were sent into Soviet Russia.'[2]

In reply to a question in the House of Commons by Labour MP, Tom Myers, on 3 March 1921, the Home Secretary, Edward Shortt, 'admitted the complicity of the Government officials in preparing this anti-Soviet propaganda for distribution in Russia.' (*The Daily Herald*, 4 March 1921) The Director of Intelligence, he said, had acted without consulting him and had been 'indiscreet'.

Fortunately for the citizens of both countries, the revelations did not prevent the continuation of the trade negotiations. Nevertheless, the campaign to sour Anglo-Soviet relations persisted.

Russian émigrés, backed by the French Government, were exploiting every avenue to sabotage the Anglo-Soviet trade negotiations. Fleet Street was inundated with press reports emanating from the Baltic countries of widespread revolts against the Soviet Government. Whilst it was undoubtedly true that there had been a revolt at Kronstadt and some minor revolts elsewhere, they had not undermined the Soviet regime.

H.N. Brailsford, an eminent journalist, who had been on a visit to Russia and the Scandivavian countries, cabled from Stockholm that

'The news that some kind of concerted insurrection has been attempted need cause no surprise. There is no military danger to the revolution . . .

. . . The fact in this case is probably that the Social Revolutionaries hoped to start a whole series of formidable risings. They have said for some months that the plan of invading Russia with British drums and French trumpets was mistaken; their rival scheme was to raise rebellion, without obtrusive Allied patronage, in Russia itself. They have had one small success among the sailors at Kronstadt, who for some time have been discontented over lowered rations . . . .
Everyone knows that last year's harvest failed.

One needs no direct evidence to establish the probability that there is in consequence terrible privation and widespread discontent. This perilous phase may last till the next harvest is gathered. The probability is that the revolution will survive much worse trials than these . . .' (*The Daily Herald*, 8 March 1921)

On 12 March 1921, H.J. Alsberg, *The Daily Herald's* Moscow correspondent reported:

'I can state definitely that the French Government is concerned in the Kronstadt affair, and that a large sum of money for the use of the mutineers has been sent by them to a certain Professor in Viborg. Supplies are also being sent under cover of the Red Cross. Every conceivable pressure is being brought on Mr Lloyd George to induce him to put off signing the agreement.

If those efforts succeed, it will mean that the agreement will be too late to become operative this summer, and that the opening of trade will be postponed for another year.

It is largely with this object that the fiction factories of Helsingfors and Reval* have been working overtime this last fortinight.'

The Daily Herald's exposure of the plots to discredit the Soviet regime greatly strengthened the resolve of those elements in Britain, and especially Lloyd George and some of his more realistic Cabinet colleagues, not to be diverted from the trade negotiations. Four days later, on 16 March 1921, the first Anglo-Soviet Trade Agreement was signed.

The Daily Telegraph, whose record was not unblemished in its reporting of the visit of the Soviet Trade Delegation and of the negotiations, suddenly developed a change of heart. Under the heading 'THE REAL SITUATION' the *Telegraph* admitted that

---

*Now known as Tallinn, capital of Estonia.

'The Kronstadt affair has been thoroughly mis-represented. The wild rumours about sanquinary encounters, tremendous gunfire, and doughty deeds are exaggerated. They are produced by men who try to replace information they cannot obtain by daring flights of vivid imagination. In loyalty to the public it is high time to bring light to bear upon the situation. Lately American anarchists deported from the United States have had a constantly growing influence on the sailors. This is so true that the Soviet Government has now given strict orders to its agents in Estonia and Latvia to refuse visas to all re-emigrants from America.' (*The Daily Telegraph*, 18 March 1921)

The eventual signing of the Trade Agreement automati-cally established a de facto recognition of the Soviet Government.

Under the Agreement:

'each party refrains from hostile action or under-takings against the other and from conducting outside of its own borders any official propaganda direct or indirect against the institutions of the British Empire or the Russian Soviet Republic respectively'

It was agreed that the Soviet Government

'refrains from any attempt by military or diplo-matic or any other form of action or propaganda to encourage any of the peoples of Asia in any form of hostile action against British interests or the British Empire, especially in India and in the Independent State of Afghanistan'

The British Government also had to undertake

'a similar particular understanding to the Russian Soviet Government in respect of the countries

161

which formed part of the former Russian Empire and which have now become independent'

Regarding the matter concerning claims,

'The Russian Soviet Government declares that it recognizes in principle that it is liable to pay compensation to private persons who have supplied goods or services to Russia for which they have not been paid'

and 'The British Government hereby makes a corresponding declaration' Under Article V, it was agreed that:

'Either party may appoint one or more official agents to a number mutually agreed upon, to reside and exercise their functions in the territories of the other, who shall personally enjoy all the rights and immunities set forth in the preceding Article (i.e. for the agreed number of nationals of each country to be afforded the usual facilities regarding the import of consumer goods for their personal use)

as well as being at liberty under Article IV

'to communicate freely by post, telegraph and wireless telegraphy, and to use telegraph codes under the conditions and subject to the regulations laid down in the International Telegraph Convention of St. Petersburg, 1875 (Lisbon Revision of 1908).

At the same time the British Government (Article IX) undertook

'not to initiate any steps with a view to attach or to take possession of any gold, funds, securities or commodities not being articles identifiable as the property of the British Government which may be exported from Russia in payment for imports or as securities for such payment'

162

Lloyd George in his defence of the Agreement reminded the House of Commons, 22 March 1921 that:

> 'It is a small world. Nations are very dependent upon each other. We are dependent upon Russia, and Russia is dependent upon us . . . . It was not done merely in the interest of Russia, but in the interest of everybody all round.' (*Hansard*, 22 March 1921, Col. 2510)

Notes

1. BROGAN D. W., *The Development of Modern France* (1870–1939) pp. 599 and 603
2. COATES W. P. and Zelda, *A History of Anglo-Soviet Relations* p. 51

13

GATEWAYS TO THE EAST

When Turkey and its Ottoman Empire collapsed in the Autumn of 1918, the Dardanelles Straits passed into the hands of the British and French Governments.

This gateway to the East was the one most frequently used to land and evacuate troops; to provide the 'White' counter-revolutionary forces with military supplies, and to enable Allied battleships to bombard coastal town and Black Sea ports. Other gateways were through Persia and Afghanistan. All three had one thing in common: they bordered on Soviet Russia.

Gateways to the East have always facinated romantics, historians and even generals, with their air of mystique, adventure and antiquity. To the new Soviet state, gateways, from recent experience, could be used to undermine its security. Consequently when, as in the case of Persia and Afghanistan, military control, in the form of a protectorate, was taken over by the British Army, the Soviet Government was naturally perturbed. In the case of Afghanistan the Tsarist Government, as part of a quid pro quo for its influence in the Balkans, accepted Britain's suzerainty in that country. It was part of the terms of the 1907 Anglo-Russian Agreement, and it remained in force until the Bolsheviks took over in November 1917 when this Agreement, together with the war-time Secret Treaties, was renounced.

In 1921 the Soviet Government signed treaties of peace and friendship with all three countries. It signed the first of these with Afghanistan on 28 February 1921, and in so doing, upset the British Foreign Office. By openly recognizing Britain's protectorate as an independent and sovereign state, the British Government somehow felt obliged to follow suit, although not until some months later. An Anglo-Afghan Treaty was signed on 22 November 1921 which recognized the complete independence of Afghanistan. Before taking this decision the British Government had sent a sharp note to Moscow reminding it of the fact that 'the Imperial Russian Government recognized that Afghanistan lay outside its sphere of influence'.

The Russo-Afghan Treaty earlier in the year had apparently touched a sensitive nerve at Britain's Foreign Office. Even if Afghanistan was an independent country, if only on paper, the Foreign Office did not like being pressed into taking decisions contrary to desires, least of all by the Bolsheviks.

A month after signing the Treaty, the Soviets came to an amicable arrangement with Turkey regarding the use and control of the Straits. It was agreed 'that Russia, Turkey, the Ukraine and Georgia, to whom belongs practically the greater part of the Black Sea, could not admit the right of any other Government to interfere in the settlement of the question of the Straits.'[1]

Although the Entente* had taken over joint control of the Straits, their relationship in this part of the world was far from cordial. Turkey also had its revolution and the days of the imperial Sultan were over. Their new nationalist leader, Mustapha Kemal, had been able to exploit the divisions between the British Foreign Office and the Quai d'Orsay. In spite of Lord Curzon's protestations, a Franco-Turkish Treaty was signed in October 1921 which recognized the new Turkish National Government.

Back home, in Europe and on the American continent, the brief post-war industrial spurt had petered out, and the expected boom had yet to arrive. Mass unemployment and the slow recuperation of the basic industries had compelled both Britain and France to trim their budgets of some of the funds earmarked for military hardware, especially the building of massive battleships. The main creditor nation was beginning to call the tune.

---

*Italy also had some responsibility over the straits, but played only a minor role and eventually withdrew from the conflicts in the area.

In August 1921 the American Secretary of State, Charles Evans Hughes, sent out invitations to a number of the world's major powers to attend a conference on arms limitations. Although the United States had refrained from signing the Versailles Treaty and from joining the League of Nations, it nevertheless felt that it had to lead the world out of its recession and at the same time prevent some of its debtors from bankrupting themselves while in the process of building up large navies.

The Washington Conference lasted from 11 November to 6 February 1922 and in the arguing and haggling that went on during this period, it reluctantly agreed to a United States proposal that a ten-year moratorium should be imposed upon the building of new capital ships, and that any under construction be scrapped; that Britain, until then the greatest naval power in the world, be restricted to the same number of battleships as the United States, i.e. five, and Japan, which in 1920–21 had been spending nearly half of its national budget on the navy, be restricted to three. There was no agreement on submarines.

Having cut back Britain's naval supremacy, the United States succeeded in breaking up the Anglo-Japanese alliance in the Pacific by pressing the British Government to join a Four-Power Treaty between the United States, Great Britain, Japan and France.

Delegations came from the host country, Britain, Belgium, China, France, Japan, Holland, Italy, Portugal, as well as the British Dominions who were tactlessly listed as part of the British Empire delegation and not as independent countries. One major country with a significant presence in the Pacific was not invited – the Russian Socialist Federal Republic. From the outset, the United States was able to dominate the decisions of the Conference in the acquiescence to her proposals by the sheer force of her economic and financial resources.

Meanwhile plans were going ahead for the preparation of a world-wide economic conference to be held in Genoa in the Spring of 1922. The meeting of the Allied Supreme Council in Cannes from 6 – 14 January was used by Britain and France to try and work out some kind of joint approach to the problems of German reparations, prospects for the economic penetration of Russia and the general economic restoration of Europe.

In April 1921 German reparations had been finally fixed by a Special Commission at the colossal sum of £6,600 million, in spite of the fact that the Germans were already in default of the initial payment of £1,000 million. There were sharp differences of opinion in the Entente on the question or reparations and its effect upon European recovery. The debate had also divided some sectors of the French Cabinet. Briand, who was at the time French Prime Minister, was prepared to meet Lloyd George's appeal for lowering the reparation commitment as part of a package deal that would include an Anglo-French Security Pact against Germany. Briand's compromise on the German question had aroused the hostility of a number of his Cabinet colleagues as well as many French Deputies. German reparations was a very emotive topic in France and he was forced to resign. His position was taken over by Raymond Poincaré, an old time hard-liner.

At the Cannes meeting of the Allied Supreme Council, Lloyd George managed to steer the discussion towards accepting the inevitability of Soviet participation. But on condition that

'If Russia attends, we should make it quite clear to Russia that we can only trade with her if she recognizes the honourable obligations of every civilized country – namely that she should pay all debts, whether incurred by the present government or by its predecessors .... That she will refrain from undertaking propaganda to subvert our institutions and social systems: and that she will join in undertaking to refrain from attacks on her neighbours'

But, Lloyd George added

'You must make it quite clear that the last obligation must be undertaken by our own friends. If we insist that Russia shall not attack her neighbours, we must also insist that her neighbours shall not attack her, and if the conditions under which alone trade is possible involve the recognition of the Russion Government, that also should be done, provided it is made quite clear that the Russian Government will undertake all the other obligations which I indicated'. (*The Times*, 7 January 1922)

Poincaré was not at all keen to give support to the Economic Conference along the guide-lines which were being proposed by the British Prime Minister. On 26 February 1922 the two Heads of State met in Boulogne. Unlike his predecessor the French Prime Minister was against the holding of the proposed Genoa Conference but had succumbed to the persuasion of Lloyd George. He nevertheless made himself absolutely clear in advance that 'there was to be no balancing of accounts as between loans made to Russia and the Soviet counterclaim for the Denikin, Wrangel and Kolchak expeditions',* and that he was against the recognition of the Soviet Regime. On the other hand, Lloyd George who was well aware that the rebuilding of Europe and the development of European trade could not be effectively realized without Russia's participation had yielded to Poincaré's demands, rather than jeopardize the future of the Entente. This was revealed in an interview given to the press:

'The fact that Russia has accepted our invitation to the Conference does not imply recognition of the Soviets by any means. Everything depends upon the guarantees and safeguards which Russia can give at Genoa. If these are satisfactory, then recognition may follow – perhaps immediately.

But I certainly shall not press for recognition of the Soviet Government if the guarantees forthcoming at Genoa are not satisfactory. I would not do that under any considerations. France and England are in agreement upon that question.'
(*The Daily Chronicle*, 27 February 1922)

The Times, 27 February 1922.

Invitations were sent out to twenty-nine European countries and they included both Germany and Russia. The Conference opened in Genoa on 10 April 1922. Among the guide-lines was a report, which had been drafted in London by a so-called Committee of Experts, laying down a long list of conditions upon which the Soviet Government 'shall accept the financial obligations of its predecessors' and for the sequestration of foreign property, etc.

During the first week of the Conference the Soviet representatives were invited, together with the Belgian, British, French and Italian delegates, to discuss the implications of the London Experts' report.

'At this meeting the Soviet delegation put forward claims amounting to £4,067,227,040 for destruction wrought on their territory both by direct foreign intervention and by the aid given to Kolchak, Denikin, Yudenich and Wrangel.' In reply, the Allied representatives handed the Russian delegation a memorandum which stated:

'1. "The Creditor Allied Governments represented at Genoa cannot admit any liability with regard to the claims by the Soviet Government.
2. But in view of the serious economic condition of Russia, such creditor Governments are prepared to write down the war debts owing by Russia to them (by a percentage to be determined later); and the countries represented at Genoa would be prepared to consider not only the postponement of the paymnts of interest upon financial claims, but also the remission of some parts of the arrears of interest or postponed interests.
3. It must be definitely agreed however, that there can be no allowance made to the Soviet Government against:
    a) Either the debts and financial obligations due to foreign nationals
    or
    b) The rights of such nationals with regard to the return of their property, and compensation for damage or loss in respect thereof." '[2]

Meanwhile the representatives of the two pariahs of

Europe, Germany and Russia, had decided that mutual interests were now far greater than recent antagonisms. Their delegations, led by Foreign Ministers Chicherin and Rathenau, met in Rapallo on Easter Sunday just seventeen miles from Genoa and signed the historic treaty which was to be the instrument that would break apart the chains of Versailles.

The two governments agreed upon a policy of economic co-operation and friendly relations, which was to continue throughout the 1920s.

The significance of the Russo-German Treaty had undoubtedly shaken the authority of the Allied inspired Genoa plans for economic subservience of the rest of Europe. Yet in spite of the new factor which had arisen from Rapallo, Lloyd George, who hoped that the conference might lead to an agreement between Russia and the other European nations, still persisted in pampering to the forces of reaction. In a speech to the Genoa delegates he warned the Soviet delegation 'that Russia without European help could not "recover for a generation"; that Europe was eager to help, but that if Russia wanted her assistance she must first renounce "the doctrine of the repudiation of the debts".'[3]

The Soviet reply was sharp and to the point:

> 'The British Premier tells me' said Chicherin 'that if my neighbour has lent me money, I must pay him back. Well, I agree, in that particular case, in a desire for conciliation; but I must add that if this neighbour has broken into my house, killed my children, destroyed my furniture and burnt my house, he must begin by restoring to me what he has destroyed.' (From the Genoa Conference pp 284/285)

'The indignation with which this treaty [Rapallo] was greeted by the Allied Powers was understandable. But it was the direct consequence of their own policy of treating Germany and the Soviet Union as inferior countries.'[4]

As for the Genoa Conference, the Soviet delegation refused to allow themselves to be browbeaten into accept-

170

ing some vague form of economic assistance in return for the economic penetration of their country. Their Government had, on 20 April, stated that without financial aid it would be unable to settle Tsarist and municipal debts and pay compensation.

The failure of the Genoa Conference to come to terms with the Soviet offer of compensation in return for financial assistance was to be a major factor in the tardiness of European recovery. The return of the British delegation with nothing to show after three months of fruitless endeavour, prompted Labour Party spokesmen to emphasize the supreme importance to Britain of the Russian market. They accused the Government of allowing the future of Anglo-Soviet trade to be determined by the possessors of Tsarist bonds and called for the full legal and diplomatic recognition of the Soviet Governement and for an extension of credits to enable an increase in that trade.

The conflict of interests reflected in the foreign policies of Britain and France towards Germany and Russia had now opened up in Asia Minor. In addition, Lloyd George was faced with a division within the Coalition Cabinet concerning his support for the occupation by Greece of large areas of Turkish territory.

'Imperial Strategy and naval communications were the grounds for his support of the Greeks and his coolness to the traditional* pro-Turkish attitude of his Tory colleagues. Hence in 1921, when the Greeks could have extricated themselves from Asia Minor, they did not do so, in part trusting to Lloyd George's support. They rejected the proposals for the modification of the Treaty of Sèvres† made at the London Conference in February, and in the Summer began a new offensive aimed at Ankara.'[5] The Russo-Turkish Agreement of March 1921 and that between France and Turkey in October had seriously weakened the Lloyd George policy for the area. C.L. Mowat, author of Britain Between the Wars 1918 – 1940, goes into some detail of the Greco-Turkish war and the Chanak crisis, describing how 'on 4 March the Viceroy of India published a memor-

*Presumably since 1918. H.S.
†Signed on 10 August 1920 . . . at which the Allies agreed to the internationalization of the Straits.

171

andum giving sympathetic support to Turkish aspirations as a means of quieting Moslem alarm in India. This, which ran counter to the British Government's policy at the time had been authorized by [Edwin] Montagu, the Secretary of State for India. Curzon, as Foreign Secretary, took up the challenge in the Cabinet and forced Montagu's resignation.'[6]

The conflict of views in the Coalition Cabinet on the affairs of the Middle East had originally flared up in 1920 when Winston Churchill sided with some of the Tory members of the Cabinet. In his dissenting Note submitted on 10 December 1920, he stated that 'we should make a definite change in our policy in the direction of procuring a real peace with the Moslem world and so relieving ourselves of the disastrous reaction both military and financial to which our anti-Turk policy has exposed us in the Middle East and in India.'[7] And on 11 June 1921 he told Lloyd George that 'If the Greeks go off on another half-cock offensive, the last card will have been played and lost and we shall neither have a Turkish peace nor a Greek Army.'[8]

According to Robert Rhodes James in his book, *Churchill, A Study in Failure 1900 – 1939*, the 'eventuality did not belie this prognostication. By the Summer of 1922 the condition of the Greek forces in Turkey-in-Asia had become desperate.

The nationalist forces of Mustapha Kemal ... swept down upon the Greeks, and thrust them relentlessly towards the sea. The Greeks reached the Port of Smyrna in chaos and rout, hotly pursued. The victorious Kemalist army turned north, and advanced upon the neutral zone at the Dardanelles created by the Treaty of Sèvres in 1920.'[9]

The Greeks tried to divert the Turkish Army by attacking Constantinople from their own mainland of Thrace. 'The Allies, still in occupation of the zone of the Straits, refused to permit the landing.' On 18 August Mustapha Kemal launched an attack on the Greeks, 'and the weight of his numbers, and the munitions imported from France and Russia, were decisive .... Turkish forces entered Smyrna on 9 September.'[10] There was panic not only among the Greek Forces, but also among their backers. Lloyd George and his pro-Greek faction were now joined by Churchill in calling for a greater determination to defend the Dardenelles Straits from the victorious Turkish Army who they believed was about to challenge the Alled forces of occupation. Chanak, at the mouth of the Straits, and held by British troops was being threatened by Kemal's Army.

Churchill's sudden change of attitude to the events in the Middle East reached common ground with Lloyd George when the latter declared: 'It was inconceivable that we should allow the Turks to gain possession of the Gallipoli Peninsular and we should fight to prevent their doing so.'

Two of Churchill's colleagues who knew him well have explained what they believe determined his change of attitude. Lord Beaverbrook* relates an occasion when:

> 'Churchill talked of the might and honour and prestige of Britain, which he said I, as a foreigner or invader, did not understand, and of how it would be ruined forever if we did not immediately push a bayonet into the stomach of anyone in arms who contested it. He was always ready to fight England's foes.'[11]

And Lord Birkenhead, a Cabinet colleague, was reported to have said to Bonar Law, 9 June 1921, 'Winston seems to have become almost pro-Greek having always hated them. I suspect the explanation is that the Kemalists are being helped by the Bolsheviks & W. will support anyone who attacks them.'[12]

In the anxiety not to lose control of the Straits, the Government decided that it would confront the Turks with a show of imperial force. According to Mowat, 'telegrams were dispatched to the Dominions outlining the critical position and inviting them to send contingents to aid in the defence of the Straits; and the next day a communiqué, drafted by Churchill, was published from 10 Downing Street recounting the matters at issue and clearly foreshadowing the possibility of war. The communiqué had bitter results. The Dominion leaders saw it before the telegram from the Cabinet, sent in cipher, had reached

*Beaverbrook was a Canadian.

them. They felt they were being asked, imperiously, to send help to Britain in a quarrel into which she had got herself without consulting them; the tender privileges of 'dominion status' seemed to be strangled by the old colonialism. Chanak was thus a crisis in the history of Britain's imperial relations, and ultimately vindicated the independence of the Dominions.'[13]

The French Government also showed no inclination to get involved in a war which they believed was of Britain's own making, and they withdrew their troops from the area. Meanwhile Churchill was still prepared to go ahead and challenge the Turks. At a Cabinet meeting on 15 September 'He was wholly opposed to any attempt to carry out a bluff without force.' Churchill not only had 'Bolshevism on the brain' as Lloyd George had pointed out a few years earlier, but also the memory of Gallipoli. This came out in a further contribution to the Cabinet discussion: 'However fatigued it might be he thought that the Empire would put up some force to preserve Gallipoli, with the graves of so many of its soldiers, and they might even be willing to do this without the co-operation of France.'*[14] Were it not for the level headedness of the British Commander-in-Chief of the area, General Harrington, Britain would have become involved in a major war. The General held up the instructions for sending an ultimatum to Mustapha Kemal demanding withdrawal from the Chanak area; thus allowing tensions to ease. On 3 October, General Harrington, together with representatives from Britain and France, met Mustapha Kemal at Mudania and after a few days of discussions the Turkish leader agreed that provided the Greeks evacuated Eastern Thrace, Turkey would recognize the neutral zone and would not occupy the evacuated territory until there had been a ratification of the Peace Treaty.†

The failure of the Genoa Conference, and of Lloyd George's attempts to unify Allied policy towards Germany and Russia, as well as the conflicts within the Cabinet over reactions to the events in Asia Minor, eventually led to the break up of the coalition. Lloyd George was forced to resign

---

*Dominion troops suffered heavy losses at Gallipoli.
†See Winston Churchill – *The World Crisis, The Aftermath*, p.437.

on 19 October 1922 and a new government was installed under Bonar Law, who decided to call for a General Election, the first since the 'Khaki' election of 1918. The Conservatives were returned with a large working majority of 345 seats to Labour's 142, with the Liberals split between the Asquith Liberals, 60 seats and Lloyd George Liberals 57.

With the collapse of the Greek army in Asia Minor, Britain still hoped that it would be able to maintain its influence in the area through its control of the Dardanelles Straits. The opportunity came soon after the election.

Towards the end of November a conference was held in Lausanne, with the primary object of reaching agreements on the Straits, as well as other areas in the near and Middle East. Both Russia and Turkey were invited, although Britain's policy from the outset had been to undermine the newly formed friendship between the two countries. Britain's representative, in outlining the Government's scheme, 'proposed the demilitarization of the Bosphorus, the Dardennelles and the Turkish Islands in the Aegean Sea, and the establishment of an International Control commission to supervise the carrying out of the terms of the agreement. This meant that Turkey would be deprived of physical means to dispute the passage of battleships belonging to non-Black Sea powers, despite the fact that the Black Sea is a closed sea and not a marine thoroughfare.'[15]

Both Russia and Turkey were suspicious of the British scheme. They did not want the Black Sea to be used once again as an area for naval and militrary hostilities. The Soviet representative, Chicherin, put forward an alternative plan which would restore Turkish sovereignty over the Straits.

> 'The Straits, in peace-time, were to be open day and night to commercial traffic, but closed to battleships, and the passage of light warships was to be permitted in special cases. In time of war the Straits were also to be open to merchant shipping, but Turkey, being a belligerent, would have the right of search. It was also proposed that the scheme would be under the control of the Interna-

tional Board representative of the . . . Black Sea States and the Great Powers, with a Turkish Chairman'.[16]

However, the outcome of Lausanne was that

'Turkey retained Eastern Thrace (including Adrianople); demilitarized zones were established on both sides of the Dardanelles (including Gallipoli and the Chanak area) and on both sides of the Bosphorus; navigation of the Straits was opened to ships of commerce of all nations in time of peace and of neutrals in time of war involving Turkey, and to warships of all nations (subject to limitations of number and size) in time of peace or Turkish neutrality; and the disposition of the territory of Mosul, with its oil-fields, which was indispute between Turkey and Iraq, was left for later negotiations (it was ultimately referred to the League of Nations and awarded to Iraq, a decision accepted by Turkey in a treaty in 1926)'[17]

Chicherin, in an interview with Arthur Ransome of *The Manchester Guardian* had complained of 'The systematic elimination of the Russian delegations from real negotiations on the Straits question' and that he and his colleagues in the Russian Government were convinced 'that lack of friendship in the British Foreign Office towards us was no longer restrained by wiser counsel in Downing Street.' (*The Manchester Guardian*, 22 February 1923)

Perhaps an indication of the thoughts of certain sections of the British Foreign Office at the time could be detected in an extract from the Diary of Viscount D'Abernon dated

'Berlin, Aug. 30, 1922. From the point of view of English policy a big question presents itself – is a large Russia desirable? America is strongly for it, presumably as a counterpoise to Japan. English interests, I think, are much more certainly against it. As long as there is a strong Russia, India is, to a considerable extent menaced. The Balkanization of Central Europe is bad, but the Balkanization of Central Asia would be unquestionable relief to English policy.

Even as regards the Black Sea and the Mediterranean, a Russia divided into different states, whose commercial interests overpowered her political ambition, would make our position far more secure than in the event of the re-establishment of a powerful Empire. A separatist policy for the Ukraine would unquestionably lead to a safer and more healthy position in the Black Sea, and would facilitate commercial control of the Straits, as opposed to central control'. (*The Daily Telegraph*, 3 October 1929)

Unfortunately for those countries bordering the Bosphorus and the Black Sea, the British Government, through its powerful navy, was able to dictate terms for the control of the Straits.

Notes

1. COATES W. P. and Zelda, *A History of Anglo-Soviet Relations*, p. 99
2. COATES W. P. and Zelda, *A History of Anglo-Soviet Relations*, p. 76
3. COATES W. P. and Zelda, *A History of Anglo-Soviet Relations*, p. 86
4. CARR E. H., *International Relations Between the Two World Wars* (1919–1939), p. 75
5. MOWAT C. L., *Britain Between the Wars* 1918–1940, p. 116
6. MOWAT C. L., *Britain Between the Wars* 1918–1940, p. 117
7. CAB 23/23 Appendix I, Greece and Middle Eastern Policy
8. CHURCHILL Winston, *The World Crisis and the Aftermath*, pp. 395/396
9. JAMES Robert Rhodes, *Churchill – A Study in Failure*, p. 141
10. MOWAT C. L., *Britain Between the Wars* 1918–1940, p. 117
11. BEAVERBROOK Lord, *The Decline and Fall of Lloyd George*, p.166
12. BEAVERBROOK Lord, *The Decline and Fall of Lloyd George*, p.267
13. MOWAT C. L., *Britain Between the Wars* 1918–1940, p. 118
14. CAB 23/31 Document 49 (22), pp.15/16
15. COATES W. P. and Zelda, *A History of Anglo-Soviet Relations*,p.101
16. COATES W. P. and Zelda, *A History of Anglo-Soviet Relations*,p.102
17. MOWAT C. L., *Britain Between the Wars* 1918–1940, p. 157

14

FROM VERSAILLES TO LOCARNO

Two months after signing the Treaty of Rapallo, Walter Rathenau, the German Foreign Minister, was assassinated by 'gangsters of the extreme Right who were the heart and soul of the Freikorps.'[1]

The struggle inside Germany since the murder of the Spartacist leaders, Rosa Luxemburg and Karl Liebknecht in 1919, had led to an all-out onslaught on the Republican Government. Morgan Phillips Price, the former *Manchester Guardian* correspondent, who had become foreign correspondent for *The Daily Herald* in Berlin, has given a detailed account of the first attempted coup d'etat* to overthrow the Republic and restore the Monarchy. In his book, *My Three Revolutions*, he says that he awoke on the morning of 13 March 1920 'to find the centre of Berlin full of troops in war kit occupying all the strategic points of the city. Soon a proclamation appeared on the walls stating that the Government had been deposed and that a new Government was being formed, headed by a former Hohenzollern official, Herr Kapp. The list contained largely unknown people, but some well-known anti-Semites. I went to a Foreign Office Press Department and found a new man in charge, a certain Mr Trebitsch Lincoln, who had once been a Liberal MP in England, then a Buddhist monk, somewhere in Asia, and had finally settled down in this sort of outfit. I met other foreign correspondents and we all agreed that, as long as this man was in that office, we would not go there. He was later replaced.'

Phillips Price then goes on to quote from his initial

---

*The Kapp Putsch

178

dispatch to *The Daily Herald*:

> 'Those who have held that the Ebert-Noske Government of Germany was little more than as camouflage for the Prussian military reactionaries have been abundantly justified. For several weeks past I have been pointing out that Noske's regular army was commanded by men who were aiming at the suppression of all forms of Labour and democratic government in Germany, and that the Ebert Government was either unwilling or unable to take steps against them – was in fact a prisoner in their hands.'[2]

Meanwhile Gustave Noske and the rest of the Government had fled to Stuttgart.

Plans for the coup had been known for some time in Allied circles, for on 5 December 1919, General Turner, a member of the Allied Mission to the Baltic had reported from Tilsit that there was 'reliable information concerning the plans of a Coup d'Etat – the object of which is to overthrow existing Berlin Government, establish a Military Dictatorship and refuse to accept the Peace Treaty. In general the plan is as follows:

> 'Spartacist riots will be arranged in Berlin and will be the excuse for the Iron Division in East Prussia and similar formations in Hanover and South Germany to march on Berlin.
>
> Ludendorf is quoted as one of the prime movers in the affair and is known to have visited the Iron Division at Mitau three weeks ago. Von der Goltz, who is now at Königsberg Headquarters, Hindenburg and Mackensen are also concerned in the movement.
>
> The date of execution is unknown but the plan is openly discussed by officers of the Iron Division and has been the underlying motive of their actions during the past weeks.'[3]

According to Sir John Wheeler-Bennett, 'the question of a Monarchist coup had actually been raised in the National

Assembly, where on 1 March, Noske had declared that while a Monarchist movement certainly existed in Germany, as indeed it did in France, the Government were confident that if the Allies were not too harsh towards the Reich, the monarchists would present no menace to the Republic.'[4]

But the complacency of the Government had not spread to the German Labour Movement. Phillips Price recalls: 'In Berlin the Trade Union Headquarters ordered a general strike throughout the country. From mid-day on, no trains or trams ran and all factories closed down . . now at last it was clear what the policy of leaving the executive government and the courts in the hands of the old régime was leading to. The strike was a complete success and after a few days the Kapp Government faded and the legitimate Government returned.

'In the meantime, however, the miners and the metalworkers in the Ruhr had risen in a body and armed themselves as volunteers of the Left. In this movement the local Majority Social Democrats took part. They issued a manifesto demanding the disbanding of all military formations of the Right, saying that they would not give up their arms until this was done. Moreover, they engaged in a successful military action, driving a Freikorps unit from Remschied into the French-occupied zone on the Rhine . . . . The Majority Social Democratic Ministers now owed their reinstatement to the fact that armed Ruhr miners had forced some Freikorps Units to leave Berlin and go to the West.'[5] And this very same Government 'while issuing warrants of arrest for the leaders of the Putsch – most of whom were already safely out of the country – granted a general amnesty to the rank and file of the conspirators.'[6] The warrants were issued through the office of President Ebert. It was therefore not altogether surprising that many in the German Labour Movement should look to Soviet Russia for a lead in the post-war struggle for economic, political and social change, and when Lenin initiated the formation of a new Socialist International, the Third – later known as the Comintern, the German Spartacist Movement and the Independent Socialist were among its first adherents.

180

The initial Congress of the Third International was, in reality, little more than a preparatory meeting of early supporters and a few observers. It was held in Moscow on 3 March 1919 during the height of the civil war and the military interventions of the Allied armies. The main Congress, in July 1920, was far more representative with delegates from 35 countries.

In France, at the Socialist Party's Annual Conference at Tours in December 1920, the majority of delegates decided to support the Communist International, but in Italy the position was reversed. After a Congress of the Italian Socialists at Leghorn in January 1921 the majority declined, and a minority group lead by Bordiga joined the new International. In August 1920 the British Communist Party was formed and it too affiliated to the Third International. The Independent Labour Party sent observers to the Congress but did not join.

Arising from the July Congress in 1920, Communist Parties were formed, not only in Europe, but in other countries of the world, the largest being in Germany created by the fusion of Spartacists with most of the Independent Socialists.

The forging of solidarity between working people in the capitalist countries with the workers of Soviet Russia, as well as between themselves, took place at a time when the attacks upon the revolutionary movements were at their height. Those who had suffered most from the War of Empires had much in common – unemployment, poverty, inflation, low wages, bad housing, as well as the severe shortage of living accommodation. The difference was one of degree. In Britain, there were over a million unemployed in February 1921 and by June it had shot up to over two million. There were revolts in India and Egypt (part of the far flung Empire) and a guerilla war in Ireland. And to add to the problems, was the low wage competition to Britain's manufacturing industry coming from new rivals in China, India and Japan. The Indian revolts against British colonial rule reached a climax in April 1919 with the Amritsar Massacre.

This terrible atrocity was carried out by a section of the British army under the command of General Dyer who gave instructions to shoot at an unarmed crowd of Indian men, women and children who had gathered at a mass protest meeting. Britain's Colonial Government had issued a prohibition order, but the Indian people were determined to use that day as a day of protest against British colonial rule. 379 people were killed outright and 1,200 were left wounded in the streets.

News of the Amritsar Massacre was suppressed for eight months. Neither Parliament nor the British public had been informed. When the news of this terrible crime did eventually surface General Dyer, although discharged from his post in the Army, was compensated to the tune of £20,000, accompanied by a vote of approval from the House of Lords.

Meanwhile, in Germany, the economic situation was rapidly deteriorating. There had been a sharp decline in the value of the Mark and in November 1922 the German Government called upon the Allies to accept a moratorium on their reparation payments of three to four years to enable them to stabilize their currency and build up their industry, particularly exports.

The German call had come at a time when France, apart from Russia, had suffered more than any other country from the war. In addition, she 'owed war debts of 18,500 million francs to the United States and 15,000 million to England.'[7] Consequently French public opinion generally did not take kindly to British critiscism of her harsh attitude of the German reparation issue, while at the same time Poincaré was exploiting the strong anti-German feeling in France to serve his purpose, as well as that of his industrial backers. He made his position quite clear in a speech on 26 June 1922:

> 'So far as I am concerned' he declared 'it would pain me if Germany were to pay; then we should have to evacuate the Rhineland. Which do you regard as better, the obtaining of cash or the acquisition of new territory? I for my part prefer the occupation and the conquest to the money of reparations. Hence you will comprehend why we need a powerful army and vigilant patriotism; you

will comprehend that the sole means of saving the Treaty of Versailles is to arrange matters in such a way that our defeated enemies cannot fulfil its conditions.'

This would explain why, according to R. Palme Dutt, 'French policy was directed to securing permanent occupation of the Rhineland and the conquest of the Ruhr', and to which he adds: 'For this purpose the reparations issue was an essential weapon.'[8]

Under the Versailles Treaty, Germany had failed to fulfil her payments and compensatory delivery of goods. And that was enough for Poincaré and some like minded allies in Belgium. On 11 January 1923, 40,000 French troops as well as some Belgium regiments moved into the Ruhr. Poincaré would have welcomed a more comprehensive Allied contingent to back his show of force, but he was fully aware of British hostility to such action and in the event the British Government remained aloof.

Egon Larsen, as a young journalist during the Weimar Era, vividly relates the German People's reaction to the events in the Ruhr.

'Responding to the enormous pressure from all sides' the German Government 'declared a total "passive resistance"' against what Larsen describes as 'the invaders in the Ruhr.' The French and Belgian actions certainly had the effect of uniting all sections of German society. 'Wherever foreign soldiers appeared, German workers downed tools. The trams stopped running, the steelworks and the factories emptied, the miners went home, farmers hid their food stocks, many shopkeepers locked up their premises' and 'civil servants shut their offices.'[9] The Poincaré plan to extract German reparations to the full began to misfire.

The financial burden created by the passive resistance movement was backed by the German Government and the Reichsbank. Inflation was already becoming unmanageable; the events in the Ruhr caused the Government to take financial measures which in turn were to lead to a rapid rise in the rate of inflation.

'At the start of the passive resistance period, one dollar cost 18,000 marks; a month later, 28,000.' By July 1923, the exchange rate for the dollar 'had reached 350,000 marks. In August it shot up to 5 million. In September it was 100 million.'[10] In other words, the country had in effect moved into a state of financial anarchy. Millions of German people, middle and working class, became victims of a Government policy which had destroyed the value of the nation's currency. But of course speculators and the great industrial magnates knew how to adapt to this fantastic state of affairs.

'Anyone such as the big bankers and industrialists who could sell goods abroad or who had any foreign currency, could, with the expenditure of only a small fraction of their foreign holdings liquidate all their debts inside Germany by paying them in nearly worthless paper money or could use the opportunity to instal new equipment at very low cost. The tendency, already existing before 1914 and increased by the war, for the concentration and cartelization of German financial and industrial life was carried a stage further by inflation.'[11]

According to Egon Larsen, some people in Germany 'even said that the state had no interest in stopping inflation because it wiped out the war-loan debts which the State owed us . . . that any revaluation of our investments was out of the question. It also meant that any private or business debts would not have to be repaid except in those now worthless banknotes.'[12]

It had become impossible for wages or salaries to keep pace with the rapid devaluation of the mark. Most working class families just could not afford to buy the basic necessities of life. Malnutrition, lack of warm clothes and adequate heating led to widespread illness and, in many cases, premature death, particularly among the elderly and children of the poorer families. As far as savings were concerned, it was the German middle class which had most to lose.

Coming out of this economic nightmare, millions of suffering, confused German people began to seek reasons for their traumatic experience. They 'tried to identify the guilts' and it was not difficult to find scapegoats, but the great industrial magnates made certain that the search for the guilty did not reach out in their direction. One such magnate was Hugo Stinnes. 'While inflation was at its worst and poverty at its greatest, Stinnes had amassed no fewer than some 4,500 enterprises, most of them bought up with bank loans, iron, steel, and electrical works, newspapers and hotels, shipping companies and cigarette factories, construction firms and sanatoria. Abroad, all over Europe, in America and East Asia, he owned oil wells, and forests, sugar plants and aluminium works, cinemas and tanneries, motor-car and margarine factories, usually acquired by means of complicated financial juggling.' Not satisfied with his stake and influence in the world of industry and finance alone Stinnes 'got himself elected to the Reichstag as an MP for the right-wing German Popular Party. There is little doubt' comments Larsen 'that these big business circles (the Krupps, the Thyssens, the Klockners and Stinnes) not only thrived in the inflation but gave it a deliberate sustained and decisive impetus.' Confirmation has come from no less a man than Hugo Stinnes himself. 'In June 1922, in fact, one day before his assassination – Rathenau . . . took Stinnes to a discussion with the U.S. Ambassador in Berlin. Stinnes wrote:

'I analysed the situation in detail. First I stated the reasons why Germany carried out her policy of inflation . . . . To acquire raw materials and export markets for our production, some capital had to be sacrificed . . . . Dreadful as the ravages of Bolshevism had been in Russia, they would no doubt have been even worse in Germany as a mainly industrial country . . . . I also told the Ambassador that the weapon of inflation would have to be employed in the future as well, regardless of the resulting great losses of capital, because only this would make it possible to provide the people with regular work . . . .'

'Thus Stinnes', who died in 1924, 'admitted that Germany's inflation had been a deliberate policy, fostered and supported by big business, by men who calmly took it upon themselves to destroy private property and whole sectors of the population with it. His explanation, that it was all done in a good cause, namely to save Germany from Bolshevism, sounds rather hollow. This was also the cause for which Hitler was soon to collect money from big business.'[13]

The runaway German inflation had undoubtedly shaken up the Allied Governments. It certainly was no mere coincidence that the main item on the agenda at the London Conference in July 1924 was the adoption of the Dawes Plan which had been thrashed out earlier in the year, whereby the whole question of German reparations and her ability to meet Allied demands was determined. The Franco-Belgian incursion into the Ruhr was an utter failure. It had defeated its objective. The French Government collected very little in reparations whilst the French taxpayer had to sustain an army of occupation in the Ruhr which achieved nothing but unpopularity with the local population. The value of the franc had sharply deteriorated and there were fears among French people that the franc would suffer the same fate as the German mark. Poincaré's Ruhr policy had by now become thoroughly unpopular and in the elections of May 1924 his administration (the Bloc Nationale) was replaced by a grouping of parties described as the Cartel des Gauches. This peculiar mixture was labelled as Left and yet did not include either Socialists or Communists. The 'Socialists refused to participate in the government; their left wing was already unhappy at the party's collaboration with the Radicals during the election campaign.'

Out of a total of 568 seats, the Cartel opposition had 266 and the Bloc National 229. The Communists had 23 leaving 47 seats to centre parties. 'The most [the Socialists] were prepared to do was to support the Radicals and their allies in policies of which they approved.'[14]

Towards the end of 1923, two Americans, Charles G. Dawes, an industrial consultant and Owen D. Young, an economist, together with three British finance specialists, had set up a Commission – headed by Dawes – to examine Germany's economic resources and financial institutions. Their report, which was published on 9 April 1924 'Recommended that Germany's currency be stabilized on a gold basis and that Germany pay an annual sum for reparations rising from 1,000 million marks in the first year to 2,500 million marks in the fifth and subsequent years.'[15] To make the Dawes Plan operate effectively American capital was needed. An initial 800 million gold marks (around £40 million) was loaned to help finance reparation debts. The plan in essence was primarily to assist Germany to pay her reparation commitments, which had in any case been reduced to a more realistic level, and thereby facilitating the payments of inter-allied debts. Collateral assurance was effected by the 'German State Railways [being] turned over to an international company which issued interest bearing bonds. A mortgage was established over part of German industry. Certain taxes were appropriated for reparations. As a final safeguard, the Reichsbank was given an international board of management.'[16]

No sooner was the Dawes Plan put into operation and the mark stabilized than an enormous amount of foreign capital, mostly American, began to flow into the country. There was, of course, a revival of international trade, industrial plants were modernized, export industries began to prosper. But at what cost? 'In fact', comments A.L. Morton, 'the whole revival was a sham, because the interest on all these loans was only paid by further borrowing: the scheme only continued to work so long as the flow of credit continued unbroken. When it ceased, a crisis on a scale never before known began.'[17]

The positive effect of the Dawes Plan was that it temporarily stabilized the German economy, as well as giving an economic boost to the rest of the capitalist world, which was to endure for the next five years. It also helped France to secure the finance for the restoration of her devastated regions and in the following year, August 1925, she responded by evacuating the Ruhr.

According to German statistician, Dr Kuczinski, about a quarter of the total German wealth in 1928, computed at between 50 to 60,000 million marks, was attributed to foreign holdings of one kind or another.* But as the debts accumulated and the payment of interest depended upon new borrowings, there was a growing fear that the flow of foreign capital would cease, and that is what eventually happened.

---

*From New York *Nation*, 7 November 1929.

Notes

1. PRICE Morgan Phillips, *My Three Revolutions*, p. 196.
2. PRICE Morgan Phillips, *My Three Revolutions*, p. 176.
3. Documents on British Foreign Policy 1919 – 1939, First Series, Vol. III, pp. 245/246.
4. WHEELER-BENNETT Sir John, *The Nemesis of Power*, p. 73.
5. PRICE Morgan Phillips, *My Three Revoutions*, p. 176.
6. WHEELER-BENNET Sir John, *The Nemesis of Power*, p. 88.
7. TINT Herbert, *France Since 1918*, p. 18.
8. DUTT R. Palme, *World Politics 1918 – 1936*, p. 57.
9. LARSEN Egon, *Weimar Eye Witness*, p. 51.
10. LARSEN Egon, *Weimar Eye Witness*, p. 52.
11. JOLL James, *Europe Since 1870, An International History*, p. 285
12. LARSEN Egon, *Weimar Eye Witness*, p. 60.
13. LARSEN Egon, *Weimar Eye Witness*, pp. 61, 63, 64, 65.
14. TINT Herbert, *France Since 1918*, p. 21.
15. MOWAT C. L., *Britain Between the Wars 1918 – 1940*, pp. 178/179.
16. WESTERN J. R., *The End of European Primacy*, pp. 387/388.
17. MORTON A. L., *A People's History of England*, p. 523.

15

THE RISE OF HITLER AND MUSSOLINI

There can be no doubt that the mass of the German people had been punished for the deeds and decisions of their political and industrial leaders. Although they had participated in a War of Empires, the Treaty of Versailles had placed the total responsibility at their doorstep. The humiliating terms, the massive reparations, the French and Belgian occupation of the Ruhr – their industrial heartland – without which there could be no German, let alone European recovery, and the catastrophic effect of the runaway inflation, provided the very seed beds upon which German fascism was to flourish during the following two decades. The German military and their political counterparts did not believe that they had been defeated. They had been 'stabbed in the back'. Nationalist movements sprouted all over the country, often in competition with each other for support and financial backing; some with their own para-military organizations. By 1923, Morgan Phillips Price was reporting how:

'The rump of the old parties is now working in close touch with a new party, the so-called National Socialist Party under Herr Hitler and Herr Eckert, who is organizing under a Fascist banner those elements of the trade unions who are tired of the cowardice of the Social-Democratic leaders. These new groups under the leadership of Hitler and Ludendorff have come out openly for a Fascist dictatorship, and by the tactics of provocation of the Socialists and Republican elements in the rest of Germany, and by attacks on Socialist

189

meetings and demonstrations, hope to ferment civil war, leading up to the seizure of power by their armed forces. During the winter of 1922–23, Hitler's storm battalions organized raiding expeditions to the industrial towns of North Bavaria. His plan of campaign is to seize power in North Bavaria or Frankenland, and use it as a base of operations against Thürlingen and Saxony, where Social-Democratic Governments are in power with the aid of Communist votes. From there the way would be open to the industrial districts of Prussia in the North. Success will very much depend on the goodwill of the German heavy industry trusts who, after the murder of Rathenau, withdrew their financial support from most of these Fascist bodies. But after the French occupation of the Ruhr, the heavy industries began again to support the Bavarian Fascists.'[1]

On 9 November 1923, Hitler and his Fascists in Munich felt confident enough to attempt a coup. But they had miscalculated the mood of the Republican Government in Berlin and the measure of support which was expected to come from von Kahr, the Bavarian Commissioner of State, and the Munich Garrison. In the street battles which followed, fourteen of Hitler's men were killed. Hitler and Ludendorff escaped but were arrested a few days later, together with Hess, Rohm and Frick. Although the Government had decided upon taking action against the leaders of the coup, they nevertheless acquitted Ludendorff – the wartime hero. Hitler and Hess were sentenced to five years in the Landsberg Fortress, but were released after only eight months. Hitler was treated as a VIP with a private room where he dictated to Hess, acting as his personal secretary, the text for the first volume of *Mein Kampf*.

It was while Hitler was in prison that the Dawes Plan, for stimulating the economy, had been set into motion. After the failure of the coup and the revival of the nation's industry, the fortunes of Hitler and the National Socialists reached their lowest ebb. They desperately needed money. Hitler through Dietrich Eckart, a writer with wealthy connections, was able to meet a number of Germany's leading industrialists among whom were Emil Kirdoff and Fritz Thyssen. He had very little difficulty in convincing them that his brand of socialism was not a threat to the principles of capitalist enterprise. They were soon assured that this new National Socialist Party was there to protect them against Bolshevism.

Kirdoff who 'was associated with the iron industry had been given the task of distributing the secret funds of the heavy industries.'[2] Thyssen was chairman oi the Vereinige Stahlwerke A.G., the largest steelworks in the Ruhr, founded by his father during the Franco-Prussian war and employing in the prosperous years some 170,000 people. Before World War I he had owned some metal mines in French Lorraine. It later transpired that Thyssen and Stinnes had during the war submitted a demand to the Kaiser that the annexation of Lorraine should be carried out by the German Government. This was not forgotten by the French, and in 1923 Thyssen was arrested and imprisoned for several months for obstructing French demands during the occupation of the Ruhr.

In his book, *I Paid Hitler*, Thyssen recalls his first meeting with him. He says he was not sure of 'the exact part which each of us took in the conversation. Yet I remember the general content. Ludendorff and Hitler agreed to undertake a military expedition against Saxony in order to depose the Communist Government of Dr Zeigener. The ultimate aim of the proposed expedition was to overthrow the Weimer democracy, whose weakness was leading Germany into anarchy. Funds were lacking. Lundedorff accepted fees for interviews which he gave to American newspaper correspondents. However, as he told me, this did not get him very far. He had already solicited and obtained the help of several industrialists, particularly that of Herr Minnoux of the Stinnes firm. For my part, I gave him about one hundred thousand gold marks.* This was my first contribution to the National Socialist Party.'[3]

In later years, Thyssen became more closely allied to Hitler personally. No major step was taken by the Nazi

---

*About £5,000.

leader without Thyssen and his rich industrial friends being first of all consulted. 'Thyssen systematically financed all election funds of the National Socialist Party. He it was who already in 1929 invited Hitler to Dusseldorf, the headquarters of the Steel trust, and there introduced him for the first time to an assembly of three hundred leading industrialists of the Ruhr ... three years later, at the beginning of 1932, brought Hitler a second time to Dusseldorf, this time in order to develop his programme for the future before two thousand German industrialists.'[4]

The twenty five point programme of the National Socialist Party, adopted in 1920 was known throughout the country. It included the union of *all* Germans, abolition of the Treaty of Versailles, that only persons of German blood to be regarded as members of the nation and that Jews were excluded, nationalization of Trusts and Combines, a conscript army, press control and a strong central power in Germany.

When the Nazis came to power in 1933 no Trusts were nationalized, private property was maintained and the concentration of capital within the narrow circle continued. The facade of National Socialism had been exposed. It was none other than the most virulent form of nationalist racialism that the people of this world had yet to experience.

In Italy, although there were not the disillusioned, as in Germany, who believed thay had been robbed of victory, there were, nevertheless, millions who had had no stomach for the war at all. Over half a million lives were sacrificed and the country was left with a war debt of 48 million gold lire. They too had war-time profiteers who made fortunes out of their misfortunes, and had to suffer the inevitable inflation. Their printing presses had been turning out paper money to such an extent that in the last year of the war the amount in circulation more than doubled. The expectation of gains, which enticed Italian political leaders to bring Italy into the war and on to the side of the Allies, had not materialized.

Repercussions from the post-war economic recession were particulary severe in the northern industrial areas. Rising unemployment, increased living costs and, for those still employed in 1919–1920, a persistent battle with the employers for a living wage led to wide-spread strikes and demonstrations. Steel, textiles and most engineering concerns had shed much of their labour force. The Metal-Workers' Union called out their men in Turin, and in Milan, automobile workers, in reply to the employers' threat of a lock-out, took over the factory and made an attempt at running it themselves.

Benito Mussolini, whose origins had been in the Italian Socialist movement, was not slow to turn the general discontent to the advantage of his newly formed 'Fascio di Combattimento' Nationalist Movement.* Mussolini, like Hitler, realized that a policy of nationalism, anti-Bolshevism and 'free' trade unions would soon bring in the financial support which he badly needed. As in the case of Hitler, his early financial backing came from the steel industry; from the brothers Perrone, who owned the Ansaldo Steel Works. It was not long afterwards that other industrialists began to appreciate his policy and sent in their donations.

His philosophy regarding fascism is illustrated by an article written in 1931 which appeared in the Enciclopedia Italiana:

'We represent a new principle in the world, the clear, final and categoric antithesis of democracy, plutocracy, Freemasonry, and the immortal principles of 1789.

The ideals of democracy are exploded, beginning with that of "progress". Ours is an aristocratic century; the state of all will end by becoming the state of a few.

Fascism is the purest kind of democracy, so long as people are counted qualitatively and not quantitatively.

The fascist conception of the state is all-

---

*It had been formed in Milan on 23 March 1919. Fascio, a bundle of rods with an axe, the token of State Power – carried by the victors in Ancient Rome before the Consuls to symbolize their power to punish – also a symbol of discipline.

embracing, and outside of the state no human or spiritual values can exist, let alone be desirable.

Perpetual peace would be impossible and useless. War alone brings human energies to their highest state of tension, and stamps with the seal of nobility the nations which dare to face it.'*[5]

Mussolini's strategy was, as in Germany, expressed in an aggressive manner out on the streets. The fascists were in the early days organized on military lines: in Fasci di Combattimento units, ready to act in the manner of the German Freikorps. Socialist organizations were systematically attacked by these fascist combat groups. Socialist councillors were beaten up and town halls occupied. The offices of *Avanti*,† the Socialist newspaper, were attacked and burnt. During 1920–1921 the 'Fascists destroyed some 120 trades union headquarters . . . while between January and May 1921, 243 left-wingers were murdered and 1,144 were seriously injured by beating, shooting and bombing.'[6] Fascist gangs were used by many landowners to attack peasant leaders who had been demanding land reforms. Rural Italy soon succumbed to the domination of Mussolini and his Blackshirts who had no difficulty in obtaining the weapons and transport needed for launching their attacks. The violence was not condemned by the Liberal Prime Minister, Giovanni Giolitti, and there was no shortage of Government officials and military officers sympathetic to their aims. Instructions had been received by the police to ignore attacks on communists and socialists. In fact, in January 1921 'the Socialist deputy, Giacomo Matteotti denounced Giolitti and the Ministry of the Interior for their complicity with the fascists.'[7]

By allowing them to fight the election of May 1921 as government candidates and in attempting to force through his policy of economies, Giolitti lost his coalition majority.

---

*According to George Lichtheim – *Europe in the Twentieth Century*, although the article was signed by Mussolini, it was 'in fact composed by a number of authors including his tame philospher, Giovanni Gentile (1875–1944) . . . Gentile became Minister of Education, President of the Instituto Fascista di Cultura and general editor of the Enciclopedia.'
†Mussolini was a former editor, 1912–1914.

The Socialists, although having the largest parliamentary representation, nevertheless refused his invitation to join the government, and the other major party, the Populists, withheld their support, leaving Giolitti no alternative but to resign in favour of Bonomi, an ex-socialist, who was called in to act as a caretaker Prime Minister.

With the help of his industrial backers Mussolini and thirty-four of his fascists were elected to Parliament for the first time. In his maiden speech he told the deputies 'that fascism stood for free-trade liberalism of the Manchester School,' and later 'spoke of returning the railways and telegraph to private ownership.' He undoubtedly knew how to solicit the support of Italian big business and the military, and to such a degree, that by 'June 1922 the army chiefs and the big men in the Confederation of Industries were urging the King to bring Mussolini into the government.'[8]

On 28 October 1922, 40,000 Italian fascists set out from Naples for a march on Rome. Neither the Prime Minister, Luigi Facta, Bonomi's successor, nor the King took steps to prevent what in fact amounted to an attempt at insurrection. Mussolini did not march, instead he took the train the following night, and by the time the fascists arrived in the capital, he was already there, installed as the new Prime Minister, having been invited to form a government. With the backing of the army, big business and the monarchy, Mussolini was able to exploit the temporary powers granted to him by an obviously impotent and divided Parliament.

In 1923 he decreed that two thirds of the parliamentary seats should go to the party which received at least one-quarter of the vote and through this mathematical manipulation the fascists were able to secure, with the help of Conservative and Nationalist deputies, a majority in the election of April 1924.

Journalist, Ninetta Jucker, has written of the great courage of Giacomo Matteotti who 'bravely stood up in Parliament to denounce the methods employed by the fascists and promised to produce evidence that would invalidate the election. A few days later he was kidnapped and stabbed to death by fascists led by the notorious squadrista Dumini.'[9]

The following year Mussolini carried out a coup d'etat which gave him full dictatorial powers. Pietro Nenni, the editor of *Avanti* was arrested and the editors of the liberal papers, *La Stampa* and *Il Corrierre della Serra* were dismissed and their papers taken over by Mussolini's nominees. In 1926 all opposition parties were suppressed and their parliamentary mandates cancelled. Opposition leaders were persecuted and many fled abroad.

'The ideals of democracy' were undoubtedly 'exploded' and 'the state of all' had become 'the state of the few' – the fulfilment of fascist ideology.

The Italian fascist movement became a prototype upon which the fascist movements of Spain, Belgium, France and Britain were to be modeled during the next decade.

Notes

1. PRICE Morgan Phillips, *My Three Revolutions*, p. 201.
2. OLIVEIRA A. Ramos, *A People's History of Germany*, p. 148.
3. THYSSEN Fritz, *I Paid Hitler*, pp. 113/114.
4. HENRI Ernst, *Hitler Over Europa*, p. 11.
5. LICHTHEIM George, *Europe in the 20th Century*, p. 159.
6. STURDY David, *Modern Europe*, p. 154.
7. JUCKER Ninetta, *Italy*, p. 85.
8. JUCKER Ninetta, *Italy*, pp. 79 and 88.
9. JUCKER Ninetta, *Italy*, p. 91.

16

GLASS HOUSE

With the replacement of the Lloyd George Coalition by an all Conservative Government, the 'interventionists' wasted no time in seeking ways and means of creating a rupture in Anglo-Soviet relations.

In April 1923 some British trawlers were seized while fishing within the twelve mile limit of Russian territorial waters. Even during Tsarist days British Governments had refused to recognize the twelve mile limit and it had been a serious bone of contention. Both Tsarist and Soviet Governments had authorized the arrest of foreign trawlers caught fishing within the specified limit, but whereas in the past, representations had been conducted in an amicable manner, in 1923 the new Government decided to exploit the incident to further the 'interventionists' cause.

All the Conservative newspapers, with the exception of *The Observer* and the Beaverbrook press (*The Daily Express* and *The Evening Standard*), were demanding the recall of Robert Hodgson, Britain's representative in Moscow, the expulsion of the Soviet Trade representatives from London, and the closing down of the Trade Mission's offices.

A statement was made in the House of Commons on 25 April 1923 by Ronald McNeill, Under-Secretary for Foreign Affairs, that the Government had decided 'without delay, to address a serious communication to the Russian Government.' The statement was inevitably interpreted by the press as a step towards the abrogation of the Anglo-Soviet Trade Agreement. At the same time, accusations were being levelled against the Soviet Government of religious persecution. Some religious bodies in Britain obviously felt embarrassed by the press outcry of religious persecution.

No British Government or official body had protested against the Tsarist pogroms and persecution of the Jews. 'We must not forget the grievance which Liberalism had against the old regime and the silence of the Orthodox Church when the non-Orthodox Church creeds, especially Jewish, were penalized or persecuted.'*

The cry of 'religious persecution' was set off by the case of a Roman Catholic priest, Monsignor Butkevitch, who had been condemned to death for high teason.

The Soviet Government's policy was against any form of religious persecution, but it would have been remarkable if the actions of the higher echelons of the Orthodox Church, in association with the Tsarist regime, had not left a legacy of hatred, prejudice or suspicion. For after all only a few years had passed since the Tsarina's adviser, Rasputin, had dominated the hierarchy of the Orthodox Church.

In its reply to the initial Note of Protest the Soviet Government accused the British Government of hypocrisy, and complained of an outside attempt to 'protect spies and traitors in Russia.' Further the reply stated that in consideration of the British Government's actions in Ireland,† Egypt and India to maintain British rule, the Soviet Government could hardly 'regard such an appeal in the name of humanity and sacredness of life as very convincing.' Hodgson replied the following day that he could not accept the Soviet Note because it impugned 'the sincerity of the British Government in its appeal for clemency.'

The Soviet reaction could have been anticipated by even the most minor of foreign office officials when Weinstein, Chicherin's deputy, expressed his Government's hopes 'that in future it (the British Government) will refrain from attempts of any kind at interfering in the internal affairs of the Soviet Republic.'

Monsignor Butkevitch had in the meantime been executed.

The Daily Herald, in its leader of 4 April 1923, put the matter in perspective when it stated:

---

*From a *Times* report of the Church Convocation at Canterbury, May 1 1923.
†In Ireland Sir Roger Casement had been executed for treason and there were the Amritsar Massacres in India.

'In spite of growing opposition to it, capital punishment in many countries exists still. Therefore, if it is "barbarous" as many voices are saying, to carry out this execution in Moscow, we are all barbarians together. We are justified, however, in demanding that so long as the death penalty is inflicted, it shall be inflicted without respect of persons. We in this country have executed bishops, even an Archbishop for treason. Why should there be such an outcry over the execution of this Russian Roman Catholic priest?

He had been found guilty of treasonable correspondence with the enemy in war-time. He was executed. To call his execution an attack on religion is nonsensical. The Roman Catholic Church enjoys wider liberty under the Soviets than it ever had under the Tsar and the Holy Synod. But religious liberty does not anywhere include exemption from the law . . .

. . . Why do they protest now? They are not moved by humanity, but by class feeling. Governments of the old order – gentlemanly governments – may butcher as they will. But if a new kind of government punishes for high treason a man who was a gentleman, a priest and a monsignor, the cry of "barbarism" goes up.

The workers, we believe, will not be misled by the spurious indignation . It is important that they should not be misled. For, as we gave warning yesterday, there are war plans afoot. The death of Monsignor Butkevitch may be exploited as part of the "diplomatic preparation" for a possible new attack on the Soviet Republic.' (*The Daily Herald*, 4 April 1923)

On 10 May, the Soviet representative at the Lausanne Conference, Vorovsky, was assassinated and two of his colleagues were wounded. His assassin was a Swiss citizen named Conradi. Two days later, *The Manchester Guardian* reported:

199

'The Conference this morning resumed its discussions without any allusion to the tragic event.

This diplomatic silence over the assassination is quite contrary to the general feeling here. Ismet Pasha this afternoon published a statement in his own name and that of his Delegation regretting the loss of a very able leader and of a great friend, highly appreciated by Ismet during the Conference.'

It appears from *The Manchester Guardian's* report that the Swiss Government had hastily made a statement prejudging the motives for the murder.

'The Federal Council says the murder is an act of personal revenge. It must be asked whether this categorical statement is not delivered too soon. Many signs, indeed, indicate that Conradi acted only for himself, but it is the task of the Judge, not of the Government, to pronounce an opinion on the guiding motives of the criminal.' (*The Manchester Guardian*, 12 May 1923)

Meanwhile in Britain, events were moving rapidly in the direction of an Anglo-Soviet military confrontation. The Under-Secretary of State for Foreign Affairs, Ronald McNeill, in answer to a question in the house of commons, stated that a British warship, HMS *Harebell*, had been ordered into the waters around Archangel with instructions 'to prevent interference with British vessels outside the three-mile limit, using force if necessary.' Many Opposition MPs had been particularly perturbed at this announcement, especially as news of the assassination of the Soviet delegate in Lausanne had come in on the same day.

The Parliamentary Labour Party, alarmed at the Government's decision to solve the fisheries dispute by resorting to the provocative application of gun-boar diplomacy and not utilizing normal diplomatic channels, sent a telegram to Moscow appealing to the Soviet Government not to allow itself to be provoked into taking 'any action which would precipate resort to force and outbreak of war until further negotiations upon the British Government's ultimatum had taken place.' The telegram concluded with the assurance –

'We work here for peace and full recognition of the Russian Gvernment, and view with alarm any possibility or rupture before all means to arbitrate and negotiate have been tried. We are responsible for debate on the Note on Tuesday next.' (from *The Daily Telegraph* 11 May 1923)

The Note referred to was a Foreign Office demand sent to Moscow on 8 May – known as the Curzon Ultimatum, calling for

. . . 'the release' of the British trawlers '*St Hubert* and *James Johnson*, as well as the crew of the latter, with the grant of suitable compensation: and an assurance that the British fishing vessels will not be interfered with in future outside the three mile limit.'
'The unequivocal withdrawal of the two communications' from the Soviet Government concerning the trial of the priests.
Within the Ultimatum was an accusation that the Soviet Government had 'flouted and infringed the preliminary condition upon which the Trade Agreement was signed' by engaging in anti-British propaganda and activities in Persia, Afghanistan and India and demanded that the Russian 'officials, who have been responsible . . . are disowned and recalled from the scene of their maleficent labours.'

In a reference to the execution of C.F. Davison and the imprisonment of Mrs Stan Harding, the Ultimatum demanded –

'that the Soviet Government should admit their liability and should undertake to pay such equitable compensation as may be awarded by an arbitrator to be agreed upon by His Majesty's Government and the Soviet Government, or failing such agreement, by the President of the International Court of Justice at the Hague, or by some other impartial person of similar standing.

It then went on to declare that unless the Soviet Government "within ten days of the receipt of the above communication ... had undertaken to comply fully and unconditionally with the request which it contains", His Majesty's Government would "consider themselves immediately free from the obligation of that agreement." [*The Anglo-Soviet Trade Agreement*][1]

According to the Soviet Government, Davison, who was executed in January 1920, was a member of the Paul Dukes secret service organization. He was accused of espionage at a time when thousands of Russians were being killed as a result of the Wars of Intervention in which Britain was one of the leading countries. Mrs Harding had been involved in espionage during the same period. She was detained 'on the basis of information supplied by Miss Margaret Harrison, an American journalist.'[2]

The 'Curzon Ultimatum' was promptly challenged by the Liberal *Daily Chronicle*, which for many years reflected the view of Lloyd George.

'To press for a remedy, to use the utmost pressure is one thing; to deliver an ultimatum is another. And the ten days' time limit attached to the British demands, allowing hardly more time than the post permits, makes it an ultimatum. The suspicion is irresistible that Lord Curzon is yielding to the Diehards in his party. Diehardism is not the spirit in which to attack the Russian problem. The Diehards are not so much indignant at British wrongs in Russia as fanatical haters of the Soviet regime. They do not resent, but rather welcome British wrongs, because they tend to bring about the rupture they desire. Lord Curzon should remember that.

Besides, what good does a rupture with Russia bring? It brings us into a complete cul-de-sac, a

202

dead end without any exit. The Russian problem will remain afterwards just where it was before. It will be equally, if not more, insoluble. And yet until some solution is found, it will continue to be out of the power of British diplomacy to frame any intelligible permanent foreign policy, and the reconstruction of Europe, upon which the welfare of this country depends, will be indefinitely postponed.' (*The Daily Chronicle*, 10 May 1923)

The alarm of the Parliamentary Labour Party was a reflection of the effect of a war psychosis that had steadily been created during the few months that the conservative Government had been in office. In the opinion of the *Daily Herald* on the same day

'Such a note sent by one great Power to another would, before 1914, have meant war. Today the only hope of avoiding a rupture of relations is that the Soviet Government may display, in the face of provocation a restraint which the Tsar's Ministers would certainly never have shown.'

In the Spring of 1923, the British Labour Movement had become aware of events that could indicate, although not prove, that the die-hards in both Britain and France were preparing for a war or some form of further military intervention in Russia. There had been a recent inspection of the Polish and Czech armies by Marshall Foch. Britain's Chief of Staff, Lord Cavan, had also inspected the Polish Army and like Foch was impressed with their efficiency. Lord French, a war-time British general, had been to Bessarabia and during the same period there had been a visit to Rumania by a British Military Mission. All these countries were along the Soviet borders.

Following the Parliamentary Labour Party telegram, Labour's National Joint Council which represented the T.U.C., the National Labour Party and the Parliamentary Labour Party, issued a declaration to the people of Britain:

'This Joint Council expresses its strongest disapproval of the terms of the Government's Note to Russia as calculated to bring about a revival of the attacks of the 'White Guards' on the Russian Government, and also a renewal of militarist efforts to resort to force instead of negotiations and justice.

It declares there may be faults on both sides, and it calls for a conference, or, in the alternative, a reference of the grievances of the respective countries to arbitration or some international court.

It protests against any rupture of trade relations with Russia, which will result not only in increased unemployment here, but also in political unsettlement, which will add to the danger of war. It therefore calls upon both the industrial and political organizations of Labour to protest immediately against the action of the Government.

The Joint Council welcomes the prompt intervention of the Parliamentary Labour Party and expresses its confidence that, in the House of Commons, the Party will defend the interests of the working classes'. (From *The Daily Herald*, 12 May 1923)

The National Joint Council's declaration and the P.L.P. telegram brought the intensification of the Government's cold war policy against the Soviet Government right into the forefront of current issues. That week-end, public meetings were held throughout the country attacking Government policy. On the Sunday, J.L. Garvin in *The Observer* reminded his readers

'that without a definite agreement between Britain and Russia, no general settlement in Europe and the East can ever be reached . . .

Lord Curzon's motion as interpreted in the Ultimatum is nothing but a policy of cutting off our nose to spite our face. . . . When Lord Curzon demands the unconditional surrender of Russia on all the mixed issues he asks the impossible. . .

204

In reply to the demand for unconditional surrender let them propose unconditional arbitration.' (*The Observer*, 13 May 1923)

The threat of an impending war inevitably had its repercussions in Russia. Arthur Ransome, *The Manchester Guardian's* correspondent, who had attended a mass meeting in Moscow drew attention to the remarks of a Diplomat from a neutral country who was with him at the meeting. The Diplomat told him:

'It is a misfortune for humanity that the Western European governments still believe that war will overthrow the Bolsheviks instead of strengthening them. The people demonstrating today were good-tempered enough, because they do not yet realize the real dangers of new wars. But if new wars are forced on these same people – and it is pure self-deception to pretend that annulment of the Agreement can have any other effect – you are utterly mistaken if you think that Russia will not fight as a single nation and as a nation bitterly resentful.' (*The Manchester Guardian*, 14 May 1923)

The first six months of the newly elected Conservative Government had also coincided with economic instability which was spreading throughout Western Europe. The American demands for the repayment of war loans, the default by Germany on the payment of reparations to France and the effects of the occupation of the Ruhr, renewed Allied fears of a return to a revolutionary situation in Germany which could spread to other countries. Stanley Baldwin, the Chancellor of the Exchequer, in an interview with the *New York Herald* said:

'The world is sitting on an anxious seat; for there is danger of revolution in France as well as in Germany.' (*The Manchester Guardian*, 8 January 1923)

Pessimism and apprehension for the future certainly

appeared to dominate the thoughts of many influential Western politicians in 1923. The failure of Poincaré's venture into the Ruhr, the devaluation of the franc and the raising of conscription to eighteen months, had created considerable unrest in France. This, coupled with the reports of a revolutionary situation in Germany, may have played a part in determining the political attitudes towards destroying once and for all time what they regarded as the source of their troubles – Russian Bolshevism. Responsibility for the recurring economic crisis, they believed, had to be placed somewhere and they had no intention of placing it at their own door. Fortunately for all concerned, the Soviet reply to the Curzon Ultimatum was restrained and conciliatory. Its main points were:

With regard to territorial waters, which included the question of fishing rights, the Soviet Government declared

> 'its readiness to take part in any international conference on this subject and to accept its findings'

Regarding the case of Mr Davison and Mrs Stan Harding the Soviet reply reiterated that they had been tried for espionage and pointed out that during the period referred to:

> 'an immeasurably greater number of Russian citizens suffered both physically and materially from actions of the English authorities in the north and south of the Soviet Republics and in the sphere of English influence. The shooting of twenty-six Baku commissars which is mentioned in this correspondence is but one of many cases of a similar nature. If the point of view of compensation be adopted, then fairness demands its application to all cases of that period, amongst them the family of Kolomitsev, to Babushkin, Karakhanian and other citizens who were confined for several years without any accusation in English and Indian prisons. . . .The Russian Government announces its readiness to compensate the fami-

206

lies of Davison and Mrs Stan Harding, if the British Government announces a similar readiness concerning the above mentioned citizens.'

'It is, however, forced to state that it has plenty of reports and documents pointing to the intense activity of agents of the British Government against the interests of the Soviet Republics in the Caucasus and in particular in localities bordering on the Central Asian parts of the Soviet Republics.'

It rejected charges of anti-British propaganda in countries of the East and declared that

'The maintenance and development of friendly connections with the peoples of the East, based on genuine respect of their interests and rights, cannot be accepted by the Soviet Government as a breach of the Anglo-Russian Agreement.

The reply concluded

'The Soviet Government therefore proposes to the British Government to accept the method of conference and to come to an agreement regarding time and place when authoritative plenipotentiary delegations of both parties could not only examine and settle disputed questions of secondary importance, but also regularize Anglo-Soviet relations in their full extent.'[3]

On the following day the Soviet reply was debated in a crowded House of Commons. In the opening speech, the leader of the Opposition, J. Ramsay MacDonald, warned the Government that 'If the Trade Agreement be torn up, there is not the least doubt about it, a state of incipient war will be created.' (*Hansard*, 15 May 1923. Col. 294)

It appeared from the debate, with the attack by the Parliamentary opposition and the pressure from all sections of the Labour and Liberal movements up and down the country, that the Government was beginning to retreat from its policy of brinkmanship. The first signal came from McNeill who used the occasion of his winding up speech to inform the House that he understood

> 'M. Krassin has suddenly arrived in London. . . .
>
> I do not know whether M. Krassin has asked, or intends to ask, to have an interview with the Foreign Secretary; But I can say this – that if he does, my noble Friend will be quite ready to see him. . . . The Foreign Secretary would be glad to see M. Krassin and to go through the whole of our claims with him, showing him, if he can, where he thinks our claims are reasonable and the way in which we complain of their being met. He would invite M. Krassin, having had that conversation, to communicate with Moscow, if he desires to do so, for instructions, and if it should be . . . that, in order to make that communication to Moscow and get instructions back, some certain amount of time would be required, the time limit mentioned in our Note would be given a reasonable extension in order to allow that be done'. (*Hansard*, 15 May 1923, Col. 318)

So the first step in the retreat was the abolition of the ten day ultimatum.

Both the Labour and Liberal Parties (including both wings*) had been united in their opposition to the government's policy. One Conservative MP, Sir Allen Smith, who was also Chairman of the Engineering and Allied Employers National Federation told the Government in no uncertain manner that:

> 'It is all very well to make a declaration which, under certain circumstances, would justify a declaration of war, and then for another Minister to get up in another Constituency, not his own, and say "Oh, but we have no quarrel whatever with the Russian people. The last thing we

---

*There had for some time been divisions in the Liberal Party between the Asquith and Lloyd George factions.

contemplate is war and the last thing we desire is an outbreak of hostilities". If you do certain acts, in accordance with all the criteria of international law, there is only one answer to these things and that is that a state of war is ipso facto produced; and if we consider that at this time, when we are so much concerned with the restoration of ourselves, as well as the restoration of Europe, we are entitled to play with fire to such an extent, I say those who are playing with fire will probably get their fingers burnt and they will howl louder than anyone else'. (*Hansard*, 15 May 1923, Cols. 361/362)

Krassin was in the House of Commons Distinguised strangers Gallery throughout the debate.

In spite of what appeared as a more restrained governmental tone, McNeill, when asked for a commitment that the Government refrain from taking any precipitate action regarding breaking off Anglo-Russian trade relations during the Parliamentary Whitsun recess without first consulting Parliament, the answer was no. 'This refusal was so unexpected and created such a feeling of anxiety in the minds of the Labour leaders' comment the Coates, 'that both Mr J. Ramsey MacDonald and Mr Fenner Brockway cancelled their engagements to attend the International Labour and Socialist Congress at Hamburg in the following week'.[4]

The Independent Labour Party, whose secretary was Fenner Brockway, quickly put out a statement warning that:

'The I.L.P. views with grave concern the attitude of the Government towards Russia as revealed in the speech of the Under-Secretary for Foreign Affairs in the House of Commons yesterday. It urges that the Russian proposal for a Conference on all outstanding issues ought at once to be accepted, and warns the Government that any rupture with Russia will arouse the most vigorous resistance on the part of organized labour. It calls upon its branches to be fully prepared to give effective co-operation in that resistance if it should become necessary and to maintain a vigorous protest against the unconstitutional disregard of Parliament foreshadowed by the Under-Secretary'.

During the Whitsuntide recess, it became apparent that there had been a re-assertion of governmental anti-Soviet policy.

'It is, in fact, entirely clear that the Foreign Secretary intends peremptorily to break off the negotiations unless M. Krassin comes to him next week with the news that Moscow has surrendered. It is also entirely clear that a complete surrender by Moscow to the Curzon demands is as unlikely as was a complete surrender by Serbia to the Austrian demands in 1914'. (*The Daily Herald*, 19 May 1923)

This 'negotiation through strength' mentality seemed to permeate British foreign policy, dominated by the thought of Great Britain still controlling, through its colonies, nearly twenty five per cent of the peoples of the world, as well as possessing one of the most formidable navies in the world.

The Observer's Moscow correspondent helped to disseminate some considerable light when he cabled his report during that week.

'Public opinion of all classes is undoubtedly behind the Soviet Government. Russia wants peace, but not peace at any price. The main interest of the population is the hope of a continuance of the improvement of living and trade conditions. This is the first Spring without war, internal disorder or famine. The expectation is widely held of an improved harvest. All classes were looking for a rapid improvement of trade as grain export grows.

Consequently, if a rupture is now forced by Lord Curzon, despite the undoubted attempts of the Russian Government to secure a peaceful settlement, two results seem inevitable. First, communists and non-communists alike, now united behind the Government in peace efforts, will support it if peace is nevertheless made impossible. The situation is similar to that of England in 1914, when national unity was secured by the conviction that the Government, having tried to prevent war, was now resisting aggression.' (*The Observer*, 20 May 1923)

Two days later it was announced that Stanley Baldwin was to become Prime Minister in succession to Bonar Law who had been compelled to resign owing to ill-health. It was hoped in some political and commercial circles that the new Prime Minister might be able to exercise a more firm and wiser counsel over his colleague, Lord Curzon.

Meanwhile, Krassin, after reporting to the Soviet Government the results of his discussions with Lord Curzon and his deputy, handed to the Foreign Secretary on 23 May his Government's reply. The following excerpts cover the main issues in dispute:

With regard to the matter of 'Territorial Waters':

'The Russian Government is ready, on the question of fishing in Northern waters, to conclude at once a convention with the British Government granting to English citizens the right of fishing outside the three-mile limit pending the settling of this question, in the shortest possible time, at an international conference, and to pay compensation for the cases in point.'

On the Davison, Harding issue:

'The Russian Government is ready to pay compensation for the execution of Mr Davison and for the arrest of the journalist Mrs Stan Harding: with the reservation, however, that this willingness in

211

no way signifies that the Russian Government recognized that there was any irregularity in the repressive measures it took against these spies, because their crimes have been proved definitely and by due legal process, and the repressive measures against them were taken before the conclusion of the Anglo-Russian Trade Agreement: in view of which their claims can in no way be regarded as a condition for maintaining the agreement.'

Concerning the matter of 'Propaganda in the East':

'As to the claims of the British Government on the question of the observation of the conditions of the Anglo-Russian Trade Agreement in the East, the Russian Government, again repelling the charge of having infringed the agreement, does not see, as far as this question is concerned, any other possibility of settling the conflict and preventing future recriminations, and of co-ordinating the differing points of view and aims of England and Russia, except by a detailed discussion of them by specially delegated representatives of both Governments.'

Referring to the trial of the priests, the Russian Government stated its readiness:

'to take back the two letters signed by Mr Weinstein'.

In conclusion, the Russian Government declared that it was:

'quite ready to reiterate the undertakings given in the Anglo-Russian Trade Agreement of 16 March 1921, or to confirm them again in a special declaration, provided that a similar declaration is also made by Great Britain.'[5]

Despite this latest effort of conciliation and compromise by the Soviet Government, Lord Curzon still demanded the removal of the Soviet representatives from Persia, Afghanistan and India. He was apparently determined to press his cold war ultimatum to the limit with a veiled threat expressed in his belief that 'the Soviet Government is losing its chance of preventing the annulment of the Trade Agreement'.

On the following morning *The Daily Chronicle* (24 May 1923), commenting on the Russian reply, believed that:

> 'This is a Note which in our opinion makes any further talk of breaking off relations quite unnecessary.'

and the Conservative *Daily Express* (24 May 1923) was convinced that:

> 'There is no reason why the affair should not now be settled swiftly and satisfactorily,'

The pressure of the TUC and the Labour Party, as well as criticisms from former Prime Ministers Asquith and Lloyd George, were by now beginning to have their effect. The latter weighed in with some sound advice in a letter to *The Daily Telegraph* on 2 June, declaring:

> 'It is time we made up our minds that the Soviets have come to stay, whether we like it or not, and that one or other of the formidable men who rule Russia is likely to rule it for some time to come. The sooner we have the courage to recognize this fact the sooner will real peace be established.'

Eventually the Government began to climb down. Agreement was reached on the first three issues, but the fourth, dealing with the matter of propaganda, had still to be resolved.

On 30 May the Foreign Office handed its latest Note to Krassin stating that '. . . Pending the conclusion of an international agreement the Soviet Government shall issue instructions to its maritime authorities to abstain from impeding the operations of British fishermen outside the three-mile limit, and that this shall be recorded in the exchange of Notes'. With reference to the case of Davison and Mrs Stan Harding, it was proposed 'that the Soviet Government shall pay the sum of £3,000 in respect of Mrs Stan Harding and of £10,000 in respect of the claim on Mrs Davison.'

The last and outstanding item referring to propaganda was now presented in the form of a request that the Soviet Government's representatives in Teheran and Kabul 'will, within a reasonable space of time be transferred to some other areas where their duties will not bring them into contact with British interests.' 'The question of recalling the two Soviet representatives was a very difficult one for Moscow because it involved the question of prestige – the prestige of a Government of a great and proud state – and, therefore, when the terms of this Note became known it seemed to many that after all the "Die-Hards" had won.'[6]

A critical assessment of this latest example of 'Curzonian Imperialism' appeared in *The Daily Herald*

'To assert a right of veto over the personnel of the diplomatic Corps in Teheran or Kabul, would be to assert a very real British suzerainty over two countries whose complete independence Great Britain has more than once solemnly recognized.' (*The Daily Herald*, 5 June 1923)

Two days later the *Herald's* correspondent pointed out that

'Four papers – the Hittim, the Ittihad, the Beharestan and the Ikdam are subsidized from the funds of the British Mission.

Now there is, of course, nothing in that. The subsidising of newspapers by foreign diplomats is common form in most countries outside Great Britain.

But it happens that the British Government is not pledged not to subsidize anti-Russian propaganda in Persia. And it happens that these subsidized papers do carry on very definite and very bitter anti-Soviet propaganda, which is – to say the least – an unfortunate coincidence.' (*The Daily Herald*, 7 June 1923)

After months of charges and counter-charges, and the exchange of Diplomatic Notes, the Curzon dictatorial 'Ultimatum' policy was laid to rest – at least for the time being. It had been rumoured that Baldwin, the new Prime Minister, had accepted the latest Soviet reply as satisfactory and had decided to end the dispute. Some weeks later, a delegation representing some of Britain's leading industrial firms, led by F.L. Baldwin, the Prime Minister's cousin, left for Russia and on their return in a press interview on 3 September, he said that 'the general impression we have brought back as to the recovery of Russia is one of hope. Recovery will be a long job unless the Government can get outside help, but if they cannot get that I am still confident that they will pull through unaided' and that 'there is a trade opening in Russia for agricultural machinery and also for all things connected with transport, both railway and motor.' Russia, said Baldwin was 'looking rather to this country for their trade necessities, believing that Britain was in a better position that any other country to extend them credits.' And to add weight to his comments he pointed out that Russia also had a favourable balance in its foreign trade. (*The Daily Telegraph*, 4 September 1923).

The subject of Anglo-Soviet relations had now become a dominant theme in the run-up to the General Election which was to be held towards the end of the year. In both the Labour and Liberal Party's Manifestos there was a similarity of approach –

'Labour's vision of an ordered world embraces the nations now torn with enmity and strife. It stands therefore, . . . for the resumption of free economic and diplomatic relations with Russia'.

And

215

'Liberals hold that the restoration of Europe is the necessary condition of the revival of our industries, and the re-establishment of peace.

They would welcome the re-opening of full relations with Russia'.

Although the Conservatives still gained the largest number of seats they were heavily outnumbered by the other parties. The results were Conservatives 258, Labour 191, Liberals 159 and Independents 7.

The Conservatives, as the largest Parliamentary group, decided to continue in office but their tenure lasted less than a month. They were forced to resign on a combined Labour and Liberal vote of 'No Confidence' and Britain's first Labour Government took over. The Prime Minister was J. Ramsey MacDonald who had a commitment to resume 'free economic and diplomatic relations with Russia.', but within a few days began to develop certain hesitations concerning this aspect of Labour's Manifesto. MacDonald also added the post of Foreign Minister to his other responsibilities. Eventually, under pressure from the rest of his Cabinet, the Soviet Government was notified on 1 February 1924 that the British Government will 'recognize the Union of Socialist Soviet Republics as the de jure rulers of those territories of the old Russian Empire'.

At last full legal and diplomatic recognition had been established.*

On 9 April 1924 a Soviet delegation arrived in Britain for a conference with the new Government on matters of commerce, industry and finance and 'inter-governmental obligations' regarding claims and counter-claims. the discussions were held at the Foreign Office under the chairmanship of Arthur Ponsonby (Under-Secretary of State for Foreign Affairs) and were opened on the 14 April.

The conference, which appeared to be making satisfactory progress on nearly all points on the agenda, eventually

---

*The Daily Herald commented on 2 February 1924 'It is a triumph of International Labour' and paid tribute to the work of Mr Coates and the 'Hands off Russia' Committee. Once de jure recognition was established, the organization became the Anglo-Russian Parliamentary Committee with Mr W.P. Coates as its first secretary.

broke down over a formula of words. On the clause dealing with compensation, the Russians insisted that 'valid claims' be replaced by 'valid and approved by the two Governments'.

According to the diplomatic correspondent of *The Daily Herald* the Russians 'felt that the use of the word valid implied that the claims were made as of right, and thus denied the validity of the act of expropriation. They could not accept it' and 'were adamant in their refusal to accept any formula which denied or questioned the right of expropriation.' (*The Daily Herald*, 6 August 1924).

Fortunately there were some public spirited Labour MPs who refused to believe that an Anglo-Soviet Agreement should break down over a form of words. Parliament was due to go into recess at the end of the first week in August and the negotiations had been dragging out over the past three and a half months. According to the Labour MP E.D. Morel,:

'A number of back-bench members of Parliament who have played a prominent part for the past four years in the public endeavour to bring about an Anglo-Russian reconciliation which should begin with recognition and be followed by a general Treaty . . . had been following the last phase of the negotiations with anxious attention.

When apprised of the lamentable upshot, six of these members proceeded by appointment to Mr Ponsonby's room in the House of Commons at 2 p.m. on Tuesday, 5 August, heard from his own lips an account of the breakdown, and made certain representations. With his knowledge and consent they at once got into communication with the Russians. At 8.30 p.m., these six members, reinforced by some twelve others, met the Russian delegation by appointment in one of the conference rooms of the House of Commons. Every section of the Party was represented. The proceedings, which lasted over an hour, were conducted partly in English and partly in French. At their close four members were chosen by their colleagues to proceed at once to Mr Ponsonby in order to place their own views and the views of their colleagues before him. They took with them a formula which seemed to them to make possible the re-opening of the shut and bolted door. By that time it was 10 p.m. (5 August). The Russians, between whom and the British Government there had been no communication of any kind whatsoever since the rupture at 7 a.m. that day, remained in the precincts of the House. The interview with Mr Ponsonby then took place with the result that at 11 p.m. the four members who had seen him were able to inform the Russians that, if the latter were willing, official negotiations would be resumed at 11 a.m. the next morning on the basis of the formula submitted. The Russians agreed. The unofficial negotiators went home to bed with the feeling that their intervention had been crowned with success and the disaster had been averted at the eleventh hour.

But these hopes were premature. Official communications were duly re-opened at the appointed hour on Wednesday. But by noon, information came to hand that a deadlock had again occured. Once more the four members met and were received by Mr Ponsonby, at 1.30 p.m., one hour and a half before the House was due to meet, four hours before the Government was due to make its declaration to Parliament. Half an hour later the four members were on their way, with others, to the Russian Agency offices in New Bond Street, carrying with them yet another formula . . . a rapid and earnest consultation between the members of Russian delegation ensued.

Then the Soviet representative rose with the words 'I accept'. The long tension was over. Unofficial diplomacy had justified itself. Englishmen and Russians clasped hands.

At 2.45 p.m., the Russian acceptance was communicated to Mr Ponsonby at the Foreign

Office. At 3.30 p.m. the final details were settled.
(from *Foreign Affairs*, August 1924)[7]

The accepted form of words put into the Treaty were
'agreed claims'. On the following day the Draft Treaties
were debated in the House of Commons but could not be
ratified for another twenty-one days until Parliament had
given the final approval. One of the most vehement
opponents of the Treaty was the former Prime Minister,
Lloyd George, who at that time held the minority viewpoint
within his own Party, but in a matter of weeks had managed
to persuade many of his colleagues to oppose the ratification.

There were, in fact, two treaties, one being a commercial
treaty and the other a general treaty. In his statement to the
House of Commons on 6 August Ponsonby explained that

'With regard to the Commercial Treaty we had
received unconditional most-favoured-nation
treatment for our goods, and in return we had
admitted the Soviet Union into our exports credit
scheme. . .'

'The Treaty then went on to make provision for
the definition of territorial waters – a question
which must be left over until we got an international agreement on this point. The line which had
been agreed to on the White Sea was a line which
satisfied their experts and would be satisfactory to
our fishermen. . .'

Referring to the claims of the bondholders, Mr
Ponsonby said 'their task was, while seeing that
British interests were safeguarded, to do nothing
that would interfere or express any opinion on the
Soviet laws and decrees'.

The British Government 'had got an admission
of liability to the bondholders from the Soviet
Government and an assurance on their part that
they would negotiate with the bondholders. He
believed that they were in process of doing so with
a very considerable number of bondholders.'

'. . . As to property claims, both sides were to

219

appoint members on a Commission, who would investigate those claims and come to a decision as to compensation'. (From *The Daily Herald*, 7 August 1924)

The Treaties were eventually signed on 8 August 1924. At the conclusion of the ceremony Ponsonby, in a spirit of goodwill, sent the following message 'to the Peoples of the Soviet Union'

'I regard the successful conclusion of an Agreement between Great Britain and the Soviet Union with satisfaction and pleasure.

I have always had a great admiration for the Russian people and throughout my political career I have striven for friendly co-operation between our two peoples. It has been a special privilege, therefore, to have been able to take a part in the renewal of normal friendly relations which have been seriously intercepted for so many years.

I believe our agreement will benefit both countries and will help in no small degree in the recovery of Europe'.

However, there were divisions within the Liberal Party over the ratification of the Treaties. In the opinion of W.P. Coates, who had become secretary of the new Anglo-Russian Parliamentary Committee, 'the decision of the Liberal Party leadership ... sealed the fate of the Draft Treaties, which in turn consitututed a powerful brake on the development of Anglo-Soviet trade.'[8]

The main opposition to the Treaties was in the section dealing with the financial arrangements and the British loan under the 'Trade Facilities Acts to British Russian Trade' which would enable the Soviet Union to purchase capital goods, such as agricultural and timber cutting machinery, merchant ships, oil refining equipment, etc. Without such financial aids, the Soviets argued, how could they discharge the claims of bondholders? A great hullaba-loo was made over the credit worthiness of the Soviet régime, but very few people at the time were aware that £68 million worth of Russian gold had been lying in the vaults of the Bank of England since the middle of the war. It had been sent to Britain during the war to stabilize the international value of the pound sterling. Although the £68 million worth of gold belonged legally to Russia, the Soviet Government had nevertheless agreed to suspend its claim until there had been a general financial settlement between the two countries.

On 10 October 1924, *The Manchester Guardian* published a letter from Christian Rakovsky, the Soviet Chargé d'Affaires, in which he said:

'There is frequent talk of the war credits granted to Russia, but it is not generally realized that large parts of the military equipment purchased therewith were used up by Great Britain and her allies and White Armies. Above all, it is generally not known that Russia gave Great Britain 40 per cent of her gold reserve, or £68,000,000 sterling to support the British exchange. This fact is absolutely unknown to the general public, but it is not unknown to Mr Lloyd George, who signed the Special Convention with Mr Bark, the Russian Finance Minister.'

It was inevitable that without Liberal support, the MacDonald Government could not survive. But in fact it was defeated on quite another issue.

On 5 August 1924, John Campbell, editor of the *Workers Weekly*, the official publication of the British Communist Party, was charged under the incitement to Mutiny Act of 1797 for publishing an allegedly seditious article. His crime was in an appeal to British servicemen not to allow themselves to be used as strike-breakers: 'let it be known that neither in the class war nor a military will you turn your guns on your fellow workers', wrote Campbell. The indictment issued under the jurisdiction of Sir Patrick Hastings, the Attorney General, was promptly condemned by many of his fellow Labour MPs, and there was an outcry from all sections of the Labour Movement. They did not expect a Labour Government, which they had only recently voted into office, to stifle free speech. Had not the Prime Minister, Ramsay MacDonald himself, appealed at a meeting in Dublin in 1912, 'Soldiers, Sailors and Airmen do not shoot the workers, turn your guns the other way'. What made matters even more embarrassing was the revelation that Campbell had been severely disabled during the war and had been decorated for exceptional bravery.

On the following day, a Labour MP, John Scurr, raised the Campbell affair in the House of Commons. In answer to his questioning, the Attorney General admitted authorizing a raid upon the paper's offices. There was a distinct mood of anger on the Labour benches, and under further questioning by a number of Labour MPs, including George Lansbury and James Maxton of the ILP, the Attorney General must have developed second thoughts on the matter for on 13 August, soon after Parliament adjourned for the Summer recess, the prosecution was withdrawn. But the matter did not end there and leading members of the Conservative opposition were anxious to question both Hastings and the Prime Minister about the dropping of the prosecution. The Conservative press lost no time in launching an attack upon the Government, accusing it of avoiding a major issue of national importance and of obstructing the due process of law. The Campbell case was debated in the House of Commons on 8 October, but on this occasion the Liberals voted with the Conservatives and the first Labour Government was overwhelmingly defeated by 364 votes to 198 on a motion of censure.

The fall of the Labour Government was not only caused by the Campbell case. In the 1920s many British workers, especially agricultural workers living in tied cottages, had to be very careful to ensure that their employers did not know that they voted Labour. As a result of press propaganda the term 'Bolshie' had become associated with Labour, and certain newspaper proprietors, having already created the 'Bolshie' bogey image, exploited it extensively to the detriment of the Labour Government throughout its nine months in office.

On 9 October 1924, Parliament was dissolved and another general election, the third during the past two years, took place on 29 October.

Notes

1. *British Sessional Papers* – House of Commons, 1923 Vol. XXV, pp. 454–519
2. FISCHER Louis, *The Soviets in World Affairs*, p. 327
3. *Soviet Documents on Foreign Policy* – Vol. I 1917 – 1924 (ed. Jane Degras), pp. 387/8/9 and 392
4. COATES W. P. and Zelda, *History of Anglo-Soviet Relations*, pp. 117/118
5. *Soviet Documents on Foreign Policy* – Vol. I 1917 – 1924 (ed. Jane Degras), p. 397
6. COATES W. P. and Zelda, *History of Anglo-Soviet Relations*, p. 124
7. COATES ex W. P. and Zelda, *History of Anglo-Soviet Relations*, pp. 166/167
8. COATES W. P. and Zelda, *History of Anglo-Soviet Relations*, p. 175

17

THE ZINOVIEV LETTER

No sooner was Parliament dissolved than MacDonald, Members of Parliament and most of the Cabinet hastened to their constituencies to embark upon a three week period of intensive electioneering. The following day was Friday, 10 October 1924. Among the piles of letters, Memos and Notes that arrived in the offices of Whitehall was a letter that was to ensure the return of a Conservative Government. It landed in the Foreign Office and was headed

VERY SECRET
EXECUTIVE COMMITTEE, THIRD COMMUNIST
INTERNATIONAL PRESIDIUM
Moscow,   September 15th 1924.

and addressed to: THE CENTRAL COMMITTEE, BRITISH COMMUNIST PARTY.

The letter was a copy, the original of which has not been seen to this day. Within its long contents were instructions to the British Communist Party to 'Strain every nerve for the ratification' of the Treaty, to form 'cells in all the units of the troops'. attract ex-servicemen 'into the ranks of the Communist Party' and to make preparations for the 'complete success of an armed insurrection', and signed:

With Communist greetings,
ZINOVIEV,
President of the Presidium of the I.K.K.I.
McMANUS,
Member of the Presidium.
KUUSINEN,
Secretary.

On 14 October, the letter passed into the hands of J.D. Gregory, Chief of the Northern Department of the Foreign Office, and the next day his superior, Sir Eyre Crowe, Permanent Under-Secretary of the Foreign Office, sent the letter to the Prime Minister, who was also Secretary of State for Foreign Affairs. MacDonald received the letter in Manchester on the 16th. He replied immediately and in his Note to the Department warned:

'that the greatest care would have to be taken in discovering whether the letter was authentic or not. If it was authentic it had to be published, and in the meantime, while investigations were going on to discover the authenticity of the letter the draft letter to Rakovsky* would be prepared so that when the authenticity was established no time would be lost in making our protest to the Soviet Government.'

MacDonald's Note was received at the Foreign Office on 17 October.

Meanwhile some newspapers had apparently been preparing the ground for the sensational news which was about to break. An early hint came from the leader of the Conservative Party, Stanley Baldwin, in an election speech at Southend on 20 October.

'It makes my blood boil, to read of the way in which M. Zinoviev is speaking of the Prime Minister of Great Britain today ... I think it is time someone said to Russia "Hands off England"'. (*The Times*, 21 October 1924)

And on the morning of 22 October, reports appeared in the *Daily Mail* and the *Morning Post*.

'Among the callers at the Conservative Central Office, Bridge Street, Westminster, yesterday, was a man who had escaped from Russia after

*The Soviet Chargé d'Affaires in London.

being sentenced to death by Zinoviev, the Bolshevik leader.' (*Daily Mail*, 22 October 1924)

The *Morning Post's* was slightly shorter, but in essence said the same thing. A few hours later, the *Manchester Evening Chronicle* received a wire from its London correspondent:

'There is a report here to which much credence is attached that before polling day comes, a bombshell will burst and it will be connected with Zinoviev.' (*Manchester Evening Chronice*, 22 October 1924)

These press reports appeared the day after Sir Eyre Crowe had sent to MacDonald for his observations, the draft* of a Protest Note to Rakovsky. The draft had been sent to his constituency, Aberavon, but as MacDonald was in Bassetlaw, his son's constituency, he did not receive it until the 23rd. He looked at the draft on the following morning, the 24th, altered it and sent it back in its altered form, 'expecting it to come back to him again with proofs of authenticity.'[1] MacDonald had not initialled the draft, which meant that it had not yet been given his final approval.

Without waiting for the return of the draft, without consulting Lord Haldane, who was deputizing for the Prime Minister while he was out of London, or Arthur Ponsonby, the Under-Secretary of State for Foreign Affairs, both of whom were near at hand, and without even any written authority from Sir Eyre Crowe, a strongly worded Foreign Office letter of protest, signed by J.D. Gregory, was sent on the afternoon of 24 October to the Soviet Chargé d'Affaires. The main part was as follows:

'I have the honour to invite your attention to the enclosed copy of a letter which has been received by the Central Committee of the British Communist Party from the Presidium of the Executive Committee of the Communist International, over the signature of M. Zinoviev, its President, dated

---

*MacDonald calls it 'the trial draft' see *The Times*, 28 October 1924.

September 15. The letter contains instructions to British subjects to work for the violent overthrow of existing institutions in this country, and for the subversion of His Majesty's armed forces as a means to that end.

It is my duty to inform you that His Majesty's Government cannot allow this propaganda and must regard it as a direct interference from outside in British domestic affairs.

I should be obliged if you would be good enough to let me have the observations of your Government on this subject without delay.'

The Foreign Office had obviously decided not to wait for a reply from the Soviet Government or even a word from the Chargé d'Affaires, for on that same day copies of the protest letter were released to the press. And that same afternoon the press received copies of the Zinoviev letter from *The Daily Mail*.

The next morning, Saturday 25 October, just four days before polling day, the British people were presented with the predicted bombshell. *The Daily Mail*, having made the most of its governmental contacts, splashed all over the front page – headings and sub-headings:

CIVIL WAR PLOT BY SOCIALISTS' MASTERS
MOSCOW ORDER TO OUR REDS
GREAT PLOT DISCLOSED YESTERDAY
PARALYSE THE ARMY AND NAVY
AND MR. MACDONALD WOULD LEND RUSSIA
OUR MONEY
DOCUMENT ISSUED BY FOREIGN OFFICE
AFTER DAILY MAIL HAD SPREAD THE NEWS

The paper was undoubtedly proud of its scoop. It certainly knew more of what was going on behind the scenes than members of the Labour Cabinet. Former Conservative Minister, Lord Birkenhead, was quick off the mark that day with lavish praise for the *Daily Mail's* generosity. Speaking at an election meeting in Brentford he said:

'It was owing to the enterprise of the *Daily Mail* that the document became known, but they did a very generous thing . . . . They alone amongst English newspapers became aware of this document, and they thought its importance was such that the mere advantage to an individual newspaper should not seriously be considered, and they decided to give it to every paper in England for simultaneous publication.' (*The Times*, 27 October 1924)

The British press that morning made full use of the *Daily Mail's* 'generosity'. *The Times*, 25 October, covered its report with 'SOVIET PLOT' – 'RED PROPAGANDA IN BRITAIN' – 'REVOLUTION URGED BY ZINOVIEFF' AND 'FOREIGN OFFICE BOMBSHELL'.

Apart from having no authority from the Prime Minister or from any member of his Cabinet, the Foreign Office did not even telephone him or send him a telegram before taking so precipitate an action. MacDonald complained to a *Times* journalist some four years later:

'I cannot to this day quite understand how for six hours when it was known I was at the end of a telephone at Aberavon, I was not informed of the *Daily Mail's* intention or of the Foreign Office's intention to send a note to Rakovsky.' (*The Times*, 5 March 1928)

A reply from the Soviet Chargé d'Affaires was received by the Foreign Office on 25 October declaring that the 'Zinoviev Letter' was a forgery., Rakovsky also stated:

'In circulars of the Communist International (which may be seen in the press, for its activities are not concealed) it is never described as the "Third Communist International" – for the simple reason that there has never been a First or Second Communist International. The signature is similarly a clumsy forgery. M. Zinoviev is made to sign himself as the "President of the Presidium of the Executive Committee of the Communist International", whereas actually he is and always signs himself officially as "President of the Executive Committee"'.

His reply was immediately released to the press and the British public were by now entitled to some explanation from the Prime Minister.

There was much criticism at the time of MacDonald's weak handling of the affair. His Cabinet colleague, Philip Snowden, recalls:

'Mr MacDonald spoke that Saturday afternoon at Swansea, and made no reference at all to the letter, which was the one thing that was in everybody's mind. His silence was taken as confirmation of all that the Tory newspapers were saying. The Labour Candidates who had to address meetings that evening were wholly at a loss what to say. Some of the more venturesome denounced the whole thing as a fraud; while others, more cautious, followed Mr MacDonald's example and said nothing unless they were questioned upon it by the audience .... The opposition press for two days had had the field entirely to themselves, and had created a state of public suspicion which it was now too late to remove.'[2]

It was not until Monday 27 October, just two days before polling day, that MacDonald broke his silence. It was at a meeting in Cardiff, but having left himself entirely in the hands of his Foreign Office officials, he was unable to state whether the 'Letter' was genuine or a forgery, even though Rakovsky had in a second Note to the Foreign Office presented an offer from the Soviet Government 'to submit the authenticitiy of the "Zinoviev Letter" to an impartial arbitration court.'[3]

The Foreign Office press release appeared to be the signal for stepping up the attacks upon the Anglo-Soviet treaties which had yet to be ratified. Leaflets, posters and other printed material with such crude and emotive headings such as 'RED BREAD FROM RUSSIA' – 'REDS NOT BREAD' and 'THE BOLSHEVIK YOKE – ITS YOUR MONEY WE WANT' were distributed. Lewis Chester, Stephen Fay and Hugo Young, in their well documented book *The Zinoviev Letter* point to the discrepency in the signatures. 'The British representative on the Praesidium of the International was Arthur MacManus. His name was spelt McManus . . . . More serious however was the use of "Zinoviev" instead of G. Zinoviev and "Kuusinen" was not secretary of the International, as the letter claimed, but merely a member of the secretariat.'[4] According to the Coates, 'The secretary was Mr Kolarov.'[5]

On Sunday, 26 October, MacManus was in Manchester and during a speech in the Ardwick Picture Theatre in which there were present both police and the press, he 'challenged the authorities to prosecute him. If he had in the "Zinoviev Letter" urged the organization of subversive units in the British army, why did not the government arrest him and bring him to trial?'[6] No action was taken.

The political bombshell must have been well prepared by the conservative Central Office early in the election campaign, for it 'had already fashioned a "Red Bogey" poster showing Ramsay MacDonald turning his back on three downcast Britishers to greet two grim-faced Cossacks. The legend ran: "SO THIS IS SOCIALISM, VOTE UNIONIST"'.[7]

Lack of decisive action by MacDonald and failure to consult his Cabinet colleagues played a considerable part in the ultimate destruction of the first Labour Government. He could have instructed Lord Haldane, the Cabinet's senior legal officer, or Arthur Ponsonby, to ensure that no action was taken until the authenticity of the 'Letter' was verified. And there were of course other Cabinet members he could have contacted in such an emergency. Failing that, he could have come to London himself, if only for a brief stay. MacDonald was also Foreign Minister, but he made no attempt to repudiate the hasty decisions of his Foreign Office officials for which he bore responsibility. Consequently. 'his supporters, till now eagerly defending the proposed Russian treaty, found themselves deserted by their chief.'[8]

The inevitable outcome of the Zinoviev affair was that the Conservatives gained a massive electoral victory. 415 seats to Labour's 152 and the Liberal's representation drastically cut from 159 to a mere 40. The Labour loss was 42, although its actual vote surprisingly was increased by more than a million, having put an extra 80 to 90 candidates into the fray. As for the Liberals, their loss of 116 seats was catastrophic reducing them to a political status from which they have not to this day recovered.

Returning now to J.D. Gregory, who was obviously a man of considerable versatility. In 1928 his name came up again concerning his partnership with a lady friend over a matter of foreign currency speculation. On 26 January, the London evening newspapers, and on the following day, the national press reported the opening of a case in which a firm of foreign bankers, Messrs Ironmonger and Company, were suing Mrs Aminto Margorie Bradley Dyne for £39,178 which they claimed was owing to them in respect of foreign currency sold by her to the bank and re-sold by the bank to her. During the course of the trial it emerged that Mrs Dyne had been intrduced to the bankers by Gregory and that he had been a partner in some of her transactions.

Immediately the trial was over, a Special Board of enquiry was set up to investigate the part played by Gregory and other civil servants in the matter. By the end of February the following conclusion had been reached:

> 'We find it difficult to see any circumstance of extenuation. He was an official of wide experience, the head of his department when these transactions began, and before they were discontinued an Assistant Under Secretary of State; yet he encouraged, instead of checking, speculative transactions on the part of those junior to himself, and even shared transactions with them. The extent and duration of his speculations were such as to involve him in serious financial embarrassment.
>
> We cannot doubt that he was conscious of the

impropriety of what he was doing, and we do not regard it as any sufficient excuse that he did not at any time make use of official information for his private ends.' (*Daily Express*, 28 February 1928)

As a result of the findings of the Enquiry, the Secretary of State for Foreign Affairs instructed that 'Mr Gregory be dismissed the Service'.

Among the first acts of the new Administration was to notify the Soviet Government on 21 November 1924 that:

'His Majesty's Government have under review the treaties negotiated by their predecessors with the Government of the USSR, and signed on August 8 last. I have the honour to inform you that after due deliberation His Majesty's Governement find themselves unable to recommend the treaties in question for consideration of Parliament or to submit them to the King for His Majesty's ratification.' (*The Times*, 22 November 1924)

It was signed by Austen Chamberlain, Secretary of State for Foreign Affairs, and gives an indication why demands by many Members of Parliament for a public enquiry into the authenticity of the 'Zinoviev Letter' was never granted. But the main reason for rejecting a public enquiry goes much deeper.

Lewis Chester, Stephen Fay and Hugo Young have provided ample evidence that the 'Zinoviev Letter' was a forgery. They discovered that the letter was composed in Berlin by Alexis Bellegarde and Alexander Gumansky, members of the Brotherhood of St George, a pro-Tsarist counter-revolutionary organization whose 'single minded aim was to keep the Soviet Union diplomatically isolated. The equation for them was simple: diplomatic contact led to trade, which led to capitalist investment which eventually would strengthen the Soviet regime and diminish the chances of ever bringing it down.' The writers say that when they wrote their book Madame Irina Bellegarde, the widow of Alexis Bellegarde, was still alive and living in London and that it was 'largely upon her evidence that the true story of the Zinoviev forgery is based. She witnessed the forgery as it was performed, and she is the sole survivor of those who did . . . but she is not the only source.' The actual forging of Zinoviev's signature was carried out by a Latvian friend of Gumansky and the Bellegardes, 'called Edward Friede, who had served with the anti-Bolshevik, Baltic "Patriotic Volunteers"'.[9]

It was Gumansky who sent the Zinoviev letter 'through the channels that led to London' where it reached Conrad Donald im Thurn, 'a former MI5 agent and a director of one of the émigré commercial concerns, the London Steamship and Trading Corporation' and he in turn contacted Major Guy Kindersley, Conservative MP for Hitchin. 'Kindersley's reaction to the news was that Conservative Party headquarters should be informed. The man he decided to contact was, logically, Lord Younger,' Treasurer of the Party and a former Chairman, who 'had virtually run the Conservative machine since 1916 . . . in 1924 he was still the dominant figure at Central Office.' He was assisted by Sir Reginald Hall, a Director of Naval Intelligence during the war, a former Conservative MP and chief Agent of the Party. According to im Thurn, it was Hall who notified Marlowe, the editor of the *Daily Mail*, of the existence of the Zinoviev letter. It appears that im Thurn had kept a diary in which he referred to 'a guarantee against loss' in return for what he had to offer. The guarantee was arranged by Lord Younger, the Tory treasurer. In the diary 'im Thurn speaks of the need to collect a total of £10,000.'[10] Eventually, he was paid a lump sum of £5,000 and was 'to get from the other source £250 a year for ten years, plus an extra lump sum of £2,500 at the end of ten years. This is to be paid to him in the Argentine, where he is to establish himself as an Argentine national.'[11]

In their *History of Anglo-Soviet Relations*, W.P. and Zelda Coates, whose book was published some sixteen years after the Zinoviev affair have written that: 'All the circumstances surrounding this notorious letter are not at present public property and perhaps never will be because those who know best about them have good reason to keep silent.'[12] Even forty years after the event, Chester, Fay and Young have had to draw attention to the fact that: 'No assistance was

233

given to us by the Foreign Office staff in our research for this book. Their official attitude is still that the Zinoviev Letter was the work of Zinoviev, although the department prefers not to answer the question direct.' The authors have further pointed out that 'In December 1966 the Zinoviev letter returned briefly to the newspaper headlines, after it had been disclosed that the Zinoviev file in the Foreign Office records was incomplete. This disclosure', they say, 'was made, remarkably in a new official edition of documents in British foreign policy. One of the auxiliary papers to the letter itself was reported missing.'[13]*

The revival of interest in the 'Zinoviev Letter' was taken a step further by the late Philip Noel-Baker, a former Minister of State at the Foreign Office. Noel-Baker in a letter to *The Times* on 22 December 1966, recalled that:

'The late Sir Walford Selby was principal Private Secretary to Mr Ramsay MacDonald in the Foreign Office before and during the 1924 election. He remained as principal Private Secretary until 1932, serving Sir Austen Chamberlain, Mr Arther Henderson and Sir John Simon. Sir Walford told me many years afterwards – I think it was during the second World War – that in 1925 the Chief Commissioner of the Metropolitan Police had assured him in confidence that, as Chief Commissioner, he had come into possession of absolute proof that the Zinoviev Letter was a forgery.'

Notes

1. SNOWDEN Philip Viscount, *An Autobiography*, p.713
2. SNOWDEN Philip Viscount, *An Autobiography*, p. 711
3. COATES W.P. and Zelda, *A History of Anglo-Soviet Relations*, p. 187
4. CHESTER Lewis, FAY Stephen and YOUNG Hugo, *The Zinoviev Letter*, pp. 134/5
5. COATES W.P. and Zelda, *A History of Anglo-Soviet Relations*, p.184
6. FISCHER Louis, *The Soviets in World Affairs*, p. 366
7. CHESTER, FAY and YOUNG, *The Zinoviev Letter*, p. 4

*See preface to *Documents on British Foreign Policy 1919 – 1939* Series 1A Vol. I. Published 29 April 1966.

8. COLE G. D. H. and POSTGATE Raymond, *The Common People*, p. 575
9. CHESTER, FAY and YOUNG, *The Zinoviev Letter*, pp. 51/52
10. CHESTER, FAY and YOUNG, *The Zinoviev Letter*, pp.71,79,80
11. CHESTER, FAY and YOUNG, *The Zinoviev Letter*, pp.178/179
12. COATES W. P. and Zelda, *A History of Anglo-Soviet Relations*, p. 181
13. CHESTER, FAY and YOUNG , *The Zinoviev Letter*, Prologue and p. 52

18

NEW POLICIES – EAST AND WEST

Within weeks of winning the election, the new Conservative administration was being pressed by powerful elements within their ranks to withdraw de jure recognition from the Soviet Government. Baldwin, however, knew that such a drastic decision would have weakened Britain's political and diplomatic status internationally, for in 1924 de jure recognition of the USSR had been undertaken by Austria, China, Danzig, Denmark, France, Greece, Hungary, Italy, Mexico, Norway and Sweden and was followed by Japan in 1925.

The United States, which remained outside the League, did not recognize the USSR* and during the Presidential annual message to Congress, on 23 December 1923, the matter of Soviet recognition was raised, but rejected by President Coolidge. The United States, he declared, was not prepared

> 'to enter into relations with another regime which refuses to recognize the sanctity of international relations. I do not propose to barter away for the privilege of trade any of the cherished rights of humanity.'

He was, nevertheless, prepared 'to make very large concessions for "the purpose of rescuing the people of Russia".'

Earlier that month, Chicherin had written to Coolidge

---

*The USA did not grant full diplomatic recognition to the USSR until November 1933.

236

'expressing his complete readiness to accept "the principle of mutual non-interference in internal affairs" and to discuss the Kerensky debts "on the assumption that the principle of reciprocity will be recognized".' His Government was

> 'ready to do all in its power to bring about the desired end of renewal of friendship with the United States of America.'

'This overture was promptly and curtly rejected by Washington where it was said there was nothing in the Soviet Note or otherwise which would warrant recognition.'[1]

The USSR was at the time going through the trials, successes and errors of its New Economic Policy, introduced by Lenin in March 1921 at the Tenth Congress of the Communist Party. It was the successor to the 1918–1920 period of 'War Communism' during which the strictest control had been placed upon the requisitioning and direction of agricultural produce, and industrial supplies and transport, considered essential for the prosecution and eventual winning of the Civil War and the Wars of Intervention.

Many bitter lessons had been learnt, particularly at Brest Litovsk* and Krondstadt† and now Lenin's policy of 'breathing space' was being applied on the economic front.

Over three quarters of the population were peasants. Most soldiers and workers in the urban areas were of peasant origin and to gain their support the policy of 'War Communism' was abandoned. Instead, there was a partial return to a mixed economy whereby the State maintained control over the 'commanding heights', i.e. the banks, heavy industry, transport, tele-communications and international trade, and the peasants and peasant farmers left free to sell their produce on the open market, thus enabling them to buy the clothes, tools and utensils which they badly needed. The NEP had provided an incentive to stimulate

---

* See Chapter 4 pp.
†See Chapter 12 pp.

food production and increase the supply of consumer goods.

Within two years production had almost doubled, whilst on the international front the door had been opened to foreign capitalist concerns by granting them concessions for the development of Russia's mines, as well as other industrial and commercial operations.

1921, the year of the famine, was also a turning point in the development of trade with the outside world. The arrival of foreign trade missions that summer provided hope for the future of international relations. The Central Union of Co-operatives – the Centrosoyous – having greatly increased their export business, particularly with Britain and Germany, successfully negotiated long-term credits with both countries for the import of chemicals, medicines, machines, machine tools and scientific instruments.

When first introduced the New Economic Policy created quite a stir in both left-wing and capitalist circles. It was interpreted by some on the left as an abandonment of 'true' socialist principles. Most politicians and business communities in the capitalist countries assessed it as an indication of the inevitable surrender to capitalist enterprise, which probably prompted Sir Robert Horne* (in October 1921) to declare:

'the best way to break down Bolshevism in Russia was to penetrate that great country with honest commercial methods'.

By 1925 the 'NEP had served its purpose: the State had re-established a stable currency; both food and goods were plentiful . . . and it had become apparent to the Bolshevik leaders that if it really intended to form a Socialist State . . . something must be done to check capital accumulations by NEP men, no less than the steady growth of a prosperous peasant class, the "Kulak" or labour-employing farmers."[2]

There were of course weaknesses in its implementation,

---

*He was Britain's Chancellor of the Exchequer at the time. Earlier in the year at the signing of the Anglo-Soviet Trade Agreement he was President of the Board of Trade.

and it did not take long for many entrepreneurs and Kulaks to exploit this transitional situation. The Kulaks, in particular, had been exploiting the new legislation, which permitted the use of hired labour and the renting of land, to enlarge their farms and extend their control over the rural areas.

In his book, *The Period of War Communism*, Lenin had called for the elimination of the Kulaks, but as a class, not as individuals. 'Our task in the rural districts', he said, was 'to destroy the landlord and smash the resistance of the exploiter and the Kulak profiteers.'[3]

This has been referred to by Walter Duranty, the American journalist, in his report of the 'intra-party struggle' during the years 1925–1928.

> 'it is significant that one of the chief points of controversy . . . which then raged among the Bolsheviks, concerned the question of expropriating the Kulaks. Both sides agreed that the Kulaks required extermination as a class, and only quarrelled about the right method and right moment . . . '[4]

It was later, during the Stalin era, that the widespread hatred of the Kulaks had become so intense that it eventually led to indiscriminate imprisonment and mass slaughter, there were many who were justifiably accused of being responsible for much of the hunger and suffering of the Russian people in the early 1920s, but there were also many injustices carried out in their name.

The relative success of the NEP and the drawing together of the two pariahs* had forced the governments of the Entente to adjust their political sights. When the Foreign Ministers of Germany and Russia met in Rapallo to sign the Treaty of Peace and Friendship, the shock waves reverberated throughout Western Europe, particularly within the French Foreign Office. Collective security, which had dominated the political thinking of France since the Armistice, was one of the first items to be built into the

---

*See Chapter 13, pp.

Covenant of the League of Nations. Under the guise of collective security there had been the economic blockade of Russia; the Cordon Sanitaire and the creation of the French inspired Little Entente – Czechoslovakia, Roumania and Yugoslavia. Rapallo was a logical reaction to the League's Collective security policies. But with the collapse of French policy in the Ruhr and changes in the governments of both Germany and France, feelers were extended with the aim of bringing Germany back into the 'family of nations'. It was the Dawes Plan which paved the way on the economic front.

According to Sir John Wheeler-Bennett 'initial proposals – tentative and secret – to the western powers for a pact of security'[5] were made by Gustav Stresemann, the German Foreign Minister, in February 1925. With the willing co-operation of Briand, the French Foreign Minister, a rapprochement between Germany and France was eventually brought to fruition at the Swiss Lakeside resort of Locarno.

The Locarno Conference opened on 5 October 1925 with representatives from Britain, Belgium, France, Germany and Italy. As Czechoslovakia and Poland had common frontiers with Germany, they too were invited to send representatives, but the main agreements and decisions of the conference were determined by Briand, Austen Chamberlain and Stresemann. They were the demilitarization of the Rhineland and mutual guarantees against attack across the Franco-German and Belgian-German frontiers, strengthened by additional guarantees from Britain and Italy, but no guarantees to the countries on Germany's eastern borders. There were instead arbitration agreements between Germany and Poland and Germany and Czechoslovakia. The door had at last been opened for Germany to enter the League of Nations, which she did in 1926, with a permanent seat on the council.

Konni Zilliacus aptly described the Pact of Locarno* as

---

*After World War II attempts were made to bring Germany back into another anti-Soviet alliance. The first through a European defence Community failed owing to French opposition. On American pressure the German Federal Republic was eventually brought into the wider North Atlantic Treaty Organization (NATO) in December 1954 and a few months later began its rearmament programme. The Soviet Union reacted with the formation of the Warsaw Pact Alliance later that year.

'the first Western Union.'[6] It was no more than a series of treaties which provided guarantees of security for the countries of Western Europe but ignored the matter of security for some Eastern European countries, and that included Soviet Russia. France did conclude, outside the Locarno agreements, new treaties with Czechoslovakia and Poland.

Britain's Conservative Government was more than pleased with the result of Locarno. Her Colonial Under-Secretary of State, Ormsby-Gore, was reported by *The Observer*, 25 October 1925, to have declared at a public meeting:

'The struggle at Locarno, as I see it was this: Is Germany to regard her future as being bound up with the fate of the great Western powers, or is she going to work with Russia for the destruction of western civilization? The Foreign Commissar was brought from Moscow to try to prevent that. The significance of Locarno is tremendous. It means that, as far as the Government of Germany if concerned, it is detached from Russia and is throwing in its lot with the Western Party.'

Lord D'Abernon, who was Britain's Ambassador in Berlin during the early 1920s, had assisted Chamberlain in the preliminary negotiations that led to Locarno. He was certainly under no illusion as to what the primary objectives of the Locarno treaties were about.

'It was apparent to those who took a world view that Western civilization was menaced by an external danger which, coming into being during the war, threatened a cataclysm equalled only by the fall of the Roman Empire. This danger arose from the sweeping success in 1917 of the revolution against the Czarist regime . . . there is little doubt that a blind persistence in the policy of maintaining the war grouping of the Allies against Germany would eventually have led to Germany being forced into close alliance with Russia . . .'

But it was the 'class-revolt propaganda, appealing to the proletariat of the world' which appeared to have the greatest impact upon Lord D'Abernon.

> 'No solution of the European problem could be tolerated by English statesmen which threatened the exclusion of Germany from the European combination and left her a prey to Russian wiles and Russian influence . . . . For the alliance of Germany with Russia, while primarily inimical to England in Asia, could hardly subsist without leaving Germany open to the penetration of Bolshevik propaganda, and if Germany was infected, could the rest of Europe – could France – remain immune?'[7]

The real significance of the Locarno conference of 1925, and the subsequent treaties, was that it laid the foundation of Western European cold war policies. Locarno was infact the first stage on the road to Munich. Both conferences, purporting to bring peace to Europe, excluded Soviet Russia, without whose presence and co-operation there could be no European security, and do much to draw attention to the reasoning that lay behind Anglo-French appeasement of Nazi Germany during the following decade.

Chicherin, in an interview in France with the correspondent of *The Observer*, was asked whether he had 'modified in any way' his 'very uncompromising criticism of the spirit of Locarno?' 'I am afraid', he replied, 'that I shall have to disappoint you. We still regard Locarno with apprehension, for we don't yet see Locarno's contribution to the cause of peace. I, for one, readily accept the assurance of the participants in the conference that Locarno is "a beginning". But a beginning of what? That only time will show.' (*The Observer*, 13 December 1925)

Exaggerated claims were made of the 'Spirit of Locarno' ushering into the world a new era of peace and the leading signatories, Briand, Stresemann and Chamberlain were each rewarded for their efforts with the Nobel Prize for Peace.

When Germany presented her application to join the League in March 1926, she linked it to a request for the removal of Allied controls having, as she claimed, fulfilled all her obligations specified in the Treaty of Versailles. The British, French and Belgian Governments thereupon instructed the control Commission to carry out an inspection of Germany's military and naval armaments. Sir John Wheeler-Bennett writes: 'Contrary to the expectation of London, Paris and Brussels, the Commission's report, a document of some five hundred pages, stated in essence that:

> 'Germany had never disarmed, had never had the intention of disarming, and for seven years had done everything in her power to deceive and "counter-control" the commission appointed to control her disarmament'.

So anxious, however, were the Governments concerned to place the final coping-stone upon the edifice of Locarno, so confident were they in the validity of Stresemann's pledges of Germany's peaceful intentions, that they deliberately suppressed and ignored this final report and issued a communiqué on 13 December 1926, that of more than a hundred questions of disarmament outstanding in June 1925 there remained now but two, that the powers had agreed to continue negotiations on these two items and that the Commission on Control would be withdrawn on 31 January 1927.'[8]

It appears that 'Stresemann played the "Rapallo bluff"' says Jon Jacobson, in his book *Locarno Diplomacy*, 'suggesting that Russia too was bidding for German allegiance and that the West could compete only by offering Germany "something positive"'.[9]

Between 1924 and 1929 foreign capital poured into Germany 'to the tune of 25,000 million gold marks, whilst the total of her reparation payment under the Dawes Plan for the same period was under 8,000 million marks. With the surplus she was able to re-equip her industries, to indulge in large public works and enterprises, to subsidize her agriculture and to rebuild her export trade.' Within that period 'the Reichswehr Budget rose from 490 million marks to 827 million.' These figures do not include items of military expenditure which were 'camouflaged as innocent items of peaceful civilian expenditure.'[10] Many of these items were concealed within the budgets of other ministries and it has been estimated that between 1924–1932 Germany spent around 3,000 million marks in this way. Together with the official Reichswehr budget, the rearmament programme included the re-birth of the German navy.

Notes

1. FLEMING D. F., *The Cold War and its Origins*, Vol. 1. pp. 44/45
2. DURANTY Walter, *Russia Reported*, pp.17/18
3. LENIN V. I., *Period of War Communism*, p.150
4. DURANTY Walter, *Russia Reported*, p.18
5. WHEELER-BENNETT Sir John, *The Nemesis of Power*, p. 177
6. ZILLIACUS K., *I Choose Peace*, p. 48
7. D'ABERNON Lord, *An Ambassador of Peace*, pp. 20, 22 & 23
8. WHEELER-BENNETT Sir John, *The Nemesis of Power*, pp. 185/186
9. JACOBSON Jon, *Locarno Diplomacy – Germany and the West 1925–1929*, p. 55
10. WHEELER-BENNETT Sir John, *The Nemesis of Power*, pp. 186/187

19

THE GENERAL STRIKE IN BRITAIN

When the French and Belgian troops moved in to the Ruhr the economic repercussions were felt throughout the British mine-owning industry. The strikes and 'passive resistance' of the German mineworkers, with the resultant shortfall in coal production on the continent, inevitably produced a temporary boom in Britain. But no sooner had the two countries evacuated the Ruhr in 1925, terminating the German 'passive resistance' policy in the area, than the extra demand for British coal ceased. The boom was over and Britain's mine-owners had made no plans in the interim period for such an eventuality. Consequently a return to the traditional measures of intimidation and pressure were used to strengthen their hands in introducing cuts in wages and a lengthening of the hours of work.

The miners appealed to the TUC for support, with the warning that this attack on them by the mine-owners was just a prelude to a general attack on the living standards of British workers. These fears were confirmed by the Prime Minister, Baldwin, who in discussions with the miners' leaders in July 1925 told them that in view of the plight of British industry:

'all the workers of this country have got to take reductions in wages to help put industry on its feet.' (*The Daily Herald*, 31 July 1925)

To strengthen the position of the mine-owners, the Prime Minister guaranteed them a nine-month subsidy, and from then on massive reserves of coal began to accumulate in various parts of the country. During this period an 'elaborate organization was set up, divided into ten areas, under Civil Commissioners, like Napoleonic prefects, who would be entitled to "give decisions on behalf of the government". Ex-Viceroys and ex-Admirals were put at the head of a voluntary strike-breaking organization, called the Organization for the Maintenance of Supplies, which was to provide these divisional generals with troops. All the machinery was ready by April 1926, to move on receipt of the one telegraphed word: "Action".'[1]

On 30 April 1926, the Miners' Federation rejected the mine-owners' ultimatum presented to them by Baldwin, which they said meant 'a uniform reduction of thirteen and a half per cent of the standard wages of the miners and further is conditional upon the extension of the working day over three years.'[2] The mine-owners immediately issued lock-out notices. On the following day – May Day – TUC leaders held an emergency Conference with the Executives of their affiliated unions. A call for a General Strike was endorsed by an overwhelming vote, 3,653,529 for and only 49,911 against. The Government reacted by proclaiming a State of Emergency.

No national newspapers were produced. Both sides, as a consequence, produced their own papers. The first to appear was the *British Gazette* with Winston Churchill as Editor-in-Chief. The paper could have been more aptly called the *War Gazette* for to Churchill it was war and the strikers were portrayed as 'the enemy'. Robert Rhodes James has described the *British Gazette* with 'its pretence to impartiality . . . an inflammatory, one-sided, highly pro-vocative propaganda broadsheet' and adds 'wild allegations of a Bolshevik plot behind the strike were published from a French newspaper.'[3]

The General Strike lasted only nine days but the TUC did not produce its own newspaper, the *British Worker*, until after the *British Gazette* had been established. The strikers, their families and supporters were not only deprived of such papers as the *Daily Herald* but were also deprived of a fair presentation of their side of the dispute by the British Broadcasting Corporation. Sir John Reith, BBC Director General, from 1927–1938, has justified the position taken by the BBC during those nine days. Referring to the illegality of the strike he says:

'the BBC, an organization within the Constitution, is unable to permit anything which is contrary to the spirit of this judgement and therefore might justify or prolong the General Strike. For this reason we refused to allow the Labour leaders to broadcast statements of their side of the case, as the Government was opposed to their being allowed to do so'.[4]

The General Strike collapsed on the tenth day after the TUC had entered into negotiations with the Government to bring it to an end. The leadership was severely criticized and it seemed to A.J. Cook, the Miners' General Secretary, 'that the only desire of some leaders was to call off the strike at any cost without any guarantees for the workers, miners and others.'[5] The dispute between the miners and the Government backed mine-owners continued until the end of the year, causing severe hardship as a result of the lock-out.

Following an appeal by the Trade Union movement for national and international support, over £1,350,000 was raised from trade unionists in many countries. Most came from the Soviet Trade Unions which had appealed to their members to contribute what they could for the British miners and their families. There was at the time an Anglo-Russian Trade Union Committee which had been set up in 1925 and an Anglo-Russian Miners' Committee during the year of the strike. The inevitable outcry of 'Moscow Gold' interfering in Britain's internal affairs was raised by the press and politicians.

On 13 June, Sir Austen Chamberlain, the Foreign Secretary, notified the House of Commons that he had:

'instructed His Majesty's Charge d'Affairs in Moscow to inform the Soviet Government that His Majesty's Government cannot pass over in silence the action of the Soviet Commissariat of Finance in giving special authorization for the transfer to this country of funds destined for the support of the general strike. He is to point out that the general strike was an illegal and unconstitutional act constituting a serious threat to established order, and that the special action taken by the Soviet Commissariat of Finance in its favour does not conduce to the friendly settlement which the Soviet Government profess to desire of the questions outstanding between the two countries.' (*Hansard*, 14 June 1926. Col. 1960)

In fact, during the period of the General Strike the TUC General Council had refused the Soviet Trade Unions' offer of financial assistance.

The Soviet Government's reply came three days later, pointing out that:

'in the Soviet Union there is not a total prohibition of the export of currency but only a restriction of the export which requires a permit in each individual case.

The Soviet Government expressing the will of the workmen and peasants of the USSR, could not forbid the trade unions which are organized by the millions of workmen of the USSR to send money abroad to render support to trade unions of another country.

At the same time the Soviet Government calls the attention of the British Government to utterances, not agreeing with real facts and not in accord with normal relations between governments, made by some members of the British Government who stated that the sum remitted to the General Council of the British Trade Unions was sent by the Soviet Government while in reality it was sent by the Central Council of the all-Russian Union of Trade Unions, in agreement with the Soviet Trade union centres.'[6]

But by now it had become apparent that the campaign accusing the Soviet Government of interfering in Britain's industrial disputes was beginning to misfire. On 16 June,

The Daily Telegraph's Parliamentary correspondent reported:

'Some Unionist members express considerable doubt as to whether it will have been possible to trace any direct connection between the Russian donations for the miners and the Soviet authorities. Failing clear proof that Russian State funds have been used for the purpose, the British Government, of course, will be unable to take any action, and in any event, it is gathered that such step as the repudiation of the recognition accorded to the Soviet Government, which is being pressed for in some quarters, would not be taken. It is the belief in well informed quarters that the Government as a whole is not disposed to contemplate such drastic action.'

The main effect of the strike was to shift the balance of power considerably in favour of the employers. The Anglo-Russian Trade Union Committee was dissolved and in 1927 the Trade Disputes and Trade Unions Act which made general strikes illegal had become part of British law. The rights and privileges of British workers after many years of struggle had received a severe rebuff. 'It was scarcely a coincidence', wrote Louis Fischer, 'that the same Parliamentary session which authorized this act also voted the diplomatic break with the Soviet State.'[7]

Notes

1. COLE, G.D.H. and POSTGATE, Raymond, *The Common People*, p. 578
2. ARNOT, R. Page, *The Miners: Years of Struggle*, p. 415
3. JAMES, Robert Rhodes, *Churchill – A Study in Failure*, p. 171
4. RENSHAW, Patrick, *The General Strike*, p. 205
5. HUTT, Allen, *British Trade Unionism*, p. 112
6. *Soviet Documents on Foreign Policy* Vol. II (ed. Jane Degras), p. 119
7. FISCHER, Louis, *Soviets in World Affairs*, p. 513

20

CHINA AND THE ARCOS RAID

Whenever Empires begin to crumble and the peoples of the colonized countries decide to liberate themselves from colonial control and exploitation, accusations of blame have invariably been diverted towards a third party. The leaders of colonial powers tend to believe that they have to convince their electorate that, as a result of the exposure of some of the worst features of their colonial or neo-colonial rule, local agitators or foreign agitators are responsible; that their actions and administrations have been for the benefit of the colonial peoples; that poverty, and the deprivation of human rights was either an exaggeration or sheer propaganda and that what went on under colonial rule in some far-flung part of the world was really nobody's business except that of the colonial rulers themselves.

Sir W. Joynson-Hicks, the Home Secretary, had (4 November 1925) 'accused the Soviet Government, without advancing any proof, of being responsible for the unrest in India, China, Persia, Afghanistan and even Africa'.* The Indian Mutiny, the Black-hole of Calcutta, the Boxer Rebellion, the Anglo-Afghan wars and the Boer War must have slipped through the Home Secretary's historical perspective. All occurred long before November 1917. His colleague, Lord Curzon, went even one better, 'in the course of a speech in the House of Lords,' the noble Gentleman, 'blamed the Soviet Government for the Irish Rising of Easter, 1916, an episode which occurred a year and a half before the November Revolution!'[1]

China was not a colony in the 1920s, it was what could be

---

*In a speech at Bournemouth.

described as a neo-colonial appendage. It had become the 'milch-cow' for a number of imperial and would-be imperial powers. The 1922 Washington Nine-Power Agreement, with its 'open door' China policy, was in reality a political device concocted by the signatories not to fight over their interests in China, but to maintain some form of status quo and to continue the joint exploitation of the Chinese people according to their spheres of influence. The old Imperial Manchu dynasty had been overthrown by the revolution in 1911, and China became a Republic in the following year under the leadership of Dr Sun-Yat-Sen. The influence of the Chinese Nationalist Party – the Kuomintang, under his guidance, spread rapidly throughout the whole country. From the very outset, the Nationalists denounced the 'unequal treaties' and set out their objective of restoring Chinese sovereignty, establishing a constitutional democracy and alleviating the appalling economic and social conditions of the many millions of their people.

It was not unnatural for political leaders of other countries who were in the throes of trying to put an end to despotic or colonial rule to be in sympathy with others trying to achieve the same ends. Some of the leaders in the American War of Independence, eminent people such as Benjamin Franklin and Tom Paine, were also active supporters of the 1789 French Revolution.

Lenin had from the beginning welcomed the Chinese Revolution of 1911 as a major step in the drive for national liberation by the peoples of 'advanced Asia' against 'backward Europe', which was 'plundering China and helping the foes of democracy and freedom' in that country.

There was nothing remarkable in the fact that after the overthrow of the Tsarist régime in 1917, Soviet Russia should be looked upon 'not as the Russian foreigner of old, but as the one ally of Chinese nationalism, ready to renounce "the unequal treaties", if not "special interests", the champions of unity and equality, of science and the welfare of the common man . . .'[2]

All territorial rights and privileges extorted from China by the Tsarist Government were initially renounced by the Soviet Government on 25 July 1919,* and on 31 May 1924 an agreement was concluded between the two countries emphasizing that it was based strictly upon terms of mutual equality.

In 1926 Chicherin, the Soviet Foreign Minister, in an interview with Arthur Ransome, the *Manchester Guardian* Foreign Correspondent, explained why his government should encourage friendly relations with the peoples of that part of the world.

> 'In general', he said, 'our relations with the peoples of the East are based on mutual friendship and on a perfectly peaceful policy free from any sort of aggressiveness. Looking over the history of the development of these relations, one may observe that we were all the time the object of attack on the part of Imperialist powers in Asia, and that our friendly relations with the national movements of the peoples of the East developed in the course of our struggle against the aggressive policy of Imperialism directed against ourselves.'

Turning to the subject of China, Chicherin told Ransome that:

> 'The Soviet Government and its agents are far from trying to develop in the Chinese people any hatred towards foreigners. On the contrary', he said, 'a free democratic China, the creation of which has our sympathy, will present far more favourable relations with all countries than a China enslaved and exploited, under the burden of unequal treaties . . . ' (*The Manchester Guardian*, 27 February 1926)

The Chinese peoples' struggle to liberate themselves from foreign domination and their own feudal War-Lords, resulted in the nationalist movement gaining control of Southern China, with Nanking as their capital. The middle region of the great Yangtse river and the provincial town of

---

*It appeared in a Soviet Government Manifesto and has since been described historically as the Karakhan Declaration.

Hankow came under their control, and Shanghai, the centre of the foreign dominated areas (the international settlements), was being threatened. In the 1920s, 'China incidents' were common headlines used to gloss over the shooting down of unarmed demonstrators and intimidating naval bombardments which left many innocent men, women and children lying dead or injured.

The British Government's 'Gun-Boat' diplomacy around the China Sea and the mouth of the Yangtse had failed to intimidate the Chinese Nationalist Movement, and the 'Mandarins' in Whitehall were blaming the Soviet Government for the Nationalists' uncompromising attitude, especially their demand for the recognition of their country's sovereignty.

The Daily Herald, 3 February 1927, reported a statement by the Foreign Minister of the Chinese Nationalists, Eugene Chen, in which he explained that the aim of the Nationalist Movement

'is the recovery of China's full independence. And until this act of historical justice has been done there can be no real peace between Chinese Nationalism and British Imperialism . . .

'Great Britain or any other Power has nothing to fear when China, under Nationalist leadership and rule, recovers her lost independence . . . The Government whose existence is implied by the modern state in China will necessarily work out the specific foreign issues involved in the recovery of China's full independence along the lines which, while asserting and enforcing Chinese authority and preserving vital Nationalist interests, will not disregard the considerations of right and justice due to foreign nationals. But in this connection a great and impressive fact must be grasped. Today, the effective protection of foreign life and property in China does not stand and can no longer rest on foreign bayonets and foreign gunboats because "the arm" of Chinese Nationalism – the economic weapon – is more puissant than any engine of warfare that a foreigner can devise . . . '

The liberation struggle of the Chinese workers from foreign control had intensified during the 1920s. On 30 May 1925 there was a big demonstration in Shanghai. 'A dozen marchers were killed and fifty wounded when they were fired upon by a detachment of International Settlement police under a British sergeant. This incident led to strikes, boycotts and demonstrations in Shanghai and many other cities. A demonstration in Canton was fired upon by French and British machine-gunners, resulting in the death of fifty two workers and students and the wounding of more than a hundred.'[3]

There was at that time about £250 million of British capital invested in the area around the Treaty ports and the Chinese Nationalists were demanding that the ports be returned to Chinese sovereignty, and an end to the granting of special privileges and immunities for foreigners.

Britain's Foreign Secretary, although admitting that the China Treaties were out of date, nevertheless, took no action to discourage the landing of additional troops in the foreign held concession areas.

It was certainly true that Dr Sun-Yat-Sen's national revolutionary party had been organized with the help of the Soviet adviser, Michael Borodin, in the same way as General Sutton, a British subject, had been 'serving with the ex-brigand and War-Lord of Manchuria, Chang Tso-Lin.'[4]

Now that the British Cabinet were again considering the rupture of diplomatic relations with Soviet Russia, the Chinese events became a very useful card to play. Chen's statement undoubtedly inflamed the imperial passions of the extremist elements in the Conservative Cabinet. Both Sir W. Joynson-Hicks and Winston Churchill as well as Leo Amery, the Colonial Minister, attacked the Soviet Government for Chen's attitude towards Britain.

On 4 February, Litvinov told foreign correspondents at a press conference in Moscow that:

'British conservative circles are trying to shift their own mistakes on to the shoulders of the Soviet Government, on the basis of ridiculous legends, and to explain the greatest liberative movement in history among China's millions by the "machinations of Soviet agents".' (*The Daily News*, 5 February 1927)

In the meantime, the Chairman of Russo-Asiatic Consolidated Ltd, Leslie Urquhart,* had on 1 February, sent out circulars to the company's shareholders urging them to press their Members of Parliament to call for a severance of diplomatic relations until the Soviet Government 'makes a satisfactory agreement on all outstanding matters including the settlement of claims.' In his appeal to the shareholders, Urquhart added 'We see today our troops sailing east to protect British lives and interests in the Chinese tragedy foisted on us by Soviet Russia ... The severance of diplomatic relations would bring the Soviets to their senses.' (From *The Times*, 2 February 1927)

A great deal of activity was going on behind the scenes to pressurize the Government to break off relations completely with the Soviet Government, and some Government Ministers, hitherto reluctant, were beginning to succumb to this pressure. A threat of action was included in a Note to the Soviet Chargé d'Affaires on 23 February 1927 by the Foreign Minister, Sir Austen Chamberlain, stating that His Majesty's Government

'consider it necessary to warn the Union of Socialist Soviet Republics in the gravest terms that there are limits beyond which it is dangerous to drive public opinion in the country, and that a continuance of such acts as are here complained of must sooner or later render inevitable the abrogation of the Trade Agreement, the stipulations of which have been so flagrantly violated, and even the severance of ordinary diplomatic relations.' (*The Times*, 24 February 1927)

---

*According to the American writers Xenia Joukoff Eudin and Harold H. Fisher, Urquhart 'was a British industrialist who negotiated with the Soviet Government for mining concessions in the Urals and what is now Kazakhstan. The project was declined by the Soviet Government 6 October 1922 as unsatisfactory'. (From *Soviet Russia and the West 1920–1927*, p. 147)

The Soviet Government had offered to meet and discuss outstanding differences but its offer was ignored. Hard-liners in the Cabinet had by now gained the upper hand, and their warlike anti-Soviet statements began to alarm some of Britain's allies. The Foreign Minister, in attempting to allay the fears abroad that Britain was considering the organization of an anti-Soviet bloc, declared 'we have never tried to do it and never shall'*, but in spite of Sir Austen's denials, the *Times* correspondent in Geneva was still able to report:

> 'the main body of the foreign journalists at Geneva are convinced that the British Note to the Soviet Government was a sort of diplomatic war, and that since then Great Britain has entirely revised her policy with regard to Poland and Roumania and is busily stirring them up against the Soviets'. (*The Times*, 9 March 1927)

It was not surprising that some responsible foreign diplomats and journalists should have become alarmed, having either read or heard of the irresponsible statements made by leading Cabinet Ministers during the previous two days. Lord Birkenhead, the Secretary of State for India, speaking at a public meeting in Portsmouth on 7 March 1927, told his audience that in Soviet Russia

> 'There is no freedom of life. There is neither justice nor law, there is no protection for religion, there is no sanctity for marriage in this home of the proletariat, in the spiritual home from which our leading Communists draw daily and weekly refreshment. They have one of the richest countries in the world. They have very nearly destroyed it. They have done more harm to the resources and to the wealth and to the trade of Russia in ten years than the Tsarist Government, with all its admitted incompetence was able to do

---

*The Daily News, 9 March 1927.

in one hundred'. (*The Daily Telegraph*, 8 March 1927)

And on the following day, his Cabinet colleague, the Home Secretary, Sir William Joynson-Hicks, was reported in the *Daily News*, 9 March 1927, to have said:

'Here in our own land, as everywhere, we had the machinations of the Russian Government seeking to destroy all that we held dear. Not content with the misery of their own country, they were seeking to extend that misery to other countries, seeking to destroy civilization, seeking to destroy what they called the "Capitalist System" and because we were the head and forefront of civilization throughout the world it was the people of Great Britain who had to bear the brunt of the first attack of the Soviet Government'. (*The Daily News*, 9 March 1927)

France, which had greatly improved its relations with the USSR in recent months, was particularly sceptical of Chamberlain's reassurances. *The Manchester Guardian*'s Paris Correspondent reported that:

'Sir Austen Chamberlain's denial at Geneva that the British Government is trying to form a combination against Russia is received here with general scepticism, equally shared by persons and papers favourable to such a combination, and by those opposed to it. One cause of the scepticism is the Italian decision to ratify the declaration of 1920 by confirming the annexation of Bessarabia by Roumania, which is universally attributed to British influence and regarded as proof that Italy is ready to join with England against Russia'. (*The Manchester Guardian*, 10 March 1927)

Whatever the restraining influences of Britain's Foreign Minister may have been, the majority of his Cabinet appeared determined to break up the diplomatic relations with the USSR, and some of his more extreme right-wing colleagues were even prepared to activate some form of military intervention. A speech in Moscow on 19 April 1927 by the Chairman of the Council of People's Commissars, commenting upon the rapidly declining state of Anglo-Soviet relations re-stated his Government's attitude to the current state of affairs between the two countries:

'The Government of the USSR in pursuance of its general policy of peace, has never refused to enter into negotiations, and considers it both desirable and possible to remove the present strained relations.'[5]

But the appeal fell on deaf ears. The Government apparently had other important matters in mind and it soon became evident that Anglo-Soviet negotiations were not among them.

It was around four o'clock in the afternoon of 12 May 1927 that some 200 uniformed and plain clothed police entered the premises of Arcos Ltd.* and the Russian Trade Delegation who were sharing the same building at 49 Moorgate in the City of London.

According to eye-witness accounts, 'the police, immediately on entering the building, took possession of the telephone exchange, disconnected all the telephones and occupied the lift and all the entrances to the building. Various groups of the police occupied the entrances to all the floors and rooms belonging both to Arcos and the Trade Delegation. Within a few minutes the whole building was in the hands of uniformed and plain clothes officers. The warrant authorizing the search was not presented before the search began. The acting Chairman of Arcos Ltd, in spite of repeated demands, was only allowed to see the warrant an hour after the search had commenced. The warrant authorized not only a search of the premises occupied by Arcos Ltd, which was subject to British law, but also those of the Soviet Trade Delegation, which was a

---

*All Russia Co-operative Societies Ltd., a British registered company established in 1920, for the purpose of conducting Anglo-Russian trade.

flagrant breach of the Trade Agreement* . . .

'One group of police officers rushed immediately to the Cypher Room of the Chairman of the Delegation of the USSR. At that time there were in the room the cypher clerks. One of them told the police officer that this room was one of the Trade Delegation offices where the cypher communications of the Chairman of the Delegation were kept, and that they the cypher clerks, were not allowed to permit any one into the room or to show the cypher communications to anyone without the express permission of the official Trade Agent, or of one of the members of the Trade Delegation or responsible official of the Trade Delegation'.[6] The police ignored the protests of the cypher clerks, who had tried to prevent their access to the cypher communications. Under Article IV of the 1921 Anglo-Soviet Trade Agreement, paragraph 3, the members of the Trade Delegation were

> 'at liberty to communicate freely by post, telegraph and wireless telegraphy, and to use telegraph codes under the conditions and subject to the regulations laid down in the International Telegraph Convention of St Petersburg, 1875 (Lisbon Revision of 1908)'

and the police action was in breach of the Trade Agreement.

The Soviet Embassy was immediately informed of the raid and the First Secretary hastened to call upon 'the Director of the Northern Department of the Foreign Office, Palairet, "who expressed complete ignorance even of the fact that the raid was taking place"'.†

The following morning the Soviet Chargé d'Affaires saw Sir Austen Chamberlain, handing him a Note which contained a detailed report of the previous days' events. According to the Coates, who have given the most explicit

---

*According to Article 5 of the Anglo-Soviet Trade Agreement, the Chairman was entitled to all the rights and immunities enjoyed by the official representatives of other foreign powers in Great Britain.
†Extract from a statement issued by the Press Bureau of the Soviet Embassy dated 15 May 1927 (COATES, Footnote, p. 270)

account of the Arcos Raid, 'there was no question that the Chairman of the Trade Delegation and his offices enjoyed diplomatic immunity and one well-known legal authority declared that such a flagrant breach of International law had not taken place in British history in the previous 200 years'.* Yet in spite of this, 'the Foreign Office, to whom the Soviet Trade Delegation naturally looked for protection, took no steps to call off the raid.

'The Trade Delegation had been asked by the police to hand over to them the keys of the safes in the offices of the Trade Delegation'. This they refused to do, 'because these offices were extra-territorial'.

There had been no information forthcoming at the time of the raid 'as to what the police were seeking, but reports appeared in the press that their objective was an important British State document. The Soviet Trade Delegation immediately issued a statement to the press declaring

> 'in view of the report in the press that the object of the search was to find a certain official State document which had been lost a few months ago, the Trade Delegation considers it necessary to declare that it knows nothing of any such document, that it has never seen it, and that there never was and there is not, such a document in the files, archives, or safes of 49 Moorgate"'.[7]

In reply to a question in the House of Commons on 13 May, the Home Secretary had to admit his part in the police operations when he said 'I know that I directed that application should be made to the Magistrate for a warrant to search the premises of Arcos Ltd., and that warrant was granted.' When questioned as to whether the premises of the Trade Delegation had also been raided he replied 'I cannot answer a question as to the exact portion of the building where the Trade Delegation is.' (*Hansard*, 13 May 1927 Cols. 800 and 803)

---

*The foreword to the Coates' book was by the Rt Hon. David Lloyd George himself who has not denied the authenticity of their reports of the Arcos Raid or of the Trade Agreements.

260

That same evening 'pneumatic drill machinery was brought to the premises to pry open strong rooms and steel boxes. The documents were examined on the spot with thoroughness and deliberation, and without haste. The search proceeded in the absence of Arcos and Trade Delegation officials, and no list of documents found or taken away was made in their presence.'[8]

Most Conservative newspapers lavished fulsome praise on the Home Secretary, in their belief that the ultimate end of Anglo-Soviet relations had at last been achieved.

Further questions on the Arcos raid were put to the Home Secretary in the House of Commons on 16 May. According to his sources of information, he reasoned 'that a certain official document was or had been improperly in the possession of a person employed in the premises occupied by Arcos Ltd, at 49 Moorgate.' That, after consulting the Prime Minister and Foreign Secretary, a warrant had been issued which 'authorized the search of the premises occupied by Arcos Ltd., and the Trade Delegation, and the search was carried out in strict conformity with the warrant. I am informed that the search only came to an end at twelve o'clock last night. The document in question was not found, but the police have taken possession of certain papers which might bear upon the matter, and the examination of those papers is still proceeding.' (*Hansard*, 16 May 1927 Cols. 915, 916)

The Home Secretary and his Front Bench colleagues were evidently embarrassed when one of their own back bench MPs, Major MacAndrew, asked 'Have any steps been taken to deal with the person responsible for this document, which has apparently been stolen?' The reply from the Home Secretary that he was not 'at present in a position to make a statement in regard to that' drew ironical cheers from Opposition MPs. (*Hansard*, 16 May 1927 Col. 915). His commitment to shed some light upon the missing document had placed the Government in a dilemma. The Diplomatic Correspondent of the *Observer* reflected this dilemma in an article on the following Sunday, 22 May:

'Students of diplomacy feel some concern that an important issue in foreign policy should be forced upon the Cabinet by the Home Office and the War Office, not by the Foreign Office and to the embarrassment of the Foreign Office. It is commonly assumed that something has now to be sacrificed to the principle of Cabinet solidarity, and the fear is growing that the victim will be the Foreign Office.

The strength of those members of the Cabinet who advocate a break with Russia is the accomplished fact of the raid on the Trade Delegation, which in their view makes a rupture inevitable. Although the issue is not yet settled, and although it is surmised that Sir Austen Chamberlain has not yet given in, one has to be prepared for the possibility of a Government announcement on Tuesday that relations have been broken off, an announcement that would have incalculable effect on British interests in many parts of the world.'

On 24 May the Prime Minister outlined the Government's justification for the Arcos raid to a crowded House of Commons. His main points were:

(1) 'The police, in collaboration with the military authorities, have been investigating the activities of a group of secret agents engaged in endeavouring to obtain highly confidential documents relating to the Armed Forces of Great Britain . . . '

(2) 'That the agents were working on behalf of the Soviet Government and that they obtained their instructions from members of the Russian Trade Delegation . . . '

(3) 'A document of an official and highly confidential character . . . was recently found to be missing, and from information secured, and supported by documentary evidence, it became clear that this document had been conveyed to Soviet House . . . Upon this information application was

made ... for a warrant for the search of the premises.'

(4) Two cypher clerks were found to be in possession of documents, one of which showed that they were in 'communication with the Communist Parties in the United States of America, Mexico, South America, Canada, Australia, New Zealand and South Africa.'

(5) And finally, the Soviet Government had been carrying on anti-British activities in China which were in breach of the terms of the Anglo-Russian Trade Agreement 'and of international comity.'

Consequently, because 'Diplomatic relations' were 'thus deliberately and systematically abused ... His Majesty's Government have therefore decided that unless the House expresses its disapproval on Thursday, they will terminate the Trade Agreement, require the withdrawal of the Trade Delegation and Soviet Mission from London and recall the British Mission from Moscow. The legitimate use of Arcos is unaffected by these decisions and His Majesty's Government are prepared, whilst terminating the privileges conferred by Articles 4, 5 and 6 of the Trade Agreement, to make all arrangements necessary for ordinary trade facilities between the two countries.'* (*Hansard*, 24 May 1927, Cols. 1842–1851)

On the following day, the Soviet Chargé d'Affaires, through the Press Department of the Soviet Embassy, denied the charges stating that 'as no evidence had been advanced by Mr Baldwin there was and could be no detailed reply.' Regarding the two employees working in the Cypher department, the reply was that one employee 'on being questioned, declared categorically that he never had in his possession a list of secret addresses. As to the documents stated to be found in the possession of another

---

*'In the six years of its existence' Arcos 'had made purchases amounting to £100 million.' (FISCHER, Louis, *The Soviets in World Affairs*, p. 505)

employee, these having been evidently taken by the police out of his pocket, the circumstances under which the search took place make it quite impossible to determine whether they were really taken by the police out of his pockets, or whether the police came into possession of them on some other occasion.'

Referring to the matter about China, the reply was 'It can be proved from the copies of all the telegrams kept in the files of the Central Telegraph Office that no such telegraphic correspondence passed *en claire**, and Baldwin must have been referring to some alleged cypher telegram decoded by a department of the British Government.' The Soviet reply then went on to point out to the Prime Minister, that, 'An admission of this character in itself sounds very strange on the lips of the head of a Government which accuses the Soviet Government of meddling with British official documents.'[9]

It was this latter statement which must have prompted Lloyd George, in the Parliamentary debate of 26 May 1927, to expose the Government's hypocrisy over the matter of spying.

'What is the first charge brought by the Prime Minister in his document? It is espionage for the purpose of obtaining information about our Army and Navy. Are we not doing that? If the War Office and the Admiralty and the Air Force are not obtaining by every means every information about what is being done in other countries, they are neglecting the security of this country. Foreign Secretaries know nothing about it. It is not their business, but it is our business to get information, Foreign Governments are getting information about what is happening here . . . it is the business of Governments to find out exactly what is being done about armaments in every part of the world. It is their business to do it. If the Soviet Government are doing it they are offending in common with every other government in friendly relations

en claire – not in code.

264

with us in the world.' (*Hansard*, 26 May 1927, Cols. 2230/2231)

Lloyd George would have known (with his lengthy experience of the highest ministerial office) probably more than any living British politician at that time, and his case was further reinforced by another former diplomat with experience in the Foreign Office, Arthur Ponsonby, who told the House,

> 'we must really face the fact, when we are getting on our high moral horse, that forgery, theft, lying, bribery and corruption exist in every Foreign Office and every Chancellory throughout the world. The recognized official attitude is to put on a mask of impassable piety, which means that you ignore the whole thing. Of course you must. This weapon is used during war because it is valuable. It is used during so-called peace because peace is used for making preparations for the next war . . .
>
> I say that I have during my career seen a document which was taken from the archives of a foreign country. I have also travelled with a spy and heard what he had to say. He travelled with me because he wanted to get information from me, and he also wanted to get from me the despatches that I carried. The more friendly he became, the more tightly I had to cling to the despatches. He was on a mission to this country in order to get a newspaper to take up the cause of a particular foreign government that he was supporting.' (*Hansard*, 26 May 1927 Cols. 2258/2259)

During the course of the Government's winding up speech Sir William Joynson-Hicks had to admit that the 'highly confidential document' which was the professed purpose of the Arcos raid had not been found. He then told the House that his Ministry knew that one of the Soviet employees, whom he described as a 'human document', was a spy. Not unnaturally, many MPs were curious to know whether this 'human document' or Soviet spy had been arrested. When questioned by Mr R. Morrison, on what the

Home Secretary 'proposes to do with the human document', Sir William Joynson-Hicks' reply was:

'Will the hon. Member leave the human document to me? I do not think it is desirable that I should announce what will be done . . . ' (Col. 2306)

A vote was then taken on a Motion put by the Parliamentary Labour Party:

'That . . . this House is of the opinion that the termination of the Trade Agreement with Russia and the severance of diplomatic relations would have serious international consequences and close a promising avenue to the restoration of trade and industry, and is, therefore, a policy to which the country ought not to be committed until a Report of a Select Committee, based upon an examination of all relevant documents and a full inquiry into the facts, has been submitted to this House,' (*Hansard*, 26 May 1927 Col. 2195)

The Party's call for a Select Committee was turned down by the Foreign Secretary, and at the end of the debate a vote was taken on the Motion of the Labour Opposition. It was defeated by 367 votes to 118.

No time was lost by the Government. Within less than a day the Soviet Chargé d'Affaires received a Note from the Foreign Secretary, dated 26 May 1927, the same day as the debate, stating that

'. . . His Majesty's Government have decided that they can no longer maintain diplomatic relations with a Government which permits and encourages such a state of things as has been disclosed. The existing relations between the two Governments are hereby suspended, and I have to request that you will withdraw yourself and your staff from this country within the course of the next ten days. I am instructing His Majesty's representative at

Moscow to leave Russia with his staff . . . '

Having thus taken this drastic step, the Foreign Secretary nevertheless felt obliged to declare that the Government

'will raise no objection to the continuance of the legitimate commercial operations of "Arcos" Ltd. in the same conditions as those applicable to other trading organizations in this country.'[10]

A few hours after the Soviet Chargé d'Affaires had received the Government's Note, both he and members of his staff were being entertained to lunch in the House of Commons by leading members of the Labour Party and the Trades Union Congress. During the following week the Government was subjected to a number of searching questions regarding the allegations of spying, especially the matter concerning the Government's claim that it knew of, and had in its possession, contents of correspondence from the Soviet Commissariat for Foreign Affairs to its Embassy in China.

'LIEUT COMMANDER KENWORTHY: May I ask, then, how the documents that passed between Moscow and Pekin were obtained – on territory not under the jurisdiction of His Majesty's Government?
SIR A. CHAMBERLAIN: I cannot prevent the Hon. and gallant member from asking, but I must, respectfully, decline to reply.
LIEUT COMMANDER KENWORTHY: Are we to understand, then, that that part of the Trade Agreement, which referred to mutual abstention from propaganda and interference in neutral territories, has been broken by His Majesty's Government?
SIR A. CHAMBERLAIN: No, Sir, the Hon. and gallant Member is not entitled to understand that, which is absolutely contrary to the facts.
LIEUT COMMANDER KENWORTHY: If that be the case, how is it possible for communications passing between Russia and another country to come into the hands of the Right Hon. Gentleman without such

267

interference?

SIR A. CHAMBERLAIN: That is a question which I have respectfully declined to answer, and I again decline, on grounds of public interest.

MR THURTLE: Is it not a fact that these documents to which reference is made were obtained by espionage on the part of the British Government?' (*Hansard*, 30 May 1927, Cols. 17/18)

There was no reply.

Refusal to reply to important and relevant questions on the grounds of security, or of 'not being in the public interest', is a device which Governmental Ministers have employed, and still do employ, as a smokescreen to cover incompetence or embarrassing political decisions which in the 'public interest' should be disclosed.*

Lieutenant-Commander Kenworthy was obviously not satisfied with the replies to his questions and during the following week asked the Home Secretary:

> 'Why the alleged spy was not arrested and pro-ceeded against'. To which Sir W. Joynson-Hicks replied that 'It has not always been found desir-able to arrest spies or proceed against them at any particular moment.' (*Hansard*, 2 June 1927 Col. 523)

Lord Parmoor, an eminent lawyer in the 1920s had pro-vided one of the simplest and most telling legal arguments during a House of Lords debate (31 May 1927) when he said:

> 'If, however, incriminating documents had been found the Courts were open to the ordinary course of criminal procedure, and anyone implicated would have been liable both to punishment and deportation.'

---

*There is at present a campaign being conducted by some Members of Parliament, Journalists and other public figures for a 'Freedom of Informa-tion Act' to counter the employment of such a device.

It is interesting to recall that not only had the Cabinet been divided on taking the ultimate decision of breaking off diplomatic relations with the USSR, but that there were also sections of the Conservative press against it.

'The rupture is now defended on the ground that there has been a discovery of a system of espionage practised by the Russians. But espionage has been practised by civilized and uncivilized nations from time immemorial. All Governments practice it. Espionage has never been used as a pretext for breaking off relations.' (*The Sunday Express*, 29 May 1927)

An American writer, Carl Manzani, in a section of his book *Cold War in the 20s*, relates that 'in 1927 in two separate areas of China, controlled by two different War Lords, the two Soviet Embassies in those areas were raided on the same day. The suspicion that someone had nudged the War Lords was strengthened when the Russian Trade offices in London were raided by the British Government within a month of the Chinese raids.'[11]

The development of Anglo-Soviet trade had undoubtedly been an obstacle for the 'interventionists' to overcome and the timing of the Arcos raid was apparently an important factor in their plans for rupturing diplomatic relations. This was referred to by Litvinov in his statement of 26 May 1927. 'It is extremely significant', he said, 'that the raid on Arcos and the Trade Delegation was made the day after agreement had been reached with the Midland Bank for financing Soviet orders to English industry up to £10 million sterling, an agreement opening further prospects for the rapid development of economic relations between the two countries.'[12]

The Soviet Chargé d'Affaires and most of his staff left London on 3 June. Their train was due to leave Victoria Station at 11 am. Hundreds of friends and well-wishers crowded into the station to see them off. There were Members of Parliament and members of the TUC General Council. The Labour Party was officially represented by Arthur Henderson and the TUC by its Chairman, George

Hicks, and Walter Citrine. Among other prominent Labour leaders who were there that morning were George Lansbury, Ben Tillett, A.B. Swales and R.C. Wallhead.

Reactionary elements within the Conservative Party were so delighted by their achievement in bringing about the severance of Anglo-Soviet Diplomatic relations that they decided to celebrate the event by holding a rally in the Albert Hall. It was held on 15 July 1927. Next morning *The Times* reported that

> 'Lady Askwith presided at a "Victory Rally to celebrate routing the Reds" . . . the speakers included M. Coty, proprietor and editor of the *Figaro*, and Maitre T. Aubert, President of The Entente Against The Third International.'

In the following year this organization met in London at the Caxton Hall. *The Morning Post* reported 9 March 1928

> 'An organization known as the "International Entente To Create A United Front Against Bolshevism" was described by M. Theodore Aubert, its founder and President at a meeting at the Caxton Hall yesterday under the auspices of the Economic League and the Anti-Socialist Union.
>
> Lieutenant-Colonel Ashley, Minister of Transport, who presided, said the Entente now had centres in thirty one countries, and was represented in Great Britain by the Economic League.'

Notes

1. COATES, W.P. and Zelda, *History of Anglo-Soviet Relations*, p. 217
2. SUMNER, E.H., *A Survey of Russian History*, p. 308
3. MOSELEY, George, *China – Empire to People's Republic*, p. 52
4. COATES, W.P. and Zelda, *History of Anglo-Soviet Relations*, p. 254
5. EUDIN, Xenia Joukoff and FISHER, Harold H., *Soviet Russia and the West*, p. 374
6. COATES, W.P. and Zelda, *History of Anglo-Soviet Relations*, pp. 268–269
7. COATE, W.P. and Zelda, *History of Anglo-Soviet Relations*, pp. 273–274
8. FISCHER, Louis, *The Soviets in World Affairs*, pp. 504–505

9. COATES, W.P. and Zelda, *History of Anglo-Soviet Relations*, p. 278
10. *Documents on British Foreign Policy, No. 215*, 1927 Vol. III, Series 1A, pp. 338–340
11. MANZANI, Carl, *We Can Be Friends – Origins of the Cold War*, p. 118
12. *Soviet Documents on Foreign Policy* – Vol. II (ed. Jane Degras), p. 210

21

THE SIEVE

The euphoria of Locarno, with its creation of a Western Union, had barely subsided, than steps were being initiated to encourage the United States, although outside the League of Nations, to participate in the League's plans for a Collective Security – Disarmament Conference.

In December 1925, two months after Locarno, a Preparatory Disarmament Commission was established. Britain, France, Germany, Italy and the United States were represented at the outset; Russia did not join in the proceedings until 1927, when a Soviet delegation led by Litvinov attended meetings of the Preparatory Commission later that year.

A resolution proposed by Poland prohibiting wars of aggression had already been passed at a meeting of the League Assembly, but like all resolutions what remained to be seen was whether there would be serious intent to tackle the problem of implementation.

For close on two years the Preparatory Commission had been engaged in talks about talks on how to avoid the main issue – that of linking collective security with concrete proposals for disarmament. It was not until the arrival of the Soviet delegation to participate in the Commission's fourth session that the fundamental issue of disarmament was brought to the forefront.

On 30 November 1927, Litvinov put forward the Soviet Government's disarmament proposals which were :

'(a) The dissolution of all land, sea and air forces, and the non-admittance of their existence in any concealed form whatsoever.

(b) The destruction of all weapons, military supplies, means of chemical warfare, and all other forms of armament and means of destruction in the possession of troops, or military or general stores.

(c) The scrapping of all warships and military air vessels.

(d) The discontinuance of the calling up of citizens for military training, either in armies or public bodies.

(e) Legislation for the abolition of military service, either compulsory, voluntary or recruited.

(f) Legislation prohibiting the calling up of trained reserves.

(g) The destruction of fortresses and naval and air bases.

(h) The scrapping of military plants, factories and war industry plants in general industrial works.

(i) The discontinuance of assigning funds for military purposes both in State budgets and those of public bodies.

(j) The abolition of military, naval and air ministries, the dissolution of general staff and all kinds of military administrations, departments and institutions.

(k) Legislative prohibition of military propaganda, military training of the population and military education both by State and public bodies.

(l) Legislative prohibition of the patenting of all kinds of armaments and means of destruction, with a view to removal of the incentive to the invention of same.

(m) Legislation making the infringement of any of the above stipulations a grave crime against the State.

(n) The withdrawal of corresponding alteration of all legislative Acts, both of national and international scope, infringing the above stipulations.' (*The Daily Telegraph*, 1 December 1927)

Taking into consideration the question of time needed to implement their proposals, the Soviet Government suggested that the plan for complete disarmament should be carried out 'as soon as the respective Convention comes into force in order that all necessary measures for the destruction of military stores may be completed in a year's time'. But if some countries were not prepared to proceed at such a pace, then the Soviet Government would agree that the disarmament programme be fulfilled, step by step, over a period of four years.

The Daily News, 1 December 1927, commenting on Litvinov's statement said that its 'essence ... was the revolutionary doctrine that the right way to bring about disarmament is to disarm'.

His resolution pinpointing the fundamental reasons for the accumulations of armaments and the urgent need for positive steps towards disarmament was attacked throughout the British press. The main points in the resolution were :

> 'The existence of armaments and their evident tendency to continuous growth by their very nature inevitably lead to armed conflicts between nations, diverting the workers and peasants from peaceful, productive labour and bringing in their train countless disasters, and whereas an armed force is a weapon in the hands of the Great Powers for the oppression of the peoples of small and colonial countries, and whereas the complete abolition of armaments is at present the only real means of guaranteeing security and affording a guarantee against the outbreak of war, this fourth session of the Preparatory Commission for Disarmament resolves :
>
> 1. To proceed immediately to the working out in detail of a draft convention for complete general disarmament on the principles proposed by the Soviet Union delegation, and
> 2. Proposes the convocation not later than March 1928, of a Disarmament Conference for the discussion and confirmation of the proposals provided in Clause 1'.

There was a general feeling in Labour and in some

Liberal circles that the Soviet proposals should have been considered. But most of the Liberal and Tory press of 1 December 1927 denounced them as 'clumsy and cynical' (*Daily News*), 'grotesque' (*Daily Mail*), 'immature' (*Daily Telegraph*), 'Soviet absurdities' (*The Times*).

The Daily Herald was one of the few papers to welcome the proposals :

> 'The Russian plan' it declared, 'cannot be lightly dismissed as utopian. Nor would it be anything but a grave folly to denounce it as propaganda. It is a plan to which, if it is rejected, some effective alternative must be proposed or the professions of the Governments, and the pledges of the peace treaties be dishonoured. Mr Litvinov, in fact, has done one of those simple things which are startling by their very simplicity. He has invited the Disarmament Commission to discuss – Disarmament! The reply of the other Governments should afford a significant revelation of their real intentions'. (*The Daily Herald*, 1 December 1927)

When Britain's Prime Minister was questioned in the House of Commons by Tom Johnston, the Labour MP, 'whether the Government is considering these proposals, and if, in view of their importance, he can give an assurance that the British delegates at Geneva will not be authorized to negative them without an opportunity having been afforded for their discussion in the House of Commons', Baldwin replied, 'The Russian proposals do not appear to have been regarded by the Committee as a practical and helpful contribution to the problem and there would accordingly be no advantage in discussing them in this House.' (*Hansard*, 5 December 1927 Col 973)

In March 1928, the Soviet disarmament proposals were raised during a further meeting of the Preparatory Commission. The Japanese representative pointed out that 'the Soviet project contradicts the Constitution of the League of Nations'. Litvinov's reply was 'Although Article 8 of the League of Nations' Covenant only mentions the limitation of armaments, it appears to us that merely minimum obligations were intended, and this Article should by no means be allowed to serve as an obstacle to further and complete disarmament, should this be desired by members of the League . . . '

Anticipating that the Soviet disarmament proposals would be rejected, Litvinov compromised with a proposition that a Draft Convention for Partial Disarmament should be considered as a first step.

The revised Draft Convention for the Reduction of Armaments was based upon the existing level of a nation's armed forces. Having divided the nations of the world into four categories, the Soviet Government proposed :

'(a) The most highly armed . . . to reduce their forces by half;
(b) the next powerfully armed by one-third;
(c) the weakest by one quarter' and
(d) that those states which were 'practically disarmed' to have their arms 'fixed under special conditions.'[1]

Opposition to the latest Soviet proposals by the three major powers in the Preparatory Commission, Britain, France and the United States, ensured their non-acceptance.

With two of the world's major powers, the USA and the USSR, not in the League of Nations, genuine attempts at disarmament, even assuming that there was a sincere desire for it, were inevitably hampered. In any case, Litvinov had put some of the League's most prominent members on the spot. Although there had been an economic upturn in the war-torn countries during recent years, the memories of the 1914–18 holocaust still dominated the thoughts of millions of people in the participant countries. The Soviets had pushed the subject of disarmament to the forefront.

With the League's Preparatory Commission bogged down by a state of inertia, the United States felt that the time was ripe to assert some form of leadership in the world. The League had, in any event, been regarded in Washington as an Anglo-French affair. Briand had proposed, in April 1927, that a pact between France and the

276

United States should be concluded. After quite a long delay, Frank Kellogg, the American Secretary of State, replied to Briand's proposals with a counter-proposal that the pact be more comprehensive and should include other nations.

The Kellogg-Briand Pact was worded in such a way as to attract the greatest number of signatories, while at the same time damping down the widespread demands for disarmament. Riddled with escape clauses, devoid of real content or commitment, imperial and non-imperial countries alike could have no qualms about being able to agree to :

> **Article 1** 'Solemnly declare in the name of their respective peoples, that they condemn recourse to war for the solution of international controversies, and renounce it as an instrument of national policy in their relations with one another'.
>
> **Article 2** 'agree that the settlement or solution of all disputes or conflicts, of whatever nature or of whatever origin they may be, which may arise among them, shall never be sought except by pacific means'.

The United States was able to exempt from the terms of the Pact any action that would conflict with the upholding of the Monroe Doctrine.* France insisted that the Pact must not include wars of self-defence or commitments to treaty obligations, while the British Government decided that 'freedom of action' to protect 'special and vital interests' wherever they may be, must be included. On 19 May 1928, it issued a statement declaring :

---

*'A principle of American policy declining any European intervention in the political affairs of the American continent . . . President Monroe declared in a message dated 2 December 1823, that the American Continents, by the free and independent condition which they have assumed and maintain, are henceforth not to be considered as subjects of future colonization by any European powers . . .'.

'The Doctrine is less popular in the Latin-American States which suspect it of being an instrument of US hegemony and economic penetration . . . The Monroe Doctrine is not international law, but a national policy of the United States.' (ex *Penguin Political Dictionary*)

'There are certain regions of the world the welfare and integrity of which constitute a special and vital interest for our peace and safety. His Majesty's Government have been at pains to make it clear in the past that interference with these regions cannot be suffered. Their protection against attack is to the British Empire a measure of self-defence. It must be clearly understood that His Majesty's Government in Great Britain accept the new treaty upon the distinct understanding that it does not prejudice their freedom of action in this respect.' (*The Times*, 21 May 1928)

The Pact had excluded wars of self-defence. This was clearly defined in the American Note of 23 June. 'If this fact had not been stipulated it was because of the "difficulties encountered by an attempt to define what constitutes an attack".'[2]

What then was left of the Kellogg Pact with all its escape clauses and no teeth to compel implementation? Disarmament had been rejected, replaced by pious words and declarations of intent to prohibit all wars of aggression. War 'as an instrument of national policy' could still be justified, thus in later years the Italian representative was able to claim that its attack on Abyssinia was not a violation of the Kellogg Pact. The first violation came in 1931. Citing the British Declaration, the Japanese Government argued that their occupation of Manchuria and Jehol was an act of self-defence and did not contravene the terms of the Kellogg Pact nor the Covenant of the League of Nations.

And while the major powers were extracting the teeth from Kellogg's Pact, a British Cabinet Minister, Lord Birkenhead, was in Berlin preparing the ground, not for peace, but for a possible war against Soviet Russia.

The Daily Express, 17 April 1928, reported from its Berlin correspondent :

'Lord Birkenhead was the guest of the Anglo-American Press Club here at luncheon today. In the course of the informal discussion after lunch, Lord Birkenhead gave it as his opinion that

Germany was giving up her policy of holding the balance between the Western Powers and Russia in favour of a closer connection with England and France.

An interview of a non-political nature with Lord Birkenhead appears in today's *Berliner Zeitung Am Mittag*. The newspaper commenting on Lord Birkenhead's presence in Berlin, declares his object in coming here "is of course, eminently political".

"Lord Birkenhead", it says, "sees in Germany a future ally in the conflict which is bound sooner or later to develop with Soviet Russia. That he should come to Berlin at the present juncture and converse with Dr Stresemann is not specially remarkable, in view of the fact that there are quite a number of problems waiting for discussion, such as, for instance, Mr Kellogg's disarmament programme, the visit of King Amanullah* to Moscow, and Anglo-Russian differences."'

Every effort was made by the British Government to exclude Soviet Russia from joining the signatories of the Kellogg-Briand Pact. Its attitude was expressed by Austen Chamberlain in the course of a reply to the United States, dated 19 May 1928 :

'Universality would, in any case, be difficult of attainment and might even be inconvenient, for there are some States whose Governments have not been universally recognized, and some which are scarcely in a position to ensure the maintenance of good order and security within their territories.'

Russia was excluded from the list of countries invited to participate in the final stages of the negotiations and their suspicions were bluntly expressed by Chicherin in a statement reported in *Izvestia* on 5 August 1928 :

'The exclusion of the Soviet Government from

---

*King of Afghanistan.

these negotiations leads us, in the first place, to the assumption that among the real objectives of the initiators of this pact there obviously was and is an endeavour to make of this pact a weapon for isolating and fighting the Soviet Union. The negotiations regarding the conclusion of the Kellogg Pact are obviously an integral part of the policy of encircling the Soviet Union, which at the present moment occupies the central point of the international relations of the whole world.'[3]

Kellogg's Pact for the 'renunciation of war' was signed in Paris on 27 August 1928 by Belgium, Czechoslovakia, France, Germany, Great Britain and the Dominions, Italy, Japan, Poland and the United States – just fifteen countries. The Latin American countries, Argentine, Brazil, Bolivia and Salvador, tied to the Monroe Doctrine, refused to take part in the procedings.

The Soviet Union made her own contribution to the renunciation of war by concluding agreements with her neighbours. She 'persuaded all of her neighbours to sign the Litvinov protocol which put the pact into effect between them and the Soviet Union. The representatives of Latvia, Estonia, Poland and Rumania signed on 9 February 1929, and Lithuania, Turkey and Persia soon followed.'[4]

Another British General Election was due in 1929 and the three major parties were again busy preparing their Manifestos to present to the British electorate. The dominant issues were unemployment and world peace.

'The promotion of peace and disarmament has been the prime object of our foreign policy and that policy has proved successful over the whole field of foreign affairs' declared the Tories. 'Labour will re-establish diplomatic and commercial relations with Russia' dominated the Party's appeal, while the Liberals' policy would be 'to re-establish normal political and economic relations with Russia at the earliest possible date.'

The pressure of commercial interests and the Trade Union Movement had forced the resumption of diplomatic relations with the USSR as a priority matter. After the signing of the Kellogg Pact, the Conservative Government felt that, in spite of its severance of diplomatic relations with the USSR, the British electorate would be taken in by the facade of having promoted peace and disarmament.

In the event, the Labour Party won 287 seats, the Conservatives 261, and the Liberals reduced to only 59. Thus, for the first time, Labour had risen to become the biggest political party in Britain, although still in a Parliamentary minority should the Liberals decide to join forces with the Conservatives. The combined Labour and Liberal votes came to 13½ million, approximately, and the Conservatives around 8½ million. A Labour Government came into office on 5 June 1929.

As in 1924, the incoming Labour Government began to retreat from its commitment of resuming diplomatic relations with the USSR. It was not until 1 October, and after pressure from the Trades Union Congress, that agreement was reached with the USSR for the resumption of full diplomatic relations.

In May 1930 a number of European Governments received a Memorandum from the French Government. Its subject was 'the organization of a System of Federal Union'. On 8 September the Memorandum and the various replies were presented in the form of a French White Paper to the League's European members. The USSR, Turkey and Iceland were not among the recipients of either the Memorandum or the White Paper.

The idea of a United States of Europe, but excluding Russia, had been pioneered by Briand who in September 1929 'proposed the creation of a United States of Europe' but to begin with a measure of Economic Union.'[5]

That this was part of a plan to isolate the USSR economically became evident when on 3 October 1930, barely a month after the French Note, a Council of Ministers, meeting in Paris, issued a decree which backed the French Government should it decide to either prohibit or restrict the importation of Soviet goods.

The Soviet Government was naturally suspicious of this move which it regarded as a first step towards the launching of an international commercial blockade against her. On 20 October 1930 she countered the French move by issuing her own decree which, in effect, excluded France from the

Soviet market.

A committee was established to supervise the operations of the proposed European Federal Union and it met in Geneva on 16 January 1931. Of the twenty seven European countries represented, twenty two were either at Prime Minister or Foreign Minister level. 'One thing is very plain' commented the *Manchester Guardian*'s special correspondent on 17 January 1931, and that is 'that the French Government is at the head of the European Combination against Soviet Russia.'

The French policy of isolating the USSR economically was somewhat diffused by Arthur Henderson, Britain's new Foreign Minister, who proposed that the matter be handed over to a Sub-Committee, which would examine the economic problems involved and at the same time look into the question of whether the League should seek the co-operation of non-members, and under what conditions. Henderson's proposal was accepted, and on 20 January 1931 the Council adopted the following resolution :

'The Commission of Inquiry for European Union, having regard to the resolution of the Assembly of the League of Nations of 17 September 1930, decides to study the world economic crisis in so far as it affects the European countries as a whole, and to invite through the Secretary-General the Governments of Iceland, Turkey and the Union of Soviet Republics to participate in this study'.

Henderson who was Chairman of the League's Preparatory Commission on Disarmament warned :

'Through failure to carry out the policy of disarmament, we may drift into the situation which existed before 1914. Mere limitation of Armaments may not be sufficient. There are some people who say that the drift has already begun, that nations are falling into the old system of alliances for warlike ends, and that these alliances are undermining the League.' (*The Daily Telegraph*, 21 January 1931)

The French plan was beginning to misfire. It had become evident that there were a number of European countries who believed that the USSR should be invited unconditionally, and did not accept the aims of France and her aides in the Little Entente – Poland and Roumania – who wanted Russia excluded.

Some form of a 'Pan-European Union' had been encouraged soon after the Briand-Stresemann discussions in 1926 – the first stage after Locarno. Based upon the Pan European Movement, which was founded in 1923, it held Congresses in 1926 and 1930 at which many leading statesmen participated. Its policy was to create a bloc of like-minded anti-Soviet European nations. The Movement proclaimed through its publication, *Paneuropa*, that Europe should 'close its economic front against Russia' and establish 'a single army against the Russian danger'; a policy which naturally had the blessing of Briand, Honorary President of the Pan-European Union.

On 4 October 1929, the *Manchester Guardian*'s assessment of Briand's Pan-European policy appeared in its weekly edition :

'He has become obsessed with the Communist danger, and the isolation of Russia has become one of the chief aims of his policy. There is reason to believe that the desire to isolate Russia has something to do with his whole proposal of a European Federation, from which his faithful henchman in the Press, M. Jules Sauerwein, declared in the *Matin* three or four months ago that Russia was to be excluded.

In this connection the recent revelations about the negotiations between French and German Nationalists are significant. It is particularly significant that Herr Arnold Rechberg should have taken an active part in those negotiaions, for it was he, as the agent of General Ludendorf, tried to induce the British and French Governments in 1919 to allow Ludendorf to reconstitute the German Army for the purpose of attacking Russia.'

283

Notes

1. COATES, W.P. and Zelda, *A History of Anglo-Soviet Relations* p. 400
2. EYCK, Erich, *The Weimar Republic* p. 176
3. EUDIN, Xenia Joukoff, and FISHER, Harold H., *Soviet Russia and the West* p. 352
4. FLEMING, D.F., *The Cold War and its Origins* Vol. I. p. 49
5. TINT, Herbert, *France Since 1918* p. 30

22

SOFT FOUNDATIONS AND THE VENEER OF CIVILIZATION

Five years had now elapsed since the inauguration of the Dawes Plan and the subsequent revival of Western economies. But the legacy of Versailles, with its ill conceived judgements on European reconstruction, rehabilitation and the many problems of German reparations still remained.

In 1929 a Committee representing both creditor and debtor countries was set up in order to reach 'a complete and final settlement of the reparation problem'. Its President was Owen D. Young, who, together with this Committee, 'began to examine anew Germany's capacity to pay and to formulate a definite Reparations settlement in place of the Dawes Plan whose first full yearly payment of 2,500 million marks became due for 1928–29.'[1]

Godfrey Scheele in his book, *The Weimar Republic*, describes how 'between 1924 and 1929 Germany was like a bottomless gulf into which foreign money poured. The Reich, the States, the Municipalities and the great industrial enterprises were all irrigated by foreign loans and because the demand always exceeded the supply, rates of interest remained phenomenally high . . .

'Estimates of total German indebtedness varies. The official German estimate given to the Young Plan Committee at Basle' says Scheele, 'was 28,500 to 30,000 million Gold Marks' and that 'Germany's total Reparations transfers between 1918 and 1931 amounted to 20,770 million Gold Marks according to the Reparations Commission's estimate, and of this amount only 5,055 millions were paid in cash or gold, the remainder in kind.'[2]

The Plan which was agreed to after a meeting of the heads of the participant states at the Hague, in August

1929, had been vehemently attacked in Germany by the Nationalist Party* and leaders of the big industrial companies. According to Fritz Thyssen, a leading opponent, 'when the Young Plan began to be enforced a number of German private banks had to suspend payment because they were not in a position to fulfil the demands of the American banks for repayment of the loans which had been granted to them'.[3]

Dr Schacht, who had become President of the Reichsbank, was one of the German economic experts on the Young Committee and he became involved in a row with Stresemann, who 'in exchange for the economic concessions of a further issue of German railway bonds in favour of the Allies . . . secured a promise of the final evacuation of the Rhineland by 30 June 1930'. This was criticized by Schacht 'on the ground that Germany had made economic concessions in return for an evacuation to which she was entitled in virtue of her fulfilment of obligations by signing the London Agreement [Dawes Plan] of 1924' and that 'by maintaining the occupation the Allies were breaking the Treaty of Versailles . . .'[4]

The Dawes Plan had undoubtedly played an important part in stabilizing and eventually boosting the German economy, especially in the heavy engineering, electrical and chemical industries which laid the foundation not only of her peacetime economy but also gave a particular boost to her armaments industry.

In actual financial terms, the Young Plan was for Germany to pay 34,000 million Gold Marks with annual payments rising from 1,700 million to 2,400 million. From 1966 onwards Germany's war indebtedness to the Allies was to be progressively decreased until final payment in 1988.

In the process of restructuring German reparations the Young Committee of experts had provided the basis for an international bank, which according to their report should 'become an increasingly close and valuable link in the co-operation of central banking institutions generally, a co-operation essential to the continuing stability of the world's

*Stresemann was a leading member of the Nationalist Party.

credit structure'. The Bank of International Settlements was founded in 1930 which in the following years was to become an international finance centre for governmental and other financial institutions.

The Committee's Report stated :

> 'In the natural course of development it is to be expected that the bank will in time become an organization, not simply or even predominantly concerned with the handling of reparations, but also with furnishing to the world of international commerce and finance important facilities hitherto lacking . . .'

Neither the Young Plan, nor this new international banking system was able to stave off the collapse of the New York Stock Market and the widespread economic slump that had consequently spread like wildfire throughout the industrialized world. Apart from a brief period in 1921 the United States had, since 1914, experienced continuous boom conditions.

In 1928 Herbert Hoover was reported to have declared that 'the outlook for the world today is for the greatest era of commercial expansion in history' and that 'unemployment in the sense of distress is finally disappearing; we in America today are nearer to the final triumph over poverty than ever before in the history of any land'. This state of euphoria was to persist right up to the eve of the crash. Speculative investing both at home and abroad had reaped massive profits. Industry had flourished to such a degree that leaders of industry, such as the President of the giant Bethlehem Steel Corporation, felt moved to declare in 1928 that he was able to 'say with confidence that there has been established a foundation upon which there may be built a structure of prosperity far exceeding anything we have yet enjoyed.' (from *The Iron Age,* 1 November 1928). His confidence must have been reinforced by an industrial colleague, the President of General Motors, who a few days earlier had been reported in *The New York Times*, 29 October 1928, to have stated that his 'standpoint regarding 1929 is based on the conviction that our general economic and industrial situation is thoroughly sound' – a combination of blissful ignorance and wishful thinking that had also permeated millions of American homes.

The vast expanse of ocean between Europe and America could not separate the interdependence of the economies. European countries, unable to meet their financial commitments through the usual trading or financial transfers, had instead been shipping vast amounts of gold from their reserves into the United States. Kellogg, the American Ambassador to Britain in 1925, was asked by an eminent British banker, 'Your country has most of the gold in the world; what are you going to do about it?' His reply was 'Bring the pound sterling to a gold basis and restore the currencies of Europe, and the gold question will settle itself.' (*The Times*, 31 January 1925)

Unfortunately for millions of American and European people, neither the fundamental malaise nor the gold question did 'settle itself'. The Wall Street crash in October 1929 was not an isolated event. It had been preceded by the beginnings of an economic recession which had started earlier in the year in Germany and parts of Central Europe.

The symptoms of an impending economic crisis had been visible for quite some time. James Joll reinforces this point in his book, *Europe Since 1870*, when he states that 'there had been some signs of an impending recession even before the crash in America : prices of agricultural produce, the staple export of most of Eastern Europe, had been falling for about a year' and that 'the fall in the prices of food and raw materials which hit the agricultural countries of Eastern Europe was accompanied by a drop in the demand for the industrial exports of the more developed countries in Western and Northern Europe. Peasants were left without markets and industrial workers without employment.'[5]

In America, too, the economy had begun to contract some months before the collapse of the Stock Market. Panic stricken speculators and ordinary shareholders unloaded just under thirteen million shares on to the New York Stock Exchange on that Black Thursday, 24 October – and during the next five days a further three and a half million. Thousands of banks had to close, many never to open again.

288

From Black Thursday until the beginning of November the average value of the shares on the New York Stock Exchange fell by around fifty per cent. The imposition of American tariffs against imports from countries, particularly those which had become dependent upon American loans, played a crucial part in triggering off the great crash. According to J.K. Galbraith 'countries could not cover their adverse trade balance with the United States with increased payments of Gold, at least not for long. This meant that they had either to increase their exports to the United States or reduce their imports or default on their past loans.'[6] This applied particularly to Germany which had re-equipped its industry with the help of foreign capital, hoping to flood the markets of the world with mass produced goods in the face of fierce competition from the other industrial countries. There was undoubtedly the need for many of the products, but productivity had greatly outstripped purchasing power. Millions of low wage workers in the industrial countries and poverty stricken peasants in the primary producing countries could not buy their mass produced goods.

Between 1925 and 1929 Germany's foreign debt had risen from £125 million (2.5 milliard Reichmarks) to £1,250 million (25 milliard Reichmarks). With the exception of Soviet Russia, which was in the midst of its first Five-Year Plan, practically the whole of Europe, North America and the various colonial dependencies were in the grip of the worst economic crisis known for many hundreds of years. The Austrian Bank, the Credit Anstalt, went bankrupt in May 1931 to be followed two months later by two of Germany's leading banks, the Darmstadter and the National.

By the end of 1931, as a result of the acute monetary situation, Britain decided to abandon its adherence to the Gold Standard and devalued the pound. Her example was followed by most of the industrial countries, aggravating still further the severe economic crisis. The problems created by the inter-Allied war debts and the German reparations were temporarily eased by President Hoover who, in June 1932, recommended that there should be a one year moratorium on the payments of the outstanding debts.

The economic, political and social effects of the slump had shaken the very foundations of the world's leading industrial countries, none more so than in Germany where unemployment had risen at such a rate that from one and three quarter million in 1929, it had increased to four and a half million in 1931, five million in 1932, and by the winter of 1932–33, six million Germans were out of work.

Britain's second Labour Government, which had taken over in June 1929, was immediately confronted with the challenge of seeking remedies to mitigate the effects of the oncoming economic crisis. The majority of British working people were looking to a Labour Government to safeguard their interests and especially their jobs. Unemployment at the time was just under 1,200,000 but by the autumn of 1931 it had risen to just under three million. The interdependent nature of the capitalist countries with their colonial and neo-colonial dependencies inevitably had serious repercussions upon international trade. Britain with its vast Empire encompassing some 500 million people, had suffered a catastrophic fall in its export trade. From £839 millions in 1929, it slumped to £461 millions by 1931. London, with sterling as the leading international currency, had for many years been the financial centre of the capitalist world. This privileged position had enabled successive British Governments to cushion their balance of payments deficits with the incomes derived from overseas investments as well as those of shipping, insurances and other financial services.

Unfortunately these 'invisible' exports or imports provided very little comfort to British industry generally, tending in the long run, if though indirectly, to export jobs and import unemployment. Investing in low wage industrial enterprises abroad had for years held back British industrial development through shortage of capital in Britain itself. And now, with the cancerous effects of the world-wide economic slump, the colonial dependencies, as well as the self-governing dominions, had been compelled to cut back their requirements from the mother country. In the case of the colonies, the massive drop in world prices for most of their primary products had severely undermined their precarious economies.

The wealth of the British Empire with its tin, timber, rubber, gold, oil and all kinds of simple and exotic food products did not save British workers from being thrown out of work, and the poverty that went with it. The pressure of the employers' federations and the financial institutions upon the Government led to cuts in the wages of civil servants and other public employees, as well as a reduction in unemployment benefits.

Part of the criticism of the second Labour Government was not so much what it did during its two years of office, but of what it did not do. It listened to the bankers and big employers and allowed itself to be intimidated by threats of cut-backs and closures and a 'run on the pound'. Its promise to raise the school leaving age to fifteen was abandoned, as was that of the seven hour day for the miners. In the Spring of 1931 the Prime Minister and Phillip Snowden, the Chancellor of the Exchequer, were advised that the balance of payments for the ensuing year would be heavily in deficit and that 'we were on the edge of a precipice'. To balance the budget and restore confidence in the pound it was proposed that there must be a cut in unemployment benefits. And it was primarily this issue which opened up the division within the Cabinet and brought about the Government's resignation. Not satisfied with bringing down the Labour Government, the leading members of the Cabinet's 'inner ring', MacDonald, Snowden and Thomas, joined forces with the Tories and a section of Liberals to form a National Government. The other members of the Cabinet, which included the Foreign Minister, Arthur Henderson, and J.R. Clynes, the Home Secretary, remained loyal to the the Party.

The National Government soon got to work. Avoiding some of the normal Parliamentary procedures, it decided to issue a series of Orders-in-Council which instituted the cuts in the pay of civil servants, teachers and other public employees, as well as members of His Majesty's Forces. In addition, the threatened reduction in payments to the unemployed was quickly put into operation. But the major resistance to the cuts came where it was least expected. It occurred in the British Navy at Invergordon, which was at the time the main harbour for the Atlantic Fleet.

In September 1931 there was a mutiny in the Lower Ranks. The insensitivity of the Government had not only instituted cuts for the Lower Ranks, which varied from between 13.6 per cent and 25 per cent, but had lessened the blow for Officers by limiting their cuts from between 3.7 per cent and 7 per cent. Naturally the naval ratings became incensed, not only by the cuts, but also by the anomalies.

The mutiny, which the sailors preferred to describe as 'being on strike' affected quite a number of ships, including the battleships *Rodney* and *Valiant*. In all some 12,000 men were 'on strike'. A mutiny in the British Fleet was world-wide news, and its effect was to undermine international confidence in Britain's ability to handle its economic affairs. Invergordon led to further pressure on the pound, which in turn was to become a major factor in the decision of the Government to go off the Gold Standard. As for the Navy, the Government announced on 21 September that, as far as it was concerned, there would be no reductions above ten per cent. It had decided not to court-martial or victimize the ring-leaders, but in spite of this assurance, thirty six were nevertheless dismissed from the Service.

The effect of the cuts was biting deep into the lives of millions of British people. In the Winter of 1932 hundreds of thousands of families were subjected to a Means Test before they could receive a mere subsistence amount upon which they were expected to live. Meanwhile, a National Unemployed Workers' Movement had organized Hunger Marches and nation-wide demonstrations culminating in a massive 100,000 gathering in Hyde Park, followed by 150,000 in Trafalgar Square on the following Sunday.

One of the many tragedies for the British Labour Movement during this period was the loss of the *Daily Herald* which the leaders of the Labour Party had allowed to pass out of the Party's overall control by transferring a majority shareholding – fifty one per cent – to the millionaire publishing company, Odhams Press.

In France the economic crisis did not really begin to grip the nerve centres of her economy until some three years after the Wall Street crash. She had, for many years, been a popular country for foreign tourists. Her unemployment at the time was minimal compared to Britain and Germany, but by the end of 1931 the effects of the economic crisis had caught up with her. The number of tourists coming into the country had begun to dwindle and her export trade was on the decline. According to J.P.T. Bury, 'the Government had intervened for the first time to limit production, starting with the vineyards'.[7] This inevitably led to a rise in unemployment. The slide into the economic abyss was further accelerated by Britain going off the Gold Standard and devaluing the pound.

The French people were due for a general election in 1932. Briand, who had dominated the French political scene since the mid-twenties, had died and his successor, Pierre Laval, after a brief period as Prime Minister was replaced by Andre Tardieu.

As in Britain, the French Government had thrown the main burden of the slump upon the shoulders of their working people. It did very little to protect the workers from the effects of unemploymentand short-time working. A Bill to give workers a week's annual holiday with pay had been rejected by the Senate. Consequently, the election developed into a bitter campaign for worker's rights and employment. With the backing of all the most reactionary elements of French society, Tardieu decided to use anti-communism as his electoral weapon. The French 'establishment' with its '200 families' was determined to preserve its privileged position from wherever the opposition came.

The first ballot was held in May and during the height of the subsequent campaigning the President, Doumer, was assassinated. The murderer turned out to be a White Russian émigré by the name of Goguloff. 'Tardieu tried to exploit the murderer's Russian birth, in the best cynical anti-Bolshevist tradition.'[8] Fortunately for the French people Tardieu and his associates were rejected.

The new Chamber of Deputies was mostly comprised of representatives from the Socialist and Radical parties. Edouard Herriot, the Radicals' leader, became the new Prime Minister, but the Socialists once again refused to join a Radical led Cabinet.

It was inevitable that the European country which would be most affected by the economic crisis would be Germany. With the rapid decline in her exports and the massive withdrawal of foreign loans and investments, hundreds of companies were forced into bankruptcy. This, together with the closure of factories all over the country, threw millions of workers on to the streets.

The Coalition Government could not muster a sufficient majority to carry on and in March 1930 was replaced by another coalition, an amalgamation of six parties, but excluding the Social Democrats and the Communists. Although the Social Democrats had the largest party in the Reichstag, they nevertheless refused to participate. The new Chancellor, Heinrich Bruning, leader of the Catholic Centre Party, tried to force through his remedy – a deflationary package of widespread cuts in governmental expenditure, cuts in wages and increased taxation.

Under Article 48 of the Weimar Constitution he declared a State of Emergency whereby Germany would be governed through Presidential Decrees. The senile Hindenburg was prepared to sign almost anything which implied strong right-wing action. Brüning called for the dissolution of the Reichstag and set a date for new elections. In addition to imposing the usual deflationary policies for stabilizing the economy, he also had plans for restoring the Hohenzollern monarchy. With unemployment at around three million and rapidly increasing throughout the country, the German people went to the polls on 14 September 1930, many disillusioned with the established political parties and their leaders whom they believed had been responsible for their economic misfortunes. When the results began filtering through on the following day it was soon realized that something sensational was about to happen. By the end of the day, not only Germany, but practically the whole world knew that Hitler and his Nazi Party had received a massive electoral boost. Six and a half million Germans had voted for the Nazis, increasing their representation in the Reichstag from twelve to one hundred and seven deputies, making them the second largest political party after the Social Democrats, who, although having lost ten of their deputies, still retained one hundred and forty three. The Communists received four and a half million votes, increasing their representation from fifty four to seventy seven.

The Nazi Party, built and nourished by millions of

Deutschmarks secretly provided by Fritz Thyssen and his industrialist friends in the Ruhr, was now at last showing results for their investments. Their Party had arrived.

The effect of the elections and the Presidential Decrees only aggravated the crisis even further with the financial collapse of the Berlin Stock Exchange and vast amounts of capital flowing out of the country. During 1931, of the many Brüning Decrees which Hindenburg signed was one which, as in Britain, cut the dole for the unemployed.

The political and social effects of the great slump had certainly revived the prospects of Hitler and the Nazi Party. The return to the years of mass unemployment, insecurity, disillusionment and general discontent gave them ample scope for exploiting the fears of a wide variety of people. The party label – Nationalsozialistische Deutsche Arbeiterpartei – The National Socialist German Workers' Party – was a useful cover to mask the real intentions of the Nazis and their financial backers.

In the Spring of 1932, Germany was in the throes of a Presidential election. Hindenburg, who had been President since 1925 was persuaded to stand again, backed by Brüning and the Centre Party. The Communist Party was represented by Ernst Thälmann* and the Nazis by Hitler.

At the first poll in March 1932 none of the candidates gained the necessary overall majority and a second poll was held a month later. The Social Democrats, having decided to refrain from putting up their own candidate, told their supporters to vote for Hindenburg. The old Field Marshal was returned with close on nineteen and a half million votes. Hitler received thirteen million and Thälmann just under four million.

Chancellor Brüning survived barely two months and was succeeded by the aristocratic representative of the Prussian Junkers, Franz von Papen. His backers had persuaded Hindenburg that Brüning was incapable of tackling the crisis. No sooner had von Papen installed himself in office than he induced Hindenburg to dissolve the Reichstag and in July 1932 there was yet another election. The Nazis

---

*Thälmann was a member of the Reichstag from 1924 to 1933. Arrested (3 March 1933) soon after Hitler came to power and sent to a concentration camp. He was murdered in Buchenwald, 18 August 1944.

received fourteen million votes, giving them 230 seats, making them the leading party in the Reichstag.

The Social Democrats had by now lost the confidence of millions of their former supporters. Their vote had slumped to only eight million, reducing their representation in the Reichstag to 133, whilst the Communist vote went up to around five million, giving them 89 seats.

The decline of the German Social Democratic Party is described in some detail by Egon Larsen, a young German reporter. In his book, *Weimar Eyewitness*, he points to 'their spineless behaviour in Prussia' as a leading contributory factor. Prussia was Federal Germany's largest autonomous State and in 1932 it was under the control of a Social Democratic Government which had the support of the Prussian Parliament. 'These Prussian ministers were as many thorns in the flesh of the new nationalist Reichs ministers' and they were removed by von Papen who had 'made Hindenburg sign a decree appointing him, Papen, "Reichs Commissar for Prussia", replacing the elected Prussian Government. It was a flagrant breach of the Weimar Constitution. On July 20, 1932, Schleicher, now Reichswehr Minister, ordered his Berlin garrison comman-der, General von Rundstedt, to take the "necessary action". This consisted in sending an officer and a few Reichswehr soldiers to the Prussian Ministry of the Interior . . . They found the Minister, Carl Severing, in his office, and ordered him to leave, threatening to use force. Severing did not resist, but declared that he was going "under duress to avoid bloodshed", and went. Just as meekly and unheroic-ally behaved the rest of the Prussian ministers, who were mostly arrested in their homes and kept overnight in an officers' penitentiary . . . The Social-Democratic Party and the trade unions admonished their members to remain calm in the face of this outrage by the Papen clique. The Communists' call for a general strike was ignored.

'Those of us who had still believed in the staying power of Germany's largest party – this was what the Social Democrats still were – felt betrayed and forsaken. They had been the creators and guardians of our Constitution, and now they had given in to unconstitutional force, yielding their offices without a fight and with hardly a murmur. The end of the Republic seemed near.'[9]

Von Papen's dissolution of the Reichstag was coupled with the lifting of the ban on the Nazi para-military Storm Troopers, the SA and the SS. Encouraged by this, armed Nazi thugs ran amok all over Germany. The 'storm troopers were using firearms everywhere . . . in Munich they tried to invade the house of the Bavarian Prime Minister; trade-union head quarters were stormed and ransacked all over the country. The worst incident happened in a small town in Silesia, where twenty seven people were killed and one hundred and eighty badly injured by shots. In Altona, Hamburg's working-class district, fourteen were killed in a gun fight between Nazis and Communists. In the night after the July elections, the East Prussian capital, Königsberg, was the scene of several murders by the SA; a former police chief and a town councillor were shot in their beds. In Upper Silesia, storm troopers broke into the home of a Communist worker and trampled him to death in front of his mother; the five culprits were sentenced to death by a courageous Judge at Beuthen – a most unusual sentence in 1932, and it had an unusual sequel:'

Hitler blamed von Papen for the Beuthen judgement. '"Now I know your so-called objectivity", he said in an open telegram. "The seed that is now growing will no longer be stunted by penalties".'[10]

Von Papen was unable to win Nazi support and once again the Reichstag was dissolved pending new elections. The November 1932 elections created quite a sensation. The Nazis lost two million votes – thirty four seats. The Social Democrats lost a further twelve seats, while the Communists gained eleven.

General von Schleicher, the former Reichswehr Minister, a von Papen rival, became the new Chancellor. Schleicher took over at a time when he believed that he could subdue the Nazi movement by placing it under his own command. Were it not for Fritz Thyssen and his industrialist friends, the Nazi party could not have survived.

Ernst Henri in his book *Hitler Over Europe*, which was first published in 1934, explains how Thyssen planned to rescue the collapsing Nazi Party.

'Thyssen persuaded . . . the two political centres of

German Ruhr capital, the "Bergbauverein Essen" and the "Nord West Gruppe derEisen-und-Stahlindustrie" to agree that every coal and steel concern had, by way of a particular obligatory tax, to deliver a certain sum into the election funds of the National Socialists. In order to raise this money, the price of coal was raised in Germany. For the Presidential elections of 1932 alone Thyssen provided the Nazis with more than three million marks within a few days ... Without Thyssen's money Hitler would never have achieved such a success, and the party would have broken up already at the time of the von Papen elections at the end of 1932, when it lost two million votes and the Strasser Group* announced its secession ... But just as before Thyssen had raised Hitler by his financial machinery, so he now rescued him by his political machinery. To bring off this coup Thyssen employed two of his political friends and agents Hugenberg (who is one of the directors of the Thyssen Steel Trust Group) and von Papen.

'In the middle of January a secret meeting between Hitler and von Papen was held at Cologne in the house of Baron von Schröder, partner of the banking house J.H. Stein, which is closely related with Flick and Thyssen. Baron Schroder is at the same time a personal friend of von Papen's. At this meeting Hitler came to an agreement with von Papen, whom he had up till then opposed in public as vigorously as possible, to form a Coalition Government together. Hitler at once went to see Thyssen; it was settled that Hitler would in any case accept a renewed invitation fïrm Hindenburg to enter the Government (Hitler had previously rejected such an invitation). The action could begin. Although, thanks to an indiscretion, the news of the meeting in Cologne got into the papers a few days later, the conspiracy against Schleicher was complete. The allied group, Thyssen-Hitler-von Papen-Hugenburg, backed by the entire German reactionary forces, succeeded in drawing to their side the son of President von Hindenburg, Major Oscar von Hindenburg, who had so far stood by his old regimental friend Schleicher. In this way the sudden fall of

*Gregor Strasser – leader of a faction within the Nazi Party. Murdered on Hitler's instructions, 30 June 1934.

Schleicher and the sensational nomination of Hitler came about . . . Thyssen had won.'[11]

On 30 January 1933 Hitler became Chancellor of a new Coalition Government of Nazis and Nationalists. His chief ministers were von Papen, Vice-Chancellor, von Neurath, Foreign Minister, Hugenburg, Minister for Economic Affairs, Goering, Air Transport and Frick, Minister of the Interior.

Egon Larsen gives a vivid account of his 'journalistic journey' on the afternoon of 30 January 1933, when he 'set out on a tour of Berlin' in his car to 'record the town's reaction . . . Outside, in the Square, groups of Communists were discussing hastily printed leaflets with the outside headline : "General Strike".' According to Egon Larsen:

'It seemed on that day the only way of stopping and toppling the Hitler government before it could establish itself firmly and get a grip on the Länder governments, the Reichswehr and the provincial police forces. Without trains, without communications, without supplies it would have been unable to govern. But a general strike would have been possible only with the co-operation of the Social Democrats and their trade unions'. Mr Larsen relates his experience on approaching the Vörwarts building where the Social Democrat paper was printed. He felt that the Party's 'printing presses were bound to have produced leaflets with some kind of indication of the Party's and the Unions' attitude . . .

'Outside the gates . . . Reichsbanner men were distributing leaflets. They read "KEEP CALM". "Don't let them provoke you"'. He 'found a Party official and asked him to explain that slogan' and was told that the Party policy was to do nothing hastily'. Egon Larsen was clearly shocked by the general apathy within the Party. 'Let the Nazi and nationalist government stew in their own juice, let them flounder and fail' he was told. 'What about a general strike as the Communists wanted it', asked Larsen, 'Never' said the official, 'we cannot join them, all they want is a Communist Dictatorship'. 'But why can't your own Unions call a general strike' he asked. The official hesitated and then admitted '"some of our own functionaries have suggested it . . . But a general strike at this point in time would mean wasting the munition of the working class. Let's wait and see"'.

In the next issue of Vörwarts, in addition to its earlier, declarations, it 'also published the grand new slogan for Germany's working class, devised by the Party boss, Breitscheid Senior: "BE PREPARED". What for, he unfortunately forgot to say . . .'[12]

The Minister for the Interior, Wilhelm Frick, soon got to work. The Vorwarts in Berlin, and the provincial Social Democrat papers were initially banned for seven days, as well as some of the papers belonging to the Centre Party. Karl Liebknecht House, the Communist Party headquarters was raided. All Communist newspapers and publications were suppressed and all their meetings and demonstrations banned. 'Yet the trade unions still ignored the Communists' frantic calls for a general strike.'[13]

On Monday 27 February 1933, five days before the National elections, the Reichstag was set on fire. Hitler, Goering and other leading Nazis immediately put the blame on the Communist Party. They were determined that the Nazi Party would gain an electoral victory and the Reichstag fire was to provide the pretext for crushing the Communists, the Trade Unions and any other opponents.

On the night of the fire, it was reported that the police had arrested a young Dutchman, Van der Lubbe, who was found in the building, equipped with firelighters and petrol-soaked rags and a Communist Party membership book in his pocket. Soon afterwards three Bulgarian Communists, Dimitrov, Popoff and Taneff, together with Ernst Torgler, leader of the Communist deputies in the Reichstag, were arrested as alleged incendiaries. Rudolf Olden, former Political Editor of the *Berliner Tageblatt*, says that Torgler 'had been picked out solely because, as the hard-working leader of his group, he had been occupied in the Reichstag building until late in the evening.'[14] The Nazis announced that they had in their possession proof – precise plans that the Communists had set fire to the Reichstag and that it was meant to be a signal for a general uprising. Their proof, with what they described as 'overwhelming material', in fact, never materialized.

The news of the fire had aroused intense interest

throughout the world, and when the trial of the alleged incendiaries opened in Leipzig some months later, the town and the court were crowded with hundreds of foreign journalists and legal experts from many countries. The brilliant and courageous defence by Dimitrov is now famous in the annals of history. His cross examination of the Nazi leaders, especially Hermann Goering, who had become President of the Reichstag, swung the trial into an indictment of the Nazis themselves. Dimitrov's counter-accusations and the effects of the wide-spread radio and press coverage compelled the court to acquit the three Bulgarians and Torgler. Although acquitted, Torgler was immediately re-arrested and taken back into prison, where he remained until he died during World War II. Van der Lubbe, a pathetic, incoherent, confused and apparently mentally deranged character was sentenced to death.

Some years later a book appeared written by Rudolf Diels, Chief of the Political Police at the time of the fire, describing the scene on the night of 27 February 1933. He had been standing next to Hitler and Goering :

> 'On a balcony projecting into the Chamber stood Hitler surrounded by a band of his faithful . . . Suddenly he started screaming at the top of his voice : "Now we'll show them! Anyone who stands in our way will be mown down. The German people have been too soft too long. Every Communist official must be shot. All Communist deputies must be hanged this very night. All friends of the Communists must be locked up. And that goes for the Social Democrats and the Reichsbanner as well."'[15]

According to the American writer, John Gunther, who had been reporting the trial : 'The fire produced exactly what the Nazis hoped for . . . The one hundred Communist deputies were arrested. A state of virtual siege was proclaimed. The provisions of the Constitution guaranteeing individual liberty were suppressed.'[16]

Until the Autumn of 1933, Hitler's policy had been to use the democratic machinery for his own electoral purposes.

This, together with the employment of his storm troopers in a reign of terror and intimidation, was to ensure the N.S.D.A.P. gaining an electoral victory. The use of the existing machinery was his cloak of political respectability, to convince his backers that he was the leader of a democratically elected government. Although on 5 March 1933, there was a high poll of around thirty eight million the Nazis nevertheless still only received forty four per cent of the vote. Having thus failed to gain an absolute majority, their Fuehrer decided that the only way he and his party could gain overall control was to throw overboard the Ballot Box.

'Once the rule of law had broken down, the veneer of civilization proved to be much thinner than had been supposed by complacent liberals and Social Democrats. Fascism also profited from the anti-communist hysteria which gripped the middle class from 1919 onwards.'[17]

Notes

1. SCHEELE, Godfrey, *The Weimar Republic – Overture to the Third Reich* p. 246
2. SCHEELE, Godfrey, *The Weimar Republic – Overture to the Third Reich* p. 195
3. THYSSEN, Fritz, *I Paid Hitler* p. 121
4. SCHEELE, Godfrey, *The Weimar Republic – Overture to the Third Reich* p. 247
5. JOLL, James, *Europe Since 1870* p. 324
6. GALBRAITH, J.K., *The Great Crash 1929* p. 162
7. BURY, J.P.T., *France, The Insecure Peace* p. 125
8. TINT, Herbert, *France Since 1918* p. 50
9. LARSEN, Egon, *Weimar Eyewitness* pp. 161/162
10. LARSEN, Egon, *Weimar Eyewitness* p. 163
11. HENRI, Ernst, *Hitler Over Europe* pp. 11/12/13
12. LARSEN, Egon, *Weimar Eyewitness* pp. 171/172
13. LARSEN, Egon, *Weimar Eyewitness* p. 174
14. OLDEN, Rudolf, *Hitler the Pawn* p. 333
15. DIELS, Rudolf, *Lucifer Ante Portas* (ex Fritz Tobias, *The Reichstag Fire – Legend and Truth* p. 85) p.193
16. GUNTHER, John, *Inside Europe* p.55
17. LICHTHEIM, George, *Europe in the 20th Century* p. 128

23

JAPAN EXPOSES THE LEAGUE

At a time when the United States and Western European countries were experiencing an acute economic crisis, the other major capitalist country and ally in the anti-Bolshevik wars of intervention, decided that the time was ripe to go in search of some Far-Eastern 'Lebensraum'.

In September 1931, Japanese troops poured into Northern China and within six months had overrun the whole of Manchuria, annexed the Chinese province of Jehol and proclaimed to the world that the captured territories would in future be known as the State of Manchukuo. As far as the Soviet Uniuon was concerned, it meant that its security could now be threatened by an aggressive Japan along some 1,500 miles of its far eastern borders as well as being deprived of the use of the Chinese Eastern Railway.*

The Japanese action had also threatened British commercial and strategic interests in the Far East, but the British Government, instead of encouraging the League of Nations to put a halt to Japanese aggression, preferred to treat the matter with restraint. Japan had challenged the League's system of collective security, but no serious action was taken. In fact there was a certain air of expectancy and hope that the Japanese desire for expansion would find its outlets over the Manchurian borders and into Soviet Russia itself. If the Japanese could stifle Chinese revolutionary movements and prevent the emergence of a progressive anti-imperialist China, that too would be welcome. The Russian 'white' émigrés in the Far East and elsewhere had been busy

---

*In 1935 the USSR sold its stake in the Railway to the Manchukuo-Japanese Government.

feeding the British press. Sensational anti-Soviet reports had been coming in from Harbin, Tokyo and Riga. Those living in Manchuria and along the borders exploited the tense situation in the area by stirring up hostility and creating incidents – hoping to provoke a Japanese-Soviet conflict – in the belief that a war would cripple the Soviet economy and lead to the collapse of Soviet Russia itself.

George Hardy, a British Trade Union leader, travelling through Northern China during the early days of Japanese occupation, relates that after a three day stop in Harbin awaiting a visa to enter the Laotung peninsular, a Japanese-controlled area of north-east China, he came to the conclusion that:

> 'Harbin was a centre of anti-Soviet intrigue by White Russians and the remnants of the defeated counter-revolutionary army of General Simonov.
>
> They earned a precarious livelihood as wreckers and spies in the employ of agents operating for many governments . . . From Harbin, saboteurs and spies were organized to cross the Soviet borders. Much damage was done.
>
> I saw some of their handiwork on the Trans-Siberian railway when the train halted behind a freight train which had been derailed as it was about to cross a bridge.'[1]

Of the Western colonial powers, Britain had by far the greatest financial interest in China, yet the welcoming prospect of a possible Japan-Soviet war appeared to override the fears for its own stake in the area. The Japanese Government was not backward in exploiting this situation. It was the first of the fascist powers to take advantage of the anti-Soviet obsessions of its imperial rivals, thus exposing the reluctance of the League of Nations and the signatories of the Kellogg Pact to take any effective action.

An indication of the attitude of some of Britain's leaders towards Japan in the 1930s is perhaps best reflected in an excerpt from Winston Churchill's speech made at the 25th Anniversary meeting of the Anti-Socialist and Anti-

Communist Union, Queen's Hall, London, 17 February
1933 :

'I do not think the League of Nations would be
well advised to have a quarrel with Japan ... I
hope we shall try in England to understand a little
the position of Japan, an ancient State, with the
highest state sense of national honour and patriotism and with a teeming population and a
remarkable energy. On the one side they see the
dark menace of Soviet Russia. On the other the
chaos of China, four or five provinces of which are
now being tortured under Communist rule'. (*The
Times*, 18 February 1933)

Japanese intentions were revealed in a Memorandum
submitted to the Emperor of Japan by Prime Minister
Tanaka. The 'Tanaka Memorandum', which was smuggled
out of Japan and first published by the *China Critic*, on 24
September 1931, had declared :

'"In order to conquer China, we must first
conquer Manchuria and Mongolia ... If we are
able to conquer China, all the other Asiatic
countries and the countries of the South Seas will
fear us and capitulate before us. The world will
then understand that Eastern Asia is ours ...
With all the resources of China at our disposal, we
shall pass forward to the conquest of India, the
Archipelago, Asia Minor, Central Asia and even
Europe ...
    It seems that the inevitability of crossing
swords with Russia on the fields of Mongolia in
order to gain possession of the wealth of North
Manchuria is part of our program of national
development ... Sooner or later we shall have to
fight against Soviet Russia ... One day we shall
have to fight against America ... "'[2]

In a report to the 17th Party Congress, 26 January 1934,
Stalin warned of the follies and dangers of such plans for

precipitating a war against the USSR.

> "'Some bourgeois politicians think that war should be organized against the USSR. Their plan is to defeat the USSR, divide up its territory, and profit at its expense. It would be a mistake to believe it is only certain military circles in Japan who think in this way. We know that similar plans are being hatched in the leading political circles of certain states in Europe . . . One such war against the USSR was waged already, if you remember, 15 years ago. As is well known, the universally esteemed Churchill clothed this war in a poetic formula – the march of fourteen States . . . You know how it ended . . . It can hardly be doubted that a second war against the USSR will lead to complete defeat of the aggressors, to revolution in a number of countries in Europe and in Asia . . . "'[3]

It was obvious that a violation of the Covenant of the League of Nations meant nothing to those countries who felt that if the invasion of a member state could lead ultimately to a war against Soviet Russia, as well as destroying the independence and emancipation from foreign control of the member state itself – so be it.

The blowing up of the railway line near Mukden on 18 September 1931 had provided the pretext for Japanese troops to march in on the following day and occupy the town. Having thus engineered the 'incident' to suit their time-table, the Japanese Government thereupon used it as a signal for the army to promptly fulfil their plan for occupying the whole of Manchuria. The Chinese Government immediately appealed to the League of Nations under Article 11 of the Covenant. On 22 September the League's Council discussed the matter, and during the debate Lord Cecil, Britain's representative, 'proposed an inquiry, and persuaded the Council to appeal to both Japan and China to stop fighting and to return their forces to their own frontiers.'[4] Instead of condemning the Japanese occupation and demanding the withdrawal of Japanese troops from Chinese territory, the Cecil proposal which had the support of US Secretary of State, Stimson, appeared to equate the responsiblity of the invader with that of the invaded, for what was in effect an act of war. This soft approach by Britain and the United States was interpreted by the Japanese authorities as an indication that the two countries would prefer to refrain from becoming involved in the matter.

On 29 January 1932, the Chinese Government appealed once again, this time to the League's Assembly, to take action which would have meant applying sanctions against Japan, but it fell on deaf ears. However, to appease international public opinion, a Commission of Inquiry was appointed under the chairmanship of Lord Lytton to investigate the matter relating to the 'dispute'.

Meanwhile, the Japanese, having seized the whole of Manchuria and changed its name to 'Manchukuo', proclaimed its independence in February 1932.

Not until fighting between Chinese and Japanese forces had spread to Shanghai, where British and American economic and political interests were involved, did the two countries emerge from their neutral stance and force the Japanese to withdraw from the area.

The Anglo-American co-operation over Shanghai must have convinced the Japanese Government that the 'open door' policy regarding China did not apply to them – Shanghai being the centre of the International Settlements. But Manchuria in the north was another matter, for it was over a thousand miles from the International Settlements and had a common frontier with Soviet Russia.

At the time of the Sino-Japanese conflict in Shanghai, the Lytton Commission* was in Manchuria, seven months after the first of the Chinese appeals to the League. Having 'spent some six weeks in Manchuria in order to ascertain the attitude of its inhabitants towards the new "State"',[5] it did not publish its report until October 1932 and, as C.L. Mowat comments, 'was sympathetic with Japanese grievances in Manchuria, but condemned the Japanese invasion, refused to accept Manchukuo's independence as genuine and proposed for Manchuria an autonomous regime under Chinese sovereignty.'[6]

---

*It was in Manchuria from 20 April to 4 June 1932.

Although the report was not adopted by the League until February 1933, it nevertheless led to Japan giving notice to quit this international body, which had failed to uphold the principles for which it was established, and from which it was never to recover.

The continued occupation of China by Japan, in defiance of the Covenant of the League of Nations, provided the green light for similar actions by Nazi Germany and Fascist Italy in the years to come. All three countries instinctively knew that so long as their motives could be attributed to, or associated with, policies of anti-Soviet, anti-Communist or anti-Socialist campaigning, the other capitalist powers would turn a blind-eye.

Anthony Adamthwaite, in his book, *The Making of the Second World War*, explains that – 'Although Britain, France and the United States had much to lose in the Far East, Japanese expansion was not yet seen as a direct threat to western commercial and colonial interests. Indeed, France was inclined to see Japan as a bastion of order against anarchy and Bolshevism.'[7] Such an inclination had also found favour in both British and American governmental circles.

Notes

1. HARDY, George, *Those Stormy Years* pp. 212/213
2. SCHUMAN, Frederick L., *Soviet Politics, At Home and Abroad* p. 243
3. SCHUMAN, Frederick L., *Soviet Politics, At Home and Abroad* pp. 244/245
4. MOWAT, C.L., *Britain Between the Wars 1918–40* p. 419
5. PELISSIER, Roger, *The Awakening of China 1793–1949* p. 347
6. MOWAT, C.L. p.422
7. ADAMTHWAITE, Anthony P., *The Making of the Second World War* p. 37

24

DECLARATIONS OF INTENT

The success of the Japanese expansionist policy in the Far East Soon had its repercussions in Europe, especially upon Germany's new rulers, who were greatly encouraged by Anglo-French passivity.

'In 1933', comments Herbert Tint, 'few western politicians suspected that Hitler might plunge the world into another war, though quite a number thought, but did not necessarily mind that he might be a threat to the Soviet Union.'[1]

Those politicians might not have desired another world war, but moves leading to a war between Germany, a major industrial rival, and the Soviet Union were to receive every form of encouragement. This dangerous game was pursued right up to the eve of World War II.

In *Mein Kampf* (My Struggle), Hitler spelt out quite clearly what would be Germany's foreign policy when he and the Nazi Party came to power. It was not long before preparations for the implementation of his policy of 'Lebensraum' which, in reality, meant the occupation of other people's territory, was set into motion.

> 'For Germany the only possibility for the carrying out of sound territorial policy lay in the winning of new land in Europe itself . . . when one would have new territory and land in Europe, this could in general only happen at the cost of Russia'. (From *Mein Kampf* – official German edition pp. 153–154)
>
> 'We stop the eternal march to the South and West of Europe and turn our eyes towards the

land in the East . . . If we speak of land in Europe to-day we can only think in the first instance of Russia and the border states under her influence. Fate itself seems here to point the way forward for us . . . The giant state in the East is ripe for collapse'. (From *Mein Kampf* – official German edition p. 743)

So long as German eyes were turned 'towards the land in the East', Western politicians were prepared to tolerate the new Nazi regime and turn a blind-eye towards an aggressive foreign policy, especially that which was directed towards its Eastern neighbours, as well as the barbarian attacks upon thousands of its own citizens. And yet it was obvious that Hitler's policy of revenge and the reconquest of lost territories could only be realized by a resort to war. There is no ambiguity in his statement when he declared :

'It is necessary to understand that the reconquest of the lost territories cannot be achieved by solemn appeals to Almighty God or pious hopes in a League of Nations, but only by armed force.' (From *Mein Kampf* – official German edition p. 708)

A clear enough declaration of intent, and to help those politicians and press lords, who for years had campaigned against Soviet Russia, put over a sympathetic pro-German policy, a specially revised and abbreviated edition of *Mein Kampf* was produced in Britain. It was first published in October 1933 (by permission of the German Government), some eight years after the original. Many of Hitler's most warlike passages were omitted, while at the same time an un-abridged French translation of the original, entitled *Mon Combat*, had been the subject of legal action in France by the German Government. The Germans had tried to secure its suppression but without success.

During the post-war years the 'Entente Cordiale' had been considerably weakened, and there were many in British influential circles who preferred to have closer ties with Germany than with France. The English edition of

310

Mein Kampf had been careful to assure British readers that the new Germany regarded Britain and the British people with great admiration and that it was France that could not be trusted. In addition to expounding the author's racial philosophy, it proceeded to exploit the existing Anglo-French colonial rivalries by pointing out that

> 'Great Britain does not desire a France, whose military power, unrestrained by the rest of Europe, might cover a policy likely one day to run counter to British interests; France's military predominance presses sorely on the heart of the world Empire of Great Britain.' (From *Mein Kampf* – English edition, p. 246)

And then went on to stir up anti-French feelings in Italy by adding

> 'Nor can Italy desire any further strengthening of France's position of power in Europe . . . any increase of French strength on the continent means restrictions for Italy's future.' (From *Mein Kampf* – English edution, p 246)
>
> 'It is these two states, Great Britain and Italy, whose own natural interests are least in opposition to the conditions essential to the existence of the German nation, and are, in fact, to a certain extent, identical with them'. (From *Mein Kampf* – English edition, pp. 246/247)

In earlier chapters of the English edition, Hitler had been careful to point out that

> 'Great Britain was the only power which could protect our rear, supposing we started a new Germanic expansion' (From *Mein Kampf* – English edition, p. 64)
>
> 'Thus the British nation will be considered as the most valuable ally in the world, as long as the world looks to the leadership and the spirit of its

people for the ruthlessness and tenacity which is determined to fight out a struggle, once begun, by every means and without regard for time and sacrifice right on to the victorious end'. (From *Mein Kampf* – English edition, p. 133)

For,

The wiping out of Germany as a power on the continent would merely bring profit to England's enemies'. (From *Mein Kampf* – English edition, p. 245)

Nazi foreign policy had from the outset aimed at placating Britain and isolating France, while at the same time preparing for expansion in the east culminating in an eventual attack upon the Soviet Union. Nazi organizations were set up in the bordering states as well as in those countries which were regarded as part of the 'German racial empire'. Terrorist methods were to be used, including assassination of political leaders opposed to Nazi aims, as part of an overall plan for a general take-over by the Third Reich when the time was ripe.

'It is common knowledge' relates Fritz Thyssen, 'that on 27 January 1932 – almost a year before he seized power – Adolf Hitler made a speech lasting about two and a half hours before the Industry Club of Dusseldorf. The speech made a deep impression on the assembled industrialists, and in consequence of this a large number of large contributions flowed from the resources of heavy industry into the treasuries of the National Socialist Parties'.[2]

Hitler's 'deep impression' on the German industrialists and the implementation of some of his policies, both home and foreign, also made a deep impression upon Thyssen's counterparts in Britain. Determining factors, which led to Britain's policy of appeasement later in the decade. Racialism, anti-Communism, anti-Socialism and anti-Bolshevism gained him many admirers within Britain's ruling circle. The fostering of racialism, especially in times of economic crises and rising unemployment, has invariably been a handy weapon used by sections of the press and unscrupulous politicians to divert attention from the root causes of the political and economic ailments.

If any western politicians, after reading *Mein Kampf*, remained unconvinced about the dangers of Nazi foreign policy, then they had only to read *The Gospel of the Twentieth Century* (*Der Mythus des Zwangzigstens Jahrhunderts*) by Alfred Rosenberg, Director of the Nazi Party's Bureau for Foreign Affairs, in which he writes :

> 'Racial honour demands territory and enough of it . . . In such a struggle there can be no consideration for worthless Poles, Czechs, etc. Ground must be cleared for German peasants'.

The "Rosenberg Plan" was based upon Hitler's conception of a racial empire – pure, unadulterated, Germanic and Aryan. It 'prescribes the end of Austria,' and the 'liquidation of Switzerland, the Germanic part of which . . . must be detached from the unnatural union with French Switzerland . . . It demands the breaking up of Czechoslovakia, in order that German Bohemia, Moravia and Silesia may be brought back to the racial fold. It demands the disintegration of Belgium, the Germanic, Flemish part of which, together with Brabant and Luxembourg, is, as in the case of Switzerland, to be separated from the French, Walloon part. It makes Flanders and Holland, the old German Burgundy, the North-Western part of the racial empire. It incorporates Scandinavia, a fragment of the Nord-Germanic race . . . It claims the Baltic and its bordering states – Finland, Esthonia, Latvia, Lithuania – for the Hitler Empire . . . It claims Western Flanders and Lorraine from France, South Tirol from Italy, South Styria from Jugoslavia, Schleswig from Denmark. The power and the sovereignty of this empire – by virtue of this new law of race – must reach out everywhere wherever even a fragment of the Germanic race has fallen, as far even as Rumania and Jugoslavia with their German colonist districts. This is the Rosenberg doctrine . . . the real political concept and meaning of the 'race manifesto' of the Nazis, for which the "Jewish problem" serves only as a cloak . . . '[3]

The attractiveness of this racial policy for powerful

313

industrialists such as Thyssen, Krupp, etc., lay in the fact that 'the map of the "Germanic racial empire" is, point for point, identical with the map of the expansion of German heavy industry. The Hitler empire is geographically nothing else but the inherent field for the productive forces of the Ruhr.'[4]

Those western politicians, press lords and public figures who were among Hitler's admirers and envied his Third Reich for the speedy and 'efficient' manner in which it dealt with political opponents and trade union leaders, were in the main the same people who had supported the wars of intervention against Soviet Russia and were prepared to ally themselves either politically, economically or militarily against the common enemy.

Michael Foot describes in his biography of Aneurin Bevan how in 1933, after Hitler and the Nazis gained control in Germany, 'Communists and Socialists were falling beneath the same lash, being kicked by the same jackboots, and the old, oft-debated, oft-spurned proposal for a united front between them to resist the onslaught suddenly appeared in a new context. A formal approach was made by the Communist International to the Executive of the Labour and Socialist International. In Britain the Communist Party and the ILP came close to agreeing on a programme of common action and both approached the Labour Party. They were promptly given the dustiest of answers. Labour's Executive issued a special Declaration, Democracy versus Dictatorship, not merely rejecting the Communist approach but insisting that no real distinction could be drawn between the Soviet and Nazi forms of totalitarianism. Both must be covered under the same sweeping clause of ban and anathema.

'But this edict did not satisfy many of those in the Labour Party most deeply shaken by the news from Germany. All over the country ad hoc meetings of local parties and trades councils were called to discuss the new situation . . .'[5]

This equating of Nazis and Communists was to persist right up to the opening of World War II and even further, to that day in June 1941, when Nazi Germany, after swallowing up most of Europe including countries in the West, launched its invasion upon Soviet Russia, for which it had been preparing for almost a decade.

Notes

1. TINT, Herbert, *France Since 1918* p. 53
2. THYSSEN, Fritz, *I Paid Hitler* pp. 132/133
3. HENRI, Ernst, *Hitler Over Europe* p. 130
4. HENRI, Ernst, *Hitler Over Europe* p 132
5. FOOT, Michael, *Aneurin Bevan, Vol. I* 1897–1945 pp. 167/168

25

DISARMAMENT AND ECONOMIC NON-AGGRESSION

When the International Disarmament Conference opened in Geneva in February 1932 the mood of the major European members was not one of compromise. They were not prepared to accept any proposals for a cut in arms.

Both the United States and the Soviet Union, although still outside the League, were invited to attend.

In his statements at the preparatory meetings Litvinov warned of the imminent danger of an outbreak of a major war, and the recent actions by Japan had confirmed his fears that such wars could lead to another world war.

Japanese artillery was still bombarding Shanghai and the surrounding coastal area when the Conference opened, but it had very little effect upon the decision of many of the leading members.

There was a proposal by the American Government for a cut in arms by one third, suggesting that, as a result, the European nations would be in a better position to settle their debts. It was supported by the Soviet Union, but made very little headway and was eventually rejected by the major European powers.

In the summer of 1933, using Article 11 of the League of Nations, Litvinov drew up a document by which he 'defined an aggressor as any state which should be the first to commit any of the following acts :

1. Declaration of war upon another state;
2. Invasion by its armed forces, with or without a declaration of war, of the territory of another state;
3. Attack by its land, naval or air forces, with or without a declaration of war, on the territory, vessels or

aircraft of another state;

4. Naval blockade of the coasts or ports of another state;
5. Provision of support to armed bands formed on its territory which have invaded the territory of another state, or refusal, notwithstanding the request of the invaded state, to take on its own territory all the measures in its power to deprive these bands of all assistance or protection'.

The Litvinov document defining aggression was signd by the Soviet Union and her neighbours, Afghanistan, Estonia, Latvia, Persia, Poland, Roumania and Turkey, and was accepted by a number of other governments. But, says Professor Fleming, 'All these initiatives by Litvinov in the direction of disarmament and limiting aggression were heavily, if not completely discounted by Western diplomats. They found it impossible to believe that the dreaded Communist state really had pacific purposes.'[1] And, of course, they had other matters on their minds. Firstly, how were they to get out of their persistent economic recession?

It was four years since the collapse of the New York banks and stockmarkets. The long awaited recovery from the great slump had not materialized. Unemployment, world-wide, was still around thirty millions (thirteen million in the USA, six million in Germany and three million in Britain). International trade had declined by more than twenty five per cent in volume and about fifty per cent in value. In some capitalist countries the general incomes of its people had fallen to almost half their pre-1929 value. And on top of this, Germany, a major capitalist country, was in the grip of a ruthless Fascist dictatorship, bent on revenge and rearmament.

This, then, was the general background to the World Economic Conference which opened in London on 12 June 1933, in which the USA, the USSR and other non-League of Nations countries, together with the League's members, took part.

The tone of the opening address by King George V was set in an appeal to reason, common sense and good intentions.

317

'It cannot be beyond the power of man so to use the vast resources of the world as to ensure the material progress of civilization. No diminution in those resources has taken place. On the contrary, discovery, invention and organization have multiplied their possibilities to such an extent that abundance of production has itself created new problems. And together with this amazing material progress, there has come a new recognition of the interdependence of nations and of the value of collaboration between them. Now is the opportunity to harness this new consciousness of common interests to the service of mankind'. (*The Times*, 13 June 1933)

As has often happened in earlier international economic conferences, the search for quick remedies took precedence over a serious diagnosis of the economic ailments. The Conference never really got to grips with the main economic problems which had plagued most of the participating countries over the past four years. The slump meant that not only the poverty stricken African, Asian and Latin American colonial or neo-colonial countries had become even more impoverished, but that millions of people in the industrialized countries had a very much reduced purchasing power. Whether it be the problems of over-production or under-consumption, in the long run it amounts to the same thing. Millions of people throughout the world, including those in the more advanced capitalist countries, were unable to buy sufficient quantities of industrial products, as well as food, to really pull those capitalist countries out of their economic decline. The situation had been further aggravated by the introduction since the war of new manufacturing techniques which had greatly improved and speeded up production. It was not a matter of needs, they were still there and increasing day by day. What was missing was the purchasing power, as well as the will to tackle the problems of poverty, unemployment and prejudice.

Litvinov gave an example of how his country, had it not been discriminated against, could have absorbed some of

318

the surplus commodities which the major industrial countries were unable to sell. The Soviet Union had offered to buy a thousand million dollars worth of goods from Western countries, but the main stumbling block had been the refusal of some countries to provide suitable credit terms.

In 1933 the Soviet Union, with a population of close on two hundred million people, could, if given the opportunity, have played a major role in helping to lift the recession. Its first Five-Year Plan was completed in just under four and a half years, raising the level of a technically and industrially backward country to one of the leading industrially developed countries of the world. But as Professor Fleming points out, 'Both domestic prosperity and military security had still to be attained, and might never be achieved if the Soviet Union were attacked by ambitious aggressive nations from the West and the East.' The discrimination was not on the grounds of credit worthiness for 'the Soviets had not defaulted on a single commercial payment.'[2]

Litvinov put forward a draft proposal for a Pact of Eonomic Non-Aggression whereby the governments represented at the Conference

> 'Recognize the cessation of economic aggression to be the most important condition for the peaceful co-operation of all States in the economic field irrespective of their politico-economic systems'
>
> . . .
>
> 'that the improvement of the present difficult economic position requires that all countries in addition to the renunciation of war as a means of solution of international conflicts should renounce completely all avowed and concealed forms of economic aggression'

. . . and that

> 'The contracting parties will abstain in their mutual relations from all forms of discrimination'

319

and will not adopt or apply in their countries any

> 'special system directed against any one country and putting this country in a worse position as regards its foreign trade than all other countries . . .'*

These were some of the main points from Litvinov's unique proposal in which the dangers of economic aggression were linked to the dangers of war. He was in particular referring to the employment of trade embargoes and discriminatory import duties which were powerful weapons in the hands of some countries to undermine the political independence and stability of others.

The recent British embargo on Soviet goods which had been countered by a Soviet embargo on British goods had once again soured relations between the two countries. For it was earlier in the year that the Soviet authorities had arrested six British subjects, employees of Metropolitan-Vickers, the well-known engineering firm, on charges of espionage and sabotage. The arrests were carried out on 12 March 1933 and the men brought to trial on 12 April.

Within hours of the arrests, Britain's Ambassador to Moscow, Sir Esmond Ovey, had cabled to Sir John Simon at the Foreign Office in London, 'It is inconceivable that Soviet Government can produce credible evidence of any criminal malpractice on the part of the Company.'[3] And a few days later, J.H. Thomas, Secretary of State for the Dominions in the Ramsay MacDonald Coalition Government, told a meeting in Swansea that : 'Public opinion in this country is satisfied the men who have been arrested are respectable and harmless British subjects engaged in their normal commercial avocations.' (*The South Wales Evening Post*, 18 March 1933)

Most of the press that week had followed the line taken by Stanley Baldwin 'that there can be no justification for the charge on which the arrests were made.' (*Hansard*, 15 March 1933, Col. 1945). Once again a campaign was whipped up to encourage the placing of a ban on all Anglo-

---

*Excerpts from Mr Litvinov's draft proposal 21.6.1933

Soviet trade.

Two of the arrested men, Monkhouse and Nordwall, were released after being detained for forty eight hours, and on 4 April, three of the remaining four men, Thornton, Gregory and Cushny, were released on bail, but the last, MacDonald, remained in custody.

The following morning, the *Financial News** in a leading article, drew attention to the fact that 'The Metropolitan-Vickers employees had scarcely been arrested when protests began in the most violent form and threats of an embargo on Russian goods started to be broadcast with complete abandon.'

The trial lasted six days and on 18 April sentences were announced. Thornton was sentenced to three years imprisonment and MacDonald two years. Monkhouse, Nordwall and Cushny were to be deported from the USSR and Gregory was acquitted.

The accused had been charged with collecting secret information concerning work carried out in Soviet military workshops, organizing failures and delays in production, undermining industries involved in military work, collecting Soviet state war secrets, working out plans for the wrecking of equipment in the event of war, hiding defects in equipment supplied by their own company, and finally, bribing Russian engineers to help carry out these activities.

Without waiting for the result of the appeal lodged on behalf of its two citizens sentenced to imprisonment, the British Government issued a proclamation which placed an embargo upon the importation of Soviet goods with effect from 26 April. Such precipitate action inevitably led to the Soviet Government retaliating. It directed all their trading organizations to ban the purchase of goods from Britain; restricted the transportation of British goods across Soviet territory, and stopped the chartering of ships flying the British flag.

On 15 May, at a meeting of the Federation of Engineering and Shipbuilding Trades, a resolution was passed condemning the trade embargo and issued a call for its immediate removal. Fortunately for all concerned, the

*5 April 1933

eventual outcome of the Metro-Vickers affair was resolved two months later when Litvinov and Britain's Foreign Minister, Sir John Simon, met at the World Economic Conference, held in London during the latter part of June. Pressure had obviously been brought upon the Foreign Office by many of Britain's industrial organizations and common sense prevailed. After meetings held at the Foreign Office on 30 June, and again the following day, agreement was reached whereby both Governments decided to remove their trade embargoes. That evening, news arrived in London that Thornton and MacDonald had been granted an amnesty and would be deported. They were in fact released just before midnight.

Meanwhile the World Economic Conference was drawing to a close, having apparently arrived at a dead end. The Litvinov proposals for tackling the current economic crisis had obviously created embarrassment among some of the major powers. An amendment to exclude from a Soviet draft references concerning economic discrimination on political grounds had been presented to the conference by Walter Runciman,* Britain's chief representative. In an attempt to shelve the problem, the Soviet proposal for an Economic Non-Aggression Pact was submitted to the Conference's Economic Commission which in turn passed it on to its Sub-Committee on Commercial policy. Thus, by adopting this tactic, the major powers were able to avoid public debate on the proposed pact.

Nevertheless, some positive results were achieved before the Conference adjourned. Contacts were made during Litvinov's stay in London between himself and Sir John Simon which led, not only to the cessation of the trade embargoes between their two countries, but also to the re-opening of negotiations for a new trade agreement. In addition, the attitudes of both Britain and France towards the USSR had undergone a temporary change, determined by the rapid development and success of Russia's first Five Year Plan, and by fears in some influential circles of the dangers arising from the new Nazi regime in Germany.

---

*Became Lord Runciman, Neville Chamberlain's emissary to Prague August 1938. See Chap. 32 pp

Notes

1. FLEMING, D.F., *The Cold War and Its Origins*, Vol I. pp. 49/50
2. FLEMING, D.F., *The Cold War and Its Origins*, Vol.I. p. 50
3. Cmd. 4286, *Russia* No. 1. (1933) No. 5.

26

THE BARTHOU PLAN
OR COLLECTIVE INSECURITY?

Hitler had never concealed his contempt for the Treaty of Versailles. Carefully feeling his way during his first few months in office, he was prepared to use the Disarmament Conference as a sounding board for the acceptance of German rearmament as well as for exploiting the divisions between Britain and France.

Germany would be prepared to disarm, he declared on 17 May 1933, providing other nations did likewise, failing that, then 'Germany must at least maintain her demand to equality'. He knew he was on safe ground here. Britain not only had no intention of disarming, but was prepared to accept German rearmament subject to limitations, which meant ignoring the Treaty of Versailles.

It was no mystery to either the British or French Governments that German rearmament had been going on for quite some time. 'It was openly admitted to our air attaché in Berlin on July 10th' comments Anthony Eden in his Memoirs, 'that Germany was manufacturing military aircraft, carrying out work on fortifications and intensifying military training.'[1]

France certainly had no intention of disarming. The French Government remained adamant that Germany should not be allowed to arm beyond the terms of the Versailles Treaty, and that was just what Hitler needed.

Having made his token gesture to the Disarmament Conference and had it rejected, he withdrew his Foreign Minister, von Neurath and his aides from the Conference, and on the same day, 14 October 1933, announced that Germany would be withdrawing from the League of Nations.

In France, the emergence of Hitler and the end of democratic government in Germany and now the German withdrawal from the League had at last brought some French politicians to their senses. None more so than Louis Barthou who became Foreign Minister in the Doumergue administration in 1934. Barthou was an experienced politician from a Conservative anti-Socialist, anti-Communist background, nevertheless he was realistic enough to see clearly the dangers of a rearmed Germany threatening the status quo in Europe. It was Barthou who initiated plans for the conclusion of an 'Eastern Pact of Mutual Guarantee' which was to include the Soviet Union. The Pact, often described as the 'Eastern Locarno' would have provided an equivalent guarantee for the protection of the frontiers of those countries in Eastern Europe, including the Soviet Union, which had been excluded from the original Locarno, as that given to Germany in 1925 by her western neighbours.

After preliminary discussions with Litvinov in the Spring of 1934, Barthou went on a tour of Eastern Europe visiting Belgrade, Bucharest, Prague and Warsaw to seek acceptance of his proposals. He was perturbed by the Polish-German Non-Aggression Pact of January 1933 and warned the Polish Government of the dangers of getting too closely involved with Hitler. He received a more sympathetic response in Prague and the Czech Government, on his initiative, gave de jure recognition to the Soviet Government. His plan envisaged the acceptance of the Soviet Union into the League of Nations with a seat on the Council.

Barthou had the support of Sir John Simon, with whom he had held discussions, as well as the new leader of the Labour Party, Attlee, who, in a speech in the House of Commons welcoming the Plan, declared that 'the Labour Party urgently hopes that His Majesty's Government will give their cordial approval to these proposals, will co-operate in pressing Germany and Poland to participate in the Eastern Pact and will agree to Russia becoming a guarantor of the Locarno Pact of 1925.' (*Hansard*, 13 July 1934, Cols. 689/690)

In 1934 the Hitler 'spirit of goodwill' towards Britain had

not convinced one group of Tory politicians of its sincerity. Its most prominent spokesman, Winston Churchill, had already reached the conclusion that the Nazi regime would inevitably threaten the future of the British Empire. Consequently, he was prepared, for the time being, to accept the association of Russia into the 'Western European System', as the Soviet Ambassador, Maisky, later revealed.

In July Churchill told Maisky (in the presence of Sir Robert Vansittart, who was at the time Permanent Under-Secretary for Foreign Affairs) that 'The British Empire is my be-all and end-all. What is good for the British Empire is good for me too; what is bad for the British Empire is bad for me . . . In 1919 I considered that the greatest danger to the British Empire was your country, and therefore I was an enemy of your country. Now I consider that the greatest danger for the British Empire is Germany, and therefore now I am an enemy of Germany. At the same time I consider that Hitler is making ready to expand not only against us but also to the east, against you. Why should we not join forces to combat our common enemy? I have been an adversary of Communism and remain its adversary, but for the sake of the integrity of the British Empire I am ready to co-operate with the Soviets.' In reply, Maisky, 'in the same spirit of frankness' told Churchill the '"Soviet people are in principle the adversaries of Capitalism. But they very much want peace, and in the struggle for peace are ready to co-operate with a state founded on any system if it is genuinely striving to avert war"'.[2]

As Maisky explains, 1934 was very much the year of the 'thaw' in Anglo-Soviet relations. Churchill and other like-minded Tories still had a considerable influence in Britain's corridors of power. Sir Robert Vansittart, with his status as a Senior Foreign Office official, had been able, if only for a brief period, to use his influence and connections in steering British Foreign Policy in the direction of the Barthou Plan. He was also a leading advocate of Russia's membership of the League of Nations. Like Churchill, Vansittart believed that Nazi Germany was potentially the greatest danger to the British Empire, and had tried to show his chief, Sir John Simon, where Britain's real security lay; especially now that Germany and Japan had left the League.

Simon, like Churchill, had great admiration for the way Mussolini was protecting the Italian ruling class. He was particularly keen to maintain cordial relations with Mussolini and harness Italy into an Anglo-French-Italian entente, hoping that a more 'respectable' looking Nazi Germany could be encouraged to join in the near future. The wishful thinking of Sir John Simon is revealed in a letter to his predecessor, Sir Austen Chamberlain, written in September 1933.

'My Dear Chamberlain,

I have just been reading a telegram from Rome which gives some account of your talk with Mussolini and of the way in which you impressed upon him the importance of a genuine Franco-Italian rapprochement. May I say how entirely I agree with you and how grateful I am to you for having the opportunity to urge this with the authority and experience which you (now that Grey has gone) alone possess. I also agree most profoundly with your reading of German psychology and with the Teutonic failing of misreading generosity and imagining that it betokens weakness rather than a warning of strength. More and more do I feel in these days that Italy is the real key to European peace. I believe that our visit to Rome and the Four Power Pact* in its ultimate form were valuable influences in the right direction ... It seems to me that the prospect of Hitlerism becoming established on a more respectable basis in Germany is great, and there are strong signs that Nazi influence in Austria will, in the end, be too strong for poor Dolfuss. If so,

---

*In March 1933 Mussolini proposed that Britain, France, Germany and Italy should conclude a Four Power Pact ... affirming 'the principle of the revision of the Peace treaties'. France's eastern allies protested because revision directly threatened their existence. The Pact was signed in July 1933 but never ratified.' (Anthony P. Adamthwaite, p. 38)

Austria is becoming a focus of terrible anxiety, and everything depends on keeping Italy on the right path . . .

Yours ever sincerely,

John Simon.'[3]

Nevertheless, in the Summer of 1934, British Foreign Policy had moved towards closer co-operation with the USSR and along the Barthou lines, and Sir John Simon had to go along with it. In declaring the Government's support for the Barthou Plan he told the House of Commons

'that an Eastern Pact of Mutual Guarantee, based on the strictest principles of reciprocity and conceived with the genuine purpose of strengthening the foundations of peace in the world - by creating a further basis for reciprocal guarantees, is well deserving the support of the British Government and of the British people.' (*Hansard*, 13 July 1934, Col. 700)

The Barthou Plan had opened up new divisions within British ruling circles. There was the powerful group of 'interventionists' whose aim was to maintain close ties with Nazi Germany and encourage Hitler in his 'Lebensraum' policy in the East. Their plans were based upon using Germany as a bulwark against Bolshevism, particularly Bolshevik Russia. And now there was a new group who believed that in the changed circumstances it would be preferable to have Soviet Russia on their side as a bulwark against Nazi Germany and thus, if though indirectly, as a potential saviour of Britain and the British Empire.

The International Disarmament Conference meanwhile had ground to a halt. It had been intermittently in session since the Spring of 1932. The British Government's attempts to get France to agree 'to concede Germany the principle of equality in armaments and to agree, to begin with, to both nations limiting their armies to 300,000 men' had misfired. 'In a note to the British Government on April

17, 1934, Barthou declared that France "refused to legalize German rearmament" contrary to the Versailles Treaty – and that henceforth "France will assure security by her own means"'.[4]

Three months later, on 25 July, the Austrian Chancellor, Dolfuss, was murdered by Austrian Nazis. It was to have been the signal for a coup d'etat by the Nazis organized from Berlin. Although Dolfuss had been responsible for the ruthless elimination of his Socialist opposition, he nevertheless was still regarded in Berlin as an obstacle to their plans for an 'Anschluss' (a joining of the two countries). The coup failed to materialize mainly because of the mobilization of Italian troops on the Austrian borders that appeared ready to protect Austria's independence. In 1934 Mussolini was not prepared to accept German expansionism right up to his own 'doorstep'.

With Japan and Germany now outside the League and the latter preparing for war, Barthou decided to canvass support, while on his journeys around Europe, for the admission of the Soviet Union into the League of Nations. Eventually, on 18 September 1934, after a gap of fourteen years, the world's largest country with a population greater than Britain, France and Germany combined, was invited to join the 'family of nations', and was immediately given a permanent seat on the League's Council. An event which was greeted with great enthusiasm at the Annual Labour Party Conference during the first week in October. In his opening address the Chairman announced on behalf of the Executive,

> 'We welcome as an event of historic importance Russia's entry in the League of Nations, and her election to a permanent seat on the Council.'

And on the following day Arthur Henderson* moved a resolution proposing that,

> 'This Conference expresses its deep satisfaction at the entry of the Union of Soviet Socialist

---

*Arthur Henderson had been President of the International Disarmament Conference when it opened in Geneva in 1932.

Republics into the League of Nations with a permanent seat on the Council of the League, believing that this historic event will greatly strengthen the League, improve the relationship between neighbouring states, render the Collective Peace System more effective, hasten a world agreement for progressive disarmament thereby creating new opportunities for effective international co-operation both in economic questions and in other fields, and assist in a general advance of the peoples of the world towards a co-operative world commonwealth'.

The resolution was carried unanimously.

Barely a week had elapsed before millions of people throughout the world, who had been encouraged by the results of Barthou's diplomacy, were to be stunned by the news that France's Foriegn Minister had been murdered. It happened in Marseilles on 9 October 1934 during a State visit by King Alexander of Yogoslavia. Both Barthou and the Yugoslav monarch were shot at close range by an assassin who was identified as a member of Ustaschi, a Croatian movement with Fascist links in Berlin, Budapest and Rome.

The removal of Barthou from the diplomatic arena resulted in the return of Laval to the Quai d'Orsay.

William L. Shirer, the American writer and journalist, who had lived and worked in France during the 1920s and part of the 1930s, describes in his massive and detailed work, *The Collapse of the Third Republic*, how Pierre Laval, who commenced his political career as a young 'extreme Left-Wing Socialist and pacifist' had 'drifted steadily to the political Right, amassing a considerable fortune as he went along and winning increasing confidence in the world of big business and finance, which he had once so unmercifully castigated.'[5] While on his road to political eminence, Laval had become an 'independent' Socialist and then finding that inconvenient, decided that he would prefer to be recognized as a 'non-party' politician. His political ambitions began to be realized in 1925 when he was appointed Minister of Public Works in the Painlevé administration and continued his political career as a junior Minister in the Briand Cabinets of 1926, but it was not until the extreme Right Wing Government of Tardieu in the early thirties that Laval achieved his ambition of attaining the highest Cabinet posts. The short lived Cabinets of that period gave him his first taste of being Prime Minister, an office which he held initially from 27 January 1931 until February 1932.

In the ensuing general election the Socialist Party gained most votes but only 131 seats. It refused to join with either the Radicals or the Communists but eventually, in the following January, joined up with the Conservative Government of Paul-Boncour, an ex-member of the Socialist Party. The marriage lasted barely two weeks. The Paul-Boncour Government was heavily outvoted on 28 January 1933 and was succeded by another Radical Government, the third since the Spring election of the previous year. Its Prime Minister was Edouard Daladier, a name, like that of Laval, which was to achieve notoriety during the rest of the decade. The Daladier administration survived just nine months. By cutting the salaries of State employees it also cut its own future and Daladier was forced to resign. His successor, Albert Sarraut, fared even worse. He lasted less than a month and resigned on the same issue. The 'fonctionnaires' were not prepared to be the whipping boys for France's inept economic policy.

The instability of French Parliamentary democracy during the early thirties, the persistent economic depression and the increasing number of financial scandals, involving prominent politicians, had created disillusionment and disgust with party politics generally, a situation which was promptly exploited by Fascist and semi-Fascist organizations. According to Shirer:

'Rowdy anti-Parliamentary Leagues had sprung up like mushrooms and while a few of them seemed to be merely offshoots of the old anti-Republicans and anti-Semitic leagues that had come and gone during the last quarter of the nineteenth century . . . most of them appeared to have a new and uglier quality that I had first seen in the Black Shirts in fascist Italy and the Brown Shirts in Germany. In France too, they were now prowling the streets in their various coloured shirts, their jackboots echoing on the pavement, beating up decent citizens and howling for the downfall of the Republic.'[6]

Shirer, who had just returned to France after an absence of four years, was obviously shocked by some of the new trends which were developing in France to an alarming degree. As an experienced journalist he soon learned that behind these organizations 'were certain powerful business and financial groups that were furnishing the money to keep them active and growing and which, on their own, while refraining from soiling the hands of their members in the hooliganism of the streets, were spreading propaganda with the aim of inducing Frenchmen to get rid of their parliamentary democracy in favour of a totalitarian regime'.[7]

The biggest and most influential of these organizations was the Croix de Feu which was founded in 1927. Its members, as in post-war Germany, were mainly discontented war veterans, and in 1931 it was experiencing a revival. It was led by a retired Lieutenant-Colonel, Francois de la Rocque, who 'quickly transformed it into a paramilitary, anti-parliamentary League, able to mobilize street demonstrators on an hour's notice and determined to stamp out Communism and pacifism and reform the Republic by curbing its erring Parliament'. On the evening of 27 November 1931 Colonel de la Rocque 'led a mob of Croix de Feu members, assisted by storm-troopers from Action Francaise and the Jeunesse Patriotes* into the great hall of the Trocadero, where thousands of persons were attending the final gala meeting of the International Disarmament Congress and broke it up'. Among some of the well known personalities on the platform were former Prime Minister Painlevé, Lord Robert Cecil, Salvadore de Madariaga and Edouard Herriot, who had been Chairman of the Congress. 'They were swept away by Colonel de la Rocque and his rowdies while other assault groups cleared out the audience and even the police who had been sent to protect it'. According to Shirer, la Rocque, 'at the time of the Trocadero riot . . . was in close touch with Laval and

---

*Action Francaise was a Royalist organization and the Jeunesse Patriotes 'an organization of street brawlers recruited mostly from the University students'. (William L. Shirer)

Tardieu, who alternated as Premiers in those days, and who gave him not only moral support but – it seems certain – financial backing from secret funds of the State, which la Rocque was trying to undermine. Private funds also were not lacking, for among his backers were such business leaders as Ernest Mercier [the electricity magnate] and Francois Coty' [the wealthy perfume manufacturer and proprietor of the Conservative daily newspaper, *Le Figaro*].

'. . . By the end of 1933, as the hostility against Parliament mounted in Paris, the Croix de Feu and its auxiliary bodies, had some 60,000 members, of whom a third were in Paris'.[8]

At the same time as the outbreak of fascism and political disorders were taking place in France, similar events were happening in Britain. Disillusionment and discontent with the MacDonald-led-Labour Government of 1929–31, the great slump and mass unemployment, and then a weak, inefficient and discredited National Coalition Government, provided ample opportunities for any demagogue to exploit the people's discontent and dig up the inevitable scapegoats. It was a wealthy former Conservative MP who switched allegiances to become a Labour Minister, and then resigned to form his own party, the New Party, who thought the time was ripe to transform Britain into a Fascist State. Sir Oswald Mosley and his New Party suffered massive defeats in the elections of 1931 and it was not until January 1932, after seeking advice from Mussolini in Rome, that the British Union of Fascists was set up. By 1934 it had about 20,000 members with about 400 branches around the country –

'Violence became the principal technique of agitation reaching its climax at a mass-meeting held at Olympia on the evening of Thursday, June 7, 1934, and attended by 15,000 people, with another 5,000 outside. Mosley, trim in his black shirt, and illuminated by spotlights on the stage, made an address which was frequently interrupted. On each occasion the spotlights were turned on the hecklers, and he (or she) was set upon by several Fascist stewards and brutally kicked and beaten as he was removed from the hall. No interference from the police checked these un-English atrocities; indeed the police were busy that evening arresting Communist and anti-fascist demonstrators out-side the hall'.[9]

Lord Rothermere, proprietor of the *Daily Mail* and a keen supporter of Mosley and the BUF from its inception, was also using his influence through the 'Rothermere Press' (with its considerable chain of newspapers) to boost the image of Hitler and Nazi Germany in Britain. On 28 November 1933 he wrote in the *Daily Mail*:

'The new bond between France and Britain would have another effect of inestimable importance. It would turn Germany's territorial ambitions in the direction where they can do least harm and most good – towards the east of Europe. Germany must have elbow-room. The gigantic reservoir of German nationalist energy is developing pressure that demands an overflow. It is to the thinly populated areas of Western Russia that the National-Socialist Government looks for an out-let. I can see no danger to Western Europe in this tendency.

. . . German expansion into Russia would free the Poles from the ever-present danger of attack by a neighbour whose Red Army in 1920 marched to the very gates of Warsaw.*

The relations between Germany and Poland have already become more friendly since Hitler came to power. Once Germany had acquired the additional territory she needs in Western Russia, the problem of the Polish Corridor could be settled without difficulty. In exchange for the recovery of the northern part of the corridor restoring her old connection with East Prussia, Germany would be able to offer Poland not only an alternative outlet to the sea through Memel but to restore to her the immense advantage she enjoyed in the 16th century of access to the Black Sea, by opening to her the great port of Odessa.

---

*It was the Polish Army aided by Britain and France which first invaded Russia in 1920 – see Chap. 10

It would also be to the advantage of those little Baltic States of Estonia, Latvia and Lithuania to have on their eastern frontier the civilized conditions of Germany instead of the constant menace of Soviet Russia . . .

. . . The diversion of Germany's reserves of energy and organizing ability into Bolshevist Russia would help to restore the Russian people to a civilized existence, and perhaps turn the tide of trade once more towards prosperity.

By the same process Germany's need for expansion would be satisfied and that growing menace which at present darkens the cloud of coming war would be removed for ever.'

This article not only reflected Rothermere's political philosophy, it was also that of a group of leading politicians known as the 'Cliveden Set'* which from 1935 until the outbreak of World War II dominated British foreign policy. Among its leading figures, including that of its hosts, Lord and Lady Astor, were Neville Chamberlain, Lords Halifax, Londonderry and Lothian, Sir Samuel Hoare, as well as Geoffrey Dawson and J.L. Garvin, editors of *The Times* and *The Observer*.†

By appeasing Nazi Germany's appetite, by 'generously' allowing, even inciting, an imperial rival to seek its 'elbow room' in Russia and other countries in the east, the Rothermere Press led the way, to be followed by other Conservative journals. They had their counterparts in France. Newspaper proprietors such as Coty and his *Le Figaro* had not only been backing the Fascist organizations to topple the Republic, but were also trying to improve Nazi Germany's image in France.

But French fears of a rearmed Germany were even greater among the mass of French people than in Britain. Consequently much of the French Right Wing press had to be a little more discreet and a trifle more diplomatic in their

---

*Cliveden was the name of the Astors' Stately Home, where British foreign policy was often initiated.
†*The Observer* was owned by Viscount Waldorf Astor and his brother, John Astor, was Chairman of *The Times*.

treatment of Nazi aspirations; anti-German feelings were far more widespread. The occupation of Paris by German troops in 1870 and the invasion of France in 1914 had not been forgotten, a factor which since 1918 had frequently threatened the cordiality of the Anglo-French Entente.

The British Government had not only condoned German rearmanent, it was actually encouraging it. It certainly had no interest in disarmament or anything to do with the Disarmament Conference. Sir John Simon had warned Parliament on 6 February 1934 that 'if a satisfactory Disarmament Agreement cannot be promptly arrived at we shall have to face the state of our own armaments . . . which will have to be re-examined' and added that 'in a new convention you will have to face some rearmament by Germany.' His statement was described by Attlee 'as a proposal for the rearmament of Germany.' (*Hansard*, Cols 988, 992 and 999)

The collapse of the long drawn-out Disarmament Conference was commented on by George Bernard Shaw in a radio broadcast the following evening. He told his listeners 'the League of Nations has set up a Disarmament Conference which, after two years of fooling has virtually ended in the confession of our Foreign Secretary, Sir John Simon, a clear-headed lawyer, that the Disarmament Conference is really an Armament Conference.' (*The Daily Herald*, 7 February 1934).

Notes

1. EDEN, Anthony, *Memoirs – Facing the Dictators* pp. 43/44
2. MAISKY, Ivan, *Who Helped Hitler?* pp. 55/56
3. ADAMTHWAITE, Anthony P., *The Making of the Second World War* p. 38
4. SHIRER, William L., *The Collapse of the Third Republic* p. 222
5. SHIRER, William L., *The Collapse of the Third Republic* pp. 172/173
6. SHIRER, William L., *The Collapse of the Third Republic* p. 181
7. SHIRER, William L., *The Collapse of the Third Republic* pp. 181/182
8. SHIRER, William L., *The Collapse of the Third Republic* pp. 185/186
9. MOWAT, C.L., *Britain Between the Wars 1918–40* p. 474

27

THE ROAD TO WAR

The road to war was now open. According to a 1937 publication by the New Fabian Research Bureau, which provides a detailed analysis of the National Government's foreign policy, British business institutions in the City of London gave 'every support and encouragement to German rearmament. Good money has been thrown after bad in a number of loans and credit schemes to release the so-called "frozen-credits" from before the slump. Aeroplane engines were sold in large quantities to Germany at a time when the Disarmament chapter of the Versailles Treaty was still supposed to be valid. Partly all this was done under the slogan "Business is Business" and "The City has nothing to do with politics". But this pretext was frequently dropped'.[1]

An indication of the attitude of some of Britain's leading industrialists appeared in the *Sheffield Daily Telegraph* on the morning of 24 October 1933 :

> 'With regard to Germany, something was bound to happen. The people there lost everything in the war. While Germany was wonderfully equipped, scientifically and industrially, she had no working capital, and the prospects of the young people since the war have been almost nil. Either they were to have Communism or something else. Hitler has produced Hitlerism as we see it today, and of the two I think it is preferable. Will the Germans go to war again? I don't think there is any doubt about it, and the curious thing about it is that I am almost persuaded that some day we

shall have to let the Germans arm or we shall arm them. With the Russians armed to the teeth and the tremendous menace in the East, Germany unarmed in the middle is always going to be a plum waiting for the Russians to take, and which we should have to defend if the Germans could not defend themselves. One of the greatest menaces to peace in Europe today is the totally unarmed condition of Germany'.

These were the words of Sir Arthur Balfour, Chairman and Managing Director of Arthur Balfour Limited, Capital Steel Works, Sheffield, and Chairman of High Speed Alloys.

In 1919 the Saar* had been put under the control of the League of Nations with France being permitted the right to exploit the valuable coalfields for a period of fifteen years, after which the local inhabitants were to decide by plebiscite the future of the territory. In addition to the coalfields, there was also an important iron and steel industry and a population of some 850,000 people, the overwhelming majority of whom were German. Under the terms of the plebiscite the inhabitants had the choice of remaining under the jurisdiction of the League, being annexed by France, or returning to Germany. In January 1935 over 80 per cent voted for a return to Germany. The vote had been considerably boosted by the intimidation and bullying of the local Nazis. This, together with the financial backing of big business organizations, ensured a massive pro-Reich vote.

'A self confident, almost cynical spirit is beginning to dominate the Wilhelmstrasse once again' commented the *Observer*'s Berlin correspondent on 3 February 1935.

The positive activities of the new German Government – the exit from Geneva, re-arming, conclusion of the pact with Poland, and the winning of the Saar victory – are regarded here as achieve-

*A region of 990 square miles bordering France and Luxembourg. Capital – Saarbrucken.

ments due to the purifying policy of a healthy "isolation"'.

And now there was to be compulsory military service, a combination of factors that prompted Litvinov to ask the League of Nations : 'What is to be done if a State demanding or seizing the right to armaments is ruled by people who have announced to the whole world a programme of foreign policy consisting not only of a policy of revanche, but also of unlimited conquests of foreign territory and the destruction of the independence of entire States, by people who, having publicly announced such a programme, far from repudiating it, continually circulate it and bring up their country in that spirit?'[2]

Neither the British nor the French Government offered a reply.

The Arms Race was once again begining to gather momentum. Led by Nazi Germany and Fascist Italy, Britain and France soon followed. Russia had to do likewise.

In an article headed 'Bankruptcy or War', H.N. Brailsford warned in the *Reynolds News*, 28 April 1935 of Germany's drive to war. Firstly, he emphasized the fact that 'Germany is the key to nearly everything that happens in Europe' and then went on to relate :

'One gathers that the return to conscription was taken very quietly and with satisfaction.

... The National Army is once more in its accustomed place, and ever since the massacre of the Storm Trooper's leaders on June 30* [1934], it is upon the army that the Nazi regime reposes ... Steadily Germany returns to something more nearly resembling the traditional pattern of a capitalist state with a conscript army. For the rest, the first effect of conscription will be to ease the economic problem.

Half-a-million young men will be taken from

---

*Brailsford was referring to the assassination of Roehm and other leaders of the SA Storm Troopers by Hitler and his rival gang of SS Storm Troopers.

the labour market and industry will be busy making uniforms, boots and arms and in refurnishing the barracks . . . Every German has been told, till the figures are as familiar as the multiplication table, that there are 12,000 hostile aircraft round his frontiers . . .

"If the others are building planes, we must build them too".

There was a rather general expectation that the great National victory in the Saar plebiscite would be the signal for a rather milder, a somewhat more liberal and tolerant epoch. It has not come. The most reliable barometer in the Nazi Reich is the treatment of the Jews. Actually a new wave of anti-Semitism has broken over them in recent months . . . The Jews, of course, are not the only sufferers. On the contrary, there has recently been one of the periodical "rounds-up" of men and women suspected of Socialist opinions or activities . . .

. . . It is then a disturbing picture that results from one's enquiries. . . There is, of course, discontent, but it has, as yet, no political significance. Work is certainly easier to come by than it was, and unemployment, thanks chiefly to rearmament has diminished.

Real wages, however, have sunk since Hitler came to power, by a full 25 per cent. The effort after national self-sufficiency has restricted imports so drastically that, for the average worker, butter and eggs are almost unobtainable.

The standard of life has sunk.

. . . Month after month exports fail to balance imports, and yet if rearmament is to continue at the present pace, the imports are indispensable. It cannot go on, and yet dare Hitler stop?

For to stop re-arming would be to face the ruin of industry, the fury of its owners, the despair of its workers.

So does its own logic drive it to choose between two forms of ruin – bankruptcy or war'.

The arms drive was given a specific boost on 4 March by

the publication of the British Government's White Paper on Defence. Falling back on the failure of the Disarmament Conference as its main excuse, the document stated that 'peace is the principal aim of British foreign policy' and 'in the present troubled state of the world the Government realised that armaments cannot be dispensed with. They are required to preserve peace, to maintain security and to deter aggression. The deliberate retardation of our armaments as part of our peace policy has brought them below the level required ... An additional expenditure on the armaments of the three Defence Services can, therefore, no longer be safely postponed.'[3]

Hitler didn't need any further encouragement. The French Government's announcement on 12 March 1936, that it was going to extend conscription from twelve months to two years, was immediately seized upon by the German Government for officially issuing a declaration four days later that it had decided to re-introduce conscription and the provision of a conscript army of thirty six Divisions (550,000) men. Von Neurath admitted that the timing of the German declaration was determined by the French announcement.*

In 1935 Britain's Foreign Office and the Quai d'Orsay were caught between a number of stools. One, should they appease Mussolini and bring him into a tri-partite pact to offset the dangers of a re-armed and aggressive Germany? Two, should they aim for a four-power pact – Daladier's dream – which would include Nazi Germany as part of a crusade against Bolshevik Russia? or three, follow the Barthou line, co-operation with the Soviet Union, while at the same time appease Italy and ensure its separation from Germany?

Laval was under great pressure in France to carry on the momentum of the Barthou Plan, and his own political future was at stake. Germany had been invited to join in the Eastern Pact of Mutual Guarantee, but had –

'let its intentions be understood – that no reply will be given to the Eastern Locarno invitation

---

*See *German Documents on Foreign Policy 1918–45* Series C. Vol. III No. 532.

until the proposed terms of the legalization of German rearmament to be agreed between France and England in London have been submitted to and considered by Berlin.' (*The Observer*. 20 January 1935)

Two weeks later, Laval and his Prime Minister, Flandin, had a meeting in London with Sir John Simon and Ramsay MacDonald. While the Anglo-French talks were in progress, the *Observer*'s Berlin correspondent reported that :

'The British desire that no pact or agreement having the character of an ultimatum directed against Germany should be concluded in London is regarded as a good sign that England is holding the scales in favour of the German thesis. Germany is the "absent partner" in the discussions for she is well aware that her growing moral and military strength has "dictated" the lines upon which the discussions must proceed.' (*The Observer*, 3 February 1935)

The result of the London Conference produced no complaints from Berlin. In a joint communiqué, the two countries :

'proposed that a general agreement freely negotiated between Germany and the other Powers should supersede the disarmament provisions of the Treaty of Versailles and that a special Air Convention should be negotiated between the Western European Powers.' (*The Times*, 4 February 1935)

Having been released from the arms limitations imposed at Versailles, Hitler's Third Reich could now, officially, join in a revived arms race by the Western Powers. The communiqué also included a proposal for a 'general settlement' based upon a system of regional pacts which would 'contribute to the restoration of confidence and the prospects of peace among nations'. It then went on to stress that

'This general settlement would make provision for the organization of security in Europe, particularly by means of the conclusion of pacts, freely negotiated between all the interested parties, and ensuring mutual assistance in Eastern Europe'.

The first of these pacts was signed at the lakeside resort of Stresa, in Northern Italy in April 1935 by the Heads of State of Britain, France and Italy.

Mussolini had previously held discussions with Laval at which the French Foreign Minister 'gave him soothing assurances that Paris and London would not seriously object to Italy's "peaceful penetration" of her "rightful sphere of influence in Africa"'. No wonder 'Mussolini returned to Rome in a jubilant mood, convinced that in return for his support, he had been given a free hand to make his move in Ethiopia.'[4]

What were these 'soothing assurances'? Earlier in the year, on 7 January, Laval went to Rome and signed an agreement with Mussolini, ostensibly to counter the threat to Austrian independence by their common neighbour. At that time, both France and Britain felt that co-operation with Italy would be sufficient to offset the danger of aggressive actions in Europe by Germany. Mussolini used the Rome meeting to get an agreement with Laval on his plans for expansion in East Africa. Anthony P. Adamthwaite refers to this meeting and says that 'The most controversial of the agreements was a secret one on Abyssinia. With minor reservations France signed over to Italy her economic interests in Abyssinia. In a private conversation with the Duce, Laval used the phrase a "free hand". The Italian leader interpreted this gloss as meaning that France would turn a blind eye to the military conquest of Abyssinia . . .

'By the Spring of 1935', says Adamthwaite, 'Italy's intentions were common knowledge. But there was no common front against her. The dominant note of Anglo-French diplomacy was conciliation. Italy was needed as a makeweight against Germany.'[5]

When the British, French and Italian delegations met in Stresa on 11 – 14 April, the security of Austria was one of the main points of discussion. The three Governments 'recognized that the necessity of maintaining the independence and integrity of Austria would continue to inspire their common policy' and cited the Anglo-French declaration of 3 February 1935 'in which the decision was reaffirmed to consult together as to the measures to be taken in case of threats to the integrity and independence of Austria.' (*The Times*, 15 April 1935). And on 27 June, Austrian independence was further assured, at least on paper, by the signing of the Franco-Italian Military Convention. Both countries agreed to undertake combined operations in the event of a German threat to her security.

Meanwhile the plans for an Eastern Security Pact – the so called 'Eastern Locarno' – by which Germany was to be included on an equal footing together with France and the Soviet Union, was negated by both Germany and Poland. It was because of Germany's refusal to participate that the Franco-Russian Pact of Mutual Assistance was eventually signed on 2 May 1935. The Pact was immediately attacked by the Nazi propaganda machine as a 'military alliance' devised to enforce the encirclement of Germany. The Franco-Soviet Pact actually left the door open for Germany, if it so desired, to join the Pact as proposed in the first instance. It was carefully worded to comply with the Covenant of the League of Nations and in an attached explanatory protocol it clearly stated :

'The two Governments put on record that the negotiations which have just resulted in the signature of this treaty were primarily entered upon in order to complete a security agreement comprising all the countries of North-Eastern Europe – the USSR, Germany, Czechoslovakia, Poland and the Baltic States bordering upon the USSR; besides this agreement there was to have been concluded a treaty of assistance between the USSR, France and Germany, under which each of these three States would be pledged to come to the assistance of any one of them subjected to an aggression on the part of one of those three States. Although circumstances have not hitherto permitted the conclusion of these agreements, which the two parties still look upon as desirable, it remains a fact, nevertheless, that the undertaking set forth in the Franco-Soviet Treaty should be understood to come into play only within the limits contemplated in the tripartite agreement previously projected.' (*The Times*, 4 May 1935)

Hitler's response came on 21 May when he declared that Germany was ready to conclude pacts of non-aggression with all its neighbours but not with the Bolsheviks. The German Government was ready to limit its armaments 'to any degree that is also adopted by the other Powers', having shown its 'goodwill to avoid an unlimited armaments race.' It had agreed to 'The limitation of the German navy ... at 35 per cent of the British navy' and as a sop for British public opinion added 'Germany has not the intention or the necessity or the means to participate in any new naval rivalry.'[6]

Britain was the only major power to accept Hitler's reassurances seriously and to such a degree that, despite its own plans for rearming, it decided to make a deal with the Nazi Government.

In May 1935, after a re-shuffle of the British Cabinet, Stanley Baldwin took over from Ramsay MacDonald as Prime Minister and Sir John Simon was replaced by Sir Samuel Hoare at the Foreign Office. Maisky, in his memoirs, commented on the fact that 'during the first world war Hoare was the British military agent at the Tsar's headquarters.'[7]

Anthony Eden, who had held the important post of Lord Privy Seal and deputy to Simon at the Foreign Office was relegated to the nondescript office of Minister without Portfolio for League of Nations Affairs. Eden had been a leading member of the group which favoured co-operation with the Soviet Union.

On 18 June 1935, after two weeks of secret negotiations, an Anglo-German Naval Agreement was signed. The signatories were Sir Samuel Hoare and Joachim von Ribbentrop for the German Foreign Office. The two parties agreed that Germany would be allowed to build a fleet of up to 35 per cent of that of the British Navy. The document then went on to declare that :

> 'In the matter of submarines however, Germany, while not exceeding the ratio of 35:100 in respect of total tonnage shall have the right to possess a submarine tonnage equal to the total submarine tonnage possessed by the members of the British Commonwealth of Nations.'

To soften the shock it was agreed that

> 'Germany's submarine tonnage shall not exceed 45 per cent of the total of that possessed by the British Commonwealth of Nations.' (*News Chronicle*, 19 June 1935)

except in special circumstances. The loophole being that she could build up to 100 per cent if she thought it was needed for her security. Germany had also agreed that 'as from now' it would 'not engage in what was called during the war, unrestricted submarine warfare'* that is, her submarines would not attack unarmed merchant ships, a commitment that was abandoned from the very outset of World War II. 'As soon as the deal with Britain was concluded', comments Shirer, 'Germany laid down two battleships, the Bismarck and Tirpitz with a displacement of over 45,000 tons.'[8]

Neither France, nor Italy were consulted despite the pious declaration at Stresa.† In France, the reaction was of bitterness and disgust at what was regarded as an act of treachery by the British Government. It was seen 'as a further appeasement of Hitler, whose appetite grew on concessions and they resented the British agreeing . . . to scrap further the Peace Treaty and thus add to the growing over-all military power of Nazi Germany.'[9]

---

*Lord Londonderry, the Lord Privy Seal, speaking for the Government in the House of Lords, 26 June 1935. (*Documents on International Affairs Vol. I.* 1935, p. 153).

†'To oppose by all appropriate means and unilateral repudiation of treaties susceptible of endangering the peace of Europe' (part of Stresa communiqué) Ex – William L. Shirer, p. 225.

Hitler had certainly never concealed his aim of driving a wedge between Britain and France. Some British statesmen must have accepted the Nazi bible – *Mein Kampf* – on its face value, and as the gospel truth, when the Nazi Fuehrer told them that 'only two states are left as possible friends for us' and they are 'Great Britain and Italy' whereas 'France's military predominance presses sorely at the heart of the World Empire of Great Britain.'[10]

Konni Zilliacus in his book, *Inquest on Peace*, written not long after the Anglo-German Naval Agreement, reinforced Shirer's assessment of its effect upon French public opinion. 'Popular resentment' in France was 'so strong' that it 'played straight into the hands of the militarists and reactionary elements in the French Government and Foreign Office, whose policy is to build up France's system of alliances, to turn their backs finally upon the League and the Collective System and therefore give Italy a free hand in Abyssinia.'[11]

The weekly publication *Time and Tide*, on 13 July 1935, reported a statement by Robert Dell from Geneva, in which he said :

> 'It is almost universal opinion on the continent that the aims of British policy are to strengthen Germany so as to counter-balance French and Russian influence, to avert German naval competition and German colonial ambitions by giving Hitler a free hand in Eastern Europe and to encourage German and Japanese aggressive designs against Soviet Russia.'

Notes

1. New Fabian Research Bureau, *The Road to War* pp. 101/102
2. *Soviet Documents on Foreign Policy* Vol. III 1933–41 (ed. Jane Degras) p. 128
3. *British Sessional Papers*, Statement Relating to Defence Vol. XIII – 83, House of Commons CMND 4827
4. ARCHER, Jules, *20th Century Caesar – Benito Mussolini* p. 116
5. ADAMTHWAITE, Anthony P. *The Making of the Second World War* p. 48
6. *Documents on German Foreign Policy* – Series C. Vol. IV pp. 176/177
7. MAISKY, Ivan, *Who Helped Hitler?* p. 62
8. SHIRER, William L., *The Collapse of the Third Republic* p. 230 F.N.
9. SHIRER, William L., *The Collapse of the Third Republic* p. 230
10. HITLER, Adolf, *Mein Kampf* (English Edition) p. 246
11. ZILLIACUS, K., *Inquest on Peace* pp. 115/116

28

THE MOSCOW TRIALS AND SUBSEQUENT PURGES

The Soviet Government had indicated on a number of occasions that it was fully aware of the 'aggressive designs' upon their country ever since the 1917 Revolution – and not only by the Germans and Japanese. Apart from the brief respite during the years of the Weimar Republic, the advent of Hitler, even before he became Chancellor, had compelled them to tighten up their means of security.

On 10 March 1938, a letter appeared in the *Manchester Guardian* from its former foreign correspondent, Morgan Phillips Price, in which he recalls 'sitting in the press gallery of the Taurida Palace' on 23 February 1918, during that 'fateful meeting of the All-Russia Soviets', when a question was put 'whether the Revolution should allow itself to be dragged into the dust by the Prussian Generals.' He remembered the situation which had been created after Radek and Madame Kollontai had 'denounced Lenin as the "betrayor of the Revolution" when he wished to sign the German terms.'* Phillips Price was convinced that 'most of what had happened since, including the dreadful blood letting' had 'its roots in what happened in 1918'. It had become apparent that the struggle for power within the Central Committee and for the leadership of the Soviet Communist Party stemmed from that 'fateful meeting'.

Although the results of Brest-Litovsk had the temporary effect of closing some of the cracks within the Central Committee for a few years, they opened up again in 1923 during the period of Lenin's severe illness. In December of that year, the fight for the leadership of the Party had got

*See Brest-Litovsk, p. 57

under way with Trotsky's attack on the policies of the Central Committee. Within a few months of Lenin's death in January 1924, the new leader of the Party, Joseph Stalin, had decided that the primary objective of the USSR was the conversion of Russia into a socialist industrial state as quickly as possible. Trotsky's priority was to spread the Revolution into other countries around the world. The Comintern, he believed, was established in 1920 for that purpose, and by the mid-1920s he had recruited most of the Committee members who supported him in 1918. He had the backing of Comintern secretary, Grigori Zinoviev, who was also leader of the 'Leningrad Group' of the Party which had revolted against Stalin and the Central Committee.

Walter Duranty, who was in Moscow at the time of the 'Leningrad revolt', says that he can 'remember the dismay in high Party circles which was caused by the news that Zinoviev had joined the Trotskyite opposition.'[1]

In December 1925, Kirov, Molotov and Voroshilov were sent to Leningrad to handle the Zinoviev affair. The result was that Zinoviev and the Trotskyite group were ousted.

Meanwhile the two pariahs of the post World War I scene had followed up their 1922 Rapallo Agreement with the signing of further Agreements to help each other both militarily and economically. In 1926, protocols were signed by General von Seeckt and Marshal Tukhachevsky, and in 1931 Tukhachevsky signed another protocol with von Seeckt's successor, General von Hammerstein, Commander-in-Chief of the Reichswehr.

Although Trotsky and some of his close associates were expelled from the Party in 1927, there were still many of his followers, including a number in influential posts, who had not given up the fight. Yet in spite of the inner conflicts, the Stalin policy of industrialization and the socialization of agriculture was set in motion during the latter part of 1928 as an integral part of the first of the Five Year Plans.

Stalin had rejected using the Comintern as an instrument for fomenting world revolution, but nevertheless believed that it should be used as a channel through which Soviet foreign policy would make contacts and alliances with the progressive forces of other countries, particularly after 1933, when Hitler and his Nazi party had taken over control of Germany. Thus the amicable relationship between the Soviet Union and Germany was brought to an end.

The new leader of a reorganized Comintern was Georgi Dimitrov, the Bulgarian Communist, who had defiantly challenged Hitler and Goering during the Reichstag Fire Trials of February 1933. But it was the assassinations of two prominent political figures in 1934 that were to have the greatest impact upon the political future of both France and Russia and their relationship with the rest of Europe. The first was that of Louis Barthou, the French Foreign Minister, who had persistently campaigned for a coalition of European countries, including Russia, to counter the growing menace of Nazi Germany, and the second was the murder in Leningrad of Kirov, a close associate of Stalin. In the case of Barthou, his carefully prepared plans for countering the threat of a re-militarized Germany had tragically been destroyed, whilst in Russia, the Kirov murder was to set off a train of events leading to the trials and purges that were to divide and inevitably weaken the Communist and Socialist movements throughout the world.

In June 1935, Zinoviev and other members of the 'Leningrad Group', who had been arrested earlier in the year, were brought to trial for complicity in the Kirov murder. The actual murder had been carried out in Leningrad by Nikolayev, a local citizen, whose wife was Kirov's personal secretary. Pending further enquiries, the others were acquitted, but re-arrested some months later on a charge of counter-revolutionary activities and brought to trial again in August 1936. This was the first of the four major treason trials held in Russia between then and March 1938. The second was that of Radek, Piatakov and fifteen others; the third was the trial of Marshal Tukhachevsky and the seven Red Army Generals in June 1937, and the fourth, of whom the most prominent were Bukharin, Rykov and Yagoda.

It had become apparent to many foreign correspondents and other eye-witnesses that the overall authority of Russia's political leaders had been gradually undermined by a powerful section of the Red Army during the latter part of the 1920s and the first half of the 1930s. In addition, sharp divisions had arisen in a number of regions between the supporters of Stalin and those of Trotsky. When Trotsky was expelled from the Party in 1927 and then exiled, he was never far from Russia's borders and was therefore able to maintain effective contact with his former accomplices. He first went to live on the Turkish island of Prinkipo near Constantinople. From there to France for a brief period in 1934, and then Norway until 1936, when he moved on to Mexico.

During the latter part of 1933, that is just after the Nazis had taken over power, 'the Soviet Government closed down German military training stations for aviation, tanks, and gas warfare at Lipetsk, Kazan and Saratov.'[2] At the banquet given for the departing German officers, regrets were expressed by Marshal Tukhachevsky over the ending of military co-operation. Confirmation of this was expressed in a Note from the German Chargé d'Affaires in Moscow, Herr Twardowski, to his Foreign Ministry in Berlin on 8 November 1933. Its subject :

'CONVERSATION WITH DEPUTY COMMISSAR FOR WAR TUKHACHEVSKY'

'Herewith is submitted the note on a conversation which I had with M. Tukhachevsky on the occasion of the farewell dinner for the Ambassador ... Although much of what Tukhachevsky stated as his opinion of political intercourse is falsely or wrongly viewed, his statements made with great earnestness, that the Red Army would never betray its co-operation with the Reichswehr to other powers, and that there is now as before the greatest sympathy in the Red Army for the Reichswehr, are significant and interesting. The personality and standing of Tukhachevsky are such that weight should be given to his words.'[3]

This Note was sent nine months after Hitler had become Chancellor of the German Government and eight months after the Reichstag Fire conspiracy.

The fate of Tukhachevsky and the Generals was finally

sealed by Eduard Benes who was Czech Foreign Minister at the time. It was in the Autumn of 1936 that Hitler tried to entice the Czechs into a non-aggression pact in order to keep them out of the plan originated by Barthou just before his assassination in 1934, for an 'Eastern Pact of Mutual Guarantee',* which would have included the Soviet Union.

In his *Memoirs*, Benes recalls 'that the German proposal would necessarily involve Czechoslovakia's denouncing her treaties with France and the Soviet Union and leaving the League of Nations.' He was prepared to negotiate a non-aggression pact provided his country maintained their existing treaties.† His 'concept of the treaty was not at all acceptable to the rulers of the Third Reich.' Consequently, the Nazi leaders 'considered the negotiations to have failed.' Benes records having 'received unofficial confirmation of this from Berlin in the second half of January 1937, together with a very confidential hint that Hitler was now engaged in other negotiations, which, if successful, would probably affect us considerably.'[4] What were these other negotiations? Benes says that Hitler's representative, Trauttmannsdorf, had 'As a slip of the tongue . . . unwittingly revealed these negotiations were with the anti-Stalin clique in the USSR, Marshal Tukhachevsky, Rykov and others. Hitler expected these negotiations to be successful and he was therefore not interested in bringing the discussions with us to a speedy conclusion. If the attempt to disrupt the Soviet Union had succeeded, the whole situation in Europe would have been transformed, but Stalin prevented this just in time.' He then adds that he 'at once informed the Soviet Minister at Prague, Alexandrovsky, of what (he) had learned from Berlin about the Mastny‡-Trauttmannsdorf talks.'[5]

Winston Churchill has recorded receiving a visit from

---

*Benes says that 'the Eastern Pact was never signed because of the united resistance of Hitler's Germany and Beck's Poland', and that all 'that remained was the Franco-Soviet Agreement.' (signed at Prague, 16 May 1935) *Memoirs of Dr Eduard Benes*, p. 24.

†Treaties of alliance between the Soviet Union and France, and between the Soviet Union and Czechoslovakia were concluded in 1935. *Memoirs of Dr Eduard Benes*. p. 7.

‡Mastny was the Czech Minister in Berlin.

Benes in 1944. He was in Marrakesh at the time, when the Czech President told him of the offer he had received from Hitler in 1935 'to respect in all circumstances the integrity of Czechoslovakia in return for a guarantee that she would remain neutral in the event of a Franco-German war. When Benes pointed to his treaty obliging him to act with France in such a case, the German Ambassador replied that there was no need to denounce the treaty. It would be sufficient to break it, if and when the time came, by simply failing to mobilize or march . . .'

'In the Autumn of 1936 a message from a high military source in Germany was conveyed to President Benes to the effect that if he wanted to take advantage of the Fuhrer's offer he had better be quick, because events would shortly take place in Russia rendering any help he could give to Germany insignificant.

'While Benes was pondering over this disturbing hint he became aware that communications were passing through the Soviet Embassy in Prague between important personages in Russia and the German Government. This was part of the so-called military and old-guard Communist conspiracy to overthrow Stalin and introduce a new regime based on a pro-German policy. President Benes lost no time in communicating all he could find out to Stalin. Thereafter there followed the merciless, but perhaps not needless, military and political purge in Soviet Russia . . .'[6]

It was in January 1937, that Joseph E. Davies, a lawyer with a strong and influential commercial backgroumd, took up his post as American Ambassador to the USSR. As the trial of Tukhachevsky and the Generals was held in camera, Davies's assessment was reached after discussions with Duranty and other American correspondents, as well as a number of Soviet politicians, including Foreign Minister Litvinov. In a letter to Sumner Welles, the US Assistant Secretary of State, he says that 'in all probability there was a definite conspiracy in the making looking to a coup d'etat by the army – not necessarily anti-Stalin, but anti-political and anti-party.'[7]

The trial, condemnation and execution of Tukhachevsky and the Generals was carried out on 12 June.

Davies refers to the reports 'of the execution of many

officials at Kharkhov, Rostov-on-Don, Sverdlovsk, Tiflis and other places', and adds that 'in Leningrad sixteen persons were shot for conspiring to murder members of the Government and wreck the chemical works. They were described as spies from the German Secret Police.'[8] In his journal of 23 November 1937 he reported that 'A military court at Leningrad sentenced to twenty five years' imprisonment two Germans convicted of espionage on behalf of the German Secret Service.'[9]

The American Ambassador attended the trial of political leaders, Bukharin, Rykov, Krestinsky and others, as well as Yagoda, the Head of the Secret Police, and according to some of the testimonies it 'would appear to indicate that the Kremlin's fears were well justified. For it now seems that a plot existed in the beginning of November, 1936, to project a coup d'etat, with Tukhachevsky at its head for May of the following year.' [10] On 13 March 1938, all the defendants were adjudged guilty. Three were sentenced to imprisonment and the remainder shot.

In June 1941, Ambassador Davies was back in America and he records, in what he describes as his 'Study in Hindsignt' concerning the 'Fifth Columnists in Russia', that it 'was in 1936 that Hitler made his now famous Nuremberg speech in which he clearly indicated his designs on the Ukraine.' He refers to the sabotage of Soviet industrial plants revealed in 'the testimony of many of the minor defendants' which had established the fact 'that, upon orders of the principal defendants, they had direct connection with the German and Japanese Intelligence Services and co-operated with them in systematic espionage and sabotage . . .' He cites the case of the 'two explosions at the Gorlovka Nitrogen Fertilizer Plants which entailed enormous property losses as well as the loss of human life.' In addition, there was 'the disaster to the Chemical plants of the Voskressensk Chemical Works and the Nevsky plant.' One of the accused 'told how he had planned and executed the wrecking of troop trains', under the direction of foreign Intelligence Services, and had 'testified as to how he had received instructions from these foreign Intelligence Services 'to organize incendiarism in military stores, canteens, and army shipments', and the necessity of using 'bacteriological means in time of war with the object of contaminating troop trains, canteens, and army camps with virulent bacilli'.'[11]

The great tragedy arising from the trials and purges in Russia during the 1930s was of the thousands of innocent people who were caught up into the waves of suspicion, rivalry and opportunism that had arisen after the Revolution and the Wars of Intervention. It had apparently been sufficient evidence, in many cases, to apply the term 'Enemy of the People' to thousands of Communists and non-Communists, for their being imprisoned and, in more extreme cases, shot.

Duranty was evidently deeply shocked by the 'reports of men and women Communists with doubtful pasts who had shielded themselves by their excessive zeal in denouncing innocent comrades. Greed, jealousy, rivalry and all manner of personal motives' were in his opinion enough to cause almost anyone to have his or her fate sealed.[12]

Yet, in spite of the trials and purges and their effect upon morale within the higher echelons of the Red Army and the public services, Hitler and his Nazi accomplices failed to establish a 'Fifth Column' in the Soviet Union as was eventually achieved in Austria, Czechoslovakia, Spain, Norway, Belgium and France.

By the time of the German invasion of the USSR in June 1941, the Soviet Government had eliminated a potential 'Fifth Column' which would have become an integral part of Hitler's invasion plan. There were no Henleins or Quislings to 'open the door' for Hitler's troops.

Notes

1. DURANTY, Walter, *Stalin and Co.* p. 87
2. EUDIN and SLUSSER, *Soviet Foreign Policy 1928–34* Vol II p. 362
3. *Documents on German Foreign Policy* 1918–45 Series C. Vol. II, No. 47 pp. 80/81
4. BENES, Eduard, *Memoirs of Dr Eduard Benes* pp. 18/19/20
5. BENES, Eduard, *Memoirs of Dr Eduard Benes* p. 47
6. CHURCHILL, Winston, *The Second World War*, Vol. I *The Gathering Storm* p. 258
7. DAVIES, Joseph E., *Mission to Moscow* p. 111

8. DAVIES, Joseph E., *Mission to Moscow* p. 149
9. DAVIES, Joseph E., *Mission to Moscow* p. 170
10. DAVIES, Joseph E., *Mission to Moscow* p. 177
11. DAVIES, Joseph E., *Mission to Moscow* pp. 180/183
12. DURANTY, Walter, *USSR* p. 230

29

PREVENTION VERSUS APPEASEMENT

By the middle of 1935, the 'interventionists' in Britain had regained their control over foreign policy. The 'thaw' was over. Apart from a few exceptions, the British establishment's policy of using Germany as their bulwark against the Soviet Union had not changed since Churchill's plea in 1919. Not surprisingly, 'Hitler's noisy beating of the anti-Communist drum evoked a sympathetic response from Western Conservatives.'[1]

The new 'Messiah' had effectively smashed Communist, Socialist and any other form of anti-capitalist movements in Germany by sheer ruthless and barbaric means. His avowed aims in applying the same means in countries to the East as far as, and including the Soviet Union, had a magnetic appeal for some of Britian's political and industrial leaders as well as their counterparts in France. So long as he continued on these lines they were prepared to co-operate by turning a blind-eye in his direction. The 'Iron Fist' of Mussolini and Italian fascism likewise attracted the admiration of prominent and influential people in the Entente countries.

The resurgence of militarism in Europe and the fears of another war were reflected in the massive campaign for peace and disarmament which had been carried out in Britain during 1934 and 1935 culminating in the National Peace Ballot. Sponsored by the League of Nations Union, with Lord Cecil as Chairman, the National Declaration Committee, closely identified with the preservation of the League and its Covenants of Collective Security, had succeeded in getting a response from over eleven and a half million people. The results of the ballot were announced on 28 June 1935.

To the question :

'Are you in favour of an all-round reduction in armaments by international agreement?'

over eleven million voted Yes.

'Are you in favour of an all-round abolition of national military and naval aircraft by international agreement?'
'Should the private manufacture and sale of arms be prohibited by international agreement?'

To both these questions, over ten million voted Yes.

It was the last question which had its greatest impact on the British public.

'Do you consider that, if a nation insists on attacking another, the other nations should combine to compel it to stop by
(a) Economic and non-military measures?
(b) If necessary, military measures?

To section (a) over ten million voted Yes, but on section (b) 6,784,368 voted Yes and 2,351,981 voted No, which meant that fifty eight per cent were prepared to accept the use of military means.

A general election was expected in the Autumn of 1935 and the Peace Ballot had projected the subjects of peace and disarmament to the forefront of national topics, at a time when Mussolini was threatening war against Abyssinia, a member of the League of Nations. Representations had already been made to the League by Abyssinia earlier in the year to investigate the preparations that were being made by Italy from within her African colonies. But no action was taken.

Meanwhile Sir Samuel Hoare with an eye on a possible election, had declared 'that Britain would fulfil its obligations under the Covenant.' On 11 September in an address to the League Assembly, he was careful to point out :

"'the League stands, and my country stands with it, for the collective maintenance of the Covenant in its entirety, and particularly for steady and collective resistance to all acts of unprovoked aggression. The attitude of the British Nation in the last few weeks has clearly demonstrated the fact that this is no variable and unreliable sentiment, but a principle of international conduct to which they and their Government hold with firm, enduring and universal persistence.'"[2]

The apparently forthright statement of Britain's Foreign Minister had obviously not deterred Mussolini from his planned African venture. He was confident that his partners at Stresa would allow him a free run in that part of Africa. On 3 October Italian forces began their unprovoked attack upon Abyssinia. The League met four days later and declared that the Italian Government had :

> "'resorted to war in disregard of its Covenants under Article 12 of the Covenant of the League of Nations.'"[3]

Article 16 specifically stated :

> 'Should any member of the League resort to war in disregard of its Covenants under Articles 12, 13 or 15 it shall ipso facto be deemed to have committed an act of war against all other members of the League, which hereby undertake immediately to subject it to the severance of all trade and financial relations . . . '

Once again the League was being put to the test. Its powers of implementing collective security and economic sanctions had been challenged. The Council, having met on 7 October, and 'noting that there has been a resort to war . . . under Article 12 of the Covenant' submitted its report to the Assembly, which met on 9th. After a two-day debate, the Assembly recommended the setting up of a Committee to co-ordinate measures which they believed necessary under Article 16.

There had been some half-hearted attempts to impose sanctions. But what, in fact, had been happening during the early months of 1935 was that a number of Governments, including France and Great Britain, had restricted the supply of arms and munitions to Abyssinia, after receiving representations from the Italian Government 'to the effect that the continuance of such supplies would be regarded as an unfriendly act.'[4] No such restrictions had been placed upon military supplies to Italy.

It was known at the time that the most effective way of peaceably bringing Mussolini to heel would have been to enforce an international oil embargo, as Anthony Eden points out in his memoirs. Such sanctions as there were did not include an oil embargo. According to Hitler's interpreter, Dr Paul Schmidt, in 1938 Mussolini told Hitler :

'If the League of Nations had followed Eden's advice in the Abyssinian dispute and had extended economic sanctions to oil, I would have had to withdraw from Abyssinia within a week. That would have been an incalculable disaster for me!'[5]

Eden, as Britain's representative for League of Nations affairs, had tried to rally support for an effective sanctions policy but his efforts were undermined by Laval and some of his own Ministerial colleagues, which included Prime Minister Baldwin and Sir Samuel Hoare.

There was obviously a strong division of opinion in Conservative circles of how best to preserve British imperial interests. The 1935 December edition of an influential publication called *The Round Table** warned :

'There is some reason for thinking that Signor Mussolini has long been convinced that the only way in which Italy could meet her essential needs for outlets for her population, and for markets and raw materials, was at the expense of the British

*A quarterly Review of British Imperial, later Commonwealth, affairs which began publication in 1910.

Empire. It is said that his idea was to build a fleet that would end the British naval preponderance in the Mediterranean; to annex Abyssinia, partly in order to settle Italians there, partly as a market and a source of raw materials, but partly in order to create a formidable army of black janissaries; and then, after building railways and aerodromes and roads in Libya leading to the Egyptian and Sudanese frontiers, to take the first opportunity created by an international crisis to seize the Sudan and Egypt and all British possessions in the Eastern Mediterranean . . .'*[6]

But in spite of this potential threat leading members of the British Cabinet were prepared, behind the scenes, to come to terms with Mussolini. But not until after the election.

Parliament was dissolved on 25 October and the Tories with the backing of most of the press, subtly played upon the British people's fear of an impending war. Foreign policy was therefore to become a key issue during the following three weeks. Support for the League of Nations and the upholding of its Covenant dominated the electoral campaign. Pointing to their support of sanctions against Italy the Government was able to show that it was upholding League principles. Baldwin was projected – with pipe in mouth – as the man of peace. The rearmament programme was played down. 'I give you my word that there will be no great armaments' proclaimed Baldwin at a meeting in the Guildhall of the Peace Society (International) on 31 October. The Conservative – National Government were returned with a huge overall majority.

Konni Zilliacus who, as previously stated, had been a member of the Secretariat of the League of Nations 'predicted that the National Government would use the Italo-Abyssinian conflict to spring a snap election, that the application of sanctions was a mere pretence designed to fool the British people into voting for the Tories, and that after the election the National Government, if returned to

---

*This is exactly what Mussolini tried to do in 1941 when his army was defeated by General Wavell in Libya.

power, would "seek the earliest opportunity to do a deal with Mussolini without demanding his previous withdrawal from Abyssinian territory'".[7] The Predictions came in his book *Inquest on Peace* written just a few months before the Abyssinian war.

The deal, also known as the Hoare-Laval Plan, emerged on 9 December, after the two Foreign Ministers had agreed to present to the League a proposal which would carve up Abyssinia, giving Italy over half of the country. The invader would be allowed 'to annex all the Ethiopian territory which she had actually occupied up to date by force of arms in her Covenant-breaking war of aggression.' As compensation, Abyssinia would 'receive an outlet to the sea' through to the port of Assab. Laval had also proposed that once Italy had taken over the allotted Abyssinian territory she should be given the remainder of the country 'to administer under a mandate.'[8] This was at a time when Mussolini's aircraft were indiscriminately bombing and dropping poison gas upon the poor defenceless Abyssinian people.

Once the news of the Hoare-Laval Plan surfaced there was an immediate outcry from the British electorate. Baldwin, under much pressure, not only throughout the country, but also within a group of his own Cabinet, eventually preserved both himself and the newly elected Government by jettisoning his Foreign Secretary, Sir Samuel Hoare, just one day before the subject of Abyssinia was to be debated in Parliament. Hoare resigned on 18 December, and the Plan was quietly abandoned.

The Italians did not have the speedy victory which Mussolini had anticipated. Their delegate at Geneva, Baron Aloisi, 'was assiduous in pressing the argument with the British, French and other delegates that Mussolini had staked his prestige on the Abyssinian adventure and that defeat would mean the overthrow of the Fascist regime. "You don't want Italy to go Red, do you?" he would conclude triumphantly.'[9] The French Foreign Minister certainly didn't. Laval had been working behind the scenes to prevent any possibility of oil sanctions being passed in Geneva. It was a Canadian representative* who proposed

---

*His name was Riddell and he was soon afterwards removed by the Canadian Government and replaced by a representative who was more in tune with British policy.

oil sanctions against the Italian Government. The subject was to be raised at the end of November but was postponed on the instigation of Laval, after he had projected a double barrelled canard : 'the Italian threat to attack the British Fleet and the French warning of a possible delay on the French side in coming to Great Britain's assistance.'[10]

The disclosure of the Hoare-Laval Plan had once again exposed the credibility of the whole fabric of the League of Nations. The weaker members no longer had faith in the League's ability to restrain the aggressor nations.

'France might have turned to Russia and worked out a military alliance' said Shirer, 'Moscow was still pressing for it. But hatred and fear of Communism, real or professed – and in France it was both – blinded the French to the necessity of this until it was too late.'[11] But there were many French people who were not blinded by 'hatred and fear', who had not succumbed to the brain washing by the Right-Wing press. The anti-fascist movement in France had been gaining considerable ground. Laval had come under attack by nearly all sections of the community and, like his collaborator in Britain, had been forced to resign. The Left in France had taken up the challenge. 'It supported sanctions against Italy, pressed for an accord with Britain, blamed Laval's deviousness and pro-Fascism for the fiasco at Geneva and insisted on Parliament approving the Franco-Soviet Pact, regardless of what Hitler thought.'[12]

But the 'hatred and fear' of Soviet Russia undoubtedly had a paralysing effect upon the French High Command to take protective action against the real enemy. In October 1934 the Quai d'Orsay received reports from their Consul-General in Cologne, Jean Dobler, that the Germans were taking steps to prepare the demilitarized Rhineland for the reception of troops and military aircraft. In his report, Dobler warned 'that new barracks, arms and ammunition depots, military garages, airfield, rail lines and roads were being hastily built.'

Under the Treaty of Versailles, the eastern bank of the Rhine was demilitarized to a depth of fifty kilometres and there was to be a military occupation by Allied forces of the western bank and the bridgeheads for a period of fifteen years. This was revised after the signing of the Locarno

Agreement, when it was decided that the Allies would withdraw from the area – which was completed by 1929 – and that the Rhineland would remain permanently demilitarized.

Instead of welcoming the conscientious and patriotic efforts of their representative in Cologne, the Foreign Office did not even bother to acknowledge his report, and, according to his testimony in 1947 before an investigating Committee of the French Parliament, 'he was given no encouragement to continue with his Intelligence work.'[13]

The matter was to lie dormant throughout most of 1935, although reports were still coming in of German preparations for moving into the demilitarized zone. While Laval was busy cooking up his plan for the Abyssinian sell-out, his Ambassador in Berlin was busy trying to warn the Government of what he was convinced were the Nazi Government's intentions regarding the Rhineland.

In his memoirs Andre François-Poncet has referred to his meeting with Hitler on 21 November 1935. 'His violence in criticizing the Franco-Soviet Pact' left the Ambassador 'with no doubt as to his future intentions. If he uttered such an indictment, then he must already have decided to retaliate, and his retaliation could be only the denunciation of Locarno and the occupation of the demilitarized zone.

'I had already instructed the Quai d'Orsay to this effect. I had advised it that Hitler's sole hesitancy now concerned the appropriate moment to act.'[14] François-Poncet had persistently warned the French Government of Hitler's intentions but his warnings and recommendations were ignored.

At the end of January 1936, the French Foreign Minister, Flandin, held discussions in London with Eden – who had just taken over from Sir Samuel Hoare – and Baldwin, the Prime Minister. The occasion was the funeral of King George V and Flandin had taken the opportunity of posing the question 'what would the British Government do if the Germans marched into the Rhineland? According to Flandin the Prime Minister replied that the British would have to know first what France would do. Flandin replied that his personal opinion was that France would resist but that on his return to Paris he would ask his Government to take an official stand and would inform Eden of it when they met in a few days at Geneva.'[15]

Eden states in his memoirs 'that the French attitude to a violation of the Rhineland was clearly a matter for the judgement of the French Government in the first instance. How much importance, I asked, did they attach to the demilitarized zone? Did they wish, for their part, to maintain it at all costs, or would the French Government prefer to bargain with the German Government while the existence of the zone still had value in German eyes? . . . I thought it desirable that the French Government, as the power directly concerned would make up their own mind about the Rhineland. If they wished to negotiate with Hitler they should do so; if they intended to repel a German invasion of the zone, they should lay their military plans. Any forcible action would depend on France'.[16]

It became evident that the Foreign Ministers were each, in turn, placing the initiative and responsibility on the other, and their governments, for facing up to what they both knew was being planned in Berlin. 'Eden knew perfectly well how important the maintenance of the demilitarized Rhineland zone was to France. Her security depended on it. And Britain's too. He was passing the buck, though, surprisingly, this is just what he accused Flandin of doing'.[17]

The British Government, according to the Eden Memoirs, was not prepared to commit itself on taking any action should the German army move into the Rhineland. Eden justified this attitude because, for his part, he was convinced that 'It was improbable that France would fight for the Rhineland'.

Hitler's divide and rule policy was succeeding. The Anglo-German Naval Agreement, and now this latest break in the Entente had convinced him that the time was ripe for moving into the Rhineland, although it appears from the records that his Generals were none too sure.

According to William Shirer, Albert Sarraut, the French Prime Minister, who had taken over from Laval at the end of January, had 'decided it was time to pin the Army down as to what it was prepared to do to meet the German threat . . . He had been considerably annoyed at the Army for

365

having suggested to the Foreign Office on 25 February that the ratification of the Franco-Soviet Pact be postponed because of its fear that Hitler would use it as an excuse to venture into the Rhineland . . . The Chamber was due to vote on ratification on 27 February and the Sarraut Government intended to push it through that day'.[18] Sarraut appeared to have very little confidence in the ability of his Commander-in-Chief, Gamelin, and the High Command, to take preventive action and Flandin had made it clear to the Belgian Government, through its ambassador, that the French Government 'will not take any isolated action' and 'will act only in accord with the co-signatories of Locarno'.[19]

This shilly shallying of the French and British Governments played right into Hitler's hands and on 7 March 1936 German troops moved into the Rhineland. A 'symbolic occupation' was how it was described by von Neurath, the German Foreign Minister. This 'symbolic occupation' was followed a few hours later by Hitler's 'phoney peace proposals'. William Shirer who was in Berlin at the time has described the 'delirious scene in the Reichstag', when the Nazi dictator, hoarse 'from nearly two hours of shouting . . . concluded solemnly : "We pledge now, more than ever, we shall strive for an understanding between the European peoples . . . We have no territorial demands to make in Europe . . . Germany will never break the peace."'[20] This ploy of Hitler's of the 'fait accompli' followed by proposals of peace and 'no territorial demands' was to become an integral part of his political strategy. Had the French and British Governments, together with other members of the League, called his bluff, taken a combined and determined stand and threatened the Nazi leader with preventive military action, the German generals might have undermined his power and authority and kicked him out of office. As it turned out the reactionary French press, which had been desperately trying to prevent the ratification of the Franco-Soviet Pact, now came out into the open and greeted the German occupation of the demilitarized zone with glee. *Le Matin* welcomed the occupation. Hitler 'had saved them from the "Communist peril"'. Plastered across its front page were such headlines as :

THE DENUNCIATION OF LOCARNO
BY THE REICH
IN HIS ELOQUENT AND IMPASSIONED SPEECH ADOLF HITLER SHOWED THE COMMUNIST PERIL

'I have', he said, 'warned France . . . I tremble for Europe'

The Socialist journal, *Le Populaire*, 'demanded that the Government limit its action to an appeal to the League and the Locarno Powers and that it show some understanding for the German move' :

> 'It was stupid to believe that a great country of more than sixty million people would put up with, seventeen years after the war, the demilitarization of part of its territory . . . Hitler has torn up a Treaty, he has broken all his promises, but at the same time he speaks of Peace and of Geneva. We must take him at his word'.[21]

The Germans had undoubtedly been humiliated at Versailles and the whole future of the Rhineland was like a festering sore in the heart of western Europe that needed a remedy. But to accept the word of Hitler, especially after his treatment of fellow Social Democrats in Germany, as well as other opponents, is beyond comprehension. *Mein Kampf* should have been sufficient warning.

On 16 March, the Council of the League of Nations met in London primarily to discuss Germany's denunciation of the Locarno Treaty and the occupation of the demilitarized zone. The Soviet delegate, Litvinov, warned the other members of the Council of the consequences of such violations of international agreements :

> 'We cannot preserve the League of Nations if we turn a blind eye to breaches of those treaties or confine ourselves to verbal protests' he declared. 'We cannot preserve the League of Nations if it does not carry out its own decisions but on the contrary, accustoms the aggressor to ignore its

recommendations, its admonitions or its warnings.

... The remilitarization of the Rhineland zone bordering on France is a question of setting up the domination of Germany over the whole European continent. I ask you, must and shall the League of Nations condone the promotion of this objective?'

He then went on to point out that the Soviet Government is

'for the creation of security of all the nations of Europe, and against a half-peace, which is not peace at all, but war.' (*The Daily Telegraph*, 18 March 1936)

As expected, Germany was condemned for her violation of the Versailles and Locarno Treaties. Strong words were used but only weak action was recommended. The 'symbolic occupation' was accepted by both Britain and France so long as the Germans promised not to build fortifications in the area.

Hitler had won a major victory, not only over the Allies, but also over his own generals, who knew that the French army was in every way better equipped and far superior in numbers. General Alfred Jodl, at the Nuremberg trials, told the Court – 'Considering the situation we were in, the French Covering Army could have blown us to pieces', and Paul Schmidt, Hitler's interpreter, records the Nazi leader having said : 'If the French had then marched into the Rhineland, we would have had to withdraw with our tails between our legs, for the military resources at our disposal would have been wholly inadequate for even a moderate resistance.'[22]

A clue to the reasoning that lay behind the Entente's appeasement of Hitler so early in his search for living space, may be found in the letter from a former British Foreign Minister to the editor of *Le Figaro*, Wladimir d'Ormesson. On 28 March 1936 Sir Austen Chamberlain wrote to d'Ormesson :

'There is a great fear of France's entanglement in the East and a general feeling that the occupation of the demilitarized zone by Germany was a certainty sooner or later ... Some of our Right wing politicians feel very much as yours do about the Franco-Soviet Pact. They regard it as almost a betrayal of our Western civilization.'[23]

Hitler's fait accompli had not only exposed the weakness of the Anglo-French Entente, it had also weakened the Belgians' faith in the effectiveness of their military pact with France. Their frontier was exposed to any further German military actions. The buffer had been removed. On 24 April 1937, on the initiative of their young monarch, Leopold III, the Belgian Government, with the backing of all sections of society, including the Belgian Socialist Party, withdrew from its Locarno commitments and declared its neutrality, a step which was to have dire consequences during the spring of 1940.

With the testimonies of German generals and other historical records it has become evident that the military occupation of the Rhineland could have been stopped. There was obviously an urgent need for a political solution to the problems of a territory which was formerly German. The legacy of Versailles may have provided Hitler with his excuse for the fait accompli, but the French people had not forgotten that it was a Germany army which had invaded France in 1914. Consequently the question of security for France along her eastern borders, and the maintenance of peaceful relations with Germany was of prime importance, not only for France, but for the rest of Europe. Hitler's gamble had shattered that prospect of peace and had instead opened up the road to war.

Notes

1. ADAMTHWAITE, Anthony P., *The Making of the Second World War* p. 43
2. *Documents on International Affairs*, Vol. II 1935 p. 102
3. *Survey of International Affairs*, Vol. II, 1935 p. 204
4. *Survey of International Affairs*, Vol. II, 1935 pp. 164/165
5. EDEN, Anthony, *Memoirs*, Vol. I, Facing the Dictators 1923–28 p. 297
6. *The Round Table* 1935–36 Vol. XXVI p. 14
7. ZILLIACUS, K., *I Choose Peace* p. 57

8. *Survey of International Affairs*, Vol II, 1935 pp. 295/296 and F.N.
9. ZILLIACUS, K., *I Choose Peace* p. 58
10. *Survey of International Affairs*, Vol. II, 1935 p. 294
11. SHIRER, William L., *The Collapse of the Third Republic* pp. 229/230
12. SHIRER, William L., *The Collapse of the Third Republic* p. 231
13. *Evenements** II (ex William L. Shirer, p. 233) pp. 469/515
14. REYNAUD, Paul, *In the Thick of the Fight 1930–45* p. 120
15. *Evenements** I (ex William L. Shirer, p. 234) p. 138
16. EDEN, Anthony, *Memoirs*, Vol. I, Facing the Dictators 1923–28 pp. 333/334
17. SHIRER, William L., *The Collapse of the Third Republic* p. 234
18. SHIRER, William L., *The Collapse of the Third Republic* p. 240
19. *Evenements** III (ex William L. Shirer), p. 240) p. 574
20. SHIRER, William L., *The Collapse of the Third Republic* p. 243
21. SHIRER, William L., *The Collapse of the Third Republic* pp. 246/247
22. SCHMIDT, Paul, *Hitler's Interpreter* p. 41
23. ADAMTHWAITE, Anthony P., (Notes on Reference No. 20) p. 103

---

*Testimonies and Documents collected by the Parliamentary Commission of Enquiry in Paris between 1947 and 1954 concerning events that occurred in France between 1933 and 1945 – referred to as Evenement. There are ten volumes.

30

SPAIN – THE TRAINING GROUND

On 16 February 1936, nine and a half million Spanish people out of a total electorate of approximately eleven million went to the polls to cast their vote for a new Government and a new Cortes. The result was a decisive victory for the recently created Popular Front Coalition.

The Duchess of Atholl*, in her book *Searchlight on Spain*, records that on the following morning at 4 am 'when the election returns which had come in had shown a Popular Front victory', Manuel Portela Valladares, head of the caretaker Government, was visited by a leading member of the former administration, the ex War Minister, Gil Robles, who had come 'to declare that nothing would induce him to submit to a Government of the Left. He therefore urged Valladares to remain in office, to suspend the Cortes and to rule as a dictator with his support.'[1] Later that day, General Francisco Franco, the Army Chief of Staff, in a further attempt to prevent the Popular Front from taking over the reins of Government, also called upon the caretaker Prime Minister and tried to press him to declare martial law. The pressure upon Valladares† was maintained with a third visit, this time by Jose Calvo Sotelo, the Monarchist leader.

Although Valladares was a rich man with a strong Conservative background, and had been offered the support of the Army, he nevertheless resisted the powerful pressures made on him and sent for Manuel Azana, leader of the Republican Left to form a Government.

Unfortunately for the Spanish electorate the composition

---

*Unionist (Conservative) Member of Parliament since 1923.

†Valladares revealed these events at a Press Conference in Paris exactly two years later, 17 February 1938.

of the new Government did not reflect the broad and progressive basis upon which the Popular Front had been formed. Firstly, the Socialists decided not to participate in the Government and, secondly, the other Parties had no direct voice in the Government's decision making, except to sustain it in office by their votes in the Cortes.

The representation of the Popular Front in the new Cortes was made up of ninety Socialists, eighty four of Azana's Republican Left, thirty seven Republican Union, the Catalan Autonomous Party (the Esquerra) thirty seven, Communists sixteen, P.O.U.M.* one and Syndicalists (Anarchists) one. Of the defeated group of Right wing Parties, Gil Robles's C.E.D.A.,† a pro-fascist movement, was by far the strongest with eighty seven deputies.

The position of the Socialists had been influenced by deep divisions within their ranks and by the decision of Largo Caballero,‡ leader of the Left wing, not to allow the Party to ally itself with the other Republican movements in a Coalition Government, thus avoiding the mistakes made following the collapse of the Monarchy in 1931. Consequently the Government was restricted exclusively to members of Azana's Republican Left and the Republican Union whose leader was Diego Martinez-Barrio. Yet in spite of the fact that there were neither Socialists nor Communists or any kind of Marxist within the Government, the *Daily Mail* correspondent, Harold Cardozo, described it as an 'extreme Left Government', an image which was to be projected by many newspapers in Europe and the USA during the coming months.

An article by George Slocombe in the *News Chronicle*, 12 March 1936, predicted some of the dangers which the new Government would be facing in the very near future.

'Undoubtedly the Government will be pressed to follow up the amnesty of the 30,000 political

---

*P.O.U.M.: Partido Obrero de Unificacion Marxista (Anti-Stalinist, pro-Trotskyite).

†Confederacion Espanola de Derechas Autonomas (Spanish Confederation for Autonomous Rights).

‡Caballero was also Secretary General of the U.G.T. – the Socialist Trade Union and had been Minister of Labour in the 1931 Government.

prisoners now crowding the gaols of Spain and Spanish Morocco by drastic financial and economic measures. The reaction of the Centre and the Right to any such measures will be violent.

A repetition of the tactics which overthrew two Left Governments in France between 1924 and 1926 may be expected. There will be secret exports of capital on a vaster scale than that which followed the fall of the Monarchy in 1931. The Bank of Spain is already accused by the Left of attempting to anticipate a financial crisis by its transfer of gold bullion to the value of 50 million pesetas to Barcelona in convenient proximity to the French frontier.

Monarchists and Conservative magnates like the famous Don Juan March, who threw the resources of his vast fortune into the struggle against the Left, and who is now in voluntary exile, have already transferred large sums of money to banks abroad.

A financial crisis, if it occurs, will be however, but the prelude to another and graver struggle: the struggle for economic power.

Spain is a country of extremes : wealth is concentrated in comparatively few hands. A small oligarchy of men control the banks, shipping, industry and agriculture . . .'

The 30,000 political prisoners to which Slocombe was referring were those men and women who were thrown into prison after the Asturian uprising in 1934. The country had been in a state of ferment ever since the enforced exile of the King, Alfonso XIII, and the setting up of the Republic in 1931.

Successive Republican Governments, by their failure to grant independence to Morocco, 'had facilitated the formation there of an ultra-reactionary shockforce – under the direct command of the so called 'African' generals such as Franco, Mola, Varela and Sanjurjo – which in its daily clashes with the Moroccan patriots was preparing itself . . . for the subsequent struggle against the Spanish people.

373

This shockforce, created by the colonialist policy, was the instrument which enabled the Spanish reactionaries to smash the peoples' movement in 1934; it later became the main instrument of the military-fascist rebellion in 1936.'[2]

During the early 1930s, even before Hitler became Chancellor, close contact between Berlin and Rome and the fascist and pro-fascist Spanish leaders had been maintained. 'In 1932 a branch of the Foreign Department of the German National Socialist Party had been established in Spain. Documents captured from its headquarters at Barcelona in July 1936 show that it had been actively engaged in smuggling in propaganda through the Embassy and Consulates, in influencing politicians, army officers and members of Chambers of Commerce, and in buying the press of the Right.'[3]

The success of Hitler and the Nazi Party in disposing of their opposition was greatly admired in Spanish Right wing circles. The Falange Espanola, founded in 1933 by Jose Primo de Rivera, son of the Spanish dictator of the 1920s, had begun to use the same terror tactics employed by the Nazis. Soon after the formation of the Falange he went to Germany 'to study the Nazi's system of organization and their methods of violence.'[4]

The Falange was well supplied with funds. Its main source of income came from Juan March, the Spanish millionaire who, like Fritz Thyssen, his counterpart in Germany, was prepared to finance an organization that would protect wealth, property, monopolies and the old order in general, irrespective of the methods employed. Hugh Thomas, in his book *The Spanish Civil War*, has disclosed that during the 1920s, Juan March 'had obtained a monopoly for the distribution of tobacco in Spain from Primo de Rivera' [Senior], and had been convicted of fraud by the Republican Government, but later made a 'sensational escape from Guadalajara Prison and thereafter used his considerable wealth (valued at £20 million sterling) to sabotage the currency of the Republic.'[5] He was one of the richest men in the world, 'the confidential agent of British capitalist circles, President of the Central Office of Spanish Industry, where he sat alongside . . . Sir Auckland Geddes of the Rio Tinto mines, and representatives of Italian,

French and German capitalist interests.'[6]

Spain had for many years been 'fertile ground' for the investment of foreign capital. The Belgians concentrated on railways and tramcars; the French in chemicals, minerals and textiles; the Canadians in hydro-electric works and 'British capital . . . controlling the entire metal industry in the Basque provinces, the naval shipyards and the copper mines including Rio Tinto.' By 1936 the Rio Tinto Mining Company, with a capital of eighteen million dollars had been making an annual profit of around four and a half million dollars, and the internationally known British armaments firm, Vickers Armstrong, had close ties 'with the Zubira and Urquijo Banks.' American capital had only recently come into the country, but by the mid-1930s had gained control of the telephone companies as well as 'nine tenths of the production of electric power in Catalonia.'[7]

Meanwhile Germany had been desperately anxious to establish a stronger economic foothold in the country. It already had a considerable stake in some of the power companies in the Levante areas, but with a rapidly expanding armaments industry, its primary concern was to gain control of Spain's rich mineral resources and a greater influence over its developing metallurgical industries.

Italian economic investments in Spain were considerably less than those of her rivals. Mussolini had been concentrating more on Africa, but by the early 1930s his influence in Spain was being stepped up politically through his support for rebel generals and politicians. In 1932 a young airman Major Ansaldo, went to Rome on behalf of his chief, General Sanjurjo, to obtain support for an attempted coup d'état. He saw Marshal Balbo who promised support should the coup be successful. The coup failed and most of the rebels were brought to trial and imprisoned. Sanjurjo and his co-conspirators were released in 1934. Another leading Monarchist who had been in constant communication with the Italian Fascist Government was Jose Calvo Sotelo, Minister of Finance during the Primo de Rivera dictatorship. Both he and Ansaldo were in Rome in 1933.

On 31 March 1934 a further secret meeting was held in Rome between Mussolini and envoys from the pro-

Monarchist and Carlist* organizations. Antonio Goicoechea, leader of the Monarchist group in the Cortes, Rafael Olzabel and Antonio Lizarza for the Carlists, together with Lieutenant General Barrera, reached an agreement with Mussolini by which the Italian Government would arm and finance them in their plans for the overthrow of the Republic. In the initial stages they were to receive '1½ million pesetas, 200 machine guns and 20,000 grenades'[8] with more to follow once the uprising had commenced. They received the money on the following day. Lizarza records in his memoirs that the Italian money was used to buy 'from Belgium, 6,000 rifles, 150 heavy machine-guns, 300 light ones, 10,000 grenades and 5 million bullets.'†

'Between 1934 and 1936, many young men from the Carlist military organization of the Requetes‡ underwent periods of military training in Italy. Stocks of arms were built up in Navarre, thanks to Italian funds.'[9] The meeting and some of the details were first revealed during the Civil War after documents had been taken from Goicoechea's house, and later admitted by the Monarchist leader.

Both Hitler and Mussolini had made themselves absolutely clear, not just by words, but by military activities, that they were on the road to war to achieve their objectives. In the mid-30s it was not just a matter of imperial rivalries, although that was still lurking in the background. Spain was to become a testing ground. Preparations for the overthrow of the Popular Front Republican Government were beginning to gather momentum, and the conspiracy was secretly becoming international in character. Germany and Italy were known supporters of a Fascist coup. What was not generally known at the time was that 'Juan March was in London and had the job of winning sympathy for the military movement in Internatonal banking circles,'[10] and that one of Franco's agents, Captain Luis Bolin, foreign correspondent of the Monarchist daily newspaper, *A.B.C.*, had commissioned a British Right wing journalist-publisher, Douglas Jerrold, in June

---

*Monarchist movement. Motto – God, King and Country.
†Antonio Lizarza – *Memorias de la Conspiracion en Navarra*. Pamplona. Gomez. p. 50. (ex Broué and Temime p. 42)
‡Requetes – Military wing of the Carlists.

1936 'to buy 50 machine-guns and half a million rounds of ammunition.'[11]

Towards the end of February 1936 General Sanjurjo, who had been in exile in Portugal, went to Germany 'ostensibly to attend the Winter Olympic Games. He and Colonel Beigbeder, Military Attache at the Spanish Embassy in Berlin . . . were said to have visited German arms factories with Admiral Canaris, head of German Military Intelligence. Canaris had old connections in Spain, from whose ports he had, in the first World War, directed submarine attacks upon Allied shipping.'[12]

According to the Duchess of Atholl, the purpose of the visit was to buy aeroplanes, and that he paid another visit to Berlin in June with General Goded, where 'both officers are said to have been received by Hitler.'[13]

But it was more than an 'idealogical crusade against Communism' that motivated the Fascist Governments to support a coup d'etat.

Hitler's 'participation' in the moves to overthrow the Spanish Popular Front Government 'is directed by motives far removed from purely political', commented *Reynolds News*, in an editorial of 10 January 1937 —

'In April 1935, a group of German financiers at Frankfurt-on-Main evolved a plan to obtain concessions for working mineral mines in Spain by means of German labour.

'In order to facilitate the scheme, the group created a vast financial trust at Dusseldorf; the Siemens and Halske concerns, Krupps, the I.G. Farben Chemical Trust and other well-known companies on whom Hitler relies for his maintenance in office.

'Powerful as it was, this new German machine was anxious to cover up its tracks, so that its intervention at any time might not be laid to Germany alone.

'It proceeded therefore to get in touch with Commander A. Serra who was then the Italian representative of the Rockefeller group, and transmitted to him at Rome the outlines of the plan.

'A report was made to the Italian Confederation of Industrial Employers, and another was presented by the Fascist Party by Signor Giuriati. Both were received with approval.

'The big Italian industrialists, having obtained the necessary capital for the adventure from various insurance companies suggested to the German consortium the creation of a special autonomous organization to exploit the Spanish mines.

The Germans, who had already made complete technical studies, reports, soundings and analyses, agreed, and all the Fascist capitalists had to do was to obtain concessions from the Lerroux or Gil Robles Governments.*

They were confident that this would not be difficult. But at the moment when the German-Italian magnates were on the point of beginning operations came the Spanish elections of February 1936.

Instead of a victory for the Fascist "Action Populaire", the electoral struggle resulted in an overwhelming triumph for the "Frente Populaire".

The People's Party had been returned with a programme which foreshadowed the early nationalization of those very mines on which the industrialists had set their covetous eyes.

There was consternation within the industrialists' ranks. They had poured out money like water in preparation for their plan; now all seemed lost.

There was, however, another way in which they could achieve their end. If they could not apply for concessions they might be able to take them.

Five months later the Spanish military revolt burst on an astonished world . . .'

France, meanwhile, in the elections of May 1936, had followed the example of Spain and voted for a Popular

---

*Alessandro Lerroux, leader of the Centre-Right stop-gap Government in the summer of 1933; joined with Gil Robles's C.E.D.A. in a coalition in 1934. Robles founded the Spanish Catholic Action Movement.

Front Government,* with Leon Blum, leader of the Socialists, as Prime Minister. By the end of 1935 anti-fascist organizations had already been formed in many countries, including Britain and France, and the creation of Popular Front Governments was but the logical development of the strong feelings prevalent at the time for the necessity to unite against the forces of fascism, following the refusal of the German Social Democrats to co-operate with the Communists during Hitler's rise to power.

Notes

1. ATHOLL, Duchess of, *Searchlight on Spain*, p. 53
2. SANDOVAL, Jose and AZCARATE, Manuel, *Spain 1936–39*, pp. 14/15
3. ATHOLL, Duchess of, *Searchlight on Spain*, p. 35
4. SANDOVAL, Jose and AZCARATE, Manuel, *Spain 1936–39*, p. 13
5. THOMAS, Hugh, *The Spanish Civil War*, pp. 64/65
6. BROUÉ, Pierre, and TEMIME, Emil, *The Revolution and the Civil War in Spain*, p. 41
7. BROUÉ, Pierre, and TEMIME, Emil, *The Revolution and the Civil War in Spain*, pp. 33 and 51
8. THOMAS, Hugh, *The Spanish Civil War*, pp. 75/76
9. BROUÉ, Pierre, and TEMIME, Emil, *The Revolution and the Civil War in Spain*, p. 42
10. BROUÉ, Pierre, and TEMIME, Emil, *The Revolution and the Civil War in Spain*, p. 87
11. ATHOLL, Duchess of, *Searchlight on Spain*, p. 70
12. THOMAS, Hugh, *The Spanish Civil War*, p. 101
13. ATHOLL, Duchess of, *Searchlight on Spain*, p. 70

---

*The Socialists became the largest party in the French Chamber for the first time with 146 seats, an increase of 49. The Communists gained 72, an increase of 62.

31

THE WAR IN SPAIN

Tension in Spain's leading towns had been building up for some time. Agents provocateurs were being used to provoke a violent response to the reign of terror deliberately created by Primo de Rivera and his marauding gangs. On 4 July 1936 shots were fired by gunmen in passing cars at a crowd just 'coming out from a Socialist meeting in Madrid, seven socialists were killed and eleven wounded. Eight days later, on the 12th, Senor Jose Castillo, a popular Lieutenant in the Assault Guards* and a known socialist and anti-fascist was assassinated by four men of Renovacion Espanola,† again in an open street in the capital.'[1] His murder was the second to be perpetrated by the fascists within a few weeks upon an officer of the Asaltos. On the following night the Parliamentary leader of the Renovacion Espanola, Calvo Sotelo, was shot in revenge by a group of Castillo's Asalto colleagues. These murders were the culmination of months of terror, assassinations and acts of provocation.

Throughout this turbulent period the Falange had maintained close contact with the military and the Civil Guard. Its actions were part of an overall strategy linked to the preparations and timing of an insurrection.

The role of agents provocateurs played an important part in those preparations. Reports of the burning of churches were extensively used by the Spanish anti-Republican press, as well as the Conservative press in other countries,

---

*The Assault Guards (Asaltos) were formed in 1931 as a Special Police Force for the protection of the Republic. It was made up of men known to be loyal to the Republic.

†A Monarchist organization.

to discredit the Popular Front Government.

The Duchess of Atholl, who was in Spain in 1936 with a Parliamentary delegation, reported that 'some churches were being used as centres for Fascist meetings and as stores for the arms with which fascists were liberally supplied.'[2] In May 1936 there had been a wave of church burning, particularly in the South, which was immediately condemned by the Government. As in Russia in Tsarist days, the church was identified by millions of poverty stricken people with the source of their oppression and there were some who, in their ignorance and frustration, were prepared to express their wrath through incendiarism. But this was only part of the story. Fascist agents were fully alive to the propaganda value of the burning of churches.

Agents provocateurs had also infiltrated into the Anarchist ranks with 'definite orders to encourage strikes.' Inevitably, the Government was held responsible for the general disorders, but 'by appeals to party and trade union leaders they were able to stop much of the church burning.'[3]

In the middle of June the Government was notified that arms and Civil Guard uniforms 'believed to be destined for the Requetes' had been smuggled into Navarre. Another 'indication that agents provocateurs were likely to be active.'[4] The capital of Navarre, Pamplona, was a Monarchist stronghold and General Mola, a close associate of Franco, was its Military Governor.

Anti-Government Generals such as Franco, Mola and Goded had been allowed to remain in key army posts. Franco, who was appointed Military Commander of the Canary Islands, had every opportunity to maintain close contact with like-minded 'African' colleagues in nearby Morocco, while Goded was given the key job of Military Commander of the Balearics, which included Majorca. These three generals 'in contact with fascist political groupings such as the Falange and the Renovacion Espanola . . . hastened their preparations for rebellion.'[5]

The Government had received plenty of warnings of the impending rebellion but they placidly allowed events to follow their course. When the Prime Minister, Quiroga, was asked by a Basque deputy, Jose Antonio de Aguirre, if it was true that he had arrested Mola a 'known leader of the conspirators', Quiroga 'took offence at these rumours and declared "Mola is a General loyal to the Republic".'[6]

The Sotelo murder was quickly seized upon by the conspirators to step up their plans for the coup. The general disquiet aroused by all the murders and attempted assassinations was fully exploited with demands for a return to 'Law and Order'.

'Over All Spain The Sky Is Cloudless' – this announcement was transmitted by the Ceuta Radio station in Spanish Morocco on the night of 17–18 July 1936. It was the conspirators' signal to set into motion their plans for the insurrection. That night the Moroccan seaport and garrison town of Melilla was taken over by fascist officers with the help of Moors and Legionaires, and on the following day, 18 July, General Franco arrived in Tetuan in a British aeroplane piloted by a British pilot, Captain Bebb, and commissioned by Douglas Jerrold, in collaboration once again with Luis Bolin. The plane had left Croydon on 11 July en route for the Canary Islands, to be placed at the service of Franco. According to Hugh Thomas, 'There were, apparently no aircraft in Spain fast enough for so delicate a journey. The Spanish plotters also considered an English pilot more likely to be trustworthy than one of their own compatriots.'[7]

On 19 July Queipo de Llano, with an army of Moors and Legionaires, crossed the Straits of Gibraltar. Shielded by German and Italian aircraft and navies, he occupied Algeciras and then Seville where he made the first of his many notorious broadcasts.

There were fascist uprisings in the garrison towns of Corunna, Saragossa, Toledo, Valladolid and Vigo and they too passed into rebel hands. Mola had yet to declare his hand in Pamplona, but one of his cloest associates, General Durlu, had seized Burgos, a traditional monarchist town. And while this was going on a fierce battle for the control of the navy was being fought in Ferrol, one of Spain's principal naval ports. Government loyalists, most of whom were of the lower ranks, refused to allow their ships to pass into rebel hands, and some traitor officers were shot, but in the end the loyal seamen were forced to submit to the rebels and they too were shot.

The rebel generals had anticipated that the coup could be achieved within a few days, but their plans and calculations had gone adrift. Most of the larger towns, including Barcelona and the capital Madrid, remained in Government hands.

'Immediately the news of the uprising in Morocco reached Madrid, huge demonstrations poured on to the streets, assuring the Government of the people's loyalty and demanding weapons ... On 18 July a delegation representing the People's Front saw the Prime Minister and demanded that arms be given to the people', but the Prime Minister, Casares Quiroga, refused to allow arms to be handed over to a people's militia, the only body which could be relied upon to defend the Republic. 'By that time, all the measures taken by the Government had failed and the rebellion was spreading through Spain like wildfire, destroying laws, institutions, lives and cities.'[8]

Eventually the Prime Minister gave way, but three valuable days and many lives had been sacrificed. In announcing his instructions for the distribution of arms, Quiroga also announced his resignation from the Government. On 20 July a new Government was sworn in under Jose Giral, (Republican Left).

The indecisive attitude of the Government during those crucial days enabled the rebels to take over twenty three towns.

Spain's Iberian neighbour, Portugal, under Dr Salazar, was also deeply involved in the conspiracy to overthrow the Republic. Salazar in 1933 had followed the example of Hitler and Mussolini and turned his country into a Fascist dictatorship. From the earliest days of the insurrection he had allowed the Hotel Aviz in Lisbon to serve 'as a relay station for telephone communications between Burgos and Seville'.[9] Spanish refugees who had been driven out of their homes and had gone over the frontier into Portugal were promptly returned into rebel hands. The Portuguese town of Caia, just inside the frontier, was used as a base for German military aircraft and during the early period of the war hundreds of tons of German military equipment was shipped into Lisbon and then transferred across the frontier into Spain. The Republican Government had no such comparable aid.

Pierre Cot, the French Minister for Air, had agreed to dispatch some military aircraft, but when the news became public the French Conservative press, backed by other Ring-wing forces in the country, uttered such a loud cry of protest that the Prime Minister, Leon Blum, backed down. Franco, through his powerful commercial backers, and 'through his agents in London and Paris also played an active part in the massive political drive to influence the Blum Government. In a conversation with the German Consul in Tetuan on 24 July 1936, referring to news that was circulating about deliveries of French arms to the Spanish Republic, Franco actually said, "Negotiations are going on to prevent those deliveries."'[10] And on the following day, 25 July, the Blum Government rejected a request for arms from the Republican Government, in spite of the fact that there was in existence an Agreement signed by the two countries in December 1935 which stipulated that Spain was to buy from France military supplies to the value of twenty million francs annually.

But it was not just French reactionary forces which compelled Blum to change jcourse. The decisive factor was the attitude of the British Government and the pressures that it was exerting behind the scenes upon a wavering Blum.

'It is important to recall' comments Michael Foot in his biography of Aneurin Bevan, 'how swift and resolute was the British Government in rejecting any idea of assistance to the Spanish Republic, how much its attitude and that of the bulk of its supporters veered towards ill-concealed sympathy with the Fascist revolt . . .'[11]

In the case of the British Ambassador to Spain, Sir Henry Chilton, it was more than just sympathy for the fascists. The American Ambassador, Claude Bowers, stated in a report to his Government from Spain 'that everything Chilton did was "intended to cripple the Government and serve the insurgents".'[12] It was Sir Henry Chilton who rang the alarm bell warning the Government that an initial dispatch of French arms was on the way to the Spanish Republic. According to Michael Foot, 'an urgent telephone call was received at the Quai d'Orsay from the French Ambassador in London. An Anglo-French meeting in

London had previously been fixed to discuss other matters. Baldwin now urged that Blum should accompany his Foreign Minister to London. This was the first step in the application of British pressure on the French.'[13] On 23 July, during the course of the Anglo-French meeting, Blum was asked by Eden 'Are you going to send arms to the Spanish Republic?' 'Yes' was the reply. 'It's your affair' replied Eden, 'but I ask you one thing, Be prudent.'

Blum was also under pressure from the Radical wing of his Popular Front Government. Two key posts in his Cabinet were held by leading Radicals, Yvon Delbos, Foreign Secretary and Edouard Daladier, Minister for War. And it was through them that the British Government was to force Blum and other members of his Cabinet to withdraw support for the Republican Government and declare their neutrality.

'At a stormy meeting of the French Cabinet on 2 August, Delbos, "in consideration of the British position", proposed an approach to "interested Governments" to secure "a Non-Intervention Pact" . . . On 7 August the British Ambassador in Paris presented Delbos with what was little short of an ultimatum. If France did not agree to ban the export of arms to Spain and a war with Germany ensued, Britain might consider herself absolved from the obligation to help France under the Treaty of Locarno . . . So on 8 August French policy was changed. All exports of arms to Spain would be stopped the next day . . . Henceforth, the Non-Intervention scheme could plausibly be presented to the world as the brain-child of the widely-respected Socialist Prime Minister of France.'[14] This respect was soon dissipated by the disgust which many people felt both in Britain and France at what could clearly be seen as an appeasement of Hitler and Mussolini and their disciples. As Foot explained, 'it was on the authority of the French Government that the Non-Intervention Scheme had been officially put forward and British Ministers were content that their own role in the affair should remain modestly concealed.' These exchanges between the two Governments 'were not public knowledge at the time', and for obvious reasons, because 'special measures were considered necessary if the unpalatable doctrine of Non-Intervention was to be approved by the Labour Movement.'[15]

According to Eden, it appeared that the French Foreign Minister was anxious to hasten the signing of the Non-Intervention Agreement and the Arms embargo. On 12 August, 'Delbos appealed to His Majesty's Government, through Sir George Clerk [Britain's Ambassador], to secure a quick agreement. Speed, Delbos said, was necessary on account of the internal situation in France. He thought that the French Government could claim to have acted with a certain courage, but it was growing daily, almost hourly, more difficult to withstand the pressure of their supporters.'[16]

Had the millions of supporters of the French Popular Front known of the secret deal that had been hatched behind their backs, which in real terms meant sacrificing Spain to the Fascists, it would have needed more than so-called 'courage' to have withstood their anger. As it was, many in the French Labour Movement as well as the influential and progressive elements in professional and academic circles, were beginning to sense that dirty work was going on behind the scenes. The news coming out of Spain had fired them with a passionate desire to help the Republican Government and the Spanish people to crush the fascist rebellion.

The Delbos appeal for 'speed' was promptly attended to for on 15 August 'the British and French Governments publicly exchanged notes, undertaking to prohibit the export of arms to Spain and to enforce this ban as soon as Italy, Germany, Russia and Portugal agreed.'[17]

Eden did not even wait until Italy and Germany had agreed. 'In the absence of Prime Minister Baldwin who was ill, he personally put through on 19 August a complete British embargo on the shipment of arms to Spain – and this at a date when Italy and Germany had not even signed the Non-Intervention Pact.'[18]

It does seem bizarre, to say the least, that Eden should state he 'had not yet learnt that it is dangerous to offer such gestures to dictators, who are more likely to misinterpret than to follow them.'[19] One would have thought that the occupation of the Rhineland, the Anglo-German Naval Agreement, the Italian invasion of Abyssinia and the declarations of intent in Hitler's *Mein Kampf*, that is, the unabridged version, would have been sufficient warning not to feed the insatiable appetites of the fascist dictators.

Foot gives an account of how the policy of Non-Intervention was sold to the British Labour Movement –

'On the 28 August an extraordinary joint meeting of the TUC General Council, the National Executive and the full Parliamentary Party was summoned. Blum's dilemma and the way he had solved it, supposedly of his own free will, supplied the main argument of the leadership. A declaration was proposed and carried "expressing regret that it should have been thought expedient, on the ground of the danger of war inherent in the situation, to conclude agreements among the European powers laying an embargo upon the supply of arms and munitions of war to Spain, by which the rebel forces and the democratically elected and recognized Government of Spain are placed on the same footing. While such agreements may lessen international tension, provided they are applied immediately, are loyally observed by all parties, and their execution is effectively co-ordinated and supervised, the utmost vigilance will be necessary to prevent these agreements being utilized to injure the Spanish Government". The National Council of Labour was instructed "to maintain its close watch upon events". Such quavering accents certainly did not match the mood outside.'[20]

Both the British and French Governments were being exposed by the very nature of the rebellion which had already become internationalized. Germany and Italy were known to be behind the insurgents. Widespread support for the sorely pressed Republican Government and the suffering Spanish people was being expressed in demonstrations, petitions and by the formation of Aid to Spain Committees throughout the two countries. 'Fascism Means War' had become a rallying call.

The Spanish people were fighting for their lives and they were being deprived of the means of defending themselves. There was an international conspiracy being waged under the label of neutrality to destroy their defensive capabilities. Apart from medical aid and messages of support, what they needed above all else was aircraft and modern weapons. It was against this background that the Socialist International and the International Federation of Trade Unions held an emergency meeting in Brussels on 28 July. With such powerful influences as Ernest Bevin, Walter Critrine and Leon Blum operating behind the International Socialist Movement, no positive steps were taken except to send representatives to Spain to assess Republican needs. There were far too many influential Socialist leaders supporting the Non-Intervention policy for the International to give a lead in the anti-fascist struggle in which Spain was being used as the sacrificial lamb.

Having forced the French Government to initiate the Non-Intervention policy the British Government naturally gave a positive reply to the French invitation to sign a Non-Intervention Agreement, and this was followed two days later by Italy. The Soviet Ambassador, Maisky, records in his *Spanish Notebooks* that on 17 August Germany 'expressed her readiness to join the Common Agreement on non-intervention only if the USSR, Italy and Portugal also participated. On 23 August the Soviet Government also joined the Agreement on non-intervention, but on condition that the Agreement should only come into force when Germany, Italy and Portugal had joined it.'[21]

The fascist countries had no intention of abiding by the Non-Intervention Agreement, for within twenty four hours of signing* 'Field Marshall von Blomberg, the German Minister of War, appointed a young staff officer, Colonel Walter Warlimont, to head the German armed forces in Spain.'[22] And on 28 August, the German Chargé d'Affaires wrote to his Foreign Ministry that the Italian Government has reserved for itself 'far reaching freedom of action for all contingencies' and that it 'is just as obvious that it does not intend to abide by the declaration anyway.'[23] Blomberg was reported to have said that Hitler 'had decided to aid Franco . . . On 26, Warlimont and Admiral Canaris visited the head of Italian Military Intelligence, General Roatta, and exchanged ideas about what had to be done in Spain. Warlimont then left for Tetuan, on an Italian Cruiser, under the name of "Waltersdorf".'[24]†

---

*24 August
†This came from General Warlimont's affidavit to the US Military Intelligence in 1946. From UN Council Report on Spain, p. 76.

Shirer was of the opinion that 'Anglo-French Diplomats and Intelligence Officers surely knew what Italy and Germany were up to. For one thing,' he says, 'the foreign correspondents in Spain, Germany and Italy kept them informed.'[25] And, one might add, it would have been difficult not to know what was going on when the British Government was in control of the geographically and strategically important port of Gibraltar, just fifteen miles north of Ceuta in Spanish Morocco, and barely three miles from Algeciras.

Alexander Werth, another eminent journalist, refers to a speech on 29 July 1936 on the Seville radio by the rebel General Queipo de Llano in which he appealed 'to Germany, Italy and Britain for arms and munitions, and announcing that once they came into power, the Nationalists would "break with France"'.

Werth then goes on to say that 'on 30 July, the very day after the General's speech, five mysterious aeroplanes were seen flying over Algeria, and soon afterwards, one of them crashed, and another had a forced landing, just before reaching Spanish Morocco. Both were military planes and the men inside were Italian officers. The inquiry made by the French authorities showed that they had been mobilized for service in Spain three days before the outbreak of the rebellion. On the very day of the Algerian incident, Delbos, the Foreign Minister, had spoken before the Foreign Affairs Committee of the Chamber with much appreciation of the assurance of neutrality received from the Italian Government earlier in the day!'[26]

The Soviet Government, although joining the Non-Intervention Committee appeared to have little faith in the implementation of the Agreement. 'It was perfectly obvious', comments Maisky, 'that not only Germany and Italy, but Britain and France as well, were trying to keep everything that had to do with the war in Spain as far away as possible from the eyes of world public opinion' and that 'the Soviet side . . . held that the work of the Committee should proceed with the widest possible publicity and therefore after the first meeting it informed British journalists in detail of all that had taken place.'[27]

The Manchester Guardian was certainly under no illusion of what the policy on 'Non-Intervention' was all about. In its editorial of 12 August 1936 it warned:

'The French proposal is not merely that no direct official assistance shall be given to the Spanish Government, which is trying to put down the rebellion, but that no traders in any country shall be permitted by their Governments to supply any arms, munitions, war materials, or even civil aeroplanes which the Spanish loyalists may wish to purchase. There is no precedent in international usage for this deliberate handicapping of a recognized constitutional and freely elected Government in its efforts to maintain its existence ... If it should turn out that the aeroplanes illegally sent by Italy to General Franco in Morocco have played a decisive part in getting the Moors across to the mainland ... while the Governments of the Western democracies have refused to permit the assistance which could legally be given by their national traders to the Spanish loyalists, their responsibility for the creation of another Fascist dictatorship in the Mediterranean would be grave indeed.'

On 28 July 1936 Manuel Carrada, a rebel officer, was captured by a detachment of Republican troops. Among the papers found in his possession were instructions for dealing with the enemy, and that included civilians, men, women and children. The Duchess of Atholl was so shocked when she saw the instructions that she decided to reproduce them in full in her book, *Searchlight on Spain*. The following are some of the main points:

'In order to safeguard the provinces occupied, it is essential to instil a certain salutary terror into the population. When the troops occupy a place, the local authorities must first be taught a lesson in respect; if they have escaped, a similar procedure must be adopted towards the members of their families. In every case the methods resorted to must be of a clearly spectacular and impressive character, and must indicate clearly that the leaders of the troops are determined to proceed with like severity against anyone who offers resistance.

'It is essential that in every town occupied, information shall be obtained from the priest or other reliable persons as to the views of the leading members of the community. If there are members of the Falange in the town, or officers or non-commissioned officers who have been able to escape the Red Terror, they are to be enlisted. Any tendency towards laxity in the performance of their duties, or signs of insubordination on the part of the troops, must be proceeded against with the utmost rigour. The same holds good for desertions. The rapidity with which we attain ultimate victory will depend on the merciless severity of the punishments meted out in such cases.

'Every town along the enemy's line of retreat and all the areas behind the enemy lines are to be considered as battle zones. In this connection, no differentiation must be observed between places harbouring enemy troops and those not doing so. The panic experienced by the civil population along the enemy's line of retreat is a factor of the utmost importance in contributing towards the demoralization of the enemy troops. The experiences of the last world war shows that accidental destruction of enemy hospitals and ambulances has a highly demoralizing effect on troops.

'After the entry into Madrid, the officers in charge of the various bodies of troops are to establsh machine-gun posts on the roofs of all the high buildings dominating their particular district, including public buildings and church towers, so that the surrounding streets are within range of the machine-guns. In the event of any opposition on the part of the populace, the streets should be put under fire without further parleying. In view of the fact that large numbers of women are fighting on the enemy side, there should be no distinction of sex in such cases. The more ruthless we are, the more quickly shall we quell hostile opposition among the population, the more quickly will the restoration of Spain be effected.'[28]*

The 'Holy Crusade' was soon in evidence in the rebel controlled areas. The instructions were meticulously carried out by the fascists in Seville, where 'General Queipo de Llano had ordered that executions should no longer, as at first take place in the prison or in the cemetary, but in various working-class areas for the express purpose of terrorizing the population.'[29]

The Madrid Council of Lawyers published a statement by its President, the internationally known Edouardo Ortega Y Casset, that the murders in Seville alone were 'not less than 9,000'. The terrorizing and the slaughter of the citizens of Seville was confirmed some months later by the Right wing French writer, Francois de Pierrefeu. On 22 February 1937 he related on Radio Luxemburg 'how he had been one of ten or twelve thousand prisoners in Seville. How he had seen men beaten till they bled, to exhort information from them, and how dozens of innocent persons were dragged out daily to their death.'

And in Malaga, Granada, Badajoz and other rebel occupied towns the same picture of terror emerged even though the 'rigid press censorship did its best to hide these horrors from the outside world.'[30] Journalists who were seen or known to be filming or reporting on the massacres were arrested. *The Daily Express* correspondent, Harold Pemberton relates on 21 August 1936 how a Spanish photographer was shot for having 'photographed a pile of

---

*First published by Arthur Koestler in December 1936 in a German version of his book *L'Espagne Ensanglantée*. He was at the time foreign correspondent for the *News Chronicle*.

'As the insurgents in fourteen months have made no attempt to prove the orders a forgery', comments the Duchess of Atholl, 'it must be presumed that they are authentic. They were not published in England until December 1937', when Arthur Koestler's *Spanish Testament* first appeared. (Duchess of Atholl)

forty one corpses, including three women, outside Seville.'

In Badajoz the slaughter was on such a massive scale that the 'Havas special agent cabled that there were corpses in the Cathedral, even at the foot of the altar, and that "the bodies of Government supporters executed en masse are laid out in rows in front of the Cathedral on the main square".'[31]

And while all this was going on, Archbishop Segura of Toledo, was proclaiming that it was 'the love of the God of our fathers that has armed half of Spain' against the 'modern monster, Marxism, or Communism, seven-headed hydra, symbol of all heresies'.

A British Member of Parliament, Sir Henry Page Croft, speaking at a meeting of 'Friends of Nationalist jSpain' –

' . . . moved a resolution expressing sympathy with the "prolonged martyrdom" of fellow Christians in Spain, and hoping for a nationalist victory . . . speaking as a member of the Church of England he thought they should pray for General Franco's victory if mankind was not to revert to the state of beasts of the jungle.

"I recognize the Generalisimo as a gallant Christian gentleman and I believe his word".' (*Daily Telegraph* 24 March 1938)

The 'gallant Christian gentleman' was undoubtedly as good as his word in the carrying out of a reign of terror upon the Spanish people. Many journalists representing Conservative newspapers and reporting the war from inside insurgent occupied territory were so shocked by the behaviour of the rebel troops that, in spite of the policy of their papers, most of which supported the rebels, they began to ignore the rebel briefings and 'hand-outs' and wrote what they actually saw.

Although the Giral Government had accepted the demand for arming the people it was still unable, by the very nature of its compositon, to give a strong lead in the fight against the powerfully armed insurgent force. There was an urgent need to knit together the individualistic groups which were determined to retain autonomous

393

control over their militia. The Giral administration had neither the authority nor the determination to unify the people in the fight against the enemies from within and without the country. A new Government was formed under Largo Caballero who combined the post of Prime Minister with that of Minister for War. To instil a greater sense of unity the Cabinet was reconstructed* to include six Socialists, three Republicans, two Communists, one Catalan Nationalist and one Basque Nationalist.

Meanwhile in Britain, to ensure support for the 'Non-Intervention' policy, 'a Labour delegation was despatched to Paris to seek confirmation of the French view in preparation for the Trades Union Congress which was to meet in Plymouth on 7 September.' The Secretary of the TUC, Sir Walter Citrine, supported by Ernest Bevin, the leader of the Transport and General Workers' Union, were thus able to cite the 'initiative' of Leon Blum, Prime Minister of France's Popular Front Government and fellow Socialist, for the Non-Intervention Agreement. 'The choice before us' declared Bevin, 'was whether or not we would take a step which in our view would lead to war . . . It is not a question of calling men out on strike and paying them strike pay, when the worst you have to face is defeat and loss of membership – it is an issue of life and death, an issue of the road that humanity is going to take for the next hundred years.'[32]

It certainly was 'an issue of life and death' for the Spanish people. Bevin then launched into his own special philosophy on war and peace. 'Peace is not determined by an incident that happens at a moment. A writer once said that the seed of all future wars is sown in the settlement of previous wars, and Europe today is at the crossroads. Cool heads, cool judgements, combined with fearless courage in facing the situation, settling it with our heads and not with our emotions, may indeed prove that in the end, notwithstanding the black cloud of dictatorship at the moment, this democracy may yet again set the feet of men upon a road that our children may call us blessed for having taken.'[33] Appeasing fascist dictators, and depriving the democratically elected Spanish Government and the Spanish people of the means to defend themselves could hardly be described as an act of 'fearless courage'.

The performances of Bevin and Citrine at the 1936 TUC Conference in Plymouth 'won the approving comment from Sir Samuel Hoare at the Conservative Party Conference that "the wise attitude adopted by the Trades Union Congress over the Spanish crisis shows that in the ranks of Labour there is a solid force of patriotic responsibility".'[34]

Had the Trade Union delegates known what had been going on behind the scenes between the Foreign Office, the Quai d'Orsay and some of Labour's leaders there would have been an almighty row, and in all possibility an entirely different decision would have been taken. As it was, the ground had been prepared for a further endorsement of the Government's 'Non-Intervention' policy at the Labour Party Conference held in Edinburgh a month later. Sir Charles Trevelyan, a former Labour Minister, and the young Aneurin Bevan were prominent among the speakers who attacked the NEC's policy. Bevan made a blistering attack upon some of his Labour and TUC colleagues and then asked the conference delegates to

'Consider for a moment the consequences that will occur in Europe if the present situation is allowed to work out to its logical conclusion? Is it not obvious to everyone that if the arms continue to pour into the rebels in Spain, our Spanish comrades will be slaughtered by hundreds of thousands? Has Mr Bevin and the National Council considered the fate of the Blum Government if a Fascist Government is established in Spain? How long will French democracy stand against Fascism in Germany, Fascism in Italy, Fascism in Spain and Fascism in Portugal? How long will French democracy stand if the French Fascists attempt a coup d'état against the French Popular Front Government, and are supplied with arms by friends in Spain? We have the suggestion that for the sake of avoiding a European war we must maintain a neutral attitude. If the Popular Front French Government is destroyed and democracy in France is destroyed, then the Franco-

Soviet Pact will soon be denounced, and democracy in Europe will soon be in ruins. That is the
consequence of this policy.'[35]

Unfortunately, Aneurin Bevan's prophetic and eloquent
appeal was not able to influence the outcome of the
conference decision. The National Executive's resolution to
support the Government's policy of 'Non-Intervention' was
carried by 1,836,000 to 519,000. The resolution had been
debated on the Monday, the first day of the conference and
two days before the arrival of two Spanish fraternal
delegates who had been invited to address the conference.
One, Senor de Asua, had given 'detailed proof of the supply
of arms to the rebeles' and an account of how the Spanish
people were '"fighting with sticks and knives against tanks
and aircraft and guns . . . We must have arms. Help us to
buy them somewhere in the world."' He was immediately
followed by Senora Isabella de Palencia, who, in a Scottish
accent acquired during her childhood years living in
Scotland, gave a passionate account of what was happening
to her people. Appealing to the humanitarian instincts of
the delgates she quietly told them '"We know that we are
holding your hand across the distance. But let me tell you,
if you wish this atrocious war to end soon, come and help us
as you have been asked, whenever you can. Think of the
precious gift that is being wasted – of the lives of our youth.
Do not tarry. Now you know the truth. Now you know what
the situation is in Spain. Come and help us."'[36]
   The appeal of the Spanish delegates stirred the conference to such a degree that Attlee and Greenwood (leader
and deputy leader of the Party) were sent 'on a special
mission to London to discuss the situation with the acting
Prime Minister, Mr Neville Chamberlain.' Having had their
meeting with Chamberlain, the 'missionaries' returned to
Edinburgh 'and on Friday they reported to the conference'
that they had 'urged upon him the necessity of ensuring
that the Non-Intervention Committee did its work effectively and received in return the assurance "that the British
representatives were fully conscious of the dangers which
would be incurred if the situation were not cleared up without delay".' In what may have appeared to be an attempt to

salvage a few consciences, Attlee concluded his report by declaring '"We are calling upon our Government, without delay, to establish the facts"; if the breaches of the Non-Intervention treaty continued, then the whole treaty must be abrogated.'[37]

The report had a negligible effect upon the Government. It was known from the very outset that the Non-Intervention Agreement had been violated by Germany, Italy and Portugal and the matter was eventually handed over to the National Executive which at its next meeting 'found no justification' in reversing the conference decision.

On 7 October 1936, which was during the week of the Labour Party conference, the Soviet Government notified the Non-Intervention Committee that in view of the military aid being supplied to the rebels it –

'Cannot, in any event, let the Non-Intervention Agreement be transformed by some of those taking part into a screen for concealing military aid to the rebels.

Consequently the Soviet Government finds itself obliged to state that if these violations do not cease immediately, it will consider itself freed from its obligations under the agreement.'

And on 23 October it issued a further Note stating that it no longer felt 'itself bound by the Non-Intervention Agreement to any greater degree than any of the other parties to that agreement.'

The battle for Madrid was now on. Franco and his rebel generals had planned for the capital to succumb within a matter of days, confident that they could starve and terrorize the people into submission.

In the journal *Die Wehrmacht*, General Sperrle, Commander of the German Condor Legion, stated: 'Our bombers had the task of opening up the way to Madrid and demoralizing the city so that Franco's troops could enter. But it was not possible to get the troops to take the route we showed them.'

The Spanish writers, Jose Sandoval and Manuel Azcarate, have described how towards the end of October the

397

'opening up' process began with 'the savage bombing of Madrid's population. Junkers, Heinkels and Capronis sowed death and destruction throughout the capital. The densely populated districts of Embajadores, Tetuan de las Victorias, Atoche and Cuatro Caminos were the worst hit'; how the fascist armies were stopped in their tracks by the people of Madrid when they 'came up against a veritable wall composed of tens of thousands of Madrid workers, militiamen and soldiers defending their city . . . By tram-car and motor lorry, by the underground railway and on foot, the people of Madrid went to the outskirts to fight or to dig trenches'. The heroic women of Madrid 'like the heroic women-folk of the Paris Commune, strove and worked to build fortifications, took over men's jobs in the factories, worked in the hospitals and field kitchens, helped in the evacuation of children, and carried coffee and refreshments to the front and to the fortification brigades'.[38]

By the end of November Republican troops and the people of Madrid had won an historic battle against impossible odds for their capital city. The cry of NO PASARAN (They shall not pass) had indeed been achieved. The rebels had sustained heavy losses. Their only consolation was the decision of Germany and Italy to give official recognition to Franco's Burgos administration, which was in future to be described as the 'Nationalist' Government. And as the war developed, so did the rebels become more and more dependent upon Hitler and Mussolini. Military aid was stepped up on a massive scale by both countries. Thousands of experienced officers and men from the Abyssinian campaign, with their tanks, guns, aircraft and other military supplies were hastily despatched to prop up the rebels. The German Condor Legion arrived in October 1936 with about 5,000 men, but this was soon increased to over 10,000, fully equipped with the most up-to-date tanks, artillery and signal units. Hundreds of German officers and non-commissioned officers were used to train and to reconstruct the demoralized rebel army.

By now, Eden and some members of the British Foreign Office were becoming alarmed at the extension of the Italian and German involvement in the Spanish war.

'The Spanish Civil War has ceased to be an

internal Spanish issue and has become an international battleground'

comments Eden in a Memorandum of 7 January 1937.

> 'It was above all important to see the Spanish problem in relation to Germany. We had received many indications that the more cautious elements in that country, of which the army and the Foreign Office had the most authority, were opposed to the Spanish adventure. The same influences had opposed the march into the Rhineland . . . If no attempt was made to check the Nazi adventure in Spain, we might be certain that on a subsequent occasion, when the Nazi Party urged extreme courses, the more cautious influences would have no opportunity to make themselves felt in Europe's other danger points, Memel, Danzig and Czechoslovakia.'[39]

Unfortunately, this late awakening by Eden was not carried forward to the logical conclusion, that 'Non-Intervention' was in fact intervention; that a victory for fascism in Spain was a victory for Germany and Italy and a threat to the security of Britain and France, as well as Russia and the rest of Europe.

From a purely military point of view, it had become quite obvious that without massive German and Italian intervention Franco and his rebels could not have survived. 'Non-Intervention' not only helped to sustain a tottering rebel army, it also shielded the German and Italian forces in Spain from being further humiliated by the Republican forces. The 'Non-Intervention' policy provided encouragement for the fascist powers to extend their spheres of influence into the Iberian peninsular.

The USSR was the only country on the Non-Intervention Committee which had heeded the call of the legitimate and democratically elected Spanish Government. Once the Soviet Government had decided that the Non-Intervention agreement had been broken, it sent the weapons which the Spanish leaders so desperately needed. Rifles, grenades, tanks, artillery and ammunition began to arrive in October and November and were used in the defence of Madrid.

At the outbreak of the war there were many refugees in Spain from the fascist countries. There were Germans who had had to flee their country after 1933 and many Italians, some of whom had been refugees ever since Mussolini's March on Rome in 1922. They were among the first of the volunteers to fight for the Republican cause. Soon afterwards they were joined by volunteers from Britain, Canada, France, Ireland, the United States and from countries of central and Eastern Europe – Bulgarians, Czechs, Hungarians, Russians and Yugoslavs. In all, they came from over fifty countries – workers and professional people from all walks of life.

The contribution of the International Brigades will forever be remembered in Spanish history and by the Spanish people. In the defence of Madrid, in the destruction of the Italian army at Guadalajara, in the battles of Jarama, Brunete, Teruel and finally, that on the Ebro. 'No one can think of these places without emotion, remembering the International Brigades, 5,000 of whose soldiers remain among us forever.'[40]

There were many obstacles which had to be overcome before the volunteers reached their destination. The French Government tried to stop them crossing from France into Spain and many had to make their way on foot during the night over precarious mountain paths across the Pyrénées. On 9 January 1937 the British Government decided to revive the Foreign Enlistment Act of 1870, whereby it became an indictible offence for British subjects to enlist in a foreign country. The punishment was imprisonment of up to two years, or a fine, or both a fine and imprisonment. The British volunteers were determined not to be thwarted. By purchasing week-end tickets to Paris, for which a passport was not required, they were able to leave the country and assemble in the French capital. From there, with the help of French comrades, they continued on their arduous journey into Spain.

The morale of the Republican forces and the Spanish people had been greatly enhanced by the arrival of the volunteers and the rapid formation of the International

400

Brigades. On 8 November 1936 the first arrivals were marching through Madrid en route for the front. They were joined by doctors and nurses from many countries. 'The first British Ambulance Unit . . . left for Spain in August 1936. Many more . . . were to follow and several cities sent their own ambulances bought with money raised locally.'[41] British miners were in the forefront of the Aid for Spain Campaign. The Miners' Federation of Great Britain and most of the miners' lodges collected thousands of pounds for the various Aid to Spain Committees and in particular for the International Brigades Dependents' Aid Fund.

Three hundred and ninety eight Britons sacrificed their lives for a cause in which they passionately believed – to stop fascism taking over Spain and the rest of Europe. Three were taken prisoner and shot, two died in Franco's prisons and three were drowned in the *SS Barcelona* which was 'torpedoed on its way from Marseilles to Barcelona – carrying several hundred volunteers.'[42]

On 28 April 1937 a report appeared in *The Times*, under the headlines

TOWN DESTROYED IN AIR ATTACK
The Tragedy of Guernica – Eye Witness Account

The eye witness was George L. Steer, *The Times* special correspondent.

'Guernica the most ancient town of the Basques and the centre of their cultural tradition, was completely destroyed yeterday afternoon by insurgent air-raiders. The bombardment of this open town far behind the lines occupied precisely three hours and a quarter, during which a powerful fleet of aeroplanes consisting of three German types, Junkers and Heinkel bombers and Heinkel fighters, did not cease unloading on the town bombs weighing from 1,000 lb downwards and it is calculated more than 3,000 two-pounder incendiary projectiles. The fighters, meanwhile, plunged low from above the centre of the town to machine-gun those of the civilian population who had taken refuge in the fields.'

'The whole of Guernica was soon in flames and at 2 am when Mr Steer went further into the town the whole of it was a terrible sight, flaming from end to end. The reflection of the flames could be seen in the clouds of smoke above the mountains from ten miles away. Throughout the night houses were falling until the street became long heaps of red impenetrable debris.

' . . . In the form of its execution and the scale of the destruction . . . the raid on Guernica is unparalleled in military history. Guernica was not a military objective. A factory producing war material lay outside the town and was untouched. So were two barracks some distance from the town. The town lay far behind the lines. The object of the bombardment was seemingly the demoralization of the civil population and the destruction of the cradle of the Basque race. Every fact bears out this appreciation beginning with the day the deed was done.

'Monday was a customary market day in Guernica . . .

' . . . The whole town of 7,000 inhabitants, plus 3,000 refugees was slowly and systematically pounded to pieces.

' . . . All the villages around were bombed with the same intensity as the town itself, and at Murgica, a little group of houses, at the head of the Guernica inlet, the population was machine-gunned for fifteen minutes.'

Steer's report also appeared in the *New York Times*. According to the town's official report, 1,654 were known to have been killed and 889 wounded. 'But the full number had not been counted before the insurgent troops entered.'[43]

As Phillip Knightley so correctly points out in his chapter on the 'Commitment in Spain', 'All the dire predictions of the effects of mass air-raids that dominated thinking early in the Second World War flowed from the bombing in

Spain.'[44]*

Steer's report was confirmed by Noel Monks of the *Daily Express* who described what he saw that night of 'the annihilation of the ancient Basque capital of Guernica.'

'I walked this evening through the still-burning town. Hundreds of bodies had been found in the debris. Most were charred beyond recognition. At least two hundred others were riddled with machine-gun bullets as they fled to the hills.

I stood beside the smouldering Red Cross Hospital at Josefinas. The bodies of forty-two wounded soldiers and ten nurses lay buried in the wreckage. They never had a chance. The wounded were killed in their beds, the nurses were killed on duty.

I stopped next above what had been an air-raid refuge. Down there fifty women and children, huddled together as the raiders swooped down on their town, were burned alive . . . ' (Noel Monks, *The Daily Express*, 28 April 1937)

The news of this outrage aroused anger and protests from people all over the world and to such an extent that the 'Fascist International' soon got to work to place the responsibility for the bombing elsewhere. On the night of 27 April 1937, the rebels' propaganda chief announced on Radio Salamanca that he had proof from eye-witnesses that it was the 'Reds' who had destroyed Guernica. Franco's officers did not take kindly to correspondents in their areas who stepped out of line and preferred their own observations to the official briefings. 'At the time of Guernica', says Knightley, 'there was one correspondent of the French News Agency, Havas, in a Nationalist prison and another under house arrest', and in his interview with Christopher Holme of Reuters, it was revealed by the Reuters' man 'that correspondents in Salamanca were at one stage offered

---

*'Later Goering, Chief of the Luftwaffe, boasted that Guernica had been a valuable experiment. It showed the ease with which undefended towns could be completely wiped out by proper bombing.' (SHIRER, William, FN, p. 285)

about $1,000 to record favourable broadcasts for the Italian radio.'[45]

Desperate attempts were made to offset Steer's report. *The Times* was attacked in Germany and its Editor, as well as its Berlin correspondent, were pressurized to suppress such damaging articles against the Germans. 'I did my best, night after night, to keep out of the paper anything that might hurt susceptibilities' wrote Geoffrey Dawson, the Editor, to his former Berlin correspondent. 'No doubt they were annoyed by Steer's first story on the bombing of Guernica, but its essential accuracy has never been denied.' (From *The History of The Times*, Vol. 4, p. 907).

The day after Steer's report, *The Times* tried to make amends to the German Government by printing a report from its Berlin correspondent. By using the official Nazi version of the Guernica bombardment as a counter to his special correspondent's report from Spain, the Editor hoped to restore the Anglo-German accord. Geoffrey Dawson, as previously mentioned, was an influential member of the 'Cliveden' set.

'It is denied that German aeroplanes bombed the town, it is asserted that no aeroplanes could go up owing to the weather, and it is further explained that if Guernica was destroyed by incendiary bombs it could have been done only by the "Bolshevists" who must be held responsible.

. . . The Berliner *Tageblatt* says that the whole thing is a manoeuvre by a section of the foreign press to distract attention from the senseless destruction by the "Reds" in their retreat.' (*The Times*, 29 April 1937)

That afternoon, in the House of Commons, Eden was subjected to a barrage of questions and protests from the opposition. He adroitly 'side-stepped questions from the opposition on the massacre at Guernica.' When asked, 'would the British Government protest? Mr Eden's only reply was to try to put the blame for atrocities on both sides.' (*News Chronicle* 29 April 1937)

On the same day there was a joint statement made by the

General Concil of the TUC and the National Executive of the Labour Party 'denouncing this monstrous crime'. But the monstrous crimes continued behind the cloak of 'Non-Intervention' and it needed more than words to stop them.*

This was clearly borne out in Geneva, when Alvarez del Vayo, the Republic's Foreign Minister, raised the matter of non-intervention at a meeting of the General Assembly of he League of Nations in September 1936. He complained that his Government, a member of the League, was regarded by the London based Non-Intervention Committee to be no more than of equal status to that of the rebels and reminded the assembled representatives that the Spanish Government, under International Law, was entitled to purchase arms for its own defence. But the League took no action, being content to leave the matter in the hands of the Non-Intervention Committee.

On 11 December, del Vayo called upon the League to take action against the German and Italian Governments which had given full diplomatic recognition to the Burgos rebel administration and warned that the Spanish war and the attacks upon Merchant Shipping in the Mediterranean was a general threat to peace. The League was still dominated by its original sponsors, Britain and France, and consequently the only step taken by the Council was to pass a resolution calling upon the London Committee to ensure that Non-Intervention was carried out.

The impotence of the League and the inability of the Non-Intervention Committee to prevent intervention was a great source of encouragement to the fascist powers. With their naval support, the rebels were able to intensify the blockade of the Republic. In the light of history it does seem extraordinary that the great British and French navies were prepared to allow the merchant ships of their

---

*Although the Labour Party National Executive eventually agreed that the provisions of the Non-Intervention agreement were being violated, there was not, according to Michael Foot, any outright denunciation. 'The Left was convinced that the crisis in Europe was moving towards a climax in which the role played by Britain's National Government was both contemptible and dangerous. But the Right-wing leadership always had some fresh reason for not acting.' (FOOT, M., p. 235)

countries to be attacked and, in many cases, sunk, without taking any effective action to protect them.

'By 6 August [1937] there had been fourteen attacks on British ships, chiefly from bombs and *HMS Hunter* had been damaged by a mine.'[46]*

Merchant ships from many countries that were lawfully carrying food and general cargo to Republican Spain were sunk without any warning. The *Djebel Amour*, a French liner, was bombed from the air and on 11 August the British destroyer, *Foxhound*, was attacked off Northern Spain. Two days later a Danish ship, the *Edith*, was sunk and on 15 August the *George McKnight*, a Panamanian registered tanker, was burnt out.

The attack on Soviet ships had begun even earlier. 'On 14 December, 1936 the Soviet steamship *Konsomol* was sunk near Gibraltar, and on 31 August and 1 September 1937 two more Soviet ships were lost, the *Timiryazev* and the *Blagoev.*' According to Maisky, the Soviet Ambassador, 'Sometimes the attacks were made by warships under Franco's flag, sometimes by submarines and aircraft "of unknown nationality". By the Spring of 1937 the situation had become so acute that the representatives of the three Scandinavian countries – Sweden, Norway and Denmark – laid a complaint on 30 April before the Committee, in which they asked for emergency measures to be taken for the defence of shipping in Spanish waters.'[47] All that transpired were expressions of sympathy. But what was particularly disturbing was the manner in which the British Navy was being used to help the fascist powers tighten the blockade around Republican Spain. It was no mere coincidence that the First Lord of the Admiralty at the time should be Sir Samuel Hoare, of the Hoare-Laval Pact. Having transferred to this important post, he was able to continue where he left off at the Foreign Office in appeasing the imperial aspirations of Mussolini. With the indirect help of the British Navy, Franco and Mussolini were considerably strengthened in their attempts to starve the

---

*By the end of 1937 there had been twenty-five attacks on British vessels, including eight on the British Navy. *SS Woodford* torpedoed by submarine, 1 September 1937, and *SS Jean Worms* sunk the following month.

Republic into submission.

Evidence of this was to find its way into the British press during the Spring of 1937 with the 'Potato' Jones story. On 18 April the *Reynolds News* printed an article by its foreign editor under the headline 'British Navy Turns Back "Potato" Jones Steamer'. Captain Jones had set out from St Jean de Luz in a 900 ton cargo boat, the *Marie Llewellyn*, laden with a consignment of potatoes for the starving women and children of Bilbao.

> He 'was not afraid of the limited powers of Franco's naval resources but he was not prepared for a British naval blockade. Had it been a Spanish cruiser looming out of the dusk which challenged his little 900 ton ship, he might have found a way out, but it was a British destroyer which made its midnight appearance by the side of the *Marie Llewellyn* while she was sailing for a Spanish port. It is true that "Potato" Jones was "warned" and "advised" in a fashion which brooked no argument to turn back from his venture, but the message which halted the *Marie Llewellyn* by flashlight and by megaphone was in English, not Spanish . . . So under sealed orders and with sealed lips "Potato" Jones returned with the *Marie Llewellyn* to the French port of St Jean de Luz.'

Neutral shipping continued to be attacked by aircraft and submarines of 'unknown nationality'. Even Eden had felt obliged to admit that 'there was little doubt that about fifteen Italian submarines were attacking ships in the Mediterranean.'[48]

On 31 August Ciano, the Italian Foreign Minister, was able to boast in his diary:

> 'The naval blockade is producing striking results: four Russian or Red steamers sunk, one Greek ship captured, one Spanish shelled and obliged to take refuge in a French port.'[49]

407

By the summer of 1937 there had been such an outcry against these acts of piracy that the 'Non-Intervention' sponsors felt obliged to take some form of action.

A conference of Mediterranean countries was held in the Swiss town of Nyon. Although non-Mediterranean countries, both Germany and Russia were included in the invitations; Republican Spain was excluded. The purpose was to stop piracy in the Mediterranean. As an encouragement to the Italians to join in policing the waters of that region of the world, the USSR was excluded from the 'police force', the excuse being that Russia was not a Mediterranean power; which must have prompted Ciano to record in his diary:

> 'It is a fine victory. From suspected pirates to policemen of the Mediterranean – and the Russians whose ships we are sinking, excluded!'[50]

The attacks on British shipping had eventually succeeded in souring Anglo-Italian relations, but only for a brief period. The cordiality soon returned after Baldwin resigned from the Cabinet and his place as Prime Minister was taken over by Neville Chamberlain. Within a few weeks, Chamberlain had restored the Anglo-Italian entente and on 16 November 1937 the British Government decided to give *de facto* recognition to the Burgos rebel administration. Britain's representative was Sir Robert Hodgson,* the former British consul in Russia in 1917. According to the authors, Broué and Temime, 'It was not long before Hodgson was wielding real influence in Burgos, and from then on efforts to reach a compromise peace were directed at securing a Nationalist victory.'[51]

The British Government still believed that by appeasing Mussolini it could prevent Italy from getting too closely allied to Germany. In fact it achieved exactly the opposite. The Rome-Berlin Axis had been forged and was being strengthened. The anti-Comintern Pact, concluded on 25

---

*It was the same Robert Hodgson whose comments concerning the murder of the twenty six Commissars at Baku is referred to in Chapter 5 – Wars of Intervention.

November 1936 between Germany and Japan, was reinforced by Italy twelve months later (6 November 1937).

In May 1937, at a time when the Spanish people were being bombed and burnt by fascist aircraft, and Franco and his mercenaries were busily engaged in terrorizing the citizens in the fascist occupied territories, another war broke out in Barcelona.

In Catalonia, and in particular Barcelona, the Anarchists had never really accepted the authority of the Republican Government. Trouble had been brewing for some time between the Catalonian Anarchists and the Catalonian supporters of the central Government. On 25 April, Roldan Cortada, a well-known leader of the Unified Socialist Party of Catalonia (the PSUC), was murdered. The Anarchists were immediately suspected of complicity in this murder, and some of their leaders were arrested.

The Anarchists were at that time in control of the Central Telephone Exchange (the Telefonica)* and were suspected of interfering with telecommunications to and from the Central Government headquarters in Valencia, as well as of general telephone tapping. The Popular Front Government was naturally perturbed that the Barcelona Telefonica should be under the control of anti-Government elements, especially as the autonomous Catalonian Government (The Generalitat) wholeheartedly supported the Popular Front and had a representative in the National Cabinet.

When a representative of the Generalitat went into the Telefonica to investigate the cause of the interference in telecommunications, he was greeted by an outburst of firing. He was not hurt, but the firing appeared to have been the signal for the ensuing military conflagration. A putsch had been engineered by 'special groups' within the FAI,† aided by members of POUM, as well as fascist agents who had infiltrated into the Anarchist ranks. A telegram despatched to Berlin by von Faupel, Hitler's Ambassador in Salamanca, later revealed that Franco had instructed his agents‡ to provoke an armed uprising. Within a matter of

---

*Was owned by the American Telegraph and Telephone Company.
†Federacion Anarchista Iberica. An influential violent wing of the Anarchist movement which did not exclude murder in pursuit of its objectives.
‡von Faupel had been told by Franco that he had thirteen agents in Barcelona.

hours the centre of Barcelona was embroiled in a bitter and bloody civil war which lasted from 3 to 7 May, during which hundreds of people were killed and over 2,000 wounded. The putsch was eventually crushed by the unified efforts of the supporters of the Republic and the inability of the FAI and their 'agents' to gain the support of rank and file members of the CNT.*

And while the bitter struggle for the control of Barcelona was taking place, the Prime Minister, Largo Caballero, was engaged in a manoeuvre to rid his administration of any communist influence by trying to set up a combined UGT and CNT controlled Government, a strategy by which he would replace the existing coalition with a 'trade unionist' Government and remove the communists in the process. The failure of Largo Caballero to support the unity of anti-fascist forces and his complacency towards what was going on in Barcelona had played into the hands of the Catalonian anarchists. As he was also the Minister of War, the Communist members of the Government decided that unless the Government was prepared to pursue what they believed to be a genuine war policy, they would withdraw from the Cabinet. In this they were supported by the Socialist Party which had lost confidence in their leader and declared that it was essential to work together with the communists in the war against the fascists.

Largo Caballero was compelled to resign and Dr Juan Negrin, the Finance Minister, was asked to form a new administration which in the event included most of the former members, with the exception of the representatives of the CNT.

With unity of anti-fascist forces being of such primary importance, the Spanish Communist and Socialist Parties on 27 August 1937 produced a programme for joint action, which included a call for combined activities and co-operation by the Communist International, the Socialist International and the International Confederation of Trade Unions, to combat the menace of fascism.

There had already been a meeting of leaders of the Communist and Socialist Internationals in June 1937, but

*Confederacion National de Trabajo – the Anarchist Syndicalist Trades Union.

the appeals for joint action did not get beyond a declaration to study ways and means 'of giving moral and material help to Spain'. The two Spanish parties hoped that by their example the two Internationals would find areas of agreement by which there would be an International United Front. Unfortunately the leaders of the Socialist International preferred to remain behind the facade of non-intervention, thus avoiding having to join the communists in a common anti-fascist campaign.

A few days after the closure of the Nyon Conference, the League of Nations met for the opening session of its Annual Meeting and, as to be expected, the war in Spain was to dominate its proceedings. Once again, the Republican Government raised, as a matter of extreme urgency, German and Italian aggression upon their country. After a lengthy debate, a resolution, supported by some thirty countries and backed by Britain and France, 'called for complete and immediate withdrawal of all foreigners from Spain.' But the resolution was not endorsed because, under the unanimity rule, Albania, an Italian satellite, and Portugal had expressed their opposition.

On 4 November, the British Government carried forward its initial proposal of July for a '"substantial" number of foreigners to be withdrawn before belligerent rights were conceded.' Chamberlain was just as anxious as Hitler and Mussolini for a speedy Franco victory and by this method lengthy negotiations would be of great advantage to the rebels in the preparations for what the fascist leaders and the appeasers hoped would be the final onslaught. 'The British scheme was adopted in principle. Instructions were given for a scheme of withdrawal to be drawn up, and a sub-committee settled down to a prolonged discussion as to the proportion of foreigners on each side to be regarded as "substantial".'[52]

Within a few days of the *de facto* recognition of the Burgos rebels, a senior British Cabinet minister was in Germany secretly engaged in talks with Hitler. The minister was Lord Halifax who, 'as master of the Middleton hunt' had been invited 'to visit an international exhibition of hunting arranged by Goering in Berlin. The invitation was unofficial',[52] but its purpose was not. On 19 November

Halifax was engaged in secret discussions with Hitler on the future of Europe.

There had been in recent weeks a great deal of speculation in the press over the direction of the Chamberlain foreign policy and on 24 November the *Manchester Guardian*'s diplomatic correspondent must have had good reason to write about 'Lord Halifax's visit to Europe', of the 'Background of Talks with Hitler' and of the 'Free Hand in Central Europe'.

On the following Sunday, 28 November 1937, the *Reynolds News* carried a feature on its front page under the headline

'GRAVE CABINET CRISIS'

'The story behind the crisis is one of political intrigue almost without parallel in the history of British politics.

'It is a story of meetings at a country house at which the Halifax plan was discussed in advance of the Lord President's German visit, of behind the scenes moves that may imperil our good relations with France.

'Clash is between two policies. On the one hand, is the group that seeks to detach Italy from the Rome-Berlin Axis by means of bribes to Mussolini; on the other, that which hopes to buy German friendship by a deal in Central Europe and a bargain over colonies. Mr Eden and Sir Robert Vansittart are the advocates of the former policy. Sir Samuel Hoare, Sir John Simon, Sir Kingsley Wood, Lord Halifax and a little coterie of powerful German sympathizers favour the latter . . .

'Looming heavily over the crisis is the perilous situation in the Far East where Japan, it is feared, is threatening a major war with Soviet Russia.

'By the terms of the Franco-Soviet Pact, France is bound to come to the aid of Russia, if the latter is drawn into a war in which a third power may render the aggressors military assistance.

'The anti-Communist alliance between Japan, Germany and Italy gives a new and graver turn to the situation.'

The *Reynolds News* then writes about how 'the plan for the Halifax visit to Berlin was worked out at a series of country house parties at the Astor home in the last weeks of September and the early weeks of October', and that 'Lords Londonderry and Lothian with General Goering were the originators.'

'The Plan . . . included the bargain by which in exchange for a "free hand" for German aggression against Austria and Czechoslovakia, and in the north, against Denmark, Germany would not put to Britain the final demands for the handing over of her former colonies and the League of Nations mandates for six years.'

The Plan also, 'included the recognition of Franco by the British Government as well as the dismantling of the machinery of the League as a possible instrument of collective security, and the ultimate entry of Germany into a League which would have ceased to be an instrument of security and become instead a platform for the aggressor powers.'

Towards the end of 1937, Britain's Foreign Minister was beginning to have doubts about the direction of British foreign policy. It had become apparent that since Mussolini's visit to Berlin in September the two dictators had reached agreement over their spheres of interest. According to German documents, 'Italy will not be impeded by Germany in the Mediterranean whereas, on the other hand, the special German interests in Austria will not be impaired by Italy.'* Although Eden says that 'no hint, of course, was publicly given of any such agreement at the time' he 'began, during the autumn months, increasingly to suspect something of the kind.'[54] As far as he was concerned, Anglo-Italian foreign policy could never be the same. The Stresa accord was over. Meanwhile, Chamberlain still believed that he could come to terms with Mussolini. Completely ignoring Eden, he initiated contacts with the Italian Government and at the beginning of 1938 decided to

*From *Documents on German Foreign Policy 1918–1945*, Series D. Vol. I, p. 1.

negotiate a new Anglo-Italian Agreement. Eden had warned him not to accept Mussolini's assurances on their face value and on 20 February he resigned, primarily because he had at last realized that the policies of Hitler and Mussolini would eventually threaten Britain and the British Empire.

On the following day Chamberlain told a crowded House of Commons that he had held up negotiations with the Italian Government until he was assured that 'the British formula concerning the withdrawal of foreign volunteers and granting of belligerent rights' had been agreed to. He then read out the message just received from the Italian Ambassador of his Government's acceptance of the British formula, and continued, that as 'we were loyal members of the League . . . it was essential that it should not be possible, if we went to the League to recommend the approval of the agreement, for it to be said that the situation in Spain during the conversations had been materially altered by Italy, either by sending fresh reinforcements to Franco or by failing to implement the arrangements contemplated by the British formula.' (*Hansard* 21 February 1938, Cols. 61, 62, 63).

'Yet . . . within two or three days of the assurance, larger bodies of Italian troops had landed in the South of Spain.' Just two days before he had signed his Treaty of Friendship and Co-operation with Italy, Chamberlain had received a list of reinforcements from the Duchess of Atholl, which had been delivered to 10 Downing Street, But no advice, no evidence of Mussolini breaking the terms of the agreement deterred him from pursuing his policy of appeasing Mussolini and sacrificing Spain in the process.

'That Italian men and material continued to arrive after the talks between Britain and Italy had commenced, was confirmed by an Italian Second Lieutenant, Gino Poggi, captured on 28 March. He stated that throughout 'this last month' pilots had been coming. Fifteen had arrived at his aerodrome at Logrono (in the north of Spain). Lieutenant Poggi gave the names of the three steamers in which the airmen were wont to come.'

He wound up his statement by saying that '"Shipments of material have very recently been accelerated owing to the fact that Mussolini wishes to finish the war in Spain"', and that '"Mussolini will declare that he is no longer sending anything to Franco, but intervention is being increased so as to trick England".'

The Duchess of Atholl states that she had seen a photostat of Lieutenant Poggi's statement and that in addition to Italian supplies, she cites that 'no less than fourteen ships, each of not less than some 7,000 tons, left Hamburg, laden with arms for Spain. A question put in the House of Commons on this subject drew the reply that the Government had no confirmation of this information.'

On 10 April 1938, the *Sunday Times* reported that 2,000 Portuguese soldiers left Morocco for Spain on 24 February, which brought their total contingent up to 7,000. 'And between 1 January and 20 March some 70,000 Moors and 8,000 negroes and others were transported from Morocco to insurgent Spain' as well as 'some hundreds of natives from French territory.'[55]

In March 1937 there were approximately 80,000 Italian and 30,000 German military personnel in Spain. If one takes into consideration the additional Italian troops, that the Duchess of Atholl had included in her list for Chamberlain to examine, this would have added at least 60,000 ground troops alone to the overall figure. So that by April 1938 there would have been around 140,000 to 150,000 Italians, 30,000 to 40,000 Germans, 7,000 Portuguese, apart from the 'Africans'. At no time between July 1936 and April 1939 were there more than 20,000 foreign volunteers on the Republican side. At the time of the withdrawal negotiations the figure was around 15,000.

A significant factor in the withdrawal strategem was the description of German and Italian 'regulars' as 'foreign volunteers'. To maintain the facade the only Italian withdrawals, which had been publicized, were the wounded, the sick and the battle weary, who were in any case due for replacement.

The tragedy was, that while the Spanish people were holding the fort in the initial stage of what really was a European war, Nazi Germany was busy exploiting the fruits of appeasement. On 12 March, 1938 Hitler's troops marched into Austria and annexed that country into the Third Reich. It opened up the route into South Eastern

415

Europe, and so long as they continued in that direction all was well as far as the British and French Governments were concerned. Schuschnigg, the Austrian Chancellor, had been threatened by Hitler 'that if he did not yield to German demands Austria would become "another Spain".'[56]

On 12 June 1938 the French Government decided to close the frontiers. This was a further blow to the Republican cause and particularly to the Catalonian region which was in the throes of a desperate fight against the rebels. Already short of military equipment, the Republican Army was now being cut off from the supply of arms sold to the Spanish Government by the USSR in the Spring of 1938, most of which had been lying in France just over the Franco-Spanish border.

The Negrin administration had bought from the Soviet Union hundreds of aircraft, 500 pieces of artillery, 10,000 machine guns, as well as torpedo boats. According to Negrin, if only a part of these supplies had arrived the People's Army could have changed 'the whole course of the battle for Catalonia and the war as a whole.'[57]

This move by the Daladier administration was part of the plan to hasten the demise of the Republican army.

French public opinion had become incensed by this action and, in the French Chamber, the Communist deputies tabled a motion demanding that the frontier be reopened. With the insurgents gaining the upper hand in Catalonia, the French Government cynically allowed a small amount of arms to trickle through most of which, by then, finished up in rebel hands. By helping Franco to victory the Quai d'Orsay and the British Foreign Office believed that it would strengthen their political and economic influence on the Iberian peninsula.

When Britain gave de facto recognition to the Burgos administration and exchanged 'agents', the Germans began to get suspicious of what was going on between Burgos and London. The Nazi Government had been financing the Burgos administration to the extent of 'ten million Reich-smarks a month, of which four million was for war materials, five and a half million for other exports and 350,000 cash credit', and to heighten the Anglo-German rivalry, 'German financiers were becoming fearful lest

Britain should step in to take her coveted iron ore. The busy officials of HISMA and ROWAK* had been occupied with the so-called MONTANA project, designed to guarantee to Germany a steady supply of Spanish minerals. The project provided for German control of no less than seventy three Spanish mines.'[58]

Hitler was in a hurry to achieve a Franco victory. He knew that Franco could not win the war without further massive help and in November 1938 'the Nazi Government hinted to Franco that the deliveries of war materials that he had requested depended upon giving up his reservations regarding the mining concessions included in the "MONTANA PLAN"'. A few days later, General Jordana, one of Franco's senior ministers, 'informed the German Ambassador that Franco accepted all the conditions laid down, simply asking, that, in return, the Fuehrer's Government should keep those conditions secret.'[59]

Meanwhile the build-up of the rebel forces was being intensified. On 13 December 1938 a massive attack was launched against an ill-equipped Republican army. The rebels broke through in the north, forcing hundreds of thousands of men, women and children to leave their homes. On foot, on donkeys, bicycles, carts, cars and lorries they travelled through the bitter nights of January, sleeping out in the open wherever they could and out of sight of enemy aircraft, towards the French frontier.

On 26 January 1939 the Republican army lost Barcelona and, soon afterwards, Gerona. Figueras, a small town in the north of Catalonia, packed with refugees and near the French border, was attacked by the Italian air force. It was a massacre, and the outcry in France against this latest barbaric onslaught on the Spanish people eventually compelled the Daladier Government to officially open its frontiers and the refugees†

---

*HISMA – Compania Hispano – Morroqui de Transportes
ROWAK – Rohstoffe und Waren – Einkaufsgesellschaft
HISMA, ROWAK and the MONTANA project were eventually incorporated into an agency – SOFINDUS (Sociedad Financiera Industria Ltda) which was to supervise Spanish-German economic affairs.
†In 1937, after the bombing of Guernica, '4,000 Basque children were admitted to Britain as refugees ... on the strict understanding that they must not be a charge on public funds. But voluntary funds flooded in'.
(BRANSON and HEINEMANN, *Britain in the 1930s*, p. 315)

were hastily herded into concentration camps, with next to nothing in the way of elementary facilities, such as water, food or even tents – they had to find their own cover.

With Catalonia now under fascist control and Republican territory shrinking, deep rooted cracks began opening up within the Republican Army. Negrin, del Vayo, the Foreign Minister, and the Communists were prepared to continue the fight. About a third of the country, including the capital, Madrid, was still in Republican hands. But defeatism had become rife within certain sections of the army as well as the administration. Colonel Casado, the Commander of the central region, which included Madrid, had, through intermediaries, been in contact with Franco trying to negotiate an 'honourable peace', 'convinced that the advocates of negotiation would benefit from British support as soon as Communist influence had disappeared.' According to the French writers, Broué and Temime, 'Casado had undoubtedly been in touch with foreign diplomats especially British ones.'[60]

President Azana had given up and sought refuge in France, and on 1 February the Cortes met for the last time in the mediaeval castle of Figueras, where the members sought 'to establish a basis for reconciliation among Spaniards and to bring the civil war to an end by eliminating all foreign interference in Spanish life and avoiding reprisals – without victors or vanquished.'[61]

Franco was not interested in reconciliation and a week later he publicized his own remedy – the Franco 'Law of Political Responsibility', which was to be so widely interpreted that it covered practically any person who had opposed the insurgency of his fascist army. His terms were 'unconditional surrender'. With Republican forces split by the defeatists, led by Casado and his collaborators, Franco was confident that victory was very near. On 22 February he sent a telegram to Chamberlain 'assuring him that his patriotism, his honour as a gentleman, and his generosity were the finest guarantees for a just peace', and a few days later 'announced that the tribunals to be set up after the Republican surrender would deal only with criminals – "reprisals being alien to the Nationalist movement"'.[62]

Franco's assurances were immediately seized upon by

Chamberlain to justify granting full diplomatic recognition to the Franco administration. In spite of the fact that the Republican Government was still in occupation of a third of the country which included Madrid, the capital, and that the war was not yet over, the British Government, nevertheless, rushed through measures to sever diplomatic relations with the Republican Government. This was done on 27 February at the same time as *de jure* recognition was granted to the insurgents, even though they were not, to use governmental terminology in 'effective control' of the country, the criteria by which diplomatic recognition is normally applied. French *de jure* recognition followed two days later. And as part of the process of accelerating the Fascist take-over a British cruiser, the *Devonshire* was sent to Minorca to help the insurgents take control of the island.

Meanwhile Casado, with the help of the FAI anarchists and right-wing Socialist deputy, Julian Besteiro, engineered a counter-revolutionary putsch in Madrid and on 5 March announced over the Madrid radio that they had formed a 'National Junta of Defence', with an appeal for 'Peace with Honour' and a 'Peace without Crimes' – slogan appeals which Casado knew had been rejected by Franco who would accept nothing less than 'unconditional surrender'.

Casado concentrated his attack on the Communists. He had already banned their newspaper, the *Mundo Obrero*, and thousands were arrested and thrown into prison. Once again the Spanish people were subjected to a civil war within a civil war. Eventually the whole of the central front collapsed, mainly through the efforts of Casado and his collaborators. But heroic Madrid was never captured, it was handed over to the insurgents.

On 28 March 1939 the Fascist army, with Italian troops in the lead, marched into Madrid. The Spanish war was over. The 'gallant Christian' was soon 'to fulfil his honour as a gentleman'. A new 'Inquisition' was set up, which led to firing squads, tortures and mass imprisonment.

Notes

1. ATHOLL, Duchess of, *Searchlight on Spain*, pp. 70–71
2. ATHOLL, Duchess of, *Searchlight on Spain*, p. 64
3. ATHOLL, Duchess of, *Searchlight on Spain*, pp. 65–66
4. ATHOLL, Duchess of, *Searchlight on Spain*, p. 69
5. SANDOVAL, Jose and AZCARATE, Manuel, *Spain 1936–1939*, p. 17
6. BROUE, Pierre and TEMIME, Emil, *The Revolution and the Civil War in Spain*, p. 97
7. THOMAS, Hugh, *The Spanish Civil War*, p. 119
8. SANDOVAL, Jose and AZCARATE, Manuel, *Spain 1936–1939*, p. 26
9. BROUE, Pierre and TEMIME, Emil, *The Revolution and the Civil War in Spain*, p. 177
10. SANDOVAL, Jose and AZCARATE, Manuel, *Spain 1936–1939*, p. 52
11. FOOT, Michael, *Aneurin Bevan, Vol. I* 1897–1945, p. 220
12. THOMAS, Hugh, *The Spanish Civil War*, p. 220
13. FOOT, Michael, *Aneurin Bevan, Vol. I* 1897–1945, p. 222
14. FOOT, Michael, *Aneurin Bevan, Vol. I* 1897–1945, p. 223
15. FOOT, Michael *Aneurin Bevan, Vol. I* 1897–1945, p. 224
16. EDEN, Anthony (Rt. Hon. Earl of Avon), *The Eden Memoirs – Facing the Dictators*, p. 403
17. EDEN, Anthony (Rt. Hon. Earl of Avon), *The Eden Memoirs – Facing the Dictators*, p. 403
18. SHIRER, William, *The Collapse of the Third Republic*, p. 284
19. EDEN, Anthony (Rt. Hon. Earl of Avon), *The Eden Memoirs – Facing the Dictators*, p. 403
20. FOOT, Michael, *Aneurin Bevan, Vol. I* 1897–1945, p. 224
21. MAISKY, Ivan, *Spanish Notebooks*, p. 29
22. SHIRER, William, *The Collapse of the Third Republic*, p. 284
23. *Documents on German Foreign Policy*, Series D Vol. III, p. 60
24. THOMAS, Hugh, *The Spanish Civil War*, p. 263
25. SHIRER, William, *The Collapse of the Third Republic*, p. 284
26. WERTH, Alexander, *The Destiny of France*, pp. 375–6
27. MAISKY, Ivan, *Spanish Notebooks*, pp. 34–35
28. ATHOLL, Duchess of, *Searchlight on Spain*, pp. 131–133
29. ATHOLL, Duchess of, *Searchlight on Spain*, p. 128
30. ATHOLL, Duchess of, *Searchlight on Spain*, p. 129
31. BROUE, Pierre and TEMIME, Emil, *The Revolution and the Civil War in Spain*, p. 184
32. FOOT, Michael, *Aneurin Bevan, Vol. I.* 1897–1945, pp. 224–6
33. FOOT, Michael, *Aneurin Bevan, Vol. I.* 1897–1945, p. 226
34. HUTT, Allen, *British Trade Unionism*, p. 140
35. FOOT, Michael, *Aneurin Bevan, Vol. I.* 1897–1945, p. 230
36. FOOT, Michael, *Aneurin Bevan, Vol. I.* 1897–1945, p. 231–2
37. FOOT, Michael, *Aneurin Bevan, Vol. I.* 1897–1945, p. 232
38. SANDOVAL, Jose and AZCARATE, Manuel, *Spain 1936–1939*, pp. 70, 76–77
39. EDEN, Anthony, (Rt. Hon. Earl of Avon), *The Eden Memoirs – Facing the Dictators*, pp 433–4
40. SANDOVAL, Jose and AZCARATE, Manuel, *Spain 1936–1939*, p. 83

41. BRANSON, Noreen and HEINEMANN, Margot, *Britain in the Nineteen Thirties*, p. 314
42. RUST, William, *Britons in Spain*, p. 10
43. ATHOLL, Duchess of, *Searchlight on Spain*, p. 189
44. KNIGHTLEY, Phillip, *The First Casualty*, p. 203
45. KNIGHTLEY, Phillip, *The First Casualty*, p. 207
46. ATHOLL, Duchess of, *Searchlight on Spain*, p. 210
47. MAISKY, Ivan, *Spanish Notebooks*, p. 165
48. EDEN, Anthony, (Rt. Hon. Earl of Avon), *The Eden Memoirs – Facing the Dictators*, p. 460
49. Ciano's Diary 1937–1938, p. 7
50. Ciano's Diary 1937–1938, p. 15
51. BROUE, Pierre and TEMIME, Emil, *The Revolution and the Civil War in Spain*, pp. 490–491
52. ATHOLL, Duchess of, *Searchlight on Spain*, pp. 211–212
53. MOWAT, C.L., *Britain Between the Wars 1918–1940*, p. 595
54. EDEN, Anthony, (Rt. Hon. Earl of Avon), *The Eden Memoirs – Facing the Dictators*, 476
55. ATHOLL, Duchess of, *Searchlight on Spain*, pp. 303–308
56. THOMAS, Hugh, *The Spanish Civil War*, p. 517
57. SANDOVAL, Jose and AZCARATE, Manuel, *Spain 1936–1939*, p. 129
58. THOMAS, Hugh, *The Spanish Civil War*, p. 487
59. SANDOVAL, Jose and AZCARATE, Manuel, *Spain 1936–1939*, p. 127
60. BROUE, Pierre and TEMIME, Emil, *The Revolution and the Civil War in Spain*, p. 527
61. SANDOVAL, Jose and AZCARATE, Manuel, *Spain 1936–1939*, p. 133
62. THOMAS, Hugh, *The Spanish Civil War*, p. 583

32

THE BETRAYAL

The abandonment of the Spanish Republic to the forces of fascism by Blum and his administrators had destroyed the very foundation upon which the Popular Front Government was established and in June 1937, France moved further to the Right with the introduction of a new Government led by Chautemps, with Blum as his deputy. Dominated by the Radicals this Government was just as ineffectual as its predecessors in confronting the expansionist moves of the fascist dictators. It lasted barely nine months, until 10 March 1938. Once again, Blum was called upon to form a Government. Unfortunately for Blum it coincided with the German annexation of Austria.

Hitler had already sensed from his discussions with Lord Halifax in November 1937 that the annexation of Austria would not be opposed by the Chamberlain Government. His instincts had been confirmed by Eden's resignation in February 1938 and by the removal of Sir Robert Vansittart, the Permanent Under-Secretary at the Foreign Office.* Both were opponents of Chamberlain's appeasement policies.

On 17 March, just four days after Hitler proclaimed Austria's province of the German Reich, Litvinov, at a Press conference in Moscow, warned of the dangers that lay ahead for the peoples of Europe, with a rcommendation for steps to be taken to avert war.

'The Soviet Government is conscious of the obligations devolving on it from the Covenant of

---

*He became Chief Diplomatic Adviser, but was kept away from foreign affairs.

the League, the Briand-Kellogg Pact and its treaty of mutual assistance concluded with France and Czechoslovakia.

I am therefore in a position to state on its behalf that it is prepared, as hitherto, to participate in collective action, the scope of which should have as its aim the stopping of the further development of aggression and the elimination of the increased danger of a new world slaughter.

The Soviet Government is prepared to begin immediately, together with other states in the League of Nations or outside it, the consideration of practical measures called for by the present circumstances.

Tomorrow it may be too late, but today the time has not yet passed if all the states, and especially the Great Powers, will adopt a firm and unequivocal stand in regard to the problems of the collective saving of peace.' (*The Daily Telegraph*, 18 March 1938)

Copies of the statement, together with a covering letter, were sent to the British, French, Czech and American Governments.

The Soviet proposal was rejected by the British Government and, in explaining the reason, Chamberlain told the House of Commons on 24 March that the

'inevitable consequence of such action as is proposed by the Soviet Government would be to aggravate the tendency towards the establishment of exclusive groups of nations which must ... be inimical to the prospects of European peace.' (*Hansard*, 24 March 1938, Col. 1406)

This extraordinary explanation has been commented upon by William Shirer. 'Apparently Chamberlain did not mind such 'exclusive groups of nations' as those joined in the Rome-Berlin Axis or in the tripartite Anti-Comintern pact of Germany, Italy and Japan, nor that group ... the so-called Four Powers of Britain, France, Germany and Italy –

which excluded Soviet Russia. Once again France took its cue from Britain and cold-shouldered the Russian proposal.'[1]

One of the very few French deputies, apart from the Communists who believed that co-operation with Russia was essential if peace was to be preserved in Europe was Paul Reynaud who had appealed for a Government of National Unity. Inevitably, there were deputies who 'protested against joining a government that included Communists.' Reynaud's reply was simple and to the point. "'It is not Stalin who enters Vienna today, who will menace Prague tomorrow. It is Hitler . . . I say today France must unite".'[2] The lack of such unity brought to an end the second Blum Government after twenty-six days of incessant internal wrangling. The new Cabinet was headed once again by Edouard Daladier, with Georges Bonnet succeeding Paul Boncour at the Quai d'Orsay.

It was not unexpected, that after his Austrian success, Hitler should decide to champion the cause of German speaking minorities in the adjacent territories and apply it to his 'lebensraum' foreign policy. There were three and a half million people of Germanic origin* in Czechoslovakia and the Nazi leader had not hidden his intentions. What he had not disclosed in *Mein Kampf*, was the timing.

As explained in Chapter 7, the rights of ethnic minorities in the newly created Czechoslovakia after Versailles was a matter which could easily be exploited by an unscruplulous neighbour. The creation of a Nazi Party in Sudetenland, where most of the ethnic Germans lived, was to provide Hitler with his 'Trojan Horse'.

Czechoslovakia was not only the gateway to the east, it was the pearl of Central Europe. With its rich mineral resources, one of the largest munition industries in the world, a well-equipped, well-trained army and with an air force of over 1,500 aeroplanes, the Czechs were a formidable force for any would be invader.

Since Hitler decided to pull Germany out of the League of Nations in 1933, the Czechs had spent some four

---

*The majority were not from Germany but were of Austrian-Teutonic origins.

hundred million dollars on a chain of fortifications as part of their plan of defence against attack from a powerful and aggressive neighbour. They were built by French engineers and based upon Maginot specifications. But above all, Czechoslovakia was allied by treaties with France and the Soviet Union. Its preservation was not only a moral obligation. It was a vital link in the chain of agreements made between Britain and France, France and Czechoslovakia, France and the Soviet Union, France with Poland, the Soviet Union with Czechoslovakia as well as France and the other countries of the Little Entente – Roumania and Yugoslavia. All these agreements were made primarily as a protection against the resurgence of German militarism and aggression and gave substance to Litvinov's earlier warning at Geneva in 1933 that 'peace is indivisible'.

Rather than accept the Soviet Union into a pact of collective security, both London and Paris were prepared to succumb to Hitler's bluff and promises of goodwill. Daladier certainly was not unaware of the direction of Hitler's foreign policy. At a meeting in London with Chamberlain and Halifax on 28–29 April, he clearly outlined what he believed were Hitler's real aspirations. He told his hosts that the complaints of the Sudeten Germans were just a pretext for incorporating Sudetenland into the Third Reich as a step towards the destruction of Czechoslovakia. 'In his view, the ambitions of Napoleon were far inferior to the present aims of the German Reich . . . Today, we were faced with the question of Czechoslovakia. Tomorrow we might be faced with that of Roumania . . . He thought it was clear that, if and when Germany had secured the petrol and wheat resources of Roumania, she would then turn against the Western powers, and it would be our own blindness which would have provided Germany with the very supplies she required for the long war which she admitted she was not now in a position to wage.'[3] But Daladier refused to accept that the old Entente of Britain and France was in itself insufficient to deter Hitler. Even without Britain the combined forces of France, Czechoslovakia and Russia would have been a sufficient deterrent. It is difficult to believe that his military advisers were not aware of the fears of the German military being caught up into a war on two fronts. Hitler's policy had been clearly laid out in *Mein Kampf*, to not only separate Britain from France, but to split apart all the opposing forces and attack them one by one. The German economy was weak. It was short of oil, iron ore and many essential foodstuffs and it could not have undertaken a war against the combined forces of Britain, France, Czechoslovakia and Russia. The Czechs alone had thirty five divisions.

Chamberlain had already made up his mind to abandon Czechoslovakia a month earlier.

> 'You have only to look at the map to see that nothing that France or we could do could possibly save Czechoslovakia from being overrun by the Germans, if they wanted to do it. The Austrian frontier is practically open; the great Skoda munition works are within easy bombing distance of the German aerodromes, the railways all pass through German territory, Russia is 100 miles away. Therefore we could not help Czechoslovakia – she would simply be a pretext for going to war with Germany. That we could not think of unless we had a reasonable prospect of being able to beat her to her knees in a reasonable time and of that I see no sign. I have therefore abandoned any idea of giving guarantees to Czechoslovakia, or the French in connection with her obligations to that country.'[4]

This statement was made on 20 March 1938. He had already abandoned Austria on 12 March when he notified the French Government that His Majesty's Government was opposed to the Austrian affair being brought before the League. And in this attitude he was fully supported by his new Permanent Under-Secretary, Sir Alexander Cadogan, who had at Chamberlain's request taken over from Vansittart. Once Vansittart had been removed from this very sensitive and influential post in British foreign affairs, Chamberlain and Halifax were able to proceed unhindered in their pro-German appeasement policy. 'Personally I almost wish Germany would swallow Austria and get it over'[5] comments Cadogan. His wishful thinking was soon brought to fruition.

Within a fortnight of the annexation of Austria, Konrad Henlein, the leader of the Nazi Sudeten Germans, was in Berlin where he was told by Hitler that 'demands should be made by the Sudeten German Party which are unacceptable to the Czech Government.'[6]

On 24 April this agent of Hitler, in one of his inflammatory speeches, presented an eight point plan for the Sudetenland which demanded from the Czech Government the recognition of Sudeten Germans as a separate legal entity within the State, as well as having 'complete freedom to profess adherence to the German element and ideology'. These were just some of the unacceptable demands which the Sudeten Nazis had been continually pressing until on 9 May Henlein decided to break off his talks with the Czech Government.

He was in London on 12–14 May, having stopped in Berlin en route, where he received instructions from the German Foreign Office. Among the instructions was one which stated that he was to 'speak of the progressive disintegration of the Czech political structure actually taking place, in order to discourage those circles which consider that their intervention on behalf of this political structure may still be of use.'[7]

Henlein was not a newcomer to London. Two years earlier in the summer of 1936 *Reynolds News* reported that 'he has visited the Foreign Office and has made contacts with quite a number of influential men in the diplomatic world.' The paper's correspondent gathered

> 'that the line he has taken with the Foreign Office representatives is that unless pressure is brought to bear on Dr Benes, President of Czechoslovakia, to make concessions to the Nazis, and, in fact, to effect a re-orientation of the country's foreign policy, he, Herr Henlein, will no longer be able to exercise a moderating influence over the Nazi elements in his party. This is of course, bluff.' (*Secret History of Today – Reynolds News*, 2 August 1936)

The Foreign Office certainly had plenty of advance warning of Hitler's plans for Central Europe.

Soon after the second Henlein trip to London, Czech intelligence was reporting that German troops were concentrating on the frontier. After an emergency meeting the Czech Government issued instructions for an immediate mobilization of their armed forces. These included the complete manning of the newly constructed fortifications as well as the call-up of technical reservists, the effect of which succeeded in pushing the reluctant British and French Governments into a situation where they felt obliged to follow suit. There was a mobilization of some classes of French reservists and a mobilization of the British Navy.

Hitler's original plans for the attack were revised by General Keitel who, on 20 May, sent him the text of a Directive stressing

> 'it is essential to create in the first four days a strategic situation which demonstrates to enemy states which may wish to intervene the hopelessness of the Czech military position.'

Both Hitler and Keitel were apparently confident that neither France nor Britain would come to the aid of Czechoslovakia, for the Directive only provided for 'minimum strength' in the West, 'limited in quantity and quality.' But they expected 'attempts by Russia to give Czechoslovakia military support.'[8]

Another experienced foreign correspondent, G.E.R. Gedye, who had spent most of the 1930s reporting on the political scene in Central European countries, was at that time based in Prague. In his book, *Fallen Bastions* (written in 1939) Gedye points out that 'after the Czechs had shown that they were going to defend themselves, British diplomatic pressure was exerted in a favourable sense in Berlin, where warnings were given that invasion might precipitate a general war in which Britain might unwillingly find herself dragged in on the side of France, Russia and Czechoslovakia. Faced by exactly the same situation as had confronted Austria two months before, Czechoslovakia had taken precisely the opposite action. The result justified her up to the hilt, there was no invasion . . . I am quite certain' says Gedye, 'that Germany neither desired nor intended to risk a general European conflict.'[9]

This has since been confirmed by leading members of the German General Staff. General Ludwig Beck, the Chief-of-Staff, in a memorandum to Hitler's new Commander-in-Chief, General Walther von Brauchitsch, insisted 'that the army prevent Hitler from going to war.' He had written a note to Brauchitsch on 5 May warning that 'a German attack on Czechoslovakia would provoke a European war in which Britain, France and Russia would oppose Germany and in which the United States would be the arsenal of the Western democracies. Germany simply couldn't win such a war.' In a further note, sent on 16 July, Beck 'demanded that the army tell Hitler to halt his preparations for war.'

> 'In full consciousness of the magnitude of such a step but also of my responsibilities I feel it my duty to urgently ask that the Supreme Commander of the Armed Forces [Hitler] call off his preparations for war and abandon the intention of solving the Czech question by force until the military situation is fundamentally changed. For the present I consider it hopeless, and this view is shared by all the higher officers of the general staff.'[10]

For the first time Hitler's bluff had been challenged. He was not sure of the extent of opposition that a German offensive into Czechoslovakia would entail. Although thwarted in this first attempt, Hitler nevertheless regarded it only as a temporary set-back and proceeded with plans for the invasion to take place on 1 October, confident that Chamberlain and the majority in the British Cabinet would not object to his Czechoslovak solution.

In France, opposition to the Nazi leader's solution was divided. Bonnet was in accord with Chamberlain, but Daladier was vacillating between pressures and doubts which Hitler was confident could be overcome. The strongest pressures came from the British Government. On Sunday, 22 May, at the height of the German-Czech crisis the British Foreign Office secretly transmitted a severe warning from Lord Halifax through its Ambassador in Paris, Sir Eric Phipps, for Bonnet's attention. Outlining the British Government's real attitude towards the current political situation, it warned that:

> the 'French Government should not be under any illusion as to the attitude of His Majesty's Government . . . in the event of failure to bring about peaceful settlement in Czechoslovakia.'
>
> That 'His Majesty's Government have given the most serious warnings to Berlin . . . But it might be highly dangerous if the French Government were to read more into those warnings than is justified by their terms.
>
> His Majesty's Government would of course always honour their pledge to come to the assistance of France if she were the victim of unprovoked aggression by Germany . . .
>
> If, however, the French Government were to assume that His Majesty's Government would at once take joint military action with them to preserve Czechoslovakia against German aggression, it is only fair to warn them that our statements do not warrant any such assumption.
>
> In the view of His Majesty's Government the military situation is such that France and England, even with such assistance as might be expected from Russia, would not be in a position to prevent Germany overrunning Czechoslovakia. The only result would be a European war, the outcome of which, so far as can be foreseen . . . would be at least doubtful.
>
> His Majesty's Government fully realize the nature and extent of French obligations but they feel that in the present highly critical situation the French Government should take full account of the preceding considerations.'[11]

France too had its powerful group of politicians, businessmen and Press 'barons' – similar to the Cliveden Set –

manipulating French foreign policy behind the scenes. Its foremost spokesman was former Prime Minister, Pierre Flandin, who had the sympathetic ear of Bonnet. Rumours were spread that the Soviet Union would not support France, should it decide to defend Czechoslovakia; that the Soviet Army and Air Force was in a weak state and could not be relied upon.

The Halifax warning had given Bonnet the excuse to follow Britain's policy and allow Hitler a free hand in his moves eastwards and both Halifax and Chamberlain must have been comforted by the fact that Bonnet had told Phipps

> 'that he would readily put any pressure on the Czechoslovak Government . . . if Czechoslovakia were really unreasonable the French Government might well declare that France considered herself released from her bond.'[12]

A week before the May crisis, Bonnet decided to probe into what action the Soviet Government would take if war broke out over Czechoslovakia. He was in Geneva for a meeting of the League of Nations Council, and during an interval he sought out Litvinov and raised the matter with him.

'"The French Government", said Bonnet, "are uneasy about the possibility of a clash between Prague and Berlin. In such an eventuality France would help Czechoslovakia . . . but it is essential that she should know what the USSR would do."

'Litvinov at once replied, "If France fulfils the obligations towards Czechoslovakia arising from her assistance pact, the USSR will also honour the obligations of her own pact."

"But from the practical point of view, how will you be able to help Czechoslovakia, since you have no common fronter? It stands to reason that you will be forced to send your troops or your aeroplanes across Polish territory or Roumanian territory . . . Is the USSR ready to oblige these two countries to consent?"

'Litvinov's answer was perfectly clear. "No. My government will neither go through nor fly over Polish or

Roumanian territory unless it obtains the consent of Poland or Roumania . . . We have not the least desire to find ourselves at war with these two countries. But for her part France has a treaty of friendship with the one and of alliance with the other. So it is she who is best placed for obtaining this right of passage."[13]

France held the key to the situation. Under the Locarno treaties it had a pact with Poland and a pact with Czechoslovakia, and in 1935 had signed a pact with the Soviet Union. If these pacts were to mean anything the French Government had an obligation to go to the help of Czechoslovakia if attacked. Litvinov had offered Soviet help, the missing link was French co-operation. But the French Foreign Office was more inclined to put pressure on Czechoslovakia to succumb to Hitler's aspirations, than upon the Polish Government to co-operate in stopping the expansion of the Third Reich. Daladier had already shown he was aware that the survival of Czechoslovakia and Poland was linked to the survival of the West. But neither he nor Bonnet were prepared to accept the Soviet Union into a comprehensive survival plan. Nor were the two Foreign Offices in London and Paris reconciled to the fact that Soviet Russia had come to stay. They still dreamed of it being overthrown, if not by themselves then by aiding another force, albeit indirectly, but nevertheless the objective was the same.

Inspired rumours had been going the rounds that 'in the interests of peace' Britain would support the transfer of the Sudetenland to Germany. The rumours had been encouraged by Chamberlain and in some 'off-the-record' remarks to a selected circle of American and Canadian journalists, at one of Lady Astor's 'informal' luncheons, he told them that 'neither France nor Russia, and certainly not Britain, would fight for Czechoslovakia in the event of German aggression, and that the Czechoslovak State could not continue to exist in its present form.' He 'left his hearers with the clear impression that the policy of Great Britain was to bring about a peaceful solution of the Sudeten problem by giving Hitler the German 'fringe' of Czechoslovakia, after which a Four-Power-Pact for the preservation of the peace of Europe would be concluded between Great

Britain, France, Germany and Italy, to the exclusion of Russia.'[14]

A similar statement had been made in confidence to a group of British journalists on 1 June and a few days later the German Ambassador notified his superiors in Berlin that the British Government would accept the secession of Sudetenland from Czechoslovakia provided that it was brought about peacefully.

Not only was this true, but by a piece of political chicanery Chamberlain had manoeuvred an invitation from the Czech Government to send an arbitrator to help 'settle' the Czech Sudeten 'problem'. The arbitrator was the shipping magnate, Lord Runciman, who was going 'in response to a request from the Government of Czechoslovakia'. That was how Chamberlain announced it in the House of Commons on 26 July – just a few days before the summer recess. Chamberlain hoped that if the Czech problem could be settled peacefully Britain and Germany might resume the kind of understanding which led to the Anglo-German Naval Treaty.

But there could have been no free dialogue between the Czech Government and the Sudeteners. Their leaders were agents of Nazi Germany and when Runciman arrived in Prague on 4 August, Shirer who was in the Czech capital noted in his diary that 'Runciman's whole mission smells, ... the Czechs know that Chamberlain personally wants Czechoslovakia to give in to Hitler's wishes.' According to Anthony Eden, 'the effect of Runciman's intervention could only be to weaken France's ally and breed hesitation among other watchful nations.'[15]

Robert Boothby*, a Conservative Member of Parliament, and former Parliamentary Secretary to Winston Churchill was in Czechoslovakia at the time of the Runciman mission. It was during the Parliamentary recess and Boothby had been writing on European affairs for a Sunday newspaper. In his autobiography he says that he went 'to find out what was going on.' In his opinion 'Runciman was up to no good' and that the Runciman mission 'spent most of their time visiting the private houses of the rich; and on the two

---

*The late Lord Boothby.

occasions when I ran into him I was unable to discover what purpose he had, unless it was to undermine the morale of the Czech Government. His subsequent report proved that this was in fact the case.'[16]

Having 'a great deal of sympathy for the Sudeten Germans' Runciman proposed that the areas in which they had a clear majority should immediately be handed over to them, which in effect meant handing over to Hitler's Third Reich.

On 18 August General Beck resigned his post as Chief of the German Army General Staff. It was a well kept secret. Although Beck was the only General to resign, his views were supported by quite a number of his colleagues in the High Command as well as some civilians, including Dr Schacht, President of the Reichsbank. There was during the summer months a conspiracy to overthrow Hitler should he launch into a war over Czechoslovakia. It transpired that General Franz Halder who succeeded General Beck as Chief of Staff, was behind the conspiracy. Halder and Beck had 'enlisted the aid of various Generals who commanded the Units stationed in and around Berlin . . . The civilian group kept the British informed of what was up and asked for their co-opeation.' William Shirer, in a detailed account of the conspiracy, records that 'On 5 September Theodor Kordt, Counsellor of the German Embassy in London, and a member of the conspiracy, secretly informed Lord Halifax of the date of Hitler's attack on Czechoslovakia (1 October), of the plans to overthrow the Nazi dictator on its eve, and begged Britain and France to stand firm against Hitler's threats until the revolt was launched. Halifax, the same day, discussed the development with Chamberlain, who was most sceptical. Neither man breathed a word to the French ally.'

By withholding this information 'neither Premier Daladier nor General Gamelin ever learnt . . . of the resignation of General Beck . . . or of the military plot to oust Hitler.' This together with the crisis in the German Army 'would have been information of the utmost importance to the French General Staff, with its constant over-estimation of the strength of the German Army.'[17]

The proposed plot against Hitler in the summer of 1938

has been confirmed by Telford Taylor, the United States Chief Prosecutor at the Nuremberg War Crimes Trials in 1946. 'Halder did indeed engage in secret conversations both within and without the army, the object of which was to head off Hitler from his risky military designs and remove him from power if necessary.' In addition to the names already mentioned, Telford Taylor says that 'officers in Admiral Wilhelm Canaris' OKW Intelligence division' were involved, as well as Dr Carl Goerdeler, the former mayor of Leipzig and Ulrich von Hassell who had been removed from his post as Ambassador in Rome. Although not actively involved, Canaris was known to have backed the conspirators.[18]

Daladier, by the beginning of September, still had reservations upon what attitude France would take should German troops march in Czechoslovakia. Nevertheless Phipps decided to wire the Foreign Office in London that:

> 'M. Daladier declares most positively that, if German troops cross the Czechoslovak frontier, the French will march to a man.'[19]

Strong words, but the French Prime Minister still had his doubts. He wanted reassurance from the British Government that if France decided to honour her commitment to Czechoslovakia it would be supported by British arms. He prompted Bonnet to ask the British Ambassador that if Germany should attack and France decided to support the Czechs, will Britain 'march with us?'. The question was passed on to Lord Halifax who, in his reply on 12 September, said that:

> 'While His Majesty's Government would never allow the security of France to be threatened, they are unable to make precise statements of the character of their future action, or the time at which it would be taken, in circumstances that they cannot at present foresee.'[20]

There was no mistaking the real implication of this reply. It reaffirmed the British Government's attitude put forward on 22 May, while at the same time ensuring that Daladier was hooked to the appeasement policy of Bonnet and the Quai d'Orsay.

At the annual Nazi rally in Nuremberg on 12 September, Hitler demanded an end to the persecution of the three and a half million Sudeten Germans. His speech was the signal for the Czech Nazis to whip up revolts in the Sudeten towns. On 14 September 1938, *The Times* reported:

> 'At Haberskirk, near Carlsbad, a crowd of Sudeten Germans besieged the gendamerie station and killed three of the gendarmes. At Swarzbach, where 4,000 Henleinists demonstrated, hand-grenades were thrown at a group of gendarmes, one of whom was seriously wounded. At Marien-bad, all shops and offices were ordered by the Henleinists to close at noon . . . In many districts telephone wires have been cut . . . '

Twenty-one Czech citizens, including Henleinists, were killed, and many more injured. The Czech Government, having declared martial law, promptly sent in troops to put down the revolts. By instigating an uprising in Sudeten-land, Hitler was employing an old stratagem which had served him so well in the past. It had also frightened the life out of a timid French Government. A message from a panicky Daladier was transmitted by Phipps to Halifax:

> 'Entry of troops into Czechoslovakia must at all costs be prevented. If not France will be faced with her obligation, viz automatic necessity to fulfil her engagement.'[21]

On the evening of 13 September, Chamberlain sent off a message to Hitler:

> 'I propose to come over at once to see you with a view to trying to find a peaceful solution. I propose to come across by air and am ready to start tomorrow . . . I should be grateful for a very early reply.'[22]

Two days later he was closeted with the Nazi leader in Berchtesgaden preparing the ground for the dismemberment of Czechoslovakia. The French and Czech Governments were unaware of this meeting until a few days later. 'I got the impression that here was a man who could be relied upon when he had given his word' Chamberlain was reported to have said soon after his return to London.[23] Hitler may have convinced Chamberlain that he was prepared to risk war to 'liberate' the Sudeten Germans, having impressed upon him that he would 'settle this question in one way or another' which, according to Dr Schmidt, Hitler's interpreter, meant 'either the other side gives in, or a solution will be found by means of the application of force, invasion or war.'[24] Whether he was in a position to carry out this threat, that was another matter, and Chamberlain, having already been advised by Kordt of the powerful opposition to Hitler inside Germany, chose to ignore it.

'It seems to be fully realized in London that Germany cannot face a major war for a couple of years yet' wrote Gedye not long after Chamberlain's visit. 'This is what an attack on Czechoslovakia would involve unless she could be forced into "neutralization" and the loss of her protective alliances.'[25] But the appeasers in Britain and France preferred to exploit the myth of Germany's overwhelming military superiority and invincibility. The subsequent spread of defeatism by the Cliveden Set and by their counterparts in France, had considerable success in instilling the fear of imminent world war should Hitler's demands not be satisfied. Czechoslovak obduracy was blamed for the European crisis.

Daladier, in one of his more determined moods, followed the Czech example and decided once again to mobilize the French armed forces, an action which the British Government reluctantly followed. At the same time, using the occasion for creating a war scare, Chamberlain had broadcast to the British people:

'How horrible, fantastic, incredible it is that we should be digging trenches and trying on gas-masks here because of a quarrel in a far-away

437

country between people of whom we know nothing . . .

After my visits to Germany I have realized vividly how Herr Hitler feels that he must champion other Germans, and his indignation that grievances have not been met before this. He told me privately, and last night he repeated publicly that after this Sudeten German question is settled, that is the end of Germany's territorial claims in Europe . . .

However much we may sympathize with a small nation confronted by a big and powerful neighbour, we cannot in all circumstances undertake to involve the whole British Empire in war simply on her account . . . '

These words of Chamberlain over the British radio during the evening of 27 September received a sympathetic response from millions of British people who had been brainwashed by the press, news reels and radio of German military preparedness to launch into a major war over Sudeten rights. They were not privy to the information which the Prime Minister and the Foreign Office had at the time of an impending military revolt by Hitler's leading Generals, who certainly knew of the weakness and the inferiority of the German army in relation to that of the French and Czech alone, apart from whatever help might come from Britain and Russia. A carefully orchestrated campaign to instil fear of Nazi Germany's invincibility, distrust of the Soviet Union and the creation of a picture of Czechoslovakia as a pro-Bolshevik country ill-treating an oppressed German minority, was applied to the policy of appeasement.

There was no shortage of prominent international personalities who in 1938 were prepared to help Hitler spread the myth of German invincibility. One such person was Colonel Charles Lindbergh who had built up an international reputation through his famous transatlantic flight in 1927.

During the summer of 1936, Lindbergh was invited by Goering to visit Germany. After ten days of lavish entertainment by the Nazi hierarchy and visits to various civil and military air establishments, Lindbergh, suitably impressed, embarked upon a programme of boosting the image of Germany military power and aeronautic invincibility. During the following two years he and his wife were the guests of many of the leading appeasers in Britain and France. Lindbergh maintained close contact with the Astors and the rest of the Cliveden set and his opinions on German military prowess, and particularly that of the Luftwaffe were much sought after.

Here was the 'world renowned expert' who, according to Harold Nicolson, MP,* a well known Tory politician and writer, 'has obviously been much impressed by Nazi Germany. He admires their energy, virility, spirit, organization, architecture, planning and physique. He considers that they possess the most powerful air-force in the world, with which they could do terrible damage to any other country, and could destroy our food supplies by sinking even convoyed ships. He admits that they are a great menace but he denies they are a menace to us. He contends that the future will see a complete separation between fascism and communism, and he believes that if Great Britain supports the decadent French and the red Russians against Germany, there will be an end to European civilization. He does not see any real possibility of our remaining in the centre between right and left.'[26]

The Germans undoubtedly gained excellent propaganda value out of the Lindberghs' many visits to their country, as well as from the appeasers in London and Paris. Following Lindbergh's meeting with the French Minister for Air, Guy La Chambre, Ambassador Phipps reported to London on 13 September 1938:

> 'M. Bonnet was very upset and said that peace must be preserved at any price as neither France nor Great Britain were ready for war. Colonel Lindbergh had returned from his tour horrified at overwhelming strength of Germany in the air and terrible weakness of all other powers. He declares

---

*He later became associated with the Churchill-Eden anti-appeasement group.

Germany has 8,000 military aeroplanes and can turn out 1,500 a month. M. Bonnet said that French and British towns would be wiped out and little or no retaliation would be possible.'[27]

Lindbergh, with the help of William C. Bullitt, the American Ambassador in Paris, had played an important role in conditioning French public opinion to accept that the only alternative to the German demands was war against a vastly superior Germany. The 'Führer found a most convenient ambassador in Colonel Lindbergh, who appears to have given the French an impression of its [the German Air Force] might and preparedness which they did not have before, and who at the same time confirmed the view that the Russian Air Force was worth almost exactly nothing'[28] wrote Colonel Fraser, Britain's military attache, in his report on 21 September. However Daladier, during a meeting with Phipps on 13 September, 'having heard of Lindbergh's report', had said that it 'seemed unduly pessimistic for he had reason to believe the Russians had 5,000 aeroplanes.'[29]

Hitler was also fortunate in having another 'convenient Ambassador' in General Joseph Vuillemin, the French Air Force chief, who like Lindbergh had received an invitation to visit Germany. He was impressively feted and chaperoned by Goering, and after visits to aircraft-construction factories, and a mighty aeronautical display by the Luftwaffe, he told Francois-Poncet, French Ambassador in Berlin, '"if there is a war at the end of September . . . not a single French plane will be left after a fortnight".' On returning to Paris on 24 August, he immediately 'went to see Gamelin, Guy La Chambre, Georges Bonnet, Daladier and President Lebrun, and repeated the same observation.'[30]

The Nazi leader's psychological campaign of undermining French confidence in their ability to carry out the treaty obligations to Czechoslovakia was evidently succeeding and the appeasers, with the backing of the press, were gaining ground in convincing the French public that war was inevitable if they did not forego their commitment to Czechoslovakia. In this they were reinforced by Chamberlain's threat to break the Anglo-French Alliance if France did not follow British policy. By inflating German military power and diminishing their own, the French Government was, in fact, doing just what Hitler wanted, enabling him once again to prove to his wavering Generals that his bluff would, as in 1936 over the Rhine affair, prove successful, without war or the humiliation of having to climb down.

General Gamelin, the French Commander-in-Chief, was fully aware of the true strength of the Czech Army and the readiness of the Czech defences. The Czech 'Maginot Line' was mainly in the Sudeten areas in the Western part of the country bordering Germany. When the question of France's military preparedness was discussed by the French Cabinet, Bonnet deliberately concealed vital passages in the Gamelin Report which stated that the French Army was 'absolutely certain of a victorious war if unhappily it were to occur'. It later transpired that Bonnet had 'at a critical moment given a wrong conception to the Cabinet of the part Russia would have played had France made up her mind to defend Czechoslovakia.' (*Manchester Guardian*, 22 September 1938).

Further to the reply which Bonnet had received from the Soviet Foreign Minister in May, Litvinov had, on 2 September 1938, again confirmed to Payart, the French Chargé d'Affaires in Moscow, Russia's willingness to fulfil its obligations to Czechoslovakia.

'We intend to fulfil our obligations under the Pact and, together with France, to afford assistance to Czechoslovakia by the ways open to us. Our War Department is ready immediately to participate in a conference with representatives of the French and Czechoslovak War Departments, in order to discuss the measures appropriate to the moment. Independently of this, we should consider desirable that the question be raised at the League of Nations, if only as yet under Article 11, with the object, first, of mobilizing public opinion and, secondly, of ascertaining the position of certain other states whose passive aid might be extremely valuable. It was necessary, however, to exhaust all means of averting an armed conflict, and we considered one such method to be an immediate consultation between the Great Powers of Europe and other interested states in order if possible to decide on the terms of a collective demarché.'

And on 21 September the Soviet Foreign Minister, in a speech to the League of Nations Assembly reported what he had already told the French Chargé d'Affaires and added:

'We valued very highly the tact of the Czechoslovak Government, which did not even enquire of us whether we should fulfil our obligations under this pact since obviously it had no doubt of this, and had no grounds for doubt.'[31]

Meanwhile, Chamberlain, having obtained Cabinet suport for his policy of pressurizing the Czech Government to meet Hitler's demands, came to an agreement with the French Government to force the Czechs to transfer to Germany territory in areas where the Sudeteners comprised more than fifty per cent of the population. In return the British Government said that it would agree 'to join in an international guarantee of the new boundaries of the Czechoslovak State against unprovoked aggression'. The guarantee was to replace Czechoslovakia's 'existing treaties which involve reciprocal obligations of a military character'. 'An assurance', which as Shirer points out, 'was made conditional on the Czechs abrogating their treaties of mutual assistance with France and Russia.'[32]

A joint Anglo-French Note was sent to President Benes stating:

'Both the French and British Governments recognize how great is the sacrifice thus required of the Czechoslovak Government in the cause of peace. But because that cause is common both to Europe in general and in particular to Czechoslovakia, herself, they have felt it their duty jointly to set forth frankly the conditions essential to secure it.'

Appreciating the fact that the Fuehrer was in a hurry to 'settle' the Sudeten problem, the two governments increased the pressure on Benes, giving him very little time for consultations before preparing his reply. The Note concluded:

> 'The Prime Minister must resume conversation with Herr Hitler not later than Wednesday, and earlier if possible. We therefore feel we must ask for your reply at the earliest possible moment.'[33]

On 22 September there was a report in the *Manchester Guardian* of the furore that was taking place in France, and in particular the French Chamber, over the ultimatum –

> 'It is stated that late last night such an ultimatum was sent to Prague warning the Czech Government that if they did not accept the London Plan they could face German aggression alone without relying on any French help. It is reported here that this French ultimatum was supported by a message from London demanding the Czechs immediate surrender ... M. Bonnet's step ... it would appear was taken without the approval of the Cabinet.'

The Czechs refused to be intimidated and in rejecting the Anglo-French ultimatum pointed out that the proposals within it were drawn up without consultations with the Czechoslovak Government and that acceptance would place 'Czechoslovakia sooner or later under the complete domination of Germany.' A prediction which tragically became a reality, for both the British and French Governments were by now determined to force the Czechs to succumb to the German demands.

'To make Prague change its mind they now resorted to the sharpest – and the shabbiest – kind of diplomatic pressure. And they compounded their deceitfulness by insisting that the Czechs, despite the threat of attack by an already mobilized Germany, refrain from even beginning their own mobilization', for fear of provoking Hitler; thus preventing them from taking the necessary steps for their defence. At the same time, both the British and French Governments were playing down their own military potential and propagating that the Czechs were in too weak a position to defend themselves. 'This duplicity' comments Shirer, 'was too much for the Chief of the French Military Mission in Czechoslovakia, General Foucher. He knew that the formal request of the Czech General Staff for military talks with the French to concert common action in case of German aggression which had been made to General Gamelin in July had gone unanswered.'[34]

But the duplicity did not end there. Dr Milan Hodza, the Czech Prime Minister and leader of the Right wing Agrarian Party, had already accepted the fact that France would renege on its treaty commitment. Without consulting President Benes he summoned Lacroix, the French Ambassador, and told him that he assumed '*a priori* that France will not march, and if you can get tonight a confirming telegram from your government, the President of the Republic will yield. It is the only way to save the peace.' Hodza told Lacroix that he was acting in agreement with President Benes and the Czechoslovak General Staff – this was later denied by Benes.

On receipt of a telegram from the French Ambassador, Daladier and Bonnet, with President Lebrun's approval, 'authorized Lacroix to tell Benes that, if his Government refused the Anglo-French terms, Britain would stand aside; that without Britain French aid would be ineffective; and therefore France would also refuse support.' Thus by clutching at the Hodza straw, Bonnet was able to interpret the affair as having acted at the request of the Czech Government 'which had decided voluntarily to accept the Anglo-French plan but wished the French repudiation for domestic political reasons.

'There is no basis for such an interpretation of this episode' for, says Telford Taylor 'the Czech military chiefs had indeed stressed the danger in taking on Germany single-handed, but there is no evidence that the Czechs were reluctant to defend themselves if France made good her treaty commitments.' Both Lacroix and Basil Newton, the British Minister in Prague, were instructed 'to make it clear to Benes that unless the Anglo-French terms were promptly accepted, Czechoslovakia would be on her own.'[35] Thus, they would be facing 'a situation for which we could take no responsibility'.*

The two ambassadors got Benes out of bed at 2 am on the Wednesday morning, 21 September to deliver their governments' ultimatum. As the French was delivered orally, Benes insisted that Lacroix should get his government to confirm in writing that it was not going to fulfil its treaty obligations.

The Czech President called an emergency meeting of his Cabinet, together with leaders of the various political parties represented in the Coalition Government, having already told Lacroix and Newton that he would give his reply later that day.

And while London and Paris were applying the pressure on the Czech Government, Hitler was receiving the representatives of Hungary and Poland in Berchtesgaden. Both Governments were prepared to co-operate with him in return for slices of a dismembered Czechoslovakia. Under Hitler's guidance, arrangements were made for publicizing their demands for Southern Slovakia and Teschen. The announcement was made on the following day. Two days later, 23 September. V.M. Potemkin, the Soviet Deputy People's Commissar for Foreign Affairs issued a warning to Poland's Chargé d'Affaires in Moscow 'that the entry of Polish troops into Czechoslovakia would be an act of unprovoked aggression, and would automatically cancel the Polish-Soviet Treaty of Non-Aggression of 25 July 1932 . . .'[36]

Gedye who, like Shirer, was in Prague during this critical period describes how 'the reactionary wing of the Czech Agrarians, Germany and reactionaries in many other countries busily circulated the story that Russia had said she was too weak to fulfil her obligations. It was even stated in a broadcast from Prague given under reactionary official influences.' He then goes on to explain why he had 'the best of reason for knowing that it was not merely a lie, but the precise opposite of the truth . . .

'On the Sunday immediately before Britain and France

---

*Halifax told Newton

445

forced Benes to agree to the surrender of the Sudeten districts, after Berchtesgaden, Benes sent for the Russian Minister to Czechoslovakia, Alexandrovsky, to see him in the Hradschin.* Russia had already been unofficially sounded as to whether, if asked formally, she would be prepared to defend Czechoslovakia if France should let her down, and had indicated that the answer would be favourable. To Alexandrovsky Benes formally put the following questions: 'If we are attacked and France comes to our assistance in accordance with the terms of our two treaties, will Russia also fulfil her obligations and furnish military aid to France and Czechoslovakia?'

'Alexandrovsky replied without hesitation, "Instantly, and with all her strength. Why do you ask?"'

'Then Benes said, "If France dishonours her signature and refuses to help, what would be Russia's advice to this country as to the right course to pursue?"'

'Alexandrovsky replied, "Denounce Germany immediately as the aggressor before the League and call for League support. Germany will automatically be branded as aggressor by refusing to obey the League's summons to state a case, as of course she will refuse. Russia will then fulfil her obligations under the League Covenant, and come to your assistance regardless of what the other League powers do."'

'After this there was a long silence between the two, broken at last by Alexandrovsky saying:

"M. le Président, is there not another question you wish to ask me regarding Russia's action should an appeal to the League be made impossible by some trickery or other?"

'Benes looked at him for a long time very steadily, but did not open his mouth. Silently Alexandrovsky rose, shook his head sadly, bowed and left.' This story was told to Gedye 'by a friend of Dr Benes of what actually happened'[37], the essence of which has been confirmed by other writers including Telford Taylor, Shirer and Wheeler-Bennett.

*Old Czech Castle which had become the Ministerial Palace of the President.

On the evening of 21 September 1938, Benes and the Czech Cabinet capitulated to the Anglo-French ultimatum. The reason being, according to the official Czech communique, 'We had no other choice – because we were left alone'. Which, of course, was not really true. Had the Soviet offer been more widely publicized and accepted, Benes might have changed the course of history, and saved his country from German occupation. He was unable to withstand the campaign against him of the 'Goebbels propaganda machine' which, according to Gedye, had been denouncing him as a 'Red', a fact very far from the truth especially when his Government, bowing to Right wing pressure, had banned 'Communist' demonstrations. On 5 September the Communist Secretary, Klement Gottwald, had warned in his paper, *Rude Pravo*, that 'Anyone who advises the Government and urges it along the way of new and ever fresh concessions is doing great harm. We consider it our duty to warn the Government against such advisers and influences; the whole people join with us in this warning.' And, in spite of governmental restrictions, huge crowds were seen marching in the direction of the Hradschin Castle, protesting against the capitulation.

Chamberlain could hardly wait for the Czech surrender to the Anglo-French ultimatum before deciding to visit Hitler once again. The Czech Cabinet meanwhile had resigned, and in the reshuffle General Jan Sirovy, the Inspector General of the Army, became the new Prime Minister, and on the same day the French military attaché, General Foucher, 'tore up his French passport and joined the Czech army.'[38]

The following morning the British press carried reports of a statement by Winston Churchill in which he warned that

> 'The partition of Czechoslovakia, under pressure from England and France amounts to the complete surrender of the Western Democracies to the Nazi threat of force. Such a collapse will bring peace or security neither to England nor to France. On the contrary, it will place these two nations in an ever weaker and more dangerous situation.'[39]

447

Later that day the British section of the International Peace Campaign delivered to Chamberlain at 10 Downing Street, a Protest Note condemning the betrayal of Czechoslovakia:

> 'We beg you urgently not to believe that a dishonourable suicide on the part of Czechoslovakia could save the peace. It would, on the contrary, be a catastrophe for Europe.'

The protest against the Government's betrayal of Czechoslovakia had reached such a pitch that the American Paramount News received an 'official' Government request – 'Please delete Wickham Steed's and A.J. Cummings' speeches from today's Paramount News.'* What happened was that the latest news reel from Paramount had dealt exclusively with the Czechoslovak situation.

> 'The issue . . . included a statement (in its original form) by Mr Wickham Steed in which he said "Has England surrendered to Germany? What is England – is it the Government, is it Parliament, is it the people? Parliament certainly has not surrendered to Hitler, for it has not been called."
> Mr Wickham Steed went on that in his opinion Hitler cannot be said to want to fight because he knows that he can get what he wants, and more than he dare ask for, merely by the threat of war.'
> 'This statement has been excised from the reel by exhibitors as has also an interview with A.J. Cummings who was questioned before the microphone and camera. . . . Mr Cummings described the agreement between Herr Hitler and the Prime Minister as "a piece of yellow diplomacy" and said that instead of our having peace as a result we have merely a state of war postponed.'
> (*The Manchester Guardian*, 23 September 1938)

No sooner had he received news of the Czech capitula-

---

*Wickham Steed had been a former editor of *The Times* and A.J. Cummings was a leading journalist during the post-war years.

tion to the ultimatum than Chamberlain notified Hitler that he would be coming over to see him – his second visit that week. On the morning of 22 September he flew into Cologne and met the Nazi Fuehrer at the old Rhine town of Godesberg.

On this occasion he was able to present Hitler with the Anglo-French plan which had been forced upon the Czechoslovak Government. According to Schmidt, Chamberlain had 'outlined a comprehensive and complicated system of agreements providing for relatively protracted handing over periods' and of a 'guarantee which France and Britain were prepared to give to the new German-Czech-Slovak frontier. Germany on her side was to conclude a non-agrression pact with Czechoslovakia.' Apparently surprised at the ease and speed at which Czech territory was being ceded to his Third Reich, Hitler replied, 'I am exceedingly sorry, Mr Chamberlain, but I can no longer discuss these matters. This solution, after the developments of the last few days, is no longer practicable.'[40] Britain's Prime Minister 'was both disappointed and puzzled at the attitude taken by the Führer . . . he could rightly say that the Führer had got from him what he had demanded. In order to achieve this he had risked his whole political career', and he was now 'being accused by certain circles in Great Britain of having sold and betrayed Czechoslovakia, of having yielded to dictators and so on, and on leaving England that morning he had actually been booed.'[41]

Hitler was neither impressed nor sympathetic to Chamberlain's personal problems and later that day told him, that instead of the time limits mentioned in the Anglo-French Memorandum, 'the Czech Government would have to surrender the area marked on the enclosed map by 1 October.'[42] He was now demanding not only the areas with over fifty per cent Sudeten Germans, but also areas where these non-Reich Germans were in 'conspicuous minorities or even where there are no Germans at all.' (*Manchester Guardian* 28 September 1938). To strengthen his hand, Chamberlain asked the Nazi leader to put his proposals in writing so that he could present them to the Czechs. Just before Chamberlain's departure Hitler presented him with a written confirmation of his latest demands, together with a map and a time limit. The Czechs were to commence evacuating the ceded territory by 8 am, 26 September, and be completely out by 28 September, two days later.

Having received a copy from Chamberlain of Hitler's revised plan and map, Daladier called a Cabinet meeting for the Sunday morning, 25 September, before leaving for London. During the meeting he was warned by his Army Intelligence Bureau that if the Czechoslovak Government accepted Hitler's Godesberg demands they would be surrendering most of her fortifications and 'Bohemia would be strangled'. The French Cabinet consequently rejected these latest demands.

That afternoon both Daldier and Bonnet flew to London for another meeting with Chamberlain and Halifax and their advisers, as well as members of the inner circle of Cabinet ministers. Daladier had by then returned to one of his more determined moods. He first of all told the gathering that Hitler's Godesberg proposals had been 'unanimously' rejected by his Government because, as he explained, Hitler wanted 'not so much to take over three and a half million Germans as to destroy Czechoslovakia by force, enslaving her, and afterwards realizing the domination of Europe, which was his object.'[43]

Chamberlain tried to reassure Daladier that Hitler only wanted to send in troops to 'preserve law and order'. The French Premier now felt that Chamberlain had overstepped the mark in his appeasement of the Nazi Fuehrer. He wanted to get back to the original Anglo-French ultimatum, for which he had Cabinet support. So once again Daladier had shown that he was fully aware of the dangers of giving way to Hitler over the Czech affair; yet he had agreed in the first instance, without consulting the Czech Government, in letting the Sudeteners – that is Henlein and his Nazi accomplices – take over control of the most important military and strategic parts of the country. In effect his opposition to Chamberlain was primarily of tactics and fear of French public opinion. Ivone Kirkpatrick, one of Chamberlain's assistants and acting interpreter at Godesberg, commenting on the British position has said that 'If we were prepared to agree to the cession of the territory, it seemed illogical to object to its military occupation . . .'[44]

They had no objections to the annexation of Czech territory so long as it was done in a 'gentlemanly' manner.

In the Appendix to the Godesberg proposals it stipulated that –

'The evacuated Sudeten German territory is to be handed over without destroying or rendering unusable in any way military, commercial or traffic establishments (plants). These include the ground organization of the air service and all wireless stations.

All commercial and transport materials, especially the rolling-stock of the railway system, in the designated areas, are to be handed over undamaged. The same applies to all public utility services (gas-works, power stations, etc.).

Finally, no foodstuffs, goods, cattle, raw materials, etc. are to be removed.'

In spite of the change of Government, the Czechs nevertheless decided to mobilize in defiance of the Chamberlain pressures, and Benes, who was still President, instructed his Ambassador in London, Jan Masaryk, to state his Government's latest position in rejecting the Godesberg proposals which were regarded as –

' . . . a *de facto* ultimatum of the sort usually presented to a vanquished nation and not a proposition to a Sovereign State which has shown the greatest possible readiness to make sacrifices for the appeasement of Europe. Not the smallest trace of such readiness to make sacrifices has as yet been manifested by Herr Hitler's Government. The proposals go far beyond what we agreed to in the so-called Anglo-French plan. They deprive us of every safeguard for our national existence. We are to yield up large proportions of our carefully prepared defences, and admit the German armies deep into our country before we have been able to

451

organize it on the new basis or make any preparations for its defence. Our national and economic independence would automatically disappear with the acceptance of Herr Hitler's plan. The whole process of moving the population is to be reduced to panic flight on the part of those who will not accept the German Nazi régime. They have to leave their homes without even the right to take their personal belongings or, even in the case of peasants, their cow.'

In conclusion, Masaryk told Lord Halifax that his

'Government wishes to declare in all solemnity that Herr Hitler's demands in their present form are absolutely and unconditionally unacceptable . . .'[45]

The main opposition to Chamberlain from within his Cabinet came from Alfred Duff Cooper, Minister of State for Naval Affairs, and Oliver Stanley, President of the Board of Trade, both of whom were convinced that the German army should not be allowed to march into Czechoslovakia and that appeasing Hitler was only postponing the evil day when war would be thrust upon Britain.

The Anglo-French meeting in London during the weekend of 25–26 September eventually got down to discussing the strength and preparedness of the British and French armies. General Gamelin was called in on the Sunday, and told the two Prime Ministers that 'France's military strength on the ground and in the air' was:

'five million men; about a hundred divisions to start with; a system of fortifications that guarantee us complete freedom of manoeuvre; an inferior air force, but still one that is in a condition to work at short range to support the army.'

He then gave his assessment of their potential adversaries:

'The German weaknesses: the high command, which realizes the dangers. A system of fortifications which is not yet finished. Important shortages of cadres; persisting difficulty in mobilization for want of adequate trained reserves. Difficulties of a long war because of the lack of raw materials, particularly oil. A superior air force . . .

The Italian weaknesses: the country's morale. The impossibility of a long-term war.'

In his estimate of 'Czechoslovakia's possibilities of resistance', Gamelin said that there were 'thirty divisions at present being mobilized, against the Germans' forty.' Later that morning, during discussions with Britain's Service Chiefs, 'General Gamelin received an important telephone call from Paris: his chief of staff, General Jeannel, had just seen the Russian military attaché, who, speaking for Marshal Voroshilov, had told him that the Soviets had at their disposal "thirty divisions of infantry, a mass of cavalry, many tank formations and the greater part of their air force ready to intervene in the west".' Gamelin immediately passed this information to his British colleagues, '"but it was clear", he observes "that the hypothesis of seeing Russia invade Poland scarcely gave our allies any pleasure at all".'[46]

Chamberlain was by now becoming worried that his support for Hitler could misfire should France reject the Godesberg proposals and stand firm with Czechoslovakia. Phipps had telephoned from Paris on 26 September to say that:

'Opinion had undergone a complete change . . . I have just seen President of the Chamber [Herriot] who confirmed the complete swingover of public opinion since Hitler's demands had become known. He assures me that an overwhelming majority in the Chamber will now be for resistance.'[47]

Hitler was due to speak in Berlin's Sportpalast that evening, and as Halifax was apparently anxious to warn him of the opposition in Britain and France, instructed his department to issue a press communiqué which included a reminder that 'the German claim to the transfer of the Sudeten areas has already been conceded by the French, British and Czechoslovak Governments.' Hoping that Hitler might take this into consideration, the communiqué added the warning, 'if in spite of all efforts made by the British Prime Minister a German attack is made upon Czechoslovakia the immediate result must be that France will be bound to come to her assistance and Great Britain and Russia will certainly stand by France.'[48]

That morning Chamberlain had sent by plane his personal adviser, Sir Horace Wilson, with a letter to Hitler appealing to him to negotiate with the Czech Government for the peaceful handing over of the Sudetenland, and without resorting to war. Chamberlain's peace at any cost policy was now at stake. If Hitler disagreed, Wilson was instructed to inform him of Britain's latest declaration of intent.

> ' . . . if the Germans attacked Czechoslovakia, the French, as they had told us and as M. Daladier has stated publicly, would feel that they would be obliged to fulfil their treaty obligations. If that meant that the forces of France became actively engaged in hostilities against Germany, the British Government would feel obliged to support her.'[49]

The outcome of Sir Horace Wilson's mission was that Hitler did not receive the latest information on the switch in Anglo-French policy until the day after his speech at the Sportpalast. Chamberlain's special emissary had failed to carry out the second and most important part of his instructions. While Bonnet, having received his copy of the Halifax communiqué, was busily engaged trying to suppress it. M. Pierre Comert, head of the press department at the Quai d'Orsay, has confirmed that 'M. Georges Bonnet had prevented it from being distributed in the departments of the Ministry and had forbidden Havas to give the press the text of the communiqué.'[50]

The German Embassy was apparently 'profoundly impressed by the change that has come over Paris in the last two days' reported the *Manchester Guardian*'s Paris correspondent. Especially by 'the mobilization and spirit of the people. This hardening of the French attitude is generally regarded to be of decisive importance in averting war, provided it is supported by a similar attitude on the part of the British Government.' (*Manchester Guardian*, 26 September 1938)

So even at this late stage Hitler could have been faced by a determined common front that would have saved Czechoslovakia and the rest of Europe from the inevitable drive to war. Instead of which, Hitler, in his speech on 26 September, in announcing his 'last territorial claim' was also able to declare how 'grateful' he was 'to Mr Chamberlain for his endeavours'.

'I think' said the Nazi leader, that Mr Chamberlain 'is convinced that Germany wants peace, but there are limits. I assured Mr Chamberlain that after this there would be no more international problems. I promised afterwards that if Herr Benes would settle peacefully his problems with other minorities I would even guarantee the new Czech State . . .

'Now for Mr Benes. He has it in his hands to choose either peace or war. He will accept my demands or we shall go and liberate our Germans.' (*Manchester Guardian*, 27 September 1938)

The newly found determination of the British and French Governments not to be browbeaten by Hitler's threats did not last very long. Although the pressure in both Parliaments for their Governments to submit no further to those threats had been increasing, at the same time, a war psychosis was being fostered by the appeasers and sections of the press. Chamberlain and Halifax had suppressed relevant information relating to the pressures put upon the Czech Government to accept the Franco-British proposals. The Government White Paper which was presented to Parliament dealing with this matter deliberately omitted the document from Prague which 'referred to the strong and continuous pressure put upon the Czechoslovak Government by the French and British representatives.'[51] Meanwhile, Germany's Chargé d'Affaires and Military Attaché in Prague cabled Berlin with alarming news:

'Calm in Prague. Last mobilization measures

455

carried out by evacuation of supplies. Operational staff has left Prague ... According to information from Italian military attaché, Prague is defended by forty seven anti-aircraft batteries, which change position every day. Press and Radio strengthen the Czech people in their belief that France, Great Britain, and Russia have already given a binding promise of military help ... According to the estimate of the military attaché here, the total call up is 1,000,000; field army 800,000.'[52]

William Shirer, who was at the time the CBS representative in Central Europe, says that 'was as many trained men as Germany had for two fronts. Together the Czech and French armies outnumbered the Germans by more than two to one.'[53] No wonder the German Generals were anxious to prevent Hitler from sliding into an all-out European war. By withholding the true picture of the relative strengths of the countries concerned, the British and French Governments were helping to intensify the war scare. Apart from the report of the German representatives in Prague, there was also one from their counterparts in Paris, who had cabled Berlin warning that:

'The French mobilization measures in continuous progress have so far anticipated total mobilization.'

They reckoned that the

'deployment of the first sixty-five divisions on the German frontier' would be completed 'by the sixth day of mobilization.'[54]

But in spite of the weakness of the German army at the time, particularly in the West, and the unfinished state of the Siegfried defence fortifications, Bonnet, backed by General Vuillemen and Air Minister, Guy la Chambre, and without consulting the over-all Chief of National Defence, Gamelin, had presented Daladier with a report which painted as black a picture as possible of the inadequacy of the French forces. The report told of the utter inadequacy of the Air Force and of the disastrous consequence that this would have upon the Army, the armament industries and for the defence of the heavily populated industrial centres. Daladier was undoubtedly affected by the report which had achieved its objective of undermining his confidence in the ability of the French Armed Services to fulfil the obligation under the Franco-Czech Treaty.

A letter written by Pierre Comert on 2 October 1938 describes Bonnet's diplomacy over the Czech affair. It also refers to the manner in which:

' . . . all M. Coulondre's telegrams announcing the certain participation of Russia were ignored. No mention of them was made to the press. Moreover GB went so far as to say in certain talks that the USSR would remain neutral. All right wing circles spread the same rumour.

Then panic rumours began to circulate on the inferiority of France's defences on the impossibility of attacking Germany . . . A whole faction at the War Ministry seconded this propaganda.

First it was the Siegfried line. It was impregnable. French regiments would be crushed in it . . .

Then it was the air force . . . on this point the campaign succeeded. M. Guy la Chambre announced that Germany's monthly production of aircraft was 2,000 against 45 on the French side . . .

On the political front . . . certain Parisian circles informed Berlin very accurately on the results of this campaign . . . '[55]

The pro-Nazi elements in France, led by Flandin, had seized the political initiative. They concentrated their attacks upon leading opponents of the appeasement policy, accusing them of war-mongering. Reynaud records that on 26 September 'Flandin published in *Le Temps* a letter in which he wrote:

'For every kind of reason ... I reject ... the military intervention of France in the struggle between the Sudeten Germans and the Czechoslovak State ... I do hope that France will not be faced by the *fait accompli* of a war which has been made inevitable, before the opinion of her legal representatives has been able to find expression in good time. Our British friends should in loyalty be told that the French Army will not be able to bear alone, or even with the support of a small contingent, the burden of land operations on three fronts ... '

'On 28th, Flandin went further. He had stuck up on the walls of Paris a placard whose text was, on the following day, reproduced by Doriot's *La Liberté*, a newspaper subsidized by the Reich. This read:

YOU ARE BEING DECEIVED
'People of France, you are being deceived ... A cunning trap has been laid for some weeks and months by secret elements in order to make war inevitable ... '[56]

Meanwhile a telegram had arrived in London from Sir Nevile Henderson, Britain's Ambassador in Berlin, stating 'unless Czechs by tomorrow notify German Government that they are prepared to send representative here on basis of acceptance of memorandum the invasion of Czechoslovakia begins Thursday or very soon after.'[57] This threat was immediately followed by a communication to Hitler from Chamberlain assuring him: 'you can get all essentials without war and without delay. I am ready to come to Berlin myself at once to discuss arrangements for transfer.'[58] And with this, his so-called 'last appeal', Chamberlain hastily made arrangements for a Four Power Conference to settle the Czechoslovak problem to the Fuehrer's satisfaction.

With tension mounting in Germany and the rest of Europe, German opponents of Hitler's Czech policy had been planning 'to arrest the Nazi leaders in Berlin and proclaim a military govenment. All the leading German

458

generals were in, or connived at, the plot: Brauchitsch, the Commander-in-Chief; von Rundstedt; Beck; Stulpnagel; Witzleben, Commander of the Berlin Garrison; and also Graf Helldorf, who was Chief of the Berlin Police.' General Franz Halder, the Chief of the General Staff, and one of the leaders of the plot, during his interrogation* after the war, 'said that he called off the plot at the eleventh hour when Chamberlain's flight to Berchtesgaden was announced. He decided that if Hitler could get away with this he could get away with anything . . . In his view Germany would have been defeated in three weeks in the event of war.'[59]

On 29 September 1938, the four Heads of State, Hitler, Mussolini, Chamberlain and Daladier met in the Bavarian town of Munich. The country, whose fate was being decided was not invited to join the quartet. There were two Czech representatives in the same building, but they 'were ushered into an adjoining room, out of sight', and there they remained from 2 to 10 pm, waiting to carry instructions back to their country. Then 'the two unhappy Czechs, [Dr Votjech Mastny, the Czech Minister in Berlin, and Dr Hubert Masarik, from the Prague Foreign Office] were taken to Sir Horace Wilson', who, on behalf of Chamberlain, 'informed them of the main points of the four-power agreement and handed them a map of the Sudeten areas which were to be evacuated at once. When the two envoys attempted to protest, the British official cut them short. He had nothing more to say, he stated, and promptly left the room.'[60] This vivid account by William Shirer of the manner in which Czechoslovakia and its peoples were handled reveals one of the more disgraceful episodes in British and French history. The so-called agreement was signed on 30 September 1938. The Nazi leader had shown his generals how to win a battle without firing a shot.

In his report to the Czech Foreign Office Dr Masarik relates that:

'At 1.30 am we were taken into the hall where the conference had been held. There were present Mr Neville Chamberlain, M. Daladier, Sir Horace

---

*He was interrogated by Nicholas Kaldor, now Lord Kaldor, the eminent economist, and former Hungarian refugee.

Wilson, M. Leger,* Mr Ashton-Gwatkin,† Dr Mastny and myself. The atmosphere was oppressive; sentence was about to be passed. The French obviously "embarrassed" appeared to be aware of the consequences for French prestige. Mr Chamberlain, in a short introduction, referred to the agreement which had just been concluded and gave the text to Dr Mastny to read out . . . '‡

The Munich Agreement stipulated that –

'the evacuation will begin on 1 October.
'the United Kingdom, France and Italy agree that the evacuation of the territory shall be completed by 10 October, without any existing installations having been destroyed, and that the Czechoslovak Government will be held responsible for carrying out the evacuation without damage to the said installations.
'The conditions governing the evacuation will be laid down in detail by an international Commission composed of representatives of Germany, the United Kingdom, France, Italy and Czechoslovakia. and that 'the final determination of the frontiers will be carried out by the International Commission . . .
'The Czechoslovak Government will, within a period of four weeks from the date of this agreement, release from their military and police forces any Sudeten Germans who may wish to be released . . . '

These were the main points in the document which sealed the fate of the Czechoslovak Republic and its people.

Dr Benes resigned during the evening of 5 October. Later that year, during a visit to the University of Chicago, when

*Secretary-General of the French Foreign Office.
†A British Foreign Office official.
‡Both William Shirer and Telford Taylor have quoted from Dr Masarik's report. Although there appears to be a slight discrepancy in the translation, the meaning is the same.

asked by Professor Fleming 'whether Russia would have supported him had he decided to fight in September 1938, he replied without hesitation. "There was never any doubt in my mind that Russia would aid us by all the ways open to her, but I did not dare fight with Russian aid alone, because I knew that the British and French Governments would make out of my country another Spain".'[61]

Before leaving for London, and rejoicing in his achievement of 'Peace in our Time', Chamberlain decided that there were still some loose ends to his policy that had to be secured. So once again, and without telling his French colleagues, he decided to seek out the Fuehrer, while he was still in a good mood, bringing with him a sheet of paper which he obviously felt confident the Nazi leader would sign. The wording was as follows:

> 'We, the German Fuehrer and Chancellor, and the British Prime Minister, have held a further meeting today and are agreed in recognizing that the question of Anglo-German relations is of the first importance for the two countries and for Europe.
>
> 'We regard the agreement signed last night and the Anglo-German Naval Agreement as symbolic of the desire of our two peoples never to go to war with one another again.
>
> 'We are resolved that the method of consultation shall be the method adopted to deal with any other questions that may concern our two countries, and we are determined to continue our efforts to remove possible sources of difference and thus to contribute to assure the peace of Europe.' (*The Times*, 1 October 1938)

Which, of course, Hitler signed. And why not, for any move which could help in breaking up the Anglo-French Entente was definitely welcome. The opposition within the Wehrmacht just melted away. Not a German soldier or airman had been lost or a gun fired, while Eastern Europe was laid bare awaiting his next move.

On 3 October 1938 the *Daily Telegraph* reported that Dr Halfield, a leading Nazi journalist, had written to the

Hamburger Fremdenblatt:

> 'The historical aspect of Munich lies in the fact
> that the firm determination of Adolf Hitler and
> the political far-sightedness of the Duce suc-
> ceeded in eliminating Soviet Russia from the
> concert of the Great European Powers . . .
>   . . . The League of Nations is dead – long live
> the European Council of the civilized great
> powers.'

Within six months of the signing of the Munich Agreement Chamberlain's 'Peace in our time' had been destroyed. The 'man who could be relied upon when he had
given his word' had torn up the agreement. On 16 March
1939 his troops invaded the rest of Czechoslovakia, occupied Prague, and pronounced Bohemia and Moravia a
protectorate of the Third Reich.

The International Commission was a sham. Not surprisingly, the Four Power guarantee promised at Munich was
never fulfilled. 'Thousands of Czech and Jewish refugees,
expelled by or fleeing from the German-occupied areas,
were turned back and refused asylum in the remaining
Czech territories. Many of them had to find whatever
shelter they could – a barn or even a ditch – in the neutral
zone along the demarcation line.' The remains of the
Czechoslovak carcass had been portioned off to Poland and
Hungary who had, as threatened, taken their slice. As for
the refugees, 'it is the business of those who made these
people refugees, Britain and France, to save them, not
ours,' said the new Czech administrators just after Munich.
'We appeal to their representatives on the Berlin Commission, we appeal direct to London and Paris for something to
be done in the way of providing an asylum for these people,
and we get no reply.'[62] The Commission had become hard
of hearing. Within a few months there were 170,000
refugees. Chamberlain expressed concern for the Sudeteners and the Czechoslovak minority problem, but not a word
for the plight of 'nearly 100,000 Czechs in Vienna' who
soon after the Anschluss 'lost all rights since Hitler took
control.' (*Reynolds News*, 18 September 1938)

The euphoria of 'Peace in our time' engendered by the Munich Agreement had affected 'even the French Socialist Party ... which passed the following resolution at a meeting held under the Chairmanship of M. Blum:

'The Parliamentary Socialist Party unanimously rejoices at the halt marked by the Munich Conference in the race to war. It expects from the understanding between the peaceful powers measures which will consolidate peace and settle all the problems on which it depends.' (*The News Chronicle*, 1 October 1938)

Vernon Bartlett had been reporting the Four Power Conference for the *News Chronicle*, and in his summary from Munich of the events of that fateful week-end, refers to the British Prime Minister's popularity in Hitler's Third Reich.

'There are plenty of Germans who are enthusiastic about Mr Chamberlain because he has helped them to extend their frontiers without fighting ... it is doubtful whether he realizes how much Great Britain is now looked upon as an ally of the Rome-Berlin Axis ...
' ... For this is the situation. Opinions will always differ as to whether it was necessary to break so many pledges to the Czechs, and so disown the rights of small nations, in order to build a bridge between the Western Powers and Germany.
'Some believe on the basis of evidence from Germany itself that a firm warning to Hitler would have removed for all time his belief that he could get his way in Europe by war, or the threat of it.
'Faced by the knowledge that Great Britain would if necessary fight, he would either have disappeared from the control of Germany or would have changed his policy.' (*The News Chronicle*, 1 October 1938)

To help him on his way eastwards, Hitler had been

presented with his additional 'lebensraum', as well as some 1,600 aircraft, 550 anti-tank guns, 2,175 artillery pieces, 43,000 machine guns and 469 tanks and armoured cars. And in a speech at the Kroll Opera House in Berlin on 28 April 1939, he was able to confirm the above figures of the Czech, General Krecji, and add to the collection 735 mortars and 591 anti-aircraft guns. This booty, together with the Skoda works which had supplied aero-engines to France and various types of military equipment to her partners in the Little Entente, must rate as one of the greatest victories of an aggressor country ever achieved by bluff and a stroke of the pen. Not only had he been given the 'Keys to Eastern Europe right up to the Black Sea' but also, according to the Welsh MP and miners' leader, D.R. Grenfell, a boost in Germany's coal production of thirty million tons a year and an extra three to four million tons annually of iron and steel.*

General Keitel openly admitted at the Nuremberg trials that 'had there been in place of the Munich Conference, a collaboration between Great Britain, France and the USSR it would have been impossible for us to strike.'[63]

The Soviet Union had every reason to be suspicious of the British and French governments, for, as Dr Benes recalls in his memoirs:

'The treaty between the four Western and Central European Great Powers concluded in Munich on 29 September 1938, was quite rightly considered by the Soviet Government to be not only a desertion of Czechoslovakia but also a desertion of the whole European policy of collective security founded on the Geneva obligations of France and Great Britain. Moreover, the exclusion of the Soviet Union from all pre- and post- Munich discussions was equivalent – in the Soviet view – to an attack against the Soviet Union and an attempt to secure its complete isolation. Moscow rightly feared that this fatal step could soon lead to a military attack by Germany against the Soviet Union.'[64]

*Grenfell made this statement during the Parliamentary debate on 5 October 1938.

Notes

1. SHIRER, William, *The Collapse of the Third Republic*, p. 311
2. SHIRER, William, *The Collapse of the Third Republic*, p. 313
3. *Documents on British Foreign Policy*, 3rd Series Vol. I, p. 217
4. FEILING, Keith, *The Life of Neville Chamberlain*, pp. 347–348
5. CADOGAN, Sir Alexander, *Diaries* (ed. David Dilks), p. 47
6. *Documents on German Foreign Policy*, Series D, Vol. II, p. 198
7. *Documents on German Foreign Policy*, Series D, Vol. II, pp. 273–274
8. *Documents on German Foreign Policy*, Series D, Vol. II, pp. 300–302
9. GEDYE, G.E.R., *Fallen Bastions*, p. 413
10. SHIRER, William, *The Collapse of the Third Republic*, pp. 333–334
11. *Documents on British Foreign Policy*, 3rd Series, Vol. I. No. 271, pp. 346–347
12. *Documents on British Foreign Policy*, 3rd Series, Vol. I. No. 286, p. 357
13. NOGUÈRES, Henri, *Munich or the Phoney Peace*, p. 59
14. WHEELER-BENNETT, Sir John, *Munich – Prologue to Tragedy*, p. 52
15. AVON, Rt. Hon. Earl of, *The Eden Diaries, The Reckoning*, p. 24
16. BOOTHBY, Lord, *Recollections of a Rebel*, pp. 126–127
17. SHIRER, William, *The Collapse of the Third Republic*, p. 335
18. TAYLOR, Telford, *Munich – The Price of Peace*, p. 715
19. *Documents on British Foreign Policy*, 3rd Series, Vol. II. No. 807, p. 269
20. *Documents on British Foreign Policy*, 3rd Series, Vol. II. No. 843, p. 303
21. *Documents on British Foreign Policy*, 3rd Series, Vol. II. No. 861, pp. 313–314
22. *Documents on German Foreign Policy*, Series D. Vol. II, p. 754
23. FEILING, Keith, *The Life of Neville Chamberlain*, p. 367
24. SCHMIDT, Dr Paul, *Hitler's Interpreter*, pp. 92–93
25. GEDYE, G.E.R., *Fallen Bastions*, p. 379
26. NICOLSON, Sir Harold, *Diaries and Letters 1930–1939* (ed. Nigel Nicolson), p. 272
27. *Documents on British Foreign Policy*, 3rd Series, Vol. II. No. 855, p. 310
28. *Documents on British Foreign Policy*, 3rd Series, Vol. II. Encl. No. 1012, p. 454
29. *Documents on British Foreign Policy*, 3rd Series Vol. II. No. 857, pp. 311–312
30. NOGUÈRES, Henri, *Munich or the Phoney Peace*, p. 89
31. *Documents on International Affairs* 1938 Vol. II, p. 225
32. SHIRER, William, *The Collapse of the Third Republic*, p. 345
33. *Documents on International Affairs*, 1938 Vol. II, pp. 213–214
34. SHIRER, William, *The Collapse of the Third Republic*, p. 345–346
35. TAYLOR, Telford, *Munich – The Price of Peace*, pp. 789–790
36. ROTHSTEIN, A., *The Munich Conspiracy*, p. 183
37. GEDYE, G.E.R., *Fallen Bastions*, p. 425
38. SHIRER, William, *The Collapse of the Third Republic*, p. 350
39. CHURCHILL, Winston, *The Gathering Storm* Vol. I. The Second World War, p. 238
40. SCHMIDT, Dr Paul, *Hitler's Interpreter*, p. 96
41. *Documents on German Foreign Policy*, Series D. Vol. II, p. 875
42. *Documents on German Foreign Policy*, Series D. Vol. II, pp. 905–906
43. *Documents on British Foreign Policy*, 3rd Series, Vol. II. No. 1093, p. 523

44. KIRKPATRICK, Ivone, *The Inner Circle*, p. 118
45. *Documents on International Affairs*, 1938 Vol. II, p. 236
46. NOGUÈRES, Henri, *Munich or the Phoney Peace*, pp. 184–185
47. *Documents on British Foreign Policy*, 3rd Series, Vol. II. No. 1106, p. 547
48. *Documents on British Foreign Policy*, 3rd Series, Vol. II. No. 1111, p. 550 FN
49. *Documents on British Foreign Policy*, 3rd Series, Vol. II. No. 1129, pp. 565–566
50. NOGUÉRES, Henri, *Munich or the Phoney Peace*, p. 198
51. TAYLOR, Telford, *Munich – The Price of Peace*, p. 883
52. *Documents on German Foreign Policy*, Series D. Vol. II, p. 976
53. SHIRER, William, *The Collapse of the Third Republic*, p. 363
54. *Documents on German Foreign Policy*, Series D. Vol. II, p. 977
55. ADAMTHWAITE, Anthony, *Document 59, The Making of the Second World War*, pp. 195–196
56. REYNAUD, Paul, *In the Thick of the Fight*, pp. 193–194
57. *Documents on British Foreign Policy*, 3rd Series, Vol. II. No. 1155, pp. 584–586
58. FEILING, Keith, *The Life of Neville Chamberlain*, p. 372
59. BOOTHBY, Lord, *Recollections of a Rebel*, p. 131–132
60. SHIRER, William, *The Collapse of the Third Republic*, pp. 379–380
61. FLEMING, D.F., *The Cold War and Its Origins*, Vol. I, p. 84
62. TAYLOR, Telford, *Munich – The Price of Peace*, pp. 912–913
63. WHEELER-BENNETT, Sir John, *Munich – Prologue to Tragedy*, p. 398 FN
64. BENES, Eduard, *The Memoirs of Dr Eduard Benes*, p. 131

33

THE INEVITABLE BOOMERANG

There was enough evidence in the Spring of 1939 to show that Poland was earmarked to become the next victim of Hitler's lebensraum policy, but the Polish ruling class still clung to the belief that by helping to overthrow the Soviet Government their country would be spared the same fate as Czechoslovakia. They had failed to grasp the real significance of Hitler's Eastern policy. The fact that he had openly declared that if he had control of the Ukraine and the Urals the German people would be swimming in a sea of plenty did not mean that he had forgotten that Poland was on his route, or that the Polish corridor and Danzig had been wrested from Germany at Versailles.

By persistently blocking Soviet attempts at creating a common anti-Hitler front, Poland had provided the appeasers in London and Paris with their main excuse for rejecting the Soviet peace proposals. She was now a victim of her own expansionist policies. The occupation of Soviet Western Ukraine and Western White Russia, German East Prussia, Danzig and the corridor, the Vilna region of Lithuania, and her portion of a dismembered Czechoslovakia had not endeared her to her neighbours.

The Soviet Union had good reason to remember that with Anglo-French support Poland had pushed her frontier over 100 miles to the east of the ethnographic Curzon Line at a time when the new Soviet Army was thoroughly exhausted by the Wars of Intervention and the Russian people were still recuperating from the ravages of those wars as well as the War of Empires. Hitler's flouting of the Munich Agreement should have been a salutary warning to Poland, as well as the countries of the West.

Ever since the signing of the German-Polish Non-Aggression Pact in 1934 Colonel Beck, Poland's Foreign Minister, had gradually been loosening his country's ties with France and moving Poland towards a closer association with Hitler's Reich. 'Both regimes were militaristic and authoritarian and shared ideological antipathy to Communism.' There had been frequent visits to Poland by Goebbels, Hanz Frank and Goering, and the Polish Ambassador, Josef Lipski, 'had ready access to an uncommonly agreeable Fuehrer, whose every public reference to Poland was conciliatory.'[1] That was until March 1939, when Hitler needed and had made full use of the Polish Government's obsessive anti-Bolshevism. But Czechoslovakia, or more precisely, the land that was Czechoslovakia, was now under his control and the occupation of Poland was an integral part of his plan for Eastern Europe. Danzig and the Corridor were but stepping stones towards the drive to the East.

From 1934 onwards, after the USSR had been allowed to join the League of Nations, Litvinov had tried to convince the British and French Governments that the road to peace lay through a genuine sense of purpose in implementing the resolutions and speeches on collective security against the forces of aggression, and translating them into positive deeds.

It had been exactly a year since Litvinov proposed collective action by the great powers for the preservation of peace in Europe. The latest victim then was Austria and now, 18 March 1939, three days after the absorption of Czechoslovakia into Hitler's Reich, the Soviet Foreign Minister proposed a six nation confrence of Britain, France, Poland, Roumania, Russia and Turkey to meet in Bucharest, emphasizing the urgent need to quickly establsh a 'Peace Front' against the drive to war. The destruction of Czechoslovakia had proved beyond any doubt that the Anglo-French policy of appeasement was an utter failure.

On 21 March Hitler presented his demands on the Polish Corridor and Danzig and on the following day German troops seized the Lithuanian port of Memel.* The follies of Versailles and Munich were now being rubbed in with a vengeance.

At the 18th Communist Party Congress in Moscow, on 10

*It had been German until Versailles and had a predominant German population.

March, Stalin called for the strengthening of peaceful as well as commercial relations between all countries, particularly those neighbouring countries, with which they had common frontiers. He warned, that '"in the sphere of foreign policy"' the Soviet Union should '"be cautious and not allow our country to be drawn into conflicts by warmongers who are accustomed to have others pull the chestnuts out of the fire for them."'[2]

The Litvinov proposal for a six nation conference was promptly rejected by Chamberlain. 'Believe it or not, the British Government turned down Litvinov's proposal as "premature"' writes Robert Boothby, 'and the Poles, idiotically and characteristically, objected to it. When Maisky subsequently told me that this was "the final smashing blow to any policy of collective security", I could only agree with him.'[3]

According to Lord Halifax, 'We could hardly in present circumstances manage to send a responsible Minister to take part in the Conference . . . We thought that to hold such a Conference as M. Litvinov suggested without a certainty that it would be successful was dangerous.'[4]

Soon after the annexation of Memel, the Goebbels propaganda machine began churning out its anti-Polish propaganda, preparing the ground, as it did during the Czechoslovak crisis period, for an eventual take over of the whole country. Headlines such as 'NAZIS SAY POLES ARE TERRORIZING GERMAN MINORITIES' which appeared in the *News Chronicle* on 28 March were a strong indication of what was likely to follow. Ian Colvin, the paper's Berlin correspondent, had been warning for some time that 'Poland was next on the German programme of aggression.'[5]*

The significance of the danger to Poland, if not to the rest of Europe, was beginning to register in Whitehall. On 31 March Chamberlain told the House of Commons that His Majesty's Government had decided to 'lend the Polish Government all support in their power. They have given the Polish Government an assurance to this effect . . . The French Government have authorized me to make it plain they stand

---

*On 28 March Colvin had flown to London from Berlin and personally warned Chamberlain and Halifax of the danger.

in the same position in this matter.' (*Hansard*, Col. 2415)

A few hours earlier, Chamberlain had conferred with the Foreign Policy Committee and 'explained how he had resisted attempts by the opposition leaders to make him include a reference to Russia in his statement.'[6]

The Polish guarantee, which had only been issued verbally, made no military sense whatsoever. With Czechoslovakia now part of Hitler's Third Reich, it was absurd to pretend that Poland could be protected from a German invasion without Soviet military help, which meant Soviet troops being allowed on Polish soil.

On the eve of Chamberlain's Polish guarantee,

> 'The Executive Committee of the International Federation of Trade Unions, at an emergency meeting in London ... called on the Governments of Great Britain, France, Russia and Poland immediately to enter into mutual guarantees ...
>
> The Executive declared that the only method of effectively preventing the domination of Europe by Germany and Italy is the formation of a Peace Front between Britain, France, Russia and Poland.' ('World Trade Unions Want 4-Power Pact' *News Chronicle*, 31 March 1939)

And a few days later the British Institute of Public Opinion announced the result of its survey 'of a representative cross-section of views of British men and women'. The question put by the British Institute was:

> 'Would you like to see Great Britain and Soviet Russia being more friendly to each other?'

Of those questioned, eighty four out of every hundred said 'Yes', only seven in every one hundred said 'No'. Nine in every one hundred expressed no opinion.

But the most significant indication of the Survey was the high vote among Government supporters for betterment of relations between the two countries. '83 of every 100 Chamberlain supporters are now anxious to shake hands with the Russians.' (*News Chronicle*, 3 April 1939)

This massive surge of support for friendly relations with the Soviet Union, especially among traditional Tory voters, was beginning to alarm some members of the Chamberlain administration, and their confidence was to be further undermined when the Italians invaded Albania on 7 April. But neither the Prime Minister nor the Foreign Secretary, when challenged on this latest act of aggression, were prepared to denounce the Pact with Italy or even to express condemnation of the Italian invasion.

Having rejected Litvinov's peace initiative of 18 March, and confronted by the widespread demand for peace talks with the Russians, the British Government eventually decided to make a move which they hoped would pacify the British public and soothe some of their own disgruntled supporters.

On 15 April it put forward a counter-proposal calling upon the Soviet Government to give a unilateral guarantee to Poland and Roumania.

'What good this would do', comments Professor Fleming, 'since Poland would not accept Russian assistance, was a mystery, but if that obstacle could be overcome London was willing for Russia to do the fighting.'[7]

Three days later, 18 April, the Soviet Union proposed an eight point plan which included a Triple Pact of Mutual Assistance for Britain, France and Russia, a Military Convention and a commitment that should there be an outbreak of hostilities 'not to enter into negotiations of any kind whatsoever and not to conclude peace with aggressors separately from one anothr and without common consent of the three Powers.' Ian Colvin, whose book deals specifically with the activities of the Chamberlain Cabinet during this period, describes the reaction of the Government's Chief Foreign Office official, Sir Alexander Cadogan, 'on the morning of 19 April' after receiving the latest Soviet proposals. 'He had to prepare in haste a minute for the Cabinet Committee on Foreign Policy that afternoon comprising his views on this development.'

'This Russian proposal is extremely inconvenient', he commented. 'We have to balance the advantage of a paper commitment by Russia to join in a war on one side against the disadvantage of associating ourselves openly with Russia.' He spoke of the limited military usefulness of Russia outside her own frontiers. Poland had just refused to be associated in a four power declaration with Russia and 'in order to placate our left wing in England, rather than to obtain any solid military advantage, we have since asked the Soviet whether they would declare that in the event of any act of aggression against any European neighbour of the Soviet Union, which was resisted by the country concerned, the assistance of the Soviet Government would be available, if desired, in such a manner as would be found most convenient. The Soviet Government now confront us with this proposal. If we are attacked by Germany, Poland under our mutual guarantee will come to our assistance, i.e. make war on Germany. If the Soviet are bound to do the same, how can they fulfil that obligation without sending troops through or aircraft over Polish territory. That is exactly what frightens the Poles.'[8]

At the Cabinet meeting later that day Chamberlain reminded the assembled Ministers that the Polish Foreign Minister had, at the time of his recent visit to London, declared that public association with Russia was 'an unnecessary provocation to Germany and one that ought to be avoided'. The latest Soviet peace proposal had undoubtedly put the Government on the spot. This was reflected in the comments by R.A. Butler, a Minister of State at the Foreign Office, who 'was anxious lest it should become "public property" that Britain and France were rejecting a Russian proposal for an alliance. The Prime Minister, who had made Attlee and Greenwood aware of his attitude in this matter, replied that "he would do his best to inculcate into them a sense of responsibility."' Lord Chatfield, the Minister for Defence Co-ordination, 'suggested that "the general view appeared to be that the political arguments against a military alliance ... between this country, France and Russia were irresistible and as such to outweigh any military advantages. For this reason in asking the Chiefs of Staff for an appreciation we must [when assessing the military capabilities of Russia's armed forces] give them strictly limited terms of reference."'

The Cabinet Committee accordingly reached the conclusion that: '"They were not, as at present advised, disposed to accept the Soviet proposal. The views of the French Government should be invited. The Chiefs of Staff Sub-Committee should prepare an appreciation of Russia's military strength, but this should not take the form of a review of the military arguments for or against accepting the Russian proposal."' It was also suggested that 'The Prime Minister was to warn the leaders of the Labour opposition to secrecy.'[9]

On 24 April, at a further Cabinet meeting, the Chiefs of Staff report was discussed. None of the Chiefs were present nor were they represented except by Lord Chatfield who read out his own summarized interpretation of the report, which was as follows:

> '"Russia, although a great power for other purposes, was only a power of medium rank for military purposes. On the other hand the Chiefs of Staff could not deny that Russia's assistance in war would be of advantage to her allies. Her assistance would be of considerable, though not of great military value and the side on which she participated in the war would undoubtedly fight the better for her help."'

In an attempt to downgrade the importance of Soviet military strength, Lord Chatfield

> 'enlarged "on the Chief of Staffs argument that despite a strength of 130 divisions she (the Soviet Union) would not be able to maintain in the field more than 30 divisions"

and that

> "the military assistance that Russia could bring to bear was not nearly so great as certain quarters represented it to be."'

From the record of the brief discussion that followed, Malcolm MacDonald* had declared that 'it would be important in war to have Russia on the Allied side and not neutral, or siding with Germany.' But this was immediately

---

*Son of Ramsay MacDonald. Dominions Secretary in Chamberlain Government. Later became High Commissioner in Canada and Governor-General of Malaya.

countered by Lord Halifax who, in his concluding remarks, expressed his firm belief that "'we ought to play for time.'"[10]

Some weeks later the Chiefs of Staff met to reconsider the military situation, and on 16 May they produced an entirely different document. It was a twelve page 'Report On The Military Value Of Russia' signed by Air Chief Marshal, Sir Cyril Newall, General Lord Gort and Admiral Sir Andrew Cunningham, deputy Chief of Naval Staff. This later report

> 'made it plain that the Russian Baltic Fleet could contain considerable enemy naval forces and interrupt to some extent supplies of Swedish ore to Germany. The Russian Army could mobilize on the Western front in the first three month of war 100 Infantry divisions and 30 Cavalry divisions, largely horsed, but comprising 9,000 tanks of high quality. Russian artillery fire power was low and communications by road and rail in a deplorable condition . . .
>
> 'In paragraphs 24 and 25, the Chief of Staff stated that:
>
> "even if war went so badly for the allies as to result in Poland and Roumania being overrun, the Russians would still contain very substantial German forces on the Eastern front . . . "

In its summary, the report stated:

> "The Russian Navy would contain considerable German Naval strength in the Baltic and would be an added deterrent to Japan in the Far East"

and

> "The Russian Air Force could produce a limited threat to Germany and Italy, if allowed to operate from neighbouring countries" moreover it "could contain more German air defence units in the East" as well as being able to provide "some assistance in strengthening the air defences of Poland."

In conclusion the report declared

> "Russia would not be a considerable supplier of
> war materials to Britain or her allies, but her co-
> operation would be invaluable in denying Russian
> sources of raw materials to Germany".[11]

Not surprisingly, the Prime Minister was anxious to
suppress the information in so favourable a report from
becoming common knowledge, especially to opposition
Members of Parliament, as well as to many members of his
own Party. By withholding selective parts of the report, it
had been made easier for both Chamberlain and Halifax to
continue with their policy of encouraging German expansionism eastwards, with the ultimate attack upon the Soviet
Union. Czechoslovakia, Poland, the Baltic States, the
Balkans, all were to be sacrificed in the process of achieving
this aim.

On 3 May 1939 Maxim Litvinov was replaced as the
Soviet Commissar for Foreign Affairs by Vyacheslav Molotov. The news came as a great shock to many people in the
West who had the highest regard for the great contribution
that Livinov had made over many years in his work for
peace and disarmament, not only in Europe, but throughout the world.

The Soviet Government was quick to give assurances that
'although M. Litvinov has resigned as People's Commissar
for Foreign Affairs, the foreign policy of the Soviet Union
remains the same.'[12]

On the following day a timely warning came from
Winston Churchill who, with all his political experience
and contacts at the highest level, was certainly convinced of
the urgent need for the Soviet Union to be allied to the
capitalist democracies in face of threats from Germany,
Italy and Japan, whom he knew were quite capable of
diverting their attacks westwards in spite of their anti-
Comintern alliance. Churchill was aware that the destruction of France was high on the Nazi leader's list, which
would leave Britain without allies should the German army
decide to change its strategy and turn westwards.

On 28 April Hitler denounced the Anglo-German Naval

Agreement and the German-Polish Non-Aggression Treaty, and demanded that Danzig be returned to the Reich. A clear enough indication of his war-like intentions and yet the Chamberlain Government had still not responded to the Soviet proposals of 18 April for a Triple Alliance.

Churchill's warning was delivered on 4 May.

'There is no means of maintaining an eastern front against Nazi aggression', he declared, 'without the active aid of Russia. Russian interests are deeply concerned in preventing Herr Hitler's designs on eastern Europe. It should still be possible to range all the States and peoples from the Baltic to the Black Sea in one solid front against a new outrage or invasion. Such a front, if established in good heart and with resolute and efficient military arrangements, combined with the strength of the Western powers, may yet confront Hitler, Goering, Himmler, Ribbentrop, Goebbels and Co. with forces the German people would be reluctant to challenge.'[13] But all the warnings, public opinion surveys and Soviet offers of alliance to stop the headldong drive to war were of no avail.

When the Cabinet Foreign Policy Committee met on 5 May the reply to the Soviet proposals – the last that Litvinov was to present – had still not been delivered. The Committee, after vacillating for almost a month, now wanted to know from the Soviet Government whether their proposals of 18 April 'still stood unaltered' (in view of the replacement of Litvinov by Molotov). What the 'Munichites' in the Government objected to was point No. 6 which emphasized that the signatories were 'not to conclude peace with aggressors separately from one another and without the common consent of the Three Powers.' They did not want to be tied down, yet, at the same time, they were asking the Soviet Union to provide unilateral guarantees. 'It was known', comments Ian Colvin, 'that Russia had been pressing for conditions that would afford her assistance if she went to war on behalf of the Baltic States. Lord Halifax said that the French "agreed with us that it would be excessive at present to extend our guarantee to the Baltic States."'[14] Having avoided the pressure to denounce Italy for invading Albania, the Government was even more determined that its cordial relations with Nazi Germany were not going to be impaired and it was 'agreed' by the Cabinet's Foreign Policy Committee that '"it was objectionable and dangerous to refer to Germany specifically by name"' particularly when having to deal with the Soviet condemnation of Nazi Germany as a potential aggressor. And the Government definitely did not want to get tied down to a 'No Separate Peace' tripartite agreement which, declared Lord Halifax, would '"be changing the whole basis of our policy and risking the alienation of our friends."'[15]

Eventually on 6 May 1939, a telegram was sent to Sir William Seeds, Britain's Ambassador in Moscow, advising him on how he should handle the vexed problem of the 'No Separate Peace' point in the Soviet proposals. He was told

'His Majesty's Government would hope that it might be possible for you to persuade Soviet Government not to press this point, which is one of obvious difficulty. Should it however appear that the point was one likely to exert decisive influence on Soviet decision as to unilateral declaration proposed, His Majesty's Government would wish that, while leaving them complete freedom for further examination of issues raised, you should do your best so to handle matter as to prevent negotiation breaking down finally on this or indeed any other ground.'

and that should the Soviet Government decide in the first instance to make a unilateral declaration,

'His Majesty's Government would be very willing to discuss with the Soviet Government any further questions which might arise therefrom.'[16]

As to be expected, the Soviet Government rejected these conditions.

It was not only the Churchill, Eden, Boothby elements within the Tory Party who were apprehensive of the outcome of the Government's policy. There were indications that this apprehension was being reflected in the reports and warnings from the Chiefs of Staff. Later that

477

month they put before the Cabinet Foreign Affairs Committee a Memorandum which covered their opinions on both
the strategic as well as the general aspects of the negotiations with the Soviet Government. The Memorandum was
specific in warning that

> 'The strategical and political aspects are closely
> related in a problem of this kind . . . A full-blown
> guarantee of mutual assistance between Great
> Britain and France and the Soviet Union offers
> certain advantages. It would present a solid front
> of formidable proportions against aggression . . .
> The whole hearted accession of Russia to the anti-
> aggression cause might influence certain waverers
> towards our side . . . If we fail to achieve any
> agreement with the Soviet, it might be regarded as
> a diplomatic defeat which would have serious
> military repercussions, in that it would have the
> immediate effect of encouraging Germany to
> further acts of aggression and of ultimately
> throwing the USSR into her arms . . . Fur-
> thermore, if Russia remained neutral, it would
> leave her in a dominating position at the end of
> hostilities.'

According to Ian Colvin, 'the Chiefs of Staff thought that an
occupation of the Baltic States by Germany would "turn the
Baltic into a German lake" and would "complete the
encirclement of Poland . . ."'[17]

Yet in spite of the warnings of the Chiefs of Staff,
Chamberlain preferred to follow hs own political judgement and willingly accepted the assessment of Lord
Chatfield that 'Russia was not a great military power' and,
as far as he was concerned, political considerations would
take precedence over the 'military and strategic considerations' of the Chiefs of Staff.

The pressure upon Chamberlain to seek an alliance with
the Soviet Union had by now become so acute that
eventually he was forced to make some kind of gesture
which he hoped would dampen down the mounting
opposition to his pro-German policies.

Lloyd George, whom one must presume knew as much about negotiating with the Soviet Union as any British politician, declared that he was 'certain that Russia will not come in unless a definite assurance is given to her that Britain and France will act, and not merely talk.' (*News Chronicle*, 13 April 1939)

In a foreign affairs debate in the House of Commons he warned –

> 'If we are going in without the help of Russia we are walking into a trap. It is the only country whose arms can get there. . . . If Russia has not been brought into this matter because of certain feelings the Poles have that they do not want the Russians there, it is for us to declare the conditions, and unless the Poles are prepared to accept the only conditions with which we can successfully help them, the responsibility must be theirs.'
> (*Hansard*, 3 April 1939, Cols. 2509–10)

Lloyd George, Churchill and Eden were in the forefront of a House of Commons attack upon the Prime Minister. From all sides of the House the demand for a Tripartite Agreement had become overwhelming, but it was not until 27 May that Chamberlain began to wilt under the pressure and agreed to enter into talks with the Soviet Union. Von Dirksen, the German Ambassador, reported to Berlin that he was of the opinion that the British Government had taken the decision 'with the greatest reluctance' after Whitehall had learn about the 'German feelers in Moscow'.[18]

In view of the urgency of reaching an agreement, the Russians naturally wanted the negotiations to be held at the highest level, but Chamberlain was in no hurry. He first of all resisted the pressures put upon him to fly to Moscow. Having reluctantly agreed to the negotiations he was determined to spin them out for as long as possible, hoping, in the opinion of the French writer, Francois Fonveille-Alquier, that 'the British and French people would be reassured by the prospect of an alliance with Moscow, but that the door would still be open to the new Munich for which Dahlerus* was feverishly working with Hermann Goering behind him.'[19]

The strengthening of Anglo-German ties had been going on throughout 1939. 'On 16 March, the day after the fall of Prague, the British Federation of Industries concluded with its Nazi counterpart a series of cartel agreements. In May the British permitted the Bank for International Settlements to send $25,000,000 of Czech gold from London to Berlin. While they haggled with Poland over the terms of a small $40,000,000 armament loan ... Robert Hudson and Sir Horace Wilson, conferred in London with Dr Helmuth Wohlthat, Hitler's economic adviser, concerning a possible British loan of $5,000,000,000 to the Reich.'[20]

According to Professor A.J.P. Taylor,† Wohlthat was in London between 18 and 21 July when he saw Hudson, the Secretary of the Department of Overseas Trade, and Sir Horace Wilson. The latter, says Taylor, 'produced a memorandum on 10 Downing Street note-paper, which, not surprisingly, has disappeared from the British records. This proposed an Anglo-German treaty of non-aggression and non-interference; a disarmament agreement; and co-operation in foreign trade.'[21]

Soviet suspicions were confirmed when they learnt that Lord Halifax had declined their invitation to go to Moscow. He had written to his Ambassador in Moscow telling him that 'it was really impossible to get away.'[22] Eden, although not a Minister, offered to take his place, but it was turned down by Chamberlain. Instead, William Strang, 'an able official but without any special standing outside the Foreign Office was entrusted with this momentous mission.' Churchill had strongly condemned 'the sending of so subordinate a figure' which he said 'was another mistake' as well as giving 'actual offence.'[23]

Strang left for Moscow on 12 June and diligently fulfilled his brief for spinning out the talks.

On 1 July the Anglo-French delegation proposed a

---

*Birger Dahlerus was a Swedish businessman, friend of Goering and some influential people in Britain. He claimed to be a neutral mediator between Britain and Nazi Germany.

†Professor A.J.P. Taylor refers to the 'prospect of a vast British loan' as £1.000 million.

formula regarding the guaranteeing of the Baltic States. But no sooner was it accepted by the USSR, than the proposers insisted upon including Holland and Switzerland on the list of countries to be guaranteed. As both these countries had persistently refused to recognize the Soviet Union, it was not altogether surprising that this addition should be rejected. There were also long drawn out discussions on what was meant by 'indirect aggression' which would bring into operation the application of the Triple Pact. Sudetenland, Danzig, the Polish Corridor, all came within that definition. But no agreement was reached. An assessment of the situation by Strang was despatched from Moscow to London on 20 July. 'The fact that we have raised difficulty after difficulty on points which seem to them unessential has created an impression that we may not be seriously seeking an agreement.'[24]

The Soviet representatives had insisted upon the Military Convention coming into operation simultaneously with that of the Triple Pact. This, together with the non-agreement over the precise definition of 'indirect aggression' brought the talks to a halt.

It was widely rumoured at the time that Germany would commence hostilities at the end of August and time was rapidly running out, but it was not until the end of July that the British Government reluctantly agreed to discuss the Soviet proposal for a Military Convention which meant getting down to the business of high level military discussions.

Hitler and his general staff were obviously aware that Chamberlain and Halifax were not looking for a successful outcome to the Moscow talks. His Ambassador in London, Herbert von Dirksen, was quick to point out, in his dispatch to Berlin on 1 August, the scepticism in London of the talks.

> 'This is borne out', says von Dirksen, 'by the composition of the British Military Mission. The Admiral . . . is practically on the retired list and was never on the naval staff. The General is also purely a combatant officer, the Air Marshal is outstanding as a pilot and an instructor, but not

as a strategist. This seems to indicate that the task of the Military Mission is rather to ascertain the fighting value of the Soviet forces than to conclude agreements on operations . . .

'The Wehrmacht attachés are agreed in observing a surprising scepticism in British military circles about the forthcoming talks with the Soviet armed forces.'[25]

The British delegation referred to by von Dirksen was announced on 31 July in the House of Commons. It was to be led by Sir Reginald Aylmer Ranfurly Plunkett-Ernle-Erle-Drax, a retired Admiral who, according to Captain Andre Beaufre, a young staff officer and a member of the French Military Mission, 'looked like a version of Admiral Rodney minus the wig . . . not very quick on the uptake.' Air Marshal Sir Charles Burnett, representing the Royal Air Force, 'was also a traditional figure . . . He liked to look back on those days in the Boer War and he was the military type made popular in France by Colonel Bramble, and found also in hunting prints.' General T.G.G. Heywood, head of the military delegation was 'extremely diplomatic and able, he possessed all the finer points required in the difficult art of negotiation.'[26]

When the Soviet Embassy 'which had to advise its Government as to the time of arrival of the mission, they naturally asked whether they would be travelling "by air".

'No that would be difficult because the mission consisted of twenty persons and their luggage.'

'By a fast cruiser?'

'Don't know. That is left to the Board of Trade.' Finally the mission left on 5 August 1939, travelling by a slow boat and arrived in Moscow on 11 August 1939.[27] They could of course have flown there in one day.

It was also the day when Hitler was reported to have told Burckhardt, the League's High Commissioner at Danzig:

'I want nothing from the West . . . But I must have a free hand in the East . . . I want to live in peace with England and to conclude a definite pact; to guarantee all the English possessions in the world and to collaborate.'[28]

Although the Admiral had no written authority to negotiate he had, nevertheless, been given secret instructions 'to go very slowly with the conversations, watching the progress of the political negotiations.'[29] And furthermore, he was told not to pass on to the Soviets any military information until a political agreement had been signed.

The Germans also knew most of the sticking points that would abort the negotiations, particularly the refusal of Poland and Roumania to allow Soviet troops on their territory, the same factor which had enabled them to destroy Czechoslovakia.

The leader of the French Military Mission was General Doumenc, a former deputy Chief of Staff, whose instructions, says Captain Beaufre 'were vague on essential points and terribly negative on the points which were bound to become crucial in the course of the negotiations.' Captain Beaufre had had the opportunity to seeing Admiral Drax's instructions from London. A copy had been presented to his delegation on 31 July. They 'recommended that we should proceed only with the utmost prudence, never pass on any interesting information, bear in mind constantly that German-Soviet collusion was possible.' In his opinion the British had 'no illusions as to the outcome of the conversations which were about to open and that they were above all anxious to gain time. All this was far away from the dreams of public opinion.'[30]

The members of the British Military Mission had been well briefed as to their role in Moscow. Air Marshal Burnett had written from the Soviet capital to his Chief of Staff in London: 'I understand it is the Government's policy to prolong negotiations as long as possible if we cannot get acceptance of a treaty.'[31]

The Anglo-French-Soviet talks which started on 12 August soon ran into the main and predicted obstacle – whether Poland and Roumania would allow Soviet forces to enter their territories. It was not until the third session, on 14 August, that Marshal Voroshilov, the Soviet Commissar for Defence, having waited for two days to see whether

either the French or the British would raise the matter, eventually asked the crucial questions. He wanted 'a clear answer' to his question 'concerning the joint action of the Armed Forces of Britain, France and the Soviet Union against the common enemy – the bloc of aggressors, or the main aggressor – should he attack.'
He wanted to know whether:

> 'the French and British General Staffs think that the Soviet land forces will be admitted to Polish territory in order to make direct contact with the enemy in case Poland is attacked?'

Did they:

> 'think that our [Soviet] Armed Forces will be allowed passage across Polish territory, across Galicia, to make contact with the enemy and to fight him in the South of Poland . . . Is it proposed to allow Soviet troops across Roumanian territory if the aggressor attacks Roumania?'

'These are three questions' said Voroshilov 'which interest us most.' After Admiral Drax had conferred 'at length with General Doumenc', the latter replied that he 'agreed with the Marshal that the concentration of Soviet troops must take place principally in the areas indicated by the Marshal, and that the distribution of these troops will be made at your discretion. I think that the weak points of the Polish–Roumanian front are their flanks and point of function. We shall speak of the left flank when we deal with the question of communications.'

Marshal Voroshilov: I want you to reply to my direct question. I said nothing about Soviet troop concentrations. I asked whether the British and French General Staffs envisage passage of our troops towards East Prussia or other points to fight the common enemy.
General Doumenc: I think that Poland and Roumania will implore you, Marshal, to come to their assistance.
Marshal Voroshilov: And perhaps they will not. It is not

evident so far. We have a Non-Aggression Pact with the Poles, while France and Poland have a Treaty of Mutual Assistance. This is the reason why the question I raised is not an idle one as far as we are concerned, since we are discussing the plan of joint action against the aggressor. To my mind, France and Britain should have a clear idea about the way we can extend real help or about our participation in the war.

(There follows a lengthy exchange of opinion between Admiral Drax and General Heywood.)

Admiral Drax: If Poland and Roumania do not ask for Soviet help they will soon become German provinces, and then the USSR will decide how to act. If on the other hand, the USSR, France and Britain are in alliance, then the question of whether or not Roumania and Poland ask for help becomes quite clear.

Marshal Voroshilov: I repeat, gentlemen, that this question is a cardinal question for the Soviet Union.

Admiral Drax: I repeat my reply once again. If the USSR, France and Britain are allies, then in my personal opinion there can be little doubt that Poland and Roumania will ask for help. But that is my personal opinion, and to obtain a precise and satisfactory answer, it is necessary to approach Poland.

Marshal Voroshilov: I regret that the Military Missions of Great Britain and France have not considered this question and have not brought an exact answer.[32]

Marshal Voroshilov had made himself absolutely clear at the outset that 'the Polish Army single-handed could not possibly withstand an attack by the powerful mechanized army of Germany; that the Red Army was willing and able to co-operate with the Polish Army in defence of Poland, but in order to do so the Red Army would have to cross Polish territory and jointly with the Polish Army, face the German Army on the Polish-German frontier.'[33]

The British and French Governments were obviously obliged to forward the Soviet requests to the Polish Government. The reply from Warsaw was that they did not need Soviet help, provided they received effective assistance from Britain and France, and that under no circumstances would they allow Soviet forces to enter their territory, but were perfectly willing to accept Soviet military supplies.

When Admiral Drax forwarded to the Foreign Office Voroshilov's request that Soviet troops be allowed to pass through Polish and Roumanian territory, Lord Halfax failed to reply.

The Anglo-French policy of prolonging the talks for as long as possible and of avoiding commitment to a tripartite agreement was eventually to boomerang back into Whitehall and the Quai d'Orsay.

After almost six weeks of abortive political haggling, followed by a further ten days of futile military talks, Soviet patience had obviously begun to run out. On 17 August, Marshal Voroshilov demanded that the talks be adjourned until he had received a definite reply. The participants agreed to return on the 21st.

Air Marshal Burnett, meanwhile, had written from Moscow on 16 August to his Chief of Staff:

> 'We consider that Russia wishes to come to some agreement with the Allies, but they fear that they cannot afford to wait until Germany has overrun Poland and fight Germany on the defensive in their own territory . . . '[34]

And on the following day, immediately the talks were adjourned, the leader of the French delgation, General Doumenc, sent a telegram to Paris warning that:

> '"The session for 21st was only fixed to avoid an impression abroad that the talks have been interrupted . . . The USSR wants a miltary pact . . . She does not want us to give her a piece of paper without substantial undertakings. Marshal Voroshilov has stated that all the problems . . . would be tackled without difficulty as soon as what he termed the crucial question was settled. It is now indispensable that I should be authorized to respond Yes to the question."'[35]

Thus, both Governments were under no illusions of the seriousness of the situation, and the determination of the Soviet Union to receive a positive reply to the all-important question. Time was rapidly running out. The military leaders, through their intelligence departments, must have known that a German invasion of Poland was imminent. Most of the harvest, by the end of August, would have been gathered. Hitler had planned the attack, known as Case White, for 1 September.

Even Bonnet at this late stage was beginning to panic while awaiting the official Polish reply to the Soviet request which had been presented by the British and French Ambassadors to the Poles.

'It would be disastrous', he said, 'if, in consequence of a Polish refusal, the Russian negotiations were to break down . . . It was an untenable position for the Poles to take up in refusing the only immediate efficacious help that could reach them in the event of a German attack. It would put the British and French Governments in an almost impossible position if we had to ask our respective countries to go to war in defence of Poland, which had refused this help.' A positive reply from the Polish Government was dependent upon the willingness of the British and French Governments to force them to give way on this issue. 'Though both Paris and London had been reckless in giving their pledges to Poland without thought of Russia, they now realized – in mid-August – that their help in the west could not save Poland unless the Soviet Union also came to her aid in the East.' Shirer was convinced that 'the French and British had only one last ace to play with the Poles: to tell them that unless they reversed their decision and agreed to accept Russian aid the Anglo-French commitments of help would be withdrawn. The formal Anglo-Polish mutual-security treaty had not yet been signed, despite Beck's urging. And Bonnet was still sitting on the political accord with Poland which he had refused to sign in May.'[36]

The appeasers still believed that they would be insulated from a westward attack by the military forces of fascism which they had helped to sustain. They had willingly put pressure on Czechoslovakia to hand over territory to Hitler and yet withdrew from exercising justifiable pressure upon the Polish Government to not only save itself but the rest of Europe from the impending holocaust. Both Governments were fully aware that Nazi Germany, like its predecessors, would take every precaution to avoid a war on two fronts. But the old obsessions, prejudices, and hatred of the Soviet Union had warped their minds as well as their judgement. And now they had thrown away the last chance of preventing World War II.

Chamberlain had been warned by the Chiefs of Staff that they were 'very anxious that Russia should not under any circumstances become allied with Germany' and that 'such an eventuality would create a most dangerous situation for us.'

Lord Halifax has recorded that Sir Robert Vansittart telephoned him on 18 August in Yorkshire and was 'very insistent that I ought to return to London the following morning.' According to Ian Colvin, 'Sir Robert, through a German diplomat in the Hague, had received information that an attack by Germany within two weeks was a practical certainty. He was guarded on the telephone and Lord Halifax, with his eye on Cricket Week and a little farming at Garrowby was reluctant to be drawn. he played for time, suggesting that Vansittart should consult with Sir Alexander Cadogan and if both agreed, "[he] would come up by the early train ... "' At mid-day, Saturday 19 August, Halifax met Cadogan and Vansittart 'at the office'. 'An RAF machine then flew Lord Halifax from Heston to Driffield and he managed some farming and cricket that week-end before going to 10 Downing Street on Monday to see Chamberlain. Halifax noted in his Confidential Record of Events that "C* tells us that he has received an approach, suggesting that Goering should come to London if he can be assured that he will be able to see the Prime Minister. It was decided an affirmative offer to this curious suggestion and arrangements were accordingly set in hand for Goering to come over secretly on Wednesday the 23rd." Among the preparations for such a conspiratorial meeting they decided

---

* 'C' was the pseudonym of the Head of the Foreign Intelligence Service – Major General Sir Stuart Menzies.

to land the Field Marshal "at some deserted aerodrome" and motor him to Chequers, where the telephone would be disconnected and "the regular household given congé." Lord Halifax anticipated "a dramatic interlude" but there was no news from Berlin next day as to Goering before the Cabinet met at 3 pm,'[37] to approve a letter that Chamberlain was going to write to Hitler.

But London was not the only capital where dramatic events were taking place. During the night of 21–22 August a report had come in from the Soviet News Agency, *Tass*, announcing that the German Foreign Minister, von Ribbentrop, would be flying to Moscow to sign a Non-Aggression Pact.

The following morning the world's press carried banner headlines that agreement had been reached between Berlin and Moscow and that a Non-Agression Pact was to be signed. The news erupted like a bombshell upon London and Paris. But by the next morning an item appeared in the *News Chronicle** which had been taken from the Soviet Press stating that 'A war by the Soviet Union against the Fascist monsters will be the justest war in the history of mankind.'

Under a headline 'RUSSIA ANXIOUS FOR A 3-POWER PACT', the paper's Mowcow correspondent reported

> 'Before hasty conclusions are drawn it must be remembered that the Soviet-German Pact is still unsigned. While Berlin reports predicted the signing tomorrow Moscow is careful to state that the talks will only begin after Ribbentrop's arrival.'

Under another heading 'DOCUMENT NOT READY' the paper pointed out that

> 'Russians in London do not believe that a docu-

---

*This paper which consistently appealed for an Anglo-French-Russian Pact had reminded its readers on the previous day (22 August 1939) –
'One cannot forget the responsibility of the British Government which failed to accept the Soviet offers of co-operation in March and April and has since on so many occasions paid more attention to German than Russian feelings.'

ment has already been prepared and merely awaits signatures along the dotted ine. Alternatively, if there is a document, it should not exclude the possibility of a British-Russian-French Treaty.'

Even at this late stage the Soviet Government had indicated to London and Paris that they were prepared to hold up the signing of the Nazi-Soviet Agreement should London and Paris join with them in a three Power Pact which would have meant Britain and France exercising their authority on the Polish Government. But neither Government availed themselves of this last minute opportunity which could have preserved the peace of Europe.

Feelers had been put out by the Nazi Government through their Ambassador, Schulenberg, in Moscow, on the possibility of a Non-Agression Pact earlier in the Summer. It was not until the Poles had finally shut the door and the British and French Governments took no action that the USSR decided to take up the German proposal.

The Pact was signed on 23 August 1939 but, as Professor A.J.P. Taylor has pointed out, it 'contained none of the fulsome expressions of friendship which Chamberlain had put into the Anglo-German declaration on the day after the Munich Conference. Indeed Stalin rejected any such expressions ... The Pact was neither an alliance nor an agreement for the partition of Poland. Munich had been a true alliance for partition: the British and French dictated partition to the Czechs. The Soviet Government undertook no such action against the Poles. They merely promised to remain neutral ... More than this, the agreement was in the last resort anti-German: it limited the German advance eastwards in case of war ... However one spins the crystal and tries to look into the future from the point of view of 23 August 1939, it is difficult to see what other course Soviet Russia could have followed ... given the Polish refusal of Soviet aid, given too the British policy of drawing out negotiations in Moscow without seriously striving for a conclusion – neutrality, with or without a formal pact, was the most that Soviet diplomacy could attain ... '[38]

Even then, the Soviet Government had left the door open for the British and French Governments by which a similar pact could have been concluded with them, but they were not interested. Instead, the verbal guarantee to Poland, announced on 31 March, was hastily confirmed on 25 August and put into a formal Treaty of Mutual Assistance.

'Never were names put to a more hollow instrument' writes Professor Fleming. For neither Britain nor France had 'the slightest power to save the life of a single Pole.'[39]

On 1 September 1939 at 4.45 am Hitler's order for the attack on Poland was put into operation. All hell was let loose.

Notes

1. TAYLOR, Telford, *Munich – The Price of Peace*, p. 188
2. *Soviet Documents on Foreign Policy*, Vol. III, ed. Jane Degras, pp. 322–3
3. BOOTHBY, Lord, *Recollections of a Rebel*, p. 103
4. *Documents on British Foreign Policy* 3rd Series Vol. IV No. 433, p. 392
5. COLVIN, Ian, *The Chamberlain Cabinet*, p. 197
6. COLVIN, Ian, *The Chamberlain Cabinet*, p. 197
7. FLEMING, D.F., *The Cold War and Its Origins*, Vol. I, p. 89
8. COLVIN, Ian, *The Chamberlain Cabinet*, p. 200
9. COLVIN, Ian, *The Chamberlain Cabinet*, p. 204
10. COLVIN, Ian, *The Chamberlain Cabinet*, p. 205
11. COLVIN, Ian, *The Chamberlain Cabinet*, p. 206–7
12. MAISKY, Ivan, *Who Helped Hitler?*, pp. 123–4
13. CHURCHILL, Winston, *The Gathering Storm*, Vol. I. The Second World War, pp. 285–6
14. COLVIN, Ian, *The Chamberlain Cabinet*, p. 210
15. COLVIN, Ian, *The Chamberlain Cabinet*, p. 208–9
16. *Documents on British Foreign Policy* 3rd Series Vol. V No. 389, pp. 443–4
17. COLVIN, Ian, *The Chamberlain Cabinet*, p. 211
18. *Documents on German Foreign Policy*, Series D. Vol. VI, pp. 616–7
19. FONVEILLE-ALQUIER, Francois, *The French and the Phoney War 1939–1940*, p. 91
20. FLEMING, D.F., *The Cold War and Its Origins* Vol. I, p. 92
21. TAYLOR, A.J.P., *The Origins of the Second World War*, p. 298
22. *Documents on British Foreign Policy* 3rd Series Vol. VI No. 5, p. 5
23. CHURCHILL, Winston, *The Gathering Storm*, Vol. I. The Second World War, pp. 303–4
24. *Documents on British Foreign Policy* 3rd Series Vol. VI No. 376, p. 426
25. *Documents on Germany Foreign Policy* Series D, Vol. VI, pp. 1033–4
26. BEAUFRE, General Andre, *1940 – The Fall of France*, pp. 97–8
27. COATES, W.P. and Zelda, *History of Anglo-Soviet Relations*, p. 616

28. *Documents on British Foreign Policy*, 3rd Series, Vol. VI No. 659, pp. 693 and 695

29. *Documents on British Foreign Policy*, 3rd Series, Vol. VI Appendix, p. 763

30. BEAUFRE, General Andre, *1940 – The Fall of France*, p. 93

31. *Documents on British Foreign Policy*, 3rd Series, Vol. VII Appendix, p. 600

32. From Ministry for Foreign Affairs of the USSR Documents and Records ed. V.M. Falin *et al.* Part 2. (Moscow 1973) No. 415 (Ex Anthony P. Adamthwaite Document No. 76 – The Making of the Second World War), p. 218

33. COATES, W.P. and Zelda, *History of Anglo-Soviet Relations*, p. 616

34. *Documents on British Foreign Policy*, 3rd Series, Vol. VII Appendix, p. 519

35. SHIRER, William, *The Collapse of the Third Republic*, pp. 435–436 and FN

36. SHIRER, William, *The Collapse of the Third Republic*, pp. 437–438

37. COLVIN, Ian, *The Chamberlain Cabinet*, p. 229

38. TAYLOR, A.J.P., *The Origins of the Second World War*, p. 318–319

39. FLEMING, D.F., *The Cold War and Its Origins*, Vol. I, p. 95

34

LA GRANDE ILLUSION

It soon became evident to Hitler that neither the British nor the French Governments were prepared to go to war over Poland. He certainly knew that Chamberlain had been desperately keen to conclude an Anglo-German Non-Aggression Pact so that Britain and the British Empire would remain outside a German-Russo war. On 28 August Sir Neville Henderson, Britain's Ambassador in Berlin, had been sounding him out on the possibility of staging another 'Munich'.

Even in September 1939, according to the military experts, Germany could not have withstood a war on two fronts − a fact which both Hitler and his Generals were agreed. Where he differed from some of his senior commanders was in his assessment of British and French foreign policy. And he was once again to judge correctly. Poland's allies took nearly three days to declare that they were in 'a state of war' with Germany while bombs were falling on the Polish people and their army was being crushed. But a 'state of war' is not the same as being engaged in a war. Hitler knew that without Soviet military help Poland could not withstand a German attack and that a Franco-British-Russian military pact would have thwarted his plans. Instead of which the Polish door had been opened for him. Even after the signing of the Nazi-Soviet Pact the door could have been closed had there been a concerted effort in Britain and France to have rid their countries of Chamberlain, Daladier and the Ministerial appeasers in their Cabinets, whose policies had contributed to the destruction of Republican Spain, Austria and Czechoslovakia and had now brought their countries to the brink of another European war.

During an emergency debate in the House of Commons on 24 August, there was absolutely no attempt by the leaders of HM Opposition to call the Government to account for its disastrous policies or to call for a vote of censure. Even if they had lost the vote, even if the supporters of an Anglo-French-Soviet Agreement within the Conservative Party had not voted with them, or had abstained, it would have at least acted as a rallying call to millions of people outside Parliament that there was at last a determined effort to prevent Hitler from achieving his objectives by collective action, and that it was still possible to prevent a major war. There were some back bench MPs who did not accept that war was inevitable.

Aneurin Bevan wanted to know:

> 'whether the mind of the Government has been closed to the possibility of entering into, not military, but political discussions with the Government of Russia immediately for the purpose of discovering the ramifications and consequences of the Non-Aggression Pact entered into with Germany and finding out whether it is not still possible to arrive at an arrangement with Russia ... It is an obligation upon the Opposition' he said, 'to obtain an assurance that this situation will not be left where it is, but that efforts will be made in Moscow, first, to explore this treaty and next, to find out how far it is possible still to enter into an Anglo-French-Soviet Pact.' (*Hansard*, 24 August 1939, Cols. 55 and 57)

There was obviously much discontent in the ranks of back bench MPs over the acquiescence of their leaders to meekly accept Chamberlain's call for unity. Eleanor Rathbone, in the same debate, said that she had 'listened with some dismay to the statement of the Leader of the Liberal Opposition [Sir Archibald Sinclair] that this was not a time for criticism', and reminded the Prime Minister and her Parliamentary colleagues that:

> 'It is less than a year ago when a scene took place

494

in this House not unlike the scene today when we seemed equally on the verge of war and many of us, and I think the country, realized that the Opposition, carried away by an impulse which overcame us all, forwent its right to criticism too far. We gave something which was too much interpreted as being a blank cheque.' (*Hansard*, 24 August 1939, Cols. 33 and 34)

Her argument was reinforced by Ellen Wilkinson, a Labour MP and one of the doughty fighters on behalf of the unemployed during the early 1930s. She refused to be intimidated by the atmosphere of crisis and rallying calls for unity behind a Prime Minister and his administrators whom she knew had played a major part in bringing the country to the brink of war. 'I cannot enter into this general atmosphere of forgive and forget as regards the present Prime Minister', she declared, adding that she did not 'believe that any criticism of the Prime Minister or his policy . . . will in any way encourage Herr Hitler to think that this nation is not united. If the Prime Minister will forgive me for saying so, I think this nation will be more united if he were not Prime Minister.' (*Hansard*, 24 August 1939, Col. 48)

In spite of the efforts of some back bench MPs to rouse their leaders to take in initiative by either forcing the Prime Minister or the Foreign Minister to fly to Moscow to save the peace, or to have gone themselves, they allowed the situation to drift and Hitler took full advantage of it.

The military historian, Sir Basil Liddell-Hart, has analysed in detail the implications of Chamberlain's policy upon Hitler and a rearmed Germany.

'For Chamberlain, the Munich Agreement spelt "peace in our time". For Hitler, it spelt a further and greater triumph not only over his foreign opponents but also over his generals. After their warnings had been so repeatedly refuted by his unchallenged and bloodless successes, they naturally lost confidence, and influence. Naturally, too, Hitler himself became overwhelmingly confident of a continued run of easy success.

'If you allow anyone to stoke up a boiler until the steam-pressure rises beyond danger-point, the real responsibility for any resultant explosion will lie with you.'[1]

But the elements that allowed the stoking up of the boiler were still around in September 1939. It does seem amazing, in the light of the historical record of the Chamberlain administration, that Arthur Greenwood,* the deputy leader of the Labour Party, could agree with the Prime Minister 'that the issue of peace and war rested in the hands of one man.' (*Hansard*, 1 September 1939, Col. 134). For that was the foundation upon which Chamberlain based his reasoning for the critical situation that prevailed in Europe on 1 September 1939 when he declared in the House of Commons:

> 'Now that all the relevant documents are being made public we shall stand at the bar of history knowing that the responsibility for this terrible catastrophe lies on the shoulders of one man – the German Chancellor, who has not hesitated to plunge the world into misery in order to service his own senseless ambitions.' (*Hansard*, Col. 127)

Chamberlain proceeded to inform the House that the British and French Ambassadors had been instructed to submit an Anglo-French Statement, a document which once stripped of its diplomatic verbiage, amounted to no more than a 'slap on the wrist' for the German Chancellor. It had been carefully worded to convey to Hitler that it was not an ultimatum but only a warning, and did *not* stipulate a time-limit. The Statement was treated contemptuously by Hitler who did not even bother to reply. He was not deterred by words which clearly showed that Poland's allies were reluctant to take action. The document stated

> ' . . . that unless the German Government are prepared to give His Majesty's Government satis-

---

*Clement Attlee, the leader of the Labour Party, had been away ill for some weeks.

factory assurances that the German Government have suspended all aggressive action against Poland and are prepared promptly to withdraw their forces from Polish territory, His Majesty's Government in the United Kingdom will without hesitation fulfil their obligations to Poland.' (*Hansard*, 1 September 1939, Col. 130)

The very fact that this was just a warning, not an ultimatum, and without a time-limit, was sufficient evidence to convince Hitler that there was obviously a great deal of 'hesitation' in Whitehall and the Quai d'Orsay. For had not Chamberlain stated in the spring of 1938 'You have only to look at the map to see that nothing that France or we could do could possibly save Czechoslovakia from being overrun by the Germans.'[2] And geography had been no kinder to Poland than to Czechoslovakia.

A few days before the German invasion, Poland had been subjected to considerable pressure by the British and French Governments to join them, together with Italy and Germany, in a Munich type conference. Not surprisingly they declined. They knew what to expect, for they had not only witnessed the dismemberment of Czechoslovakia, but in the words of Winston Churchill, Poland 'with hyena appetite had only six months before joined in the pillage and destruction of the Czechoslovak State.'[3] Nevertheless they still believed their allies would honour the agreements and come to their rescue. They were soon to be disillusioned. Under the Anglo-Polish Treaty, Article I stated

'Should one of the contracting powers become engaged in hostilities with a European Power in consequence of aggression by the latter against that contracting party, the other contracting party will *at once* (own emphasis) give the contracting party engaged in hostilities all the support and assistance in its power.'

For close on three days absolutely nothing militarily was done to help the Polish people and the Polish Army in their hour of need. While Hitler's bombs were smashing up their homes and cities, and their army was being crushed, the appeasers in London and Paris were still trying to do a deal with Hitler. The Nazi Fuehrer was prepared to collaborate with Chamberlain, but the occupation of Poland came first. Consequently, Chamberlain's final note to Hitler delivered at 9 am on 3 September – this time with a time-limit of two hours, was also ignored. The note stated:

> ' . . . that unless not later than 11 am British Summer Time today, 3 September, satisfactory assurances . . . have been given by the German Government and have reached His Majesty's Government in London, a state of war will exist between the two countries as from that hour.' (*Hansard*, 3 September 1939, Col. 292)

The hesitant French Government timed their warning to expire at 5 pm, six hours after that of the British, so that in effect sixty hours had elapsed since the German invasion.

Thus, by the evening of 3 September 1939, the people of Britain and France and their Governments were 'in a state of war', a war, which in its first eight months, has been described as the 'phoney war', the 'sitzkreig' and in France as 'la drole de guerre', the strange war, which indeed it was.

Basil Liddell-Hart has assessed that at the time of the German invasion of Poland 'the Poles and the French together had the equivalent of 130 divisions against a German total of ninety eight divisions, of which thirty six were virtually untrained and unorganized . . .

'On the surface', he adds, 'it would appear that the French had ample superiority to crush the German forces in the West, and break through to the Rhine. The German Generals were astonished, and relieved, that they did not do so.'[4] Just as they were 'astonished and relieved' in March 1936 when their forces marched into the Rhine, and again in 1938 when German troops were allowed to march into Austria and Czechoslovakia.

William Shirer has described in some detail the facade surrounding the allied 'offensive' to help the Poles. Being a foreign correspondent from a neutral country he had been able to travel and observe what was going on in both France and Germany.

'The French', he reports, 'met little opposition, as the German covering forces withdrew towards the Siegfried Line eight miles north of the frontier . . . There was no serious fighting . . .

'The French had an overwhelming superiority in men, guns and tanks. Against their fully armed eighty five divisions, the Germans had thirty four divisions, all but eleven of which were reserve units with little training and lacking adequate arms, munitions and transport. All the Panzer divisions, all the motorized divisions had been reserved for Poland . . .

'Fortunately for the Germans a serious attack was never mounted nor did the highly cautious French Generalissimo ever contemplate one. By 12 September the French forces had moved forward some five miles on a fifteen mile front and occupied twenty deserted villages. General Gamelin, thereupon commanded them to halt and on that very day, 12 September, to prepare to beat a retreat to the safety to the Maginot Line should the Germans attack through Belgium.'

'The battered Poles protested against such monumental inaction . . . There was no action in the air except for a few reconnaissance missions . . .

'Not a single German tank or plane or division was diverted from Poland to reinforce the West.'[5]

General de Gaulle, who was at the time Colonel in Command of the Tank section of the 5th Army, described the 'offensive' in his memoirs as no more than 'a few demonstrations'. An even more severe critic was Captain Beaufre, who believed that 'contrary to all logic – since logic indicated that we should have attacked to take the pressure off Poland – nothing was happening . . . Gamelin, true to type, decided to do nothing more than make a gesture . . . So much for our help to Poland.'[6]

Shirer further records

'Along the ninety miles of the Rhine which separated France and Germany and their armies

499

not a shot was fired.' He had 'on the morning of 10 October gone up by train from Karlsruhe to Basle on the German side of the Rhine' and noted in Diary

> "No sign of war and the train crew told me not a shot had been fired on this front . . . We could see the French bunkers and at many places great mats behind which the French were building fortifications. Identical picture on the German side . . . They went about their business in full sight and range of each other. For that matter, one blast from a French '75' could have liquidated our train. The Germans were hauling up guns and supplies on the railway line, but the French did not disturb them. Queer kind of war."

It was not only Gamelin who was 'true to type'. The 'gesture' was part of the facade to hoodwink the British and French people that they were really helping the gallant Poles. Although Winston Churchill was brought into the British Cabinet as First Lord of the Admiralty, the reins of Government still remained in the hands of Chamberlain and Halifax, and in France, Daladier and Bonnet were still at the helm. The leaders of both Governments felt that they had been drawn into the wrong war by mistake, and the British Foreign Office, according to the Cadogan Diaries appeared anxious to rectify that mistake. That 'mystery man' Dahlerus,* the Swedish industrialist and friend of Goering had been busily engaged travelling between London, Berlin and Berchtesgaden many months after war had been declared. There were members of the Cabinet, including Churchill, who, during the early weeks of the war, were deliberately kept in the dark about the secret negotiations that had been going on between the Munichite section of the Government and Berlin. Contacts were made with both Hitler and Goering, and when they had failed to achieve the desired results, those contacts were switched to

---

*See Cadogan Diaries, pp. 202, 204, 205, 220, 224, 228, 229, 236, 241

some dissident Generals. Sir Alexander Cadogan, Permanent Under-Secretary of State at the Foreign Office, says he 'told H [Lord Halifax] . . . He mustn't listen too much to Winston [Churchill] on the subject of "beating Germany". We must try every means of helping G [Germany] to beat herself . . . '[8] These undercover negotiations with the enemy were to continue on and off throughout the 'phoney war' period.

'The idea of letting Hitler rip against the Soviet Union, on the basis of a deal with him, . . . did not die with the outbreak of war', comments Konni Zilliacus, 'it reappeared as the idea of "switching the war" during the period of the "phoney" war.'[9]

Sir Alexander Cadogan, close associate of the Cliveden Set, has indicated in his diaries the real aspirations of British foreign policy up to and including the 'phoney war'.

Both Whitehall and the Quai d'Orsay, together with sections of the press, had deliberately created an impression that the Polish Army was much stronger and more efficient than it really was. Gamelin was reported to have said that it was capable of withstanding a German assault for up to six months. At the same time, while suppressing the opinions of some of the more objective military experts, and projecting the image of a comparatively weak and inefficient Soviet Army and Air Force which would not last more than a few weeks against the mighty German military machine, the Munichites were not only deceiving their own people but also themselves. Wishful thinking had replaced military and political judgement with disastrous consequences.

By the time Britain's contribution of two divisions to the Allied cause had taken up their position on the Western front at the end of September, Poland had collapsed. In fact, the Polish Government had fled over the border into Roumania on 15 September. An SOS to Britain was sent out over the Warsaw radio on 19 September. The following morning the *News Chronicle* reported that a 'British message of goodwill to Warsaw broadcast by the BBC last night brought the following radio reply from the President of the city:

"The brutal bombardment of towns, the destruc-

501

tion of hundreds of churches, hospitals and private dwellings, and the murder of thousands of women and children are being carried out mercilessly.

I feel, therefore, entitled to make a new appeal to you.

When will the effective help of Britain and France come to relieve us from this terrible situation?

We are waiting for it."'

But the Polish people were to wait in vain.

In his testimony at Nuremberg General Franz Halder confirmed that:

'The success against Poland was only possible by our almost completely baring our Western border. If the French ... had used the opportunity presented by the engagement of nearly all our forces in Poland they would have been able to cross the Rhine without our being able to prevent it and would have threatened the Ruhr, which was decisive for the German conduct of the war.'[10]

Another American writer and journalist, Joseph P. Lash, in his book *Roosevelt and Churchill 1939–1941*, has referred to excerpts in General Halder's diary that the 'Fuehrer will not take it amiss if England were to wage a sham war' and that a 'decision against evacuation shows that he expects France and England will not take action.' Lash comments that 'his [Hitler's] expectations were fulfilled. The French strategy of "static defence" while the Polish army was being destroyed seemed to be a "miracle" to the German High Command, which shared Hitler's hope that Anglo-French passivity was a prelude to another Munich. There were statesmen in London and Paris who were thinking along such lines.' He then goes on to relate that on 11 September 1939 'a despatch had come into the State Department Cable room in Washington from the appeasement-minded US Ambassador in London, Joseph Kennedy. It was marked "Personal for the President and the Secretary of State" and contained Kennedy's account of a talk he had had with the King and Queen and with Sir Samuel Hoare, British Lord Privy Seal and confidant of Prime Minister Neville Chamberlain. Hoare felt that after Hitler cleaned up Poland, which he was expected to do in four to six weeks, he would then propose to call this war off and come to some agreement with Britain and France. Having been in the forefront of the appeasement policy, Sir Samuel did not recoil at the prospect.'[11]

But Sir Samuel Hoare must have become oblivious to the fact that Hitler's foreign policy was not only based upon anti-Bolshevism. His hatred of France had not abated – she had never been forgiven for the humiliation of Versailles. His wooing of Britain through the appeasers was an integral part of his policy of splitting up the alliance and isolating Britain.

With the Polish Army disintegrating and Hitler's troops rapidly moving on to Warsaw, the Soviet Red Army, on 17 September, moved into the eastern part of the country and reoccupied territory that had been wrested from their country by Polish troops in 1921. Inevitably, there was an outcry of 'stab in the back' from most of the press, but coupled with the hostile statements were some interesting observations such as that in the Conservative *Daily Telegraph*'s editorial of 18 September:

'Reading between the lines, it is plain enough that the Russian Government is alarmed at the rapidity of the German advance and the threat it offers to Russia's western frontier. The new Russo-German non-aggression pact is worth no more and no less than Herr Hitler's agreements with Austria, Czechoslovakia and Poland, and Stalin cannot watch the German steam-roller crashing over prostrate Poland without an uneasy suspicion that the driver may forget to stop. Stalin has presumably read *Mein Kampf*. If so, he has no doubt noted Herr Hitler's conviction that Germany's true field of expansion is to be eastward; that what he covets most in Europe is the granary of the Ukraine ... The presence of a powerful

Russian army on his eastern frontier will immobil-
ize a large part of Herr Hitler's forces at a time
when they are needed in the West . . . '

And on 20 September Robert Boothby, during a debate in
the House of Commons, warned that any hasty judgement
upon Russia's actions would be most ill-advised and
contrary to Britain's national interests.

'I think it is legitimate to suppose that this action
on the part of the Soviet Government was taken in
sheer self-interest, and from the point of view of
self-preservation and self-defence. After all, what
effect has the action taken by the Russian troops
during the last three days had? It has pushed the
German frontier with Russia considerably westward of where it would have been had the
Russians taken no action at all . . . In my view the
Russians are now face to face with one of the most
formidable military machines that the world has
ever seen; and for my part, although I do not
condone the Russo-German pact itself, I am
thankful that Russian troops are now along the
Polish-Rumanian frontier. I would rather have
Russian troops there than German troops.' (*Hansard*, 20 September 1939, Cols. 995–996)

That morning there was a report in the *News Chronicle*
from its war correspondent, William Forrest, despatched
from the Polish-Rumanian frontier which gave a graphic
account of what happened when the Soviet troops entered
that part of Poland

'Not a shot has been fired, not a bomb dropped,
and villagers and townspeople freed from the
terror of the air are hailing the Red Army as
deliverers. Russian troops themselves are contributing to this feeling of relief by telling the people
that they have come as friends and comrades.
Many inhabitants in this part of Poland are Jews,
whose number has been swelled by thousands of

504

Jewish refugees fleeing before the German advance. Their joy at finding themselves saved from the fate that awaited them at Nazi hands can well be imagined.' (*The News Chronicle*, 20 September 1939)

The Soviet Government was well aware that Russia was still the primary target of Hitler's 'lebensraum' policy. Having tried for many years to initiate a policy of collective security and failed, it had consequently taken the precautionary action of safeguarding its own borders against the threat of invasion. It therefore, according to Basil Liddell-Hart, 'lost no time in securing strategic control of Russia's old-time buffer-territories in the Baltic. By 10 October [1939] it had concluded pacts with Estonia, Latvia and Lithuania which enabled its forces to garrison key-points in those countries. On the 9th conversations began with Finland.'[12]

Notes

1. LIDDELL-HART, Sir Basil, *History of the Second World War*, pp. 6–7
2. FEILING, Keith, *The Life of Neville Chamberlain*, p. 347
3. CHURCHILL, Winston, *The Gathering Storm*, Vol. I, The Second World War, p. 271
4. LIDDELL-HART, Sir Basil, *History of the Second World War*, p. 19
5. SHIRER, William, *The Collapse of the Third Republic*, pp. 496, 497, 498
6. BEAUFRE, General Andre, *1940 – The Fall of France*, pp. 146–7
7. SHIRER, William (Ex Berlin Diary, p. 234), *The Collapse of the Third Republic*, p. 514
8. *The Diaries of Sir Alexander Cadogan*, (ed. David Dilks), p. 228
9. ZILLIACUS, K., *I Choose Peace*, p. 68
10. SHIRER, William, *The Collapse of the Third Republic*, p. 503
11. LASH, Joseph P, *Roosevelt and Churchill 1939–1941*, pp. 21–22
12. LIDDELL-HART, Sir Basil, *History of the Second World War*, p. 43

35

THE WAR IN FINLAND

In 1939 the Finnish-Soviet border stretched from the Arctic Ocean to the Gulf of Finland, 800–900 miles, through Karelia to the Karelian Isthmus where the border at some points was no more than twenty miles from Leningrad, Russia's most important seaport and second largest city.

'The Soviet had not forgotten the dangers which Leningrad had faced in 1919', wrote Winston Churchill in Book II of *The Gathering Storm*. 'Even the White Russian Government of Kolchak had informed the Peace Conference in Paris that bases in the Baltic States and Finland were a necessary protection for the Russian capital.'[1] There were very few people alive in 1939 who were better informed than Churchill of the strategic importance of the approaches to Russia in the regions around Leningrad and Murmansk.

Before the Russian Revolution Finland was part of the Tsarist Empire.* She had been allowed a degree of autonomy but had yet to experience full independence. This came in December 1917 when 'the Council of People's Commissars in full accord with the principles of the right of nations to self determination' gave Finland the right to exist as an independent state, and on 4 January 1918 it was officially confirmed by the Soviet Government.†

There was at the time in Helsingfors (Helsinki), the capital, an unstable coalition government comprised of Social Democrats and anti-Socialist parties with strong pro-German elements. It had only been in existence since October 1917 and when, on 11 January, it became known

---

*Before 1809 it was part of an enlarged Sweden.
†See Chapter 8, p. 109.

that a massive order for arms had been placed in Germany by certain right-wing members of the Government, the coalition broke apart. The effect of the disclosure was to set into motion a chain of events which were to have the most tragic consequence for the Finnish people.

It began with an attack by the White Guards, an élite military corps recruited from the middle and upper classes, upon the headquarters of both the Socialists and the Trade Unions. This provocative action was immediately counter-ed by thousands of Finnish people who came out into the streets and demonstrated in support of their political and Trade Union leaders. The country rapidly moved into a state of civil war. The White Guards were 'reinforced by Finnish officers from the disbanded Russian Imperial Army and, later, by the Jaeger Battalion* from Germany.'[2] A climax was reached on 22 January when the coalition Government was overthrown. The pro-German members fled from the capital, some to Germany, while others moved into the north-western region of the country where Finland's ruling class and their White Guards were predominant.

A new Government formed by the Executive of the Social Democratic Party immediately embarked upon programmes for economic and social change. Many acres of agricultural land were handed over to the peasants; the old traditional links between Church and State were severed, and new laws governing the conditions of employment were introduced. The old feudal structure was at last being demolished. An agreement was reached with the Soviet Government over the difficult task of clarifying the frontier between their two countries, and as part of the agreement the Soviets transferred to Finland the Arctic port of Petsamo and its outlying districts (which had been within the Tsarist Empire) because, according to Molotov some years later, Russia 'considered it necessary to let Finland have an ice-free ocean port.'†

After the Russian Revolution the British and French Governments looked to Finland to provide an important

---

*Was formed 1915–1916 when 'about 2,000 young Finns were sent for secret training in Germany.' (Wendy Hall, p. 105)
†From Molotov's statement to the Supreme Soviet, 29 March 1940.

507

link in the chain of countries which were to form the 'Cordon Sanitaire', for they knew that the Finnish ruling class, as in other European countries, were desperately keen to prevent the Bolshevik 'disease' getting a grip upon their peasantry and working class.

A leading advocate of the 'Cordon Sanitaire' was the well-known Finnish aristocrat, Baron Gustave Emil von Mannerheim. He had been so enamoured by life under the Tsar that most of his early and middle years were spent in the service of the Royal Household, and then later as a Tsarist general. It was not until the collapse of the Tsarist Empire and the demise of the Kerensky Government that Mannerheim hastened back to Finland to play his part in the preservation of the power and authority of Finland's middle and upper classes. Having collaborated with the colonizers of his country he now saw himself as the country's saviour from Bolshevism.

With the return of Mannerheim to lead the Finnish White Guard and with the support of 30,000 German troops under General von der Goltz, preparations were made for a coup d'état. The manner in which this coup was planned was not unlike that in Spain in 1936. Mannerheim was the Finnish 'Franco' dependent upon foreign troops to overthrow a government that represented the majority of the Finnish people. He and his entourage established their base at Vaasa, a small sea-port on the Gulf of Bothnia some 230 miles north-west of Helsinki, where they formed a rival Government. The German army meanwhile had taken over the Aaland Islands which they used as a staging post for their landing on the south-west corner of Finland from where they captured the naval base at Hango and then seized Helsinki.

As in the case of Franco, Mannerheim who had been out in the wings at Vaasa, awaiting the call, was eventually able to ride 'victoriously' into the capital alongside his benefactors. In recognition of his contribution to the fight against Bolshevism he was decorated by the Kaiser with the Iron Cross.

The Finnish civil war between the White Guards and the Red Guards, the people's militia, was brought to an end and, as in Spain, thousands were held in detention camps

508

and many were executed on trumped up charges of being traitors. Out of about 80,000 taken prisoner, 30,000 were either killed or died from ill treatment.

The old Parliament was dissolved and the ninety one Social Democrat members were excluded from the new Diet – no more than a rump body 'dominated by the pro-German element, which . . . favoured the organization of the army on German lines and with some German direction.'[3]

D.N. Pritt, K.C., who was a leading authority on international law and a British Member of Parliament, states in his book, *Must the War Spread*, – 'Though Finland was technically neutral, she was compelled to allow Germany the use of Petsamo as a submarine base from which to attack British and neutral Scandinavian shipping. It is worth noting', he adds, 'that in July 1918, in the British House of Commons the Government acknowledged that the Finns were doing this and admitted that the Soviet Government who had ceded territory originally to the Socialist Government had protested strongly.'[4]

During the Wars of Intervention there were many Finnish White Guards who regarded the whole of Karelia as their territory and collaborated with the anti-Bolshevik counter-revolutionary forces in that area.

'Amongst the students and amongst the White Guard there was founded at this time a Greater Finland Movement, the Academic Karelia Society, which believed that the borders of Finland ought to be extended in this direction and worked for the day when it should be possible.'[5]

Meanwhile Mannerheim, after a brief period as Regent, returned to his country estate from where he sent 'an open letter to President Stahlberg urging him to launch war on the Soviet Union, seize St Petersburg and set up a more moderate Russian Government.'[6] Although his proposal was rejected, Helsinki, nevertheless, was being used by the 'White' Russian General Yudenitch to prepare an army for the first of his attempts on Petrograd. A British naval squadron had been standing by in the Gulf of Finland ready to help and Churchill had, on 13 June 1919, called upon the Finish Government to provide further assistance.

Retirement obviously did not suit the restless Mannerheim, and in October 1919 he was in London. He had already made contacts with British army chiefs, and on 12 January 1920, *The Times* reported from its correspondent in Stockholm

> ' . . . it is expected that General Mannerheim will be designated as Commander-in-Chief of the United Forces of the Baltic States and Finland to assume the offensive against Bolshevism. General Mannerheim, who is expected back in Finland from Paris, has, it is added, obtained a promise of both military and financial assistance in organizing the contemplated offensive against the Bolsheviks on a front which is eventually to extend from Murmansk to the Black Sea.'

This grandiose plan did not materialize. Instead there was the Polish invasion of the Ukraine on 26 April and the abortive Wrangel offensive in the Crimea in October, both of which failed in their objective.

In 1924 General Sir Walter Kirke, who later became Commander-in-Chief of Britain's Home Forces, led a Military Mission to Finland, and under his direction there began the construction of the Mannerheim Line, a series of military forts similar to those of the Maginot and Siegfried Lines, and built across the Karelian Isthmus to a depth of thirty to thirty five miles.

During the 1920s, about the time of the rise of the German Nazi Party, a parallel movement was developing in Finland. Known as the Lappos, this Finnish Fascist organization was created out of the White Guards and the German trained Jaeger Battalion, which provided the backbone of the Finnish General Staff. The Lappos operated in the same way as the German Nazis by campaigns of terror and intimidation. They gained their name and notoriety after the destruction of the Socialist headquarters at Lapua. They broke into the Helsinki Parliament buildings, attacked Opposition MPs and demanded special powers. The pro-German Peter Evind Svinhufvud, when he became President in 1931, was only too pleased to grant them. Left wing Socialist and Trade Union leaders were

510

dismissed from their posts, the Left wing press was banned and the Left Socialist parties and the Communist Party were dissolved. A reconstructed Right wing Social Democratic Party was allowed to exist and its leader Vaino Tanner was to become the Ebert* of Finland. It was also in 1931 that Mannerheim returned to public life as Chairman of the Finnish Council for Defence. The Army Chief of Staff was General Wallenius, an open supporter of the Lappos, who had been involved in the kidnapping of former President Stahlberg and his wife.

From then until the end of the 1930s Finland's political life was dominated by pro-German Right wing Governments which needed no lessons in the art of suppressing Trade Unions and political opponents. In October 1933 there was a secret meeting between a representative of the Finnish Protective Guards (successor to the White Guards), leaders of Sweden's Nazi Movement and Hermann Goering at Castle Rockelsta, the home of Count von Rosen, Goering's brother-in-law.

Three years later, Mannerheim was on an official visit to London as the guest of the British Government.

'He was taken to Salisbury Plain to see British tank manoeuvres, was conducted over Woolwich Arsenal and went for a tour of the various Vickers-Armstrong works, finally ending up with a visit to the Bristol Aircraft Company's factory.

He was at the same time officially entertained to dinner by the British Government at Lancaster House, The guests included the Chief of the Imperial General Staff, the Permanent Under-Secretary of State for War, the Secretary of the Army Council, the Director-General of the Territorial Army, the Director of Military Operations and Intelligence, the Chief of the Air Staff, the Director of Operations and Intelligence at the Air Ministry, the Permanent Secretary of the Air Ministry and various other officers. The munitions industry was represented by Sir Charles

---

*See Chapter 6, pp. 94–95

511

Craven of Vickers-Armstrong, with colleagues from the Birmingham Small Arms Company and the Bristol Aircraft Company. A third group of guests was composed of Foreign office officials who included . . . Mr Gordon Vereker'* who, as Pritt points out, was 'Counsellor at the British Embassy in Moscow during the Anglo-Soviet negotiations of 1939. Also present were Mr Duff Cooper, then Secretary of State for War, and Lord Plymouth, at that time Chairman of the Non-Intervention Committee and now [January 1940] Chairman of an "Aid-Finland" organization.' The Federation of British Industries was represented by Sir George MacDonogh 'who combines the offices of President of the Anglo-Finnish Society and of Vice-president of the Japan Society.' And there was also 'General Burt, who had retired from the army in 1920; in 1918 and 1919 he had been Chief of the British Military Mission acting against the Soviet Union in Latvia and Lithuania.'[7]

On the occasion of this visit Mannerheim was created a Knight Grand Cross of the British Empire.

And while the Spanish Republican Government was being denied arms under the 'Non-Intervention' Agreement, licences were being granted for the sale of British Blenheim bombers to Finland.

It was in 1938 and in 1939, when public attention was focussed upon the events in Spain, Czechoslovakia and Munich, that discreet negotiations were being conducted in London and Helsinki. In the summer of 1939, at a time when Lord Halifax was refusing the Soviet invitation to go to Moscow to negotiate a tripartite agreement, General Sir Walter Kirke was paying another visit to Finland, during the course of which he inspected the Mannerheim Line and visited Finnish air bases where he had the opportunity of seeing the recent delivery of Blenheim bombers. When the news of General Kirke's visit was disclosed six months

*He later became Britain's Minister in Finland.

later, the Government denied that he was on an official visit, or that he was there to advise the Finnish army. On the 14th December 1939 George Strauss, the Labour MP:

> 'asked the Secretary of State for War whether his attention has been drawn to the announcement by the Soviet foreign broadcast that General Sir Walter Kirke was in Finland in the first half of this year advising the Finnish army; and will he state the nature of the mission, and how long he was in Finland?
>
> Sir V. Warrender: General Sir Walter Kirke was in Finland from 18th June to 22nd June this year. His visit was purely of a private nature.' (*Hansard*, 14 December 1939, Col. 1275)

It was against this background, as well as Hitler's Lebensraum policy, that the Soviet Government, on 14 October 1939, proposed to the Finnish Government that in order to safeguard the security of Northern Russia and in particular 'the safety of Leningrad', it needed measures:

> '1. To make it possible to block the opening of the Gulf of Finland by means of artillery fire from both coasts . . . in order to prevent warships and transport ships of the enemy from penetrating the waters of the Gulf . . .
> 2. To make it possible to prevent the access of the enemy to those islands in the Gulf . . . which are situated west and north-west of the entrance to Leningrad;
> 3. To have the Finnish frontier on the Isthmus of Karelia . . . which frontier is now at a distance of thirty two kilometres from Leningrad – i.e. within the range of shots from a long-distance gun – moved somewhat further northwards and north-westwards.'

To achieve these ends the USSR asked the Finnish Government to cede 'in exchange for other territories, the islands of Suursaari, Seiskari, Lavansaari, Tytarsaari and Koivisto, part of the Isthmus of Karelia, from the village of Lippola to the southern border of the town of Koivisto and the western parts of the Kalastajassarento – in total 2,761 square kilometres . . . '

In exchange the USSR offered to cede to Finland the 'districts of Repola and Porajarvi to the extent of 5,529 square kilometres.'[8] This exchange, says Liddell-Hart, 'even according to the Finnish White Book, would have given Finland an additional 2,134 square miles in compensation for the cession to Russia of areas totalling 1,066 square miles.'[9]

The Soviet Government also proposed that the Port of Hango, which was in a strategic position at the south-easten corner of Finland and at the mouth of the Gulf, should be leased to them for a period of thirty years; the purpose of which was to create 'a naval base with coastal artillery capable of blocking by artillery fire, together with the naval base Baltiski,* access to the Gulf of Finland.'[10]

Far north, 'in the Petsamo region, where the frontier was badly and artificially drawn',† the Russians proposed an adjustment which, Liddell-Hart records, 'was apparently designed to safeguard the sea approach to Murmansk by preventing an enemy establishing himself on the Rybachi peninsular.' He has explained in his chapter on the Finnish war that 'an objective examination of these terms suggests that they were framed on a rational basis, to provide a greater security to Russian territory without serious detriment to the security of Finland. They would, clearly, have hindered the use of Finland as a jumping-off point for any German attack on Russia. But they would not have given Russia any appreciable advantage for an attack on Finland. Indeed, the territory which Russia offered to cede to Finland would have widened Finland's uncomfortably narrow waistline.[11]

The Finns agreed to some of the Soviet proposals, but the main ones which they turned down were the leasing of

*Baltiski was situated on the opposite coast in Estonia.

†Sir Basil Liddell-Hart describes this northern part of the frontier as 'a straight line running through the narrow isthmus of the Rybachi peninsular and cutting off the western end of that peninsular.'

Hango and the moving of the Karelian Isthmus frontier back to a distance where its guns would be out of reach of Leningrad.

The reason stated for not leasing the port of Hango was that it would be contrary to Finland's 'policy of strict neutrality'. However, the Russians had not forgotten that Hango had been captured by a German army in 1918.

D.N. Pritt, whose book was first published in January 1940, has effectively countered the false impression that the Russians and the Germans had become real allies as a result of the Non-Aggression Pact. The Soviet Government, he states, 'would know quite clearly that if Russia were involved in a war with Germany one of two things was bound to happen: either the Finnish army under Mannerheim would as they did in 1918, invite the German forces to enter Finland, or else the German forces, without waiting for the formality of invitation, would occupy Finland as a preliminary to an attack on Russia.'*[12]

Just a few days after the opening of negotiations *The Daily Mail*'s Special Correspondent predicted that:

> 'If President Kallio ... can obtain a definite assurance of military as well as moral and financial aid Finland may stand firm.' (*The Daily Mail*, 17 October 1939)

On 31 October the Soviet Foreign Minister, Molotov, reported to the Extraordinary Fifth Session of the Supreme Soviet the situation concerning the negotiations with the Finnish Government. In his report he explained:

> 'With a Soviet naval base at the southern entrance to the Gulf of Finland, namely at Baltiski Port, as provided for by the Soviet-Estonian pact of Mutual Assistance, the establishment of a naval base at the northern entrance to the Gulf of Finland would completely guarantee the Gulf of Finland against hostile attempts on the part of other States. We have no doubt that the establish-

---

*Which is exactly what happened eighteen months later.

515

ment of such a base would be in the interests not only of the Soviet Union but also of the security of Finland herself.'

and expressed the hope

'that Finnish public men will not yield to anti-Soviet pressure, or to incitement from any quarter.'[13]

With Mannerheim back in Supreme Command of the Finnish Army, the Soviet Government was naturally concerned that Finland might allow foreign troops once again to use her territory as a spring-board to invade northern Russia. By 13 November the negotiations had become deadlocked.

On 26 November the Soviet Government, according to its own records, received a report from Red Army headquarters that four of its soldiers had been killed and nine wounded that afternoon 'in the vicinity of Mainila' by 'artillery fire from Finnish territory.' In a strongly worded note of protest to the Finnish Government Molotov stressed 'the fact that during the recent negotiations with M. Tanner and M. Paasaviki,* it had directed their attention to the danger arising from the concentration of large regular forces in the immediate proximity of the frontier near Leningrad.' In view of this warning and of what had just happened, he proposed that 'the Finnish Government should, without delay, withdraw its troops on the Karelian Isthmus from the frontier to a distance of twenty to twenty five kilometres.'[14]

The Finnish Government replied the following day denying that its troops had fired on the Soviet troops and 'that a check from three observation posts had shown the shots were fired from the south-east on the Soviet side of the frontier. Perhaps there had been an accident during Soviet artillery practice? However, Finland was ready to join Russia in a joint investigation of the matter and to

---

*M. Tanner was Foreign Minister and M. Paasaviki was a former Prime Minister

discuss a mutual withdrawal of troops from the border.'[15]

On 28 November Molotov rejected the Finnish proposal for a mutual withdrawal pointing out that 'there can, indeed be no question of equality in the situation of the Finnish and Soviet troops. The Soviet troops do not constitute a menace to Finland's vital centres, as these troops are posted hundreds of kilometres away from those places, whereas the Finnish troops, stationed at a distance of thirty-two kilometres from Leningrad – a vital centre of the USSR, with a population of three and a half millions – menace that town directly. It is needless to stress the fact that actually the Soviet troops cannot be withdrawn anywhere, since their withdrawal to a distance of twenty to twenty-five kilometres from the frontier would mean that they would have to be posted in the suburbs of Leningrad, which would be absurd from the point of view of the safety of the city . . . ' That day the Soviet Government denounced the 1932 Russo-Finnish Non-Aggression Pact. The ultimate rupture came on 29 November when the USSR recalled 'its political and economic representatives from Finland,' after reporting the continuation of 'attacks on the Soviet troops . . . not only on the Karelian Isthmus but also in other parts of the frontier between the USSR and Finland,'[16] and on the 30th launched an attack on the Finnish lines.

'When the Winter War came', comments Douglas Clark in his book, *Three Days to Catastrophe*, 'it was widely held in the West to prove that in terms of political cynicism and territorial appetite there was little to choose between Communist Russia and Nazi Germany. But, of course, the story of these negotiations and of the Winter War itself proves the contrary. Whereas Hitler's negotiating technique was to demand more and more, Stalin and Molotov bargained seriously for a compromise. Twice they modfied their proposals; and their patience was less easily exhaustible than Hitler's. They were ready to spend time and effort in finding a peaceful solution. Fifty-two days elapsed between their first diplomatic approach to Helsinki and the Mainila incident.

'Nor, as events were to show, did the Russians want more than they asked for.'[17]

On 3 December the Finnish Government officially appealed to the League of nations 'to summon the General Assembly on account of Soviet aggression.' Having lain dormant during the invasions of China, Abyssinia, Spain, Austria, Czechoslovakia, Albania and Poland, the moribund League suddenly sprang into life.

A Finnish writer, Jukka Nevakivi, in a book published in 1976, has described the manner in which preparations were made behind the scenes by certain politicians and officials in Paris, London, Geneva, Washington and Helsinki to exploit the Soviet-Finnish dispute for their own ends long before it resulted in a war.

Within a few days of the opening of the Soviet-Finnish negotiations Lord Halifax in a letter to Lord Chatfield, Minister for Defence Co-ordination, demanded 'the immediate delivery of the artillery tractors recently ordered by the Finns.' He told his Cabinet colleague on 17 October –

'You will know all the political and strategic reasons that make it urgently desirable for us to do what we can to strengthen the position of Finland at this time.'

Apparently, 'Gripenberg [Finland's Minister in London] . . . embarrassed Butler by telling him frankly that the Finns considered the growing Russian strength the greatest danger to Europe, and expressing a wish that Britain would take a more uncompromising stand against Russia.'[18]

The day before the outbreak of the Russo-Finnish war, 29 November, the Secretary-General of the League of Nations, Joseph Avenol, was in Paris 'on a private visit.' That day Finland's Minister in Paris, Harri Holma, reported that 'he had met the United States Ambassador, William C. Bullitt, who since the summer had been warning him of the dangers threatening Finland. The Abassador had on the same day lunched with the Secretary-General . . . and he now told Holma that it would be advisable for Finland to submit the conflict to the League immediately.'[19]

Avenol and Bullitt were both keen to put the Soviet Union in the 'dock'. According to Jukka Nevakivi, 'the

Finnish representative to the League, Rudolf Holsti,* had in fact mentioned as early as October that the Secretariat was interested in the matter.' Nevakivi goes on to say 'the Secretary-General tried to exploit the Soviet aggression against Finland and the sentiments which is aroused to activate the League of nations.' Bullitt, who had been behind Lindbergh in 1938 propagating the invincibility of the Nazi war machine, and, 'himself well-known for his aversion towards the Soviet Union, was inspired after realizing that the Secretary-General had a tangible aim in deliberating the Finnish question . . . As the crisis on the following day was developing into an armed conflict, the Ambassador had reiterated his point of view to the Finnish Minister and promised to prepare the ground by influencing Premier Daladier, both directly and through the White House.'[20]

On the morning of 1 December, Avenol, who had just returned to Geneva, discussed the Soviet-Finnish conflict with Holsti and told him that in his opinion 'the majority of the member states would support Finland', adding that 'although the League might not be able to give material help to Finland . . . the universal importance of its support was not to be underestimated.'[21] He may have had good reason to feel confident, but there were many countries, including Finland's closest neighbours, the Scandinavian countries, who were perturbed by Finland's decision to approach the League before being consulted. On '11th December the French Minister to Copenhagen was told by M. Munch, the Danish Foreign Minister, that Finland had not consulted Denmark, Norway and Sweden . . . and that they all opposed the move.'[22]

Soon after the Finnish Government presented its appeal, the League's Executive Committee (i.e. the Council) met to discuss the matter and to prepare their recommendations to the General Assembly. Britain, France and Russia were

---

*Holsti had proposed, 18 October 1939, that Finland should appeal to the League. He was Finland's Foreign Minister 1937–38. In 1937 there was a visit from a German U-boat Squadron to Finnish waters. Two months later 'Holsti's trip to Berlin raised yet again in the Soviet press the spectre of White Finland sliding into the Nazi camp.' (See *Finland In The 20th Century*, by D. G. Kirby, p. 117)

permanent members of the Council, but from the outset the Soviet Government had made it clear that it would not participate in the League's deliberations on the Finnish affair. *The Manchester Guardian* (11 December) pointed to the dilemma of the League's hard-liners that:

> 'a unanimous vote would be required to exclude Russia from the League. It is not thought in League quarters that this would be possible with the present membership of the Council.'

Consequently the next step was to get rid of the old Council.

'Some recommendations' explains Pritt, 'had to be made to the Assembly by the Council, i.e. by the old Council' but, he adds, 'This final difficulty was avoided by the Council handing over the consideration of the dispute to a special Committee – called the "Committee of Fourteen" – created for that particular purpose.' It could be argued that the Soviet Union should have gone to Geneva to present its case, but it obviously had no confidence in the Committee's ability or desire to examine the matter in an impartial manner, when only four of the 'Committee of Fourteen' held 'normal diplomatic relations with the Soviet Union.'[23]

In spite of the unanimity ruling, only seven of the fourteen recommended to the Assembly full implementation of Article 16 of the Covenant which stated: 'any member of the League which has violated any covenant of the League may be declared to be no longer a member of the League by a vote of the Council concurred in by the representatives of all the other members of the League represented thereon.' Article 16 also made it obligatory upon League members to immediately sever all trade, financial and personal connections, with a proviso that if the Council proposed participation in military counter-measures, then in such circumstances the passage of military personnel and equipment of the other member states should be allowed. Ironically Poland, which had not appealed to the League over the German invasion of her territory, was represented in Geneva by a delegate from an émigré Government based in Paris. He was one of the leading advocates for the full implementation of Article 16.

As to be expected, 'the expulsion of the Soviet Union, an

obsession of Avenol, was finally realized'[24] but, according to Vernon Bartlett in the *News Chronicle* on 15 December, 'the League members are not unanimously happy.' In fact, most European countries, and they included the Scandinavian, Baltic and Balkan States, as well as Holland, Switzerland and Hungary either abstained or were absent. Neither Afghanistan or Iran voted. It was left to the delegate from Mexico to remind the Assembly that 'the League existed rather to settle disputes on the basis of right and law than to provide the screen behind which political interests could take shelter.'

The press, meanwhile, had relegated the war against Germany to the back pages. All eyes were to be focussed on little Finland fighting the Goliath. A 'Switch the War' campaign was being organized. 'Major Kermit Roosevelt [a cousin of the American President] who had offered his services to the British Army on the outbreak of war, was relieved of his duties and promoted to Colonel in Command of a British volunteer brigade to fight against the Russians. Lady Astor tried to enlist American war correspondents as recruiting agents, and a British officer told Drew Middleton of the Associated Press: "We'll all be marching against the Russians in the Spring".'[25]

Arms and aircraft earmarked for use against the Germans were sent instead to Finland.

'In France', says Shirer, 'the war against Germany was for the moment forgotten and Stalin replaced Hitler as the great enemy ... Pressure mounted quickly in the press and Parliament for France, which had done so little to help Poland, to come to the aid of Finland. Shipment of arms to the beleaguered country began on 13 December. And on the 19th, at a meeting of the Allied Supreme Council, Britain and France agreed to step up the despatch of war material to Finland.'[26]

General Sikorsky who had escaped from Poland with three destroyers and two submarines offered them to the Allies for use against the Russians in the Arctic Ocean around Petsamo and Murmansk.

Francois Fonveille-Alquier describes in his book, *The French and the Phoney War 1939–40*, how the French planned to switch the war. Thirty fighter planes had already been

521

taken from combat service and sent to Finland. He refers to a meeting between Captain Paul Stehlin who 'had just been transferred to fighters', and the principal private secretary of Guy La Chambre, Minister for Air. 'The Minister told him that the Government had decided that France, together with England, would come to the aid of Finland with all the three Services participating, particularly the Air Force. General Gamelin had been told to send a military mission to Marshal Mannerheim and to make preparations for allied intervention.'

Stehlin, having been told that he was to represent the Air Force, went to see his chief, General Vuillemin, who appeared to lack enthusiasm for the Finnish plan.

'It was from General Bergeret, his assistant and a future Minister of Pétain, that the Captain was to learn the real nature of his mission. Bergeret led him with a great deal of mystery in front of a map hidden behind a curtain bearing in big letters the word 'SECRET'. Stehlin could see on it two huge arrows, coming together in the neighbourhood of Moscow, one starting from Finland, the other from Syria. It was the famous pincer movement which was to have crossed the European Isthmus from the Baltic to the Black Sea.' Bergeret explained to his visitor:

> '"Henceforth Russia is the associate of Germany
> . . . It is then by striking at the Soviet Union that
> we shall deprive Hitler's Germany of the re-
> sources that she needs, and at the same time keep
> the war away from our frontiers. General
> Weygand commands the armed forces in Syria
> and the Lebanon and he will proceed in the
> general direction of Baku in order to stop petrol
> production; from there, Weygand's troops will
> veer northwards to meet the armies which set out
> from Scandinavia and Finland on their way to
> Moscow".'[27]

Phillip Jordan,* who for many years in the 1930s had been Foreign Correspondent for the *News Chronicle* and then

---

*He was Atlee's Public Relations Officer from 1947 until he died in June 1951.

later its Foreign Editor, has confirmed Fonveille-Alquier's report of the proposed Allied attack upon the USSR. In his book, *Russian Glory*, he gives a vivid account of his visit to Weygand's Headquarters in Syria during the early months of 1940.

'They were at war with Germany, with the most formidable fighting machine that the world had yet known; and yet they were pre-occupied with and consumed by a desire to destroy the Soviet Union and to deal with Hitler later, and at their leisure.

Of such criminal folly I had evidence in the early months of 1940 when I visited Syria at the invitation of General Weygand to inspect and see for myself something of the French war effort in that country.

There can be no harm in saying now that the old gentleman was infinitely more concerned with the hope of an attack by the Allies on Russia then he was concerned with the necessity of beating the Germans . . .

The first and largest maps I saw in his head-quarters were not maps of Turkey, and how to go to its aid; were not maps that might the quicker have enabled the French in Syria to damage the actual enemies' influence in that part of the world; but were maps showing how best and most easily British and French troops could move up to the Armenian plateau and attack the oil wells of Baku.

He had sent French airplanes to take aerial photographs of both Baku and Batoum, and he would show these photographs with the same sort of excited pleasure that a ruined debauchee will exhibit indecent photographs to the curious.'[28]

This was the same Weygand who had been sent by the French Government in 1920 to help the Poles plan their invasion of the Ukraine.

At last the golden opportunity had arisen for the Allies to carry on where they had left off twenty years ago; 'the old delusion of 1918–1920 that one combined push, one last intervention could topple the Bolsheviks from power – again started to affect the Allied leaders.'[29]

Lord Plymouth, the former Chairman of the 'Non-Intervention' Committee, was appointed President of the Finland Fund. Sir Walter Citrine, General Secretary of the TUC, who had in 1936 been praised by Sir Samuel Hoare for his 'patriotic responsibility' in supporting the Government's denial of help to the Spanish Republican Government through its Non-Intervention policy, was now openly calling for all forms of assistance to the Finnish Government. On 7 December the TUC General Council called 'upon the free nations of the world to give every practicable aid to the Finnish nation in its struggle.' Quite a contrast to its declaration of 28 August 1936 when Spain was being attacked by the Germans and Italian armies and air force. Citrine led a delegation to Finland in January 1940 and on his return passed on Mannerheim's urgent request for aeroplanes, guns and men. He records in his Finnish Diary: 'On our return [8 February] I said publicly on behalf of the Delegation that the next six weeks or so might well be critical for Finland. We knew that would depend on factors largely outside the control of the Finnish Government. We tried to convey this to quarters where its significance would be properly understood.'[30]

It had undoubtedly been understood well in advance of his return, for on 5 February the Allied Supreme Council had decided to send 100,000 men to fight in the Finnish war.*

The plan was to be put into operation the following month and linked to the occupation of the Gallivare iron ore fields in northern Sweden, a few miles from the Finnish frontier. Gallivare provided most of Germany's iron ore requirements, and the movement of troops to Finland was to be interpreted as part of the war against Germany.

---

*'In February Sir Paul Dukes arrived in Finland to investigate possibility of British aid ... Dukes was among the few Englishmen who received an invitation to visit Mannerheim at the Finnish HQ.' (RODZIANKO, Paul, *Mannerheim*, pp. 209–210)

In 1923 he was accused by the Soviet Government of running an espionage organization in Russia, (see Chapter 16 p. 202)

Gallivare happened to be on the route to Petsamo and northern Finland.

To implement their decision the Allies needed the co-operation of the Norwegian and Swedish Governments, for the iron ore was transported across both countries to the Norwegian ports of Narvik and Lulea. When the proposition was put to them, both countries adamantly refused to allow their countries to be dragged into the war and were determined to maintain their neutrality. They knew that to permit their countries to be used as transit camps would provoke a German attack. Unfortunately for the Norwegians the Germans had anticipated the Allied moves by landing troops in Norway, as well as in Denmark.

Meanwhile the Finnish war, aggravated by an extremely severe winter, had taken a heavy toll of Russian and Finnish lives. During the early stages of the war the Finns had achieved some initial success, but as Sir Basil Liddell-Hart has explained, an 'effect of Finland's early successes was that it reinforced the general tendency to underrate the Soviet military strength.'[31]

On 1 February the Russians launched a massive frontal attack upon the 'impregnable' defensive positions. 'As the fortifications were pulverized, tanks and sledge-carried infantry advanced to occupy the ground, while the Soviet air force broke up attempted counter moves. After little more than a fortnight of this methodical process a breach was made through the whole depth of the Mannerheim Line . . . once a passage was forced, and their communications menaced, eventual collapse was certain.'[32]

While the Allied governments were contemplating violating Norwegian and Swedish neutrality, the Finnish Government decided that it had no alternative but to sue for peace, which it did on 6 March.

'In the radically changed circumstances, particularly after the disastrous collapse in the Summa sector of the Mannerheim Line on 12 February, the new Soviet terms were remarkably moderate.'[33]

On the evening of 12 March, the Peace Treaty between the Finnish and Soviet Governments was signed in Moscow. The Winter War was at an end.

The appeasers in London and Paris were stunned by the

news of the cessation of the Finnish War, for only the previous week (5 March) they had replied to the Finnish Government's request 'for men and material'. The reply, drafted by General Sir Edmund Ironside,* Chief of the Imperial General Staff, had 'disclosed the exact strength of the military forces which, in the cheerfully optimistic view of the Allies, would be coming to Finland's help in the coming weeks.'[34]

Sir Alexander Cadogan refers to the request in his diary when Gripenberg saw Lord Halifax and asked for: '(1) 50,000 men in Finland in March . . . (2) 100 bombers at once (3) promise that our force be employed anywhere in Finland and (4) assurance that we shall act in spite of Sweden.'[35]

Plans for intervention and for switching the main war had to be abandoned. Both Chamberlain and Daladier were accused by many of their supporters of doing too little and too late to help the Finns. The two Prime Ministers were clearly incensed that their Foreign Ministries had not been informed by the Finnish Government of its decision to come to terms with the Russians. Both felt aggrieved that they should be treated in this manner; Daladier in particular had 'personally telephoned Helsinki to try to hasten its formal request for armed intervention by the West.' Without even consulting his allies in London he had 'assured the Finns that France agreed to everything they asked for and was ready to brush aside any obstacles put up by Norway and Sweden.'[36] After a heated debate in the Chamber of Deputies Daladier resigned – 239 had supported him but 300 had abstained on a vote of confidence.

Chamberlain, meanwhile, had been addressing his critics in the House of Commons. 'Any suggestion that the Allies, this country and France, in any way failed in their obligation to do their utmost to assist Finland in her need', he indignantly declared, 'is one which cannot for one moment be maintained.' To convince the MPs of the veracity of his statement he read out a detailed list 'of the war material which before the war ended we had given or undertaken to give to the Finnish Government' –

---

*General Ironside, Commander in Chief of the British Intervention Forces in Archangel in 1919. (See Chapter 9, p 116)

	Promised	Sent
Aeroplanes	152	101
Guns of all kinds	223	114
Shells	297,200	185,000
Vickers Guns	100	All sent
Marine Mines	500	400
Hand Grenades	50,000	All sent
Aircraft bombs	20,700	15,700
Signalling Equipment	1,300	800
Anti-tank rifles	200	All sent
Respirators	60,000	All sent
Great Coats	100,000	All sent
Battle dress suits	100,000	All sent
Anti-tank mines	20,000	10,000
Ambulances	48	All sent

(*Hansard*, 19 March 1940 Cols. 1834, 1836, 1837)

In order to reinforce his case Chamberlain revealed that the Allied Governments 'were prepared to send a fully equipped army of 100,000 men to assist the Finns and protect Sweden against a threatened German invasion. The expedition were ready to leave at the beginning of March. It would have arrived in Scandinavia during this month and April. The formal request for assistance, it was hoped, would have resulted in Norway and Sweden admitting the passage of our troops. It was never made . . . ' (*The Daily Telegraph*, 20 March 1940). What he failed to reveal was that passage had been refused by the Scandinavian countries and that he and his military chiefs were about to violate their neutrality.

On the same day, just prior to his resignation, Daladier told the French Deputies that his Government had despatched to Finland 145 aeroplanes, 496 guns, 5000 machine guns, 400,000 rifles, 200,000 hand grenades and 20,000 rounds of ammunition.

The campaign to switch the war away from Germany on to an anti-Soviet course was eventually to lead to the erosion of the very foundations upon which allied security depended. 'For Great Britain and France to provoke war with Soviet Russia when already at war with Germany seems the product of a madhouse.'[37]

527

Notes

1. CHURCHILL, Winston, *The Twilight War*, Book II *The Gathering Storm* Vol. I, *The Second World War*, p. 425
2. HALL, Wendy, *The Finns and Their Country*, p. 106
3. HALL, Wendy, *The Finns and Their Country*, p. 107
4. PRITT, D.N., *Must the War Spread*, p. 110
5. BACON, Walter, *Finland*, p. 136
6. CLARK, Douglas, *Three Days to Catastrophe*, p. 57
7. PRITT, D.N., *Must the War Spread*, p. 132
8. *Soviet Documents on Foreign Policy*, Vol. III, ed. Jane Degras, pp. 382–383
9. LIDDELL-HART, Sir Basil, *History of the Second World War*, p. 43
10. *Soviet Documents on Foreign Policy*, Vol. III, ed. Jane Degras, p. 383
11. LIDDELL-HART, Sir Basil, *History of the Second World War*, p. 43–44
12. PRITT, D.N., *Must the War Spread*, p. 211
13. *Soviet Documents on Foreign Policy*, Vol. III, ed. Jane Degras, pp. 396–397
14. *Soviet Documents on Foreign Policy*, Vol. III, ed. Jane Degras, p. 401
15. CLARK, Douglas, (ex *Mannerheim Memoirs*, p. 320), pp. 11–12
16. *Soviet Documents on Foreign Policy*, Vol. III, ed. Jane Degras, p. 402
17. CLARK, Douglas, *Three Days to Catastrophe*, p. 28
18. NEVAKIVI, Jukka, *The Appeal That Was Never Made*, (F.O. 371/23692/510), p. 32
19. NEVAKIVI, Jukka, *The Appeal That Was Never Made*, (F.O. 371/23692/510), p. 53
20. NEVAKIVI, Jukka, *The Appeal That Was Never Made*, (F.O. 371/23692/510), p. 53–54
21. NEVAKIVI, Jukka, *The Appeal That Was Never Made*, (F.O. 371/23692/510), p. 54
22. CLARK, Douglas, *Three Days to Catastrophe*, p. 50
23. PRITT, D.N., *Must the War Spread*, pp. 223–224
24. NEVAKIVI, Jukka, *The Appeal That Was Never Made*, (F.O. 371/23692/510), p. 56
25. KNIGHTLEY, Phillip, *The First Casualty*, p. 226
26. SHIRER, William, *The Collapse of the Third Republic*, p. 516
27. FONVEILLE-ALQUIER, Francois, *The French and the Phoney War 1939–40*, pp. 151–152
28. JORDAN, Phillip, *Russian Glory*, p. 21
29. KNIGHTLEY, Phillip, *The First Casualty*, p. 226
30. CITRINE, Sir Walter, *My Finnish Diary*, p. 190
31. LIDDELL-HART, Sir Basil, *History of the Second World War*, p. 45
32. LIDDELL-HART, Sir Basil, *History of the Second World War*, p. 46
33. LIDDELL-HART, Sir Basil, *History of the Second World War*, p. 46
34. CLARK, Douglas, *Three Days to Catastrophe*, p. 169
35. *Sir Alexander Cadogan, The Diaries of* (ed. David Dilks), p. 257
36. CLARK, Douglas, *Three Days to Catastrophe*, p. 162
37. TAYLOR, A.J.P., *English History 1914–1945*, FN pp. 571–572

36

SHATTERED DREAMS

Soon after the ending of the Finnish War thirty six French Communist Deputies were brought to trial 'for having between 27 September and 5 October 1939 taken part in the formation and functions of a group of workers and peasants and promoting action and propaganda directly, and indirectly, on the instructions of the 3rd International.'* It was held in camera and conducted by a military tribunal.

Since the signing of the Nazi-Soviet Pact the Communist Party and their papers, *L'Humanité* and *Ce Soir*, were banned. Throughout the winter months, and particularly during the Soviet-Finnish war, a campaign had been conducted through the press and radio against leaders of anti-fascist movements, describing them as 'Muscovite' traitors and accomplices of Hitler. On 19 March 1940, Sarraut, the Minister of the Interior, announced that 2,778 electors had been deprived of their voting rights, 11,000 were under investigation, 3,400 militants were arrested, of whom 1,500 were either detained in concentration camps (where they were to join Spanish Republicans and anti-fascist Germans and Italians) or transferred into 'special labour camps for military undesirables.'[1]

When the trial of the Deputies opened the defending Counsel demanded the appearance of Daladier and Bonnet as witnesses. The application was rejected. The reason given was that Cabinet Ministers were not permitted to either appear or give evidence in legal actions. However, since the opening of the trial the Daladier Government had collapsed and Daladier had been replaced by Reynaud,

---

*From *Le Telegramme*, a northern regional newspaper, 5 April 1940.

although retaining the post of Minister of War, but Bonnet was no longer a Minister. Consequently on 3 April another application was made for Bonnet to appear in court. The Defence were particularly anxious for him to attend as he had been Minister of Justice in the previous administration and there were now no legal grounds for non-attendance, but this did not deter Bonnet who sent a certificate to the court which stated that he would be unable to attend owing to ill health, and it was readily accepted. Under normal circumstances the court would have adjourned until the witness had recovered and declared fit to attend.

Two days later the Deputies were given the maximum sentence of five years in prison and were deprived of their political and civil rights.* On 9 April the recently appointed Minister of Justice, Serol, signed a decree which provided for the death sentence of Communists accused of treason. Having declared the country to be in a State of War, the Government was able to issue emergency decrees without consulting the French Chamber.

The Allies, meanwhile, by not taking up the Soviet offer of a tripartite agreement had played right into Hitler's hands. Once Poland had been destroyed he was able to boast, on 23 November 1939:

> 'For the first time in history we have to fight on only one front. The other front is at present free. But no one can know how long it will remain so.'

and, he significantly added:

> 'We can oppose Russia only when we are free in the West.'[2]

On 8 April 1940 the 'Phoney War' came to an abrupt end. Hitler's troops, instead of continuing eastwards, turned towards the west. The dreams of the appeasers had been shattered. Norway was the first western country to be invaded, followed by Denmark the next day.

---

*The Deputies were eventually released in November 1942.

Norwegian waters had been mined and the Norwegian coast was being policed by British warships on Churchill's instructions. This was part of the plan to cut off Germany's supply of iron ore from Gallivare. But in spite of Britain's naval supremacy, and heavy German naval losses, the Germans struck first. With the aid of their Norwegian agent, Vidkun Quisling, leader of the fascist fifth column, the German army quickly gained control of the major Norwegian ports and then occupied key strategic positions in the country. British troops did not land in Norway until a week later. After bitter battles and heavy military losses, they were forced to withdraw.

Once again there was an inquest in Parliament on the conduct of the war. Although the Admiralty and Churchill in particular, who was First Lord of the Admiralty, were held responsible for the Norwegian debacle, the MPs' attack, supported by public opinion, was principally directed against Chamberlain.

During the course of the Parliamentary debate, held on 7–8 May, it was revealed that the Government had dispersed what was described by Chamberlain as the 'Anglo-Finnish Force' – 'The force which was designed for the assistance of Finland.' It had contained a specially trained battalion to operate on skis, in addition to others that were expected to fight under arctic or semi-arctic conditions. All had been dispersed, and in a tone of righteous indignation, the Prime Minister declared:

> 'It is as well not to forget that for the transport of the Anglo-Finnish forces a substantial amount of shipping was required and for a considerable time that shipping was kept standing idle until it should be required.' (*Hansard*, 7 May 1940 Cols. 1078, 1079)

Thus, shipping desperately needed during a period of losses resulting from German submarine attacks, had been laid up awaiting a call from Mannerheim which never came.

At that time the Government had a massive majority of around 240, but when the Labour Opposition pressed for a vote, a group of thirty five Conservative MPs which

531

included former Ministers Amery, Hore-Belisha and Duff Cooper, as well as Boothby, MacMillan, Nicolson, Admiral Sir Roger Keys and Brigadier-General Spears, joined the Labour and Liberal Opposition and voted against the Government, and there were many others who abstained. 281 voted for the Government with 200 against. One of the most critical and effective speeches came from the former Prime Minister, Lloyd George. He reminded the House that the Prime Minister had:

> 'appealed for sacrifice. The Nation is prepared for every sacrifice so long as it has leadership, so long as the Government show clearly what they are aiming at and so long as the nation is confident that those who are leading it are doing their best. I say solemnly that the Prime Minister should given an example of sacrifice, because there is nothing which can contribute more to victory in this war than that he should sacrifice the seals of office.'
> (*Hansard*, 8 May 1940, Col. 1283)

Chamberlain, in reply to his critics, lamely appealed for a closing of the ranks, but it was too late. By 9 May the number of Tory rebels, led by Leo Amery, had swollen to sixty and they laid down conditions that they would only support a National Government which included the Labour and Liberal leaders and did not have Chamberlain as Prime Minister. On the 10th, the architect of Munich was forced to resign and Churchill became Prime Minister.

In spite of a change at the helm Chamberlain, nevertheless, retained a senior position in the new Cabinet – Lord President of the Council – and some of his leading lieutenants still held high office. Halifax remained in charge of the Foreign Office, Sir Kingsley Wood, who had been Air Minister, became Chancellor of the Exchequer and Sir John Simon gained the highest legal ministerial position, that of Lord Chancellor. Clement Attlee and Arthur Greenwood, leader and deputy-leader of the Labour Party, were brought into the Cabinet. 'Of the thirty-six leading ministerial posts filled by 15 May, twenty one went to men who had held office under Chamberlain.'[3] Not until many months later – 22 December – was Lord Halifax* replaced at the Foreign Office by Anthony Eden.

Ironically, an announcement was made that the House of Commons would adjourn from 9 until 21 May, with the provision that it could be recalled by the Speaker if necessary. The next day, 10 May, the day of Churchill's accession to the premiership, the Germans launched a massive and simultaneous attack upon Holland, Belgium, Luxembourg and France.

The French Parliament, too, had decided to adjourn, from 26 April until 16 May, and on the 17th, the eighty-four year old Marshal Pétain, France's Ambassador in Spain, bade forewell to his friend General Franco and left Madrid to return to France. He had been invited to join the Government and on 19 May was appointed Vice-President of the National Council.

Henri Amouroux in his book, *Pétain Avant Vichy*, describes the reactions and ambitions of 'Pétain, the victor of Verdun'. Within five days of the German attack Pétain had reached the conclusion that the war against Germany was already lost† and that it was a major error for France to have entered the war in the first place. Whether it was nostalgia that determined the French Government to recall the old Marshal is difficult to say. Certainly Reynaud hoped that together with Weygand, regarded as 'Foch's right hand man' during World War I, they would have 'enough prestige to revive the morale of the army'.[4]

Having taken over the premiership from Daladier, Reynaud dismissed the ineffectual Gamelin and replaced him with Weygand; 'Wizard' Weygand, as some of the Right-wing press in Britain began to describe him. His appointment came just a few days after the Germans broke through the French lines at Sedan.

On the evening of 25 May, at a meeting of the War Committee, Weygand had raised the issue of the 'necessity of saving the French Army so that it could put down

---

*He was however placed in the most important post of Ambassador to the United States and his colleague, Sir Samuel Hoare became Ambassador to Franco Spain.

†He was reported to have said on 15 May 'La guerre peut-etre considerée somme perdue'. (Henri Amouroux, p. 229)

anarchy and revolution at home.' He was reported to have told the Committee '"We must conserve the means of keeping order in the country".' According to Shirer, Weygand 'seemed as much concerned with fighting the phantom of a red revolution in Paris, a revolution of which there was not the faintest sign, as with fighting the Germans. To preserve the army not so much to resist the enemy, which he now deemed hopeless, as to maintain law and order in the stricken country became an obsession with him.'[5]

General de Gaulle had apparently arrived at a similar conclusion. He has recalled in his memoirs:

'I went on June 8th to make contact with General Weygand at the Chateaux de Montry. I found the Commander-in-Chief calm and master of himself. But a few moments of conversation were enough to make me realise that he was resigned to defeat and resolved upon an armistice.'

And with an air of resignation Weygand had said:

'"Ah! If only I were sure the Germans would leave me the forces necessary for maintaining order . . .".'[6]

Within a few days of the Nazi blitzkreig upon the West the rot had set in, with Hitler's fifth column operating both within the Western armies and behind the lines. Rumours of a German attack had been circulating in Belgium since January 1940 and had created panic among some of its political leaders.

'Spaak, the Socialist Foreign Minister, had been responsible for leading Belgium down the blind alley of neutrality. Now, frantically, he was, like the King and his military adviser, demanding that the allies come to the aid of Belgium – if the Germans attacked.'[7]

On 14 May Cadogan reports in his diary that Reynaud sent a message to Churchill telling him that the Germans had 'broken through at Sedan and imploring air raid, which we can't give in great measure.'[8] The hundreds of military aircraft sent to Finland would undoubtedly have been invaluable at this critical stage of the war.* Later that day the Dutch army was instructed to lay down its arms, the Queen and her Cabinet having already left the Hague on the 13th aboard a British destroyer to seek exile in Britain. The following morning Holland capitulated. Two weeks later, after a series of fierce battles, Leopold the King of the Belgians, without consulting either Britain or France, surrendered his army to the German High Command. The capitulation was immediately repudiated by his own Cabinet, but it was too late, the deed had been done. Leopold's surrender was denounced by Reynaud in a broadcast on 28 May as an 'act without precedent in history'.

With Belgium and Holland isolated, the German army was now able to concentrate its forces upon France and within two days motorized Panzer divisions had driven through the Ardennes, having already by-passed the 'impregnable' Maginot Line. France was on the verge of collapse. On 27 May it was

'officially announced in Paris that fifteen French Generals had been relieved of their Command. They include generals in command of armies, as well as of Army Corps, and also several divisional Commanders and Chiefs of big Service Units.' (*Manchester Guardian*, 27 May 1940)

This drastic shake-up in the French army was ordered by Reynaud who, on 21 May announced that the German break-through had followed

'incredible mistakes which would be punished. The mistakes include the failure to destroy bridges over the Meuse, across which the German motorized troops were able to pass.' (*Manchester Guardian*, 27 May 1940)

---

*In December 1939 Labour MP, George Strauss, 'asked the Secretary of State for Air why the aeroplanes sent by British firms to Finland are not required by this country for the purposes of the present war?' The Minister avoided a direct reply. (see *Hansard*, 13 December 1939)

On the day of the Reynaud shake-up of the French army, changes were also being carried out in Britain's High Command, the most important of which was the retirement of General Sir Walter Kirke, Commander-in-Chief, Home Forces, whose place was taken by General Sir Edmund Ironside, Chief of Staff.

From 10 May until 17 June the French army and its Government had been subjected to the most humiliating defeat at the hands of an enemy ever experienced throughout the entire history of France. By 20 May the Germans were in Abbeville, at the mouth of the Somme, having split the Allied armies – Belgian, British and French – in the north, from the French armies in the south. When the Germans in their strike westwards reached Brittany, Rennes, the capital, was taken without a shot being fired in defence of the town, and 'the entire General Staff of the French tenth Army along with several hundred officers surrendered to a German corporal. At Clermont-Ferrand General de Laclos and all his officers and men waited until the Germans arrived and then surrendered.'[9] And in Cherbourg, 'thirty thousand French soldiers surrendered in a matter of hours.'[10]

France as a nation had disintegrated; riddled with fifth columnists, collaborators and corruption – political and financial, the defeatist politicians and generals were ready to hand over the country to the invaders. The French people, millions of whom had held such high hopes for the future of their country with the advent of the Popular Front Government in 1936, had become bitterly disillusioned. The results of appeasement, and in many cases open collaboration with the Fascist countries by political leaders, had now been exposed. A political cancer had eaten into the very fabric of French society. Millions of French workers and peasants had lost their homes, their families, their livelihood; they, together with their sons at the front, were the real victims of a war which could have been avoided. Shirer gives a heart-rending account of the 'plight of the refugees, utterly disorganized, eight million of them milling about on the highways and byeways below Paris, without shelter, begging to buy food and water or pillaging for it, desperate to survive, to keep out of the clutch of the onrushing Germans but with no definite place to go except in the general direction of the south, stopping only when the log-jams prevented further progress or when enemy planes machine-gunned them as they dived for the ditches to try to save their miserable lives.' It was, he adds, 'a terryfing reminder to the leaders of the Government and the High Command that the stricken French nation was falling apart.'[11]

With the capitulation of the Belgian army, the British Expeditionary Force was cut off from its allies in the south, and on Sunday, 26 May, 'Operation Dynamo' was put into operation. This was the signal for the evacuation of British and a section of the French forces in the north-eastern area to retreat towards the coast and board whatever vessels they could in a dash for the British mainland. 222 British naval vessels and over 600 other craft were employed in this massive operation, the news of which stirred the admiration of people all over the world. Throughout the following week – until 4 June – 338,000 troops, including 115,000 French were evacuated. During the early days of the evacuation there had been a heavy bombardment by German aircraft and long-range artillery upon evacuating ships with many casualities, and then, suddenly, the rapidly advancing German Armoured Corps was given instructions to halt. Basil Liddell-Hart in his description of 'the escape of the British Expeditionary Force in 1940' says that it 'was largely due to Hitler's personal intervention. After his tanks had overrun the north of France and cut the British Army from its base, Hitler held them up just as they were about to sweep into Dunkirk – which was the last remaining port of escape left open to the British. At that moment the bulk of the BEF was still many miles distant from the port. But Hitler kept his tanks halted for three days. His action preserved the British forces when nothing else could have saved them.'[12]

A number of writers and historians have written about the 'inexplicable order given by Hitler himself, on the advice of Rundstedt, to halt the Panzer divisions just as they were closing in on Dunkirk.'[13] Professor Alan Bullock refers to the fact that 'the possibility of such an evacuation might well have been denied to the British if Guderian's tanks had not been ordered to halt a few miles south of Dunkirk on 24 May.'[14] Hitler certainly still believed that he could come to terms with some of Britain's political leaders, if not with Churchill. He had been kept well informed by Goering's Swedish friend, Dahlerus, since August 1939 of the prospects of neutralizing Britain, once he had consolidated Germany's position in Western Europe, in preparation for the fulfilment of his main ambition, the occupation of Russia. Barry A. Leach, in his book, *German Strategy Against Russia, 1939–1941*, writes that Hitler 'clung to the hope that a serious set-back would "bring the British to their knees" and that they would then be ready to reach an agreement with Germany as he had always predicted.'[15]

On 4 June Churchill announced in the House of Commons that although the evacuation from Dunkirk was a 'miracle of deliverance' the British had suffered a 'colossal military disaster'. All their heavy military equipment had been left behind. '880 field guns, 310 guns of a larger calibre, about 500 anti-aircraft guns, 11,000 machine-guns, nearly 700 tanks and some 45,000 motor cars and lorries. These losses', writes Basil Collier in his book *Arms and the Men*, left the people of Britain 'with only enough modern equipment in the United Kingdom for about two divisions.'[16]

This latest disaster, together with the losses in Finland, were to denude British servicemen of essential military supplies in the months to come; whilst France had lost 'nearly all the army's motorized transport and armour and half of its modern artillery.'[17]

At midnight, 10 June, Allied foreign policy suffered a further humiliating rebuff when Italy, which had been consistently wooed by both the British Foreign Office and the Quai d'Orsay since the 1935 Stresa Conference, decided to throw in her weight behind her Axis* partner and declare war on both France and Britain. The next day, with the German armies converging on Paris, Reynaud, accompanied by de Gaulle, left the capital driving westwards through

---

*On 26 September Japan joined the Rome-Berlin Axis. The Soviet Government was told by Ribbentrop that the pact was 'directed against the American warmongers'. Although it was primarily to intimidate the United States which was beginning to move towards helping Britain, it was also directed towards the encirclement of the Soviet Union.

roads overflowing with refugees. It took them over three days to reach Bordeaux, which was to become the provisional home of a reconstructed Cabinet.

In an attempt to stiffen resistance Reynaud announced that France would fight on 'even if it was in one province only, even if it was in North Africa only'. In addition to retaining the post of Premier he took over that of Foreign Minister, with Paul Baudouin as his Under-Secretary and Yves Bouthillier, Minister of Finance (both regarded as defeatists), together with a newcomer to the Cabinet, Jean Prouvost, the millionaire proprietor of *Paris Soir*, *Paris Match* and other influential publications. The one and only encouraging newcomer was Charles de Gaulle who had commanded the 4th Armoured Division and had recently been promoted from Colonel to Brigadier-General. He was appointed Under-Secretary at the Ministry of Defence. The Vice-Premier was Camille Chautemps, a close associate of Laval.

Meanwhile, on 13 June, Paris was declared an 'open city', and town after town followed suit. With Pétain and Weygand preparing for the capitulation, Laval and Bonnet attacking those deputies and ministers who wanted to carry on the fight, Reynaud and his handful of 'fight on' colleagues were completely undermined, having already lost any semblance of control over the country. The spread of defeatism had been deliberately encouraged by many leading politicians and senior army officers.

'The Fifth Column in France had been whispering stories about a separate peace for a good long time' wrote the *Manchester Guardian*'s Paris Correspondent. He remembered 'how on the day Reynaud made his famous speech at the Senate announcing the fall of Arras and Amiens, it was hinted that President Lebrun was all in favour of a separate peace.' He was reported to have said that '"Once Paris is taken you'll hear a lot more about it".' The Correspondent, who had been an eye-witness to many of the events that led to the capitulation, was obviously not impressed by Reynaud's choice of Cabinet colleagues. He described Reynaud as a man:

'full of good intentions' who 'lacked great dyna-

mic vigour and failed to inspire the people . . .
Even with Mandel* as Minister of the Interior, he
continuously compromised. There were no spectacular arrests among the Fifth Columnists whose
names were on everybody's lips. What is worse,
Reynaud did not choose his own people well.
Astonishing influences began to assert themselves
in his "fight on" Cabinet. This Cabinet was not
perhaps as "fight on" as it was first believed to
be . . .

And there were some strange appointments in
the Cabinet itself. Defeatism, pro-Italianism, pro-
fascism. France-is-an-old decrepit nation tenden-
cies were all represented in the War Cabinet of M.
Reynaud . . .

Pétain, very much under Spanish influence,
expected Germany to offer France honourable
peace terms, believing that these could be discussed as between soldiers.

All these men . . . tipped the balance heavily
against Reynaud, Mandel, Marin and Dautry, who
are believed to have been the chief advocates of
resistance . . . ' (*Manchester Guardian*, 25 June 1940)

While Weygand and Pétain had been spreading the tale
of the 'enormous disproportion' between the French forces
and those of the enemy, General Colson, the Army's Chief-
of-Staff, had disclosed to General Spears on 26 May that
'despite the German superiority in numbers of divisions,
the French Army had demobilized three classes – 750,000
men – on the eve of the German offensive.'[18]

Apart from a few senior officers of the calibre of General
Georges, Commander-in-Chief of the North-Eastern forces,
most of France's military leaders had been affected by a
state of inertia induced during the period of 'phoney war',
or what General Andre Laffárgue has aptly described as 'a
"doctrine of minimum effort" on both the army and the
home fronts.'[19]

On 14 June 1940, Hitler's troops entered a deserted Paris.

---

*Mandel of Jewish origin, was arrested on 17 June 1940 and thrown into
prison and murdered on 21 June 1944 by Pétain's militia.

Not a shot had been fired in its defence.

'No attempt was made to destroy the great factories in the industrial belt, which provided most of the armaments. Thus the Renault works, which turned out tanks and trucks, and the Schneider-Creusot works, which turned out guns, were abandoned intact, and soon would be working for the Germans.'[20]

It was the day that Reynaud arrived in Bordeaux, and at the Cabinet meeting that night he was immediately put under pressure by the defeatists to call for an armistice. Two days later at 10 pm, 16 June, he eventually succumbed to their attacks and resigned. The President thereupon called upon Pétain to form a new Government.

Pétain must have confidently anticipated the outcome of the battle in the Reynaud Cabinet for, within record time, he had presented his list of Ministers to President Lebrun. 'There was a rush of defeatist politicians and defeated generals towards the Marshal's office', comments Shirer, as well as 'a loud clamour amongst some of them for important posts in a government resolved to surrender. Pierre Laval . . . was among the first.'[21] Just as Hitler in his early days had shielded behind the senile Hindenburg, so did Laval establish himself under the cloak of the eighty four year old Pétain.* Together with Chautemps, the Vice-Premier, he had been working behind the scenes to prevent the Cabinet moving to North Africa where it could carry on the fight.

The very nature of Pétain's Government was soon revealed by its ready acceptance of Hitler's terms. Pétain had already made an approach to Hitler through his friend, General Franco, who assured him that the Fuehrer would be 'generous', and announced over the radio on 17 June that he had called for a cease fire.

On 22 June, at 7 pm, in the forest of Compiègne, and in the very same wagon-lit which had been used in 1918, General Huntzinger, on behalf of the French Army and its

---

*In 1937 the German Ambassador to Franco had sent a note to Berlin that 'Laval was of the opinion that the salvation of France lay in a Pétain Government and that the Marshal was determined to assume this responsibility . . . He is in touch . . . with Pétain.' (From German Foreign Office papers captured after the war – ex Shirer p. 464).

Government, signed the Armistice Agreement. It could hardly be described as an agreement for it was none other than Hitler's ultimatum to surrender – his revenge for the French ultimatum of 1918 and for Germany's humiliation at Versailles. The 'generous' terms were disclosed to Weygand the night before. The whole of northern France which covered the Channel ports, the western coastal areas down to the Spanish frontier at Hendaye including La Rochelle and Bordeaux, and the inner region from Tours to St Nazaire; all were to be occupied by the invaders. France's Navy, Army and Air Force to be disarmed, and all military equipment to be surrendered. Within the terms was a clause which stated that all anti-nazi German refugees residing in France must be handed over to the occupying authorities. And under Article 20, the French prisoners of war, of whom there were around one and a half million, would remain Germany custody until the end of the war.

The Manchester Guardian's Paris Correspondent recalled that 'The pro-Fascist clique in France imagined their "jour de gloire" had arrived.' He described his journey out of Paris to Bordeaux and remembered 'the hundreds of men and women to whom I spoke on my way to Bordeaux; not one of them would have subscribed to the German Armistice terms.'

France's Third Republic was dead. Destroyed from within and without. Even its motto, Liberté, Egalité and Fraternité had been replaced by Pétain to become Travail, Famille et Patrie. Whose country? That he failed to define.

On 4 October the Pétain Government, now installed in the Spa town of Vichy, decided to emulate the Nazis. It issued a decree that all Jews of foreign origin were to be arrested and sent to concentration camps, and on 17 May 1941 it was announced in *Le Telegramme* that 5,000 Parisien Jews had already been despatched to the concentration camps.*

There have been many inquests on the fall of Paris. Had

---

*Between 1940 and 1944 there were 'mass deportations of persons for political and racial reasons' in transports 'each of which consisted of from 1500 to 2500 deportees'. In 1940 there were three transports; 1941 – 14; 1942 – 104; 1943 – 257 and 1944 – 326 transports. (From *Trial of the Major War Criminals*, Vol. I, p. 51, Nuremberg

the French capital become a second Madrid, with leaders to rally the people, as was the case in Spain, France might have survived. The *Reynolds News* Foreign Correspondent, 23 June 1940, portrays the French people as 'bewildered and betrayed' with 'no time to reform their ranks under the slogan "They Shall Not Pass".' He says that 'the leaders of France were determined Paris should not be a second Madrid. That would have meant a Workers' Government in France.' For behind the old Marshal Pétain 'were the sinister pro-Fascists, who had always looked to Fascism to protect their class interests – Bonnet who sold Czechoslovakia, Laval who betrayed Abyssinia, Flandin, Chiappe* and many others who had always shown their sympathy with the Axis powers. Pacifist elements in the Socialist ranks did not make the situation easier.'

And while the French Army was being destroyed by Hitler's Panzer divisions, the shock waves had at last aroused the pro-Churchill elements in the British Cabinet to try and salvage something out of the wreck of Anglo-French diplomacy.

Feelers were being extended to Moscow to test the possibilities of a rapprochement. It was suggested in Whitehall that Sir Stafford Cripps, a former member of the Labour Party Executive who had for some time campaigned for greater Anglo-Soviet co-operation, be sent to Russia to help improve, in the first instance, trade relations. *The London Evening Standard*, encouraged by its proprietor, Lord Beaverbrook, a close friend of Churchill, had been pushing this line for some months.

On 17 June an article, written by Michael Foot, appeared in the *Evening Standard* in which he stated:

'When the Russians made their pact with the Nazis, the *Evening Standard* refused to believe the glib host of diplomatic correspondents who assured the public that a military alliance had been signed between the two powers. One of these

*There was a report at the time that Chiappe was appointed by the Nazis to become 'the head of some kind of Security Council for the Paris area.' (*Manchester Guardian*, 25 June 1940)

diplomatic correspondents had seen the document with his own eyes.

Later when the Russians went to war to seize bases in the Baltic, the *Evening Standard* refused to join the clamour in which almost all the British press engaged. The true blues, the pale pinks, . . . the dull greys . . . all these schools argued (or caterwauled) for action against Russia. *The Evening Standard* refused to do so, and was vituperated for the refusal.

We can see now what monumental folly such action would have been. It would have spelt the irrevocable ruin of this country . . . our concern is still to extract from these events an understanding of Russia's policy. Whatever the methods employed, this is the core. Ever since Russia entered the League of Nations when Hitler was first trumpeting his hatred of Bolshevism from a seat of authority the root aim of Russia's rulers has been the same. To avoid single-handed combat with a major power. And of course, the most menacing power was always Nazi Germany . . . [Stalin] did not tell the Russians after the conclusion of his pact with the Nazis that he had brought the Russians peace in their time. He called for more vigorous peace measures.'

Thus, with the backing of the Beaverbrook Press, the ground was being prepared, even at this late stage, for Russian help to stop any further moves by the Nazi armies. And as most of the Foreign Office officials were not trusted in Moscow, the name of Cripps had been leaked to the press as a likely representative. Cripps was originally sent to Moscow in June 1940 as a special envoy, but the Soviet Government insisted, before entering into negotiations, that he should be empowered with the official British governmental status of Ambassador. After a few weeks delay this was agreed to by Churchill, and Cripps replaced Sir William Seeds as HM Ambassador to the USSR.

Despite overwhelming victories over the countries of Western Europe, Hitler still maintained reservations for extending his conquests into Britain. There had of course been no 'phoney' war at sea; Britain's navy, merchant vessels and fishermen had suffered many casualities during the eight months of 'sitzkrieg' in Western Europe. Under Churchill's guidance Britain had concentrated on blockading Germany and had inflicted considerable damage to her maritime force.

'It is one of the most extraordinary features of history', says Liddell-Hart, 'that Hitler and the German Supreme Command had made no plans or preparations to deal with Britain's opposition. Stranger still, nothing was done during the long interval, of nearly nine months, before the great German offensive in the West was launched in May 1940, nor were any plans made even after France was obviously crumbling and its collapse assured. It thus became very clear that Hitler was counting on the British Government's agreement to a compromise peace on the favourable terms he was disposed to grant, and that for all his high ambitions he had no wish to press the conflict with Britain to a decisive conclusion.'[22]

Having gained his lebensraum in the West, Hitler was determined to exploit to the full the economic and industrial resources of the newly occupied territories for the eventual attack upon Russia. But before committing the German Army to a time table for the invasion of the Soviet Union, Hitler decided to wait a few weeks to see whether he could come to terms with Britain. His hopes were dashed on 3 July when the British navy opened fire on the French fleet in Oran. He nevertheless waited a further two weeks, and on 19 told the Reichstag,

' . . . it almost causes me pain to think that I should have been selected by Fate to deal the final blow to the structure which these men have already set tottering . . . Mr Churchill ought perhaps, for once, to believe me when I prophesy that a great Empire will be destroyed – an Empire which it was never my intention to destroy or even to harm . . .

'In this hour, I feel it to be my duty before my own conscience to appeal once more to reason and common sense in Great Britain as much as elsewhere. I consider myself in a position to make this appeal since I am not the vanquished begging favours, but the victor speaking in the name of reason. I can see no reason why this war must go on.' (*The Times*, 20 July 1940)

His appeal was ignored by Churchill, who had already stirred the British people in a speech declaring that the Government was determined to defend Britain, the British Empire and its Commonwealth of Nations. In his anxiety to neutralize Britain before launching his attack on the Soviet Union, the Nazi leader decided to bomb Britain into submission. He was obviously reluctant to carry out 'Operation Sea Lion' (code name for the invasion of Britain) after confiding to Admiral Raeder that

'The invasion of Britain is an exceptionally daring undertaking, because even if the way is short this is not just a river crossing, but the crossing of a sea which is dominated by the enemy.'[23]

Hitler's policy had always been to ensure that there was no intervention from the countries of Western Europe before turning eastwards. Professor Alan Bullock points out that 'on 3 September 1940, when General Paulus took over the office of Quartermaster-General of the Army, he found a skeleton operational plan for the offensive already in existence and this was completed by the beginning of November. The plan was presented to Hitler by General Halder on 5 December, and Hitler then gave it his approval, stressing that the primary aim was to prevent the Russian armies withdrawing into the depths of the country and to destroy them in the first encounter.'[24]

It was during the late summer of 1940 that the German High Command began the movement of their troops towards the East.

Meanwhile in the attempt to subdue his rear, Hitler issued instructions for the aerial attack on Britain and on 12 October there was a directive from him stating that he had

' . . . decided that from now until the Spring, preparations for Sea Lion shall be continued solely for the purpose of maintaining poltical and military pressure on England.'[25]

In the summer of 1940 and throughout the autumn and winter of 1940–41 the Luftwaffe concentrated their attacks upon Britain's major cities and ports. London, Liverpool, Coventry, Birmingham, Cardiff, Swansea, Southampton, Plymouth and many other towns and cities were continually attacked until the spring of 1941. During the most critical phase of the Battle of Britain 'from July until the end of October the Germans had lost 1,733 aircraft . . . while the RAF lost 915 fighters.'[26] On one day alone, 15 September, 185 of Hitler's Luftwaffe were shot down. Without the command of the air and sea, Operation Sea Lion could not have gone ahead. And while German bombs were raining down upon the British people Hitler was still dangling the carrot in front of the British Foreign Office. Cadogan records in his diary, Tuesday 10 September 1940, that he had a 'long talk with H[alifax] and later Strang, about further "peace" offer through a certain [Dr Ludwig] Weissauer in Switzerland.' Hitler knew that his 'peace' initiatives had a certain attraction among the many Munichites who still held influential positions in the Foreign Office and in Churchill's Cabinet. But on this occasion Cadogan and Halifax were obliged to discuss the matter with Churchill now that he was Prime Minister. Cadogan comments that the question was 'not of what to reply, but how to reply.'[27] He says that the Prime Minister read to them his reply and that it was 'alright'. What was alright he doesn't say. Three months later Halifax was removed to Washington.

The Soviet Union was undoubtedly aware of the significance of Hitler's military successes. Their expenditure on defence was increased to almost a third of the total budget. Arms production was speeded up and around the middle of September reports were coming in 'that the Russian propaganda service had switched to a line of anti-German talk within the Red Army. This showed the Russians' suspicious reaction to the first increase of the German forces in the East, and their promptness to prepare their troops for a Russo-German conflict.'[28]

Hitler's plans for the invasion of Russia were gathering momentum. Following the Halder report of 5 December he received on 18 December Directive 21, otherwise known as 'Barbarossa', the code name for the invasion. The 'final text' received Hitler's approval on 3 February 1941. 'The military plan', says Liddell-Hart, 'was coupled with a large-scale economic "Plan Oldenburg" for the exploitation of the conquered Soviet territory. An economic staff was created entirely separate from the general staff.'[29]

On 17 March Hitler held a conference with his leading generals to discuss the implementation of operation 'Barbarossa' and emphasized that he was against 'Halder's concept of obtaining substantial help from the satellite states by stating that only German, and to a limited degree, Finnish forces could be relied on. In the plan for 'the far north two mountain divisions were to secure Petsamo and if possible take Murmansk. Further south, a German infantry division and an SS brigade and supporting formations were to drive for Kandalaksha and the Murmansk railway.'[30] The German High Command had for a long time regarded Leningrad as a much easier target to capture than Moscow.

Ever since the Wars of Intervention, Soviet leaders had cast anxious eyes upon the activities and attitudes of countries ranged along her extensive borders, many of whom had been part of the 'Cordon Sanitaire' of the 1920s. They knew that it was not only from Finland where the Germans would launch their invasion. The attack would come, of that they were convinced, what they were not so sure of was Hitler's time-table. In July 1940 the Soviet Union took back the former Russian territories of Bessarabia and North Bukovina which the Allies had presented to Roumania in 1918 – both border areas.

Operation 'Barbarossa' was very much in Hitler's mind when he invited the Roumanian Foreign Minister, Manoilescu, to Vienna on 29 August and forced him to accept the ceding of a very large slice of Transylvania to Hungary. Meanwhile, Jodl, Chief of the Wehrmacht Operations Staff, was instructed by Hitler to make thorough preparations for the occupation of the Roumanian oil districts immediately.

Five armoured and three motorized divisions were to be ready for action by 31 August, while at the same time 'parachute and airborne landing troops' were to be committed 'for the quick local protection of the most important parts of Roumania.'[31]

On 6 September 1940, King Carol abdicated and General Antonescu, leader of the 'Iron Guard', the Roumanian Nazi organization, became Prime Minister, but by the end of the month had turned the country into a dictatorship. From then onwards Roumania was to play a prominent part in the Nazi conspiracy and in the preparations for the attack upon the Soviet Union. In a document produced at the Trial of the Major War Criminals, Antonescu states:

'Hitler emphasized that Rumania should not remain out of this war, as in order to get back Bessarabia and northern Bukovina she had no other way but to fight on the side of Germany. He added to this that in return for our help in the war Roumania could occupy and administer other Soviet territories up to the Dnieper.'[32]

On 22 February 1941, Schulenberg, the German Ambassador to Moscow, announced that 680,000 German troops were now in Roumania, and on 1 March Bulgaria was forced to sign a pact with Germany which would allow German troops to travel through its territory. In fact she had no option because German troops soon began marching in, taking up positions along the Bulgarian border with Greece. Yugoslavia, surrounded by both Germany and Italy, and led by a reactionary Government under the Regent Prince Paul, accepted Hitler's ultimatum to join the tripartite pact of Axis satellite countries – Hungary, Roumania and Bulgaria – which had been signed in November 1940. This tie-up with the Axis powers created a furore among the Yugoslav people and on 27 March the Government was overthrown.

The Yugoslav revolt had apparently caused Hitler to revise his time-table for the invasion of Russia, for 'on 3 April 1941 orders were given delaying the "Case Barbarossa" for five weeks.'[33] And on 5 April, the Soviet Union, encouraged by the events in Yugoslavia, signed a non-aggression pact with the new Government. Hitler meanwhile had summoned his military chiefs to an emergency meeting. According to Shirer, it 'was so hastily called that Brauchitsch, Halder and Ribbentrop arrived late.' Working himself up into a terrible rage, Hitler told them that 'the Belgrade coup had endangered both Marita* and, even more, Barbarossa. He was therefore determined, "without waiting for possible declarations of loyalty of the new government, to destroy Yugoslavia militarily and as a nation. No diplomatic enquiries will be made and no ultimatums presented." Yugoslavia would be crushed with "unmerciful harshness". He ordered Goering then and there to "destroy Belgrade in attacks by waves", with bombers operating from Hungarian air bases.'[34]

During the first week of April 1941, rumours were circulating in Britain and in many other countries that the Germans were massing their forces very near the Soviet frontiers. There were also reports 'that the German Government were encouraging the formation and strengthening of Russian 'White' organizations in Germany . . . At the end of April, *Pravda* itself stated that 12,000 German troops fully equipped and with tanks and artillery had arrived in Finland.'[35] And it was during the May Day celebrations that the Soviet Military Chief, Marshal Timoshenko, told the crowds in Red Square 'the international situation is very tense and fraught with all kinds of surprises. Therefore the entire Soviet people, the Red Army and Navy, must be in a state of fighting preparedness.'[36]

The Soviet Government had shown an awareness of the German troop movements since the beginning of April, and this had been reflected in their press and radio broadcasts; whilst in Britain the rumours of a German attack upon Russia had stirred up the old prophesies in some newspapers of the poor prospects of a Soviet survival against a German onslaught. The Foreign Editor of the *Daily Express* wrote:

'Against the reformed Panzer divisions from the

---

*Operation Marita – code name for the attack on Greece.

rest of Europe few military authorities would allow the massed Russian Army more than three months before capitulation if they fought alone.' (*The Daily Express*, 1 May 1941)

On Sunday, 4 May, a few lines appeared in the *Observer* in its column, The World's Week. Under a heading 'Russia as Cynosure' it referred to the current rumours and stated:

'All eyes are focussed on Russia, because Hitler's eyes are known to be focussed on Russia. Last week *Pravda* announced that a German mechanized division had just arrived in Finland, and Mr Mikoyan, the Russian Commissar for Foreign Trade, announced that in future no war supplies (munitions, aircraft parts, machine tools, explosives or poisons) would be allowed to pass through Russian territory: that is neither from Japan to Germany nor from Germany to Japan.'

German Generals, and particularly Chief of Staff, had been nurtured on the military doctrine of Count Alfred von Schlieffen: to avoid involvement in a simultaneous war on two fronts.* Thus, while preparing for the invasion of Russia they would have set in motion plans for securing their rear, and that is precisely what they did.

On the evening of Saturday, 10 May 1941, an aeroplane was heard circling around a fairly remote area of Lanarkshire in Western Scotland. It was not a British plane and there had been no air raid warning. The plane crashed and exploded into flames. The pilot who had managed to extricate himself landed by parachute and in doing so broke an ankle. He was found by a farmer, handed over to the army and taken to Maryhill Barracks, Glasgow, as a German prisoner of war. The prisoner gave his name as Oberleutenant Alfred Horn, 'stated that he was on a "special mission" to see the Duke of Hamilton and had intended to land at Dungavel.'[37] He had crashed twelve miles from his destination – the stately home of the Duke of

*See Chapter 2, p. 36

Hamilton, a Wing-Commander in the Royal Air Force.**

The Duke arrived at the Barracks the following morning. After an initial cross examination it transpired that the Oberleutenant was none other than Hitler's Deputy, Rudolf Hess. The Deputy Fuehrer had known Hamilton for some time although the Duke denied it.* According to his son 'Hamilton had no recollection of having seen him before, and the prisoner immediately asked that Hamilton should speak to him alone. The other officers were requested by Hamilton to withdraw, which they did.'[38]

Forty-eight hours elapsed between the landing of Hess and the Government's announcement of his arrival, but during this period there had been a great deal of activity behind the scenes. The first move came from Berlin with an announcement over the German radio 'that Hess, "apparently in a fit of madness", had taken possession of an aircraft contrary to Hitler's orders and had disappeared.'[39] The British Government meanwhile had called upon Ivone Kirkpatrick, a senior Foreign Office official, who had been First Secretary at the British Embassy in Berlin and one of Chamberlain's assistants at Munich, to interview the prisoner. He was thereupon flown to Scotland and had his first meeting with Hess on the morning of 13 May.

Kirkpatrick's Chief, Sir Alexander Cadogan, records in his diary for Monday, 12 May, that he had a meeting at the Foreign Office with Anthony Eden who told him that he 'had got text of German announcement.' They then went to see the Prime Minister who 'already had text of an announcement, which included remark that H[ess] had come here "in name of humanity". This won't do' says Cadogan 'looks like peace offer, and we may want to run the line that he has quarrelled with Hitler.'[40]

The sudden arrival of Hitler's Deputy had apparently created panic among the Munichites in the Cabinet, as well as some non-Munichites, including Churchill. Their immediate reaction was to hush up the affair. Using the war

---

**'As it happened, Hamilton . . . was on duty that Saturday evening at a Sector Operations room and had spotted the Messerschmitt plane off the coast as it came in to make a land-fall shortly after 10 pm.' (SHIRER, *Rise and Fall of the Third Reich*, p. 835)

†See *Trial of the Major War Criminals*, International Military Tribunal, Nuremberg, Vol. XXXVIII, Documents in Evidence 116 – M, pp. 174–5.

time censorship of the press and radio, Churchill and a small group of Ministers and officials were able to completely black out news of the Hess arrival until Monday evening, 12 May, and even then there was not a word of Hamilton's involvement.

According to Cecil King, the newspaper proprietor, not even Duff Cooper, the Minister of Information, had been informed of the Deputy Fuehrer's arrival. He first 'heard of Hess's disappearance – from the German wireless – and not until 10 pm or so on Monday that he heard from the Prime Minister of his arrival in this country.' Duff Cooper told Cecil King 'that he had not yet seen a transcript of what Hess had said.'[41]

On the following morning, with the panic temporarily over, the British people were to read in their newspapers that Hitler's Deputy had landed in Scotland. It was headlined in *The Times* –

'HITLER'S DEPUTY ESCAPES TO BRITAIN'

The next day the paper's diplomatic correspondent reported:

'What is quite certain is that he has not come on any mission from the German Government . . . He is believed first to have become more and more disgusted by the trickery and the shamelessness of Hitler's entourage.' (*The Times*, Wednesday 14 May 1941)

Not until Thursday, 15 May, was it disclosed that 'Hess had hoped to land on the Duke of Hamilton's estate'.

In May 1941, the USA was still a neutral country with foreign correspondents in both London and Berlin. Consequently the *New York Herald Tribute*, free from censorship restrictions, was able to report on 15 May under the heading

'HAMILTON AIDED PRE-WAR MOVES FOR NAZI AMITY'

'The Duke of Hamilton, whom Rudolf Hess was attempting to see when Nazi deputy-leader crashed in Scotland, has been identified in British press as a former member of the Anglo-German Fellowship, an organization designed to foster friendship between Britain and Germany. The fellowship was dissolved before the war . . .

The thirty-eight year old Duke, formerly known as the Marquess of Clydesdale . . . met Hess several times before the start of the war in 1939 in connection with flying and skiing, in which both were interested. They also were together at Germany's Olympic Games serving as officials.'

The paper had received a wire from its Berlin correspondent the previous day stating:

'While emphasizing that the German Government knew nothing of these plans, the spokesman said Hess had expected to fulfil the peace mission in about two days and return freely to Germany, with gasoline (and presumably a plane) furnished by the British . . .

The spokesman said Hess "considered discussions with Churchill useless, because he [Hess] had expressly observed that he had no wish to confer with the British Prime Minister under any circumstances".'

And in a later edition it disclosed that:

'Reports from Germany said that Hess, in letters he left behind, had indicated his intention of flying to Great Britain to confer with the Duke whom he had met at the Olympic Games in 1936 and at other times. The German statement said Hess hoped to effect a truce between Germany and England. It added that Hess indicated he expected to return to Germany in two days . . .

Some time ago Hess wrote to the Duke, and it is assumed that at that time he made certain suggestions similar to those in some of his public speeches in Germany, that a continuance of the war would be disastrous for both England and Germany. It was his belief that the Duke would be likely to have influence in English circles opposed to the Churchill Government and interested in securing a negotiated peace.' (Joseph F. Evans Jnr. Late City Edition *New York Herald Tribune*, 15 May 1941)

Once the Soviet Government was aware that the Germans were actively engaged in preparations to invade their country, the disclosure of the Hess mission would undoubtedly have heightened their suspicions that a secret deal might be realized between Britain and Germany. The American writer, Trumbull Higgins, comments:

'Whether or not this mission was undertaken with Hitler's tacit consent, the Soviets had little reason for accepting at their face value either the embarrassed German or non-commital British announcements concerning the Hess flight . . . there is no doubt that the Fuehrer would have gladly accepted any reasonable opportunity to obtain a free hand in Eastern Europe on the very eve of Barbarossa.'[42]

That week Kirkpatrick held three lengthy interviews with Hess – on 13, 14 and 15 May*, and on 9 June, Lord Simon† (formerly Sir John Simon), who had met Hess in Berlin in the mid-1930s when he was Foreign Minister, had a secret three hour interview with him. So secret in fact that it was decided to hold the meeting in a country house in Hampshire. According to Hamilton's son:

'It was considered vital that no one should know that a Minister had seen Hess so that there should be no rumours about peace negotiations. Simon

---

*See *Trial of the Major War Ciminals*, International Military Tribunal, Nuremberg, Vol. XXXVIII, Documents in Evidence 117–M, 118–M, 119–M, pp. 177–184

†An account of this interview was produced by Dr Siedl, Defence Counsel for Hess, at Nuremberg. See Vol. XL, Documents in Evidence Hess–15, pp. 279–292.

and Kirkpatrick [who was there to assist] assumed the pseudonyms of Doctors Guthrie and Mackenzie respectively.'[43]

The next day Sydney Silverman, the Labour MP asked the Prime Minister

'whether he can now state the results of the investigation into the purpose of the arrival in this country of Rudolf Hess; whether Hess brought with him any proposals indicating how the problems of Europe might, in his view, be solved; whether any reply to such proposals, has been made or is contemplated; whether such proposals or reply would be published; and whether he will indicate the general lines of the government's own proposals for the settlement of Europe after the war, so as to repair its ravages and prevent its recurrence?

Mr Churchill: I have no statement to make about this person at the present time; but His Majesty's Government have of course, kept the United States Government informed on the subject of his flight to this country.

Mr Silverman: Is the House to infer that this prominent Nazi leader came to this country without any serious purpose whatsoever; and if he had such a purpose, why are the people of this country not entitled to know what it was?

Mr Churchill: I have no statement to make.' (*Hansard*, 10 June 1941, Col. 29)

A week later there was a report in the *Manchester Guardian* (18 June 1941) under the heading 'HESS AND THE GERMAN SECRET SERVICE' stating:

'Sir Patrick Dollan, Lord Provost of Glasgow, has been rebuked by Dr G.B. Henderson in a Ministry of Information lecture at Glasgow on his statement about why Hess came here with peace proposals, believing that he would get in touch

with peace party leaders in this country and that
he could return at will to Germany . . . '

There was one Minister who was obviously not satisfied
with the official report released during the first few days of
the Hess episode, and had embarrassed the Government by
expressing his views in public. On 15 May, the Minister for
Labour and National Service, Ernest Bevin, was at a
luncheon at the Holborn Chamber of Commerce and in a
speech to his fellow diners was reported to have said:

'From my point of view Hess is a murderer. He
was the man who collected every index card of
every trade union leader in Germany . . . and
when the time came they were either sent to
concentration camps or murdered . . . My own
views on this adventure I will not express beyond
saying that I do not believe that Hitler did not
know that Hess was coming to England.'[44]

Louis Fischer recalls that when he was in London 'several
months' after the Hess landing, he:

'discussed the Hess riddle with Foreign Secretary
Anthony Eden, Home Secretary Herbert S. Morrison, Clement R. Attlee, Deputy Prime Minister,
Professor Harold Laski, Labour leader and publi-
cist and others.
   The pieces of evidence I gathered made the
picture quite clear. Hess knew of the coming
assault on the Soviet Union. Hitler's *Mein Kampf*,
which Hess helped to write, was not anti-British.
It stressed Germany's need of the Ukraine and of
an arrangement with Britain by which Germany
could seize that rich area. What was more natural,
then, than that the Nazis should seek an arrangement with Britain when they were about to attack
Russia? . . . Hess remembered the appeasing
British lords who visited him before the war. He
believed they still had influence.'[45]

The Russians would also have known that Hess had collaborated with Hitler in the writing of *Mein Kampf* and that he and his Fuehrer had agreed many years ago that:

'Great Britain was the only power which could protect our rear, supposing we started a new Germanic expansion.'[46]

They did not believe that Hess had come to Britain for 'humanitarian reasons' or in a 'fit of madness'.

When Lord Beaverbrook, a senior Minister and close friend of Churchill, and Averell Harriman, Roosevelt's special envoy, were in Moscow in September 1941 they had a number of meetings with the Soviet leader. Harriman noted that at one of the meetings:

'Stalin asked about Hess and semed much interested in Beaverbrook's amusing description of his talk with Hess and his size-up of the situation. Stalin indicated that he thought Hess had gone not at the request of Hitler, but with the knowledge of Hitler, to which Beaverbrook agreed.

The net of Beaverbrook's statement was that Hess had come thinking that with a small group of British aristocrats a counter-Churchill Government could be set up to make peace with Germany which would be welcomed by the majority of the British. Germany with British aid would then attack Russia.'[47]

But it was not only a small group of aristrocrats who wanted to make peace with Hitler. There were in addition a number of potential British Petains, Lavals* and Cotys who could have provided the foundation for a British Vichy type administration.†

During the concluding stages of the Trial of the Major

---

*Pierre Laval was brought to trial on 4 October 1945, sentenced to death and executed by firing squad on 15 October.
†See 'ENGLISH CONNECTIONS AND THE POSSIBILITY OF UTILIZING THEM' from *Documents on German Foreign Policy*, Series D. Vol. XII, No. 500, pp. 783–787 (Appendix I)

War Criminals at which the 'Judgement' of the International Military Tribunal was proclaimed, it was said:

'Until his flight to England, Hess was Hitler's closest personal confidant. Their relationship was such that Hess must have been informed of Hitler's aggressive plans when they came into existence. And he took action to carry out these plans whenever action was necessary.

With him on his flight to England, Hess carried certain peace proposals which he alleged Hitler was prepared to accept. It is significant to note that this flight took place only ten days after the date on which Hitler fixed, 22 June 1941, as the time for attacking the Soviet Union. In conversations carried on after his arrival in England Hess wholeheartedly supported all Germany's aggressive actions up to that time, and attempted to justify Germany's action in connection with Austria, Czechoslovakia, Poland, Norway, Denmark, Belgium, and the Netherlands. He blamed England and France for the war.'[48]

The Prosecuting Counsel, Lieutenant Colonel Griffith-Jones, was obviously under no illusion regarding the real purpose which lay behind the Hess flight to Britain when he told the Tribunal:

'nobody who held the position that the defendant did at that time – in charge of the foreign organization, Deputy to the Fuehrer, having been made designate successor Number 2 only a year ago – never in that position could he have been kept in ignorance of those preparations and those plans ... my submission, therefore, is that the only reason he came to England was not humanitarian at all, but purely, as I say, to allow Germany to fight her battle against Russia on one front only.'[49]

And there appears to be no evidence for *The Times'* assertion that Rudolf Hess escaped to Britain and that he had 'become more and more disgusted by the trickery and shamlessness of Hitler's entourage'. There was certainly none at Nuremberg. In fact, Hess was proud of his Third Reich and of its leader. As for its entourage, he was an integral part of it. On 31 August 1946, he told the Tribunal:

> 'I was permitted to work for many years of my life under the greatest son whom my people has brought forth in its thousand-year history. Even if I could, I would not want to erase this period of time from my existence. I am happy to know that I have done my duty to my people, my duty as a German, as a National Socialist, as a loyal follower of my Führer. I do not regret anything.
> If I were to begin all over again, I would act just as I have acted . . . '[50]

But the real purpose of the secret visit of Hitler's deputy had apparently stirred some British journalists to question the motives, as well as the timing. For example, on 21 June 1941 an article appeared in the *News Chronicle* under the heading 'WHY THE LULL?'. It was written by Ronald Walker, the paper's Air Correspondent. He had taken note of the fact that:

> 'Since 10 May the Germans have not made a large-scale bombing raid on Britain. This is the longest period of quiet since the night bombing of this country began last year.
> The people ask why. Without being inside the Command of the Luftwaffe, it is impossible to know the full answer to the problem of Nazi air inactivity on their northern front.
> During the past six weeks there have been spurts of activity, but nothing on the scale of the major raids which ended with the attack on London on 10 May.'

In the same edition, the paper drew attention to a statement which had been broadcast over the German radio in its English propaganda transmission of 20 June:

'"the reason for the somewhat lighter activity of the German Luftwaffe over Britain may soon become apparent to a surprised world".'

The next day the *Sunday Times* reported the 'mobilization of a large number of Finnish troops and the increase of the German effectives in Finland from two to four or even five divisions.'

That very morning, 22 June 1941, just a few minutes before sunrise, over three million German soldiers and airmen, together with Finnish troops in the north and Roumanian, Hungarian and Italian troops in the south, launched a massive attack upon the Soviet Union along a 1,600 mile front extending from the North Cape to the Black Sea. Thousands of tanks, aircraft, motorized vehicles, and the most up to date military equipment were used to blast their way into the heart of Russia.

That night Churchill made his historic broadcast in which he declared Britain's support to the people of Russia and their Government.

'We have offered to the Government of Soviet Russia any technical or economic assistance which is in our power and which is likely to be of service to them.'

And in conclusion he stressed:

'The Russian danger is therefore our danger, and the danger of the United States, just as the cause of any Russian fighting for his hearth and home is the cause of free men and free peoples in every quarter of the globe.
    Let us learn the lessons already taught by cruel experience.' (*The Times*, 23 June 1941)

It was a speech that did much to strengthen the morale of the peoples of both countries in their fight against the common enemy.

Nevertheless, there were still many influential people in

Britain and the United States of America who welcomed the military clash of the giants of Europe. One such person was an American Senator, Harry S. Truman, who, on the day after the German invasion, was reported in the *New York Times*, 24 June 1941, to have said:

> 'If we see that Germany is winning the war we ought to help Russia, and if Russia is winning we ought to help Germany and in that way let them kill as many as possible.'

And in Britain, a prominent member of the British Cabinet expressed similar sentiments. It was revealed by the President of the Amalgamated Engineering Union, Jack Tanner, in an address to the TUC's annual conference on 2 September 1941:

> 'There are people in high places who declare that they hope that the Russian and German armies will exterminate each other, and that while this is taking place we, the British Commonwealth of Nations, will so develop our Air Force and the other armed forces that if Russia and Germany do destroy each other we shall be the dominant Power in Europe. Now this point of view has been expressed quite recently by a Cabinet Minister, a Member of the present Government, a gentleman who holds a very important position, none other than the Minister of Aircraft Production, Colonel Moore-Brabazon.* Such an attitude I think everyone here will agree is a terrible danger. And it is a crime against the people of this country and the people of Russia who, during these last three months, have suffered so terribly ... Unless Russia is successful the possibility of complete victory so far as we are concerned is very much less certain, and it is true to say that one is conditional upon the other. If Russia succeeds, then we

*Colonel Moore-Brabazon was removed from office by Churchill, but not until February 1942.

succeed; if Russia fails, then we fail. Well, I hope that that would not be the case. But we are vitally concerned in the success of Russia as an essential factor in the triumph over Nazism, and that being so, it is necessary that we let it be known that we will defeat any plot that may be in process of formation that would withhold full and adequate aid to our allies ... because the impression is still very strong that certain elements desire to switch the war against Russia, and that impression is natural and will naturally be confirmed when statements are made by an important Minister such as I have referred to.'

In conclusion, Tanner reminded the delegates that:

'The Unions are entitled to know what support is being given to Russia.' (from *Trades Union Congress Report*, 1941, pp. 250–251)

Until September 1941, support was mainly in the form of good wishes, ably expressed by David Low in a famous cartoon which appeared in Lord Beaverbrook's *London Evening Standard* on 8 September. Bouquets of flowers and messages of 'GOOD LUCK' and 'HEARTFELT ADMIRA-TION FROM BRITAIN' are shown being presented to Russian troops in the front line of the battle against the German Army and the Russian reply, 'THANKS COM-RADE – BUT I'D RATHER IT WERE SOMETHING TO FIGHT WITH'. Harold Nicolson recorded in his diaries that 'supplies of war materials from Britain through the Northern Russian ports were not to become effective for many months.'[51] In fact, it was not until later that year, after considerable public pressure had been exerted upon the Government, that the promise of supplies to the USSR was to become a reality.

EPILOGUE

During the War of Empires and the Wars of Intervention, thirty million Russian people were either killed or died of starvation, and in World War II over twenty million Russian people suffered the same fate. Yet it has been said in the West that at the end of World War II the Russians had a massive army poised ready to overrun Europe. It has also been said that the Russians had become paranoic, that they were over obsessed with security, and as a consequence had nobody but themselves to blame if they felt insecure.

Lord Russell of Liverpool, who was Deputy Judge Advocate General, British Army of the Rhine, and Legal Adviser to the Commander-in-Chief at the trials of German war criminals in the British Zone of Occupation, writes in his book, *The Scourge of the Swastika*:

> 'The war against the Russians was fought with more savagery and barbarity than anywhere else, and it has been contended by German counsel at a number of war crime trials that the Hague Conventions did not apply to the war between the USSR and Germany . . .
> 'From the moment the German troops entered Russia until the last Nazi had been driven out, from the Russo-German border to Smolensk, from Smolensk to Stalingrad, from Stalingrad to the Crimea, and from thence to Kharkov, wherever the German soldier or the SS men set foot, crimes of unimaginable brutality were committed against old men, women and children in their

564

thousands.'[52]*

When the atomic bombs were dropped on Hiroshima and Nagasaki in August 1945, the Russians had reason to believe that they were used, not just as a means of terminating the war against Japan, but as a threat to themselves. The Anglo-American consultations and plans for the manufacture and subsequent dropping of the atomic bombs were conducted in such secrecy, that the Russian Government was completely unaware of what the American and British Governments were planning until the sensational news of the destruction of the two Japanese cities burst upon a shocked world.

The death of President Roosevelt in April 1945, and his replacement by Truman, had within days changed the Roosevelt policy of peaceful co-existence and co-operation with Soviet Russia in a post-war world, to one of cold war and military confrontation.

Thus, although an ally 'to save the world from Fascist tyranny', Russia had, once again, become the 'enemy'.

Notes

1. BONTÉ, Florimund, *Le Chemin de l'Honneur*, p. 307
2. DE MENDELSSOHN, Peter, *The Nuremberg Documents*, p. 242
3. CALDER, Angus, *The People's War, Britain 1939–1945*, p. 86
4. AMOUROUX, Henri, *Petain Avant Vichy*, p. 229
5. SHIRER, William, *The Collapse of the Third Republic*, pp. 709 and 737
6. DE GAULLE, Charles, *War Memoirs – Call to Honour 1940–1942*, pp. 60–61
7. SHIRER, William, *The Collapse of the Third Republic*, pp. 552–553
8. CADOGAN, Sir Alexander, *The Diaries of* (ed. David Dilks), p. 283
9. SHIRER, William, *The Collapse of the Third Republic*, p. 847
10. LUKACS, John, *The Last European War – September 1939–December 1941*, p. 274
11. SHIRER, William, *The Collapse of the Third Republic*, p. 749
12. LIDDELL-HART, Sir Basil, *History of the Second World War*, p. 74
13. SHIRER, William, *The Collapse of the Third Republic*, p. 731

*See Appendices II and III 'MURDER AND ILL-TREATMENT OF CIVILIAN POPULATIONS OF OR IN OCCUPIED TERRITORY AND ON THE HIGH SEAS'. A confirmation in detail of Lord Russell's descriptive account of what happened to the peoples of Russia and the rest of Europe during World War II.

14. BULLOCK, Alan, *Hitler, A Study in Tyranny*, p. 537
15. LEACH, Barry A., *German Strategy Against Russia, 1939–1941*, p. 48
16. COLLIER, Basil, *Arms and the Men, The Arms Trade and Governments*, p. 233
17. SHIRER, William, *The Collapse of the Third Republic*, p. 733
18. SHIRER, William, *The Collapse of the Third Republic*, p. 727 and FN
19. WILLIAMS, John, *Ides of May*, p. 93
20. SHIRER, William, *The Collapse of the Third Republic*, p. 751 and FN
21. SHIRER, William, *The Collapse of the Third Republic*, p. 816
22. LIDDELL-HART, Sir Basil, *History of the Second World War*, p. 87
23. BULLOCK, Alan, *Hitler, A Study in Tyranny*, p. 545
24. BULLOCK, Alan, *Hitler, A Study in Tyranny*, p. 549
25. BULLOCK, Alan, *Hitler, A Study in Tyranny*, p. 546
26. LIDDELL-HART, Sir Basil, *History of the Second World War*, p. 108
27. CADOGAN, Sir Alexander, *The Diaries of* (ed. David Dilks), p. 325–326
28. LIDDELL-HART, Sir Basil, *History of the Second World War*, p. 144
29. LIDDELL-HART, Sir Basil, *History of the Second World War*, pp. 146–149, 150–151
30. LEACH, Barry A, *German Strategy Against Russia, 1939–1941*, pp. 162 and 164
31. *Documents on German Foreign Policy* Series D. Vol. X, pp. 566–7 FN
32. International Military Tribunal, Nuremberg, *Trial of the Major War Criminals*, Vol. VII, p. 163
33. International Military Tribunal, Nuremberg, *T.M.W.C.* Vol. VII, p. 143
34. SHIRER, William, *The Rise and Fall of the Third Reich*, p. 824
35. COATES, W.P. and Zelda, *History of Anglo-Soviet Relations*, p. 663
36. COATES, W.P. and Zelda, *History of Anglo-Soviet Relations*, p. 664
37. International Military Tribunal, Nuremberg, *T.M.W.C.* Vol. XXXVIII Document 116–M, p. 174
38. HAMILTON, James Douglas, *Motive for a Mission*, p. 158
39. HAMILTON, James Douglas, *Motive for a Mission*, p. 160
40. CADOGAN, Sir Alexander, *The Diaries of* (ed. David Dilks), pp. 376–377
41. KING, Cecil, *With Malice Towards None – A War Diary*, p. 129
42. HIGGINS, Trumbull, *Hitler and Russia, The Third Reich in a Two Front War, 1937–1943*, p. 114
43. HAMILTON, James Douglas, *Motive for a Mission*, p. 182
44. *Keesings Contemporary Archives*, Vol. IV, p. 4601
45. FISCHER, Louis, *The Great Challenge*, p. 42
46. HITLER, Adolf, *Mein Kampf* (English edition), p. 64
47. SHERWOOD, Robert E., *The White House Papers of Harry Hopkins*, Vol. I, pp. 391–392
48. International Military Tribunal, Nuremberg, *T.M.W.C.* Judgement, Vol. I, p. 284
49. International Military Tribunal, Nuremberg, *T.M.W.C..*, Vol. VII, p. 143
50. International Military Tribunal, Nuremberg, *T.M.W.C.*, Vol. XII, p. 373
51. NICOLSON, Harold, *Diaries 1939–1945* (ed. Nigel Nicolson), p. 173
52. LIVERPOOL, Lord Russell of, *The Scourge of the Swastika*, pp. 127–128

APPENDIX I

Copy of a document submitted to Hitler on 12 May 1941.
(Two days after Hess crash landed in Scotland)

MEMORANDUM WRITTEN BY
DR ALBRECHT HAUSHOFER

'English Connections and the Possibility of Utilizing Them.

The circle of English individuals whom I have known very well for years, and whose utilization in behalf of a German-English understanding in the years from 1934 to 1938 was the core of my activity in England, comprises the following groups and persons:

1. A leading group of younger conservatives (many of them Scotsmen). Among them are: The Duke of Hamilton, up to the death of his father Lord Clydesdale, conservative Member of Parliament; The parliamentary private secretary of Neville Chamberlain, Lord Douglass.*

    The present Under State Secretary in the Air Ministry, Balfour.

    The present Under State Secretary in the Ministry of Education, Lindsay (National Labour)

    The present Under State Secretary in the Ministry for Scotland, Wedderburn.

    Close ties link this circle with the Court. The younger brother of the Duke of Hamilton is closely related to the present Queen through his wife; the mother-in-law of the Duke of Hamilton, the Duchess of Northumberland,

---

*The spelling of Lord Douglass appears to be a misprint and should have read Dunglass.

is the mistress of the robes; her brother-in-law, Lord Eustace Percy, was several times member of the Cabinet and is still today an influential member of the Conservative party (especially close to former Prime Minister Baldwin). There are close connections between this circle and important groups of the older conservatives, as for example the Stanley family (Lord Derby, Oliver Stanley) and Astor (the last is owner of *The Times*). The young Astor, likewise a Member of Parliament, was parliamentary private secretary to the former Foreign and Interior Minister, Sir Samuel Hoare, at present English Ambassador in Madrid.

I have known almost all of the persons mentioned for years and from close personal contact. The present Under State Secretary of the Foreign Office, Butler, also belongs here; in spite of many of his public utterances he is not a follower of Churchill or Eden. Numerous connections lead from most of those named to Lord Halifax, to whom I likewise had personal access.

2. The so-called 'Round Table' circle of younger imperialists (particularly colonial and empire politicians), whose most important personage was Lord Lothian.

3. A group of the 'Ministerialdirektoren' in the Foreign Office. The most important of these were Strang, the chief of the Central European Department, and O'Malley, the chief of the Southeastern Department and afterwards Minister in Budapest.

There was hardly one of those named who was not at least occasionally in favor of a German-English understanding. Although most of them in 1939 finally considered that war was inevitable, it was nevertheless reasonable to think of these persons if one thought the moment had come for investigating the possibility of an English inclination to make peace. Therefore when the Deputy of the Fuhrer, Reich Minister Hess, asked me in the autumn of 1940 about possibilities of gaining access to possibly reasonable Englishmen, I suggested two concrete possibilities for establishing contacts. It seemed to me that the following could be considered for this:

A. Personal contact with Lothian, Hoare, or O'Malley, all three of whom were accessible in neutral countries.
B. Contact by letter with one of my friends in England. For this purpose the Duke of Hamilton was considered in the first place, since my connection with him was so firm and personal that I could suppose he would understand a letter addressed to him even if it were formulated in very veiled language.

Reich Minister Hess decided in favor of the second possibility; I wrote a letter to the Duke of Hamilton at the end of September 1940 and its dispatch to Lisbon was arranged by the Deputy of the Fuhrer. I did not learn whether the letter reached the addressee. The possibilities of its being lost en route from Lisbon to England are not small, after all.

Then in April 1941 I received greetings from Switzerland from Carl Burckhardt, the former League of Nations Commissioner in Danzig and now Vice President of the International Red Cross, whom I had also known well for years. He sent the message that he had greetings to pass on to me from someone in my old circle of English friends. I should please visit him sometime in Geneva. Since the possibility existed that these greetings were in connection with my letter of last autumn, I thought I should again submit the matter to the Deputy of the Fuhrer, though with the reservation (as already last autumn) that the chances of a serious peace feeler seemed to me to be extremely slight. Reich Minister Hess decided that I should go to Geneva.

In Geneva I had a long conversation with Burckhardt on 28 April. I found him in something of a quandary between his desire to support the possibilities of a European peace and the greatest concern lest his name might somehow be involved with publicity. He expressly asked that what went on be kept strictly secret. In consideration of the discretion enjoined upon him he could only tell me the following:

A few weeks ago a person well known and respected in London, who was close to the leading conservative and city circles, had called on him in Geneva. This person, whose name he could not give, though he could vouch for his earnestness, had in a rather long conversation expressed the wish of important English circles for an examination of the possibilities for peace; in the search for possible channels my name had been mentioned.

I for my part informed Professor Burckhardt that I had to expect the same discretion with regard to my name. Should his informant in London be willing to come to Switzerland once more and should he further be willing to have his name communicated to me in Berlin through confidential channels, so that the earnestness of both person and mission could be investigated in Germany, then I thought that I, too, could agree to taking another trip to Geneva. Professor Burckhardt stated that he was willing to act as a go-between for this in this manner: It would simply be communicated to England through an entirely safe channel that there was a prospect for a trusted representative from London, after he himself had given his name, to meet in Geneva a German also well-known in England, who was in a position to bring such communications as there might be to the attention of the competent German authorities.

My own conversation with Professor Burckhardt furnished a number of important points regarding the substantive part of possible peace talks (Burckhardt has not only been in England during the war – for example, he had a long and detailed conversation with Halifax – but he also has frequent contact with the English observer in Geneva, Consul General Livingston, who likewise is one of those Englishmen whom the war does not please). Burckhardt's general impression of the opinions of the more moderate groups in England can be summarized as follows:

1. The substantive English interest in the areas of eastern and southeastern Europe (with the exception of Greece) is nominal.
2. No English government that is still capable of action will be able to renounce [the aim of] a restoration of the western European system of states.
3. The colonial question will not present any overwhelming difficulties if the German demand is limited to the old German possessions and if the Italian appetite can be curbed.

All of this, however – and this fact could not be stressed seriously enough – under the assumption, which overshadowed everything else, that a basis of personal confidence could be found between Berlin and London; and this would be as difficult to find as during the Crusades or in the Thirty-Years' War. As matters stood, the contest with 'Hitlerism' was being considered, by the masses of the English people, too, to be a religious war with all of the fanaticising psychological consequences of such an attitude. If anyone in London was inclined toward peace, then it was the indigenous portion of the plutocracy, which was able to calculate when it, along with the indigenous British tradition, would be destroyed, whereas the nonindigenous, mainly Jewish element, had already in large part completed the jump to America and the overseas dominions. It was Burckhardt's own and deepest concern that if the war continued for a considerable length of time every possibility that the reasonable forces in England would force Churchill to make peace would disappear, since by that time the whole power of decision regarding the overseas assets of the Empire would be taken over by the Americans. Once the remainder of the indigenous English upper class had been eliminated, however, it would be impossible to talk sense to Roosevelt and his circle.'

(From *Documents on German Foreign Policy*, Series D. Vol. XII, No. 500, pp. 783–787)

Dr Albrecht Haushofer was the son of Dr Karl Haushofer, Professor of Geopolitics (from 1921) and pioneer of the Nazi political and racial philosophy. Hess was a close friend of the Haushofers. He was one of the Professor's earliest pupils at Munich University and introduced Hitler to the Professor during the early 1920s.

APPENDIX II

MURDER AND ILL-TREATMENT OF CIVILIAN POPULATIONS OF OR IN OCCUPIED TERRITORY AND ON THE HIGH SEAS.

From the *Trial of the Major War Criminals before the International Military Tribunal*, Nuremberg – 14 November 1945–1 October 1946. (Vol. I. pp. 47–50)

In the USSR, i.e. in the Byelorussian, Ukrainian, Estonian, Latvian, Lithuanian, Karelo-Finnish, and Moldavian Soviet Socialist Republics, in nineteen regions of the Russian Soviet Federated Socialist Republic and in Poland, Czechoslovakia, Yugoslavia, Greece and the Balkans (hereinafter called 'the Eastern Countries') and in that part of Germany which lies east of a line drawn north and south through the center of Berlin (hereinafter called 'Eastern Germany').

From 1 September 1939, when the German Armed Forces invaded Poland, and from 22 June 1941, when they invaded the USSR, the German Government and the German High Command adopted a systematic policy of murder and ill-treatment of the civilian populations of and in the Eastern Countries as they were successively occupied by the German Armed Forces. These murders and ill-treatments were carried on continuously until the German Armed Forces were driven out of the said countries.

Such murders and ill-treatments included:

(a) Murders and ill-treatments at concentration camps and similar establishments set up by the Germans in the Eastern Countries and in Eastern Germany including those set up at Maidanek and Auschwitz.

The said murders and ill-treatments were carried out by divers mean including all those set out above, as follows:

572

About 1,500,000 persons were exterminated in Maidanek and about 4,000,000 persons were exterminated in Auschwitz, among whom were citizens of Poland, the USSR, the United States of America, Great Britain, Czechoslovakia, France, and other countries.

In the Lwow region and in the city of Lwow the Germans exterminated about 700,000 Soviet people, including 70 persons in the field of the arts, science, and technology, and also citizens of the United States of America, Great Britain, Czechoslovakia, Yugoslavia, and Holland, brought to this region from other concentration camps.

In the Jewish ghetto from 7 September 1941 to 6 July 1943, over 133,000 persons were tortured and shot.

Mass shooting of the population occurred in the suburbs of the city and in the Livenitz forest.

In the Ganov camp 200,000 peaceful citizens were exterminated. The most refined methods of cruelty were employed in this extermination, such as disembowelling and the freezing of human beings in tubs of water. Mass shootings took place to the accompaniment of the music of an orchestra recruited from the persons interned.

Beginning with June 1943, the Germans carried out measures to hide the evidence of their crimes, They exhumed and burned corpses, and they crushed the bones with machines and used them for fertilizer.

At the beginning of 1944 in the Ozarichi region of the Byelorussian SSR, before liberation by the Red Army, the Germans established three concentration camps without shelters, to which they committed tens of thousands of persons from the neighbouring territories. They brought many people to these camps from typhus hospitals intentionally, for the purpose of infecting the other persons interned and for spreading the disease in territories from which the Germans were being driven by the Red Army. In these camps there were many murders and crimes.

In the Estonian SSR they shot tens of thousands of persons and in one day alone, 19 September 1944, in Camp Kloga, the Germans shot 2,000 peaceful citizens. They burned the bodies on bonfires.

In the Lithuanian SSR there were mass killings of Soviet citizens, namely: in Panerai at least 100,000; in Kaunas more

573

than 70,000; in Alitus about 60,000; at Prenai more than 3,000; in Villiampol about 8,000; in Mariampol about 7,000; in Trakai and neighbouring towns 37,640.

In the Latvian SSR 577,000 persons were murdered.

As a result of the whole system of internal order maintained in all camps, the interned persons were doomed to die.

In a secret instruction entitled 'the internal regime in concentration camps', signed personally by Himmler in 1941 severe measures of punishment were set forth for the internees. Masses of prisoners of war were shot, or died from the cold and torture.

(b) Murders and ill-treatments at places in the Eastern Countries and in the Soviet Union, other than in the camps referred to in (a) above, included on various dates during the occupation by the German Armed Forces:

The destruction in the Smolensk region of over 135,000 Soviet citizens.

Among these, near the village of Kholmetz of the Sychev region, when the military authorities were required to remove the mines from an area, on the order of the Commander of the 101st German Infantry Division, Major-General Fisler, the German soldiers gathered the inhabitants of the village of Kholmetz and forced them to remove mines from the road. All of these people lost their lives as a result of exploding mines.

In the Leningrad region there were shot and tortured over 172,000 persons, including over 20,000 persons who were killed in the city of Leningrad by the barbarous artillery barrage and the bombings.

In the Stavropol region in an anti-tank trench close to the station of Mineralny Vody, and in other cities, tens of thousands of persons were exterminated.

In Pyatigorsk many were subjected to torture and criminal treatment, including suspension from the ceiling and other methods. Many of the victims of these tortures were then shot.

In Krasnodar some 6,700 civilians were murdered by

poison gas in gas vans, or were tortured and shot.

In the Stalingrad region more than 40,000 persons were tortured and killed. After the Germans were expelled from Stalingrad, more than a thousand mutilated bodies of local inhabitants were found with marks of torture. One hundred and thirty-nine women had their arms painfully bent backward and held by wires. From some their breasts had been cut off and their ears, fingers, and toes had been amputated. The bodies bore the marks of burns. On the bodies of the men the five pointed star was burned with an iron or cut with a knife. Some were disembowelled.

In Orel over 5,000 persons were murdered.

In Novgorod and in the Novgorod region many thousands of Soviet citizens were killed by shooting, starvation, and torture. In Minsk tens of thousands of citizens were similarly killed.

In the Crimea peaceful citizens wre gathered on barges, taken out to sea and drowned, over 144,000 persons being exterminated in this manner.

In the Soviet Ukraine there were monstrous criminal acts of the Nazi conspirators. In Babi Yar, near Kiev, they shot over 100,000 men, women, children, and old people. In this city in January 1942, after the explosion in German headquarters on Dzerzhinsky Street the Germans arrested as hostages 1,250 persons – old men, minors, women with nursing infants. In Kiev they killed over 195,000 persons.

In Rovno and the Rovno region they killed and tortured over 100,000 peaceful citizens.

In Dnepropetrovsk, near the Transport Institute, they shot or threw alive into a great ravine 11,000 women, old men, and children.

In Kamenetz-Podolsk Region 31,000 Jews were shot and exterminated, including 13,000 persons brought there from Hungary.

In the Odessa Region at least 200,000 Soviet citizens were killed.

In Kharkov about 195,000 persons were either tortured to death, shot, or gassed in gas vans.

In Gomel the Germans rounded up the population in prison, and tortured and tormented them, and then took them to the centre of the city and shot them in public.

In the city of Lyda in the Grodnen region on 8 May 1942, 5,670 persons were completely undressed, driven into pens in groups of 100, and then shot by machine guns. Many were thrown in the graves while they were still alive.

Along with adults the Nazi conspirators mercilessly destroyed even children. They killed them with their parents, in groups, and alone. They killed them in children's homes and hospitals, burying the living in the graves, throwing them into flames, stabbing them with bayonets, poisoning them, conducting experiments upon them, extracting their blood for the use of the German Army, throwing them into prison and Gestapo torture chambers and concentration camps, where the children died from hunger, torture, and epidemic diseases.

From 6 September to 24 November 1942, in the region of Brest, Pinsk, Kobren, Dyvina, Malority, and Berezy-Kartuzsky about 400 children were shot by German punitive units.

In the Yanov camp in the city of Lwow the Germans killed 8,000 children in two months.

In the resort of Tiberda the Germans annihilated 500 children suffering from tuberculosis of the bone, who were in the sanatorium for the cure.

On the territory of the Latvian SSR the German usurpers killed thousands of children, whom they had brought there with their parents from Byelorussian SSR, and from the Kalinin, Kaluga, and other regions of the RSFSR.

In Czechoslovakia as a result of torture, beating, hanging, and shootings, there were annihilated in Gestapo prisons in Brno, Seim, and other places over 20,000 persons. Moreover, many thousands of internees were subjected to criminal treatment, beatings, and torture.

Both before the war, as well as during the war, thousands of Czech patriots, in particular Catholics and Protestants, lawyers, doctors, teachers, etc. were arrested as hostages and imprisoned. A large number of these hostages were killed by the Germans.

In Greece in October 1941, the male population between sixteen and sixty years of age of the Greek villages Amelofito, Kliston, Kizonia Mesovunos, Selli, Ano-Kerzilion and Kato-Kerzilion were shot – in all 416 persons.

In Yugoslavia many thousands of civilians were murdered.

APPENDIX III

MURDER AND ILL-TREATMENT OF CIVILIAN POPULATIONS OF OR IN OCCUPIED TERRITORY AND ON THE HIGH SEAS.

From *The Trial of the Major War Criminals before the International Military Tribunal, Nuremberg* – 14 November 1945–1 October 1946

In France, Belgium, Denmark, Holland, Norway, Luxembourg, Italy and the Channel Islands (hereinafter called the 'Western Countries') and in that part of Germany which lies west of a line drawn due north and south through the center of Berlin (hereinafter called 'Western Germany').

Such murder and ill-treatment took place in concentration camps and similar establishments set up by the defendants, and particularly in the concentration camps set up at Belsen, Buchenwald, Dachau, Breendonck, Grini, Natzweiler, Ravensbrück, Vught, and Amersfoort, and in numerous cities, towns, and villages, including Oradour-sur-Glane, Trondheim, and Oslo.

Crimes committed in France or against French citizens took the following forms:

Arbitrary arrests were carried out under political or racial pretexts: they were both individual and collective; notably in Paris (round-up of the 18th Arrondissement by the Field Gendarmerie, round-up of the Jewish population of the 11th Arrondissement in August 1941, round-up of Jewish intellectuals in December 1941, round-up in July 1942); at Clermont-Ferrand (round-up of professors and students of the University of Strasbourg, who were taken to Clermont-Ferrand on 25 November 1943); at Lyons; at Marseilles (round-up of 40,000 persons in

577

January 1943); at Grenoble (round-up on 24 December 1943); at Cluny (round-up on 24 December 1944); at Figeac (round-up in May 1944); at Saint Pol de Léon (round-up in July 1944); at Locminé (round-up on 3 July 1944); at Eysieux (round-up in May 1944) and at Moussey (round-up in September 1944). These arrests were followed by brutal treatment and tortures carried out by the most diverse methods, such as immersion in icy water, asphyxiation, torture of the limbs, and the use of instruments of torture, such as the iron helmet and electric current, and practised in all the prisons of France, notably in Paris, Lyons, Marseilles, Rennes, Metz, Clermont-Ferrand, Toulouse, Nice, Grenoble, Annecy, Arras, Béthune, Lille, Loos, Valenciennes, Nancy, Troyes and Caen, and in the torture chambers fitted up at the Gestapo centers.

In the concentration camps, the health regime and the labor regime were such that the rate of mortality (alleged to be from natural causes) attained enormous proportions, for instance:

1. Out of a convoy of 230 French women deported from Compiègne to Auschwitz in January 1943, 180 died of exhaustion by the end of four months.
2. 143 Frenchmen died of exhaustion between 23 March and 6 May 1943, in Block 8 at Dachau.
3. 1,797 Frenchmen died of exhaustion between 21 November 1943 and 15 March 1945, in the Block at Dora.
4. 465 Frenchmen died of general debility in November 1944, at Dora.
5. 22,761 deportees died of exhaustion at Buchenwald between 1 January 1943, and 15 April 1945.
6. 11,560 detainees died of exhaustion at Dachau Camp (most of them in Block 30 reserved for the sick and the infirm) between 1 January and 15 April 1945.
7. 780 priests died of exhaustion at Mauthausen.
8. Out of 2,200 Frenchmen registered at Flossenburg Camp, 1,600 died from supposedly natural causes.

Methods used for the work of extermination in concentration camps were:

Bad treatment, pseudo-scientific experiments (sterilization of women at Auschwitz and at Ravensbrück, study of the evolution of cancer of the womb at Auschwitz, of typhus at Buchenwald, anatomical research at Natzweiller, heart injections at Buchenwald, bone grafting and muscular excisions at Ravensbrück, etc.), gas chambers, gas wagons, and crematory ovens. Of 228,000 French political and racial deportees in concentration camps, only 28,000 survived.

In France systematic extermination was practiced also, notably at Asq on 1 April 1944, at Colpo on 22 July 1944, at Buzet-sur-Tarn on 6 July 1944 and on 17 August 1944, at Pluvignier on 8 July 1944, at Rennes on 8 June 1944, at Grenoble on 8 July 1944, at Saint Flour on 10 June 1944, at Ruisnes on 10 July 1944, at Nimes, at Tulle, and at Nice, where, in July 1944, the victims of torture were exposed to the population, and at Oradour-sur-Glane where the entire village population was shot or burned alive in the church.

The many charnel pits give proof of anonymous massacres. Most notable of these are the charnel pits of Paris (Cascade du Boi de Boulogne), Lyons, Saint-Genis-Laval, Besancon, Petit-Saint-Bernard, Aulnat, Caen, Port-Louis, Charleval, Fontainebleau, Bouconne, Gabaudet, Lhermitage Lorges, Morlaas, Bordelongue, Signe.

In the course of a premeditated campaign of terrorism, initiated in Denmark by the Germans in the latter part of 1943, 600 Danish subjects were murdered and, in addition, through the German occupation of Denmark, large numbers of Danish subjects were subjected to torture and ill-treatment of all sorts. In addition, approximately 500 Danish subjects were murdered, by torture and otherwise, in German prisons and concentration camps.

In Belgium between 1940 and 1944 tortures by various means, but identical in each place, were carried out at Brussels, Liege, Mons, Ghent, Namur, Antwerp, Tournai, Arlon, Charleroi, and Dinant.

At Vught, in Holland, when the camp was evacuated about 400 persons were murdered by shooting.

In Luxembourg, during the German occupation, 500 persons were murdered and, in addition, another 521 were illegally executed, by order of such special tribunals as the so-called 'Sondergericht'. Many more persons in Luxembourg were subjected to torture and mistreatment by the Gestapo. Not less than 4,000 Luxembourg nationals were imprisoned during the period of German occupation, and of these at least 400 were murdered.

Between March 1944 and April 1945, in Italy, at least 7,500 men, women, and children, ranging in years from infancy to extreme old age were murdered by the German soldiery at Civitella, in the Ardeatine Caves in Rome, and at other places.

BIBLIOGRAPHY

ADAMTHWAITE, Anthony P., *The Making of the Second World War*, Allen and Unwin, London 1977.

AMOUROUX, Henri, *Pétain Avant Vichy*, Fayard, France, 1967.

ARCHER, Jules, *20th Century Caesar – Benito Mussolini*, Bailey Bros. and Swinfen, Folkestone, 1972.

ARNOLD, General Henry H., *One World Or None*, Masters and Way, New York, 1946.

ARNOT, R. Page, *The Impact of the Russian Revolution in Britain*, Lawrence and Wishart, 1967.

ARNOT, R. Page, *The Miners: Years of Struggle*, Allen and Unwin, 1953.

ATHOLL, Duchess of, *Searchlight on Spain*, Penguin Books, 1938.

BACON, Walter, *Finland*, Robert Hale and Co., 1970.

BEAVERBROOK, Lord, *The Decline and Fall of Lloyd George*, Collins, 1963.

BENES, Eduard, *The Memoirs of Dr Eduard Benes*, Allen and Unwin, 1954.

BEAUFRE, General Andre, *1940 – The Fall of France*, Cassell, 1967.

BITHELL, Jethro, *Germany – A Companion to German Studies*, Methuen, 1932.

BLACKET, P.M.S., *The Military and Political Consequences of Atomic Energy*, Turnstile Press, 1948.

BONNEFOUS, Edouard, *Histoire Politique de la III Republique*, Press Universal, Paris, 1959.

BONTÉ, Florimund, *Le Chemin de l'honneur*, Editions Sociale, France, 1970.

BOOTHBY, Lord, *Recollections of a Rebel*, Hutchinson, 1978.

BRANSON, Noreen, *Britain in the 1920s*, Weidenfeld and Nicholson, 1975.

BRANSON, Noreen and HEINEMANN, Margot, *Britain in the Nineteen Thirties*, Weidenfeld and Nicholson, 1971.

BROGAN, D.W., *The Development of Modern France – 1870–1939*, Hamish Hamilton, 1940.

BROUÉ, Pierre and TEMIME, Emil, *The Revolution and the Civil War in Spain*, Faber and Faber, 1970.

BULLOCK, Allan, *Hitler, A Study in Tyranny*, Odhams, 1952.

BUNYAN, James, *Intervention, Civil War and Communism in Russia April–December 1918*, J. Hopkins Press, Baltimore, 1936.

BURY, J.P.T., *France 1814–1940*, Methuen, 1949.

BURY, J.P.T., *France, The Insecure Peace*, MacDonald/American Heritage Press, 1972.

CADOGAN, Sir Alexander, *Diaries* (ed. David Dilks), Cassell, 1971.

CALDER, Angus, *The People's War. Britain 1939–1945*, Jonathan Cape, 1969.

CARR, E.H., *The Bolshevik Revolution 1917–1923*, Macmillan, 1964.

CARR, E.H., *International Relations Between the Two World Wars (1919–1939)*, Macmillan, 1947.

CARR, William, *A History of Germany*, Edward Arnold, 1969.

CHAMBERLIN, W.H., The Russian Revolution 1917–1921, Vol. II, Macmillan, New York, 1954.

CHESTER, Lewis, FAY, Stephen and YOUNG, Hugo, *The Zinoviev Letter*, Heinemann, 1967.

CHURCHILL, Winston, *The World Crisis: The Aftermath*, Thornton Butterworth, 1931.

CHURCHILL, Winston, *The Gathering Storm Vol. I. The Second World War*, Cassell, 1948.

CHURCHILL, Winston, *The Twilight War Book II, The Gathering Storm Vol. I. The Second World War*, Cassell, 1964.

CIANO, Count Galeazzo, *Diaries 1937–1938*, Methuen, 1952.

CITRINE, Sir Walter, *My Finnish Diary*, Penguin Books, 1940.

CLARK, Douglas, *Three Days to Catastrophe*, Hammond Hammond, 1966.

COATES, W.P. and Zelda, *A History of Anglo-Soviet Relations*, Lawrence and Wishart Pilot Press, 1943.

COBBAN, Alfred, *A History of Modern France*, Jonathan Cape, 1965.

COLE, G.D.H. and POSTGATE, Raymond, *The Common People*, Methuen, 1938.

COLLIER, Basil, *Arms and the Men, The Arms Trade and Governments*, Hamish Hamilton, 1980.

COLVIN, Ian, *The Chamberlain Cabinet*, Gollancz, 1971.

D'ABERNON, Lord, *An Ambassador of Peace*, Hodder and Stoughton, 1929.

DAVIDSON, Basil, *Germany, What Now?*, Frederick Muller, 1950.

DAVIES, Joseph E., *Mission to Moscow*, Gollancz, 1943.

DE GAULLE, Charles, *War Memoirs – Call to Honour 1940–1942*, Collins, 1955.

DUNSTERVILLE, Major-General L.C., *The Adventures of Dunsterforce*, Edward Arnold, 1920.

DURANTY, Walter, *USSR. The Story of Soviet Russia*, Hamish Hamilton, 1944.

DURANTY, Walter, *Stalin and Co.*, Secker and Warburg, 1949.

DURANTY, Walter, *Russia Reported*, Gollancz, 1934.

DUTT, R. Palme, *World Politics 1918–1936*, Gollancz, 1936.

EDEN, Anthony (Rt. Hon. Earl of Avon), *Memoirs – Facing the Dictators*, Cassell, 1962.

EDEN, Anthony (Rt. Hon. Earl of Avon), *The Eden Diaries – The Reckoning*, Cassell, 1965.

ELLIS, C.H., *The Transcaspian Episode*, Hutchinson, 1963.

EUDIN and SLUSSER, *Soviet Foreign Policy 1928–1934* Vol. II, Pennsylvania State University Press, 1967.

EUDIN, Zenia Joukoff and FISHER, Harold, *Soviet Russia and the West*, Stanford University Press, California, 1957.

EYCK, Erich, *The Weimar Republic*, Oxford University Press, 1964

FEILING, Keith, *The Life of Neville Chamberlain*, Macmillan, 1947.

582

FISCHER, Louis, *The Great Challenge*, Jonathan Cape, 1947.

FISCHER, Louis, *The Soviets in World Affairs*, Vintage Books, New York, 1951.

FLEMING, D.F., *The Cold War and Its Origins* Vol. I, Allen and Unwin, 1961.

FONVEILLE-ALQUIER, Francois, *The French and the Phoney War 1939–1940*, Tom Stacey Ltd., 1973.

FOOT, Michael, *Aneurin Bevan – Vol. I. 1897–1945*, MacGibbon and Kee, 1962.

FULLER, Major-General, *War and Western Civilisation*, Duckworth, 1932.

GALBRAITH, J.K., *The Great Crash 1929*, Hamish Hamilton, 1955.

GEDYE, G.E.R., *Fallen Bastions* Gollancz, 1939.

GRAVES, General W.S., *America's Siberian Adventure*, Peter Smith, New York, 1941.

GUNTHER, John, *Inside Europe*, Hamish Hamilton, 1936.

HALL, Wendy, *The Finns and Their Country*, Max Parrish, 1967.

HAMILTON, James Douglas, *Motive for a Mission*, Macmillan, 1971.

HARDY, George, *Those Stormy Years*, Lawrence and Wishart, 1956.

HENRI, Ernst, *Hitler Over Europe*, J.M. Dent, 1934.

HIGGINS, Trumbull, *Hitler and Russia, The Third Reich in a Two Front War 1937–1943*, Collier/Macmillan, 1966.

HITLER, Adolf, *Mein Kampf* (abridged English Edition), Paternoster Library, 1933–37.

HITLER, Adolf, *Mein Kampf* (German Edition), 1936.

HOBSON, J.A., *Imperialism – A Study*, Allen and Unwin, 1902.

HOUSE, Colonel, *The Intimate Papers of* (arranged as narrated by Charles Seymour), Ernest Benn, 1926.

HUTT, Allen, *British Trade Unionism*, Lawrence and Wishart, 1941.

IRONSIDE, Edmund, *W.E. Ironside – Archangel 1918–1919*, Constable, 1953.

JACKSON, Robert, *At War With the Bolsheviks*, Tom Stacey Ltd, 1972.

JACOBSON, Jon, *Locarno Diplomacy – Germany and the West 1925–1929*, Princeton University Press, 1972.

JOLL, James, *Europe Since 1870 – An International History*, Weidenfeld and Nicholson, 1973.

JORDAN, Phillip, *Russian Glory*, Cresset Press, 1942.

JUCKER, Ninetta, *Italy*, Thames and Hudson, 1970.

KENNAN, George, *Soviet–American Relations 1917–1921*, Faber and Faber, 1956.

KEYNES, J.M., *Economic Consequences of the Peace*, Macmillan, 1919.

KING, Cecil, *With Malice Towards None – A War Diary*, Sidgwick and Jackson, 1970.

KIRBY, D.G., *Finland in the 20th Century*, Hurst, 1979.

KIRKPATRICK, Ivone, *The Inner Circle*, Macmillan, 1959.

KNIGHTLEY, Phillip, *The First Casualty*, Andre Deutsch, 1975.

LARSEN, Egon, *Weimar Eyewitness*, Bachman and Turner, 1976.

LASH, Joseph P., *Roosevelt and Churchill – 1939–1941*, Andre Deutsch, 1976.

LEACH, Barry A., *German Strategy Against Russia 1939–1941*, Oxford University Press, 1973.

LENIN, V.I., *The Period of War Communism 1918–1920*, Lawrence and Wishart, 1937.

LICHTHEIM, George, *Europe in the 20th Century*, Weidenfeld and Nicholson, 1972.

LIDDELL HART, B.H., *History of the Second World War*, Cassell, 1970.

LLOYD GEORGE, David, *The Truth About the Peace Treaties*, Gollancz, 1938.

LLOYD GEORGE, David, *War Memoirs Vols. V and VI*, Ivor Nicholson and Watson, 1936.

LOFTS, Nora and WEINER, Marjorie, *Eternal France, A History of France 1789–1944*, Hodder and Stoughton, 1969.

LUKACS, John, *The Last European War, September 1939–1941*, Routledge and Kegan Paul, 1977.

MACARTHUR, General Douglas, *Reminiscences*, Heinemann, 1964.

MACCARTNEY, C.A., *Hungary – A Short History*, Edinburgh University Press, 1962.

MAISKY, Ivan, *Spanish Notebooks*, Hutchinson, 1966.

MAISKY, Ivan, *Who Helped Hitler?*, Hutchinson, 1964.

MANZANI, Carl, *We Can Be Friends – Origins of the Cold War*, Topical Books, New York, 1952.

MAYER, Arno, J., *Politics and Diplomacy of Peacemaking*, Weidenfeld and Nicholson, 1968.

MENDELSSOHN, Peter de, *The Nuremberg Documents*, Allen and Unwin, 1946.

MONTAGU, Ivor, *The Youngest Son*, Lawrence and Wishart, 1970.

MONTGOMERY, Field-Marshal, *The Memoirs of Field Marshal Montgomery From Yalta to Potsdam*, Collins, 1958.

MORTON, A.L., *A People's History of England*, Gollancz, 1938

MOSELEY, George, *China – Empire to People's Republic*, B.T. Batsford, 1968.

MOWAT, C.L., *Britain Between the Wars 1918–1940*, Methuen, 1955.

NETTL, J.P., *Rosa Luxemburg*, Oxford University Press, 1969.

NEVAKIVI, Jukka, *The Appeal That Was Never Made*, C. Hurst and Co, 1976.

NICOLSON, Harold, *Diaries and Letters (1930–1939)* (ed. Nigel Nicolson), Collins, 1966.

NICOLSON, Harold, *Diaries 1939–1945* (ed. Nigel Nicolson), Collins, 1967.

NOGUÈRES, Henri, *Munich or the Phoney Peace*, Weidenfeld and Nicholson, 1965.

OLDEN, Rudolf, *Hitler the Pawn*, Gollancz, 1936.

OLIVEIRA, A. Ramos, *A People's History of Germany*, Gollancz, 1942.

OWEN, Frank, *Tempestuous Journey – Lloyd Goerge, His Life and Times*, Hitchinson, 1954.

PELLISSIER, Roger, *The Awakening of China 1793–1949*, Secker and Warburg, 1967.

PHILLIPS, Price Morgan, *Germany in Transition*, The Labour Publishing Co, 1923.

PHILLIPS, Price Morgan, *My Reminiscences of the Russian Revolution*, Allen and Unwin, 1921.

PHILLIPS, Price Morgan, *My Three Revolutions*, Allen and Unwin, 1969

POKROVSKY, M.N., *Brief History of Russia Vol. II*, Martin Lawrence, 1933.

PRITT, D.N., *Must the War Spread*, Penguin Books, 1940.

REED, John, *Ten Days That Shook The World*, Lawrence and Wishart, 1961.

RENSHAW, Patrick, *The General Strike*, Eyre Methuen, 1975.

REYNAUD, Paul, *In the Thick of the Fight 1930–1945*, Cassell, 1955.

REYNOLDS, E.E., *Nansen*, Penguin Books, 1949.

RHODES, James Robert, *Churchill – A Study in Failure*, Weidenfeld and Nicholson, 1970.

RIDDELL, Lord, *Intimate Diary of the Peace Conference and After, 1918–1923*, Gollancz, 1933.

RIOS, Fernando de los, *What is Happening in Spain*

RODZIANKO, Paul, *Mannerheim*, Jarrolds, 1940.

ROSKILL, Stephen, *Naval Policy Between the Wars Vol. I. 1919–1929*, Collins, 1968.

ROTHSTEIN, A., *The Munich Conspiracy*, Lawrence and Wishart, 1958.

RUSSELL, Lord (of Liverpool), *Scourge of the Swastika*, Cassell, 1954.

RUST, William, *Britons in Spain*, Lawrence and Wishart, 1939.

SANDOVAL, Jose and AZCARATE, Manuel, *Spain, 1936–1939*, Lawrence and Wishart, 1963.

SCHEELE, Godfrey, *The Weimar Republic – Overture to the Third Reich*, Faber and Faber, 1945.

SCHMIDT, Paul, *Hitler's Interpreter*, Heinemann, 1951.

SHERWOOD, Robert E., *The White House Papers of Harry Hopkins, Vol. I*, Eyre and Spottiswoode, 1948.

SCHUMAN, Frederick L., *Soviet Politics, At Home and Abroad*, Robert Hale, 1948.

SHIRER, William L., *The Collapse of the Third Republic*, William Heinemann Secker and Warburg, 1970.

SHIRER, William L., *The Rise and Fall of the Third Reich*, Secker and Warburg, 1960.

SILVERLIGHT, John, *The Victors' Dilemma*, Barry and Jenkins, 1970.

SNOWDEN, Viscount Phillip, *An Autobiography*, Ivor Nicholson and Watson, 1934.

STURDY, David, *Modern Europe*, Gill and Macmillan, 1974.

SUMNER, B.H., *Survey of Russian History*, Duckworth, 1944.

SUNY, Ronald Grigor, *The Baku Commune 1917–1918*, Princeton University Press, 1972.

TAYLOR, A.J.P., *Englsh History 1914–1945*, Oxford University Press, 1965.

TAYLOR, A.J.P., *The Origins of the Second World War*, Penguin Books, 1964.

TAYLOR, Telford, *Munich – The Price of Peace*, Hodder and Stoughton, 1979.

THOMAS, Hugh, *The Spanish Civil War*, Eyre and Spottiswoode, 1961.

THOMSON, David, *England in the 20th Century*, Penguin Books, 1965.

THYSSEN, Fritz, *I Paid Hitler*, Hodder and Stoughton, 1941.

TINT, Herbert, *France Since 1918*, B.T. Batsford, 1970.

TOBIAS, Fritz, *The Reichstag Fire, Legend and Truth*, Secker and Warburg, 1963.

TROTSKY, Leon, *The History of the Russian Revolution Vol. I*, Gollancz, 1932.

ULLMAN, Richard H., *Britain and the Russian Civil War 1917–1921 Vol. II*, Princeton University Press, 1968.

WATSON, Robin, *Georges Clemenceau*, Eyre Methuen, 1974.

WERTH, Alexander, *The Destiny of France*, Hamish Hamilton, 1937.

WESTERN, J.R., *The End of European Primacy*, Blandford Press, 1965.

WHEELER-BENNETT, Sir John, *Munich – Prologue to Tragedy*, Macmillan, 1948.

WHEELER-BENNETT, Sir John, *Nemesis of Power*, Macmillan, 1953.

585

WILLIAMS, John, *Ides of May*, Constable, 1968.

WITTRAM, Reinhard, *Russia and Europe*, Thames and Hudson, 1973.

WOOD, Anthony, Europe 1815–1945, Longmans Green, 1964.

ZEMAN, Zbynek, *The Masaryks – The Making of Czechoslovakia*, Weidenfeld and Nicholson, 1976.

ZILLIACUS, Konni, *I Choose Peace*, Penguin Books, 1949.

ZILLIACUS, Konni, *Inquest on Peace*, Gollancz, 1935.

ZILLIACUS, Konni, *The Mirror of the Past*, Gollancz, 1944.

ZIMMERN, Professor Alfred, *The League of Nations and the Rule of Law 1918–1935*, Macmillan, 1935.

NEW FABIAN RESEARCH BUREAU, *Road to War*, Gollancz, 1937

History of the Communist Party of the Soviet Union, Foreign Language Publishing House, Moscow, 1939.

Penguin Political Dictionary, Penguin Books, 1939.

Socialist Annual for 1908.

NEWSPAPERS AND PERIODICALS

The Daily Chronicle

27 February	1922
10 May	1923
24 May	1923

The Daily Despatch

4 June	1920

The Daily Express

6 September	1919
24 May	1923
28 February	1928
17 April	1928
21 August	1936
28 April	1937
1 May	1941

The Daily Herald

2 January	1920
30 April	1920
11 May	1920
19 May	1920
24 June	1920
28 February	1921
4 March	1921
8 March	1921
11 March	1921
12 March	1921
4 April	1923
10 May	1923
12 May	1923
19 May	1923
5 June	1923
7 June	1923
2 February	1924
6 August	1924
7 August	1924
31 July	1925
3 February	1927
1 December	1927
7 February	1934

The Daily Mail

22 October	1924
25 October	1924
28 November	1933
17 October	1939

The Daily News

19 January	1905
23 January	1905
9 October	1920
5 February	1927
9 March	1927
9 March	1927
1 December	1927

The Daily Telegraph

18 March	1921
11 May	1923
2 June	1923
4 September	1923
16 June	1926
8 March	1927
1 December	1927
3 October	1929
21 January	1931
18 March	1936
18 March	1938
24 March	1938
3 October	1938
18 September	1939
20 March	1940

The Evening Standard

17 June	1940
8 September	1941

The Financial News

5 April	1933

The Manchester Evening Chronicle

22 October	1924

The Manchester Guardian

20 November	1917
12 December	1917
9 January	1918
3 May	1920
8 January	1923
22 February	1923
12 May	1923
14 May	1923
10 October	1924

587

27 February	1926	3 February	1935
10 March	1927	4 May	1941
4 October	1929		
17 January	1931	*Reynolds News*	
12 August	1936	28 April	1935
24 November	1937	2 August	1936
10 March	1938	10 January	1937
22 September	1938	18 April	1937
22 September	1938	28 November	1937
23 September	1938	18 September	1938
26 September	1938	23 June	1940
27 September	1938		
28 September	1938	*The Sheffield Daily*	
11 December	1939	*Telegraph*	
27 May	1940	24 October	1933
27 May	1940		
25 June	1940	*The South Wales*	
25 June	1940	*Evening Post*	
18 June	1941	18 March	1933

The Morning Post

5 October	1920	*The Sunday Express*	
9 March	1928	29 May	1927

The News Chronicle

22 June	1933	*The Sunday Times*	
19 June	1935	10 April	1938
12 March	1936	22 June	1941
29 April	1937		
1 October	1938	*The Times*	
1 October	1938	12 January	1920
31 March	1939	10 May	1920
3 April	1939	2 June	1920
13 April	1939	8 July	1920
22 August	1939	25 August	1921
20 September	1939	7 January	1922
20 September	1939	27 February	1922
15 December	1939	1 May	1923
21 June	1941	21 October	1924
		27 October	1924
		28 October	1924
The Observer		22 November	1924
4 January	1920	31 January	1925
4 July	1920	14 October	1925
13 May	1923	2 February	1927
20 May	1923	24 February	1927
25 October	1925	9 March	1927
13 December	1925	16 July	1927
22 May	1927	5 March	1928
20 January	1935	21 May	1928
3 February	1935	18 February	1933

13 June	1933
4 February	1935
15 April	1935
5 May	1935
28 April	1937
29 April	1937
14 September	1938
1 October	1938
20 July	1940
14 May	1941
23 June	1941
8 August	1945
24 November	1954
10 October	1961
22 December	1966

L'Humanité
18 February	1920

La Liberté
16 June	1920

Le Telegramme
5 April	1940
17 May	1941

New York Herald Tribune
15 May	1941

New York Times
29 October	1928
24 June	1941

Saturday Review of Literature
15 June	1946

Time and Tide
13 July	1935

Izvestia
5 August	1928

DOCUMENTS

BRITISH CABINET DOCUMENTS
CAB 23/14 10 November 1918. 500A p. 300
CAB 23/23 Appendix I, Greece and Middle Eastern Policy
CAB 23/31 Document 49 (22)

BRITISH SESSIONAL PAPERS, House of Commons
Cmnd. 1846 (Russia No. 1) Vol. XXV (6–10) pp. 491/495
1923 Vol. XXV pp. 454–519
Cmnd. 4286 (Russia No. 1) (1933) No. 5
Cmnd. 4827 11 March 1935, Vol. XIII – 83. Statement Relating to Defence

DOCUMENTS ON BRITISH FOREIGN POLICY HMSO
1st Series Vol. III
Series 1A Vol. III
3rd Series Vols. I, II, IV, V, VI, VII

DOCUMENTS ON GERMAN FOREIGN POLICY HMSO
Series C Vols. II, III, IV
Series D Vols. I, II, III, VI, X, XII

SOVIET DOCUMENTS ON FOREIGN POLICY (ed. Jane Degras)
Vol. I 1917–1924 Royal Institute of Foreign Affairs/Oxford University
Press 1951
Vol. II 1925–1932 Royal Institute of Foreign Affairs/Oxford University
Press 1952
Vol. III 1933–1941 Royal Institute of Foreign Affairs/Oxford University
Press 1953

INTERNATIONAL MILITARY TRIBUNAL, NUREMBERG
Trial of the Major War Criminals, Nuremberg
Vols. I, VII, XII, XV, XXXVIII, XL, 1947

DOCUMENTS ON INTERNATIONAL AFFAIRS
1935 Vols. I, II, Oxford University Press, 1937
1938 Vol. II, Oxford University Press, 1943

SURVEY OF INTERNATIONAL AFFAIRS
1935 Vol. II, Oxford University Press, 1936

GREAT SOVIET ENCYCLOPAEDIA Collier/Macmillan, 1981

KEESINGS CONTEMPORARY ARCHIVES
Vol. IV Keesings Ltd, 1940–43

THE ROUND TABLE
1935–1936 Vol. XXVI Macmillan, 1936

PARLIAMENTARY REPORTS – *HANSARD*

10 February 1920
22 March 1921
15 May 1923
15 May 1923
15 May 1923
14 June 1926
5 May 1927
13 May 1927
16 May 1927
16 May 1927
24 May 1927
26 May 1927
26 May 1927
26 May 1927
30 May 1927
2 June 1927
15 March 1933
6 February 1934
13 July 1934

13 July 1934
21 February 1938
24 March 1938
31 March 1939
3 April 1939
24 August 1939
24 August 1939
24 August 1939
1 September 1939
1 September 1939
1 September 1939
3 September 1939
20 September 1939
14 December 1939
19 March 1940
7 May 1940
8 May 1940
10 May 1941